54480

HN
65
.H56

Hollander, Paul.

Soviet and American
society

Soviet and American Society

SOVIET AND AMERICAN SOCIETY

A COMPARISON

PAUL HOLLANDER

New York
OXFORD UNIVERSITY PRESS
1973

. . . Liberal beliefs did not seem capable of self-defense, and you could smell decay. You could see the suicidal impulses of civilization pushing strongly. You wondered whether this Western culture could survive universal dissemination—whether only its science and technology or administrative practices would travel, be adopted by other societies. Or whether the worst enemies of civilization might not prove to be its petted intellectuals who attacked it at its weakest moments—attacked it in the name of proletarian revolution, in the name of reason, and in the name of irrationality, in the name of visceral depth, in the name of sex, in the name of perfect instantaneous freedom. For what it amounted to was limitless demand—insatiability, refusal of the doomed creature (death being sure and final) to go away from this earth unsatisfied. A full bill of demand and complaint was therefore presented by each individual. Non-negotiable. Recognizing no scarcity of supply in any human department.

. . . This liberation into individuality has not been a great success. For a historian of great interest, but for one aware of the suffering it is appalling. Hearts that get no real wage, souls that find no nourishment.

Both the U.S.A. and the U.S.S.R. were, for Sammler, utopian projects.

—Saul Bellow, *Mr. Sammler's Planet*

Contents

Acknowledgments

I am thankful to a number of people who read the manuscript (or parts of it) and made helpful suggestions for improvements.

The list must begin with Charles Page who invested an extraordinary amount of time, energy, and concern in reading and improving several drafts over a period of several years. His comments and criticisms encompassed the entire range of responses to a manuscript: from major substantive and theoretical suggestions to painstakingly detailed and specific comments on style and presentation. It is beyond doubt that without his efforts this would be a far poorer book in every respect. To be the recipient of such dedication revived pleasurable recollections of my graduate student days when he was my department chairman and teacher.

Six people, in addition to him, read the entire manuscript and gave it the benefit of their particular knowledge, and intellectual common sense. Two foremost students of Soviet and American society respectively, Alex Inkeles and David Riesman, made many valuable comments on various aspects of the book. Howard Elinson, Peter Kenez, Stanley Milgram, and William J. Wilson also read the entire manuscript and communicated their responses and suggestions in the form of extremely useful and detailed written comments.

Individual chapters or other parts of the book (related to their particular interests and expertise) were also read by Isaiah Berlin,

Nathan Glazer, Milton Gordon, Gayle D. Hollander, Sam Kaplan, Michael Lewis, Seymour Martin Lipset, Murray Melbin, Hans Speier, Randal Stokes, Curt Tansky, and Janet Vaillant. They too shared with me their insights into the issues discussed in these chapters or parts of the book.

Mrs. Ann Lindsay and Mrs. Manuela Krueger at Oxford University Press were most pleasant editors to work with and their efforts greatly improved the manuscript. Mrs. Lindsay also prepared the index. Mr. Sheldon Meyer, executive editor at Oxford University Press, was considerate and helpful in all transactions between the Press and myself and conveyed to me a sense of intellectual concern I rarely sensed before in the publishing business.

Preface

The circumstances under which an author undertakes the writing of a comparative study of American and Soviet society may interest the reader. This being a largely interpretive work, he might wish to know something about the author's background, qualifications (or lack of them), and the sources of his views and values, or at any rate, his perception of the sources of his views and values.

It is unusual for the preface of a scholarly or social scientific volume to contain the author's reflections about the relationship between his social and personal background and the message and meaning of the work to follow. Prefaces to such books customarily contain tributes to the generosity of foundations, academic officials, colleagues, students, wives, children, and neighbors. Although I do hope *not* to set a new trend in this regard, I cannot list the numerous sources of research funds which made the writing of this book possible, since I sought no special funding. At the same time, I wish to note here that during the early stages of writing and thinking about the book, I was a research fellow at the Russian Research Center of Harvard University, which meant a reduced teaching load, a truly stimulating intellectual atmosphere, and generally excellent working conditions. While this did greatly facilitate writing, it was not an arrangement arrived at on account of this study. There have been many individuals over the years who read the manuscript or parts of it and made valuable comments. They are listed under the acknowledgments.

Despite the absence of the conventional justifications noted above, I intended to write this preface for several reasons. One was to find a final outlet for the persistent apprehension about attempting a study of this kind, an undertaking which invites a certain amount of skepticism. Most problematic was to decide what should actually be included in this comparison and what periods to encompass or touch on within the vague designation of contemporaneity. I ended up including what most sociologists would consider the "major institutions" in both societies and probably also what most of them would regard as their major "social problems." Even so much of importance has been omitted both by choice and necessity. "Limitations of space" is, of course, an old excuse for incompleteness and superficiality in scholarly books, for questions not raised and for those raised which had not been answered. In this particular case, the excuse seems somewhat more plausible than in some others. It is not simple to compress into one medium size volume a comparison of two such societies as the American and Soviet.*

It should also be noted here that this book does not represent the fulfillment of long-standing intellectual or personal aspirations. On the contrary, I drifted into this project. I was originally asked by a publisher to write a short text on Soviet society for a paperback series. I felt at the time that, although such published overviews of Soviet society had not been numerous, some excellent works were available and that I could not offer much that was original to justify the undertaking. Subsequently, it occurred to me that there were no books, either for the "college market" or the general reader, which compared Soviet and American societies. Such an undertaking seemed more of a challenge, not only because of its novelty, but also because in the professional sense of the word I was not a student of American society; my specialization lay in the field of Soviet studies. A sociologist by training and resident of this country since 1959, I succeeded in persuading myself that a combination of individual

* The difficulties of such an undertaking are also suggested by the absence of comparative studies of this kind, especially of a sociological nature. While this book was in press a volume written by a British geographer, W. H. Parker, was published under the title: *The Superpowers: The U.S. and the Soviet Union Compared* (New York: Wiley, Fall 1972). It is primarily concerned with the physical setting, resources, and economy of the two societies.

scholarly efforts and the "anthropological" perspectives and perceptions of the newcomer might make up for the deficiencies in more
formal or specialized training.

Alerting the reader to the connections between my biography and
professional activities (such as this book) should not be taken to imply
either a view that my biography somehow validates my intellectual
work (lending to it some special aura of authenticity) or that, on the
contrary, I consider it a series of traps and pitfalls which threaten its
validity. Correspondingly, I believe neither that the self-conscious
assertion of one's values necessarily enriches one's work, nor that an
awareness of them must make it hopelessly subjective. This being the
case, it is not easy to dispose of the problem.

At a time when commitment, passionately embraced and com-
batively expressed, is an emerging cultural norm among many American intellectuals, including social scientists, it may seem both quaint
and passé for a sociologist to treat his readers to his thoughts on the
likely sources of subjectivity or partisanship in his work. In the minds
of many, fierce subjectivity is associated with commitment and the
latter with relevance; in turn, objectivity or its pursuit is paired with
hypocrisy and irrelevance. If in the past it had been customary to
caution about the undesirable effects of certain types of personal experience on an author of a social scientific work, today, increasingly,
intellectual and scholarly authenticity is sought and found in the
directness of experience, including that which derives from the par-
ticularistic perspective of group membership.

This author is a more or less conventional sociologist who believes
that the *pursuit* of objectivity is desirable, even if it is unattainable,
because it is less likely to lead to oversimplification or distortion than
simpleminded espousals of commitment and the underlying certi-
tudes. It is the belief in the desirability of this pursuit that has led me
to ponder the influence of my background and present way of life
on this book.

I was born in Budapest, Hungary which I left in November 1956
following the defeat of the Revolution. Between 1956 and 1959 I
studied in England. I received a Bachelor of Arts degree in sociology
from the London School of Economics and Political Science in 1959.

Since my arrival in this country in 1959, my social and physical environment has been almost exclusively academic, as I have passed
through the stages of graduate student and faculty member at differ-

ent universities. From time to time, I felt uneasy about viewing American society from this vantage point, restrictive of one's vision in some ways, liberating in others. Not that I subscribed to the belief that academia is an ivory tower that seals its occupant from reality. Academic life represents a segment of reality, but so does being a car salesman, social worker, truck driver, corporation executive, or steel worker; yet, it cannot be denied that, at least as far as students and tenured faculty are concerned, academic life is more sheltered and secure than the "outside world," the punishments for poor performance are milder, and that those inhabiting this universe often have more leisure (or at least greater choice in the use of their time) than people in other occupations. Enclosure in this setting has, doubtless, deprived me of some experiences, impressions, and contacts which might have added depth, color, or complexity even to a book that does not claim to, and cannot possibly rest on the accumulation of personal experience.

It is hard to decide what is likely to have made a greater impact on this book: the 12 years spent in academic settings in the United States or the first 24 years of my life in Hungary. In Hungary, I witnessed the systematic and purposeful transplantation of Soviet institutions and policies developed under Stalin, and over the years I had come to dislike the process and its outcome. (More will be said about this below.) I also observed closely the Revolution in 1956 and its crushing by Soviet troops. Readers concerned with objectivity and impartiality may wonder, in view of these circumstances, if I might not be disposed to stress in writing about Soviet society only its unappealing features and by contrast praise the virtues of my new homeland. Would not my past experiences create an irresistible pressure for double standards of judgment? It could further be argued that I proved my partiality by choosing to live in the United States in preference to Hungary (that is, a society in many ways resembling the Soviet one). It could also be suggested that any person leaving his native country and settling in a new one is under great internal pressure to justify the wisdom of his choice to himself and cultivate favorable attitudes toward the society of which he has become a member.

The possibility that it is difficult to produce respectable sociological analysis of a society about which one feels critical (or of one which elicits some positive sentiments) raises interesting questions in the light of certain intellectual trends in the United States today. Anal-

yses of American society written by highly critical and alienated authors have been increasingly respected and respectable, and, more and
more a degree of estrangement is taken for granted on the part of
those who write about American society. By contrast those who might
be laudatory of some aspect of American society tend to be viewed
with suspicion and their soundness of mind or intellectual credentials
are often called into question; thus, alienation *in the American context* is seen, by and large, as a wholesome quality and a veritable precondition of insight and authenticity.

When Alex Inkeles and Raymond Bauer published their study
of Soviet society *(The Soviet Citizen,* 1959) based largely on interviews with Soviet refugees, many readers and critics were apprehensive about their conclusions. It was suggested that their findings might
have been seriously compromised by obtaining their information
from people critical of and disaffected from the society which they
described. Other eye-witness accounts by individual émigrés or es-
capees from communist countries have also often been viewed with
similar misgivings; how could we give much credence to the reports of
people who obviously disliked the society they had formerly lived in?

Similar apprehensions are noticeably absent in regard to American
society. It has yet to be proposed that alienation from American society disqualifies social scientists from writing about it. An unfavorable disposition toward American institutions does not seem to render
untrustworthy the accounts of critics, in or outside the social sciences. Nobody questions the validity of the analyses of American
society provided by such obviously discriminated, and hence justifiably alienated groups as American Indians, blacks, or Mexican-Americans. On the contrary, sometimes it is suggested that only blacks (or
other deprived groups) are qualified to provide authentic accounts
of their lives and problems, and of the institutions which impinge on
them. Nobody seems to fear that in such instances perceptions and
judgments are distorted because of the obvious and understandable
bias of the oppressed toward the social system and environment which
had mistreated him. Few would suggest that victims of racial discrimination take a balanced view toward discrimination or the institutional arrangements which produce or tolerate it; thus, it seems also
natural that women teach and cultivate women studies; blacks, black
studies; ethnics, ethnic studies. Jews have yet to be cautioned about
the danger of getting involved with studies of nazism or anti-Semitism

in view of their personal concern with such matters. If this is the case with such groups and individuals, no less, and possibly more disposed to personal involvement (with the subject matter of their study), the scholarly hazards take on manageable proportions in the case of a former Hungarian citizen who writes about Soviet society. This is not to say that my background had no impact on this book, but only that it is an open question to what extent some of my personal experiences (relevant to an understanding of Soviet institutions) improved or weakened the intellectual undertaking.

As noted earlier, I am neither a native-born American nor a former Soviet citizen, although being a former Hungarian citizen makes me more a "product" of a Soviet- than Western-type society. Perhaps the most fundamental lesson of having lived in Hungary in a turbulent historical period (which encompassed Hungary's becoming an ally of Nazi Germany, World War II, the persecution of Jews, liberation by the Red Army, the imposition of Soviet-style government, the 1956 Revolution and its defeat) was that social injustice and narrow limits on personal freedom are not unusual or deviant conditions of social existence.

Being a stranger to American society inevitably added something to my perceptions of this country; at any rate, *before* many features of the United States came to be taken for granted with the passage of years. I had a miscellany of preconceptions and expectations, some of which were confirmed, others dispelled by experience. I expected skyscrapers to be predominant, and found instead flimsy little wooden houses accommodating, it seemed, most of the population. I did hear stories in Hungary about manual workers coming to work in their big cars and indeed found this to be the case. I was surprised that even people not particularly well-off put on clean shirts every day. I was not prepared for the kind of "friendliness" which expressed itself, for example, by virtual strangers calling me by my first name; at first I was deeply touched by this. On the more serious side, I was unprepared for the bitterness associated with the race problem, had no conception about the nature and manifestations of violence in urban areas, and did not anticipate the widespread disaffection and even despair among students and intellectuals, in relation to their society. I had no inkling of the bizarre religious beliefs and practices to be found in this country or of the problems created by the wastefulness of consumers and the consumer goods industry. I was equally unprepared for the phenomenon of "identity problems" (or "crises") and the difficulties encountered in the relationships of the older and younger generations, supported by the cultural devaluation of the old and the veneration of youth. In short, my knowledge and anticipation of American social conditions was very spotty even though I was not completely unprepared for what I found.

Along with the unexpected and unpleasant impressions, I found that there was much personal freedom in this society. Although I had behind me three years of life in England, and thus my standards of comparison were no longer rooted exclusively in an East European perspective, I still found much to appreciate in this regard. Even a subsequent growth in my understanding of the defects of American society could not subvert this initial impression that there was much freedom here—perhaps too much—for the good of some groups in society or even society at large. Nevertheless, my preference for the American political system over the Soviet (and other similar ones) has not, for example, predisposed me to predict that it would be more durable than the Soviet, or led me to believe that societies should only be evaluated by this dimension (that is, the availability of certain political and personal freedoms). The personal and political freedoms such as exist in the United States are perfectly compatible with, say, poverty, neglect of the old or the inequities of the welfare system. Correspondingly, I remain mindful of such advantages of Soviet society as full employment, a more muted presence of economic inequalities, and a less contradictory system for socializing the young. Indeed a lack of close contact with the Soviet realities (as reflected in the conditions experienced in Hungary up till 1956) made the unappealing features of Soviet society more abstract and unreal, less apt to provoke indignation and emotional criticism. More than that, at times, the spectacle of social cohesion, stability, and a seemingly well-ordered society (such as the Soviet) appeared almost refreshing (from a safe distance) compared with the disorder and apparent instability of the United States.

Because my economic and social circumstances have improved since I left Hungary, the question may also be raised about the seriousness of the effects of the comfort or discomfort of one's living conditions on the appraisal of the society which provides or withholds them. More fundamental still is the difference in occupation; in Hungary after finishing the Gymnasium (a type of secondary school), I had a

series of unenviable jobs and statuses (political exile, laborer in forestry and agriculture, private in a labor battalion of the army, construction worker, industrial trainee), whereas in the United States I
became a graduate student, Ph.D. recipient, and university professor.
Must such changes in one's way of life impinge on consciousness to a
degree that precludes honest judgment and clear perception of the
pluses and minuses of each society? On the one hand, it is clear that a
high or higher standard of living per se does not lessen the propensity
to social criticism, as is demonstrated by the social background and
standard of living of many vocal social critics of American society
today. On the other hand, it is also true that many such people take
their material comforts and personal freedoms for granted, since, as
a rule, they have no basis for comparison in a more disadvantaged
past. The important difference, from a social psychological standpoint,
is that in my case, conditions *improved* and it could be plausibly argued that a society that allowed me to enhance my social and material
position is bound to be viewed favorably. It is, after all, difficult to feel
strongly that a society can be very bad if it allows the particular individual a certain amount of achievement. While it is undoubtedly
tempting to generalize from one's particular situation to social conditions as a whole, there are factors which keep in check such tendencies
both in my case and in general.

Concerning negative attitudes toward the Soviet system (based on
personal experiences in Hungary), the reader may be interested to
know that my critical attitudes emerged in my mid teens, well before
my family and I suffered any disadvantages and even before we could
foresee them. I can trace the beginnings of my distaste for the system
to exposure to Party propaganda in the second half of the 1940's, to
its self-righteous, strident tone and its obvious lies, as well as to the
cult of Stalin and his Hungarian alter ego, Rakosi. Another seemingly trivial factor that bestirred critical sentiments in me was the
spectacle of expensive American and British cars parked around the
Party headquarters, ministries, and the secret police headquarters
leading me to wonder about the nature of commitment to social justice and equality on the part of the users of these vehicles. The spectacle of "salami tactics," that is, the gradual (slice by slice) elimination
of political parties and their leaders opposed to the Communist Party
deepened my misgivings about the system, which initially, had looked
very appealing to me. Not too far from where I lived in Budapest, I

also witnessed the visible expansion of the "State Security Organs" (housed with unintended symbolism in the former headquarters of the Hungarian Nazi, or Arrow-Cross Party Building) which kept adding new buildings and whole blocks to its complex; thus, by the time I finished the Gymnasium and found myself barred from entering the University of Budapest (by virtue of being exiled to a small village with my family, because of a "capitalist" grandfather), my attitudes toward the system had crystallized. Exile and deprivation from higher education did not substantially alter my attitudes, except in one respect. During my exile in the village and subsequent years in the army and construction work, I found increasing evidence that the society being built was no more popular with peasants and workers that with declassé exiles of bourgeois (or middle-class) origins. I welcomed this evidence, since, not unnaturally, I was relieved to find confirmation of my value judgments.

It is more difficult to settle the question of the impact of relatively favorable personal experiences in this country on my capacity as a professional sociologist to observe and analyze American society. It might be noted here, however, that having spent the entire period of my life in the United States in academic settings, I have been continuously exposed to an intensely critical social environment in which a widespread attitude, both among colleagues and students, was one of skepticism, if not vehement denigration, of many dominant American institutions and values. It would have been surprising if I had not absorbed some of the native intellectuals' capacity for social criticism and their heightened sensitivity to the ills of their society. There is, of course, a fair amount in this book, to indicate that whatever favorable dispositions or predispositions I have had toward this society, they have not blinded me to its many failings, and problems, and especially to the perception of personal unease and unhappiness that sometimes seems to be endemic. At the same time, life in the academic setting deprived me of the type of experience and personal contact which in Hungary allowed me a better understanding of society as a whole and provided me with a deeper, broader, and more vivid sense of its wrongs; thus, many of the defects and injustices of American society have remained relatively abstract.

In the end, the search for the roots of one's views and values becomes futile insofar as even if unearthed, these roots will not greatly help us in assessing the validity of these views, although the links between social background and intellectual concerns are always interesting to observe. It is difficult to generalize about the best combination of personal experience and professional concerns, or about the benefits and liabilities of distance versus intimate personal involvement with the subject matter. One must finally abandon the self-conscious search for the best balance between subjectivity and objectivity, involvement and detachment, partisanship and skepticism.

The pressure of intense value commitments on one's work (scholarly, intellectual, social scientific, or all three) represents a threat insofar as it pushes toward the obliteration of the dividing line between ideas and actions (or opinions and behavior), a dividing line that is the critical safeguard of intellectual (as well as political) freedom. It is a major premise of liberal Western political values and ideals that such a dividing line exists or should exist and that it provides the basis for the free expression, pursuit, and circulation of diverse ideas. At the same time, we also feel deeply that authenticity lies in acting on our ideas, in doing what we believe in and hence crossing the boundary between ideas and actions. No theoretical or ideological formula will resolve the tension between these two sets of attitudes. We must accept this tension and the troublesome fact that there are compartments in life and in one's attiudes, which, regrettably, are neither perfectly integrated with, nor efficiently insulated from one another.

Leverett, Massachusetts   *Paul Hollander*
February, 1973

Soviet and American Society

1. Introduction: Perspectives and Perceptions

The Problems of the Comparison: Theoretical and Methodological

One does not have to search for long to find reasons for a comparative study of the United States and the Soviet Union. Theoretical and practical justifications abound.

Few undertakings can be more stimulating than the analysis of societies which came into existence abruptly and therefore had an observable beginning. Both the United States and the Soviet Union are such societies.[1] The first started with the settlement of people on a thinly populated continent; the second with a revolution. We know, of course, that neither represents an absolute beginning: the first settlements and colonies in what became the United States were influenced by the experiences and aspirations of the people who founded them, as were the founders by the values and aspirations of the societies from which they came. Similarly, the October Revolution in Russia, though also aiming at a completely clean break, was preceded by a chain of events, traditions and institutions which shaped its character and that of subsequent social arrangements. Critical in both instances were the deliberate efforts to transcend the framework of continuity and custom, to construct new societies and establish new social relationships. In one instance, people physically removed themselves from their old societies to accomplish this; in

3

the other, they proceeded by the revolutionary destruction of the institutions of the old society. In both cases there was an unusual accumulation of frustration and dissatisfaction with the known social arrangements and, correspondingly, deliberate efforts were made on a large scale to bring about new ones. Moreover, both the settlers and the revolutionaries were motivated by well-defined ideals, not merely impatience with the status quo or the pursuit of change for its own sake. Although there is little substantive similarity between the ideals of the Puritans and 18th-century American revolutionaries, and the Russian revolutionaries of the 19th and 20th centuries, the attitudes of these diverse groups have an important, if obvious, common core: the belief that it is possible to alter society fundamentally, that radical new departures in human affairs are feasible and that accumulated historical antecedents of injustice, oppression, and privation can be undone by human will and exertion.

A comparison of these two societies within the limits of a single volume is a formidable task and in some respects beyond the purview of a single author or a single discipline. Yet the undertaking is encouraged and stimulated by what has always been an important (if sometimes forgotten) tradition in sociology: the comparison of large-scale, complex societies in pursuit of theoretical generalizations.

While we certainly cannot do full justice to the topic, there are good reasons why it is nevertheless worthwhile to make the attempt. The arguments in favor of comparative studies are familiar, particularly for students of sociology. Thus it is frequently noted that we can understand our own society better by comparing it with others because of the detachment gained by finding out that the familiar and seemingly "natural" features of our own society are but one of many possible modes of social organization. It is also argued that theoretical propositions about the uniqueness or universality of any social institution require making comparisons, implicitly or explicitly. We need not belabor the point, especially since there is at present an increase in comparative studies in sociology and a renewed realization of the insights they can yield.

As for this study, an additional reason for comparing American and Soviet society is the inspiring absence of such inquiries, at least on the part of sociologists.[2] While fragmentary comparisons of the two countries have been undertaken by many journalists, politicians, and ideologues, scholars have been more reticent.

Sociological comparisons are usually motivated by more than idle curiosity. Most typically they serve to vindicate theoretical propositions. In comparing societies we seek to uncover similarities or reveal and sharpen our perception of differences. Invariably there is some theory behind a comparison and points to prove. The present undertaking is no exception.

In the present intellectual and political atmosphere of the United States it would have been following the path of least resistance to organize the evidence and argument of this book around the theme of increasing similarities between the two societies—around some variety of the theory of *convergence*.[3] The assurance that both our virtues and vices are rapidly spreading among the nations of the world holds much fascination for many Americans and they have been truly generous in their willingness to share both of them with an often unwilling world. The American mass media have, for some time, been filled with reports suggesting growing similarities between the United States and the Soviet Union. Characteristically such reports emphasize that the Russians are "coming around" to American tastes, fashions, and ways of doing things, they are discovering the profit motive, principles of capitalist business management, the advantages of cars, supermarkets, washing machines, miniskirts, air pollution, and other blessings of the contemporary American way of life.* Forerunners of this outlook appeared as early as the 1930's in such films as *Ninotchka* which provided the Hollywood version of some of the main propositions of the convergence theory. *Ninotchka* related the decline of the ideological commitment of a solid Soviet commissar (played by Greta Garbo), and some of her fellow functionaries assailed and overwhelmed by the material and emotional temptations of the West in Paris. Then as now it was a firmly held American belief that exposure to a high standard of living brings an erosion of political militancy and ideological rigidity, that under every austere communist functionary lurks the pleasantly corruptible opportunist ready to embrace the soft life, and finally, that simple human sentiments triumph over political bar-

* An excellent example of this outlook was provided by the special section of *Life* magazine devoted to the 50th anniversary of the October Revolution (November 10, 1967) which included references to Russian youth as "swinging, critical, cocky" and also "gay, uninhibited, hip," among other manifestations of the American (or universal) tendency to find in the unfamiliar setting that which is familiar.

riers, proving that people are basically the same all over the world.*

Similar underlying dispositions feed, at a more sophisticated level, into the convergence theory, which has supporters among liberal intellectuals (including some social scientists), politicians, and journalists. Its appeal lies in its theoretical sweep, simplicity, and optimistic message.[5] However, the term "convergence" is no longer favored, not even by those who uphold the thesis it denotes, because of its association with an oversimplified economic determinism and also because events have failed so far to bear out the predictions of the theory. The theory arose in part as an over-reaction to the changes that had taken place in Soviet society in the recent years—in particular the decline of mass terror and improvements in the standard of living—and acquired plausibility as these changes were translated into inexorable trends.

The inclination to accentuate the similarities between the two societies is also strengthened by the fact that many Americans have become tired of the cold war, which is to a large extent rooted in the clash of differences. If one accepts the notion that the United States and the Soviet Union are becoming increasingly similar, the specter of cold war pales and political differences earlier viewed as irreconcilable appear soluble.

Whatever its appeals, the theme of convergence will not figure prominently in this book. This may complicate our task at a time when no new and persuasive models or theories are readily available, and when many of the designations used in the past to set the two societies apart—for example, democratic versus totalitarian, capitalist versus socialist, pluralistic versus monolithic—have been found unsatisfactory. Thus we are today at a somewhat uncomfortable juncture: although the old models and conceptions of the two societies (and the USSR in particular) remain valid in part, they insufficiently accommodate all the facts, while new models of similar scope have not yet arisen.[6] This state of affairs in scholarship is an

---

* Reminiscing about the years 1929-30, a British journalist, Claude Cockburn, recalled that ". . . Wall Street men . . . looked upon the USSR with a minimum of alarm, as in effect just another fast developing area with a big trade potential . . . there was something undeniably irksome in the American evaluation of the situation—as though the Revolution and the doctrines of Marxism-Leninism were puerile incidents, temporary deviations from the ultimate forward movement of the world alongside business-like American lines."[4]

appropriate reflection of the nature and degree of change in Soviet society during the past decade.

The task of comparing the two societies is further complicated by the fact that we do not have at our disposal equal amounts of information about them. Much more information is available about the United States than about the Soviet Union. This problem has for a long time confronted every student of Soviet society. There are at least three types of limitations on information about Soviet society. One is the limitation of Soviet statistics; there are no published figures on crime (on a national basis), or alcoholism, suicides, the prison population, and many other statistics which are available for the United States. The second is the limited coverage of Soviet sociological studies, attitude surveys, and public opinion polls, which are also often unreliable in their sampling and burdened by the close association between data-gatherers and the officialdom. It is, for example, quite unlikely that Soviet citizens would feel free to discuss their political attitudes with an interviewer representing or closely associated with a government agency, even if such surveys were undertaken. Thirdly, no outside observers are allowed to do field research or to study empirically any aspect of contemporary Soviet society. Correspondingly, access to archives and official documents remains severely restricted. It should be noted, however, that on the whole the situation has substantially improved since the reign of Stalin, when no sociological inquiries whatsoever were allowed, when the number and freedom of movement of visitors from abroad was sharply curtailed and when the freedom of expression of Soviet citizens was totally stifled.

Today another problem, in addition to that of unreliable and spotty information, confronts the student of Soviet society. This is the difficulty of maintaining a good grasp of the changes (mostly non-political) that have taken place since the death of Stalin and the removal of Khrushchev. Sometimes it appears that we know more of certain aspects of Soviet society under Stalin than of the more recent past and the present. There are several reasons for this. One is simply that the accumulation of historical knowledge takes time. Another is that Stalin's Russia, assisted by the German occupation and the breakdown of controls during World War II, "produced" more refugees than recent regimes. It was these refugees who provided much of the data and the fundamentals for our thinking about life in the Soviet Union in the 1930's and '40's and even the early '50's. These former Soviet citizens made it possible for the few western sociologists interested in Soviet society to conduct large-scale interviews they could not have carried out within the USSR itself. Unfortunately, but not surprisingly, there have been no comparably systematic, comprehensive, and informative studies of Soviet society since the Harvard Project which used the information obtained from these former Soviet citizens.[7]

We also know more today about many aspects of the Stalin period because revelations about it have become semi-legitimate in the Soviet Union. Thus a number of important Soviet writers, politicians, and retired military officers have testified about the bygone era in a manner in which it is not possible to deal with the present.[8]

The study of Soviet society under Stalin was also facilitated by a widely accepted theoretical framework. Most studies of Soviet society (including the Harvard Project) and its political, economic, and cultural institutions were based on the concept of totalitarianism.[9] Today there is far less agreement on the most fruitful theoretical approach to Soviet society, which has changed sufficiently in recent years to raise doubts about the applicability of the totalitarian model but not enough to justify casting it out completely.

Of course the problem of change is not peculiar to the USSR. Both Soviet and American societies are dynamic, making it difficult to capture their enduring qualities. Yet this is precisely the task which must be attempted. Since this is not an historical study we cannot afford to compare the various stages of development of the United States with those of the USSR. What we are interested in are *contemporary* American and Soviet societies and the institutions peculiar to each. Our goal is to analyze their more durable and most characteristic social institutions and practices. This does not mean that we ignore change. Yet the focus will be on the most persistent features. For example, we shall not be concerned with the fluctuations in the organizational structure of the Soviet Communist Party but with the overall role of the party in Soviet political and social life. Thus we shall emphasize the sociological and social-psychological significance of the fact that there is *a* party, whereas in the United States there is no such single party nor any other political entity similar to the Communist Party of the Soviet Union.

Although attention will be focused on the contemporary scene, to the extent that its understanding necessitates knowledge of antecedent events and developments, we shall move back into the past. For instance, we must know about Stalinism in order to comprehend present-day Soviet society and the extent to which it has become de-Stalinized.

In addition to the methodological problems noted we must also be aware of two predispositions which can endanger such a comparative undertaking, especially when one of the societies is familiar and the other much less so. The first temptation is to attribute radical differences to the unfamiliar society, to perceive it as a unique, exotic environment to which few of the expectations relevant to one's own society apply. The other temptation is of a more sophisticated and basically different kind, and theoretically minded sociologists are perhaps more prone to it than any other group. This is the reluctance to entertain the possibility of truly sharp differences between various societies, sometimes combined with the propensity to project the features of the known social environment to the less known or unknown. Why are some sociologists, in contrast to anthropologists, or historians, more susceptible to the temptation to view alien societies in terms of their own? Sociologists, and particularly those among them sensitive to the principles of the functional requirements of social existence, are looking for theoretical generalizations. They are, in varying degrees, professionally committed to discovering similarities between any two societies—industrial or otherwise.* They can claim more theoretical sophistication as they discover more similarities at the most unexpected places, between the most disparate social systems. While most sociologists have probably given up the search for infallible laws of the Comtean type, the quest for ever-present functional regularities continues. It is, and perhaps rightly so, a measure of analytical insight to point out that seemingly diverse customs, institutions, and social practices are only manifestly different variations of essentially similar functions, or functionally equivalent responses to the requirements of different

---

* But of course industrial societies are especially tempting targets. Why this should be so is not quite clear since nobody has suggested that all tribal or feudal or agrarian societies had converged on one another, or that all traditional societies were alike. As Bendix observed: "The industrial societies of today retain aspects of their traditional social structure that have been combined with economic development in various ways. . . . The idea of tradition and modernity as mutually exclusive is simply false. . . . Modern industrial societies retain their several, divergent traditions."[10]

social systems. The vast number of seemingly trivial empirical studies notwithstanding, sociology by its very nature has a built-in preference for focusing upon the general rather than the unique. The latter is more the domain of history than of sociology.[11]

What then can be said about our interest in what is unique to American and Soviet society respectively—an interest we maintain along with the interest in their similarities? The most obvious point to make is that even the theoretically minded sociologist must be interested in those regularities and recurrent features of human interaction (and their structural, institutional results) that are peculiar to one society. Understanding one society and perceiving the differences between it and others is an essential stepping-stone to broader generalizations. It is as necessary to explore the varieties of social organizations as their uniformities.

At the same time it must be noted that, as techniques of communication and physical mobility develop, it is becoming more difficult to conceive of uniquely distinctive or autonomous societies. As is frequently noted, in this century different societies are becoming more and more involved with each other. Yet divergent lines of historical development and the effects of different physical environments do not vanish in a few decades, however rapidly contemporary technology is diffused and however extensive the network of communications.[12] Moreover, the spectacular development of the means of communications and transportation has been accompanied by the development of powerful countertechniques to control and thwart communications and to prevent the movement of people.* Thus, despite the miracles of modern communications we know, for example, little more about life in Tibet, or Sinkiang, or the rural parts of South Africa, or even Albania than was known half a century ago (and, needless to say, the inhabitants of these areas know even less about life in the United States than we know about them). Censorship, jamming, centralization, and monopolization of the means of communication effectively restrict the free circulation of ideas; and there are ingenious systems—sometimes called iron curtains—to prevent the free movement of people. We live in an age when satellites orbit the earth and jet planes carry (some) people to almost any corner of the world, while others are prevented from movement,

* George Orwell was one of the few who realized this as early as 1944 and who resisted the false visions of a world united by benevolent technology.[13]

sometimes even into the next village, by administrative restrictions, police controls, barbed wire, watchtowers, and mines. The free flow of communications and the free movement of people need more than technical implements: they also require political-institutional facilitation or simply freedom.

The decline of the cold war, as much as its rise has provided motives for reassessing the differences and similarities between the two societies. Fearful of the possibility of a violent resolution of the strain between them, we plead for a better understanding of what they have in common, for the defeat of hostile stereotypes, for the triumph of reason over emotion. By attempting to compare the two societies as dispassionately as we can, we may conclude that neither is quite as vicious or unjust as propagandists proclaim.

Yet the decline of the passions of the cold war also endangers the reasoned perception of the differences between the two countries. This is more of a threat to American than to Soviet people. Americans sometimes seem to hold the view that the corollary of friendliness is identity, or at least similarity.* Hence the belief that there will be no significant improvements in international relations until we realize that Soviet people are "just like us."†

Notwithstanding the improvements in their relations, the United

---

* Geoffrey Gorer's comments on this subject are highly relevant here: "Apparently to persuade Americans that war between their country and the USSR would be disastrous, many 'liberals' feel it to be necessary to paint a completely unrealistic picture of Russian society as practically identical with that of America, except for a few technological developments; to admit that Soviet society is markedly different in form and in values from American society is wilfully to imperil the peace. . . . For the internationalists . . . the 'one-ness' of the world is a universal Americanism."14

† An organization devoted to promoting face to face meetings between Russians and Americans (The Citizens Exchange Corps, in New York) ran advertisements which asked: "Do the Russians have horns?" implying perhaps humorously that such drastic misconceptions prevail and are at the root of tension between the two nations. It is hardly surprising that for those who intially assume Russians to be totally different, the shock of discovering that this is not the case often results in the conversion to the opposite viewpoint, namely that the Russians are exactly like us. The same initial, subconscious assumption of total differences between Russians and Americans was behind the advertisement of a television program designed to convince the viewer that this was *not* the case: "Can the Russian keep up with the Joneses? Do you picture the typical Russian citizen as a servant of the state, toiling in a drab collective vineyard? Look again. He lives in a comfortable apartment. His wife enjoys a day at the stadium or an afternoon of boating [Apparently it was felt that this would be a revelation to Americans— P. H.]. Tonight you get a candid view of 'Ivan Ivanovich' as ABC News takes you on a visit with a typical Russian family."15

States and the USSR remain in highly competitive positions.[16] They are competing for political and military power, prestige, scientific achievements, and influence in diverse parts of the world. They are even competing in some measure for the loyalty of their own peoples; they are trying to persuade one another's population about the advantages and virtues of their respective social systems. They are also vying for influence among the so-called uncommitted nations, eager to convince them that the American or Soviet way of life is superior and offers the most appropriate model for changing and modernizing their societies. For many years Soviet leaders have proclaimed that they consider themselves engaged in economic and cultural competition with the United States. Reluctantly and slowly the United States accepted the challenge. Thus during the last fifteen years comparisons of our technological, scientific, and military achievements, economic gains (or losses), and systems of education with Soviet ones have become widespread. Such comparisons affect our perception of our foreign and even domestic policies.

American Perceptions of the USSR and the Cold War

American perceptions of the Soviet Union are inseparably linked to the fluctuations of the cold war and to the American attitudes toward it. The intensification of the cold war tends to be paralleled by a more negative attitude toward the Soviet Union, just as its thaw is followed by a more favorable one. Less self-evidently, even the internal structure and domestic institutions of Soviet society are appraised according to the current state of the cold war. Three major phases might be discerned. There was World War II and its immediate aftermath, a time of unquestioning friendliness brought about by the antinazi alliance. Not much was generally known about the Soviet Union except that the Soviet people suffered and fought heroically in World War II. In 1945 enthusiasm and comradeship were still dominant. Critical analyses of Soviet society or politics were scarce. The euphoria of wartime cooperation played a part in extravagantly optimistic appraisals of the relationship and the similarities between the two societies.[17] This period of ignorance and uncritical admiration soon gave way to the cold war. The "classical" cold war years were those between 1946 and 1953, when Soviet aggressiveness and expansionism were most clearly revealed, particularly by the establishment of the Eastern European satellite states and the Korean War. Those were the years of unmitigated hostility and McCarthyism. Yet it was in this period that some of the best American works on Soviet society were written.[18] After Stalin's death and the emergence of the Sino-Soviet conflict came a gradual revision of American conceptions of the cold war, by both policy makers and the American people at large and pre-eminently among intellectuals. Interestingly enough, belief in the decline of the cold war was based primarily on domestic changes in the Soviet Union.[19] Stalin's death, followed by the official Soviet rejection of many of his policies, the decrease of coercion, greater emphasis on improving the standard of living, more contacts with the outside world, and the Soviet affirmation of peaceful coexistence with the United States (justified by the mutual possession of nuclear weapons) were the major factors leading to the conclusion that aggressive Soviet intentions in international politics had waned.

More recently a new and, one might truly say, *radically* revised view of the cold war has emerged in the United States. It has found a ready, indeed enthusiastic, acceptance among some segments of the intellectual-academic community. This new interpretation increasingly shifts the responsibility for the cold war to the United States —an interpretation that inadvertently coincides with the long-standing official Soviet position. Much of the currently fashionable cold war revisionism has been tied, both chronologically and psychologically, to the Vietnam War and the alienation it has inspired or confirmed. The revisionists simply cannot believe that if American foreign policy was wrong (criminal, bankrupt, or irresponsible) in regard to Vietnam, it could have been otherwise in different historical situations, especially if communism was at issue. Moreover, they prefer to view the American involvement in Vietnam as "fitting into a pattern"—something determined rather than accidental. This being the case, it is imperative to find parallels, other instances of wrongheadedness (or worse) in American foreign policy.

The major thrust of the revisionist argument is that the cold war has no sound basis growing out of genuine, unavoidable conflicts of interest between the two societies. On the contrary, it is the creation of various vested interest groups (American, that is), and it results from a distorted vision of the world. In this perspective the cold war has grown out of a myth, a hysteria, or the alleged American tendency to dichotomize the world into forces of good and evil.[20] There are, of course, many shades and emphases of the argument, and divergent views as to which aspect of American society is primarily to be blamed.

The Soviet position on the origins of the cold war is similar to the revisionist, except that it denies *any* Soviet responsibility or contribution, whereas the revisionists do not hold the USSR *totally* blameless. At the most exoteric, popular level (and particularly in communications directed outside the USSR) it is maintained that the only obstacle to peaceful coexistence is American aggressiveness, the expansionism of the ruling circles, the greed of capitalism, the hysterical (and by implication, unjustified) apprehensions about Soviet policies. At the more esoteric level Soviet ideologues will not deny that there is an authentic conflict between the two social systems rooted in their different political, economic, and ideological structure which disposes them to mutual hostility and friction. In this perspective true reconciliation between the socialist and capitalist systems is barred by the ironclad logic of historical laws.

Those Americans blaming the United States for the outbreak (or prolongation) of the cold war rest their case on two types of propositions: economic-political and ideological-characterological.

Among the first type we find assertions to the effect that the cold war is good for business; the United States being dominated by the military-industrial complex (or the power elite), welcomes the international tensions resulting from the cold war since they help to justify huge military expenditures. It is also asserted that the cold war is a useful device for the ruling classes to divert attention from unsolved domestic social problems by conjuring up false external threats.[21] Another variant is that the American political establishment needs unifying ideologies and myths; anticommunism and its derivative, the cold war, fits the bill by creating a negative consensus.

Secondly, it is often alleged that Americans, and especially the ruling elites, are basically aggressive, militant, and determined to spread the American way of life. Furthermore, Americans are full of crusading zeal and convinced of the superiority of their society over others—a proposition that seems less and less plausible by the beginning of the 1970's. Among these characterological explanations we also encounter the proposition that Americans are prone to neurotic defensiveness and thus are apt to overinterpret everything as threatening.*

We shall not, at this stage, attempt a detailed refutation of these points. Some of them can be neither proven nor disproven, others have some truth to them, still others are obviously wrong. Their major weakness is that in accounting for the origins of the cold war, they do not take sufficient notice of the nature of Soviet foreign policy and ideology in postwar Europe and elsewhere.

In the current, more relaxed state of the cold war† (that is, in comparison with the late 40's, early 50's, or the time of the Cuban missile crisis in 1962) a much discussed American political attitude has also begun to reassert itself—at any rate in relation to the Soviet Union. We refer to pragmatism and the related reluctance to perceive or acknowledge the reality of ideological commitments and their role in political conflict. Skepticism about the importance of ideology as a determinant of Soviet political conduct is most noticeable among the more educated segments of the American public. On the other hand, the belief in the importance of ideology, usually couched in unsophisticated terms, is primarily a preserve of the more fanatical and less educated, since such belief provides a con-

---

* Erich Fromm is among those who try to explain anticommunism on the basis of the flaws of American society *and* personality.[22] Dismissing anticommunism as a neurotic, hysterical, or obsessional attitude comes most easily to those who are convinced of the fundamentally corrupt nature of American society, and who, therefore, identify anticommunism with the personal and social malaise inherent in American life. For example, Edgar Friedenberg believes that "People in this country certainly fear and hate what they learned to respond to as Communists. . . . It seems to threaten their claim to status, for example. . . . This threat of communism—it implies loss of virility, a loss of individual identity as defined by achieved status in a competitive society. . . ."[23] In other words, Friedenberg (as many other intellectuals) scorns the idea that communism might be a threat *because* it is the neurotic, competitive, status-anxious Americans who define it as such. This attitude naturally precludes the examination of any evidence that might confirm the alleged delusion. It also explains the often astonishing ignorance of many so-called liberals of the thoroughly illiberal institutions and practices of various communist regimes. Thus a proper understanding of communism remains at best a matter of indifference to many liberal intellectuals in America, who tend to assign the whole topic to paranoid and/or status-anxiety ridden right-wingers, Pentagon generals, fundamentalist preachers and other disreputable groups. (A smaller group has actually succeeded in reactivating their youthful commitments to communism of some sort, with the help of the Vietnam War and the doubts and deprecation of American society it has inspired.)

† Despite the war in Vietnam, American-Soviet relations have not deteriorated significantly; areas of cooperation have been preserved and in some instances enlarged as exemplified by President Nixon's visit to Moscow in 1972.

venient focus for the attribution of boundless malevolence to the enemy. It is easier to explain what is seen as a total, relentless effort for world domination and the spread of the Soviet system, on the basis of evil doctrines, such as the ideas of "atheistic communism" than on any other grounds.

Those taking a milder view of the Soviet system and the intentions of its leaders prefer to question the seriousness of ideology, which they view as a façade or rationalization. They explain Soviet behavior in terms of national interest, balance of power, and traditional political, historical, geographical, or economic objectives; these are more conventional and more easily understood as well as less threatening. We will discuss some of the factors that influence American perceptions of the Soviet Union, particularly among intellectuals. This is a difficult area about which to generalize since there is a good deal of diversity, though probably less than generally assumed.

Among the factors which influence the perception of Soviet society* by American intellectuals, none is more important than the fear of being identified with the reactionary right-wing movements and their spokesmen, who are obsessed by communism. This fear explains, in part, that, although "fellow traveling" has long been unfashionable, the predominant attitudes among intellectuals toward the Soviet Union range from benevolent neutrality to noncommittal detachment or mild distaste. For the liberal intellectual a strongly critical stand toward Soviet society (and more generally toward matters concerning communism, domestic or foreign) poses the painful dilemma of joining the ranks of the John Birch Society, Texas oil millionaires, white supremacists, the Ku Klux Klan, fundamentalist crackpots—the whole array of groups who have made anticommunism their main preserve and preoccupation. Numerous liberal intellectuals have taken strong anti-Soviet stands, but by and large this attitude does not come easily and naturally to many of them,[24] for it has been tainted by indelible association with figures like Robert Welch, the late Senator Joseph McCarthy, Governor George Wallace—figures with whom they understandably enough wish to avoid any association.†

---

* This also applies to the judgements made of other Communist countries, whether they are in the Soviet or Chinese sphere of influence.

† Diana Trilling observed: ". . . for so many Western intellectuals political probity

More favorable attitudes toward the Soviet Union have also been gaining ground in the last decade as a result of the split between the apparently more moderate Soviet and the seemingly more militant Chinese factions. (This development however did much to discredit the USSR among more radical leftists.) In the light of the comparison with China, but also because of internal change, the USSR came to be viewed as less threatening and more rational. The American involvement in Vietnam also enhanced the image of Soviet moderation since the Soviet Union, unlike the United States, did not resort to sending troops in support of its protégé, limiting herself to the shipment of weapons and other essential supplies. Many intellectuals, in proportion to their growing alienation from American foreign policy in Southeast Asia, have been taking a more skeptical attitude toward the threat of communism in general, and, by extension, toward the threat represented by the Soviet Union. Moreover, the Vietnam War has contributed to a merciless re-examination of American society and polity,* and, as noted above, to a re-evaluation of past American policies to fit the present mood. It has become by no means unusual among intellectuals to discover the roots of the current American intervention in Vietnam in a long-standing "characteristic" American attitude of pugnaciousness, naïveté, misguided idealism, and self-righteousness.[27] Not surprisingly, those Americans who devalue American institutions and policies cannot be totally unsympathetic to the foreign critics of the same policies and institutions. And the more impassioned the domestic critic the more difficult he finds it to avoid feeling some affinity with those who second his views from abroad, no matter how alien those voices might be to him on issues other than the critique of American society.

All this raises the broader question of the relationship between the intellectuals' role as critics of their own society and their attitude

---

rests essentially in demonstrating one's anxiety about the threat from the Right; the abrogation of human rights under the dictatorship of the Left is allowed to disappear in a generalised disapprobation of Communism; or, another way to put it is that the threat of armed conflict between the democracies and the Soviet Union overrides the principled opposition to Communist totalitarianism, which, for the sake of convenience, as it were, is presumed to exist in a different moral context. . . ."[25]

* As Susan Sontag put it: "Beyond isolated private disenchantment or despair over America's betrayal of its ideals, Vietnam offered the key to a systematic criticism of America."[26]

toward other societies. Often it seems that the combination of domestic social criticism with a critical stand toward the shortcomings
of other societies is difficult, if not impossible. The reasons are fairly
clear. First, American intellectuals know the defects of their own
society best. Second, they feel more responsible for correcting social
injustices in their own country than elsewhere. They may also feel
that while their efforts have limited effect at home, they are totally
incapable of influencing the course of events in other societies.
(There are, of course, occasional exceptions when a spectacular atroc-
ity or threat arouses intellectuals to join international protests. Most
typically these are incidents involving the mistreatment of other
well-known intellectuals abroad.)

A critical stance toward other societies, including the Soviet
Union, is often also blocked by a fear that seems to haunt American
intellectuals more than those of other countries, namely the fear
of self-righteousness. It is almost as if only a position of perfect moral
rectitude and domestic harmony would make the criticism of others
justifiable.* How can we rebuke Soviet leaders for, let us say, stifling
the freedom of expression as long as our cities are full of festering
slums and Negroes are treated as second-class citizens? How can we
reproach the Soviets for withholding, for instance, the right to travel
abroad from its citizens as long as we fail to provide adequate medical care for our poor? Such questions have a compelling emotional
force even if the issues at hand are totally unrelated, insofar as racial
discrimination or poor medical care will not cancel out totalitarian
restrictions on free speech or travel.

In particular, many American intellectuals are inhibited in their
criticism of Soviet society by the fact that its spokesmen tirelessly
condemn the same defects of American society they are also sharply
critical of: racial prejudice and discrimination, unemployment,
commercialism, the banality of the mass media, defects of the educational system, and many others. Such a convergence of critical

---

* A similar point was made by Arthur Koestler.28 This attitude, the fear of self-
righteousness, leads to what might be called an "inverse double standard." Those with a
heightened sense of criticism of their own (American) society seem to feel that they
cannot apply the same standards to other societies. This is justified by suggesting that
the defects of other countries are taken for granted, whereas they expect more from
America. Actually, those arguing in this vein tend to expect *less* from American society,
which they reject with passion and bitterness, reserving their capacity for moral indignation for *her* faults alone.29

views cannot but blunt the perception of the defects of the Soviet system, which in any event appear irrelevant for those whose primary concern lies with their own society. It should be stressed that the fear of self-righteousness, "giving the benefit of the doubt," and even benevolent neutrality do not resemble attitudes widespread among American intellectuals in the 1930's and early 1940's. The contemporary posture is different both in style and substance. What we encounter today is at best (or at worst, depending on one's viewpoint) a reserved sympathy toward the Soviet Union rather than the boundless admiration of the old-fashioned fellow traveler. Unrestrained fellow traveling is almost as discredited today as "hard-line" anticommunism or "red baiting." If any Communist power commands the admiration of the most alienated intellectuals or of aspiring revolutionaries, it is not the Soviet Union but mainland China, Cuba, or North Vietnam. In the eyes of many extreme left-wing intellectuals the Soviet Union has become an established bureaucratic, postrevolutionary society unduly concerned with things material, avoidance of world war, and accommodation with the United States. Even when pro-Soviet sympathies linger on, strong emotional response is evoked by the feats of more active and authentic revolutionary movements, governments, and situations: Latin American guerrillas, the Vietcong, Castro's Cuba, the Chinese "cultural revolution," and some of the picturesque radical regimes of the Third World.* The comment made by H. Stuart Hughes about Jean-Paul Sartre is applicable to these American intellectuals: "Like Lenin before him, Sartre discovered the underdeveloped world when he needed it most to buttress a faith that seemed increasingly inapplicable to European conditions."[30] Pro-Soviet sentiment in the United States today is diluted and caught in the crossfire of old disappointments and new loyalties even on the part of those who are most prone to such attitudes. Revolutionary romanticism can no longer conveniently focus on what used to be called the "socialist motherland."

It would both simplify explanations and confirm one's sense of objectivity if one could suggest that distorted perceptions, Ameri-

---

* Evidently it is very difficult for most people to reject their own society without idealizing another. And the less known a society the easier it is to idealize it, to impose expectations and hopes on it. Fellow traveling resembles romantic love which is also enhanced by distance, ignorance, illusions, and unattainability of the object.

can and Soviet, complement one another like mirror images.[31] However, except for a few similarities, such as the attribution of aggressive intent (at the high, political rather than the popular, or personal level), the forms and sources of distortions are as different as the amount and kind of misinformation that generally prevail in the two societies. Insofar as the mass media are the major source of information about foreign lands in both countries, many of the distorted perceptions can be traced to them.

The Soviet mass media are part of the political apparatus and thus instruments of its purposes. Even allowing for the fact that the mass media in the United States are not overwhelmingly friendly toward the USSR, they cannot be characterized—at least during recent years—as carrying out a systematic campaign of misinformation or criticism of the Soviet Union. It is of course more difficult to generalize about the content of the American mass media than about the Soviet, since the former are relatively heterogeneous while the latter are among the most monolithic of Soviet institutions. In general the political content of the American mass media is a mere fraction of that of the Soviet. And finally it must be pointed out that the importance attributed to ideas and ideological indoctrination in the Soviet Union is unmatched in the United States. Consequently, misrepresentations of American life are far more systematic, deliberate, and comprehensive than the other way around.

Although they are not as neatly separated in time as the historian or sociologist might wish, a set of American perceptions and stereotypes typical of the cold war period and another of the post-Stalin period may be distinguished. The characteristic cold war perceptions stressed relentless Soviet hostility growing out of a political system determined to expand its influence by open conquest or camouflaged subversion. Domestically, Soviet society was seen as terroristic, ruled by a small group of autocrats (subordinated in turn to a ruthless dictator, Stalin), indifferent to the needs of its people living in abject poverty. At a more primitive level, the Soviet people themselves were sometimes viewed as dedicated, fanatical Communists, a strange, incomprehensible, godless breed totally different from Americans. These perceptions lost their preeminence and grasp on American imagination although they survive, more or less intact, among many right-wing conservative elements of the population.

In recent years, and particularly in the last decade, there has been a greater fragmentation of opinion about the Soviet Union. On the whole the pendulum has swung away from the cold war stereotypes. Few Americans would maintain today that the Soviet Union is a poor, backward nation whose citizens are totally different from Americans. On the contrary, the Soviet Union is often presented (in the mass media) and seen by many, as a country of growing affluence and goodwill. For some of the left-wing critics of American society the superiority of Soviet accomplishments is a natural complement to their rejection of American institutions. In their perspective, Soviet society is more efficient, less wasteful of talent and resources and, above all, more "responsible" in taking care of the material needs of its members. They are particularly impressed by Soviet progress in industry, science, and education. The appeal of the latter persists even among those who no longer cherish an image of Soviet society as the embodiment of social justice. For others the differences between the two societies seem to be diminishing at a rate much more rapid than factual information, well-grounded social theory, or even intelligent speculation would warrant. Sometimes it appears as if Khrushchev had been more successful in persuading Americans than his own people of the imminence of the Soviet Union's "catching up" with American society. For Khrushchev and his successors (as well as for his predecessor, for that matter), "catching up" had a singularly limited meaning.[32] It referred to the growth of production and the corresponding improvement in the standard of living. However, quite different and even conflicting interpretations can be attached to catching up. From the American standpoint the prospect is desirable (except in relation to military matters) as long as it refers to the attainment of high levels of material prosperity accompanied by political maturity and a settled, healthy hedonism which distracts from belligerence and hostility. From the Soviet standpoint, while catching up also entails the attainment of American standards of living, technology and efficiency, the political implications are not necessarily peaceful. At one extreme they entail the famous Khrushchevian "burial" of American power, influence, and social order in an unspecified, though far from friendly, manner. In a less threatening form it implies the improved ability of the Soviet Union to challenge the United States in all the varied arenas of "peaceful coexistence." However, for more optimistic (or naïve) Americans catching up has come to represent the attainment of American social values and even political arrangements. Without knowing it, many Americans are orthodox if inarticulate economic determinists who, not unlike old school Marxists, believe that the economic basis shapes the political superstructures. If their own society, industrially advanced and rich, produced democratic institutions, surely, as other societies improve their economies, they must also develop similar institutions.

During the last decade there has been a general decline of political criticism of Soviet society in the U.S. except for the protests over discrimination against Jews and imprisoned intellectuals. This decline is in part a result of the belief that the democratization of Soviet political life is more or less preordained and largely a matter of time. On the other hand, many Americans have by now taken for granted the loss (or continued absence) of political freedoms as the price paid for rapid Soviet modernization. Moreover, this argument runs, people in such a country have no conception of or interest in civil liberties, which for them remain empty abstractions. What they care for are material satisfactions, improvements in their standard of living. Thus Soviet institutions are appropriate for Soviet conditions, democracy being the privilege of a few lucky countries in the West.

While it might be argued that such ideas are limited to a minority of the educated, most Americans do seem to accept the view, disseminated by the mass media and embraced by foreign policymakers, that the Soviet Union today is less hostile toward the United States than ever before, that it has become a "mature" industrial society providing more freedoms and more material satisfactions to its citizens.

We will try to evaluate these perceptions, partly by implication, in the rest of this book.

Soviet Perceptions of the United States: Official

Significantly, Soviet perceptions of the United States divide into official and unofficial (or popular) perceptions. The existence of clearly defined official images of the United States is in itself among the important differences between the ways the two societies perceive of and relate to each other. In the United States no official, centrally formulated, and exclusively legitimate doctrine on the nature of Soviet society is systematically fed to the population by means of governmentally run mass media. Even insofar as American mass media are critical of the Soviet Union (and they have become much less so in the past decade) the amount of time, space or attention devoted to the systematic and detailed exposure of the defects of Soviet society is a mere fraction of the corresponding Soviet efforts to present a highly and explicitly unfavorable portrait of the United States.[33]

It is also noteworthy that although there is a division between official and popular perceptions of the United States in the Soviet Union, the popular ones tend to be private while the official ones are public. Thus Soviet perceptions of the United States could also be divided into public (official) and private (unofficial). This division accurately reflects the scarcity of legitimate and *publicly voiced* differences of opinion on ideologically sensitive matters.

There has been far greater continuity and stability in official Soviet perceptions of the United States than the other way around, particularly with regard to the level of hostility maintained.* Not even the decline of the cold war and the doctrine of coexistence have brought a fundamental change to the tone and style of the Soviet mass media and official statements concerning the United States. The doctrine of peaceful coexistence has been supplemented by the proposition that there can be no amity and peace in the realm of ideas. There the struggle not only continues but intensifies.[35] This proposition makes possible the continued attribution of relentless hostility to the United States, the leading imperialist power, and justifies the corresponding Soviet response. In particular, it is alleged that the forces of imperialism have substituted ideological subversion for other, more naked and blatant forms of aggression —or rather, added them to their arsenal on a larger scale—which in turn demands militant vigilance on the part of the Soviet Union.

Soviet perceptions of American society at the official level seem

---

* Thus much truth remains in the observation made two decades ago: ". . . in the strange realm of Soviet political mythology America resembles more closely . . . Orwell's 1984 than the country we know. The America in Soviet propaganda is ruled by force and fraud. Its handful of rulers pull the strings to which their subjects dance like puppets. Its domestic policy is one of exploitation and oppression . . . its foreign policy . . . [one of] deception and aggression."[34]

to depend more on ideological premises than on experience.* Naturally we do not know what the political elite, those who define the official viewpoint, really think about the United States.[37] There might be, of course, a difference between their innermost convictions and feelings and their public utterances. Yet their actions and policies tend to suggest a substantial congruence, if not a perfect fit, between public utterance and private belief. Both the official image of and the policies toward the United States are colored by hostility, apprehension, suspicion, and caution. This image is also shaped by an apparent belief that American attitudes, policies, and institutions are historically determined products of an unjust socio-economic system that is doomed in the long run and the demise of which is to be hastened. The belief that American society, whatever its present attractions and comforts, is in an historically determined state of decline, is the cornerstone upon which a whole set of Soviet perceptions of the United States rests. It is this underlying vision which helps to explain and which underlies many specific Soviet perceptions. This perspective in turn is at the root of the most crucial differences between the ways the spokesmen of the two societies look at each other's lands. Few even among those Americans unsympathetic toward the Soviet Union assert with confidence that the Soviet Union is in a state of decline, much as they would wish that to be the case. But, in any event, intense hostility toward the USSR is no longer preponderant in the United States, neither among spokesmen of the government nor among scholarly specialists and journalists. On the contrary each of these three groups has adopted a perspective that is basically optimistic concerning the future of Soviet society. Today the prevailing opinion in the United States is that things are, on the whole, getting better and not worse in the Soviet Union (whatever temporary setbacks there might be), in the spheres of both economic development and personal-political freedoms. Soviet society is typically viewed as becoming more affluent,

* However one interesting pragmatic explanation has also been suggested to account for the outpouring of hostility toward the United States: "A strong residue of Protestant ethics, causes Americans to regard all hostility to them as being at least in some measure brought about by their own faults. . . . It is quite possible to exploit this tendency to self-accusation by setting into motion a steady barrage of hostile actions accompanied by expressions of hatred. The natural reaction of the victims, if they are Americans, can be and often is, bewilderment, followed by guilt. Thus is created an atmosphere conducive to concessions whose purpose is to propitiate the allegedly injured party."[36]

modern, and liberal. Those of its characteristics which have been viewed critically tend to be seen as being in the process of change or modification. Such a perspective is diametrically opposed to the Soviet one on the United States. Adam Ulam, in a discussion of the Western views of the Russian Revolution (and of the social system that emerged from it), points out this fundamental asymmetry of perceptions:

> how unequal are the terms of the dialogue between East and West. Would a Soviet historian or philosopher reciprocate his liberal western colleague's attitude and grant that, whatever its crimes and present deficiencies, capitalism in the last 20 years has shown an amazing power of adjustment and vitality? Or that it is likely to reform itself still further and cease entirely to be an oppressive and hostile force?[38]

There is one significant inconsistency in the Soviet presentation of the United States. It is the result of the conflict between the themes of "catching up with" or "burying" the United States. Popularized by Khrushchev, these obviously conflicting alternatives have been present in Soviet official thinking well before he made them a dominant theme of his political pronouncements. For the Soviet leaders the United States is at once an adversary and a model.[39] Although such an attitude has parallels in the psychology of personal relationships, it hardly enhances consistency in political propaganda and ideological discourse. Yet it can be argued that the Soviet Union merely wants to catch up with the United States in a few areas of productivity and technological efficiency, a desire that implies no imitation or acceptance of the American social order or institutional arrangements. For example, it is sometimes admitted that American food production or computer technology offer some lessons to be learned, as do the techniques of highway construction and the production and distribution of consumer goods. The question of the extent to which high productivity, efficiency and the abundance of consumer goods is linked to the noneconomic, nontechnological aspects of American society is avoided. In effect, the Soviet proponents of catching up are saying that it is possible to transplant selectively certain features of the American social system. But they are also saying implicitly that a basically corrupt and decadent society can nevertheless offer techniques and institutions worthy of emulation. Thus in this compartmentalized vision of the United States technological-organizational superiority has "coexisted" with moral inferiority, with the image of a crisis-ridden society. Indeed crisis has for decades been the watchword in the Soviet appraisals of the United States. In the past the impending (or actual) economic crisis was stressed, more recently the moral-spiritual. This shift has reflected not only a greater sense of realism on the part of Soviet observers but possibly also the ever-increasing attention Soviet ideologues have been paying to ideas as social forces, at the expense of economic processes and institutions.

The major purveyor of the official images of the United States are of course the mass media, which have been relentlessly and ceaselessly disseminating negative conceptions of American society except for the period of wartime alliance. (By contrast, the far more apolitical American mass media regard as their main business the provision of entertainment. Political propaganda is rarely entertaining and the American communications and entertainment industry fears few things more than boring its audiences.)

A principal characteristic of the official Soviet perceptions of American society (fully reflected in the mass media) is the tendency to project upon it characteristics of the Soviet social-political environment. Not surprisingly it is the unappealing features of Soviet society which are projected onto the American, without acknowledgment of the process which may in part be subconscious. Thus time and again Soviet spokesmen credit American society with political conditions which actually exist (though are, of course, officially denied), in the Soviet Union. These include the absence of political choice or alternatives; a high degree of police surveillance and coercion; a politically apathetic and intimidated populace; a highly centralized decisionmaking process; a frantic, ongoing effort on the part of the ruling groups to present a façade of political democracy and popular participation; a closely integrated institutional network harnessed to the service of the political objectives set by a small elite;* the absence of freedom of expression and political organiza-

---

* A curious view of the role of ideology in American politics (obviously patterned after the Soviet experience) was reflected in the observation of a Soviet citizen reported by Lewis Feuer: ". . . when I lectured on 'Contemporary American Thought' [this of course was in the Soviet Union], one questioner asked me about the influence of such Catholic philosohical journals as the *American Ecclesiastical Review*, *New Scholasticism*, and *Thought*. When I replied that their influence was small, he was extremely skeptical,

tion. At the root of these claims is not so much deliberate distortion or malevolence, but a genuine inability to conceive of political systems or arrangements which offer more choice and freedom than do the Soviet ones. In particular Soviet officials appear unable to grasp the nature of political pluralism, or understand its feasibility. For example, Soviet spokesmen find it difficult to believe that, say, a demonstration of American Jews, or former Cuban, Hungarian, or Polish refugees in front of the Soviet embassy or UN mission in New York may take place without the instigation or blessing of the American government. Soviet citizens do not demonstrate in front of the American (or any other) embassy on their own initiative. Similarly an attack on any Soviet policy in the *New York Times* (or in any other major American newspaper) tends to be interpreted as the voice of the State Department or White House, since the notion of an autonomous press is not quite comprehensible in a society that has had no such press for half a century, if not longer. In other words, Soviet spokesmen cannot conceive of any spontaneity in the American political process (except for such events as riots). Their perspectives are colored by the deeply ingrained habits and experiences of the manipulation of the masses and public opinion; they seek, and succeed in discovering, the same in the United States.[41] An example of this process was reported by the historian James Billington, after a prolonged stay in the Soviet Union: "The State Department's earnest attempt to dispel this belief [that President Johnson must have been behind John Kennedy's assassination—P.H.] by translating the report of the Warren Commission into Russian ironically convinced many Russians of Johnson's guilt. They are inclined to assume that lengthy legal arguments by government commissions are always lies. 'Why, the Warren Report is almost as long as the proceedings of our purge trials' one Russian told me."[42]

Soviet visitors and journalists often report on their return from the United States the anxieties and fears of "ordinary Americans" intensely worried about public meetings with Soviet citizens, or about being followed, spied upon, and compromised by such contacts.[43] Such reports accurately reflect the traditional apprehension of "ordinary Soviet citizens" about contacts with foreigners. It must, however, be noted that such anxieties have been on the decline in the

and said that after all President Kennedy was a Catholic, and that consequently, the importance of Catholic ideology must have increased."[40]

last decade, although the Soviet government continues to preach vigilance (mistrust) toward foreigners often alleged to be spies "under the masks of tourism."[44]

Soviet spokesmen also tend to project onto the United States the degree of politicalization of life that prevails in the Soviet Union. They seem to believe that the American people are subjected to a relentless propaganda barrage, that political indoctrination is in high gear, that American universities and the government work hand in hand in devising the latest move in ideological warfare,* that everything the United States government does is carefully planned and calculated for political effect. Tourism is another good example. As a Soviet newspaper article pointed out: ". . . tourism is a means of propagandizing the Soviet way of life." It is a matter of historical record that this has indeed been a Soviet policy and that from its earliest days, the regime has expended enormous efforts to present visitors from abroad with the most carefully selected aspects of Soviet life and to deprive them from seeing others.[46] It is then not surprising that the same Soviet writer claimed that "this writer has seen how the capitalist countries do this. Some of them even build model villas for a dozen working-class families and tourists are brought there from other countries, especially the socialist countries, to see, as they say, how wonderfully their workers live."[47]

In the light of such beliefs it is easy to appreciate the attitudes of a group of Soviet engineers on a tour of the Ford plant in Detroit as related by an American tour guide:

> We . . . passed the huge parking lot [of the plant] filled with cars, when I noticed a wave of excitement. . . . The one who spoke the best English addressed me with a smile: "Do they prepare themselves like this to impress all their visitors? Or is it just for us?" "What do you mean?" I asked. "The impressive number of cars. It's a flattering illustration of Ford's capacity for production." [The guide assured him that the cars belonged to the peo-

* A good example of this somewhat paranoid tendency is found in an article that details the gigantic psychological warfare campaign being launched in the United States to desecrate the 50th anniversary of the October Revolution! Among other things, the article asserted that at Columbia University alone 400 doctoral dissertations were written between 1960 and 1964 on "anti-communist problems." In the same article American specialists on Soviet affairs are described as "probing for spots [in the Soviet system— P. H.] where infections could be introduced."[45]

ple who worked at the plant.] The Russian grinned with irony. "You are kidding," he said, "so many cars?" . . . "Look," I said, "it's easy to check. You ask the first worker in the assembly line whether he owns a car; he'll tell you." The Russian made a sadly cunning grimace. "Of course he will," he said. "We know that old trick. The plant is well prepared for our visit. Every worker has learned by heart how to answer our questions. Unless he wants to be fired or arrested he'll have to give the proper answer." . . . "O.K.," I said, "if you wish, I'll wait with you on the parking lot until the workday is over. You approach people the moment they unlock their cars, and ask them." The Russian looked amused, as if playing with a child. "What do you take me for?" he asked, "an idiot? It's simple to stage such a show. I don't hold Americans for bunglers. If you do something you do it well. You are a big nation and you know how to deal with other nations." . . . "What makes you think they would waste so much energy preparing for your arrival?" "My friend," said the Russian solemnly, "Ford is the pride of America. A nation's pride is a serious matter. We don't blame you for anything when a state's pride is at stake. But please don't take us for fools. . . ." The other Russians nodded earnestly with comprehension and in total agreement.[48]

Even outside the political sphere there is no shortage of projections. For example, Soviet analysts see the American family as the last and perhaps only escape from the pressures (political and economic) of larger society where the individual can withdraw and lick his wounds, so to speak.[49] By coincidence Western observers (as well as many Soviet citizens) have regarded the Soviet family as one of the few apolitical havens of the harassed citizen in Soviet society. It is, of course, quite possible that the family has such properties in both societies.

To sum up: The opinion makers of Soviet society see American society as profoundly lacking in social justice, characterized by enormous inequalities of wealth and a ruthless exploitation of the masses, whether they are aware of it or not. Vast sections of the population, and Negroes in particular, live in abject poverty (the existence of black middle classes is rarely mentioned in this context.) The government (as a rule undifferentiated as to federal, state, or local) is unresponsive to popular needs. Political democracy exists only in the hypocritical rhetoric of the spokesmen for the system; in reality, the decisive inequalities of political power are hidden, often poorly, behind a façade of representative institutions. Political institutions are controlled by the wealthy.[50] Not only economic and political but also personal and social relationships are distorted, dominated, and undermined by pecuniary motives signifying the accelerated erosion of moral standards, also revealed in the proliferation of escape-seeking hedonistic activities.[51] Moral decay and overall decadence are reflected in family instability, crime, juvenile delinquency, sexual perversions, alcoholism, and drug addiction. Life is dehumanized, brutalized; trust, true friendship, emotional warmth, are rarities. People are haunted by a variety of fears, anxieties, and apprehensions: unemployment, a drop in the standard of living, interest payments, fierce competitiveness, the threat of nuclear war (that might be unleashed by their reckless leaders) and the multiplicity of social-political tensions and conflicts.

The American social system is doomed not only because of its social costs but also because of its growing inefficiency, wastefulness and irresponsibility, because of its misuse of human and material-natural resources, its dehumanized science and technology which becomes more and more subordinated to the military machine and the insatiable profit and power hunger of its amoral elite.*

Soviet Perceptions of the United States: Popular

As we noted earlier the unofficial or popular perceptions of the United States are sufficiently distinct from the official to be discussed separately. It is not easy, however, to pinpoint the precise boundary between the two.

It would be tempting to suggest that the Soviet popular perceptions of the United States are diametrically opposed to the official ones, and represent a reaction against them. This is however not the case, as far as the majority of people are concerned. There is a substantial continuity between the official and popular conceptions of the United States. This is as understandable as is the possibility of a reaction formation against the official stand. No people can be systematically bombarded by a steady stream of propaganda with im-

---

* While a few years ago most liberal intellectuals in America would have considered such a critique of America both unfair and propagandistic, today it might be difficult to distinguish it from the rhetoric of the New Left, such has been the sweep of alienation in the late 1960's and early 1970's.

punity over a long period of time, especially when there are few competing channels of information.* After decades of exposure to the official perceptions and stereotypes of American society *all* Soviet perceptions of it are bound to be permeated in some manner by the official viewpoint. The question is: to what degree and in what respects?

Perhaps the closest approximation of the truth is that the popular perceptions represent a distorted mirror image of the official one, unconsciously incorporating its contradictions and ambiguities. This often becomes apparent in private conversations with Soviet citizens and is frequently reported by American travelers and scholars. It is in such conversations that the whole range and depth of the ambivalence toward the United States, more concealed in the official manifestations, becomes apparent.[53]

The material standards of living provide a good example. It is axiomatic that Soviet citizens in conversations with Americans exhibit the most intense, often wistful, curiosity about the material aspects of American life. Westerners, and Americans above all, are bombarded with precise, factual questions about their income, living conditions, their apartment size, the durable goods they possess, and the price of food, clothing, and all the necessities and luxuries of life. While this attitude implies, and often clearly expresses, an undisguised admiration of American affluence, the Soviet interlocutors, sometimes in the same breath, also deplore American materialism.

Although occasionally great wealth is attributed to every American (except Negroes), on the whole Soviet people have a fairly realistic estimate of American living conditions and of the relative ease and comfort of daily life in the United States. Women in particular appreciate the availability of labor-saving devices in the home, the simplicity of shopping, the abundant choice of goods, and the fact that most wives do not have to combine full-time outside employment with the burdens of primitive housework. Unshared apart-

---

* Let alone first hand experience. The number of Soviet citizens who get to see the United States is a mere handful and their trips are rarely, if ever, undertaken on their own initiative. Rather, they visit the United States in various official or quasi-official capacities and are screened with extreme care. As a rule some member(s) of their families are left behind for a good measure. In 1968 115 Soviet citizens came to the United States (in six groups; group travel is also one of the precautionary measures against ideological contamination and defection). By contrast, about 20,000 Americans visited the USSR in the same year.[52]

ments and private houses are pre-eminent among the features of American life which evoke admiration.

Projection is also a characteristic of the popular perceptions. Since a portion of the official information is received with skepticism and since there is not enough solid information with which to fill in the gaps left by the nonacceptance of the official viewpoint, many areas of American life are vague and hazy. Not surprisingly these gaps are filled by transferring the features of the familiar social environment to the unfamiliar. For example, American travelers reported that some Soviet citizens believed that the freedom to travel outside the United States was a privilege rather than a right. Some even expressed surprise on learning that movement *within* the United States was entirely unrestricted. Some Soviet citizens found it difficult to imagine that Americans can get along without internal passports. "But how do you identify yourself?" one asked insistently.[54]

Thorough as Soviet propaganda is, it cannot present detailed accounts of every aspect of American society. Nor would this always be advisable since specific, factual information may work against the negative image that is to be conveyed. Vague accusations and innuendoes are often more helpful. For example, Soviet propaganda insists that there is no freedom of press in the United States, but it is vague about the exact details of the mechanisms of control. In light of this it may not be surprising that some Soviet citizens believe that in the United States the government appoints or removes newspaper editors.[55] This assumption fits well both the official portrayal of the lack of freedom of the American press *and* the Soviet citizen's own knowledge of Soviet society where the government does indeed appoint or remove newspaper editors. Soviet citizens also fill in the gap between the official images of the United States and the unknown details of American life when they inquire about the nature of restrictions imposed on Americans to prevent them from listening to Soviet broadcasts. (The jamming of Western radio broadcasts has been a longstanding Soviet policy; even in those periods when jamming was suspended, Soviet citizens were discouraged from listening by the authorities.)

In general, on subjects other than the standard of living and consumer goods, Soviet popular perceptions of the United States reflect, for the most part, incomprehension and ignorance. Conceptions of American political life are particularly quaint, though perhaps not much more than the "ordinary American's" beliefs of Soviet political life. Popular Soviet perceptions, like the official ones, show the difficulty of grasping the complexities of political and cultural pluralism. The very concept of voluntary association (perhaps even that of voluntarism) is one that creates endless perplexities for Soviet citizens. The same applies to American political opposition and dissent, which are puzzling to the Russians because they are both legitimate and spontaneous.

Not a few Soviet citizens assume that American workers are staunchly opposed to the "system," and that practically the whole populace (and the workers in particular), have been opposed to the war in Vietnam, unleashed by the proverbial ruling circles. Often the extreme right wing is seen as the most powerful sector in American politics since its characteristics and public statements approximate most closely the picture traditionally presented of the reactionary political forces dominating American society. Soviet citizens, less surprisingly, have trouble understanding the separation of church and state, of parties and government, federal and state government, the powerlessness of the federal government in many spheres of life, local autonomy, and the role of trade unions. However, in general these are not subjects which provoke much discussion or curiosity.

The majority of Soviet citizens seem to agree with the official condemnation of "American aggressiveness" (given more credibility in the context of Vietnam), and many seem to believe that the United States is a militaristic nation that may provoke a new world war.

Not surprisingly, Soviet people also disapprove of the spiritual decay and the coldness in human relationships that are supposed to prevail under capitalism—a view which does not square too well with their image of the friendly, informal, good-natured "ordinary American," considered in some ways similar to the correspondingly good-natured Soviet man.

Of course many Soviet intellectuals and scientists have a far more sophisticated view of the United States.[56] They are well aware that the apealing features of American life cannot be reduced to shiny cars, good roads, or comfortable homes. They envy and admire intellectual and personal freedom, especially the freedom of expression and travel. Yet even among the better-informed groups American political, cultural, and value pluralism often goes unnoticed.

All groups of Soviet people think well of Americans as people, "despite" the system under which they live. (American evaluations of Soviet people make similar allowances for the differences between the "Russian people" and their government.)

On the whole Soviet people are much more interested in the United States than Americans are in the Soviet Union. There is something paradoxical about this in the light of the long-standing efforts of the Soviet government to denigrate the United States and to immunize its people against the attractions of the American style of life. It is also interesting to note that while ample information about the Soviet Union is available in the United States (including that which is disseminated by the Soviet government itself), not many Americans, except for some students and specialists, take advantage of this situation. In contrast the paucity of varied and objective information about American society is paralleled by a voracious popular curiosity about all things American.

Popular Soviet perceptions of America, though they embody several of the official stereotypes, are far more favorable than the official ones. Appreciation of the American standard of living, leisure activities, and creature comforts are more impressive than those more abstract features of American life, which are known only through the gloomy accounts of the official media. At the same time some American consumer goods, some output of the mass media, and people exemplifying American values and attitudes do reach the Soviet Union, and they all have a direct and generally favorable impact.

Ambivalence is the dominant theme of both the official and the popular perceptions of the United States. Soviet observers, official and unofficial, fluctuate between feelings of inferiority and superiority. In their eyes the United States is a measure of the failures as well as the accomplishments of Soviet society.

Publicity and the Images of American and Soviet Society

In conclusion, it should also be pointed out that the images of the two societies held by their respective members, while strongly colored by ideology and propaganda, are also influenced by more subtle cultural differences toward publicity and collective self-exposure. As we well know, the United States is an immensely publicity-conscious, publicity-oriented society. A more limited sense of personal privacy (or a greater openness) has its counterpart in the public realm, slanted toward sensationalism and exposure. Much of the indigenous publicity in the United States concerning American society might be described as scandal-minded, or, on a more serious level, problem-oriented. The commercialism of the mass media and their quest for the eye-catching and sensational supply some of the motivation for this. Other motives are provided by a long-standing tradition of social criticism. American society and its domestic analysts and critics do, as a rule, a far better job at exposing its defects than the most venomous foreign critics, including Soviet ones, could.[57] Indeed, a large proportion of Soviet critiques of American society relies on American sources.* By contrast, Soviet society is not publicity-oriented, except in a narrow, "programmed" sense: social criticism is rarely lurid, sensational, or scandal-oriented. These Soviet attitudes can only in part be explained by the traditional Russian political habits of secrecy, reinforced by periods of totalitarian paranoia. There is also a different cultural orientation toward publicity and self-exposure, at any rate on the collective or societal level. Even on the personal level there is a sense of propriety that curtails delving into what is considered impure, indecent, or scandalous. A Russian intellectual, Piotor Dolgorukov, observed bitterly over a hundred years ago:

> Many of our compatriots say: "There is no need to tell the truth about Russia to a foreigner; the sores of the Fatherland should be hidden. . . ." People who want to hide and conceal their sores are like the critically ill who prefer to suffer and die rather than ask the help of a skilled doctor who could cure them. . . . For Russia this doctor is publicity.[60]

These differences affect profoundly the images of the two societies throughout the world. We do not intend to suggest that there is a

---

* Which are, not infrequently, permeated by a breast beating quality. For instance, an advertisement in the *New York Times* proclaimed: ". . . We, the American people—We: affluent, corrupt, dehumanized, brutalized, chauvinistic, racist, white America—who share guilt for U.S. policy and for the atrocities . . ."[58]; a book by Fred J. Cook entitled *The Corrupted Land* was advertised as "A Searing Indictment of America's Social Morality," presumably because that is just what readers were to find appealing, or at least readers of the *New York Times*. A recent arrival from Europe noted that social protest ". . . is a new industry, a new way of making money and accumulating affluence. Three things are necessary to start this business: a pen, a guitar, and a free society as one's professional space. Written protests bring decent livings, vocal protests bring millions. One who knows how effectively to exhibit his social misery and anguish rapidly becomes a millionaire."[59]

dearth of information outside the Soviet Union on the unappealing features of Soviet life. There is, however, a lack of vivid, or detailed information about them. We do not lament the absence of this kind of information; we must, however, observe that it is a gap of particular importance in a comparative assessment of the images of American and Soviet society. Poverty, oppression, urban decay, and rural stagnation, abuses of public office, political dissatisfaction, and social conflicts are not recorded by reporters (foreign or domestic) in the Soviet Union; nor are they depicted in photographs, films, or television tapes. Whatever may or may not be wrong with Soviet society, whatever disturbs the Soviet citizen and the various groups in his society is not conveyed to worldwide (or domestic) audiences as is the case with the ills of American society. This factor helps to explain not only certain Soviet perceptions of American society, but also in part the worldwide phenomenon of anti-Americanism, coupled with a comparatively mild or neutral position toward Soviet society, even though it is easy to find as many grounds for criticism and moral indignation in relation to the Soviet Union as to the United States. The highly unfavorable self-images disseminated by the American mass media may also account for the paradox pointed out by Jacques Barzun: "As a nation whose citizens seek popularity more than any other kind of success it is galling (and inexplicable) that we, the United States, are so extensively unpopular."[61]

Ideas are weapons, as generations of Soviet leaders have believed. The control of mass media and publicity is more than an irrational reflex of a sensitive political system. In the final analysis, the finer points of the freedom of expression and criticism score less than visible portraits of misery, injustice, and despair. The different degrees of free publicity in the two societies exercise a powerful influence on their images, both within and without.

2. Political Institutions and Practices

Nothing sets the United States and the Soviet Union apart more clearly than their political institutions and practices. Here basic differences are revealed both by cursory observation and detailed analysis. The two political systems may be contrasted, with various degrees of precision, in terms of pluralistic versus totalitarian, democratic versus authoritarian, permissive versus rigid, chaotic versus overorganized, two-party system versus one-party system, electoral rule versus pseudoelections, constitutional government versus the dictatorship of the proletariat.* Distinctions of this kind can convey only a fragment of complicated political realities and institutional arrangements. If we were pressed to summarize the principal differences between the two political systems we would favor calling the American imperfectly pluralistic and the Soviet imperfectly totalitarian.

It can also be argued that the political differences between the two societies are not as sharply defined as any of these dichotomies

* The concept of mass society, is sometimes loosely applied to both the U.S. and the U.S.S.R. However, each of our two societies satisfy only one of the most widely used definitions of mass society: in the United States "elites are readily available to influence by non-elites" (while Soviet elites are certainly not), whereas the "non-elites in Soviet society are readily available for mobilization by elites" (which is not the case in the United States).[1]

suggest. After all in every society coercion is the business of government, power is always concentrated in relatively few hands, and people everywhere are restricted by their political-institutional environment. It could further be argued that democratic government—based on the principle of widespread political participation—is technically impossible in modern mass societies. Moreover, social and economic inequalities also affect political participation and access to power in all modern societies. In the light of such observations, differences in the distribution of and access to power may appear more a matter of degree than of kind. However, if our criteria are the legitimacy of organized opposition to the government in power, the presence of institutionalized opportunities for changing the government and the attitude of the government toward dissent and criticism, we are likely to conclude that the differences between the American and Soviet polity are not merely matters of degree. Such criteria will also make it apparent that the formalities of a democratic constitution, the rituals of mass political participation and the persistent affirmations of popular government—all present in the Soviet Union—create neither political democracy nor a pluralistic society.

The Conceptions and Functions of the State

A comparison of the American and Soviet political system may usefully begin by looking at the major repository of political power in all modern societies, the state.* It will be of particular interest to outline the dominant ideas of each society in regard to the proper role of the government. The principal difference between the American and Soviet conceptions is, in brief, that the American view assigns far more limited functions to the state than does the Soviet. This in turn is related to differing basic premises about social order and conflict. The Soviet view, rooted in Marxism, stresses the ever present nature of social conflict created by the clash of class and economic interests. The state is an instrument of the ruling class and a symbol of both this endemic conflict and its repression. Without such a strong regulatory agency society would fall apart under the

---

* As will be seen later it is among the characteristics of the Soviet political system that the power of the state is shared with that of the party, and that often the two are inextricably intertwined.

pressure of conflicting socioeconomic interests. As Engels said (Lenin quoted him approvingly):

> The state . . . is a product of society at a certain stage of development; it is the admission that this society has become entangled in an insoluble contradiction with itself, that it is cleft into irreconcilable antagonisms it is powerless to dispel. But in order that these antagonisms, classes with conflicting economic interests, might not consume themselves and society in sterile struggle, a power seemingly standing above society became necessary for the purpose of moderating the conflict, of keeping it within the bounds of "order." . . .[2]

While Soviet theorists have claimed that the existence of the state in Soviet society is no longer required by conflicting class interests, they have advanced other justifications for its vigorous survival. In the first two decades of Soviet rule it was the surviving social groups hostile to the Soviet system; this was followed by the intensification of class struggle on the part of these stubborn remnants who were supported by the external enemies of the Soviet Union under conditions of "capitalist encirclement." More recently, while the encirclement of the Soviet Union by hostile powers can no longer be claimed,* the continuing machinations of the imperialist powers (led by the United States), the menace of the "Maoist clique," as well as the survivals of antisocial attitudes among the population, may be invoked in explaining why the state has not shown any signs of "withering away," as Marx and Engels hoped it would after the abolition of private property and the liquidation of antagonistic social classes.[3] It has further been argued that the state has acquired new functions, economic and educational, unforeseen by Marx.[4]

In general Soviet spokesmen use two types of arguments in accounting for the existence of the state. One applies to Soviet society (and other "socialist" countries), the other to capitalist ones. In the former the state is a basically friendly and constructive force exercising coercion with great restraint against a handful of antisocial individuals. In other words, it is engaged in repression on behalf of the majority against a tiny and ever shrinking minority. By contrast in

---

* We may not rule out however that the theme of encirclement may revive in a new form. This at least was suggested by the Soviet diplomatic, military, and propaganda responses following the serious border clashes with China along the Ussuri River in March 1969.

capitalist societies, the state is a thoroughly repressive force, alienated from the rest of society, a cancerous growth, so to speak, a ruthless organ of power with no constructive functions other than the protection of the interests of the parasitic ruling minority. As will be seen later, these conceptions of the Soviet and capitalist state are questionable both with reference to Marxist propositions (concerning the conditions for the existence and disappearance of the state) and also in the light of such observable realities as the discrepancy between the size of the coercive apparatuses of the most advanced capitalist societies and those of the socialist ones, especially the Soviet Union.* The difficulties of the Soviet position concerning the state were clear to Rosa Luxemburg as early as 1918. In prophetic words (which also fully apply to contemporary "socialist" dictatorships in the "Third World") she warned:

> Socialist democracy is not something which begins only in the promised land after the foundations of socialist economy are created; it does not come as a sort of Christmas present for the worthy people who, in the interim, have loyally supported a handful of socialist dictators. Socialist democracy begins simultaneously with the beginnings of the destruction of class rule and of the construction of socialism. It begins at the very moment of the seizure of power by the socialist party. It is the same thing as the dictatorship of the proletariat.[6]

The American conception of the proper role of the state, deriving from a broader Western European liberal tradition, is diametrically opposed to the Soviet-Marxist point of view. While it does recognize the potentials of social conflict (though not necessarily along economic class lines), its major premise is that the persistently repressive regulation of conflict is avoidable through compromise. Furthermore this tradition postulates that a peaceful reconciliation of interests

* Reading Engels on the subject allows for only two conclusions. Either his theory was wrong or Soviet society has continued to be riddled with conflicts to be repressed. He said (and again was approvingly quoted by Lenin): "When at last it [the state] becomes the real representative of the whole of society, it renders itself unnecessary. As soon as there is no longer *any social class* to be held in subjection . . . nothing more remains to be repressed and a special repressive force, a state, is no longer necessary. The first act by virtue of which the state really constitutes itself the representative of the whole of society—the taking possession of the means of production—this is at the same time, its last independent act as a state."[5] [Emphasis supplied—P. H.]

is possible through institutional devices which enable different segments of the citizenry to have a share, at least periodically, in political power. Such assumptions about conflict and order, in turn, are based on a basically more optimistic outlook concerning the possibilities of social harmony and a community of interests within society.* How realistic these assumptions are is another question. Here we merely wish to stress that they underlie the American conceptions of the state and the role of government and thereby affect political arrangements.

In the American political tradition the state is seen as a necessary evil at best and a menace if it becomes a vehicle for the concentration of power. The fear of the concentration of political (as opposed to economic) power has haunted American and Western European political thinkers for centuries and prompted them to devise institutional safeguards against it.[7] At the same time, as Marxist critics have often noted, less attention has been paid to the *political consequences* of the concentration and inequalities of *economic power*.

The contrasting conceptions of the role of the state have been among the factors which lead to noticeable differences in the practices of the American and Soviet governments. In empirical terms the contrast can be stated not so much as a matter of democracy versus dictatorship but, more informatively, as a discrepancy in the conceived responsibilities of the state in the two societies. In the United States, until the 1930's, the state (that is, in the American context the state and federal governments) limited its responsibilities primarily to negative, defensive tasks: the prevention of large-scale domestic disorder (police functions), defense against foreign powers (military), and a *minimal* regulation of economic and educational affairs and tax collection. These restrictions on the functions of the state were in part the outgrowth of the desire to eliminate obstacles from the path of private economic activities. To a large degree the individual was assumed to be able to take care of all his needs and interests in free and equal competition with his fellow citizens. Un-

---

* However, in Western-liberal political thought there is no anticipation of a utopian stage of *total harmony* that will completely preclude coercion; at the same time, while the concentration of political power is deemed undesirable, a measure of coercion is viewed as a more or less unalterable feature of any organized society. By contrast in the Soviet-Marxist vision the realities of extreme coercion and concentrated power give way —in an unspecified future—to the total disappearance of coercive power and to a social order of unsoiled harmony.

der no circumstances did the American government—on either the state or the federal level—undertake to assure that equality of opportunity in fact existed; it was assumed. While this is no longer the case, the residues of the traditional conceptions of the role of the state continue to influence its newly assumed activities. Welfare programs, for example, are still inadequate and grudgingly administered. Nevertheless, although the ideals concerning the properly limited functions of the state are still cherished by many,[8] its actual functioning has changed considerably. Under economic and political pressure (depressions, recessions, unemployment, the arms race, and more recently, urban riots) the realization spread that, for the sake of reasonable political stability, the government cannot remain inactive in economic life. It has also been increasingly recognized that political rights and freedoms can be rendered meaningless unless they are supported by at least a minimal equality of opportunity, or by the minimal assurance of "positive freedoms." The findings of sociology and political science, as well as common sense experience, confirmed that political participation, or at any rate orderly political participation, can hardly be expected from those deprived of basic material satisfactions, educational opportunities and some sense of dignity. People under such conditions tend to be unwilling or incapable of making use of their theoretically existing political rights and freedoms.[9]

Thus we may, over a long period of time, observe a certain amount of convergence between the American and Soviet conceptions of the proper functions of the state in economic affairs. It is important, however, to realize that the growth of the functions of the state in the economic life of a society may in itself be irrelevant from the standpoint of political democracy. For example, the nationalization of certain basic industries does not necessarily threaten political freedoms. What is of crucial significance is the political-institutional framework in which government control of certain economic affairs takes place. Sweden and Britain are no less democratic than the United States for having nationalized railroads and public utilities, and the United States has not become a dictatorship for providing school lunches.

The following chart summarizes the important social activities and institutions subject to governmental control and concern in the United States and the Soviet Union respectively:

THE UNITED STATES CONTROLS			THE SOVIET UNION CONTROLS		
Total or near total	*Partial or limited*	*None or virtually none*	*Total or near total*	*Partial or limited*	*None or virtually none*
Military forces	Economic production & distribution	Religious life	Military forces	Domestic travel	
Postal services	Political participation & organization	Leisure activities	Police forces	Religious life	
	Education	Social mobility	Postal services	Family	
	Mass media	Sports	Economic production & distribution	Leisure activities	
	Family (i.e., divorce laws, birth control)	Domestic travel	Political participation & organization	Social mobility	
	Firearms	Youth organizations	Education	Arts & literature	
	Health, drugs	Child rearing (except for the legal requirement of compulsory schooling)	Mass media	Child rearing	
	Rents & housing		Foreign travel		
	Working conditions		Firearms		
	Retirement		Health, drugs		
	Arts & literature		Retirement		
	Foreign travel		Working conditions		
	Police forces*		Rent & housing		
			Publishing		
			Sports		

* There are innumerable private police forces in the U.S.; in addition, each small town and municipality has its own police which are largely free of state and/or federal controls and jurisdiction.

It should be stressed that our chart, generally, understates the differences. For instance, to say that both the American and Soviet governments exercise a "limited control" over the arts is perhaps literally true but does not do justice to the enormous discrepancies in the amount of concern and control. In the United States the government has very little influence on the arts, due in part to the correspondingly limited material support it can give or withhold from artists. Legislation can influence the content of the arts (for example through censorship) but the law is rarely used for that purpose. In contrast, "partial" control in the Soviet context means that *occasionally* works of art which displease the regime reach the public and hence the control is not total. Similarly "limited control" over foreign travel in America means that people must get a passport from the federal government if they want to go abroad—a routine procedure. Tens of millions of Americans hold passports, that is, practically everybody who wants to have one. Once in a while the State Department "lifts" somebody's passport to prevent him from going abroad—such cases receive much indignant publicity and the restrictions are generally rescinded. The same applies to State Department efforts to prevent Americans from going to certain countries considered unfriendly (for example, Cuba, North Vietnam, and so on). These prohibitions (stamped into passports) prevented few if any of those who wanted to visit those countries concerned. Soviet citizens, even those few who have passports, must surrender them upon return from abroad. To conclude, in almost all spheres cited "partial" control in the USSR means a great deal more than "partial" in the United States.

The Party and the Two-Party System

The exercise of totalitarian power* requires a specific instrument in addition to the general strengthening of the various organs of state, and especially the coercive ones. The Communist Party of the Soviet Union (referred to below as the party) became this unique instrument of political power in the USSR. Subsequently it has also become a model for other totalitarian and highly authoritarian societies, its organizational structure having been the most successful "export" of the Soviet system.[10]

It is very important to grasp the difference between political parties and the party. Political parties in pluralistic societies (that is, societies *not* organized around one binding set of values and permitting the promotion of a multiplicity of political interests) represent different groups. They embody the ideological preferences of only a part of the population. (Hence the term "party.") They represent different conceptions of the preferred forms of social and economic organization. The leaders of political parties in pluralistic societies, such as the United States, are usually aware that they cannot claim the loyalties of the entire population, not even that of a great majority. Political parties in pluralistic societies (unless they represent totalitarian

* The concept of totalitarianism will be more fully discussed in Chapter 3. In the meantime we are using it to refer to political systems characterized by highly concentrated power, legitimated by the intense ideological commitments of the ruling elite promoting drastic social transformations.

movements and ideologies) make no serious attempt to appear as the representatives of the "general will." Certainly in a two-party system like the American the strata of the population to which each party appeals are broader than in a multi-party system, like the French or Italian. However, in both the two- and multi-party systems politicians recognize that their respective goals are not the only ones that can be pursued legitimately and they acknowledge alternatives, even if they view them with distaste or animosity. Even more significant is the fact that in pluralistic societies, like the American, politicians are aware of the changeability of power relations and positions. The possession of political power is not and cannot be taken for granted: elections eliminate the certainty of permanent positions of power. (The insecurity of the Soviet politician is of an altogether different nature and his removal from power more unpredictable.) In addition, in American society political parties are not the only effective organizations the citizen can join in order to promote his political, economic, or ideological interests. In the United States, as in other pluralistic societies, many other forms of association are available. Furthermore the citizen can join several of these simultaneously in the pursuit of his varied interests.

Another significant difference in the nature of political affiliations is the quality of the ties that bind the citizen to his political party in the pluralistic and totalitarian society, respectively. Affiliation with democratic parties involves only a partial, limited commitment.[11] Neither joining, nor expulsion, nor voluntary withdrawal is likely to make a great impact on the life of the individual. In American society, partly because of the relatively low level of politicization, it matters very little whether or not the citizen "belongs" to a political party. In the Soviet Union joining or being expelled from the party is surrounded by rituals, and each represents either a significant gain or a corresponding loss of privilege. Likewise party politicians in the two societies are a very different breed. The American politician is "essentially a civilian. He does not distinguish between himself and his antagonists in the military categories of 'friend' and 'enemy.' He acts on the premise that he will always share power with competitors. Both he and his competitors operate under a shared set of rules which limit the modes of competition."[12] This is how Stalin described the Communist Party of the Soviet Union: "In our Party . . . there are about 3000 to 4000 first rank leaders . . . our Party corps of generals. Then there are about 30,000 to 40,000 middle rank leaders who are our Party corps of officers. Then there are about 100,000 to 150,000 lower rank Party command staff who are, so to speak, our Party's non-commissioned officers."[13] While the figures would be different today and Stalin may no longer be quoted in the USSR as the major authority, his description aptly captures both the hierarchical principles and the vanguard image of the party, which have *not* been repudiated. In Lenin's view, belonging to the party is a full-time occupation, a total commitment for life.[14] Thus among the crucial differences between the party and the political parties in the United States is the expectation of total commitment and rigid organizational discipline on one side, against limited commitment and little discipline on the other. Moreover the ideal party member in the Soviet Union believes that the party can take care of all his problems and interests. The adherent of democratic parties has no corresponding expectations. This difference is closely related to the fact that in the United States politics is not viewed by most people as the major arena in which the life of the citizen is determined.

These considerations impose an altogether different code of behavior or "operational code"[15] and organizational structure on the American political party, even after it has achieved a dominant, governing position. In the United States as in other pluralistic societies, it is a normal and acceptable condition for political parties to be out of power. Hence *their character is not determined by the exercise of power but rather by their social base.* They are oriented toward a limited exercise of power which has important institutional and organizational implications: when they attain power (upon becoming the governing party) they do not feel obliged to transform the instruments of government, although they may modify them. The American (and the pluralistic) political party continues to work within a relatively stable institutional framework which is not altered significantly, no matter what party is in power. This sets the tone of the relationship between the state and political parties in America, and in pluralistic societies in general. The corresponding relationship is fundamentally different in the Soviet Union where party and state are inextricably mixed and interwoven, and the party is the major instrument of power. To be sure there is still a division of political labor: the various organs of the state have not disappeared. While the duality of state and party control is characteristic of Soviet government—and is one of the sources of the colossal bureaucratization of the system—the primacy of decision making rests with the party, and all significant appointments are made through party channels.[16] In the United States, even after one of the political parties achieves victory in the national elections, local officials may still be recruited from the nationally defeated party since preponderance in the Congress or in the presidential election does not guarantee local supremacy.

For the American citizen the presence of competing political parties is a natural, easily understandable phenomenon. He does not expect any one party to be an able and fair spokesman for all since he is aware that there is a multiplicity of views and interests which seek political expression and representation. It is far more difficult for him to understand the logic and reality of a one-party system. We must therefore turn our attention to the question: how does a one-party system such as the Soviet one arise? What makes it stable and acceptable? To what degree must it be acceptable for the majority of citizens? Can there be so much "unanimity" in any society that all its interests are taken care of by one political entity, such as the Communist Party of the Soviet Union?

The Uniqueness of the Party as an Instrument of Power

Ruling through one party may be viewed as a new, twentieth-century concept of exercising power arising out of the need to intensify and extend control over society. In particular, it stems from the need to possess a monopoly of a stable, permanent, and unchallenged source of power and to make use of it for the greatest variety of tasks. The Communist Party of the Soviet Union (as other Communist and totalitarian parties) is singularly well suited for this purpose.

The novelty of the party as an instrument of power (rather than as an expression of socio-political or economic interests) lies in the effort it represents, namely *to overcome the division between formal and informal devices of power*, formal and informal methods of social control. The party is capable of performing functions which the state cannot. It is an intermediary between the supreme holders of power, the party leaders, and the population at large. The party consists of what might be called a multitude of part-time civil servants, part-time propagandists, part-time informers, part-time political cheer leaders.

(There is also, of course, a hard core of paid full-time functionaries.)

As originally conceived the party is formed of an elite whose commitment to the political order is rooted in ideological conviction rather than in narrowly defined material interests. While in principle this remains the precondition of membership, ideological commitment today is more characteristic of Communist party members *in non-Communist societies* than in those where the party is in power. Unlike a specialized employee of the state, the party member's functions are not specifically circumscribed or limited to his working hours; they are highly diffuse, indeed all-embracing.* Unlike the employees of the state or police, or police state, who exercise specialized coercive functions, the party member is free of such obligations. His political and control functions are more informal and therein lies the potential strength of his role. (This description refers primarily to the rank-and-file member, or the low-echelon part-time functionary. The case of the full-time functionary is different; enmeshed in the bureaucratic apparatus, he is separated by a wider gulf from the ordinary citizens and society at large.) Coercion itself is not the task of the party members, though of course they are free to recommend it to the "appropriate" or "competent" authorities, the "organs of the state"—euphemisms which refer to the state security organs (or secret) police. The readiness to invoke coercion is often associated with the concept of "vigilance" which is among the important qualities of the party member.

The party as an instrument of power can also be viewed as serving the purpose of overcoming the dispersion and weakening of power as it radiates from the center to the peripheries, or to the local levels. The local cells (branches, or primary organizations) of the party are supposed to relay and replicate the power emanating from the center, or from the top. To achieve its ideal of control the party has to

---

* According to the 1961 Rules of the CPSU (Communist Party of the Soviet Union), a party member is obliged to work for the creation of communism; to serve as an example of the Communist attitude toward labor; to raise labor productivity; to put party decisions into effect; to explain party policy to the masses; to take an active part in political, economic, and cultural affairs; to master Marxist-Leninist theory; to combat bourgeois ideology and religious prejudice; to promote socialist internationalism; to safeguard the party against infiltration; to guard party and state secrets; to develop criticism and self-criticism; to select personnel for assignments by impersonal Leninist criteria; to obey party and state discipline; to assist in the military strengthening of the Soviet Union—to name the most important.[17]

prevent the attrition or dilution of power resulting from the process of transmission over physical and social distance. In theory the party must make the power and the instructions of the Center directly felt at all social and geographic levels. (In practice the dilution of power and control does occur and in some remote corners of the vast country the authority of the party is sometimes weak.)[18] This purpose is served by the dispersion of its members in every territorial unit, locality, social or economic institution, social stratum, or ethnic group. No single conventional bureaucratic state organization can aspire to achieve comparable levels of control. Membership in such organizations is limited by specific qualifications, formal criteria and training, which tend to limit the incumbent's usefulness as an agent of control, separating him from the social setting he is supposed to blend into.

The party has radically changed its character during the half century of Soviet rule. From the beginning its bureaucratization was predetermined (because of the Leninist obsession with intra-Party controls and centralization), but it did not become a fully developed bureaucracy until Stalin's rule. To the extent that full-time, paid functionaries constitute a small minority in it,[19] it is fully bureaucratized only at the top. In proportion to its bureaucratization the party has lost some of its vitality and capacity to fulfill the controlling, motivating, and mobilizing functions. In 1966 these problems were discussed with considerable candor in an article of *Kommunist*, the theoretical journal of the party, in connection with "Party Work in Institutions of Higher Education." The article criticized the party organization at Moscow University for its failure to attract new activists and for allowing its activities to become routinized. It also took to task the academics for their apolitical attitudes:

> There are still some Communist scholars who try to avoid active public work, who concentrate on work in learned councils and in their departments. At report-and-election meetings they frequently object when they are nominated to Party bureaus. . . .
>   . . . It is our task to try to have all Communist teachers themselves [that is, those who belong to the Party—P. H.] take the initiative, introduce a fresh stream into Party work and seek and find a creative approach to examining vital problems in the life of the university. . . . At present the bulk of Party work falls upon a small number of Communists who are enthusiasts. For example in the mechanics and mathematics department for the last 15 years

the same 25 to 30 scientists have been elected to the department Party bureau over and over. Of course these comrades deserve the deepest respect. Their civic conciousness is very high. Nevertheless such a situation is intolerable. For when Party work becomes the domain of a narrow group of *aktiv* members it gradually begins to pall. And the work itself often suffers from this. From being essentially creative, Party work becomes a succession of habitual acts, mainly monotonously repetitive organizational measures.[20]

The party as an instrument of power should be distinguished from the state on several grounds. First, it is the supreme decision-making and policy-making body (not, of course, the party as a whole, but its Supreme leader, Lenin, Stalin, or Khrushchev, or a small number of leaders, the members of the Politbureau or Presidium). Secondly, the party provides an ideological basis or "legitimation" for all policies. Thirdly, it exercises control over their execution; fourthly it participates in the semicoercive mobilization of the masses.[21] The state, including even its coercive organs, is subordinate to the party.

There have been periods in Soviet history when the coercive agencies of the state reigned supreme and were subordinate only to Stalin. On local levels this supremacy was expressed by the secondary role played by the party organizations and functionaries compared with that of the secret police.* Even then, however, the supremacy of the party continued to be claimed.

The party is also a "state within a state" since in its internal structure it replicates many state functions. Thus departments of the Party

* "As the Great Purge of the mid-thirties gathered momentum, the Party apparatus found itself increasingly subject to NKVD harassment. . . . While the right of appeal through Party channels remained on the books during the thirties, at the height of the Great Purge it became virtually meaningless. Acting under instructions from Stalin himself the troikas of the NKVD [three man tribunals—P. II.] dispensed their own brand of quick justice, and no distinctions were made between Party and nonparty members. . . . This should not be understood as meaning that the NKVD functioned without any Party guidance. But it was Party guidance in a special sense. The Party was essentially a pseudonym for Stalin and the Party apparatus merely communicated his wishes. The unique position of the NKVD derived from the fact that it became Stalin's special instrument to watch the Party as well as other sectors of Soviet life. . . .
. . . Even at the height of the purge, Stalin maintained the fiction of 'the leading role of the Party.' "[22]

Such historical antecedents help to understand the measures which were taken after Stalin's death to ensure true party control over the "state security organs" and to reestablish its dominance over all areas of life.

Central Committee deal with agriculture, industry, propaganda, culture and science, education, foreign relations, defense, appointments, and other matters. Hence the party, and especially its upper echelons, can also be viewed as the supreme or commanding bureaucracy of all bureaucracies existing in the Soviet Union.[23]

There is no comparable political bureaucracy in the United States. American party bureaucracies are highly limited in scope and exist usually only at times of election campaigns. They are composed largely of unpaid part-time workers. American parties exercise their power through elected representatives who are not full-time party officials, but rather individuals relying on local support who chose to affiliate themselves with one of the parties, and who may even switch party allegiances. Local "party organizations" in the United States are dormant much of the time, their activity is intermittent and publicly manifests itself mainly at election times and around election issues, many of which are highly localized and often totally unrelated to long-range party policies or platforms.

The Party as a Unifier of Elites

Unlike American political parties, the Communist Party of the USSR fulfills important functions in the distribution of status and privilege within Soviet society. The Soviet system of stratification and the party are closely related. The conception of the party as a unifier of elites is relatively new[24] and differs considerably from the original Leninist vanguard image of the party. According to the latter, the party is a chosen vehicle of history, an embodiment of historical consciousness and an instrument of universal justice. The party was seen as the unique organization of the proletariat, of an exceptionally class- and politically conscious elite of disciplined professional revolutionaries (or professional politicians, if there was no revolution at hand) who had joined the party because of their ideological commitment. The party changed its character in the 1930's under Stalin when the vanguard role came to be limited to the very narrow top echelon, and the party was transformed into an entity more difficult to define, an institution with new functions and features. From this stage onwards party membership became a symbol of privilege and status already achieved in some, not necessarily political, sphere of life.

If earlier membership was a precondition of privilege, since Stalin it has become more a reflection of it. The majority of those who are encouraged to join the party are important, substantial members of society, not unlike English citizens who receive titles annually from the monarch for their contributions in diverse areas of life. While there are many obvious differences between receiving such English titles and becoming a party member,* the similarity lies in the institutionalization of social recognition. The changed nature of the party, from an organization of dedicated, ideologically committed political activists to that of substantial citizens paralleled the shifting emphasis from ideological commitment to performance that occurred under Stalin in the course of the "restratification" of Soviet society. Before the thirties, the major criteria for admission into the party were ideological commitment, distinction in the political struggle and appropriate (peasant or working class) social background. Since Stalin, while manifestations of political loyalty and ideological commitment have remained relevant criteria for membership, membership itself has become the tool with which to generate or strengthen the loyalties and commitments of those viewed as functionally important. They include members of such nonpolitical elites as factory managers, engineers, scientists, kolkhoz (collective farm) chairmen, army and security police officers, famous artists and sportsmen, exceptionally productive workers—in short, experts in any field of activity useful for the regime and its prestige.† For the regime their member-

* One difference is that the number of people so honored is much smaller in England, usually in the hundreds per year. Another is that the prestige rewards are much higher in the English case. It should be remembered, however, that prizes, titles, and monetary rewards are also given annually in the Soviet Union for outstanding achievement of various kinds (for example, Lenin prizes, or earlier their equivalent, Stalin prizes).
† The political importance of occupations can be assessed from their saturation with party members. Indeed an expert on the subject, T. H. Rigby, uses the term "Party-restricted occupations." "These include not only full-time party officials, but also members of government executive bodies, the heads of government departments and directorates from city level up, and the directors of state-owned enterprises, in none of which the number of nonparty members exceeds one percent. Other occupations, which may be called 'virtually party-restricted,' since non-communists may range up to perhaps 5%, include judges, army officers, probably the police, and most recently kolkhoz chairmen. . . ." Elsewhere he notes that "In 1964 65% of all platoon commanders were communists [that is, party members—P. H.] and 90% of all company and battery commanders. At higher levels the party saturation must have been virtually complete." The actual number of Party members in the armed forces (including the border guards, but probably not the state security organs, or the political police) is close to 900,000.[25] Total party membership is approximately 15 million of a total population of over 240 million.

ship became a form of political identification; hence they were co-opted.

In this way political and functional components of status were united. From the point of view of the rulers, bringing these elites into the party makes them more controllable and at the same time creates a sense of obligation, since membership is both useful and honorific. From the point of view of the elite, membership improves career opportunities and can be an important asset in upward mobility. The changing composition of the membership reflected these new functions of the party:

> The problem was to get reliability and skill in the same person. . . . The working and peasant class component [of the Party membership] represents an exceptionally small fraction of the working and peasant classes themselves . . . the intelligentsia . . . make up at least 50% of the membership. The proportion of members in various professions is generally at least 30% and ranges as high as 80-90%. Membership is particularly expected of those with responsibility.[26]

These proportions* illustrate the transformation of the party, from an ideologically committed, revolutionary elite to an "establishment" of vested interests, from a crusading minority bent on radical social change to a privileged elite interested in the maintenance of the status quo and improving the efficiency of the existing system.†

There is no comparable institution in the United States that unites the strata of the powerful, privileged, and influential. Certainly the American political parties do not consist of elites. They are a shifting alliance of partially committed, loosely affiliated social strata, ethnic, interest, and pressure groups. At the same time members of certain elite groups, such as professional politicians, lawyers, and business-

---

* According to more recent Soviet figures: ". . . workers in the CPSU as of January 1, 1968, amounted to 38.8%, peasants (collective farmers) to 15.8% and employees to 45.4%.[27] It must be noted in evaluating these figures that not all those in the "worker" or "peasant" category are necessarily manual laborers but many can be foremen in plants or chairmen of collective farms. But even if the figures are accepted at face value the "employee" category represents almost half of the membership.

† In discussing the transformation of the character of the party it should also be recalled that during the purges of the 1930's many of the most committed, revolutionary members of the party were deliberately and systematically exterminated—a circumstance that had an incalculable effect not only on the party but on Soviet society and its subsequent development.

men do have a dominant position within the two major political parties in the United States.

The Metaphysical Conception of the Party

The complex role the party plays in Soviet society—so much at variance with the Western conceptions of political parties—might be better understood by a brief examination of the origins of the idea of the party and of what we call its metaphysical image.[28] The Communist Party of the Soviet Union arose in response to specific political needs and Lenin's perception of them. Its elitist character reflected Russian socio-political conditions, in particular the difficulty of organizing and mobilizing the peasant masses. Lenin viewed the gap between the minority of educated, active, and politically conscious revolutionaries and the sluggish, backward, and passive masses as virtually unbridgeable. Only an elite, with a clearly defined identity, using authoritarian methods seemed capable to the early (as well as latterday) leaders of carrying out the desired transformation of Russian society. The concept of "democratic centralism" was used to justify the militaristic hierarchy of the party which did not allow the questioning of the commands of the superiors. Gradually, over the decades of Soviet rule, the image of the party became transformed from a politically and historically conscious vanguard into an infallible metaphysical entity.

The Soviet conception of the party is reminiscent of the tendency of some social theorists to exaggerate the discontinuity between the individual and the group, or the individual and society. The corresponding Soviet propensity is most vividly revealed on those occasions when party leaders are denounced and accused of grave errors, even unspeakable crimes*—without any critical reflection on the nature, the integrity, or the organizational foundations of the party itself. No matter what individual leaders have done the party as such has remained infallible and always correct in its policies. This is all the more puzzling since individual leaders are always extremely closely identified with the party while in power. It has never been adequately

---

* In point of fact hardly any top leader (except for Lenin) escaped subsequent denunciation, removal from power or even physical extermination. The list of those once distinguished and extolled and later vilified includes Trotsky, Bucharin, Kamenev, Radek, Tomsky, Zinoviev, Yezhov, Stalin, Zhdanov, Beria, Molotov, Zhukov, Malenkov, Kaganovich, Khrushchev, and many others.

explained by the ideological authorities what distinguishes the party from its members, leaders, and policies. The party never identifies with its mistakes: they are rapidly assigned to a few individuals and a new party line (or policy) is introduced repudiating the particular policy together with the particular leader. Thus the party dissociates itself from mistakes committed earlier in its name, on its behalf. The opposite is true for successful policies, and the real or alleged accomplishments of the regime for which the party and its leaders in power (at any given time) are quick to take credit.

The claim of infallibility and the metaphysical image of the party are ceaselessly promoted in Soviet literature and mass media. The party is discussed in quasi-religious terms as a mysterious entity that embodies the will of history, selects the most capable leaders, perceives and speaks for the interests of all citizens, chooses the wisest policy, and appears something of a divine incarnation, divorced from the fallibility of the humans who compose it. Thus a contrast between personal fallibility and collective infallibility is established.* (The *Collective* is another of the quasi-metaphysical entities of Soviet life and ideological discourse; it will be dealt with later in this chapter in connection with criticism and self criticism.)

The Western observer (and the nonbeliever), will not find a persuasive Soviet explanation of the infallibility of the party. He will wonder what its unchallenged authority derives from and how it can claim infallibility when so many of its leaders and policies were in error for so long. This question becomes particularly pressing with reference to the activities of leaders like Stalin who piled "error" upon "error" for decades, without apparently infringing on the qualities of the party itself.

The Cults of Personality and Problems of Legitimation

To what degree is the cult of personality an intrinsic part of the Soviet political system? What, if anything, are its equivalents in

---

* This traditional conception of the nature and role of the party appears to be well preserved and deeply entrenched even in the post-Stalin and post-Khrushchev period, viewed by many as a less ideologically oriented and more rational one.

A recent article outlining the role of the party in contemporary Soviet society noted "Who else but the Communist Party, the proprietor of Marxism-Leninism, can fulfill the task of a really scientific, objective investigation of socialism and the extraction of correct conclusions for practice?"[29]

America? Is it a product of the megalomania of individual leaders (and their sycophants) or is it essential for the functioning of the system?

The phrase itself—the cult of personality—is of Soviet coinage and is a characteristic expression of the official distaste for publicly confronting unpleasant political realities. It appears to have been designed to distract attention from certain aspects of the Soviet political system. Introduced in the process of de-Stalinization, it refers to the quasi-religious worship* of the supreme leader and to the extraordinary concentration of arbitrary power in his hands. For Soviet citizens, terror and repression are associated with the "cult." The choice of the phrase, which avoids direct reference to Stalin himself, (although specifically designed to characterize *his* misdeeds) may spring from the lingering, partial identification of the post-Stalin leaders with Stalin. The mitigating nuances implied by the phrase contribute to this impression. Certainly Stalin's rule and the specific mistakes attributed to him (even by his Soviet critics) are most inadequately described as "the *cult* of personality," even if it were made explicit that it was the cult of *Stalin's* personality. Thus it seems that one of the functions of the phrase has been to distract attention from the very consequences of the "cult": the immense concentration of power, rule by coercion, and the extermination of millions of Soviet people.†[31]

Cults of personalities or persons are by no means unknown in the United States but they tend to be manifested outside the realm of politics. Many major film and television stars, football players, musicians, are the victims or beneficiaries of a cult of personality. Their fans worship them, collect personal relics, crowd into movie theaters and rock festivals, imitate their clothing and hair styles. Such cults

---

* The nature of this worship is well exemplified by the following statement: "Thank you Stalin. Thank you because I am joyful. Thank you because I am well. . . . Every time I have found myself in his presence I have been subjugated by his strength, his charm, his grandeur. I have experienced a great desire to sing, to cry out, to shout with joy and happiness. . . . I shall be eternally happy and joyous, all thanks to thee, great educator, Stalin. Everything belongs to thee, chief of our great country. And when the woman I love presents me with a child the first word it shall utter will be: Stalin."[30]

† The reluctance to fully assess the damage done by Stalin to Soviet society intensified in the mid- and late 1960's. More than that, there has been a gradual rehabilitation of Stalin. Among others, his sterling qualities as commander in chief during World War II have been rediscovered.[32]

are often fanned by deliberate publicity, but in the final analysis it is the public reaction to the individuals in question that creates the cult. Such a cult is far removed from the world of politics. The cult of Stalin was primarily a cult of him as a political leader. That his "personality" was also an object of compulsory adulation was secondary in the context of Soviet history. If all the unappealing aspects of Stalin's rule had been limited to the cult of his "personality" there would have been no need for de-Stalinization.

Indeed if the implications of the phrase were primarily "personal," it would be more applicable to the United States and to the publicity that surrounds American presidents. Here we have a cult of personality largely divorced from the cult of the person as a politician or statesman. This cult focuses on his nonpolitical activities, his hobbies, likes and dislikes, and even on members of his family. While this type of cult and the associated publicity is apolitical in its manifestations, it can and often does enhance political power, for example by increasing popularity with voters.*

Western texts on Soviet political institutions (perhaps unwittingly accepting the Soviet view that Stalin's cult of personality was a mere aberration and not an intrinsic characteristic of the Soviet system of government) rarely discuss the cult of personality as a political institution. Developments since the death of Stalin lend some support to this position since there have been no comparable cults of other leaders who followed him. Yet in some form the cult of personality has been a discernible part of the Soviet institutional fabric from its very beginnings. Its importance lies not only in the practices of personal dictatorship, but also in the compulsion of the system to derive its authority and legitimation from one man even under conditions of collective leadership. This was certainly the case under Lenin and Stalin; it was less pronounced but still perceptible under Khrushchev. Since his removal the legitimating functions of the cult of personality shifted from the living leaders to the dead founder Lenin. Today virtually no policy or ideological proposition can be made without invoking his authority.[33] Thus the compulsion to derive

* However it should also be noted that such a cult of the president, on the part of a segment of the public or the mass media, may coexist with his vilification by another segment of the public or mass media. Thus, in addition to the favorable attentions of the mass media, both Presidents Johnson and Nixon were subject to considerable public denunciation and satirizing.

legitimation from some great leader-figure persists.* It is still not sufficient for present-day leaders to take a position or suggest a policy on its own merit or on the basis of anticipated popular approval. The extraordinary number and frequency of references to Lenin have the function of a mystical incantation.† The practice suggests the persistence of a measure of doubt on the part of the leadership in regard to its own legitimacy.

In the American political system legitimation is not derived from personalities, especially not from living leaders. In the United States the major sources of legitimation are the Constitution, the laws, the Congress, or references to popular desires and values, to public opinion. It does not, of course, follow that personalities are unimportant in American politics. On the contrary, paradoxically enough, personalities are more important in American political life than in the Soviet, despite the absence of phenomena similar to the Soviet "cult of personality." The importance of the personality of the American politician is an indicator of the low level of politicization of society at large and the political actors themselves. It indicates that vast sectors of the American electorate are less interested in the principles and programs which a given politician espouses than in his personal characteristics, nonpolitical attributes, and attitudes. This low level of politicization is also reflected in the American practice of switching back and forth from political to nonpolitical occupations. For example, in the Soviet Union it would be inconceivable for an actor—a counterpart of a George Murphy or a Ronald Reagan —to aspire to high political office (though he might be seated on one of the Soviet nondecision-making, pseudorepresentative bodies: the Supreme Soviet or some local Soviet), or for a lawyer to run for office in the middle of his career, or for some respected retired citi-

---

* Another interesting post-Stalin device of legitimation is the frequent official use of the expression that "life itself" demands, requires, urges, or justifies a given measure. The expression has been used with increasing frequency over the last years and has been added to the many clichés employed by the Soviet propaganda apparatus. Obviously, "life itself" can make no demands and the expression is therefore rather meaningless. The expression may imply that not only the policies of the party, or the desires of the leaders dictate policy, but also the burning issues of the day, or certain pressing social realities. The term may represent implicit opposition to the weight of dogma or the inertia of established routines and practices.

† For example, "The Moscow movie program in the anniversary week [that is, the centennial of his birth—P. H.] contained 64 movies about Lenin, which was about three times more than the average. (Twenty-two 'art' films and 42 'documentaries.' ")[34]

zen to decide to embark on a political career. One of the crucial differences in recruitment to political office in the two countries is that
the period of training and preparation is much longer in the USSR
than in America. The training is also much more bureaucratized and
institutionalized.

The American politician's "cult of personality" is closely tied to
the basis of the American political system, its pluralism, and the inherent competition for power. American aspirants for political office
seek popularity actively because they need it in order *to gain* power.
They also need a local territorial political basis from which to launch
their careers, since officeholders are elected (or appointed by people
elected). The popularity and acceptance which the American politician seeks are not limited to matters of policy, to issues and principles. He courts the voters and tries to appeal to them as a "total
personality" rather than as a specialized political figure. This mode
of appeal may be a response to the impersonality and anonymity ascribed to contemporary mass societies like the American. Perhaps it
has become more important for the voter to view his political representative as a total person, and to be treated by him as such—at least
symbolically—than to let him fulfill a specialized, functionally specific, political role. But the enhanced importance of the personality
of the politician and political leader (or of the aspiring one) may
also be accounted for by the weakening of intermediate groups and
relations which mediate between the masses and the elite or the
masses and the state.[35] Such developments almost inevitably increase
the psychological significance of the leader or leaders. Another possibility is that the preoccupation with the personality of the politician
reflects the greater accessibility of the elites, who must open (or pretend to open) even their personal lives to public scrutiny, since doing
otherwise might seem undemocratic, aristocratic, or snobbish, especially in a society which subscribes to egalitarian values.

The fact remains, however, that the personalization of political
issues has trivialized American political life; it has introduced the
concept of "image" into politics; it has on many occasions distracted
attention from important political issues and contributed at times to
the electoral victory of unqualified candidates.

In the Soviet Union, little is known about the personal life and
attributes of politicians. Their "total personality" is hardly an asset
in the drive for power since Soviet politicians are not compelled to

seek popularity on any broad scale. They may be concerned with their acceptance among certain important elite groups—among the military, the security police, industrial managers, scientists—but on the whole the quest for popularity is not a major preoccupation of Soviet politicians. Popularity-seeking usually emerges, if at all, *after* power is attained. The Soviet polity is designed to function without popular support. In fact, there is hardly any mechanism in the Soviet Union by which to elicit or measure popular support, or the lack of it.

In the USSR, then, the cult of personality emerges *after* power is seized; it is a by-product of a commanding position already achieved, a tribute paid to the ruler.* The situation is quite different in the United States. Although sometimes the president is an object of a "cult," this may have relatively little bearing on his exercise of power. (For example President Kennedy was the subject of something of a "cult," yet his power remained seriously impaired, especially with relation to Congress.) In the United States, as in some other Western societies (such as the United Kingdom, with reference to the monarch) there are personality cults which have limited political relevance and are generated by nonpolitical sources, such as the commercialized mass media. Politicians in the United States do not control the mass media: using it for the generation of their "cult" is a matter of expense and connections, but not command. Thus on several counts the two types of "cult" reflect some of the fundamental differences between the two societies, namely, those relating to pluralism and totalitarianism.

Criticism and Self-criticism

Criticism and self-criticism constitute a Soviet political institution and a mechanism of social control that has no counterpart in American social or political life. It has two forms. One is the public meeting of a given "collective": a cell or branch of the Party or the youth organization (Komsomol), of coworkers in a factory, farm, office, or unit of the armed forces. In Soviet ideological discourse the collective

---

* Most recently, for example, new light was shed on the hitherto unknown or unmentioned military accomplishments of Brezhnev in the book of General Grechko.[36] Similarly Khrushchev's military genius in World War II was brought to light during the period of his consolidation of power.

is the second most sacred social entity, following the Party. Most frequently, it is a "community" of coworkers or members of the same organizational unit of society. The collective consists of a group of people who work closely together—either in production or in some political organization or educational institution—and who are presumed to be vitally interested in each other as citizens *and* "total personalities." In theory, Soviet society is composed of these interlocking, brotherly units. At meetings of the collective, individuals may be criticized by their fellow members for shortcomings of work, political attitudes, or personal life. The person criticized is expected to respond by criticizing himself in turn and to express his determination to correct the deficiencies noted.

The second form of criticism and self-criticism appears in the mass media, the press in particular. It tends to be more impersonal and focuses on institutional malfunctioning (especially red tape, waste, and inefficiency) rather than on individual failings. Criticism in the press, whether it is made by the readers (that is, from "below" in the revealing official terminology) or by journalists engaged in constructive criticism* may be viewed as a stunted counterpart of the opposition in pluralistic societies who criticize the power-holders with respect to their policies and their execution. Since the Soviet political system does not permit opposition, it needs some substitute feedback mechanism. Criticism in the press fulfills this function to a very limited degree. It also provides an outlet for the expression of the nonpolitical frustrations of the citizen.[38]

Criticism and self criticism—especially in the group setting—occupies a borderline position between the formal and informal devices of political control, a circumstance that perhaps accounts for their neglect on the part of Western students of Soviet political institutions. As a rule, criticism and self-criticism are initiated and fostered by the party, both at high and low levels.

We can conceptualize criticism and self-criticism in various ways.

---

* Stalin's distinction between constructive and destructive (or permissible and impermissible) criticism persists. He said: "It is necessary to make a strict distinction between destructive, anti-Bolshevik self-criticism that is alien to us and our Bolshevik self-criticism which aims at the propagation of party-mindedness, the strengthening of Soviet power, the improvement of our construction, the consolidation of our economic cadres, the arming of the working class."[37] It has remained the prerogative of the leaders in power to decide what kind of criticism (or self-criticism) is harmful or beneficial to Soviet power.

From a theoretical standpoint we might describe it as an instrument of societal self-examination, an institution intended to express the "collective super ego." In the course of criticism and self-criticism members of the group criticize one another and themselves for their shortcomings defined with reference to supposed societal or collective interest. In the spirit of Durkheim, we might also suggest that this kind of criticism is a vehicle for the expression of "collective sentiments," an institution for the articulation of commonly held values and norms, which are challenged whenever the individual fails to fulfill his social obligations and responsibilities. When described in this manner, criticism and self-criticism may not appear peculiar to Soviet society and totally alien to American society. The practice has some resemblance to a gathering of the faithful, to the meeting of a small religious sect, or a group-therapy session in which participants are also expected to criticize one another. These resemblances however are superficial. The practice is inconceivable in the United States because it cannot be dissociated from the party which initiates and informally controls it and which itself has no functional equivalent in American society. It is also difficult to visualize it in this country because the American value system (and the attitudes it reflects and reinforces) is highly individualistic and does not encourage public self-exposure unless defined as a form of therapy. The public admission of error or personal misbehavior is distasteful and humiliating for most Americans,* and there is no established authority in American life that can compel such self-humiliation. Here we must emphasize the differences between American attitudes toward the group and the Soviet attitudes toward the collective. Despite all that has been said about the American propensity for "joining," "togetherness" and "other directedness," the individual's affiliation with the group is generally looser and more superficial than it is in the Soviet Union. The collective in Soviet society tends to be equated with the primary group—and a politicized one at that—the members of which are supposed to interact as total personalities rather than as

---

* It has to be pointed out however that, from the late 1960's onward, there has been a spectacular decline of the values of privacy and individualism and an associated emergence of what might be called a "therapeutic collectivism." The new popularity of group-therapy and sensitivity-training shows that Americans are also quite capable of public self revelation and of the drastic redefinitions of personal dignity associated with such practices. However all this has been largely apolitical.

incumbents of narrowly defined roles. From the regime's point of view group participation is essential to the ritual of criticism and self-criticism because it provides an opportunity for a shared identification with the official values and attitudes which are articulated and expressed in the process. Participants at such meetings (unless the size of the group makes this impossible) are expected to contribute to the criticisms. The number of people to be criticized—and who are to criticize themselves—is usually small, sometimes only one individual per meeting, and therefore group involvement is largely restricted to people joining in the process of criticism. Group presence is also necessary in order to expose the passive spectators to the party line and its specific application to individual cases. Finally, the presence of a group and its alignment with the critics serve to isolate symbolically the person criticized who emerges as a lonely deviant, at least temporarily outcast from the collective and society.

Ideally the collective is not permissive, and the criticisms its members direct at one another must transcend the bonds of friendship or kinship. In short, effective criticism and self-criticism presupposes to a considerable extent the politicization of interpersonal relations. This is how an authoritative article presented the issue:

> Principledness is molded under conditions of demandingness, criticism and self criticism, when the relationship between the workers is built on the foundation of communist ideals. Unprincipledness, the flouting of party and national interests appear more often when the Leninist principles of work with the cadres are violated, when the workers approach one another in terms of friendship [or] the spirit of fellow countrymen* and so forth. Then conditions are inevitably created for mutual praise, mutual forgiveness, for fawning and servility.[39]

Criticism and self-criticism in the group setting demonstrate the insignificance and powerlessness of the individual in the face of the group and the inescapable need to conform. Its "rules" are not codified, nor are the areas of behavior that can be subjected to criticism clearly defined. It is precisely this aspect of the institution that makes it, potentially at least, a highly flexible and useful instrument of social control. Criticism and self-criticism sessions offer wide opportunities

---

* The Russian expression is: "coming from the same locality."

to attack the most diffuse personal shortcomings, particularly those which do not call for legal-coercive intervention—although public criticism may be a prelude to such measures. The most frequent targets of criticism are shortcomings in work, excessive individualism (or poor relationship with the collective), deviant personal opinions, violations of "socialist morality" (for example, indulgence in extramarital relationships) and insufficient participation in public-communal affairs. Because of its wide scope and relative informality, criticism and self-criticism may also be viewed as attempts to enlist the help of all citizens in the tasks of social control.

While potentially a formidable tool of social control, there is little evidence that criticism and self-criticism had a wide impact on attitudes and behavior. For one thing, it lends itself to a ritualistic application: people can go through the motions without genuinely participating. It is probably most effective in social settings most rigidly controlled by the party, where individuals have a vested interest in demonstrating their political-ideological virtue and feel strongly motivated to contribute to the maintenance of conformity. Thus the more politicized the social environment, the more likely that such sessions will take place and the more seriously they will be taken. For example, we would expect more such sessions at a party school than on a collective farm.

Criticism and self-criticism are never directed at the highest authorities, or the supreme powerholders, neither in the group setting nor in the press. This omission is one of the paradoxes of the institution, especially in a highly centralized society where even most of the localized shortcomings have their origin in high-level policy decisions. A top official, however, can (and often is expected to) be criticized *after* his removal from office, when the floodgates of criticism are officially swung open by his successors. This happened to Khrushchev whose shortcomings suddenly came to light after his removal from power, following many years of total immunity from criticism. It was found that his agricultural policies were wrong, his architectural tastes poor, his preference for concrete over brick mistaken, his support of the biologist Lysenko wrongheaded, and even his military contributions to World War II (earlier much praised) were seen in a new, critical light. None of these criticisms could have been aired while he was in power and thus in a position to make the mistakes. Being in power and especially at the top, by definition confers a degree of infallibility to the leader in Soviet society which endures exactly as long as his power.

At the same time the press does fulfill some genuinely critical functions by attacking local shortcomings, waste and bureaucracy. In recent years criticism of this type has become bolder, although top level policies (but not their execution) are still immune from it.

Elections

In neither of the two countries do elections fulfill the function of putting into power people who represent all the diverse interests of the innumerable subgroups in the society. In both societies there is such a multiplicity of social, political, ideological, economic, and ethnic interests that their faithful representation among the political decision-makers cannot be accomplished—not, at any rate, on the national level. Moreover, the effort to achieve such representativeness would lead to fragmentation and chaos, preventing effective government. In huge heterogeneous modern societies the representation of diverse interests in the political decision-making body can only be approximated. Thus the issue of political representation in such societies boils down to the question: how much choice, how many alternatives are possible for the citizen who wants his interests best served? Between what can he choose? How far or how close will be the alleged representatives of his views and interests from what he considers his true interests and views?

In the realm of electoral politics the difference between the United States and USSR can be summed up easily. In the United States there is *some* choice and a limited range of alternatives; in the USSR there is none. It is also significant that a vast number of political or administrative positions are filled by election in the United States and by centralized appointment in the Soviet Union. It is in fact one of the strengths of the democratic process in the United States that so many local officials are elected, rather than appointed from above.[40] In the United States the political representation of the citizen has a local, regional basis which is not purely symbolic. Congressmen need the approval of their constituents in order to be elected and therefore cannot afford to disregard their views and interests completely, to say the least. However, the constituents carry unequal weight: some groups among them are better organized than others; some have

more money to contribute to the expenses of an election campaign;*
some care more, others less, about politics—hence the voice of the
electorate is better heard in some cases than in others. The existence
of only two major political parties further narrows the effective expression of group interests not encompassed adequately by the programs of these parties. Furthermore, as critics of the American political system often point out, the differences between the two parties
on some major policies are small. Distortion of the electoral process
results also because a large proportion of Americans do not vote,
particularly in local elections.† The major accomplishment of the
American electoral system is not that it accurately represents the
interests of every major group and stratum in society. More modestly,
it establishes for the politician a measure of dependence on popular
sentiment (as expressed in voting) and thereby inhibits him from
total disregard of the wishes of citizens, thus limiting the abuse of
political power.

The Soviet electoral system is at first sight a most puzzling institution, for the voter has no opportunity to select among alternatives.
There is only one set of candidates and the only choice the voter has
is to vote or not to vote for them. By "not voting" we do not mean
abstention. The Soviet voter has very limited opportunities to abstain
from voting. All the organizations and agencies of the state swing into
action at election times to make sure that all those eligible to vote do
so. Entire army units are marched to polling stations, convalescing
hospital patients are taken to vote, workers of the same place of employment cast their vote together. Sometimes residents of the same
block join forces.‡ Not voting for the official list of candidates can

---

* This is not to say that any simplistic correlation can be drawn between social class
and the nature of political commitments and affiliations, or between wealth and political persuasions. Nor can it be assumed that the rich will always support the status quo
or the political party most likely to favor the rich (the Republicans in recent history).
Thus for example many among the rich have given massive financial support to McGovern despite his tax proposals aimed at income redistribution. It was also reported that
in the 1972 presidential primaries McGovern "received a plurality or majority of 'high
income' votes cast in Wisconsin, Massachusetts, Ohio, Michigan, Oregon, California and
New Jersey."[41]
† Whereas in presidential elections approximately 65% of the electorate participates,
in mid-term Congressional ones only 40-45% cast their ballot. In local and municipal
elections the turn-out is still lower.[42]
‡ "The invalid is visited in his home by a representative of the local electoral commission, accompanied by a portable ballot box; the isolated weather observation team
sends its votes from the northern frozen wastelands by radio. The network is so all-
inclusive and so carefully articulated that it is virtually impossible to avoid voting."[43]

only be accomplished by going to the polling station, entering the booth, and crossing out the candidates' names. In contrast, voting for the official candidates can be done simply by folding the ballot and putting it into the ballot box in full view of the local election committee.[44] This procedure makes it obvious and public if the voter wishes to register his disapproval of the officially nominated candidates, and few Soviet citizens avail themselves of the opportunity to make their dissent so fully known.* Soviet election figures testify to the startling unanimity of popular choices:

> The announcement, for example, of the 1962 elections to the USSR Supreme Soviet solemnly proclaimed that 99.95% of all eligible voters cast ballots in the elections and that 99.47% voted for "candidates of the Communist and non-Party Bloc" to the Council of the Union and that 99.60% provided the same endorsement to the Council of Nationalities. . . . These statistical triumphs were widely heralded in the Soviet press as a "majestic demonstration of the unity of the Soviet people."[45]

From the official Soviet point of view none of this is surprising since the Soviet people are (supposedly) convinced that the Communist Party of the USSR and its candidates represent their interests most faithfully and effectively—hence they vote for them with predictable regularity.

Why, then, is it necessary to hold elections if the Communist Party and its candidates (to the local provincial, republic, and All-Union Soviet) can count on being elected by the entire Soviet voting population every year? What are the functions of elections under these conditions of apparent unanimity and social-political harmony? From the official descriptions, Soviet elections appear to be days of public rejoicing, gay occasions for the spontaneous affirmation of social solidarity and enthusiastic approval of the system. People sing and dance on the streets,† contemplate with satisfaction the achievements of the past and indulge in delightful anticipation of yet greater fu-

---

* The significance of the "missing one percent" (those abstaining) is discussed by Gilison. He argues that they, along with the still more minuscule proportion of voters against the official candidates, are the dissenters of Soviet society. We cannot, however, rule out the possibility that such figures may represent official conceptions of the appropriate number of nonvoters and dissenters and not necessarily their actual numbers.
† For example: "Like a big joyous holiday, the Muscovites greeted the day of elections to the USSR Supreme Soviet. From early in the morning songs and gay voices resound in the streets of the capital."[46]

ture achievements. Against this official vision of the function and atmosphere of Soviet elections one may counterpose a more somber one. Probably there is a measure of popular satisfaction present since it is a public holiday. On the other hand, it is likely that most Soviet citizens view elections as a ritual which has little to do with their fate or with making political choices. There is very little, if any, expectation of choice to begin with—and this would temper disappointment or cynicism over the character of the electoral process.

What about the function of the elections for the rulers and the Soviet system? Elections are a part of the paraphernalia of popular democracy to which the Soviet regime has always paid lip service (for example, the Soviet Constitution of 1936 upholds almost every imaginable political right). It is a measure of the appeal of the slogans of democracy that few societies today, including the USSR, can abandon at least the pretense of being democratic. Obviously, the leadership does not view elections as having significance for the distribution of political power or for gauging public opinion. They are more likely to view them as rituals* that may provide people with an illusion of participation, or as an occasion for pseudoparticipation and the physical mobilization of the masses, trained to affirm unconditionally the candidates and the policies they symbolize. In keeping with Pavlovian behavioristic principles, Soviet leaders may believe that if people are made to "participate" in elections over a long period of time, they will learn to respond positively to these periodic exercises and perhaps will be persuaded that their action must have some political significance. If people have no choice but to vote for the party for decades, they may conclude that they favor it. This interpretation is especially plausible when the electorate has had very little experience of more meaningful elections. We do not know, of course, to what degree elections have helped to cement the loyalties of the Soviet people. It is clear, however, that they have an important ideological function for the leaders, who have persisted in staging them year after year.

* Durkheim wrote of rituals:

". . . The rites are a manner of acting which take rise in the midst of assembled groups which are destined to excite, maintain or recreate certain mental states in these groups. . . ."

". . . beliefs are active only when they are partaken by many. A man cannot retain them by a purely personal effort. . . ."[47]

Mobilizing the Masses

The mobilization of the masses, a paramount function of the Soviet political system, is not a comparably significant feature of the American system. The physical mobilization of the populace involves bringing together large numbers of people for symbolic, ritual or ceremonial functions, exemplified by the numerous meetings, rallies and marches which take place in the Soviet Union. We are not, of course, suggesting that such political getherings do not take place in the United States. They do but on a much smaller scale, much less frequently than in the Soviet Union, and rarely at the initiation or command of the government. (Presidential inauguration ceremonies come closest to the Soviet type of assemblies.) Political crowds in this country often gather at election times or when participating in protest, but people are virtually never brought together *by the government* with the explicit purpose of symbolizing national unity or for the endorsement of government policies. In the USSR such gatherings take place routinely for example on May 1, November 7 (the anniversary of the October Revolution), and during elections.* Hundreds of thousands of people are brought together in a particular area to listen to speeches by political leaders and to parade before them. Participation is not voluntary but highly organized, based upon place of work or study, or upon such mass organizations as the Young Pioneers (a politicized equivalent of scouts) Komsomol, trade unions, women's organizations, and athletic groups. Meetings on a smaller scale take place at work or school, often in connection with current domestic or foreign political events.

Differences in the physical mobilization of masses supply crude, but useful and highly observable indices of different political styles and systems.† There is, in general, a discernible correlation between the scale and frequency of the physical mobilization of people by

---

* There are many other occasions as well. For instance: "The draft Programme of the CPSU was discussed on a truly country-wide scale. Nearly 73 million people attended the meetings devoted to the draft and over 4,600,000 of them spoke on it."[48]

† Thus for example during his visit Castro criticized the Allende regime in Chile for its failure to fill a stadium to its capacity of 80,000. "In Cuba, Mr. Castro said, he could assemble half a million people on less than a day's notice."[49] It is of course a good measure of the extent to which Allende's regime remains democratic, that he could not duplicate such feats.

political agencies and other characteristics of the polity. Elaborately organized mass rallies in particular are among the properties of totalitarian systems, presumably emphasized for at least two purposes. One is the need to provide secular rituals, to create or recreate social solidarity (or some semblance of it) by the physical proximity of large numbers of people surrounded by political symbols (flags, banners, torches, red stars, swastikas, hammers, and sickles, as the case may be, the pictures of leaders, painted slogans, music, and so on). It seems to be the assumption that external unity and uniformity, an apparent characteristic of large crowds, can create an internal unity of sentiments and values.* A second purpose may be to produce a sense of participation in the affairs of the nation or society. In totalitarian society like the Soviet Union, such a sense of participation does not arise easily and spontaneously since the masses are systematically excluded from the processes of political decision-making and are instead integrated into elaborate structures of compliance and conformity. They can only "participate" by assent to the policies promulgated by their leaders. The masses in such societies are also physically far removed from their leaders. Mass gatherings and marches provide virtually the only opportunity to establish a minimum of physical "contact" with them, to be addressed by them directly. The gathering of huge crowds of people in apparent enthusiastic support of political symbols also helps to convey the impression of unity and unanimity to the potential dissenter or skeptic in the crowd. Since a pluralistic ignorance of each other's feelings and political dispositions operates in huge crowds, people are under a powerful situational pressure to appear supportive of the political symbols displayed and institutions represented. These gatherings are highly organized and the chances of spontaneous crowd behavior are nonexistent, especially since the citizens participating have had a long schooling in overt conformity and have strongly internalized the knowledge of the risks involved in the public display of dissent. Nontotalitarian societies like the United States have neither the organizational-institutional mechanisms for

* Once more Durkheim suggests an explanation of these policies: ". . . Society cannot make its influence felt unless it is in action, and it is not in action unless the individuals who compose it are assembled together and act in common. . . . There can be no society which does not feel the need of upholding and reaffirming at regular intervals the collective sentiments and the collective ideas which make its unity and its personality. Now this moral remaking cannot be achieved except by the means of reunions, assemblies and meetings. . . ."[50]

regularly assembling huge crowds nor the political-ideological mo
tives for doing so.

The persistent Soviet effort to create a sense of popular participa
tion in politics—whether by elections, rallies, marches, or meetings—
cannot be considered a total success. Behind the motions of such
participation the Soviet masses (as well as most of the intelligentsia)
have developed a profoundly apolitical attitude. An experienced visitor to the Soviet Union provides an excellent description of these
attitudes:

> . . . Russians hardly discuss foreign affairs because they hardly
> discuss politics of any sort, foreign or domestic. The kinds of peo-
> ple, who, in the course of a dinner party in New York, would be
> certain to trade opinions about the pressing domestic and interna-
> tional issues of the day demonstrate, in Russia, scarcely any inter-
> est in similar matters.
>
> Russians talk enthusiastically about art, love affairs, the mush-
> room season, the nature of the soul, the merits of herring and po-
> tatoes, the appearance of English boots in a new shop—about
> everything except governmental affairs. In this most political of
> nations where according to Marxist-Leninist theory and the ex-
> hortations of all media and public communications everything
> from tennis to clothing styles, genetics to whaling is imbued with
> political purpose and meaning . . . in this most political of
> worlds, almost no one talks about politics of any kind. . . . The
> Moscow intelligentsia are preoccupied almost entirely with mat-
> ters in which they are *personally* involved: their work, their fam-
> ily and friends, their material comfort and intellectual stimula-
> tion—their private lives in their intensely private worlds.
>
> . . . Russians have . . . never developed a tradition of politi-
> cal involvement, a tradition which evolved as a matter of course
> in Western countries where participation in politics (in the kind
> of political processes that never existed in Russia) was possible
> and meaningful, to however limited a degree. . . . Russians are
> uninterested in politics . . . because the kinds of information, de-
> bate and excitement—the political give-and-take which presup-
> poses a public conflict of parties, points of view and interests—
> which make the stuff of politics in the West are lacking in the So-
> viet Union. Politics are dull when but a single point of view is
> publicized. They are meaningless to citizens who play no role
> whatsoever in their determination. (Why is it, I often ask Rus-
> sians, there is so little interest in the relations between Kosygin

and Brezhnev, and in who will succeed them? "What's the use of interest" is the usual answer, "when we are told nothing of what goes on at the top and have no control at all about what happens there? There could be a new leader tomorrow, and we might never know how and why it happened, much less have some say in it. That's why no one cares.") And politics are distasteful when this single point of view is preached relentlessly, every day in every way, as gospel.[51]

Similarly, a *New York Times* Moscow correspondent, Henry Kamm, observed: "The result of this sustained cradle-to-grave barrage of stridently one-sided propaganda, unrelieved by the expression of differing views, has been an almost total deafening of political receptiveness. . . . The never-ending wave of agitprop (agitation and propaganda) has produced the most nonpolitical large nation on earth.[52]

The point is an important one, because it helps to explain both the stability of the Soviet political system and the nature of its legitimacy that has endlessly puzzled Western observers. "If the Soviet system is so unpopular how can it persist?" some people would ask. "But if it's popular why the secret police and why the lack of free expression?"—others would counter. Only two answers seemed possible: either the system must rest on naked police terror or else it must be popular and legitimate. Needless to say these are not the only alternatives. There is a type of legitimacy that rests on the inability to conceive of alternatives (to the status quo), or on the impossibility to implement such conceptions even if they had existed and on the resigned acceptance of the remoteness of the government and political power from the ordinary citizen. There is no evidence of a critical or even questioning spirit among the vast majority of Soviet people, including the educated. As a Soviet intellectual put it:

> Most people, meaning *the* people, simply can't conceive of political democracy. They understand quantitative changes perfectly well: more or less suffering, a tighter or looser squeeze, a harsher or more benevolent leader. But only within the system, with someone up above giving or taking back. . . .
>
> Take censorship, for example. . . . You can't have a label for a vitamin bottle or a toothpaste box printed without the censor's stamp—not to speak, of course, of a single word in any publication whatsoever. The control is *total*. Yet nobody mentions censorship.

If the staffs of the censorship offices were ordered to march in some parade, carrying a banner saying "Soviet Censorship Is the Most Democratic in the World!" people would see nothing peculiar in it.[53]

Reports in the Soviet press bear out these observations. Alongside the praise of the loyalty and dedication of the Soviet masses, there are recurring complaints about their unconcern with political matters and their lack of political knowledge. For example, in a study of young factory workers it was found that:

> . . . Many young men and women are seriously studying the works of K. Marx and V. M. Lenin—either independently or in higher schools and political enlightenment circles. And yet only one-third of the respondents read political literature regularly, and to the questionnaire query on whether they know the history of the working class many replied: "I don't know it" or "I have only a poor knowledge of it." . . . Every worker, including young ones, should know the history of his class and the history of the Leninist Party, so that his convictions will be unshakable and militant.[54]

Another aspect of essentially the same problem—overexposure to politics and pseudoparticipation—is reflected in a letter by a member of a local party bureau published in *Pravda*:

> . . . Each of us is obliged to attend in the course of one month: two sessions of the Party bureau, one meeting for all Party members in the garage, two sessions of the People's Control group and one general meeting each of the shop Party organization's Communists, the column trade union and the brigade.
>
> To this we must still add the quarterly meetings of the People's Control groups and of the Party organization aktiv, conferences, etc. Add participation in ad hoc commissions and People's Control inspections—sometimes lasting several days—and there goes your week! All our month's free days turn out to be taken up by volunteer work.
>
> Of course each of us has a family, too, for which time must be allotted.*[55]

---

* A former Soviet journalist describes the time-consuming adult political education programs as follows: 'The Party educational network' . . . operates every year from October to June, like an adult-education institution spread across the entire country. In every office, workshop, scientific laboratory, restaurant, cinema studio, taxi garage, collective farm—in short, everywhere—one day a week is called political instruction day.

The attempted escape from politics of ordinary Soviet people is also suggested in a study of the favorite topics of the readers of the daily newspaper *Trud*. The four most popular topics were found to be: Feuilleton (apolitical, humorous sketches or features); everyday life, that is, questions of morality and pedagogy; legal questions (which tend to be apolitical, for example, concerning alimony); and sport. These preferences contrasted sharply with the large amount of space allocated for other less popular topics.[57]

Despite election turnouts which are low in comparison with the Soviet (and also many Western European) figures, and despite the absence of institutionalized mass rallies, there is far more effective political participation in the United States than in the Soviet Union. While "membership" in American political parties does not mean very much (nor is it necessarily a good measure of political concern and participation), the vast number of voluntary organizations, associations, campaigns and ad hoc committees is a good indicator of the extent to which Americans believe in voluntary political organization and collective action. Many of these groupings, though often manifestly apolitical, are partially political in character and provide channels for political participation at the local or national level. This is not to say that there is anything like equal access to political power and decision-making.* As we noted earlier, political participation in the United States is by no means equally distributed across class lines or socioeconomic categories. For instance, involvement in local voluntary organizations is primarily a middle-class custom. There is far lower working-class participation in elections. This is no mystery. There is a relationship between the level of education and the range

On that day, people stay behind after work for an hour or maybe two, to absorb the wisdom of the Party. . . . Few people actually enjoy this political training. Should there arise the slightest opportunity to miss a lesson, the average student is likely to seize it without hesitation. . . . But few people make the mistake of flatly refusing to take part. . . . The Party has a handy label to attach to any such dissenters: 'Refused Political Instruction.' It is a dangerous label to carry round, when it is glued to one's career."[56]

* A rather unique effort was made by President Nixon shortly after his election in December 1968 to broaden the base of political participation in the United States: "Charles Dillon Stengel ('winner of numerous pennants'), Elvis Presley ('first commercial recording "That's All Right Mama" ') . . . are among 80,000 Americans who have been asked by Richard Milhous Nixon . . . to 'recommend exceptional individuals for executive positions in the Federal Government.' They received the invitation by virtue of the fact that their names appear in *Who's Who in America*. . . ."[58]

of concerns which transcends the individual and his most immediate needs and circumstances. Higher levels of education tend to broaden such concerns. Also, higher living standards and greater material comforts allow more time and psychic energy to be channelled outside, away from the self. (They can, however, also create narcissistic self-centeredness and unconcern with the world outside. It is not quite clear under what conditions will one or the other outcome follow. Interest in the self, as against matters public or political, is influenced by many factors in addition to levels of material comfort or affluence.)*

Probably a different set of explanations applies to the political apathy of the more prosperous American working classes (who might also be classified as lower middle-class) on the one hand and to the real poor, especially the ethnic poor and the hard core unemployed on the other. There are basically two reasons for abstaining from political participation. One might be called "negative apathy," that is, the belief that participation is meaningless and ineffectual and will not change a bad situation. "Positive apathy," on the other hand, means that people do not participate because they are not particularly dissatisfied or troubled by their condition, they think they can afford to be unconcerned. Until recently, at any rate, both of these attitudes accounted for the limitations on political participation in the United States. It takes a great sense of resentment and frustration for workers, such as those in the construction industry, to become politically active even intermittently. From the mid-1960's political participation (of various types) has increased among many different groups in American society in response to a wide range of frustration which included the war, inflation, crime, racial problems, and student unrest.

---

* The importance of social class in political participation finds new support in a recent study which showed that social and political participation had less to do with race (that is, the black and white dimension) than with socioeconomic status. In fact, when whites and blacks of similar socioeconomic status were compared, blacks scored somewhat higher.[59]

3. Political Extremism and Coercion

Political Extremism in the United States

Our discussion of this subject is by necessity limited to the United States since political extremism, and the social movements reflecting it, do not exist in the Soviet Union. A discussion of "extremes" is possible only if there is a political spectrum ranging from one extreme to another through a central core of moderation. There is no such spectrum in the Soviet Union since that would presuppose a politically pluralistic society. Whatever the divisions within the Soviet political elite, they are more a matter of speculation than of hard evidence. Even insofar as diligent reading between the lines and Kremlinology* can establish differences of opinion within this elite, they are still a far cry from any sort of extreme. And if there are political extremists in the population at large, they are unorganized, inaudible, and deprived of any expression of their views.

A discussion of political extremism in the United States, however, is important in order to give a balanced picture of American political life, which we presented earlier as basically moderate, not unlike that

---

* The attempt to interpret Soviet political developments on the basis of highly circumstantial evidence, or esoteric, indirect, and sometimes trivial information (for example, to gauge the relative standing of members of the leadership from seating arrangements, or from the order in which their names are printed after official announcements, and so forth.)

of other political democracies. But moderation is certainly not the only tendency in American political life. Surrounding, and occasionally entwined with, this mainstream of moderation is a variety of extremist groups and movements ranging from admirers of Adolf Hitler, George Wallace, or Robert Welch to those of Mao, Castro, Che Guevara, Eldridge Cleaver or Angela Davis. Groups and movements of this type also engage in the competition for power, but not exclusively or primarily (as the case may be) through legitimate, institutionalized means. In fact, their impatience with and unwillingness to participate through such means is in part responsible for their powerlessness, and this in turn intensifies the alienation that is a mainspring of extremism.

As in any other society the presence of extremist political movements indicates the intense discontent of some groups and individuals. They feel that they are (or expect to be) in a position of disadvantage or deprivation, and they are (or claim that they are) so threatened by their social environment that they seek radical social change without concern for the methods by which to achieve it. However, their sense of threat need not always indicate only objective conditions accounting for it, such as poverty, police repression, or loss of social status. Unmet expectations of a utopian or quasi-utopian quality may provide the basis for the sense of threat, frustration, and anger which motivate political extremists. This is especially applicable to the left-wing radicals in American society today, but also to their counterparts in other Western societies:

> One of the most striking aspects of rebellion in Western capitalist countries is the fact that apart from the American blacks, supporters of rebellion in these countries . . . belong to privileged groups which, in contrast to the masses involved in the production process, have no immediate need to earn their own living. . . . Indeed, one of the prerequisites for the presence of radical revolutionary movements in highly industrial countries, so far from being poverty and social oppression is the very affluence which makes a good and secure social status a matter of course rather than a worthwhile goal.[1]

The propensity to violence, varying in degree and expression, is noticeable among almost all extremist groups, regardless of their ideological differences. This tendency used to be more pronounced among the right-wing than among the left-wing groups. This is no longer the case.

For example, there is a striking similarity between the justifications offered by elements of the New Left for abandoning democratic procedures (that is, for turning from "protest to resistance" as their spokesmen say) and the attitudes of the right-wing Minutemen who ". . . lost patience with American reliance on the ballot. . . . 'the time is past when the American people might have saved themselves by traditional political processes' the militantly ultra-conservative group says. . . ."[2] On the other hand, in 1967 Baynard Rustin, a prominent figure of the civil rights movement ". . . said wearily that he recently had to damp down the revolutionary enthusiasms of a group of New Left students at Howard University in Washington by explaining that conditions for a successful guerrilla war in the United States hardly exist."[3]

We will examine briefly three characteristic expressions of political extremism in the United States today and the movements associated with them: the John Birch Society, the Black Power movement, and the Radical New Left.

A major extremist group of the Right is the John Birch Society. It is given to alarmist rhetoric and small-scale, quasi-conspiratorial political activity at the local level (for example, efforts to gain control of local governments, school boards, library committees). On the other hand, to date there has been no evidence of physical violence instigated by the Birch Society. Nevertheless, the group amply meets the criteria of extremism in its views and policies, its paranoid delusions of social and political events and trends, and its open hostility to democratic procedures and principles. It favors the imitation of communist methods[4] as, for example, using front organizations, tight organizational discipline, and preoccupation with secrecy. The Society apparently also believes, as do communists, that ideas are deadly weapons and therefore concentrates its efforts on the dissemination of political propaganda, much of it designed to reveal the extent of communist domination already achieved in the United States. It follows closely the bizarre pattern associated with the late Senator Joseph McCarthy. For example, a leader of the Birch Society asserted that President Kennedy "had 'collaborated' with Premier Khrushchev to stage a sham embargo of Cuba" and that Chief Justice Earl Warren was a "pal" of the latter. The paranoid character of members' beliefs is also reflected in their preoccupation with such seemingly innocent and nonpolitical matters as the fluoridation of water and mental health programs. For Dr. Revilo Oliver, the above quoted spokesman for the society, "fluoridation was a pilot study for totalitarianism." He also noted that 55 senators "were now kept in line by blackmail made possible by highly trained and expert call girls."[5]

The propensity for imagination and strange fears are not a monopoly of the Birch Society. A spokesman for the Christian Crusade, another right-wing organization long obsessed by fantasies of internal subversion, said that "music by the Beatles and a number of folk singers was part of a 'Communist master music plan.' The Beatles' beat is designed . . . to 'hypnotize American youth and prepare them for future submission to subversive control.' "[6] In a similar vein a legislative proposal in Wisconsin (aimed at some interstate cooperation in the care of mental patients) was met by a barrage of right-wing objections charging that ". .'. the mental health movement in the United States was a 'front' for a 'hidden plot' to 'brainwash' the American people. . . ."[7]

As such statements indicate, the extreme Right in America is permeated by astonishing fantasies and irrational fears. While there is a tradition of paranoid style in American politics,[8] it is not self-evident why extremists should focus on such curious targets as mental health, fluoridation, and Beatles music, and rank them among the forces of subversion. A combination of personal insecurity, status anxiety, lingering traditions of fundamentalism, limited education, and rapid social-political change (inside and outside the United States) maintains this peculiar reservoir of fear and delusion.

It is possible that the nonviolent character of the Birch Society is related to its social basis, which is more middle-class and marked by better education than that of the Ku Klux Klan and the Minutemen, among others. The latter concentrates its energies on the paramilitary training of its members, purportedly to be in a state of readiness to fight a guerrilla war in case the country falls under communist occupation. This movement, too, is impressed by some of the communist tactics and strives to copy them: "The Communists are winning by infiltration, subversion, and psychological warfare. We must turn our enemies' own tactics against them."[9] Despite such differences, Birchites, Minutemen, the KKK, and the many similar groups of the Right are in basic agreement on the nature and sources of

menace to American society, in particular the growth of the Federal
Government, domestic communist subversion, and the moral degen-
eration of American life. They are, as C. Vann Woodward has put it,
"One-idea men with uncommonly angry minds, dark suspicions, conspiratorial fantasies and feelings of persecution. . . ."[10]

As noted above, frequently fundamentalist religious notions find
their way into the hodgepodge of right-wing ideology. Thus in 1967
James S. Greenlee of Los Angeles ("Evangelist and God's Watchman
for America") joined the presidential campaign with the following
announcement, by no means exceptional in its message or style:

> I want to be President of the United States . . . so I can lead the
> way in solving our great nation's THREE TOP PROBLEMS: The Ne-
> gro Problem, the Communist Problem, and the Liquor and Drink
> Problem. I know how those THREE TOP PROBLEMS can be solved
> under God's guidance. . . . I urge that 51 huge Patriotic and Re-
> vival and Reformation Rallies be held in America's large cities
> during the next five months. . . . I will fly to fifty of these great
> rallies and address them and will sing a number of TIMELY and
> Suitable Songs, which I have written. . . . The evil Communists
> claim they will dominate the world by 1972 and they will have a
> Communist Dictator in the White House . . . by 1969. We must
> arise, move, and work fast and prevent the ungodly Communists
> from reaching their goals. . . . America has had a Negro Prob-
> lem ever since the first Negroes were brought to our country. . . .
> However, during the past 6 and ½ years our Nation's Negro Prob-
> lem has gotten 10 times worse. . . . If I am America's President
> for 4 years . . . I will offer to Congress, when God leads, a plan
> which, if adopted and used would solve our great Nation's Negro
> Problem permanently and satisfactorily.
> Our Nation's liquor and drink problem (which has grown worse
> and worse since liquor was legalized over 30 years ago) needs
> solving real soon. When it is solved the rising crime rate will
> diminish, the alarming rising divorce rate will diminish, and
> homosexuality and other gross immorality will quickly be
> diminished.
>   The only way to solve our Nation's liquor and drink problem
> . . . is to hastily return America to National Prohibition. . . .
> Like Jefferson I am a champion of States Rights and Free Enter-
> prise and Individual freedom. Like Wilson I am a Christian and
> a man of prayer and undaunted courage. Like Franklin D. Roose-
> velt, I will blaze some new and needed trails. . . . Like Lincoln

I believe in a Government of the people, by the people, and for the people. . . . Ye Christians and Freedom-loving Americans let's move fast and get our country quickly out of the evil Communist quicksand and re-anchor our Country on the rock and right foundation where our founding ancestors anchored it, before that fast sinking sand drowns and dooms America.[11]

Despite its manifest absurdities the quotation incorporates many themes and apprehensions widely shared among right-wing movements. Foremost among them is the notion of America in decline, ripe for Communist subversion. The Communist threat is coupled with the Negro threat and placed in a broader context of rampant immorality, in this case, primarily heavy drinking, accompanied by crime, divorce, and homosexuality. There is an appeal to the American past and its values to which we must return in order to overcome the evils of the present. Recommendations on foreign policy (not quoted) include the overthrow of communism in China and Cuba, seen as requiring little effort. Frequent references to God complete the picture, as in much of right-wing sentiment and propaganda.

The comparatively recent Black Power movements do not readily fit into a conventional right-left continuum. Extremist they are but not exactly along the lines of the Right and Left dichotomy. The reason is the uniqueness of the problems of Negro Americans. Unhappily, but understandably, black extremists have borrowed from the Right its racism, a long-standing right-wing preoccupation not only in America but also in Europe. The cultivation of racial pride has in fact become a major activity of black extremists, who, reacting to the claims of white supremacy have produced their own myth of black moral, physical, and cultural superiority. But the black extremist movements also have much in common with left extremism of both the "new" and "old" varieties particularly with respect to the critique of American capitalism. Thus, for example, Stokely Carmichael said that "the 'real' reason the United States was fighting the Vietnam war was to 'serve the economic interests of American businessmen who are in Vietnam solely to exploit the tungsten, tin, and oil which rightfully belong to the Vietnamese people and to secure strategic bases surrounding China.' "[12] Black Power advocates and the extreme Left share an unqualified and generalized rejection of American society (including its liberal elements) and an apparent belief in the "purifying" functions of revolutionary violence that will one day bring down the "system" too corrupt for remedy or reform.

The black extremists' stress on violence appears to be stronger at times than that of white Left extremists, perhaps largely for psychological reasons.* Physical and verbal violence for some of them has apparently become an essential form of self-expression and a proof of having survived the white man's efforts to "emasculate" them. The inclination to verbal violence often provides an exaggerated impression of the reservoirs of physical violence behind it. It is yet to be ascertained however how close or causal has been the link between urban riots of the last few years and the type of verbal violence which Stokely Carmichael, H. "Rap" Brown, LeRoi Jones, Eldridge Cleaver, and many others have indulged in. There is some evidence to suggest that the slum riots have been more a result of spontaneous crowd behavior touched off by some relatively trivial incident (though of course backed by the massive experience of deprivation) than of deliberate planning on the part of the advocates of Negro violence.[13]

In the late 1960's and early 1970's new patterns of violence have begun to replace the slum riot. These were sometimes defined as "urban guerrilla warfare," consisting mostly of attacks on policemen attributed to Black Panthers and a smaller but allegedly more violent group called "Black Liberation Army." Though numerically small, and split into factions, the Black Panthers attracted the attention of the mass media (as well as of the police and the courts) because of their violent and strident rhetoric and avowed revolutionary commitment. Whether or not Black Panthers have engaged in unprovoked attacks on the police has been a matter of heated debate. (There is however at least one well documented case of an unprovoked police attack on them, that is, the 1970 Chicago raid.) At the same time it is unquestionable that they have made violent verbal attacks and agitation against the police a major activity. For example, a 16-page bulletin of the "People's News Service" (dated January 31, 1970) had four cartoons depicting policemen as pigs—out of a total of

---

* There are, as far as we know, no paramilitary organizations of the (white) New Left similar to those of the Black Panthers, who wear uniforms, are given ranks, carry weapons, and engage in drills. On the other hand, the violence proneness of the white Weathermen seems to be a match for that of the Panthers even though the former wear no uniforms and have fewer militaristic paraphernalia.

five cartoons in that issue. Orientation toward violence is also reflected in their organizational patterns,* a predilection for ranks,
titles (field marshals, ministers, and so forth), uniforms, and weapons.
Also characteristic of the Panthers, as distinct from many other black
extremist movements, is their willingness and desire to collaborate
with white radical groups, particularly those committed to ultra-
leftist, Maoist principles. To what extent this attitude is exploitative
and opportunistic is difficult to assess. Certainly from the Panthers'
point of view, such associations have been beneficial: they have
brought financial and legal support, a largely good (or at least neutral) press in much of the liberal media and popularity on the
campuses. Also noteworthy have been the efforts of the Black Panthers to identify with totalitarian societies and movements across
the globe, from Cuba and North Vietnam to China and North Korea.

The roots of black extremism are easy enough to discern.† Centuries of humiliation and deprivation resulting in a low status created an enormous fund of resentment among Negroes. Characteristically, these resentments found more forceful expression *after* some
measures had been taken to remedy the situation, from the mid-
1950's onwards. But improvements have been slow and much of the
civil rights' legislation ineffective, while the new expectations have
increased at an accelerated pace. The abundant grievances of Negroes are translated by the extremists into an implacable, totalistic
hatred of American society and its institutions, norms and values,
including those not responsible for or relevant to racism. The rejection of American, and indeed Western values and life styles, is also
manifested in a cultural escapism of some Black Nationalists: in their
cult of a heroic past, African hair styles, names, clothing, and languages. Doubtless all this is a part of the quest for dignity, of the effort
to find a new sense of identity.

Of all extremist movements in present-day America, Black Nationalism and Black Power are the most understandable since they spring

---

* "The Panthers are organized along strict para-military lines. Power in the organization is concentrated wholly at the top. The party has never held an election of its officers, never held a convention and never debated basic policy. Individual members
have no right with respect to the party bosses. They are liable to summary purge with
no right of appeal for any reason deemed appropriate. No internal factions, or even
differing points of view are tolerated. . . . The leadership has the right to criticize the
rank and file and the rank and file has the right to criticize itself."[14]
† Ethnic and racial discrimination are further discussed in Chapter 8, Social Problems.

from groups effectively excluded from citizenship and society for the longest time in the history of the nation (except for the American Indian) and whose impatience and alienation is the most justified.

The radical New Left, with its various subgroups, which include SDS, Weathermen, Yippies, militant antiwar groups, radical feminists, Maoists, and so on, must be included in a survey of contemporary political extremism in the United States. Two characteristics of the New Left must be noted at the outset: one is the imprecise nature of the term "New Left," which is used to cover a variety of groups, individuals, and attitudes. Secondly, while the youthfulness of the adherents is often stressed—and is indeed a major component of its "newness"—the New Left does attract many people "over thirty," the mythical demarcation line beyond which integrity crumbles and corruption sets in, according to some New Leftists.

Furthermore, the New Left has also been attractive to some elements of the Old Left, old in the personal and in the organizational sense. Thus, for example, at the New Politics Convention (the Chicago gathering of the New Left in 1967) several organizations and individuals associated with the Old Left, including the American Communist party, were also in attendance. Angela Davis, a young heroine of the New Left is at the same time a member of the Communist party. This is not to say that there are no significant differences, generational as well as political and ideological, between the New Left and its predecessors. The New Left does in fact have more youthful adherents than the old used to have, especially among college students or dropouts. The New Left is marked by a more romantic approach to politics than the old; it is less well organized, less disciplined, and perhaps also more passionate than its predecessors. Its ideology is no longer safely anchored in the guidelines emanating from what was once the center of international communism, namely the Soviet Union. While the Soviet ideological tutelage that characterized much of the Old Left had its disadvantages, it provided more stability and discipline than the free-floating and groping ideological eclecticism has imparted to the New Left.

The middle-class background of the supporters of the New Left has made a distinct imprint on the movement including the close association between generalized political demands and the quest for freedom in the most personal sense of the word. Social and political goals are intensely personalized. Indeed a striking characteristic of many of the radicals being discussed here is the deliberate attempt to link the personal and political realms and even to account for personal problems by political factors. For example some members of the Venceremos Brigade (a good sample of committed young New Left radicals who volunteered to cut sugarcane in Cuba) had this to say on the subject:

> I am beginning to understand how very thin is the line between neurosis and oppression, and consequently how in the most profound way the solution to what formerly seemed our most personal problems is deeply political.

Difficulties in personal relationships have also often been blamed on social arrangements:

> We had all been taught to relate to people in their social roles. . . . In Cuba this was not the case. . . .

> Not long ago I was in pieces. All the experiences of my life had conspired to fragment my understanding. . . . I suffered from the prime American problem: middle class consciousness, the inability to feel.[15]

The cult of commitment shades into the cult of strong feelings: moral indignation is valued precisely because it stems from emotion.* A major focus of protest of the New Left is depersonalization, bureaucratization, routinization, "the multiversity"—in short, attitudes, situations, and institutions lacking in individualized emotional content and meaning. New Left terminology also reflects the rejection of technology: "the machine" is a favored term of opprobrium, IBM and computers a symbol of the horrors of modern American life. Thus the New Left's objections to American military activity in Vietnam are strongly colored by distaste for mechanization, impersonality, and massive reliance on technology. As if it were somehow more virtuous to kill with a rifle or poisoned bamboo stick

---

* This however need not be taken to mean that New Leftists are ready to wax indignant over *every* indignity and injustice men suffer. The capacity for moral indignation of the New Left (as of most political movements) is highly partisan and selective. Mortar shells fired at random by the Vietcong into densely populated civilian areas may rate a shrug (perhaps implying that, well, wars are horrible and these things just happen), but American bombs dropped upon peasant huts (accidentally or not) are met with outcries of rage and indignation, justified in themselves, but indicative of the double standards applied. Examples of this kind could be multiplied.

than with a shell or bomb. It could, however, be argued that more complex weapons are more destructive, hence more objectionable.

Folk music and songfests often accompany New Left protest meetings. The physical closeness of sit-ins is relished in part, it seems, for the symbolic closeness it creates among the participants. The poor are admired and romanticized for leading more authentic lives unencumbered by gadgets and property, in contrast to the lifeless phoneys of middle-class suburbs. Disorder is often equated with freedom, eccentric clothing with defiant individuality, an unkempt appearance with independence from oppressive convention. On the edges of the New Left, and frequently intermingling with it, as is the case of the Yippies, are the arty, bohemian, or hippy subcultures who fully share the New Left's alienation from society but espouse different, and largely hedonistic, means to express it. The New Left, then, is many things to many people: sincere dedication to social justice and frenzied political activism for some, sheer negativism for others, a quest for personal meaning in life, a quasi-religious experience, and a pursuit of sustaining group ties.* Many of its followers belong to a

---

* Many of these objectives and attitudes, but especially the longing for community and for a fundamentally apolitical ecstasy and escape from stifling rationality are reflected in some of the accounts of the most memorable experiences of members of the Venceremos Brigade in Cuba:

"Everybody loves Saturday night. A vision of a new society. What started out as a USO type concert . . . ended as the most genuine group ecstasy I've ever seen. . . . Here people are high on their lives all the time. A group called Los Bravos charged in from back, parting the crowd, sounds of deep drum, a bell, a guitar, and sticks, charging deep rhythm. Everyone went wild. The men, squatting on their haunches, jumping up, singing in time, big grins on their faces. An actual physical force seemed to surge through the room, men dancing with men, women with women, everyone's hands on everyone's shoulders, a huge snake line forming and chugging around the hall: lawyers, translators, drivers, cane cutters, students, waiters, an absolute frenzy of brotherhood and excitement. . . ." Another brigade member perceived the Cubans as follows: "Do the Cubans ever get tired? On 4, 5, 6 hours of sleep all they do is cut cane and dance. Singing while they cut, while they sweep the floor, and then dancing with the broom. . . . The Cubans are like superthyroid freaks; the men will make music and dance and screw around at the drop of a hat." And one more vision of communal frenzy: "At lunchtime . . . the whole crowd spilling out onto the lawn, falling down sweaty, screaming at the top of their lungs, rolling down the hill . . . that much unadulterated emotional give is almost unbearable. I begin to really conceive of being part of a current, that in the process of a revolution you are both very important and very small; we are talking about something bigger than all of us, and that is the transformation of an entire people, the liberation of that kind of energy we saw this evening, the beginning of building the new man. . . . High on the people! Woooiiieeeeeeeee!!"16

generation to which frustration comes quickly, ambiguities are intolerable, moderation is alien; a generation which despises authority and takes a permissive and affluent environment for granted.[17]

The New Left views American society largely in terms of a more or less traditional Marxist social criticism, but without its systematic emphasis on the role of the working class in the projected revolutionary rejuvenation of society. Stress on participatory democracy is a somewhat novel ideological theme, its practice however does not combine easily with scorn for procedure and high levels of intolerance. There is also a growing fascination with violence, sometimes abstract and verbal, sometimes acted out.* Where real power is lacking, words are a heady substitute. From peaceful protest (particularly of the war in Vietnam) the New Left has been shifting to civil disobedience, to more active forms of resistance, such as the destruction of draft records, attempts to blockade the induction centers, the Pentagon or university administration buildings, hoping to bring them to a "grinding halt." Dramatic and potentially violent confrontations are favored as gestures of defiance. There is a cult of activism, much of which is verbal, or symbolic; it manifests itself in the outpouring of magazines, pamphlets, speeches, debates, "underground" newspapers and movies, vigils, fasts, marches, rallies, sit-ins and guerrilla theater. However in the late 1960's the most radical among leftists, in particular the Weathermen, moved to acts of calculated violence, such as the bombings of corporate offices, induction centers, army barracks, campus buildings, and other Establishment symbols. Some New Leftists on trial also began to develop tactics of courtroom disruption, designed both to provoke sanctions from the judges to make what they considered the repressive nature of the courts obvious, and to politicize and discredit the legal process in general.

The New Left remained so far an amorphous collection of groups and individuals (mostly from the campuses), torn by internal dissension and not, as a rule, pursuing limited, specific political objectives. While grass-roots community organization has been favored by most

---

* Despite their crusade against depersonalization many New Leftists consistently depersonalize, indeed dehumanize their enemies (an all too obvious example is the calling of policemen "pigs"). This is, of course, a time-honored device of hate mongering. As Huxley noted: "All propaganda directed against an opposing group has but one aim: to substitute diabolical abstractions for concrete persons. The propagandist's purpose is to make one set of people forget that certain other sets of people are human."[18]

of its adherents, only a small proportion of its efforts have actually been channeled to such activities.[19]

The New Left's rejection of American society rests primarily on moral grounds. Moral rejuvenation is as much sought after as is social-institutional transformation. The quest for social justice somewhat pales in comparison with the thirst for "Gemeinschaft," the ideal community in which people care for each other, but which no longer exists, having been destroyed by the merciless, competitive individualism and manipulativeness of American life. The New Left does not measure its ideals against either societies of the past or other contemporary ones. It tends to be ahistorical* but implicitly (or explicitly) assumes that American society is the worst of all possible societies, past or present.

The anticapitalism of the New Left differs from its predecessors in being more romantic, more antitechnological, and in stemming more from an anarchic, undisciplined longing for a vaguely formulated ideal of personal freedom, sense of community, and meaning to life, than from the more conventional Marxist critiques of political and economic institutions.[21] Capitalism is disliked not so much for retaining excess profits or for exploiting the masses, as for creating false values, bureaucracies, depersonalization and materialism, instead of brotherly love and spiritual enrichment. An interesting aspect of the New Left rhetoric is the protest against being manipulated* by elites (commercial, academic, industrial, or military) although the very existence of the New Left and the rich variety of the social criticisms it offers is a living proof of how little effect this alleged manipulation has had on so many.

A characteristic that distinguishes many supporters of the New Left from other extremist groups is a diffuse sense of guilt and distinctly negative self-conceptions. Many New Leftists feel guilty of being middle class in relation to the poor, of being white in relation

---

* "For the study of history teaches that other periods have, broadly speaking, not been much better than one's own. This is why the moralist and the revolutionary regard history as a reactionary discipline, the story of big failures and small successes. The study of history is the breeding ground of scepticism; the less the moralist knows of it, the more effectively will he pursue his mission with an untroubled conscience."[20]

* Not that manipulativeness is alien to New Left movements. The Students for Democratic Society, for example, have admitted on many occasions the pursuit of "issues" in themselves of little importance to the radical activists, but which were used to "mobilize" other students often for bloody confrontations with the police.

to the blacks, of being American in relation to the "Third World."*
Once more the candid and insightful accounts of members of the
Venceremos Brigade provide interesting and perhaps exceptionally
vivid illustrations of these attitudes:

> White people . . . came to Cuba with only the most fragile sense
> of themselves as people. . . . They were often paralyzed with
> shame and despair over the values which a competitive, individ-
> ualistic and racist middle class culture has instilled in them.

> I am all fucked up. Too many problems I have to deal with. I am
> amazingly selfish. . . . That's certainly how we are taught in a
> capitalist society, and I am a child of capitalism. Even thinking
> myself crazy is part of my self indulgence.

> . . . hostility and confusion developing among brigadistas. Blacks
> and whites are not relating too well. Women's Liberation people
> are regarded by almost all others with biting sarcasm. . . . Every-
> one is just so untogether. Someone has been writing "Off the Peo-
> ple!" and "Off Chicks" on the tents. . . . The Cubans must be
> tearing their hair out trying to deal with us.

> I am starving to learn discipline and consciousness from los
> Cubanos. . . .

> . . . You don't argue with a black—anything you say will be at-
> tacked as racist. The other white move is to attack the other "lib-
> eral" whites and ally themselves with the blacks. . . . The whole
> thing was about what slobs we were. The Cubans were disgusted
> about ,. . . the way we made a mess, leaving clothes around; and
> the amount of water we used taking long showers in a boat with
> a limited supply. And as the Cubans cleaned the bathroom we
> continued to bicker about who was guilty.

> The white caucus meeting was the most diseased, frightening
> meeting I have ever seen. The central force in it was fear—every-
> one was scared shitless of himself and the next person. "Heavy po-
> litical raps," blind individualism, and the general impression of a
> Lewis Carroll novel. One girl finally stood up in tears and pleaded

---

* Some of these attitudes appear with special intensity among Jewish intellectuals, who,
in addition to the characteristics mentioned above, also feel uncomfortable about being
Jewish.[22]

with everyone to please stop hating each other and try to listen and trust. She was almost hysterical. . . . The meeting left me bottomless. For the first time in my life I felt deep in my gut a real, powerful shame of my whiteness. It is a paralyzing feeling.[23]

Some of these attitudes were also poignantly reflected in the 1967 National Conference for New Politics.[24]

A pervasive sense of guilt and frustration produces strong doses of hostility. Its main targets are the middle classes, authority figures (parents, university and government officials, policemen, judges), and moderate-liberal politicians and intellectuals.

Extremist movements in contemporary American society, black or white, Right or Left, have more than enough features in common to make the concept of extremism meaningful. First there is an interesting symmetry between the factors which contributed to the emergence of both the right and left extremism of the last two decades. It has been noted many times that the failures of American foreign policy in the cold war period and in particular the frustrations of the Korean War gave rise to McCarthyism, the Birch Society and other similar movements of the Right.[25] Correspondingly, the emergence of the New Left is intimately connected with the frustrations of the war in Vietnam, which provided a new rallying ground for the forces of the *Left*. The reason for this contrast must be sought in the different stages of the cold war in the late 1940's and early 1950's as against the 1960's. After World War II the cold war burst upon the American public as an unpleasant surprise; especially disturbing was the recognition that American military force was not, in practical terms, omnipotent and American foreign policy rather ineffective as a means of national self-assertion. But after Stalin's death the American public has slowly come to believe that the cold war has waned. It appeared that Soviet expansionism (of which the Korean War was considered a prime example) had lost its force following domestic liberalization in the Soviet Union and the splintering of the international communist movement, no longer spearheaded by the USSR. Furthermore, McCarthyism did much to discredit anti-Communist attitudes and movements (which intensified at the time of the Korean War); subsequently the preoccupation with communism lost its relevance for large segments of the American public, especially in comparison with the situation in the late 1940's and early 1950's. Under these conditions, American involvement in Vietnam provoked the most vocal response from the Left and those potentially sympathetic to it. Not only has it been a distant, frustrating and costly war which has achieved few of its goals, but it came at a time when public belief in the necessity of fighting Communist regimes and movements has generally declined, and when the money absorbed by the war has been badly needed for domestic reform and federal programs. Furthermore, in contrast to Korea, Vietnam was not a clearcut case of fighting Communist expansion. Much of the domestic opposition to American intervention has been directly related to the initially questionable degree of North Vietnamese involvement and to the fact that the guerrilla war was in part a civil war. In contrast, however, to the frustrations of the extreme Right at the time of the Korean War, the New Left was frustrated not because the U.S. did not win in Vietnam but because it intervened in the first place.

Right and left extremists are *both* profoundly attached to a conspiratorial model of American society.[26] This similarity is often overlooked because of the better established nature of right-wing paranoia and a persisting impression that left-wing thinking is generally more rational. For the right wing, the dark forces are the Federal Government (heavily infiltrated by Communists and Fellow Travelers), rabble-rousing radicals, "bearded college professors," "pseudo-intellectuals," in league with (or recruited from) Jews, Negroes, labor leaders, Eastern bankers, and newspaper editors. For the New Left, the actors in the conspiracy are different, but their power and malevolence are as great and their motives as sinister. In the eyes of the New Left those controlling and manipulating American society are the big businessmen (particularly in war-related industries—an echo of the old image of the warmonger munition manufacturers), the fanatical "cold warriors" in the State Department, White House, Pentagon and CIA, supported by corrupt, dehumanized "establishment intellectuals" bought off by fat federal agents or the pleasure of being on the fringes of power or both.

Conspiracy models of politics are suggestive of high levels of personal insecurity and free-floating hostility in search of targets. Believers in conspiracies insist that they are the chosen few who are aware of the true nature of given threats, the magnitude of which eludes the majority. The threats are carefully concealed, which makes it difficult to combat them. This perception leads to feelings of tension and apprehension on the part of those who "discovered" the threat. Secondly, the attribution of conspiratorial intent and activity makes it easier to focus hatred on the conspirators: by definition they are sinister, camouflaged, insincere, and cowardly.

Extremists of different persuasion also have in common an impatience with the democratic political process and the compromise, bargaining, and piecemeal accomplishments it entails. For them, democratic political arrangements are either ineffectual or mere façades, concealing the hidden realities of ruthless power and unscrupulous self-interest. Impatience with democratic procedures also derives from intensity of political commitments. These preclude respect for "the rules of the game" which come to be viewed as trivial in the light of the evils the extremist perceives and wants to eliminate. Intense commitments are also the basis of strong moral indignation, susceptibilty to emotional appeals, self-righteousness, and impatience with opposition.

Extremists also share an abhorrence of complexities because of their overriding attachment to one or a few values, ideas, or fears. They crave and believe in simple solutions, be it to crime on the streets or the war in Vietnam. They also value the purity of feeling and moral conviction more than dispassionate rational discourse.

Again, most extremists tend to harbor a profound hatred of bureaucracy, that symbol of impersonality, lack of forthrightness, and the unnecessary complication of life. They share a desire for brotherhood, community and in-group feeling antithetical to the workings and ethos of bureaucracy.

Despite their numerical weakness, extremist groups are a significant factor in American society today. They are vocal, articulate, much publicized, and organized to different degrees. They are also often disruptive and destructive and they contribute deliberately to the polarization of the political spectrum, and to undermining political stability. The extremists' intolerance and propensity to violence are a threat to the democratic process. On the other hand, extremist movements often do draw attention to serious social problems and injustices and help to speed up innovation and reform.

It is difficult to conceive of any large-scale, complex, heterogeneous society without some extremist groups, provided freedom of expression and organization prevails. As long as their violence is mostly verbal* and their appeals limited to small minorities they do not pose a serious challenge to democratic institutions.

The Techniques of Control and Coercion

The exercise of political power and the threat of coercion are rarely separable. Coercion serves to exact obedience and conformity. Its presence, especially on a large scale—when directed at the majority of citizens in a society—indicates a disjunction between values and behavior on part of those subject to it.† Coercion points to a gap between what people think they should (or should not) be doing and what they are actually doing (or not doing). People under coercive governments are forced into certain patterns of behavior while in democratic and more permissive societies they can follow to a far greater extent their values and impulses unaffected by government pressure and control.

There is a striking difference between American and Soviet society with regard to the number and intensity of governmental controls the citizen is subject to. As we noted earlier this contrast is closely related to the areas of life which are matters of concern or indifference to the respective governments. Political leaders and ruling groups in the United States traditionally have operated on the assumption that there is sufficient consensus, at least on major issues, to permit the functioning of the political system without too many controls, especially of coercive kinds. Soviet leaders on the contrary developed huge and highly differentiated apparatuses of coercion, reflecting their belief that social order would be seriously endangered without them—a belief which in turn suggests their perception of potential

---

* There was of course a great deal of physical violence as well as angry rhetoric in the 1960's. In addition to slum riots and campus disturbances there were the assassinations of President and Senator Kennedy, Martin Luther King Jr., Malcolm X, Medgar Evers, and George Lincoln Rockwell, leader of the U.S. Nazi party. Evidence so far suggests that these were not the products of extremist plots but the actions of single individuals who, however, shared much of the outlook, values, and fears of the adherents of such movements.

† It is of course also possible that the rulers misperceive the situation with regard to the necessity of coercion. It may be speculated that when in a given society there appears to be a coercive apparatus excessively large in relation to the actual or potential dissent or opposition, such an institution is either a "cultural lag," surviving from times when there was a greater justification for it, or it is a reflection of the continued unease of the rulers about their own legitimacy.

hostility and dissent among the ruled. It is not easy to decide to what degree such perceptions are the products of ideologically induced delusion and fear, or an accurate estimate of social-political realities. Possibly the Soviet political system would survive in a largely unaltered form even if the coercive establishment were dismantled, if dissent were allowed to express itself and larger areas of free choice for the citizen were made available. But it is also possible that if the potentials of coercive sanctions were removed, and political dissent allowed to surface, disintegration of the present institutional structure would set in. We simply do not know enough of the disposition of the Soviet masses to make any such prediction.

The presence and size of coercive institutions also tell us something about the presumed and actual results of political socialization. A system that is more successful in inculcating certain beliefs, values and internalized prohibitions is less likely to need the threat of coercive sanctions to secure conformity of its citizens. If so, political socialization must be more effective in the United States since American coercive institutions* are far smaller and less specialized than the Soviet ones, and because the American political system permits an almost unlimited freedom of dissent.

While conformity does not have to be ensured by the threat of force insofar as most Americans are concerned, it is also true that the American political system has a far greater tolerance for nonconformity, disorder and conflict than the Soviet (and many others, including some nontotalitarian societies). That relatively high levels of commitment to the political system prevail is all the more remarkable since the political conditioning of the citizen in American society is a seemingly haphazard, poorly organized, uncoordinated and decentralized affair while in the Soviet Union it is vastly more elaborate, systematic, centralized, and thorough.

In discussing the differences between political coercion in the United States and the Soviet Union it will be helpful to recall the profound historical differences in the origins and development of the two societies. Although, as we pointed out earlier, there is similarity between some of the founding ideals of the two social systems, the concern with democratic procedures, due process of law, respect

---

* We do not include the military forces among the coercive institutions since in both societies their primary task is to face external threats (real or imagined).

for individual rights, fear of the concentration of political power, and the like, were certainly not among the preoccupations of the founders of Soviet society. Nor did Russian social-historical conditions favor such preoccupations and their translation into political practice. The Soviet regime as we know it today grew out of historical events each sufficiently violent to preclude the possibility of government by consent, given the combination of both genuine external and internal threats to the system *and* the ideologically generated sense of threat of the leadership. The October Revolution of 1917 (in itself not especially bloody) was followed by the years of the civil war. There was more violence when in the early 1930's the regime decided upon the forced collectivization of agriculture. The culmination of internal violence was reached in the middle and late 1930's during the notorious Purges, which cost millions of lives. They were launched in part to eliminate Stalin's political competitors, but became a bloodbath comparable in proportions (if not in the type of victims, and the methods of their liquidation) to the Nazi massacres a few years later. After World War II another purge followed, less well documented than the first ones, costing probably hundreds of thousands of lives. Since Stalin's death, massive coercive violence has receded. Much, if not most, of this violence cannot accurately be called "revolutionary," insofar as it did not contribute to the establishment of Soviet power or the defeat of its real enemies, which took place during the revolutionary transformations of the 1920's. By the time political repression reached its peak, in the 1930's, 1940's and early 1950's, the regime was well established, institutionally solidified and its power uncontested by domestic enemies. In regard to military threats from abroad, domestic terror was irrelevant to them —it actually weakened Soviet society (and its armed forces) when Hitler struck in 1941.

During the formative periods there were no comparable social-political upheavals in the United States; neither "nation building" nor domestic social revolution offered justification for large-scale governmental coercion (with the exception of the subjugation of Indians). While the physical elimination of political competitors has not been characteristic of the struggle for political power in the United States, a more diffuse yet personalized violence has been a part of political life, reaching a new height in the assassinations between 1963 and 1968. Yet such criminal violence has not been part of the institutionalized ways of conducting political business.* The murders were neither sanctioned nor approved of by any political party, movement, or organization; they were the acts of (possibly deranged) individuals outside the mainstream of political life. These assassinations belong perhaps not so much to a discussion of political conflict and coercion as to a consideration of the more general problem of violence in American life (see Chapter 8).

In the Soviet Union politically motivated and ideologically justified violence has hardly ever been committed by isolated individuals† outside the framework of political institutions; rather it has emanated from a huge, governmental machinery of coercion. Moreover, there is a crucial difference between the two societies pertaining to the individual's access to the instruments of violence, and firearms in particular. In the United States the government does not have a legitimate monopoly over the means of violence, unlike the situation in most contemporary societies. On the contrary, since the (18th-century) Constitution upholds the citizen's right to bear arms, firearms have always been within the easy reach of every adult (and often minors). This fact has had regrettable consequences for public safety, facilitating criminal violence and probably also the more recent politically motivated murders. Not only is it possible in the United States to legally acquire small arms like pistols, shotguns, and rifles, far more lethal items of clearly military purpose are also on sale, such as machine guns, submachine guns, mortars, and antitank weapons. Such a state of affairs would be inconceivable in the Soviet Union (even in most nontotalitarian countries) where the state retains an unquestioned monopoly of the means of violence, and where no anachronistic historical justifications can be advanced to call such a monopoly into question, as they have been in the United States.

The relative weakness of the specialized and politically oriented coercive institutions in the United States reflect these traditions and conditions. The military forces, while big and powerful, have not been an important factor in domestic politics, although they are at times called upon to suppress large-scale disturbances and riots—in itself significant in that it reflects the absence of a specialized police

* According to some observers the murder of the president symbolized the vulnerability of authority and thereby contributed to a decline of the respect toward it. At the same time the successful assassination of the best protected American encouraged further violence against figures and symbols of authority.

† Tsarist Russia is, of course, another story.

force to deal with such situations.* (Military conscription, and the resulting large standing armies, are of quite recent origin in the United States, dating from World War II.) The Federal Bureau of Investigation, which, besides ordinary (or nonpolitical) crime, is concerned with political subversion, was founded in 1924. The Central Intelligence Agency, another governmental organization concerned to some degree with political subversion in relation to espionage, came into existence after World War II. There are in addition the special units of many large urban police departments which deal with subversion. Moreover the recently revealed domestic activities of the military intelligence services are also politically relevant. Yet none of these organizations, or their combined strength and influence, is a "match" for their Soviet counterparts in regard to their numbers, freedom of action, the power to intimidate, freedom from public scrutiny and criticism, and historical roots which in the Soviet Russian case go back to the early 19th century.† We have of course no detailed comparative information on the size of the various Soviet political police forces (the "state security organs," as they are usually called by Soviet spokesmen), the number of informers per thousand population, number of political prisoners,‡ the number and nature of places of detention, and so forth. There are, however, creditable estimates and some figures which illuminate the differences between the size, differentiation, and range of activity of coercive institutions in the two societies. Clearly the FBI, with approximately 17,000 employees,[28] limited power to arrest and none to detain, is not especially formidable compared with the Soviet KBG§ (called at various times Cheka, GPU, OGPU, NKVD, MVD, MGB). This has, according to conservative estimates, at least half a million uniformed and civilian members.[29] Its power was virtually unlimited under Stalin and is still enormous, although it was brought under more effective control by

* Many countries, including the Soviet Union, maintain special police forces (or gendarmes, riot police or political police) to deal with such disorders.

† The first Russian political police, the so-called "Third Section" was established in 1826.

‡ According to Sakharov, the famous Soviet nuclear physicist, "Most political prisoners are now kept in a group of camps in the Mordvinian Republic, where the total number of prisoners, including criminals, is about 50,000."[27]

§ The abbreviation stands for the Russian words of "Committee of State Security"—the unassuming designation which refers to one of the most powerful organizations ever established to assure political conformity in any society. There is also, of course, a regular police force to deal with nonpolitical matters.

the Party oligarchy. Characteristic of the scope of the Soviet coercive establishment under Stalin was its control over economic enterprises (linked with labor and concentration camps and the mobilization of millions of inmates).[30] The KGB still has regular contingents armed with heavy weapons and maintains garrisons all over the country. Its members wear special uniforms, receive regular, as well as specialized military training, and are provided with salary and living conditions superior to those of the regular armed or police forces.[31]

Not only is the KGB vast and highly differentiated, it is probably also the most efficient of all bureaucratic organizations created by the Soviet system:

> This efficiency is possible because a single organization [the KGB] has total control over where Russians work and live, as well as what they legally read and publicly say. Ordinarily, the inherent muddle of Soviet bureaucracy might give some measure of delay, if not protection, to potential victims: a decision to dismiss a man from his job, for example, might not be co-ordinated with revocation of his residence permit in a coveted major city. But Russia's most competent and prodigally financed central agency, the KGB serves as co-ordinator in all matters of this importance.[32]

A well-known feature of the Soviet system of coercion has been the concentration or "corrective labor" camps. While reduced in number and somewhat humanized in comparison with conditions under Stalin,* they still exist, though we do not know the numbers they ac-

---

* Scattered information reaching the outside world suggests that conditions in some camps are not much better than they used to be; for example, a smuggled out manuscript by an imprisoned Soviet engineer describes "the horrors of the slow journey to the prison . . . packed in sealed compartments, nearly suffocated, 'like fishes on the sand.' The author who emerged from his imprisonment almost deaf and suffering from intestinal disease describes a life of hunger, cold and the cruelty of the guards. . . ."

Another account describes these conditions in a particular camp: "The great majority of the prisoners are on semi-starvation rations. Theoretically we are to receive 2300-2400 calories daily but we are lucky if we get 1500 because the products are of low quality, especially in spring and summer before the new crop. The herring is rotten and smelly. The dried potatoes, macaroni, barley and meat are infested with worms. We are forced to fulfill our work quota 100%. At the type of jobs we do we use up 3500 to 4000 calories. Try to survive on that if you can!! Most of the male prisoners are invalids. . . . Medical aid is virtually nonexistent. . . . There are no drugs and the prisoners are not allowed to receive any from their families—not even vitamins. . . ."

Finally from another description of Soviet camps for political prisoners: "The system of educating by hunger is also unprecedented. . . . We have the right to receive two packages a year after completing half our sentences 'with good behavior.' The camp

commodate.[34] Many are also used for the detention of common and economic criminals, "parasites" (that is, individuals capable of work who have no regular job) and other socially undesirable elements whose cases may or may not have political implications. Under Stalin concentration camps served a triple purpose, combining the inculcation of fear in the population at large with the confinement and liquidation of politically unreliable elements (as defined by the changing criteria of the day), as well as the extraction of some economically useful labor. Concentration camp prisoners made a contribution to most major construction projects during the industrialization drive (and later), opening up remote areas of the North and Far East, building roads, railroads, canals, digging for gold, harvesting timber, building new factories, and so on.[35]

Characteristic of the scope of Soviet coercive controls is the severe limitation of travel by Soviet citizens outside the USSR, and less severe but still significant restrictions on movements within the country.[36] The freedom to travel outside the country is not a right but a privilege to be earned by "good conduct," or it is an accessory of high social status. The freedom to emigrate is virtually nonexistent. On rare occasions members of families are allowed to reunite abroad (with those who either left in the 1920's, before the rigid system of control and denial of exit was established, or with those who left during the disruptions of World War II). Those granted such permissions are most often elderly.* Correspondingly a huge network of controls has been built up to prevent unauthorized departures; a special arm of the state security organs, the border guards, exists more for the purpose of preventing unauthorized exits of Soviet citizens than thwarting entries by spies or other subversive elements. As an extension of these measures, the Soviet government also engages in an intensive propaganda campaign to persuade its people that those who intend to leave (or who have left the country illegally) are the dregs of humanity and that only people of ignoble character would contemplate such acts.[37] Soviet officials also put strong pressure on individual defectors abroad to induce them to return; occasionally

---

diet has made half the people ill . . . the camp doctors openly state, 'We are the Cheka [the secret police—P. H.] first and doctors second.' "[33]

* In 1971 several thousand Soviet Jews of different ages were allowed to emigrate to Israel. It remains to be seen if this was an unusual deviation from long-standing policies or the beginning of a new approach to travel and emigration.

physical force is employed in such undertakings.[38] For the Soviet authorities any inclination to leave the country is an intolerable act of treachery and every defector or escapee an embodiment of rejection of what they conceive to be the historically most advanced and best society. Besides the ideological and psychological motives, prevention of free movement across frontiers is an important instrument of maintaining overall social-political stability: it removes alternatives from the life of the potentially discontented citizen and compels adjustment to the society he must live in.*

The major instrument of control of domestic travel is the domestic passport, or personal identity book, which every Soviet citizen over sixteen must carry with him. (This document also includes information regarding employment, training, marital status, and the like.) In it changes in address, both permanent and temporary, are registered by the police. Restrictions on domestic travel have varied through Soviet history, but it is safe to say that for the most part there were some in force. In particular, permissions have been required to settle in border areas, Moscow, and several other major cities.

In the United States there are hardly any legal (or effective extralegal), restrictions on travel inside or outside the country, as we noted earlier. The possession of a passport is legally defined as a right, not a privilege or reward. Americans are not required to register with the local police when they change residence, nor are there any restricted regions in the United States to which the citizen can only move with special police permits. Americans can visit countries openly hostile to their own (for example, Cuba, North Korea, North Vietnam). Draft evaders can also leave the country without difficulty by crossing into Canada, a political-military ally of the United States allegedly dominated by American power. By contrast, if Soviet draft evaders or deserters succeeded in escaping into any one of the neighboring socialist countries (which is highly improbable) they would be returned immediately to Soviet jurisdiction, since the Soviet Union exercises a far greater degree of control over its allies than does the United States.

---

* While legal departures from the USSR are exceedingly difficult and rare (except for those on official missions) illegal ones are punished with utmost severity. "Flight abroad or refusal to return from abroad to the USSR" is listed among "Especially dangerous crimes against the state," that is, treason, espionage, aiding the enemy, and conspiracy for the purpose of seizing power.[39]

Several factors account for the differences between the severity of political controls in the two societies. Some have to do with the different conceptions of the state, discussed in the previous chapter. Others include the divergent conceptions of political opposition and criticism, which in the United States are regarded by the authorities and most citizens as normal and legitimate, whereas in the USSR they are equated with treason or a cancerous growth to be removed swiftly and decisively. Nor has the competition for political power in the United States—especially at the national as distinct from the local level—resulted in the physical elimination of opposing factions, and rarely even in their imprisonment. The number of people subjected to coercion or persecution for their political beliefs, associations, opinions, or activities over the last 50 years probably would be in the range of thousands—even if the localized and essentially unlawful harassment and intimidation of Negroes in the South is included. (It should be noted here that many of the generalizations about political pluralism in the U.S. had and still have a more limited applicability to the South.) The number of those killed for political reasons during this period may not exceed one thousand even if we included the victims of lynchings, industrial violence, and recent urban riots.* The corresponding figures in the Soviet Union run into millions. At the height of the McCarthy era, the most recent period of evident political repression, the most severe sanctions applied to those labeled as "anti-American" or "Communist" (labels which were somewhat comparable in character to the Soviet charges of "antistate," "antiparty" or "antipeople") were typically the loss of employment, demotion, or social ostracism, rather than imprisonment, let alone loss of life.† Even in the postwar trials of American

---

* Whether or not the latter is political violence proper may be argued, since the political motives of rioters are open to question, although their behavior is obviously highly relevant to and consequential for American domestic politics.

† The relatively low level of official violence and its decline are also shown in the number of executions in the United States over time: (the only executions in which political factors clearly played a part were those of the Rosenbergs).

Number of executions in the United States per period:[40]

1930-39	1667	1963	21
1940-49	1284	1964	15
1950-59	717	1965	7
1960	56	1966	1
1961	42	1967	2
1962	47		

Communist leaders, although they were accused of attempts to over-throw the government, only medium-length prison sentences were imposed. The relative leniency of coercive measures in the United States is also illustrated by the comparatively few and mild sentences imposed on urban rioters in recent years. Most of those arrested in riots were either released without charges filed (a practice virtually unknown in the Soviet Union where arrests tend to be self-justifying), or charges were dismissed, or sentences imposed but suspended.*[41]

Some further significant differences emerge between the coercive practices of the two societies by comparing prison and labor camp populations. These comparisons are qualified by fluctuations in different periods, and by some statistical uncertainties. Alex Inkeles, restricting his analysis to the years 1930-1955 (and thereby opting for a smaller sum total), concludes that:

> At an average of only 5 million inmates [per year in the Soviet Union] and 15 years of operation, we still get 75 million life years of total human waste. These were, generally speaking, people who would be considered criminals nowhere but in the Soviet Union. Their crimes consisted mainly in being in the wrong social category, such as kulak, peasant or son of a priest, of having received letters from abroad, of telling the wrong joke, of working in the wrong place, of having the wrong friends or enemies.[42]

Inkeles also notes:

> The United States has a highly punitive system, whose typically long sentences gives this country, proportionately, one of the largest prison populations in the world. Nevertheless, the federal and state prisons of the United States in 1935 had a prison popu-

---

"There have been no executions in the United States since 1967" it was reported in the *New York Times* (December 21, 1969, p. 28). The same article also noted that capital punishment can be imposed in the Soviet Union for ten types of crime including counterfeiting, large scale theft of state property, rape, and some classes of murder.

At the same time, there has been an increase from the early 1960's in the number of those killed by the police in the course of urban riots of various types as well as in the number of policemen killed while on duty.

* It might, of course, be argued that the mild penalties reflected a collective, societal guilt feeling toward the American Negro, whose rioting was seen by many as an understandable and justified expression of frustration and despair. The Soviet regime has at no point been inhibited by analogous considerations from dealing harshly with any group of violators of social order and public security.

lation of less than 150,000.* If we add 100,000 in county and local prisons on short-term sentences the grand total would still be
only one-twentieth the estimated Soviet forced labor camp population. Indeed if the 5 million estimate is correct, and even if the
rest of the world imprisoned people at the high rate prevailing in
the United States, which it does not, then on any typical day in
the late 1930's there would have been more inmates of Soviet concentration camps than in all the prisons of the rest of the world
combined.[45]

The preceding comments highlight the crucial difference between
the American and Soviet approach to coercion. The Soviet use of objective criteria (or of extremely broad and flexible categories noted
earlier[46]) in defining political crimes meant that people were susceptible to punishment not for what they did but for what they were;
they were held responsible for their *potential* actions extrapolated
from such objective criteria as social background and contacts.
Thereby the dividing line between attitude, opinion, and belief,
on the one hand, and action or, behavior, on the other, was diluted,
indeed frequently demolished. (Nor for that matter were the assessments of attitude and belief, based on so-called objective criteria always, or even predominantly, correct.) With the passage of time, as
more and more people have been brought up under the Soviet system, it has become less tenable to assign political unreliability on
such a priori grounds as the occupation or income of parents and
grandparents. Yet even today some categories of people are more
vulnerable to coercion than others regardless of their actual behavior: for example, people who have relatives abroad, or the relatives
or close friends of those who have been arrested for political reasons,
and unemployed intellectuals (the latter is a very small group, to be
sure).†

---

* In 1960 the United States prison population had not changed significantly compared
with 1935, especially if the growth of the population is also taken into consideration.
There were, in 1960, 229,306 inmates in state and federal prisons and reformatories and
almost 120,000 in local jails and workhouses, bringing the prison population to a total
of roughly 350,000.[43] Comparative Soviet figures for the 1960's are not available though
we can state with some certainty that there are no longer millions in forced labor
camps. On the other hand, as noted before, there is some new evidence to indicate that
the treatment of political prisoners has not significantly improved, contrary to the
widespread belief to that effect—widespread at least in the West.[44]

† The case of Brodsky, the unemployed poet, is a good example of this. He was characterized by the judge who sentenced him to forced labor as a person who ". . . systemati-

In the United States the possibility of becoming a victim of coercive measures on purely a priori grounds, such as opinions, associations, or kinship ties is remote. People may be prosecuted for efforts to overthrow the government with violence, but this must be demonstrated by some action and is rarely inferred from attitudes and opinions.[48] In addition, the cumbersome legal machinery of the American system of government allows considerable freedom even for those accused of such action.* Long pretrial detentions, common in the Soviet Union even today, are exceptions rather than the rule in the United States, particularly in political cases. They are, however, more likely to happen to poor people arrested for nonpolitical reasons who cannot raise the bail money.

American coercive institutions do not operate on a preventive or prophylactic[49] principle, except in times of such an emergency as a declared war.† Indeed the definition and perception of what constitutes an emergency is the crucial difference between a democratic and totalitarian society, as well as a democratic and totalitarian movement. Totalitarians, in or out of power, conceive of far more situations as emergencies and feel correspondingly more often and more intensely threatened than democratic politicians or leaders.[50] In the outlook and policies of totalitarian leaders defensiveness and aggressiveness are inextricably mixed. What for them is vital and legitimate self-defense may strike the observer as an act of flagrant aggression.

Preoccupation with secrecy is another characteristic of the totalitarian techniques of coercion. It grows out of an exaggerated aware-

cally does not fulfill the duties of a Soviet citizen with regard to his personal well-being and the production of material wealth, which is apparent from his frequent change of jobs. He was warned by the agencies of the MGB . . . he promised to take on a permanent job . . . he continued not to work . . . he wrote and read his decadent poems at evening gatherings. . . ."[47] In the summer of 1972 Brodsky was allowed to leave the Soviet Union, a step which represents a new departure in the handling of political dissenters.

* Including the freedom to escape. This of course is possible for those released on bail as exemplified by the case of Eldridge Cleaver, the Black Panther leader, an avowed enemy of the American social and political system, who made his way to Algiers while out on bail. A number of Weathermen also jumped bail.

† Thus the Vietnam war did not result in any curtailment of domestic civil liberties, including contact with Vietcong or North Vietnamese representatives. It has also been possible for sympathizers of the Vietcong to organize or attend rallies supporting the Vietcong and display its flag; there have been collections of money, blood, and other articles for the Vietcong and North Vietnam.

ness of threats. Thus, the notion of the official secret is enormously inflated and extended in Soviet society, and its violation invites severe punishment.[51] For example, figures relating to a very large proportion of industrial production and the system of transportation are treated as secrets. In Soviet terminology "spying" may refer to the most innocent "information gathering" or inquiry, especially by a foreigner,[52] to queries which in the United States would be readily answered by both officials and private citizens. Much of what Western tourists consider innocent photography is prohibited by Soviet authorities often for reasons difficult for the outsider to fathom.[53] In the United States taking pictures of many military installations can be readily accomplished and is rarely prohibited. It would be inconceivable in the Soviet Union to see the names and numbers of military units displayed on the gates and fences of military establishments (frequently seen in America), or to have a newspaper conduct a critical study of secret services as the *New York Times* did of the CIA a few years ago.[54]

There is a sharp discontinuity between the Stalin and post-Stalin period with regard to Soviet coercive practices and policies, but since approximately 1966 there has been a resurgence of a more active stifling of dissent and a new effort to restore and solidify overt conformity which had been somewhat weakened in the process of de-Stalinization under Khrushchev. De-Stalinization itself came to a halt; the condemnations of Stalin ceased or became muted and cautious, and the exploration and revelation of the errors and tragedies of his regime were ended. The post-Khrushchev leadership has apparently decided that a deepening awareness of the nature of Stalinism could seriously undermine the legitimacy of the system, that more and more Soviet people might question a system which permitted a single individual to assume such power and wield it in such a destructive and arbitrary manner. But the recent waves of repression do differ from the older ones: first, the numbers affected are a fraction of the victims of past repressions; secondly, coercion is primarily directed at actual critics of the regime rather than at potential dissenters; finally, the forms and substance of protest and dissent themselves are new and bolder than at any time since the 1920's. Hence—as a Soviet dissenter himself observed, the major thrust of Soviet coercion in the post-Khrushchev period has been directed against unorthodox ideas and their small band of carriers, against people who think differently, or who think at all, and whose spiritual world cannot fit into the Procrustian bed of Stalinist standards which the KGB defends so assiduously. . . . Insofar as the seed of all change is hidden in the uniqueness of the individual, they have attempted in the first place to standardize him, to kill originality in him. . . . Captain Kazakev of the KGB, who was sent . . . to check to what degree I had been "reeducated" . . . confessed to me quite sincerely: "It's too bad we can't see what you have in your head. If we could do this and throw out everything which stops you from being a normal Soviet citizen, there would be no need for all this conversation." . . . It is very important to silence the man who first cries out: "The King is naked"—before others pick up the cry.[55]

In comparison with the vast campaigns of intimidation of the past, the new ones have been more selective; the victims tend to come from narrower strata of the population: primarily from among the urban intelligentsia, literary as well as scientific.* The coercive strategies of recent years seem to center on selective intimidation and on removal from circulation of the outspoken critics, rather than on campaigns of mass terror. These tactics have also been facilitated by the relatively homogeneous social background of the suppressed and by the incipient anti-intellectualism and well-developed anti-individualism of the Soviet "man on the street" who is either indifferent toward the fate of the persecuted deviants, or actually gleeful.

Dissent and its handling over the last few years have had some other novel features. The new dissenters raised fundamental questions about the legitimacy of the present political system, its historical roots and its continuity with the institutional arrangements created by Stalin. Thus one critic stated:

. . . Communism is the highest flowering of the spiritual world of the individual. A man is not a soulless automaton or a robot who can live by a defined program. . . . The meeting of thoughts, the contest of views, the crossing of ideas—that is the lever which always has and always will drive mankind forward. The greatest material saturation, without the unfettering of thought and will

* But there have been exceptions such as Yakhimovich, the articulate and critical kolkhoz chairman from Latvia who wrote indignant letters to the Politbureau and was duly arrested.[56] Another unusual dissenter has been Grigorienko, the former high-ranking military officer and inveterate idealist.[57]

is not communism. It is merely a large prison with a higher ration for the prisoners.[58]

The conflict between the official materialism and the dissenters' idealism was also revealed in the following recollection of a prisoner: "the KGB officer from Kiev [and others] were all 're-educating' me. 'Well, what did you want? You had a good job, an apartment. . . .' " They spent several hours trying to prove that a man has nothing more than a stomach and so many meters of intestines.[59]

But the rejection of the implicit materialism of the official code of values is not the only point of collision between the protesting intellectuals and the regime. Perhaps still more important is the fact that they do, or pretend to, take seriously the official values in their most idealistic version and base their criticism of the regime on them, demanding that the leadership live up to them—rather than discard them.* For example, one of the victims of a round-up of Ukrainian intellectuals defended himself on the basis of the Soviet Constitution and the Code of Criminal Procedure, quoting these documents point by point with regard to both the proper procedures of arrest and trial and the legitimacy of the charges brought against him. It was in the same spirit of commitment to the basic values, but not the daily practices of the regime that another protestor (kolkhoz chairman Yakhimovich) commented in his letter to Suslov, member of the Politbureau:

> You know Article 125 of our Constitution perfectly well; I shall not quote it. I only want to recall the thought of V. I. Lenin to the effect that "we need full and true information; and truth should not depend upon the question of whom it should serve. . . ." Ideas cannot be murdered with bullets, prisons or exile. He who does not understand this is no politician, no Marxist.[60]

---

* This demand, of course, is by no means unprecedented historically. Revolutionaries have often demanded that a given society translate its proclaimed values into practice, to do what it preaches. This is also very much the case in the contemporary United States, where the Constitution and the Declaration of Independence still serve as a value basis for many rebels, including large numbers of youth, who want society to return to its founding ideals. They take these values seriously and insist on putting them into practice completely and without delay. This at least is the case in regard to the critiques of racism and in regard to poverty. In the same spirit it is demanded that society assume greater responsibilities for the welfare of the citizen, broadly interpreted.

It may be debated whether or not this statement represents a pious wish or a correct description of reality. True enough, ideas cannot be murdered, but their carriers can be, and they have been silenced many times in history, particularly in the history of the Soviet Union. This is especially the case when they are only a handful surrounded by the many who are both indifferent to the ideas in question and traditionally intimidated by state power. Perhaps in the very long run Yakhimovich is right: ideas do survive periods of repression.

There are other differences in the official handling of the new types of dissent in the Soviet Union. Certainly in comparison with the methods of Stalin, recent measures have been mild: apparently none of the known dissenters has been executed; nor has systematic torture been reported (such as was used during interrogation and in preparation for trials in the past). A new and somewhat more human form of repression has been revived, namely, confinement in mental hospitals. (This practice may have some symbolic significance: as if the regime wanted to convey the idea that political deviance after 50 years of totalitarian regimentation amounted to insanity.) Many intellectuals brought to trial in recent years disputed the judge and prosecutor and did not plead guilty—in sharp departure from the behavior of defendants in the courts under Stalin. These trials were also given some publicity in contrast with the highly secret trials of the past; and not many relatives of the defendants have been arrested, as they would have been earlier. On the other hand, many similarities remain between the contemporary and past methods of handling political offenders. There is the same long pretrial detention and the assumption of guilt—reflected in the press—before the verdict, or even the trial itself; the defense is still largely symbolic;* the sentences are predetermined; and the trial continues to serve didactic and publicity purposes. The charges brought against the defendants are about as vague and unspecific as they used to be; they relate to attitudes, beliefs, and values rather than to actions or behavior. People continue to be punished for their ideas if they diverge from those officially sanctioned.

---

* A recent Soviet article analyzing the problematic role of the defense in Soviet courts (without reference to political cases) noted that "It is a commonly held opinion that if the defense counsel's position does not coincide with the decision of the court, then the defense counsel is in the wrong and deserves to be rebuked." It also pointed out that "Some say the defense council is an assistant of the court."[61]

It is tempting to conclude the discussion of coercion in Soviet and American society by proposing a paradox: Soviet society is far more coercive but less openly violent than American society. If people in any society are sufficiently intimidated* they will not organize protests and street demonstrations. There will be no heads to crack for the police, no occasion for throwing tear gas, no photographs of demonstrators being dragged to police vans. In American society there is probably more violence—both political and nonpolitical—than in the Soviet Union, and often it is not easy to separate the political from the nonpolitical forms of violence. Are (mostly young) Negroes looting stores or throwing rocks at policemen and firemen engaged in political violence? Perhaps not, but (as we noted before), their violence is politically consequential and symptomatic. Violence and permissiveness are conjoined in American society, the latter allowing relatively free expression to the former. In the Soviet Union violence is far more institutionalized and hence better controlled. As has been frequently observed, mass violence is not proportional to an underlying set of grievances. Thus in the United States the Black protest movement arose at a time of undeniable improvements in Negro life, but also at a time when persisting hardships and disadvantages are felt as more and more intolerable.

In the Soviet Union there is no single disadvantaged group in a comparable position. Indeed, political or economic disadvantage is, in some ways, distributed in a more "egalitarian" fashion, largely unrelated to ethnic criteria and not always determined by social background either. Thus neither a particular social class or group (nor Soviet society as a whole) has held intense expectations, making demands on the regime comparable to those of the black poor in Amer-

---

* Levels of intimidation and highly revealing public behavior toward the police can be gauged from the experiences of an American scholar who was arrested on the street in Moscow: "Thus it was certainly strange that a person could be dragged, shouting and scuffling, from the sidewalk fronting a big hotel, on a busy street, without causing a single citizen to display curiosity or to alert a foreign embassy or news service."[62] To be sure the incident occurred in 1963 and it is conceivable, though not very likely, that in the late 1960's or early 70's attitudes of passers-by would be different. More recently— in the early 1970's—at least some members of certain groups in Soviet society (Jews, intellectuals, Catholics in Lithuania) displayed more defiant attitudes toward the authorities. Such occasions, however, remain rare and the numbers of people involved very small. By contrast the verbal and physical abuse of the police in the U.S., especially in urban slums and on the campuses, has become a regular occurrence and attempts by the police to arrest suspected criminals or rioters often precipitate serious disturbances.

ica. The expectations of Soviet citizens are modest and manageable. A mixture of potential coercion and slow economic improvements seems adequate for maintaining stability in the foreseeable future with little overt violence.

Pluralism and Totalitarianism

Pluralism and totalitarianism remain, in our view, the most useful single concepts for explaining and understanding the principal differences between American and Soviet political institutions.* Totalitarianism refers to the extension and maximization of state controls, the "penetration" of the state (and its various political agencies) into society, and the resulting deliberate identification of state and society. Russian historical tradition facilitated the emergence of the strong autocratic state. Spontaneous social forces have been weak in Russia for many centuries. For the most part people were unable or unwilling to organize their own groups and associations and saw

---

* The usefulness of both concepts has recently been challenged by several American social scientists. Totalitarianism in particular has come under heavy criticism both by those who have come to believe that it has *never* been a useful concept and by those who think that it has been rendered obsolete by social change in the Soviet Union.[63] The applicability of pluralism to American society in turn has been questioned most forcefully by C. Wright Mills and his numerous followers.[64] Note that the growing denial of pluralism in American society by one group of social scientists has been paralleled by an increasing imputation of pluralism to the Soviet by another group.[65] Indeed the search for signs of pluralism (however feeble or minor) in the Soviet Union has been just as determined and purposeful as the pursuit of data to prove its nonexistence in the United States! These two endeavors have been carried on by different groups of scholars, yet they spring from the same underlying "Zeitgeist," which prompts many American intellectuals to approach their own society in the most critical spirit and other societies fearful of being critical—increasingly haunted by the specter of self-righteousness. "Totalitarianism" carries such negative connotations as regimentation, repression, and thought control, whereas "pluralism" tends to be associated with democracy, freedom, and group autonomy. The propensity to impute pluralism to Soviet society may also be associated with a theorizing impulse which seeks to maximize the common characteristics of *all* industrial societies and which tends to operate on the premise that they must all, sooner or later, become assimilated to the Western model of industrial society, which is indeed pluralistic. Among those who question this assumption, George Fisher has argued forcefully that "a fully modern society might be able to develop along a nonpluralist path" and that under Stalin "the system had little use for politicians with solid economic skills. A generation or less after that it appears that the system needs just such skills in order to run a far more modern society. What has changed is not the monism of the system but the tasks with which it deals."[66]

no point in doing so. The promotion of legitimate group interest through peaceful political means was a basically unfamiliar procedure even before the Soviet regime was established. A Soviet party official put it this way (in a very private conversation with a visitor from abroad):

> Our country has no civil tradition. The taste for association, for organising communal life together, for getting to know each other and taking decisions together, never really existed in Russia. Between the czar and the moujik there was nothing; equally, between one moujik and another there was nothing except for essential personal relationships. We were and we remain a huge body, colossal even, but shapeless and deprived of articulation, of that political fabric on which modern states of Europe were built. The Revolution failed to make the Russian articulate because the experiments of Lenin's soviets were quickly stifled.[67]

Although historical antecedent and tradition facilitated the establishment of a totalitarian regime, they have made it neither inevitable nor wholly explicable.

Soviet totalitarianism resulted from a variety of factors, among which the motivation and disposition of the early Bolsheviks was important. They wanted to make the state as powerful as possible in order to create an instrument for the radical transformation of society. This attitude cannot be reduced to the desire for modernization. Even if it could, rapid modernization can rarely be contemplated without recourse to repressive means of government. As Samuel Huntington has noted, "However it occurs, the accumulation of power necessary for modernization makes the future of democracy rather bleak."[68] Their conceptions of this transformation were, in turn, informed by their absorption of Marxism-Leninism and its application to Russian social-historical conditions. Soviet totalitarianism was "launched" by the early Bolshevik leaders who combined in their outlook an alluring vision of the future (free of all forms of exploitation, want, and injustice), a hard-headed approach to power politics, and an emphasis on elitist conspiratorial organization that was nurtured by the repressive atmosphere of Tsarist Russia. The formative period of the Bolshevik movement was one of illegality and of intricate maneuvering to avoid police detection. The habits of secrecy still characteristic of Soviet political transactions can be traced back to that period.*

Every definition of totalitarianism[70] stresses the historically unprecedented expansion of state power and the multiplication of political controls. This expansion of controls has two bases: one is a set of *values* (an ideology or secular religion) which underlie the conviction that ends justify means, that coercion is necessary, that all and any opposition is treasonable (in relation to the goals envisaged), and that politically unorthodox thoughts are as dangerous as acts. The second basis of totalitarian controls is technological. The maintenance of an elaborate controlling and coercive apparatus requires technical means of communication, transportation, and violence. These must be fairly advanced for the maintenance of totalitarian controls over a large territory and population. Perhaps it was possible to establish and maintain totalitarian controls in a city state such as Geneva under Calvin[71] without modern technological devices; it is clearly impossible in a large nation state.†

Another way to "operationalize" the concept of totalitarianism is in terms of the areas of life with which the state or the government is concerned (which was discussed in the previous chapter). In the USSR, in contrast to the United States, there are hardly any areas of life toward which the state is indifferent.‡ The spirit of totalitar-

* According to some historians the roots of the Soviet propensity to secrecy, and its associated xenophobia, go back to the historical isolation of Russia enhanced by its embracing Eastern Orthodoxy rather than Western Christianity.[69]

† For example, the control of population movements across the border, the so-called Iron Curtain, is impossible without modern technology. This unique feature of totalitarian societies requires devices like mines, barbed wire, telecommunications, high-powered binoculars and reliable, long-range firearms. Similar equipment is required for the maintenance of concentration camps. The develoment of cheap electronic devices has opened up new possibilities for the totalitarian control of privacy. The latter has however been sparingly used so far as a generalized medium of information gathering, which in the USSR is still done largely by human agent. Listening in on telephone conversations and mail censorship are more widely practiced. The small number of private telephones in use in the Soviet Union[72] contrasts with the much more widespread use of television and cannot be explained by technological or economic factors alone, if at all. A much more likely explanation is the fact that television represents one-sided, centralized, controlled communications, while private telephones are instruments of diffuse, decentralized, and (theoretically) private communications.

‡ Typical in this respect is the official attitude toward sports. For example "Leonid Brezhnev, First Secretary of the Communist Party called today for improvements in Soviet sports following disappointing performances by Soviet athletes at the Olympic Games."[73] What is significant is that the head of state himself took up the matter. The

ian controls, and particularly the careful thought given to the definition of subversive ideas, is illustrated by the following account of a Westerner who spent many years in the Soviet Union.

> Russian intellectuals . . . have developed an extremely keen sense about what will be considered "un-Soviet" and why. . . . A young Estonian writer who had seen *Elvira Madigan* [abroad] . . . told me why it could never be shown in Russia. I, too, felt it couldn't: it was too "anarchistic" and too "pessimistic," and it made too much of the power of love and complexities and weaknesses of human nature . . . it provoked too many thoughts about human motivation that had nothing whatever to do with the class struggle, materialism, the whole Marxist explanation of the psyche and society. But I had missed, said my Estonian friend, one of the film's most dangerous flaws: the discredit it cast on the officer class and the obligations of patriotism and military service. "The Soviet Army and Soviet officer corps are absolutely sacrosanct, and funnily enough, this often extends to other armies so that our people won't get 'queer' ideas. So when a Swedish officer deserts, our censors think carefully about what effect it might have on people's respect for military authority in general."[74]

It is also worth pointing out that in the Soviet Union political jokes carry almost the entire burden of social and political criticism. In the United States political jokes are neither very numerous nor important as such vehicles.

The difference between the two systems may also be stated as one in the degree of politicization. In the United States most of the activities of the citizen are not seen as politically relevant. In the USSR they are. In a pluralistic society political factors are not the most important in determining the life of the citizen. This means that most personal decisions are made without reference to political-ideological factors.

This situation imposes a certain amount of strain on the individual who is typically unguided and unaided by political institutions in making his choices and decisions, and who frequently finds himself outside any institutional, organizational context. Consequently

---

official approach toward sports has always stressed, on the one hand, its function in adding to the prestige of the regime (in international competitions) and, on the other, in improving the endurance, health, and physical efficiency of the population with a view to military preparedness and better performance at work.

a pluralistic society is more likely to breed diffuse personal insecurities than does a totalitarian one. Insecurities in a totalitarian society are more clearly focused and more standardized. Thus for example the individual can be reasonably certain that conformity will be rewarded—at least to the extent of attaining basic economic security—and nonconformity punished. Good and bad behavior are clearly defined and enforced by the authorities as best they can.

Pluralism means, as noted above, that political power has many sources and not all of them reside in the state, the government, or a ruling party.[75] It means that there is competition for power—although not all compete and even those who do are unequally equipped for such competition. It also means that the social order is subject to legitimate challenges and pressures on the part of dissatisfied citizens;* that they can legitimately organize and strive to change the existing constellation of power. Pluralism makes it possible, for example, for opponents of the Vietnam war (and indeed of the entire American military establishment and foreign policy) to denounce and demonstrate against the army with impunity, to disrupt and prevent its recruitment on campuses, and force numerous universities to stop or curtail military research and abolish the ROTC programs. Such acts would of course be inconceivable in the Soviet Union (indeed in most other nations), where respect for the armed forces, if not spontaneous, is enforced and public expressions of hostility toward them are not tolerated. Nor would a Soviet citizen (unless perhaps intoxicated) risk the consequences of verbal abuse of the police of the kind largely accepted in the United States, where such insults on officials are viewed as inseparable from the right to free expression and therefore entitled to protection by the Constitution and the courts. Pluralism, and the rule of law associated with it, also means that a civilian employee can disconnect the telephones of an Air Force Base if the Air Force does not pay the bill† (even if the base in question is con-

* This point is supported by Gabriel Almond and Sidney Verba who found that the majority of Americans believed that they could exert some influence on both local and national politics.[76] Their survey was carried out in the early 1960's and it is possible that in the late 1960's the proportions of those who do and do not believe this to be the case would have been different, in view of problems appearing beyond the control of the citizen, namely, inflation, war, and racial unrest. In any event "beliefs" in themselves would be insufficient indicators of effective political participation.
† "Frustrated in attempts to collect a bill for $41,000, the president of a telephone system unplugged an Air Force installation this week. Edward Streigel head of Gem State Utilities stepped into a manhole two blocks from his office in Grand View, Idaho, and

nected with vital defense systems) without fear of being jailed for sabotage. Similarly, it protects the mayor of a small town who has towed away and impounded a car belonging to the army and who sues the Federal Government successfully to pay the charges.[78]

Pluralism means that those opposed to the political system (and who frequently denigrate its legal-political safeguards and institutions) can nevertheless take advantage of this system, in and outside the courts. Thus, for example: "The Federal Communications Commission ruled today that a New York radio station that editorially attacked the W. E. B. DuBois Clubs as being 'controlled by American Communists' must give the group radio time to answer."[79] Pluralism also means that the government does not control the press and mass media and therefore the latter can mount campaigns of criticism of the government, and, wielding the powerful instrument of publicity, can expose the abuses and errors of the government, including its coercive organs. A leading newspaper reports: "An employee of TVA said today that a Secret Service agent recently interrogated him because of a report that he had made 'strong statements' concerning President Johnson. . . . Referring to the interrogation Mr. Ferris said, 'Is this the sort of intimidation that a private citizen should have to put up with? Must we fear knocks on our doors late at night?' "[80] Perhaps in part because of the national publicity given to the incident by the *New York Times,* Mr. Ferris was not afraid of knocks on his door at night.* Had he been, he would not have made public statements on the attempted intimidation for a major newspaper nor would a major newspaper concern itself with the incident if it had been routine and acceptable. (By contrast, "Where there is no freedom, complaining of its absence is severely forbidden."[84])

---

cut off communications to two Titan missile silos for an hour and 15 minutes. . . . He has been ordered to submit a written report to the state agency . . . to explain his action. . . . 'They ought to pay their bill like anyone else . . .' his attorney quoted Mr. Streigel as saying. 'If they don't the farmers and ranchers in Idaho will have to pay it for them."[77]

* It might in fact be argued that one of the most important consequences of pluralism is permissiveness in the political arena which explains the attitudes of those among the population who define themselves (and are defined as such by the rest of society) as political deviants. In the light of such considerations one can understand "Mark Rudd Seeking A Draft Deferment As a Revolutionist"[81] or "Antiwar Group Asking Fort Dix For Permit to Stage Show"[82] or a leader of the Socialist Workers Party trying to distribute antiwar literature at a military base while attending the trial of an enlisted man who had done the same thing and was acquitted.[83]

A pluralistic society also provides the setting in which political dissidents engaged in some spectacular or photogenic form of protest can count on considerable publicity by the mass media. The story below is a good example of this phenomenon:

> Proclaiming victory for their gesture with cheers and raised fists, 15 antiwar veterans ended their occupation of the Statue of Liberty yesterday.
>
> "Wow, we were in there a day and a half and the Government would not touch us" shouted one of the fatigues-clad men at a jubilant feast in a midtown restaurant where they went to celebrate. . . .
>
> "Look" he [Al Hubbard, the director of Vietnam Veterans Against the War—P. H.] shouted . . . "the Liberty 15 has been asked to go on the 'Today' show. What do you say?" "Right on" shouted back the veterans as they laughed and drank their beer. "We also got an invitation for a talk show on WRVR, an FM station, but we are hedging" Mr. Hubbard said. "I think we'll be hearing from the 'Cavett Show.' "[85]

Pluralism cushions the impact of authority because the power of the government is neither unquestioned nor undivided, as various groups keep a watchful eye over its exercise. In the final analysis it is again pluralism (and the related rule of law) that helps to understand the case of the late radical prisoner, Samuel Melville, accused of setting off bombs in various Manhattan office buildings, who requested permission to read his favorite radical magazine (*Ramparts*), and whose request was granted by a court.[86] It is also pluralism which makes it possible for the Mayor of Seattle to refuse to cooperate with the Federal authorities in raiding the Black Panthers' headquarters, and also his denouncing the plan as "smacking of gestapo style tactics."[87] Similarly the freedoms created by pluralism protect (perhaps unwisely) the distribution of manuals on explosives and guerrilla warfare by a book salesman.[88] It is the embattled, still surviving, rule of law which explains why intruders on the grounds of the presidents' homes outside Washington were not detained: "We had to let them go," said the secret service director, James J. Rowley, "because present Federal laws do not specifically bar unauthorized entry to Presidential compounds outside Washington. The bill which he requested would do so and also would outlaw noisy demonstrations aimed at disrupting Presidential business."[89]

Trivial as some of these examples might appear they do express aspects of pluralism frequently taken for granted while they also exemplify the enlargement of personal freedom pluralism makes possible.

Pluralism in America evolved out of the Western European cultural-political tradition and a fortunate combination of natural and human resources, as well as from conscious political designs. Totalitarianism in the USSR emerged from a violent revolution, civil war, the legacy of political-economic backwardness, and the ideological compulsions of a small elite. It can be viewed both as a response to the desire for rapid modernization and as the malformed practical expression of high ideals.

4. The Nature and Propagation of Values: Advertising and Propaganda

It is among the commonplaces of social science that a reasonable understanding of societies cannot be attained unless their major values are grasped and their influence on behavior ascertained. Social scientists are interested not only in what people typically do, but also in what they would like to do, what they value and what they believe in. Correspondingly, social institutions are examined with reference to both their actual functioning and what they are supposed to accomplish.

It has been widely observed that social institutions and values are inseparable[1] and interdependent. The current sociological approach to this relationship might be compared to the position modern medicine has reached concerning the duality of body and mind. While primitive healing methods have always recognized the interdependence between the two, Western scientific medicine, inspired by positivism, prided itself until recently upon separating the two spheres.[2] In both cases—body and mind, social institution and value—the distinction is based on two levels of observation rather than on irreducible, qualitative differences between the two types of phenomena.

The "observation" of values is, of course, a complicated matter. Though many contemporary American sociologists habitually talk about "societal values" or "dominant systems of values," there are no reliable procedures to ascertain the nature and influence of these values in large and complex societies such as the United States and the Soviet Union.* Such difficulties are similar to those encountered at the individual level. The fundamental complication arises out of the tendency of human beings to pay verbal tribute to certain values without otherwise incorporating them into their behavior. The relationship between profession of values and behavior is obscured by the widespread inability of people to live up to their own values. More from personal experience than from sociological theory we are familiar with situations in which a wide gulf separates our values from our actions, our aspirations from our achievements, what we think we should do from what we actually do.[4] The same applies at the societal level. Social institutions diverge from the values in whose spirit they are supposed to function.

Thus, the assumption that what people do is a reflection of what they want or value, bears re-examination, especially in the light of the popularity of functional theories of society. The latter suggest an unrealistically high level of congruence between individual and social values, and between values and institutions. But the inculcation and acceptance of values need be neither a smooth nor self-evident process. As Barrington Moore notes:

> Cultural values do not descend from heaven to influence the course of history. . . . To maintain and transmit a value system, human beings are punched, bullied, sent to jail, thrown into concentration camps, cajoled, bribed, made into heroes, encouraged to read newspapers, stood up against the wall and shot and sometimes even taught sociology.[5]

The problem of congruence, both between personal values and their attainment, and between personal and social values, is particularly acute in modern societies, even in those which do not place many external constraints on individual behavior. It may be that both the techniques and the substance of socialization in modern, secular, and mobile societies create a poor fit between personal aspi-

---

* The difficulties of ascertaining the dominant values of complex societies is aptly captured in this comment: "What is presented as the 'central value system' of a society often turns out to be little more than the individual sociologist's own prejudiced view of the society in which he lives . . . many sociological and psychological accounts of moral values fail to distinguish between the values that are asserted in a formal way and the values which actually guide behavior in everyday situations."[3]

rations and socially framed opportunities.[6] Perhaps a major cause of conflict between values and behavior in such societies is to be found in inflated expectations of one kind or another. As will be seen later, both the United States and the USSR inculcate, in different ways and to different degrees inflated expectations in their citizens.*

The unearthing of individual values presents problems as great as the discovery of those assumed to characterize society as a whole. Most individuals formulate their values in a more simple, rudimentary manner than the official or self-appointed spokesmen of their society. Moreover, most people evince some bewilderment when called upon to summarize their major value commitments—even when the word "value" is translated into simpler, more concrete terms.[7] For most people, their values are either self-evident or unclear, or unattainable and as such pointless and painful to articulate. People are also inclined to define their values according to what they perceive to be the expectations or trends current in their society—which is not the same as accepting or internalizing them.

Thus, the discernment of values is a difficult task, both at the societal and individual level. At the former, problems arise because of the presence of multiple sets of values, nurtured by different subgroups and subcultures of society; at the latter, difficulties are encountered because neither observed behavior nor personal professions of value commitment are reliable guides.

Owing to these limitations, we will focus attention on the major institutions in each society engaged in the dissemination and propagation of values, namely, political propaganda, commercial advertising, formal education, and religion. We shall also try to sketch the major values of each society† on the basis of what their authoritative spokesmen tell us about them.

Some warnings are in order here. The usefulness of different sources in ascertaining major values is qualified. Printed matter, and the mass media in general, are a less reliable guide to popular values in the USSR than in the United States. In the latter, much of what gets into print is produced largely in response to actual or an-

* However, in the Soviet case social realities (and the appropriate authorities) keep in check the growth of expectations to a far greater extent than in American society.

† We prefer to use the term "major values" to "value system." Most values, both on the societal and individual level, do not add up to a system, that is, to a well-integrated, consistent, and cohesive whole. On the contrary, values held by individuals as by societies are often strikingly contradictory, unintegrated, and compartmentalized.

ticipated public demand and interest, in response to the fluctuations in the nation-wide or local markets of taste. In the Soviet Union, the contents of printed matter and the mass media are determined by the political-ideological elites and by their persisting desire to re-educate and mold the masses. The Soviet policies toward the free circulation of ideas reflect the official assessments of the importance of ideas in general. The more seriously they are taken (in any society) the more likely it is that the authorities will be concerned with their dissemination and potential effect. In pragmatic Anglo-Saxon societies, the United States included, ideas are not taken too seriously and it is widely felt that, as a rule, there is a considerable distance between ideas and action, theory and practice. Thus ideas are viewed as relatively inconsequential in themselves. This is exactly the opposite of the Soviet, or the Leninist, position which explicitly treats ideas as "weapons." If ideas are weapons, they must be carefully controlled lest they fall into the wrong hands; unorthodox ideas are to be suppressed. In the Soviet-Leninist perspective there is no sharp dividing line between ideas and action, opinions and behavior. One can easily lead to the other, hence the unauthorized dissemination of ideas is as dangerous as the illegal possession of arms, and both are treated with similar gravity.[8]

Reliance on the sources described above will make the assessment of minority values difficult; in the United States as in the USSR, certain minorities have an unequal opportunity to express their variant or deviant views, while others have much better chances.* The problem is virtually universal: in every society the desire and facility for articulating values, value judgments and commitments are unevenly distributed, depending largely on the level and type of education received and on the intangibles of motivation. For example, the people in the United States who write letters to their congressmen, or the local paper, or New York Times, are doubtless unrepresentative of the population as a whole as are the people most frequently interviewed on television.

The problem of sorting out dominant from deviant (or variant) values in Soviet society is additionally complicated by the fact that

* On the other hand it might also be argued that in many instances certain militant, though not necessarily powerful, minorities may have a better chance to express their values (with the help of the mass media) than do the more conventional majorities. This, at any rate, often is the case in the U.S.[9]

the dividing line between legitimate and illegitimate, permissible and impermissible value orientations is sharply drawn. The "dominant" values of Soviet society are obviously dominant in the legal-political sense; what is more difficult to ascertain is the extent to which they "dominate" private beliefs or popular attitudes.

Commercial Advertising and Political Propaganda

Commercial advertising in the United States and political propaganda in the USSR are among the most visible aspects of life in the two societies. They seem to set the tone of much that is most readily observable. Should the proverbial visitor from Mars try to summarize his most striking visual impressions of the two countries, the massive evidence of advertising in one and propaganda in the other would be among the features cited as "characteristic." They are indeed. Even if their significance could be limited to the realm of visual perceptions, we would have to deal with these phenomena which are obviously the products of the "culture" in the anthropological sense. If advertising or propaganda were merely one of the many strange and quaint ways in which societies dress themselves up, or one of the interesting but unessential games of make-believe their members play, we might dismiss them as unrelated to more "basic" and important social realities and institutions. But this is not the case. American commercial advertising and Soviet political propaganda are not just wasteful games or forms of aimless display, although they often appear to be no more than that. Each is closely linked to more important institutions and values in each society, predominantly economic in the United States and primarily political in the USSR. Both cost immense sums of money, involve the time of hundreds of thousands (if not millions) of people, and are often viewed as the mainstay of economic and political institutions respectively.

The annual cost of advertising in the United States was over 15 billion dollars in 1965 and close to 20 billion in 1970.[10] The Soviet expenditure on propaganda has never been revealed, but it is not unreasonable to assume that it might approximate that for American advertising. If we could compute only the cost of "television time" devoted to political propaganda in the USSR we would arrive at large amounts. Another obvious item would be the value of work that goes into the planning, execution, and participation in propaganda campaigns including the time spent at rallies and meetings. The high cost of such efforts is exemplified by the estimated 200 million dollars spent on the 1957 Moscow Youth Festival.[11]

American commercial advertising and Soviet political propaganda are similar in many respects. In particular, each illuminates in its own way the major values of its society and some of the popular attitudes toward them.

First and foremost, we are interested in what the two phenomena have in common. We suggest that both attempt to capture and express these major values, though with different degrees of deliberateness and success. Political propaganda in the Soviet Union is a highly planned, centralized, and government-controlled enterprise which has tried consistently and systematically to inculcate attitudes and values deemed desirable at any given time by the political leadership.[12] Its forms and goals derive from the principles of Marxism-Leninism, or, more precisely, from the reigning interpretation of these principles. American advertising by contrast has not relied, at least consciously, on any set of philosophical principles, nor has it been directed by or related to the government or any political entity.[13] Instead, commercial advertising in America tries to draw out the implications of some of the prevailing major values, to perceive popular aspirations, and to mount its "campaigns" accordingly. While many people, and especially the most severe critics of commercial advertising, sometimes have the impression that it creates values ("false values" it is usually said), it would seem more appropriate to say that advertising exaggerates, modifies, or distorts existing values, rather than deliberately creates new ones. This is profoundly different from the procedures of Soviet political propaganda. The latter appears to rest—for the most part—on the assumption that people must be persuaded about things they do not believe in, or about things they do not wish to do. Its approach most frequently entails exhortation to effort: the vast, probably overwhelming proportion of Soviet propaganda has been directed toward the physical reconstruction of Soviet society and toward inducing active support of policies entailing some measure of sacrifice or deprivation. Such goals can in no way be equated with the major effort of American advertising, namely, to persuade people to consume more—an orientation that builds upon pre-existing, or at least latent attitudes, many of them obviously hedonistic. The contrast may be focused more sharply by suggesting that while the major thrust of Soviet propaganda has consisted of persuading people to defer gratifications, American advertising aims at precisely the opposite: to develop an intolerance of such deferrals and to deepen and enlarge the desire and impatience for gratification.[14]

Thus, both American advertising and Soviet propaganda, each in its own way, are pressed into the service of dominant values, the difference lying both in the substance of the respective values and in the sense in which we can call them dominant. The nature of the "domination" which the two sets of values exercise over the lives and attitudes of people in the two societies differ as profoundly as the substance of the values. In the American case we can speak of dominance because the values in question are to a large extent accepted and internalized, assimilated into behavior which they influence in a discernible manner. They are, for example, the value of success or achievement, expressed in the desire to multiply and cherish material possessions, to be competitive in the marketplace of accumulation or interpersonal relations.[15] On the other hand, the dominant values of Soviet society are most characteristically "dominant" because they are upheld by the political leadership and are supported by all the political institutions of society. They "dominate" because they are the only legitimate set of values, because the articulation and dissemination of competing values are not tolerated. For example, the supremacy of society over the individual, or public over private interest, is among such dominant values which cannot be considered as fully internalized or incorporated into the behavior of the majority of Soviet citizens. Likewise the idea of the primacy of the collective over the individual (especially when his family interests are also included and counterposed to those of the collective) cannot realistically be considered as an internalized and deeply accepted value dominating Soviet popular attitudes. Yet it is dominant in the other sense: it is the basis of Soviet social institutions, it is the prescribed and only legitimate disposition. (We are not concerned at this point with the extent to which behavior deviates from such ideal patterns.)

The most striking similarity between American advertising and Soviet propaganda lies in their corresponding *pervasiveness* and *omnipresence*. While in the United States it is virtually impossible to escape exposure to advertising, Soviet society is similarly remorseless in enveloping all life situations of its citizens with the messages of political propaganda. The degree of saturation attained in the United States is such that even the most minimal participation in social living compels contact with advertising.* Indeed, one simply cannot conceive of situations and settings which have not been penetrated by advertising. Shunning the mass media is not enough. Streets and buildings of both cities and villages, roadsides, remote landscapes, even the skies, carry messages about the virtues of one product or another. Avoiding inhabited regions is insufficient since billboards penetrate the heart of the countryside and reach any locale traversed by people. Theoretically only a hermit, living in the heart of a forest and obtaining his supplies from nature (or from outside civilization) could hope to remain isolated from the inducements to consume some product or service. American advertising has achieved unparalleled total and systematic coverage of the entire population. Soviet political propaganda can boast of similar coverage, although it is likely that remote areas in the USSR are not as efficiently covered as their counterparts in the United States, partly because the land area of the Soviet Union is almost three times that of the United States, and partly because of the less developed nature of the Soviet system of communications. Yet it might be argued that such disadvantages are offset by the presence, or frequent visits, of the personal carrier of Soviet propaganda messages. The "agitator" who sells his ideological wares in the home is not unlike the traveling salesman in America, except for one important difference: he cannot be brushed off or refused admittance to the house and has to be listened to with forebearance dictated by prudence.†

Advertising and propaganda use essentially the same methods: the mass media, static visual images (billboards, slogans, and symbols painted on walls), and traveling salesmen. Soviet propaganda has one additional advantage over advertising in the United States: it also

---

* Improbable as it seems, according to one account, "The amount of advertising that the average American sees and hears is supposed to be 1500 messages a day."[16]

† The number of agitators is difficult to ascertain in part because it fluctuates depending on the presence or absence of particular political events or campaigns. Their numbers may range from hundreds of thousands to 3 million (or more) according to different estimates in different periods. "Agitation is carried on almost anywhere, and very often takes place in the field during a rest break or during the lunch hour at a factory shop. There are also permanent places for agitation called 'agit-points' where literature, film projectors, tape recorders and other aids are kept, and where scheduled sessions are held. These are often in clubs and Houses of Culture."[17]

has at its disposal the entire system of formal education from nursery to university. At the same time, unlike American advertising, it has failed to enlist to a corresponding degree the help of the social sciences, psychology in particular, which might give an edge of efficiency to American advertising over Soviet propaganda. It is interesting to ask why Soviet propagandists have not utilized more fully the services of psychologists or sociologists, and have instead relied predominantly on party functionaries and journalists untrained in the finer arts of influencing the mind. One reason may be the less developed state of Soviet social psychology, attitude surveys, and testing; it may also be the case that Soviet leaders have considered propaganda too important to be left in the hands of scholarly specialists and are unwilling to allow anyone but the party to handle it.*

Soviet propaganda, and much of political propaganda in general, face more difficult tasks than advertising not only because it urges effort and sacrifice rather than relaxation or luxury, but also because it often deals in less tangible appeals and concepts. It is more difficult to provoke enthusiasm about overfulfilling the five-year plan or the moral and material support of a "national liberation" movement in some distant corner of Africa or Asia—that may in turn require belt-tightening for the citizen—than to persuade him about the desirability of a huge refrigerator or a powerful car.

Both advertising and political propaganda tend to make claims which can neither be proved nor disproved—or at least the implications of their claims are misleading. They both misrepresent reality by its denial or selective presentation, or by substituting "ought" for "is." In advertising the distortion of reality is usually related to the alleged effects of buying some goods or services. In propaganda, misrepresentations may concern either the nature of the social environment (presented, for example, as just, blissful, invigorating, or friendly), or the individual's future in society (portrayed as both materially and spiritually fulfilled). Most frequently Soviet propaganda depicts the implausibly fruitful results of work, loyalty, or discipline, while advertising portrays the similarly, if not more improbably, miraculous results obtained by some type of consumption. The two types

* This state of affairs has been changing as illustrated by one important collection of writings on propaganda. Among the 31 contributors at least a dozen had an academic status or affiliation; in other instances political and academic affiliations were intertwined, while a small majority of contributors clearly belonged to the Party apparatus or worked in journalism. Also noteworthy was the presence of an essay on "Social Psychology and Political Propaganda" authored by a professor trained in philosophy.[18]

of persuasion are at one, in that they offer solutions for every human need and problem: advertising by means of the appropriate purchase, propaganda by means of appropriate attitude and exertions. If a person lives according to the precepts of the party, or Marxism-Leninism, as expounded and applied by the propagandist, his life will be a good one. Correspondingly, the impression conveyed by advertising is that those who respond to its multiple appeals cannot fail to be satisfied and happy. To be sure the components of the two types of happiness or fulfillment are markedly different. In the American advertising version they most frequently are: youthfulness, vigor, aggressiveness, masculinity, feminine beauty, prestige, influence, high social status, high earning power, good taste, popularity, and sex appeal. In the Soviet version the components of happiness are a sense of community, satisfaction in work, discipline, loyalty, dedication to the party, knowledge of ideology, and the like. In each case the components enumerated derive from the major values (official or dominant) upheld in the two societies. Thus both American advertising and Soviet political propaganda support the dominant system of values: the former more indirectly and less self-consciously (but probably more effectively) and the latter directly and deliberately.

The two institutions are also similar in their reliance on slogans, repetition, and saturation. While the technique of repetition common to both suggests that the appeals are not entirely rational (why repeat that which is obviously and clearly acceptable and persuasive?), Soviet propaganda tries to affect its audience primarily on a conscious rather than sub- or semiconscious level, which is the preferred technique of American advertising.[19] Soviet propaganda campaigns may entail fraudulent claims, dubious promises, and hate-mongering, yet they are somewhat more "above board" than their American counterparts in advertising. The deliberate American effort to prompt people to act on the basis of motives and impulses of which they have little or no awareness* has no easily identifiable Soviet equivalent. Thus the two methods of persuasion differ in that

---

* Richard Hoggart has observed that "At bottom the case against advertising is the same as that against political propaganda, much religious proselytizing and any other form of emotional blackmail. The case is this: that advertising tries to achieve its ends by emotionally abusing its audiences. Recognizing that we all have fears, hopes, anxieties, admirations, insecurities, advertisers seek not to increase our understanding of these feelings, and so perhaps our command of them, but to use their existence to increase the sales of whatever product they happen to have been paid to sell. . . ."[20]

Soviet propaganda is blatant, crude, and often obviously fraudulent, but addressed to an audience assumed to be somewhat more rational, though hardly more autonomous. American advertising is more refined, surreptitious, and underhanded, based on the model of the irrational consumer who will buy a product because of its associations, because of fears and anxieties which he may or may not be aware of. At the same time American advertising cannot and does not *claim* respect as does Soviet propaganda, which is an essentially spiritual rather than secular undertaking in regard to its objectives, notwithstanding its simpler techniques. According to a knowledgeable Western student of Soviet society:

> . . . In substance, advertising in America, however vulgar and stupefying, is innocuous compared to Party propaganda. If large sections of America resemble a giant supermarket for the hawking and selling of goods, all Russia is an even larger revival meeting where the mind and soul, damnation and salvation, are the issues. Here it is not mere goods and services that are being hawked, but nothing less than cosmic goals and a total explanation of man, society and history—together with the Party's advertisement for itself as the sole interpreter of these matters, and therefore the sole source of wisdom, truth and happiness.[21]

The point also highlights an issue which is often falsely dichotomized both in the West and in the USSR, namely that of coercion versus persuasion, or coercion versus propaganda. In Soviet society the two are not mutually exclusive but supportive. Propaganda (and the persuasion it attempts) is coercive in two senses: on the one hand it is monopolistic: there are no alternative sources of information or argument; on the other hand these attempts at "persuasion" are always integrated with the entire institutional network, including the coercive apparatus, which is ready to back up "persuasion" with punitive and coercive sanctions whenever needed.

The vast streams of both American advertising and Soviet political propaganda easily break down into a few simple themes and messages incessantly repeated with or without variations. In advertising the basic themes are more diversely camouflaged and displayed than in propaganda, which assaults its audience with dogged monotony. Hence advertising is occasionally entertaining and even humorous. This can hardly be said of Soviet propaganda, which is almost uniformly boring (an exception, the Soviet humor magazine, *Krokodil,* sometimes provides humorous propaganda).

Advertising and propaganda also have in common the distortion of language. To convey their message, each relies on disfiguring ordinary language, changing the conventional meaning of words, coining new phrases, and indulging in exaggeration.* Such techniques reflect the underlying objective of altering accepted frames of reference. They grow out of the desire to replace conceptions of reality as they can be experienced with a make-believe world which the advertiser and propagandist wish to force on their audiences. The greater the urgency of persuasion the more pressure there is for the introduction of terms and concepts difficult to validate by ordinary, everyday experience. In advertising, linguistic "innovations" often also serve as attention-getting devices, sometimes to distinguish specific products. In propaganda, most typically two goals are served by distortions of the language: to cover up unattractive aspects of social-political realities (for example, to call police terror "administrative measures"), and to personify abstractions for emotional stimulation (for instance, the Party or the Enemy).[23]

Further similarities can be noted in the dissemination of propaganda and advertising messages. Soviet propaganda campaigns tend to be completely centralized: they are planned at the highest levels of the Party's propaganda apparatus and spread through the country simultaneously. Local campaigns launched on local initiative and applying to a limited sector of the country of population are rare. Advertising campaigns for a given product are similarly centralized and

---

* Also characteristic of American advertising is the effort to transcend what common sense would consider its natural boundaries and the attempt to exploit current social or political themes, issues or motives. The first objective is manifest in the copywriters' desire to convince the consumer that a particular product is not merely a specific item of consumption but an inordinately diffuse panacea (this is exemplified in the technique of using the expression "the world of" X product or service). The second objective is manifest in harnessing every prevailing "trend" to a particular sales pitch. Thus an advertisement for *Glamour* magazine (primarily concerned with fashions, cosmetics and entertainment) proclaimed: "Commitment and Involvement Is In" (*New York Times,* February 6, 1968). Another advertisement (in *Psychology Today,* October, 1969, p. 73) offered for sale the "Official Harvard Strike Shirt." Promoters of "movement jackets" were willing to provide "a different color jacket for instant recognition" (*Massachusetts Daily Collegian* November 23, 1970, p. 10). Such ads demonstrate an infinite flexibility in the pursuit of the dollar.
Themes of social consciousness and activism have also begun to penetrate the world of the soap opera, hitherto reserved for the pseudoconflicts of personal life.[22]

disseminated simultaneously, at least for major products. The same slogans from the same source advertise a soft drink in a small midwestern town and New York City at any given time.

Neither advertising nor propaganda can offer hard evidence of specific results. Advertisers and their clients (under competitive pressures) have made more determined efforts to measure results than political propagandists—and the effects of advertising campaigns are more amenable to measurement than those of political ones. Thus, probably more is known about the results of advertising, though not about the exact relationship between the magnitude and nature of the effort and its results. Curiously enough, Soviet propagandists seem less concerned with devising measures of the success of their work. Nevertheless, one can state with some certainty that neither of the two types of persuasion is a total failure even if not proportional to the ambitions of those who devise them.

It does appear that Soviet propaganda has been successful in inculcating if not all the desired attitudes, at any rate the notion that the system is legitimate and irremovable.[24] Even disaffected members of Soviet society have adopted many of the official perspectives and values. Advertising also has such residual results, that is, the inculcation of attitudes of which the target of advertising is not aware.* Neither propaganda nor advertising can be successful if the claims put forward are patently and demonstrably fraudulent and if there is strong group pressure against them.

The final similarity between the approaches and implications of American advertising and Soviet propaganda is their impersonality and effort to standardize attitudes. More "individualistic methods" symbolized by the door-to-door salesman and the visiting agitator make little dent on this impersonality. In practice these more "individualized" approaches also become standardized: both the salesman and the agitator typically recite their messages in a mechanical way, without much regard to the differences among their audience, which they do not and cannot know well. The "personal touch" of the

* For example, it is not inconceivable that in the U.S. many among the most impatient youthful critics of the world of business, competition, and manipulation (such as being attempted by advertising) developed their own craving for instant solutions of social problems, and their intolerance of frustration, at least in part as a result of their exposure to the advertising, they doubtless despise.

American salesman, just as the pseudocomradeship of the agitator, are both feeble and, for the most part, futile attempts at personalizing an essentially impersonal situation. In any event, both advertising and propaganda remain largely impersonal because of the unavoidable predominance of the mass media in the dissemination of their messages. Such a predominance has been a mixed blessing from the point of view of the Soviet regime:

> As the accessibility to the media has increased, exposure has become more and more privatized. The artificially supportive context of earlier days, collective listening and the agitator who guided discussions after programs or newspaper readings, has gradually begun to disappear. As people have less and less contact with officials who try to guide their exposure patterns and reactions, they become somewhat freer in their choices regarding the media. To some extent liberated from official scrutiny, people can now more easily choose not to expose themselves to media, and they can react to political messages in private or in the company of trusted friends . . . A second possible dysfunctional effect of the mass media comes from their capacity to penetrate the population so rapidly with news. When fewer people were informed of events, sudden changes in the Party line were not as noticeable.[25]

Both advertising and propaganda are presumed to create as their residual by-product an endemic "credibility gap" between the entire social world and the individual, a certain numbness and skepticism regarding the pleasures and promises proffered by both advertising and propaganda. What Richard Hoggart, the English critic of the mass media, said of their effect on the British working classes, could be extended to Americans and Soviet people bombarded respectively by advertising and propaganda:

> Today he is so bespattered by ceaseless esoteric voices, is invited so frequently to feel this, this and this, to react to this, to do that, to believe this—that in recoil he often decides to feel none of these things, neither the glories, nor the horrors. He goes dead to it all. He develops a strong patina of resistance, a thick and solid skin for not taking notice. When the voices, especially those of the Press, really have something important to speak to him about, he

gives them the old smile and continues to read the funny bits. They have cried "wolf" too often.[26]*

Important differences remain, however, between the functions and forms of commercial advertising and political propaganda. The functions of advertising are predominantly economic while those of Soviet propaganda are political.[28] Advertising tries to multiply needs (in order to increase consumption) while propaganda tries to restrict many of them (in order to establish or strengthen conformity and make certain deprivations acceptable). Finally, the philosophical and methodological foundations are also profoundly different: in the case of advertising, applied social science is harnessed to material greed, while Soviet propaganda rests on the bedrock of Marxist-Leninist dogma and ideology.

By comparing Soviet *propaganda* with American *advertising* we did not wish to convey the impression that the former is absent or insignificant in the United States. There is, of course, plenty of political propaganda, but it is far less pervasive and homogeneous than the Soviet version. American political propaganda is fragmented (among the two major parties, smaller ones, pressure groups, and local interests). Much of it is periodic (related to election campaigns), and it can be far more easily evaded than either advertising or Soviet propaganda. It does not command the resources of either government or powerful commercial interests, though the latter do support it covertly during elections and on some other occasions. Since it does reflect the varied political values of a pluralistic polity, its analysis would call for an examination in terms of different types of political propaganda—a task that cannot be accomplished in this survey of the two societies.

The "Success Digest"—A Case Study of American Popular Values

Every year a vast number of books and magazines are published in the United States which constitute, what might be called the self-

* Yet Soviet propaganda continues to count on the credulousness of its audience as the following shows: ". . . Buchwald's columns are often reprinted in Russian newspapers, although they're usually run there not as comic flights of fancy about Nixon & Co. but as straight news dispatches from Washington. A while ago for instance Buchwald wrote a column in which he revealed that a top-secret Government study, the Dawk Report, had recommended that the State Department be shut down because its duties had been taken over by 'the Defense Department, the CIA and Henry Kissinger,' and Russian readers were presented with this as the truth."[27]

improvement literature. The "Success Digest"[29] chosen for examination here, is a collection of advertisements for self-improvement or self-help books.* Similar (or the same) books can be found advertised in other media, including various mass circulation magazines. The "Digest" brings together in one publication advertisements for books on a wide range of topics in anticipation of a variety of consumer needs. More significantly, as the title indicates, all advertisements in the booklet offer assistance for the accomplishment of success, the pinnacle of the popular value "system" of most Americans. We can be assured that the interpretations of success in a booklet of this kind will not be unduly esoteric. Moreover, the pamphlet also fits into the long-standing American tradition of the self-improvement literature. It deviates from this tradition in one important respect: by offering the achievement of success, not by hard work and strenuous effort, as similar pamphlets did in the past, but by easily acquired techniques and gimmicks.[30] We can learn from the "Digest" not only about the popular conceptions of success (and its accessories) but also those of failure. Unfortunately no comparable document exists to aid us in a survey of Soviet popular values and aspirations.

In treating the values inferred from the "Success Digest" as widespread, we are supported by the results of various scholarly efforts aimed at the codification of American values.[31] These studies confirm that what we are dealing with here are more than the bizarre products of the imagination of advertising copywriters.

While the preoccupation with success cuts across class and status groups, the books advertised in the *Success Digest* are addressed primarily to the unsuccessful or less successful, to those with limited education, who are more susceptible to the encouragement and impersonal advice of dubious experts. The presumed typical readers of these publications seem united by their lack of self-confidence, insecurity, and their hope of gratifying their desires by passing the regular, institutionalized pathways to success (that is, education, special skills, or advantages of birth). They are apt to believe that short cuts to success exist and are available to everybody, and that disadvantages of birth can be compensated for by certain techniques. Such beliefs reaffirm the great American dream, the American mystique of success and equal opportunity.

---

* An effort to find out the approximate circulation of this booklet from the publishers met with refusal.

It could be argued that the desires and frustrations which the titles advertised reflect are not peculiarly American: people all over the world wish to be healthy, rich, sexually satisfied, liked by their fellows, and at peace with themselves. What is, however, peculiarly American is the belief that all this can be attained by anybody, by the simple expedient of learning a few easy methods and by taking to heart the advice of a few experts.[32] This belief is, of course, closely linked to the American value of egalitarianism. Indeed, the emergence and appeal of these books are best understood as a product of the clash between the value of egalitarianism, the belief in the equality of opportunity, and the limited accomplishments of the majority. It is this clash, experienced by so many, which inspires these books. The similarly widespread American belief in the manipulability of the self and the environment offers further clues to understanding the self-improvement literature. The conflict between these beliefs and social realities, presumably, creates a sense of nagging doubt, the doubt that one is not living up to his opportunities and to his innate, if hidden, potentials. Since self-improvement (rather than changing institutions) is offered as the solution, the books imply that the fault lies with the self—its ignorance, sluggishness, lack of initiative, imagination, and drive—and *not* with the social environment.

The authors of the books advertised seem to assume that the potential reader is extremely credulous, if not downright gullible[33]— despite his lifelong exposure to the extravagant and unverifiable claims of commercial advertising. One would expect that a measure of skepticism, immunity, or invulnerability to these improbable claims and promises would develop. Yet one book promises: "You will overshadow others like the towering oak overshadows the sapling, like the giant overshadows the dwarf"; another offers: "For once 'ego-power' is yours—there are no limits to what you can have. Your wishes will be granted quickly and automatically."

These examples of contemporary self-improvement literature have little in common with the Protestant Ethic. On the contrary, they imply that Americans have a strong distaste for effort. They also appeal to the American belief in the unlimited changeability of human character and personality: "Lifelong habits and mannerisms . . . will vanish for good—new attitudes and skills become permanently implanted." Such books could not be written and advertised without assuming that Americans are, or fear to be, in poor health and are intensely dissatisfied with their income, job, personality, sex life, intellect, level of education, and interpersonal relations.*

The image of human nature conveyed by the contents of the "Digest" is a modification of what is implied by the "American Dream." The modification is presumably designed to accommodate the potential reader, who did not or could not take advantage of the offerings of American society. Human nature as seen by the writers of the "Digest" has practically unlimited potentialities which somehow were denied expression because of bad luck, ignorance, or merely the lack of pertinent information.

The existence of the books described in the "Digest" also suggests that their authors and sponsors credit Americans with a tremendous respect for the printed word emanating from the expert who usually assumes the mantle of *scientific* authority. In the following paragraphs we will examine what the books claim to remedy by presenting a few examples of each of the three major types.

First, are the *money-making' books* which promise to "skyrocket" or substantially increase income or earning power. Characteristically, they do not propose to accomplish this by the acquisition of some specific, testable skill or by the learning of some occupationally useful knowledge. Success, apparently, is seen as due to more intangible skills, talents, and inspirations, and is to be gained by short cuts, tricks, simple techniques—gimmicks. This belief largely corresponds to the outlook of the frustrated, the alienated, the unsuccessful, who themselves lack tangible skills, profitable occupations, and higher education. For the poorly educated and unsuccessful, success appears to be elusive, mysterious, often unfairly attained, and not the result of any clear-cut criteria or qualifications. Approximately one-third of the 66 titles advertised in the booklet are directly concerned with the problem of how to make more money, but a far larger proportion touches on the issue by including greater earning power among the many other benefits the reader will reap from the particular book. For example, a volume on *Sleep Learning* promises to help, among many other things, in "sales training" and "financial success." But

---

* A revealing list of major current American fears (called "The New Seven Deadly Sins") was compiled by a popular magazine. They were: chastity, poverty, anonymity, age, failure, ugliness, and constancy. They were to replace the old ones such as lust, pride, avarice, and so on, which according to the article, "quickly passed away during the 60's" (*Esquire*, December 1966.)

even books concerned with the most diffuse personal problems like *Advice From a Failure* refer to finances ("How to understand the real reasons behind 'money' problems and how to deal with them.") *Power English Teaching Machine,* while dealing with issues far broader than making money, includes among its benefits "New power in business! . . . statistics prove that when you increase your Word-Power, your Earning-Power shoots right up alongside it!"

In *How to Write for Money,* the author proposes that turning writing into a profitable occupation requires neither talent, nor education, nor ideas, nor literary ambitions. ("How to write without any unusual inspiration—really, actually, without a thought in your head except money!") The book is a remarkable example of American cultural-intellectual egalitarianism. Writing is presented as accessible to all and viewed simply as a device for making money without effort. ("There is really nothing to it. . . . You will find it as simple as scribbling a few words on a postcard. Simpler even! . . . it need not even be grammatically correct! . . . Writing is the one big profession in which you need no formal training. Even a high school education is not necessary.") By contrast the "writers' schools" appeal to artistic creativity in the first place rather than to the love of cash.[34] *How to Write for Money* stresses the composition of "short paragraphs" which, however, ". . . can bring in money hand over fist—$3000 here, $1500 there . . . week after week!" Other titles among the money-making books include *The Successful Investors' Guide* ("Never before has the opportunity for the independent investor been so great"); *How Any Woman Can Make $10,000 a Year in Real Estate* ("a great new book that puts any woman on the threshold of gigantic earning power" . . .); *How to Build a Second Income* ("hundreds of profitable, low-budget, spare-time ventures"); *How to Have More Money to Spend* ("71 ingenious (but perfectly legal) ways . . . to get out of debt"—implying that "ingenious" is often thought of as not legal). These and many other titles all have in common the claim to offer easy, fool-proof techniques accessible for anyone; most of their authors are described as ambitious, self-made men, who got rich as a result of having struck on some simple idea no one else discovered before, and their motives are often presented as highly altruistic, that is, wanting "to share" their "secrets."

The second type of books described in the *Success Digest* are those on *health and sex.** They include *Painless Way to Stop Smoking, Good-bye Allergies, Reduce and Control Weight Via Self-hypnosis* ("It will be like a miracle, as almost overnight you turn sorrow into joy, failure into success, hate into love, anger to benevolence, distrust to faith, weakness and impotence into boldness, strength and vitality—boredom and apathy into hearty zest and interest!"); *The Secret of Instantaneous Healing* (concerned with both physical and mental health written by the founder of the Church of Life in Southern California); *How to Live to Be a Hundred* (". . . pump up to ten, twenty, even forty, years of vibrant health into your body! . . . simply by putting your locked-up health power to work . . ."); *Fit at Forty and Over, Sex and the Mature Man* (for readers ". . . who are being plagued by one of the most demoralizing . . . conditions . . . [the] fear of impotency!"); *The Marriage Art* (". . . can help both men and women to improve their sexual performance"). These and other books in this group all share the promise of maximizing physical fitness and sexual potency—just as others promise to expand earning power—by some simple technique.

The third major category consists of *self-expanding books,* which might also be called manuals of interpersonal manipulation. In these books success is synonymous with the ability to dominate, control, and manipulate others, preferably while retaining and increasing their love, affection, or respect. Like most "self-improvement" publications, they promise the best of all possible worlds: for example, a beneficial increase of aggression without alienating others, illustrating one of the most paradoxical of all American aspirations: the simultaneous value placed on being aggressive *and* on being liked and popular.[35] There is another contradiction barely concealed in these messages. While all the desired and promised improvements of character, intellect, and personality (and the attendant improvements of status, income, and prestige) are supposed to come about as a result of seemingly rational procedures—by learning facts and techniques, by understanding or discovering—the end products are often

---

* Such publications might have been eclipsed by more recent and more explicit ones, for example the best selling *The Sensuous Woman* by "J"—*The First How-to Book for the Female Who Yearns To Be All Woman* (New York, 1969) and its companion volumes, *The Sensuous Man* and *The Sensuous Couple.*

portrayed as miraculous, wondrous, incredible, or breathtaking (the words "secret" and "magic" being used very frequently). The books clearly aim at the irrational hopes, fears, and superstitious attitudes of the reader. Often this type of book represents itself as a cure-all, covering not only the restoration of self-confidence and the removal of a wide assortment of psychic disturbances, but also of physical illness. For example, the *Programmed Course in Self-Hypnotism* offers "a more dynamic, commanding personality, freedom from tension and worry, a better vocabulary . . . , a more powerful . . . memory, restful sleep . . . , the knack of getting along better with others, power to hypnotize others, new sexual harmony and a happier married life, reduction of excessive smoking and drinking, increased powers of concentration, relief from aches and pains." *Getting Through to People* is frankly exploitative. It promises ". . . in just one hour, the secret of how to command and dominate everyone you meet!"; it also purports to describe ". . . techniques of practical psychology, sound as a dollar, universally valid [for instance] . . . a simple action that gets a person to 'open up' and pour out his or her deepest, most private feelings. It lets you peer into the deep recesses of his mind and emotions. . . . Then you know how to get what you want from him." *The Intelligent Woman's Guide to Man-Hunting* is another illustration of the apparent American belief that everything can be reduced to techniques, no matter how intimate, intricate, and private. In the perspective of this *Guide,* a potential husband becomes an article of consumption to be acquired, an object of deliberate manipulation similar to those of commercial transactions. We are confronting here another contradiction in American values: that between romantic love and attraction on the one hand, and interpersonal manipulation and calculation, on the other.[36] It is safe to assume that this book—like most of the others—is addressed to the sizeable group of "losers" (unmarried women in this case) so defined by the dominant values of society—according to which women ought to be married after a certain age. One clue to what group of readers the author has in mind is this sentence: "Dr. Ellis discusses the art of conversation, tells you why you frequently appear to have little or nothing to say in the presence of males and helps you to overcome that problem." The volume *Egoefficacy* offers "The new way to maximize personal effectiveness" which includes: "precontrolling the

minds of others to make them respect and admire you on sight."
In particular, it wishes to teach the reader

> How to honestly help others—while helping yourself even more!
> . . . how to counter attack the sixteen ways others may challenge
> your authority . . . how to instantly expose the weaknesses of
> other people—and use them to increase your own power . . . how
> to make friends, acquaintances, even perfect strangers your "silent
> partners," cutting you in for a share of their income without your
> having to contribute a nickel! . . . How to employ the "royal
> method" of always seeming to be just and fair—while you may
> actually be just the opposite.

It is difficult to avoid the conclusion that there is an affinity between
sharp business practices and a generalized manipulativeness. As long
as it is practically legitimate to sell a product by all means of deception, it is a small step to extend the same logic to "selling oneself" to
other people.[37] As with products, the person following the advice of
Egoefficacy tries his best to appear something he is not. *The Million
Dollar Personality* is another classic of its kind, a manual on how to
be devious without being caught. It was written by a J. V. Cerney,
described as "one of the most powerful behind-the-scenes operators
of all times." The suggestions of this book make explicit what is often implicit in the operative values of American commerce and business (and sometimes in interpersonal relations). For example,

> make a stingy employer actually pay you more than other people
> doing the same job . . . land much bigger orders from your small
> clients . . . organize your business so one person is doing the
> work of two and loving it . . . gain the active support and pa-
> tronage of really rich men . . . land an executive job with a big
> corporation even if you do not have the education and are past
> middle age . . . find an excellent marriage partner no matter
> what your looks, income, family, status or age . . . make a spouse
> work harder at *sexual adjustment* . . . get a mate sexually ex-
> cited any time you want to . . . be able to move in any circle of
> society to the extent that you actually have an invitation every
> night . . . prevent unwanted or too frequent visits by your fam-
> ily without hurting anyone's feelings . . . borrow money or
> things from friends or neighbors and actually make them happy
> about it . . . get even with those above you who come to you for

advice . . . immediately establish in the mind of everyone that you are a superior person . . . win the admiration of better educated people . . .

This is perhaps as good an example of the caricature of the "American Dream" as we can get. *Social Awareness, Poise, and Gracious Living* helps to ". . . discover the simple tricks and easy rules business and social leaders, prominent socialites, and political dignitaries, lawyers, diplomats, and society matrons use to act, dress, talk, and handle themselves in even the most difficult or exalted social circumstances." Books like this suggest that social intercourse is a good deal more complicated and intimately tied to status and manners than the still current values of egalitarianism would have us believe. They also indicate that such social values, no matter how widely accepted, prepare the individual inadequately to meet the social realities of status distinctions and manners appropriate for them.

The Anatomy of Success introduces the key concept of "the power of positive selfishness" and assures the reader that "Every man has within him the elements of success." *Change Your Life With Positive Action* ". . . will destroy that senseless feeling of 'inferiority' at one blow!" *Effective Speaking, Double Your Power to Learn, The Magic Power of Your Subconscious Mind* ("why it is your right to be rich"—written by a minister of the Church of Divine Science), are other examples of the self-expanding literature.

We cannot exclude the possibility that some of these books may be less fraudulent than the *Success Digest* makes them appear. Even if this were the case, the manner in which they are advertised remains significant. We can assume that advertisers would not persist in using a language and certain recurring messages had they proven to be ineffectual and without appeal. Despite its distortions, exaggerations, and crudeness, the *Success Digest* embodies major elements of widely shared American values, however disfigured they have become in the process of being popularized by advertising.

How would the Soviet reader react to such publications? The question is, of course, entirely hypothetical, but nonetheless instructive to ponder. From what we know about Soviet people and society we can attempt a speculative answer that will further illustrate the gulf separating many American and Soviet values. To be sure, it would be pointless to speculate about Soviet popular reaction to the books concerned with multiplying income by some commercial activity or gimmick, since engaging in such activity would presuppose a radical overhauling of Soviet society, including the establishment of private enterprise. Even so, we feel that the messages of the *Success Digest* would produce bewilderment and some revulsion among Soviet readers, primarily because their preoccupation with personal success is far more limited. "Success"—the conspicuous rise of the individual expressed in the rapid acquisition of wealth and status—is not even a nostalgic daydream for most Soviet citizens, who are still at the stage of wanting to acquire *necessities* rather than the *symbols* of material and social success. Self-respect in Soviet society has a lot less to do with being successful at maximizing income, consumption, or popularity than it does in American society. The books depicted in the *Digest* owe their appeal to conditions which barely exist in the Soviet Union: widespread insecurity and diffuse anxieties bred by social and psychic mobility (an American phenomenon very different from insecurity generated by political pressures); the related myth and reality of opportunity; the relative permissiveness of social structure (which prompts the individual to blame himself for failure), and extreme competitiveness. In the absence of such conditions, the *Digest* has little to offer to the Soviet reader.

More specifically, Soviet readers, no matter how ambitious and "upwardly mobile"—how educated or uneducated they might be—are fully aware that no secret, magic, trick, or step-by-step technique can rapidly multiply their income. Notions of magic may survive in remote peasant communities, but this is not the kind that creates susceptibility to the claims of advertising. While conceptions of shortcuts to success may be just as illusory in the United States as in the USSR, what makes the difference is that in the former some segments of the population believe in them, while this is most unlikely to be the case in the Soviet Union.

As to the appeal of the health and sex books, there is reason to believe that it would be limited since Soviet people seem less preoccupied with health—physical, mental, or sexual—than are Americans. We do not know whether or not this is so because Soviet people enjoy better physical or mental health than do Americans. More likely it is a result of a greater degree of unself-consciousness and lack of self-centeredness, of a disposition more casual and stoic toward the self.[38]

The third category of books, focusing on *success via interpersonal manipulation* would be the most certain to be rejected as repulsive on ethical grounds, both traditional Russian and contemporary Soviet. The deliberate creation of façades for the personality, the teaching of how to pretend, impress, show off, gain respect, money, or power by clever techniques (rather than by the intrinsic qualities of the individual), the various ways of legitimating deception—all of these clash with what we know of Russian character and culture. The Soviet system itself, no matter how manipulative, hypocritical, or deceptive it has been, has not instilled in the population the *values* of manipulation and deception. On the contrary, openness, frankness, the revelation of the self to the collective, striving for authenticity through effort and work—such have been a part of the official values. There is little evidence that Soviet society has generated an intense preoccupation with personal success, or has fostered the habit of invidious comparison with others. Finally the *Success Digest* would be unacceptable or irrelevant to Soviet society because of its residue of fatalism, in part a heritage of a traditional peasant society, in part bred and reinforced by an overorganized totalitarian one.

The Values of the "Counterculture"[39]

It would be thoroughly misleading to imply that in the 1960's and 1970's the values of the *Success Digest* still adequately or exhaustively symbolize, represent or reflect the predominant currents in American life, stretching in serene historical continuity from the beginnings of American society to the present. Nor would it be satisfactory to say that today, as in the past, such dominant values (the derivatives or caricatures of the Protestant Ethic) have been challenged only by minor subcultures. The present-day challenges to these values are of a different order. They intensified so significantly since the early 1960's that the "subcultural" values can no longer be regarded as marginal or minor. Nor are the major deviant values any less codified, articulated, or less effectively disseminated than those we have viewed as the dominant ones until now. At the same time it has been noted that these (new) values are hardly original and resemble those of the bohemians.[40]

For the most part the values of the "counterculture" are radically and diametrically opposed to the cluster of values associated with

work, success, status, and acquisition. First and foremost those alienated from the hitherto dominant values and institutions of American society reject materialism, acquisition, the cult of status symbols
(as well as social status itself), and financial success. Moreover routinized occupations (especially commercial and business ones), and
often work itself, are held in contempt. Correspondingly, competition, competitiveness, and individualism form another cluster of values which are abhorrent, especially to the alienated young. Among
them individualism is being replaced by a new veneration of community and togetherness, indeed a new tribalism; achievement orientation is supplanted by escapism, idleness, or reflection or some
communally oriented occupation (such as social work of some kind).
Freedom, spontaneity, unrestricted full expression, and openness are
extolled; manipulation, adjustment and discipline deplored. Reason
and intellect are regarded with suspicion, feelings and sensations are
revered, as is subjectivity and personal experience of almost any
kind. An intense reaction against fragmentation, specialization, and
differentiation (on almost any ground) underlies the values of the
counterculture that pursues a vision of totality and integration never
attained either at the personal or social level.

Interestingly enough, the counterculture itself bears the imprints
of the dominant culture of "straight" society, no matter how furi-
ously and vocally it rejects it. Thus the "new" revulsion from any
kind of differentation and hierarchy is solidly rooted in old-fashioned
American egalitarianism such as we also identified in the *Success Digest*. The glorification of youth and novelty is common to both "culture" and "counterculture," as is the love of publicity and indifference to privacy. There is also an unmistakable link between the
offerings of the "self-expanding books" reviewed earlier, and the
aspirations of those who will clutch at every straw—chemical or other
to "turn on." And there is similarity between the belief in techniques
set forth by the authors of the *Success Digest* (and countless other
commercial enterprises) and the earnest gropings of those who seek
shortcuts to "meaningful" social relationships and an understanding
of one's self by engaging in the popular practices of "sensitivity training" and varieties of gimmicky group therapy. In all such endeavors
the solid, all-American faith in miraculous techniques (available to
all), and in instant solutions to all problems, shines through. There
is not an unbridgeable gulf between those who believe in instant

communities and those who hope (or pretend) to effect an instant change in their lives by a new hair dye or motor vehicle.* And in the longing for community (which, after all, is defined by many as a group in which everybody likes everybody) one may also detect the echoes of a more conventional pursuit of popularity, as eagerly sought by the readers of the *Success Digest,* as by those who read the "underground" press and swear by Theodore Roszak, Timothy Leary, or Charles Reich. Nor is it difficult to trace an affinity between the once dominant forms of individualism and the current narcissistic concerns with identity[42] (and the frequently resulting self-centeredness and self-indulgence) which are also among the hallmarks of the counterculture.

Equally noteworthy has been the relationship between the "culture" of the counterculture and of that of society at large. We have in mind here the expressive and artistic aspects of the counterculture, preeminent among which has been rock and folk music and associated mass gatherings. Two features of rock music in particular are significant for the student of the counterculture and the attitudes it shelters or reflects. One is the deliberate "mind blowing" or escapist character of much of rock music and its affinity with drug-induced escape. The other is the inability or unwillingness of the rock music establishment to fend off incorporation into the entertainment industry or "mass culture."†

* The faddism, constant novelty-seeking and lack of persistence of the counterculture was criticized by Jonathan Kozol: "Each book, each author, each new fashion, each new Interesting Idea, serves not as a strong or catalytic passage of rededication . . . but rather as the justification for desertion of those things which we have undertaken.

"Some of the men and women in the counterculture put it to me in these words: 'I used to be into that race and conscience bag. I'm out of that now. I'm in a new bag. I'm into communes.' Or 'I'm into growing natural organic foods—' or 'I'm living on the land.' It is not that each of these things might not be a thing worth being 'into'— it is the idea which these people often have that they are freely choosing each thing they get 'into,' and that to be 'into' something only for the length of time it takes to try and fail at it is of any worth to other human beings."[41]

† "Anyone who has traveled with these musicians or simply sat for an afternoon in their dressing room can testify to the contemptuous and paranoid view they hold of this country. 'Grab the money and run' is their basic philosophy. . . . The freebooting of these rock bandits ought to end forever the idea that the counterculture is founded on some genuine ethical ideal, or that it marks in any significant way a break with the prevailing capitalist system. . . . A generation which rejects its inherited culture with such facility will inevitably reject or betray its own youth culture with the same jettisoning zeal. Counterculture is largely anti-culture: one step more and it becomes non-culture."[43]

In short, the rejection of the dominant values of American society is tempered, unwittingly, by the absorption of some of the same values by those who wish to radically remake them.

Despite their proclaimed and actual estrangement from American society most of those who are associated with the counterculture are not active politically, at any rate in the usual sense of the word. This largely apolitical ethos is aptly captured below:

> . . . No one in Berkeley is ready for anything at this time [that is, for revolutionary action—P. H.] Most of our friends wake up at noon and get stoned by three in the afternoon, the rest of the day spent in the Mediterranean Cafe going from table to table looking for newspapers to read. Everyone thoroughly informed of national and international events, everyone casting around for night drugs, something to perk up lives of waiting, then at night doing these drugs and going over to Bongo Burger to talk about what they are on.[44]

The social base and the carriers of these values are easily identifiable. The counterculture is primarily campus-based (though it spills over into neighboring rural or urban "communes"); its carriers are the prosperous (or once prosperous) children of the middle and upper middle classes; educated, or part educated (in the case of dropouts), urban, and suburban. They are people for whom life in a secular, technological, individualistic, and competitive society has become empty and intolerable; who can afford to take for granted goals which earlier provided meaning to the lives of millions, such as material satisfaction, consumption, social status, education, and achievements associated with work. Permissiveness, affluence, free expression, mobility, and the rejection of the routines of an industrial society combined to give rise to the counterculture—a mixture of romanticism, anarchism, escapism, primitivism, and longing for the long overdue elimination of all conflicts from life and a foolproof answer as to its meaning.

"On Communist Morality, A Popular Outline"— A Case Study of the Official Soviet Values

There are no Soviet equivalents of American publications like the *Success Digest*. "Success" as such is neither an official value nor a popular preoccupation in the USSR. It is not even a meaningful concept in itself unless its components are specified and stated. (In the United States "success" conjures up instantly widely shared associations, for instance, high income, some tangible achievement and a degree of fame). Therefore we are not suggesting here that the book *On Communist Morality* is the Soviet equivalent of the *Success Digest*. We selected it from a vast literature of its kind[45] because it is typical of Soviet propaganda concerned with dissemination of official values. In a sense, of course, *On Communist Morality* is also concerned with success as it is implicitly defined by the molders of the New Soviet Man. "Success," from their point of view, is attained when the individual lives according to the tenets of Marxism-Leninism (as currently interpreted), when his behavior conforms to the codified version of the official Soviet values: *The Moral Code of the Builder of Communism*.[46] The *Success Digest* and the *Popular Outline* have in common a concern with self-improvement—they contain messages and exhortations pertinent to the formation of the desirable personality, enumerating its attributes very explicitly. The *Success Digest* does so by responding to what the authors assume to be the popularly sought components of success; the *Popular Outline* pursues a similar objective by explicating the official moral imperatives. The two publications are similar in another respect: *On Communist Morality*, like the *Success Digest*, is aimed at a rather unsophisticated audience. It strives for simplicity of expression and its style is relatively lively by the standards of Soviet propaganda, possibly resulting from the campaign of the early and mid-1960's aimed at developing more engaging forms of persuasion.[47] This is how the book starts out:

> Dear Reader! We live in interesting times. Participating together with the whole Soviet people in the building of Communism we are witnessing magnificent events which will resound for centuries. One space ship after the other soars up assailing the skies and wrests from nature its secrets.
>
> We win one battle after the other in the building of the new society in which we wish to live and work.[48]

In spite of a less stilted style and a brief section devoted to denouncing the cult of personality (pp. 36-38) there is little in the book that might not have been written and published at almost any time since the establishment of Soviet society. (Even the persuasiveness of the criticism of Stalin's cult of personality is greatly reduced by elevating Khrushchev to the pedestal of moral authority, whose words are often quoted or referred to, as was appropriate while he was in power.) This publication is, indeed, a popular outline, presenting the official values in their most diluted and acceptable form. With a few exceptions the morality advocated is undistinguishable from much of what school-children, boy scouts, or listeners to Sunday sermons hear (or used to hear) in the United States.* The value prescriptions of the book divide into two groups: those which are not peculiar to the Soviet system and are not specifically based on Marxism-Leninism; and those which can be derived from specific Soviet policies or Marxism-Lenism, or both.

Conveniently for our present purposes the official Soviet value system, or at any rate, its major propositions and demands, have been codified and were enunciated at the 22nd Party Congress in 1961 as part of the new Program of the CPSU, called the *Moral Code of the Builder of Communism.* The author of *On Communist Morality* interprets the significance of the *Moral Code* as follows: "The commandments of the *Moral Code* do not consist of abstract, artificial demands; they are scientifically formulated precepts which govern the conduct of man who builds the new society. The *Moral Code* represents the concretized basic principles of communist morality."[51] Another publication, devoted almost exclusively to a discussion of the new *Moral Code,* adds a further dimension to its importance:

> In the Program of the CPSU for the first time the code of communist morality has been exhaustively formulated. This fact is remarkable. In the past, moral demands existed in the form of public opinion; they were expressed in the approval or disapproval of one or another human action. Most of the pre-proletarian forms of morality emphasized primarily "the demands on what not to do" and said relatively little about what to do. Our moral

---

* ". . . We are confronted with the fact that, to a striking degree, the specific principles of communist morality . . . resemble those of bourgeois ethic. . . . In going through the enumerations of the highest moral values given in Soviet ethical philosophy it is difficult to find a single moral idea . . . that is not common to Western ethics."[49] Adam Ulam observed along the same lines: ". . . all that one can safely say 50 years after the Revolution is that a believer in Victorian middle class values can be heartened by the present scene in the USSR. In what other society are the virtues of thrift, hard word, social cohesion and discipline so greatly encouraged, prudery and decorous public manners strictly enforced, the young and intellectuals kept firmly in their place as in the land of the Soviets?"[50]

code indicates both what is to be done, and what is not. Its positive aspects are thus richer, broader and fuller insofar as the perspectives of the future are more majestic than the remnants of the past against which we have to wage war. For the first time in history communist morality is summarized in a clearly defined code.[52]

We may wonder, after perusing the *Moral Code,* wherein lies its historic significance, since little or nothing in its content differs from the moral prescriptions of the past. Perhaps, as the Soviet leaders saw it, the significance of the document lies in the fact that, for the first time, many of the official values have been designated as a *moral* code. The official view of the current stage in the development of Soviet society presented in the preamble to the *Moral Code,* provides one of the clues: "In the course of transition to communism, the moral principles of society become increasingly important; the sphere of action of the moral factor expands and the importance of the administrative control of human relations diminishes accordingly.[53]

The statement is only in part a product of wishful thinking; it also reflects the shift that occurred after Stalin's death to less coercive policies. This shift indicates the official recognition that after more than four decades of Soviet rule, the conformity of the masses has come to be based on a greater acceptance of Soviet values; the statement also reflects the official desire to foster a value-oriented (rather than coerced) conformity.

The *Moral Code of the Builder of Communism* consists of these principles:

1. Devotion to the communist cause; love of the socialist motherland and of other socialist countries.
2. Conscientious labor for the good of society—he who does not work, neither shall he eat.
3. Concern on the part of everyone for the preservation and growth of public wealth.
4. A high sense of public duty; intolerance of action harmful to the public interest.
5. Collectivism and comradely mutual assistance: one for all and all for one.
6. Human relations and mutual respect between individuals—man is to man a friend, comrade, and brother.
7. Honesty and truthfulness, moral purity, modesty and unpretentiousness in social and private life.

8. Mutual respect in the family, and concern for the upbringing of children.
9. An uncompromising attitude to injustice, parasitism, dishonesty, careerism and money-grubbing.
10. Friendship and brotherhood among all peoples of the USSR; intolerance of national and racial hatred.
11. An uncompromising attitude to the enemies of communism, peace and the freedom of nations.
12. Fraternal solidarity with the working people of all countries, and with all peoples.[54]

Despite the presumed intention to provide a highly generalized code, those drafting it had to be selective. Those values included in the *Moral Code* presumably needed reaffirmation: they could not yet be taken for granted; solemn social ideals require periodic reaffirmation in most societies, whatever their political structure. Codified social values tend to represent unattainable demands and ideals, the full realization of which is not seriously expected even by the codifiers or the value-forming elites themselves. Thus, for example, the demand for honesty and humane relations belongs to this category of never-fully-realized-ideals which have to be periodically affirmed in order to narrow the gap between ideal and actual behavior.

There are, however, certain specific value prescriptions in the *Moral Code,* the presence of which is surprising in view of the nature of Soviet society and the educational efforts of several decades. For example, as of 1961, "parasitism, careerism, and money-grubbing" were still sufficiently evident to be worthy of mention (in this most generalized statement of moral principles) persisting after almost half a century of Soviet social environment. Similarly, the injunction "intolerance of actions harmful to the public interest"—would hardly have been stated if the antisocial actions referred to had disappeared.

Let us now examine more closely the ideals advocated in the *Code* and at the same time note the extent to which they can also claim acceptance, in Western, including American, societies.

"Devotion to communist cause, love of the socialist motherland," and the like, would be acceptable in spirit to most Americans, who are also supposed to be (and are) patriotic without referring to their country as either mother- or fatherland. Of course the "devotion to communist cause" is another matter.

"Conscientious labor for the good of society," and so forth, would produce partial agreement, especially the notion that "he who does not work neither shall he eat." Americans are supposed to be a hard-working people and their veneration of work is—or has been—supported by the Protestant Ethic and the traditional values of American society. There would be disagreement as to what constitutes work, which is more broadly defined in the United States than in the Soviet Union.

"The preservation of public wealth" would also receive a sympathetic hearing among Americans provided an agreement could be reached as to what should legitimately be in the public domain. Probably there would be considerable consensus about the desirability of protecting national parks and forests, for instance. By the same token, "intolerance of action harmful to the public interest" would also meet approval if only public interest could be clearly defined—a task that tends to be more difficult in a pluralistic society.

"Collectivism and comradely mutual assistance," and so on, would be acceptable for most Americans if the words "collectivism" and "comradely" were deleted. Americans favor "mutual assistance," in principle even though its realization is often difficult in a society as competitive as the United States.

"Humane relations, mutual respect," and so forth, would be warmly welcomed particularly by the representatives of most religious faiths in the United States.

"Honesty and truthfulness, moral purity, modesty and unpretentiousness in social and private life" would be accepted in this country as laudable in principle; in practice, modesty and unpretentiousness are among the less lived-up-to values, often displaced by the operative value of conspicuous consumption and the marketing orientation toward personality[55]—neither of which is conducive to modesty or unpretentiousness.

"Mutual respect in the family . . . concern for the upbringing of children" would be upheld without any reservation in the United States.

"Uncompromising attitude to injustice, parasitism, dishonesty, careerism and money grubbing" lump together values that are differentially ranked in the United States. The rejection of dishonesty and injustice are shared, of course, as they are in all cultures (although their definitions vary substantially). It would be another matter with careerism and money-grubbing, which, if graced by more appealing terms (for example, achievement orientation and high earning power) would certainly not be opposed in the United States—nor in the USSR, for that matter.

"Friendship and brotherhood among all peoples of the USSR, intolerance of national and racial hatred" as a *general* value would not be rejected by most Americans. "Hatred" of any type is not considered to be a socially acceptable feeling; even the most extreme racists disclaim the hatred of Negroes, and only a minority of Black militants publicly endorse the hatred of whites.

"An uncompromising attitude to the enemies of communism, peace, and freedom of nations" could not claim the assent of many Americans with respect to communism, but peace and freedom, again in general terms, are endorsed by most people everywhere.

"Fraternal solidarity with the working people of all countries and with all peoples" would probably be met with lukewarm approval or indifference, perhaps with mild incomprehension but hardly firm rejection, in the United States.

There are three themes which are more peculiarly Soviet and Marxist-Leninist in the *Code:* collectivism and its various desired manifestations; the emphasis on work as the supreme molder of character, rather than as a means to something else (though it also has an instrumental aspect—as a means to building communism); and the demand for uncompromising attitudes (literally: implacability) toward the political enemy and toward behavior officially defined as undesirable. Yet even some of these themes are to some degree present among American values, especially in their traditional puritanic incarnation.

Soviet ideologues are not entirely unaware of the generality of the moral principles and value prescriptions they advocate as unique. The fact that values and ideals similar to theirs are also upheld elsewhere, including capitalist societies, is dismissed with the claim that such values in capitalist societies are not *genuinely* held, that only lip service is paid to them and that they are alien to the spirit of such societies, whereas in the Soviet Union they are genuinely held and made meaningful:

> Honesty and truthfulness are elementary norms of morality which should guide individuals as well as entire nations. However, in societies based on exploitation, and particularly in contemporary bourgeois societies honesty and truthfulness are merely a façade.

Bourgeois morality demands honesty and truthfulness from the workers. But when it comes to their own behavior the capitalists talk about these qualities only when it serves their purposes.

The simple norms of morality and justice, which under the rule of exploiters become distorted or shamelessly trampled upon, are transformed by communism into inviolable, vital principles which are applied both to the relations between individuals and nations. Communist morality includes the fundamental moral norms which were created by the masses of many nations in the course of the thousand years of struggle against oppression and moral degradation.[56]

On Communist Morality does present at one point what is intended to be a systematic summary comparison between the values (or moral principles) of socialist (Soviet) and capitalist society. The basic principles of Communist and bourgeois morality are listed as follows:

COMMUNIST

Collectivism: We work together and must help one another. The misfortune of my comrade is my misfortune.

The love of work: I work for myself, for the people and the better I work the better we live.

The love of the motherland: My country is my life! I cannot think of her otherwise than as a son.

Honesty: I do everything for the good of my country and people and in doing so there is nothing to conceal from my comrades.

Modesty: I am a member of the collective and all I do is done in accord with my comrades.

Principledness: Lawlessness and the violations of social order harm our common effort—the building of communism. Therefore I will not tolerate it.

Optimism: I believe in the justice of our cause, in the strength of the people capable of solving any task. I believe that the present generation will live under communism.

Hatred of the oppressors: I cannot think of my life without freedom and free work. Therefore I hate the oppressors and parasites.

BOURGEOIS

Individualism: It is my well-being that counts, other people are not my concern.

Parasitism: It is better to sponge on someone else than let others sponge on you.

Unprincipledness: The most important [goal] is to make more money, it does not matter how, money has no smell.

Falsehood: A man cannot tell the truth since, as a rule, deception is required for success.

Secrecy: It is better to keep one's plans secret otherwise they might be frustrated.

Indifference: Why bother to get into the depth of life, it is easier and quieter to glide on the surface.[57]

As is often the case, Soviet perceptions of things Western—and American in particular—include conspicuous doses of projection. In this list of bourgeois vices the most striking projective-attribution is the trait of secrecy frequently observed by visitors to (and students of) Soviet society, and even in prerevolutionary Russia. Indifference (or apathy) is also among the characteristic attitudes of Soviet people similarly commented upon by visitors and castigated by Soviet sources alike.[58] It is also clear that decades of total deprivation of free expression compelled millions of Soviet citizens to repeat "falsehoods" rather than "tell the truth." Such a capacity for simulation results unavoidably from the necessity of hiding true feelings and paying verbal tribute to official policies and values.[59] Political repression and the Soviet official insistence on the ritualistic expressions of conformity are hardly the most effective way to inculcate strong attachment to principles. We have shown elsewhere that one of the outstanding characteristics of the "New Soviet Man" is adaptability rather than strong commitment to principles.[60]

Despite the high level of generality and the near-universal acceptability of many of the official Soviet value prescriptions, the *Popular Outline* leaves little doubt that in the final analysis these values are strongly politicized: *their application* is determined by political-ideological criteria. This is illustrated by the discussion of "happiness":

The concept of happiness is associated with the concept of communism in the minds of our people. When we are dreaming about happiness we are dreaming about communism. And the Party, as if to confirm the rapidly approaching realizability of our dreams, solemnly declared at the 22nd Congress of the CPSU that the present generation will live under communism.[61]

Thus at one level happiness is equated with communism and with the building of communism, both of which are defined by and identified with the party. The nature of communist society itself is ill defined and vague: it will be a society in which the principles of the *Moral Code of the Builder of Communism* will apply and triumph. This *Code,* however, is one which derives from the nature of communist society. Some parts of the *Code* itself are outright tautological and circular: for example, dedication to *communism* and *Communist* attitudes to labor are among the values of the builder of *communism.* The confusion regarding the distinctiveness of the morality appropriate for communism is further increased by the fact that it is indistinguishable from the morality appropriate for citizens of the current, *socialist* stage of Soviet society.

The concrete examples used to illustrate the feelings of Soviet citizens in a state of happiness merely suggest that they anticipate or live up to the value prescriptions found in the *Code:*

> Describing the life of his parents, participants in the revolution, L. Podvoiski, engineer in the "Hammer and Sickle" factory related: "Shortly before the death of my father, in 1948, mother and father had a picture taken of them. Both were grey and thin, an open volume by Lenin in their hand. On the back of the photograph they wrote to us, their four grown-up children: 'Children. Throughout our entire conscious life we tried, with all our strength, to serve our country, to justify with honest work and revolutionary struggle the lofty calling of the member of the Bolshevik Party. We have been happy. Follow the same correct path where you will find strength, joy, and happiness.' "[62]

The message here is twofold. On the one hand, happiness can be found amidst hardship, effort, and struggle, and need not be associated with comfort, security, and tranquility. On the other, service to the party, however arduous, is equated with happiness—a highly politicized if unspecific condition. Another story relates the case of a girl, who because of some profiteering with a winning lottery ticket lost the confidence of her fellow workers, who stopped speaking to her. The moral of the story: "Money itself does not create happiness. Happiness is not a commodity. It cannot be bought or sold."[63]

Again and again, personal examples and quotations from outstanding Soviet figures—Khrushchev and Dzherzinsky among them—bring home the message that happiness is dedicated work within and for the collective, the nation, or motherland under the guidance of party and government, that work of any nature, when integrated into the common effort, lends meaning and fulfillment to life. Thus, the Soviet version of happiness, or a successful life, rests on the three pillars of a society-wide group solidarity, committed work (the meaning of which is predicated partly on its future results), and unquestioning acceptance of national-societal objectives as defined by the party leadership of the day. On these premises, the *necessity* of subordinating personal interests and desires to politically defined collective goals is transformed into the virtue of lifelong, fulfilling service to society.

5. Social Values
in Education, Religion,
and Death

The Social Role of Education in American and Soviet Society

A comparison of the agencies engaged in the inculcation of social values in the two societies strongly suggests that they are far better integrated and coordinated in the USSR than in the United States.[1] Thus, for example, the messages disseminated by American commercial advertising—although they derive from and reflect certain elements of the dominant values—are often at cross purposes with some other major values such as the schools, colleges, and religious institutions try to inculcate. Yet sometimes it is argued that the values mirrored in advertising are merely the exaggerated version of the more generalized, dominant social values, rather than genuine alternatives to them.[2] Those in advertising would also claim that their messages do not distort, caricature, or contradict true American values, but present them in a lively, contemporary format. Despite such arguments it seems to us that the spirit and substance of advertising and the surviving traditional values espoused by much of the educational system (and religion) do not mesh. In particular there is a conflict between the complex of traditional and allegedly still dominant values, called the Protestant Ethic, and the ascendant values of secular hedonism, sometimes subsumed under the name of the "Leisure Ethic."[3] Moreover, the Protestant Ethic is being eroded by two forces: the more conventional, secular hedonism upheld by much of "Middle

America," and also, more recently, by the ethos of the youthful "counterculture." The prescriptions of the Protestant Ethic have been gradually receding from the everyday, to the ceremonial plane. The vitality of these values becomes particularly questionable if we recall that in their original formulation was included the notion of worldly asceticism—a quality in rather short supply in contemporary American society.

In both Soviet and American societies formal education has some features in common with political propaganda. As we might expect from the emphasis placed on political training in the USSR,* political propaganda and formal education are far more closely integrated there than in the United States.[5] Like propaganda, education aims at inculcating certain attitudes and values but its hoped-for effect is a long-term one. In Soviet society some aspects of education and propaganda have been assigned the same task, namely, the nurturing of loyalty toward the regime and the development of a character structure most responsive to the demands made on the population by the leadership. For example, in discussing the 1968 All-Union Teachers Congress, *Pravda* wrote:

> The Soviet teacher is a soldier on the ideological front. Following the instructions of the April plenary session of the C.P.S.U. Central Committee, he is called upon to use the entire arsenal of educational resources to inculcate in his charges ideological staunchness, Soviet patriotism, proletarian internationalism, the ability to resist all forms of bourgeois influence, alien views and morality.[6]

However, Soviet education also emphasizes training in specific, functional skills and the dissemination of basic information about the physical world that has no immediate political or ideological relevance.† The continued importance of both education and propaganda in Soviet society derives from the long-standing desire of the regime to transform not only the institutions of society—that was accomplished, by and large, in the twenties and thirties—but also the

---

* This emphasis is well illustrated by the existence of a vast network of adult political education which encompasses close to forty million people, most of them not members of the party.[4]

† In fact, Soviet education is probably more concerned with inculcating specific skills and knowledge than the American which is increasingly becoming "personal growth" oriented and focused on the encouragement of free expression and spontaneity.

individual who has not kept up with the institutional changes and often remains hidebound, recalcitrant, or indifferent.

The politicization of education has produced some interesting results in the Soviet Union, particularly because certain subjects and disciplines—namely the social sciences and humanities—lend themselves to politicized treatment far more readily than others. This circumstance, combined with the higher monetary rewards offered to scientists and engineers than to other professionals, has led to an attrition of talented people in the humanities and social sciences, and to the immense popularity of the sciences. Thus Fred Hechinger observes:

> the humanities have assumed a second rate flavor. The huge thirty-story main complex of Moscow State University on Lenin Hills is the exclusive domain of mathematics and the sciences. The humanities are quartered in a labyrinth of old, early 19th century buildings downtown.
> Reflecting this symbolic, external downgrading, the humanities attract many rejects and youngsters of lesser talent or ambition, including those who will become tomorrow's conservative party hacks. . . .
> The lowly station of the humanities is, for the moment, self-perpetuating. Because they cannot attract the best students and are unable to hold out sufficient promise of distinguished careers, they find it difficult to inspire superior effort and scholarship. It is fair to say that most of the research and scholarship in the humanities and social sciences dealing with the last three hundred years is third-rate. The further back in time, the better the scholarship. . . . In so safely remote a field as archeology Soviet scholarship tends to be brilliant.[7]

It is sometimes assumed by Western observers of the Soviet Union that the generous official support of education is bound to lead to the creation of a more liberal political order.[8] True enough, an effectively politicized education (just as effective propaganda) seems to reduce the need for coercion. Yet we must note that the ample support of *both* of those institutions existed even under Stalin. Then the powerful propaganda apparatus and expanding educational institutions coexisted with campaigns of terror, and they did not preempt the role assigned to coercion. Thus, as we noted before, the dilemma, coercion versus persuasion, is false or at least vastly oversimplified. Yet both Soviet spokesmen and Western students of Societ society often contrast coercion and persuasion as if they were two distinct techniques of political administration in the Soviet Union. Although these two methods differ in degree, to regard them as the diametrically opposed ways of exacting conformity is plainly wrong in the Soviet, as in any other totalitarian, context. The contrast would be more appropriate if we substitute the use of terror for coercion. Terror and persuasion are indeed opposites. Rulers resort to terror when they are impatient and unwilling to delay or diminish the achievement of conformity and obedience. Persuasion implies delay and possibly incompleteness in the enforcement of conformity. This is precisely what happened in the USSR after Stalin's death. Terroristic methods for exacting conformity were abandoned partly because the new leadership was not obsessed with the attainment of *total* conformity, and partly because the necessity of extinguishing all dissent seemed less urgent. There were, of course, other reasons too: the rulers' own desire for a degree of personal security, and the apparent recognition that terroristic methods of government were neither necessary nor very efficient. This, however, is not to say that they shifted from methods of coercion to those of persuasion. Persuasion hardly exists in a situation in which the alternative to being "persuaded" is to be coerced. The current emphasis on persuasion means that the regime prefers to defer coercive sanctions longer than did Stalin. Yet in the final analysis persuasion to conform is followed by coercion to do so.

Both education and propaganda in the Soviet Union have a coercive character, insofar as they are government monopolies which simultaneously restrict access to unorthodox ideas and make exposure to the officially approved ones inescapable.

Formal education in the United States does little to inculcate government-approved ideas or to foster conformity to the policies pursued by the authorities. Whatever efforts are to be found in this direction—for example, courses designed to increase patriotism, civic consciousness, or anti-Communist attitudes—are limited to primary and secondary schools and are given at the pleasure of local authorities and communities.[9] Institutions of higher education, quite to the contrary, have increasingly become the settings for the generation and dissemination of critiques of the "Establishment" and most policies of the government; indeed, many campuses have become the settings for political countercultures over which the government has no effective control.

In both the United States and the Soviet Union education enjoys high prestige and is the major single potential instrument for upward social mobility, for the majority of the population. At the same time, in each society there are minorities for whom education is not the single major determinant of high status, while even in their case it is *among* the factors which enter into it. Thus in the Soviet Union high status can still be achieved by moving up the party apparatus* or through some exceptional accomplishment in productivity; correspondingly, being rich is a source of high status in the United States regardless of the ways the wealth was achieved, and regardless of the educational attainments of the wealthy individual.

In the Soviet Union approaches to education in the 1920's were marked by innovation, experimentation, and permissiveness. From the 1930's onward, in line with the growing totalitarian regimentation of society, these approaches were replaced by striving for uniformity, strict discipline, emphasis on the authority of the teacher, and a generally more conservative educational philosophy. In comparison with American high school and college students, Soviet students have to take more courses and are given very limited choices among subjects taught. At the university level training is far more specialized than in the United States.

The expansion of the system of public education took place under different historical conditions in the two societies. In the USSR the process of economic modernization, which created the need for literate and skilled workers and highly trained specialists stimulated the development of the educational system. In the United States the ideology of egalitarianism supplied the main motivation for the creation of free public schooling, including the state universities, city and community colleges.

The two systems of education differ in several important respects. Soviet education is highly centralized, government-controlled (under the Ministry of Education), and politicized. The curriculum is virtually the same in every school (of the same level and type), and neither local communities nor local educational authorities have any authority to determine its content.[10] This is not to say that the qual-

---

* It should be noted however that the party provides its own formal education to functionaries in the form of party schools the attendance of which may range from a few months to several years. It is also true, that as we pointed out earlier, the party increasingly absorbs the educated into its ranks.

ity of education is the same everywhere. As noted elsewhere (chapter 7) there are striking differences between urban and rural schools, and even between those in different urban areas. The big cities of European Russia (as well as some Siberian ones such as Novosibirsk and Irkutsk) provide better educational opportunities than do most other regions. There are also higher dropout rates in rural areas. Nor is the prestige of various institutions of higher education the same. Universities, which are the most prestigious, constitute only a small proportion of the total number of institutions of higher education: 40 out of over 700.[11] While such differences have their counterpart in the United States, the prestige of secondary school teachers is much higher in the Soviet Union than in American society despite the fact that teaching is poorly paid, not only in comparison with American teachers' salaries but also in comparison with those of many skilled workers in the Soviet Union. Soviet popular preferences for white collar occupations sometimes override the concern with material rewards.

Soviet schools are closely integrated with politicized youth organizations, such as the pioneers and the Young Communist League. From the earliest age a consistent effort is made to bring to bear the weight of the collective on the pupils both for disciplinary purposes and for academic competition.[12] Soviet education accurately reflects a strong anti-individualistic bias and collective pressures are systematically developed to bring in line those who are "deviant" in the broadest sense of the word: the poor students, the difficult or troublesome ones, eccentrics, or those who show early signs of antisocial attitudes. The Soviet educational system is also geared much more consciously to fulfill the needs of the national economy by teaching skills which are needed, rather than preparing for occupations which are popular. The extent to which the needs of the economy take precedence over the preferences and interests of students and the associated manipulative approach toward vocational guidance was revealed with striking candor in a recent article written by the president of the USSR Academy of Pedagogy:

> What is needed here is a system of active measures to exert an influence, to mold the students' aptitudes and interests and instill in them a view of their personal futures that would fit the real needs and possibilities of our society. . . .

> From the first grade on it is necessary to instill a particular regard for those worker occupations experiencing the greatest labor shortage.[13]

Apparently these objectives have been less than perfectly realized, since there are continued official complaints about problems of placement and the unreasonable preferences of Soviet students who ignore the needs of society and economy.*

American education is at every level far less homogeneous and uniform. Differences between states, regions, and private and public schools are enormous. Local pressures, resources, and traditions play a great part in determining the content and quality of education in both private and public institutions. Perhaps only one feature of American education can be generalized with some confidence: its relative permissiveness, observable not only in comparison with Soviet education but with Western European education as well. Several factors provide partial explanation of this phenomenon. Possibly the most important is the American practice of delaying intellectual maturation (or maturation in general?). As things stand now, it appears that in many, perhaps most, cases the first serious encounters with the world of disciplined learning take place at the college level. Secondary schools provide some preparation for the college, but probably in most of them academic standards remain low. American high schools, with the important exception of the minority of "elite" schools, (both public and private) allow students so much choice (among courses) that most high school students can avoid studying many important subjects (for instance, foreign languages, world history, geography, certain sciences) which are not matters of choice in Europe. Another American objective of secondary education, the development of social skills, also leaves its stamp on the curriculum. Numerous nonacademic subjects and activities fill time at the expense of more demanding learning. Until recently even the college years were associated in popular imagination with carefree social life, fun, and competition for popularity, rather than earnest preparation for an occupation. Perhaps these features of American

---

* In suggesting praiseworthy occupational aspirations one article asked plaintively, ". . . is it not exciting to become, say, an installation worker on the construction of the Plavinas or Riga Hydroelectric Stations? Is it not honorable to assemble radios that are famous the world over, to take part in the irrigation of one's own collective farm land, to erect new houses, schools, and hospitals in one's own city or settlement, to become a master of field cultivation or animal husbandry?"[14]

education, secondary as well as undergraduate, are related to the American idealization and cult of youth, the socially sanctioned period of irresponsibility and good times.[15] It is also likely that the lingering (and recently resurgent) anti-intellectual tradition of American life has something to do with the relatively light scholarly burdens imposed on the young in school and college. For many the truly committed academic life starts in graduate school.

The seriousness with which Soviet students, in contrast, approach education has several sources. One is a tradition of popular reverence for education which continues to be encouraged by the authorities. Another is the obvious and vital usefulness of maximizing one's education. Specialized knowledge in Soviet society is not only an assurance of higher status and standard of living, it may also offer a measure of freedom from political and ideological pressures and a materially and culturally better life in a major urban area. More important still, there is not yet a sizeable segment of Soviet youth that takes material security and access to higher education for granted, as do hundreds of thousands (if not millions) of Americans. It is also of importance that in Soviet society an increasingly popular American alternative to higher education—dropping out—is largely foreclosed except in some rural areas. The Soviet alternative to higher education (and its privileges) is unglamorous, routinized, low income jobs. Dropping out in the United States is appealing because it need not be arduous or impoverished, because it often implies freedom from all social obligations (as conventionally defined, at any rate), and it can be abandoned at any time when the usually middle-class youth has had enough of it and the security of "bourgeois" life styles (and the associated educational and occupational routines) become once more attractive or at least acceptable.

Student Unrest and Education in America[16]

It is no longer possible to discuss American education—and especially higher education—without reference to student unrest; that is to say, matters which are predominantly political rather than academic and intellectual.

There are two major schools of thought which dominate the endless discussions of the alienated young, and the rebellious students in particular. Those out of sympathy with the radical activists tend to explain their behavior and social criticism as an expression of personality problems. They ask in effect: "What is wrong with these people?" "Why do they behave in such eccentric, pathological, or destructive ways?" "What emotional frustrations do they act out in the political arena?" This approach may implicitly, though not necessarily, ignore or invalidate social criticism by focusing on and discrediting its carriers.

At the other extreme are those who wish to pay little attention to the actual behavior and social characteristics of student activists and focus exclusively on the targets of their protest. This attitude is widespread among liberal academics and intellectuals and also, understandably enough, among those segments of the middle-classes who raised this generation of white radicals. They assure us that the sole source of the protests are the wrongs of society. Thus student activism can be approached by concentrating attention either on the activists themselves or on the broader social environment they criticize and of which they themselves are the products. Although there is no inherent incompatibility between these two perspectives, as a rule they are used separately depending on the desire to denigrate or glorify student radicalism. Yet it is almost impossible to understand social movements without understanding their participants—in addition to knowing about the targets of their protest and the substance of their social criticism. One has to examine what shared experiences unite those who are attracted to a social movement. Neither a Marxist nor a sociologist can, legitimately criticize people for reflecting the imprint of their social background and environment. Which comes close to suggesting that every society gets the type of revolutionary it deserves.*

Both approaches contain important and compatible truths. On the one hand there is sufficient corruption, injustice and irrationality in American society to justify and nourish protest movements, including extremist ones. At the same time there is also a good deal of free-floating resentment, frustration with the "human condition" (not peculiar to life in contemporary America), thirst for moral certainties and readiness to project upon the world dissatisfactions with

* As Leopold Tyrmand put it: "The quality of a revolutionary is inversely proportional to the system he fights against—the more oppressive and cruel the system, the more heroic and self sacrificing is the rebel; in other words the better and more indulgent the system, the more flippant the revolutionary."[17]

the self, among the young revolutionaries and their supporters. These psychological predispositions are in turn strengthened by finding much to reject—by any standard—in the world outside. Still it would be difficult to account for the student radicalism of the 1960's and 1970's merely by suggesting that it emerged in response to the ills of society. With the exception of the Vietnam war, every reason for being alienated from American society had been present (often in a more virulent form) before the 1960's without provoking a similarly widespread protest on the part of the young.

It is among the peculiarities of the "student revolution" that its demands and programs range from the most idealistic, universalistic, and ambitious to the most trivial and self-serving. Thus the student radicals want to liquidate every form of injustice and repression along with foreign language requirements; they sincerely wish to endow every human being with unlimited opportunity for creative self-development, as well as to eliminate dormitory regulations and the grading system. The contradictions which beset the ideas and behavior of student radicals (and the counterculture of which they are a part) are difficult to overlook. Perhaps the most important contradiction is between the quest for community (a most pervasive and basically apolitical desire) and for limitless self-expression, untrammeled individualism, hedonism, and autonomy.* The pursuit of community frequently overshadows the political programs and purposes of the radicals, (as was also noted in Chapter 3) who often confuse a crowd with a community. Occupation of academic buildings and associated marches and rallies are among the devices by which temporary "communities" of great intensity are created, which are fortified by shared danger and defiance and enlivened by the actual physical proximity of the participants. As was reported by a student in the "historic" occupation of University Hall at Harvard: "What was most euphoric, however, was us and what we were to each other. For those few hours we *were* brothers and sisters. . . . You had to

---

* But by no means the only contradiction. Even the most violence prone and destructive radicals take for granted certain basic services and securities, as pointed out by Nathan Glazer: "The young radical guerrillas now engaged in the sabotage of social organization take it for granted that they will be provided with complex means of transportation and organization, and with food, clothing, and shelter and medical care. The easy availability of these things is based on a system they deride and which in their confusion they want to bring down not realizing that they themselves and all those they wish to help would thereby be reduced to misery."[18]

realize, whatever your politics and whatever your tactics, that we were very beautiful in University Hall, we were very human, and we were very together."[19] Such sentiments also help to explain why ostensibly serious occasions of political protest so rapidly take on the coloration of a carnival or fiesta, complete with guitars, exotic costumes, folk singing, and "guerrilla theater."[20] A good deal of the student revolution no doubt springs from nonpolitical sources*—which makes the revolution's intensity and occasional political naïveté easier to understand. For example, as observed by an English sociologist, many of the revolutionaries demand to be well treated by what they define as a dehumanized, monstrously repressive system:

> On the one hand, the least injustice or illiberalism perpetrated by the Establishment is vociferously decried (quite right, too—but it seems to imply that the Establishment can be expected to be fair and liberal, and that there is some point in protesting *within* the order dominated by it); yet at the same time a "revolutionary" mystique . . . [is] commanded, on the argument that current institutions are *so* slanted that nothing can be achieved within them. . . . Thus the current order . . . is expected to protect carefully the rebel's legal rights, but at the same time to look on benignly and with affectionate understanding when the rebel bypasses legality in the interests of higher principles. . . . It has the mad logic of a family quarrel. These are emotionally most exhausting rebels. They demand to be loved by the order against which they are raising their hand . . . they wish to play within and outside the old rules all at once according to convenience. . . . The premise for appealing to the rules, however, is that the present arrangements are not so terrible after all, and can be expected to protect even those wishing to subvert them. . . . The society which is declared rotten is also solicited for support, and failure to receive it, or enough of it, is bitterly resented rather than tough-mindedly expected.[22]†

* Often among these motives one also finds a free-floating readiness for commitment, a predisposition to find a cause that can give meaning to life. David Riesman has observed: "I see many young people today who expect to *fall* into a commitment or into an identity or into a meaning for their lives, the way romantic young people expect to fall in love. They are unwilling, often, to extend themselves in order to find themselves."[21]

† Or, as Leopold Tyrmand put it more tersely: ". . . the hero of our time demands all possible privileges from the order he tries to shatter. He claims the right to ruin it without any responsibility, and as a matter of fact, even asks for the *right* to annihilate from those he desires to annihilate. Their resistance he calls oppression."[23]

Student radicals admire political systems they hardly know and which they would flee in despair if they lived under them and were given a chance to do so. They project their permissive, libertarian fantasies on highly bureaucratized, regimented, and puritanical regimes, such as the Cuban, Chinese, or North Vietnamese, upon societies where the concept of "student power" would at best be met with incomprehension* and where the avoidance of regular work (or "dropping out") would result in being dispatched to a labor camp set up for such "antisocial parasites." The element of the exotic and unknown (or partly known) is important in explaining the attraction of these countries and of that of the heroes of the student radicals. As Lewis Feuer has noted, "What Lawrence of Arabia was with his primitivist and guerrilla mystique for the English middle-class alienated youth in the twenties and thirties, Che Guevara of Cuba and Bolivia is for the estranged youth of the mid-sixties."[24]

It is also noteworthy that while the radical students reject virtually all the institutions of society they know, they concurrently profess a deep faith in the essential goodness of human nature—an attitude that is no less illogical because it has many historical precedents. It is as if the character of institutions could be conveniently separated from the character of humans who create and perpetuate them.

The student activists seem unaware of a yet more fundamental paradox of their situation. Student protest movements flourish only in those societies of the Western world that they consider to be the most oppressive. Thus one cannot rule out the possibility that the existence of vigorous student protest movements is as much a measure of the permissiveness of a given society than that of the intensity of the grievances that are being protested. Factors considered to underlie student radicalism in America—that is, Vietnam, racism, and ethnic poverty—are hardly issues in a number of Western European countries which nevertheless have experienced highly similar forms of student protest. At the same time a number of the other factors often invoked to justify youthful alienation can be found in greater abundance in the "socialist world" (including the USSR) without

---

* It is also ironical that the kind of university or school the radical students want does not (yet) exist anywhere in the world, but *least of all* in their model countries (such as Cuba, China, North Vietnam, or those in the Third World). Instead, it is in our repressed, dehumanized, unresponsive society that the radical students' dream of transforming the university (and higher education in general) has come closest to realization.

producing significant student protest: for example, highly bureaucratized social and educational institutions, great concentrations of
political power, the (total) exclusion of students from decisions that
affect their lives (both at the university and outside), the functioning
of the university as a training ground for "military-industrial complexes," compulsory military service for *all* students, and so forth.
While efficient and resolute repression explains most easily the absence of any sustained student protest in these societies (and especially the Soviet Union), different levels of expectation on the part
of the young provide further explanations of the apparent docility of
these students. Thus, student unrest is also a measure of intense expectations. Student revolutionaries often proclaim goals that can be
described as utopian and aspirations which ignore historical experience and social scientific evidence concerning social organization and
human behavior.* For instance, many student radicals believe that
the eradication of all inequalities of wealth, power, and status could
be accomplished rapidly if the resistance of some evil men could be
broken, or the masses could be aroused from their torpor or people
would simply listen to their conscience, or some spectacular acts of
violence were committed. The ambiguities of the situation of the
American (and Western European) student revolutionaries are particularly obvious to those who have experienced the workings of
genuine police states and who have also witnessed genuine revolutionary situations. A Czech writer had this to say about Western student radicals:

> They live in a romantic dream world in which their radical rhet-
> oric is perfectly consistent with their apparently sincere faith in
> freedom and justice. But do they really think they could apply
> their radical Utopia in a real world and still respect their liber-

* "Affluence joined with permissiveness during the years of growing up has generated
a low level of tolerance for frustration among our college age young. Objects which
were desired were quickly granted by parents, and punishment was deemed illegitimate
in the schools, in the home, and we might add, in our universities . . . the lesson
learned is that *denial* is not legitimate. Exposure to debunking, muckraking and criticism of the present, without the personal experience or historical knowledge of much
worse conditions results in a rather gloomy, even morbid outlook.
    . . . Gloominess is also fed by the belief . . . concerning the perfectibility of society,
a belief not balanced by an appreciation of the inherent difficulty in perfecting the nature of man himself. When the belief in perfectibility is joined with a low level of
tolerance for frustration, we have a situation in which the desire for change is easily
aroused."[25]

tarian commitments? Do they really think their Utopias could be benign if their revolutions were not comic-opera coups on indulgent campuses but real ventures in the exercise of power?[26]

American student revolutionaries characteristically fluctuate between visions of total powerlessness and omnipotence. At times they seem to believe that breaking a few windows or burning down some buildings will topple what is, according to them, a diabolically efficient and gigantic system of repression; at other times they claim to be totally helpless (which in turn often justifies their use of violence as a "last resort"). It is likely that there is a link between the feeling of powerlessness and feeling entitled to be powerful, between the frustrated desire for power and the propensity to violence. For some of the sons and daughters of comfortable middle and upper middle-class families, occasional and spectacular acts of violence are exhilarating, fulfilling the cravings for intensity and excitement. Living dangerously is attractive to those who do not *have to* live dangerously and who want to live down their middle-class background and the softness associated with it:

> The tough high school kids must be shown . . . that the radicals were not wimpy intellectuals—soft, privileged hippies—but real fighters, gang members in their own right. . . . In Detroit, for instance, Weathermen would take red flags to working class beaches in order to start fights. . . .
>
> What Weatherman demands—and where its adherents find much of its appeal—is a total commitment to the revolution . . . radicals must abandon their comfortable hip existence . . . and submit themselves to disciplined lives as revolutionaries. They must purge themselves of all elements of the hated "white skin privilege. . . ."[27]*

The attractions of violence were also reflected in a report of a "national war council" of the Weathermen that was held in late 1969 in Michigan:

* Feuer's explanation of the violence-proneness (verbal or otherwise) of the alienated intellectual may apply here: "The intellectual too often suffers from a Hamlet complex: he often feels that intellect has disabled him, unmanned him, feminized him, deprived him of the capacity for will and action; he wishes to recover his manliness, to have his every word transmuted to action. His neo-primitivism is a rebellion against what he feels his intellect has done to emasculate him. The cult of violence is a reversion to the primitive rites of passage from adolescence."[28]

A 20 foot long poster adorned another wall of the ballroom. It was covered with drawings of bullets, each with a name. Along with the understandable targets like Chicago's Mayor Daley, the Weathermen deemed as legitimate enemies to be offered, among others, the *Guardian* (which has criticised Weatherman) and Sharon Tate, one of several victims in the recent mass murder in California. "Honkies are going to be afraid of us," Dohrn insisted. She went on to tell the war council about Charlie Manson. . . . "Dig it, first they killed these pigs, then they ate dinner in the same room with them, then they even shoved a fork into a victim's stomach! Wild!" said Bernadine Dohrn.[29]

Not even those most sympathetic to the Weathermen's social critique of America could confidently argue that attitudes, such as those reflected in these quotations, can best be explained with reference to the political aspects of American society and the defects of its institutions. It is more likely that basically nonpolitical motives provide a key to understanding *this kind* of revolutionary orientation; thus from the *Harvard Crimson:*

I like the Weathermen because I hate everyone else [wrote a sympathizer of the Movement]. . . .
    I have a great natural sympathy for crazy anarchistic action, preferably action that offers no further risk of guilt. I would like to blow up big stone banks, tip over the Washington Monument. I used to sit every morning when I was 14 years old in a big gothic chapel dreaming of machine gunning the headmaster and deacons when they walked out of the front door.
I also like disorder, chaos, riot and entropy. . . .[30]

And finally from the same publication:

We have an irreconcilable tension in our existence, all the way from breakfast to bedtime. Blowing up a bad thing will relieve much of that tension. So that the preceding sentence does not become evidence for any of the rampant psychological reductionist theories about radicals, it should be pointed out that the psychological problems most of us have are directly capitalism's fault.[31]

It is possible that the white radicals' penchant for violence (often expressed in their desire to identify themselves with truly tough groups and movements, such as the Black Panthers, the Vietcong, guerrillas in Latin America, or Algerian revolutionaries) may in part be explained by conditions which create in some modern men and women a longing for heroism, unrelated to any particular form of political persuasion or commitment. Hans Speier's comments made thirty years ago on hero worship may provide clues to understanding this phenomenon:

> Modern hero worship is a safe and underhanded way of obtaining vicariously what life refuses to give freely. Hero worship is a worship of active unbridled life. . . .
>   . . . Worship of the heroic may be a substitute for action from which they are barred by circumstance, fear and convention.
>   . . . Modern hero worship comprises three main components; first the primeval veneration of strength and freely chosen risks in defiance of Christian and middle class ethics; second the specific misery created by the clash of socially approved values of work, humility and self-sought happiness as a right with a life experience in which aspirations are curbed, desires censored and in which risks are ubiquitous but imposed; third, the passivity which modern civilization promotes as it catches man in its incomprehensible web of anonymous, depersonalized "forces" and "relationships."[32]

Violence is also often resorted to in order to confirm the situation as the radicals see it, that is, to make "repression naked" or to bring into the open "latent repression."

Much of the violence discussed above seems more a form of self-expression (or therapy, as Irving Louis Horowitz suggested)[33] than an effective means of political struggle. If this were the case, the following proposition of the poet Karl Shapiro may have some truth in it: "We have the most inarticulate generation of college students in history and this may well account for the mass outbreak of physical violence. They have no more intelligent way to express themselves."[34]

It is against this background of unrest, protest, disruption, and violence—anticipated and actual—that one must look at the problems and characteristics of American education in the second half of the 1960's and in the early 1970's.

Several results of the conditions sketched are already apparent despite a decline in the volume and intensity of violence over the last two years. One is the overall devaluation of academic, scholarly, or intellectual activities. Campus unrest, at a minimum, distracts from learning and sometimes forcibly prevents it (as in the case of coercive strikes, and bomb threats). Further, a highly politicized college, or high school is a place where mistrust rises between student and teacher, student and student, student and administrator, administrator and faculty. It is also a place where free expression declines and where the politically powerful (that usually means whoever can mount a sit-in or classroom disruption) can, to a large extent, determine what views may or may not gain public expression.* Academic freedom suffers further when, in response to student unrest, political forces outside the university begin to interfere, often repressively.

Interest in learning also declines when political slogans and programs dominate the atmosphere, when the taking of courses and passing exams come to be seen as meaningless and trivial activities viewed against a background of the world outside waiting to be redeemed, as it were.[35]

Another consequence of unrest and violence (actual or potential) is that frequently faculties and administrators are intimidated and tend to respond with thoughtless alacrity to a wide variety of student demands (pertaining to curriculum reform, participation in academic decision-making, grading, and the like) in the hope of averting confrontations. Under such circumstances, issues are not decided or discussed on merit but, rather, decisions are weighed with a view to maintaining tranquility on the campus.[36]

A combination of the political turmoil on the campuses,† the anti-intellectual trends in educational innovation (to be discussed below) and the growing search for therapy and identity through education is accompanied by a loss of interest in training for specialized occupations, especially those associated with the sciences, business, and administration. These developments could have more serious effects in the long run than the highly publicized acts of violence. If current trends continue there may be a significant decline in the number of qualified people whom institutions of higher education are able to

* In the late 1960's on many, if not most, of the best-known campuses moderate, or conservative speakers did not stand a chance of delivering an address without disruption, if at all. The same held for most government officials and a few social scientists accused of racism.

† It should be noted however that, despite impressions often created by the mass media, the great majority of college students are no more radical than the adult population and are moderate and even conservative on many issues, according to many opinion and attitude surveys.[37]

produce, people who know how to read and write and spell, and who acquire the skills necessary for running even the most "dehumanized" industrial society, let alone a more humane and rational one.

The Crisis of Authority in American Education and Society

There is probably no other area of life (save the family) where the crisis of authority is so evident and consequential as in the sphere of education. As David Riesman has pointed out:

> Since 1950 the decline in the weight and authority of adults chronicled in *The Lonely Crowd* has proceeded even further. Now attending high school and college are the children of the self mistrustful parents who felt themselves revealed in books like *The Lonely Crowd.* . . . The young react to the loss of adult legitimacy with even greater self-mistrust, confusion and rebellion.[38]

It appears that the number of "self mistrustful" adults employed by educational institutions is especially great. An increasing number of teachers at every level (but probably more in the colleges) feel unsure of themselves, full of self-doubt. They wonder if they have anything worthwhile to transmit to their students, or the right to impose any demands on them.* Correspondingly more and more young people question the ability and competence of their teachers, and the value of their knowledge and expertise. The two attitudes complement and feed upon one another, and it is difficult to say in what order they emerged. The uncertainty of teachers (as of the older generations in general) is a reflection of a more profound sense of confusion and bewilderment. It is as if suddenly in the late 1960's the full impact of secularization finally hit educated Americans, who are now desperately looking for sustaining values and are not finding them. The crisis of adult authority in the schools as in the family is also supported by the general cultural veneration of youth, youthfulness, and novelty, which has intensified in the last decade, and presumably had some relationship to the growing uncertainty

---

* At the same time the system of education—especially the high schools—is criticized for being overly authoritarian and for inculcating docility. This criticism is difficult to reconcile with the widespread antiauthoritarianism of students, with their reflexive "antiestablishment" attitudes and their propensity to call into question and reject many of the values and attitudes the schools are supposedly inculcating. If American schools train for docility they seem to do a poor job of it.

about the values, standards, and experience of the past. People who are unsure of themselves often cannot exercise authority; they are, as a rule, disenchanted with their own past and predisposed to look for something new and redeeming in the future, which is to be created by the young. It is almost as if the more self-doubt among the adults, the more lavish the glorification of the young and the more romantic the hopes pinned on them.*

A new incarnation of the noble savage has emerged: it is the untutored young, or children (in or out of school) revered for their innocence, spontaneity, intuition (real or imaginary), and freedom from knowledge and experience.[39] The writings of many distinguished and fashionable experts on education are eulogies of children perceived as being mistreated, bullied, oppressed, misused and miseducated by evil or merely stupid and incompetent adults (their teachers and parents). As many adults aspire earnestly to prove themselves worthy of the confidence (or at least attention) of the young, curious double standards evolve in the colleges and universities. For example, increasingly teachers accept the belief of many students that grading (or any other form of standardized evaluation) is demeaning, destructive (of creativity) and de-individualizing. Yet at the same time increasingly insistent demands are being made (and met) to have teachers evaluated by students, and more vigorously than students have ever been evaluated. Perhaps from an educational standpoint the most serious consequence of these trends has been the growing reluctance of teachers and educators to make demands on students. More and more teachers want to be accepted and loved by their students rather than respected for their knowledge and competence. One result is a trend toward the reduction or elimination of requirements, the willingness to abandon or soften grading[40] (or any other standardized or rigorous form of evaluation), and the growing abandonment of lectures as a mode of teaching (viewed as too authoritarian by many students and also some teachers). Correspondingly the maturity, judgment, and intellectual ability of students tends to be overestimated.

* To be sure, the enthusiasm of much of the mass media, many educators, anxious middle-class parents, and so forth, is not universally shared. There is also today another vision of youth held by the older and less educated, working and lower middle-class Americans: it is an undifferentiated vision of troublemakers, parasites, pampered rich kids who make no contribution to society whatsoever, and who badly need some discipline.

The mushrooming of "independent studies," while in many ways an appealing development, is another product of the trends noted above. They are usually justified with reference to the unique, individual needs of students although it is rarely spelled out what these needs encompass: intellectual, occupational, or emotional matters? It is also frequently asserted that "no two students have the same educational needs." The implications of these beliefs are quite momentous. They reflect a culture that lost its self confidence to such an extent that it deems nothing worthwhile enough (with the exception of reading and writing) to insist on being transmitted to the young. If it is granted that each student is the best judge of his educational needs then clearly there is no longer any agreement on what constitute core areas of learning or essential information about the world to which all students should at least be exposed. Turning formal education into a do-it-yourself endeavor, or an eclectic, totally individualized free-for-all also means that no attempt will be made to motivate the unmotivated. Raising the question of how good a judge a high school or college student is of his own educational needs is no longer legitimate among those in the forefront of educational innovation; such a question merely suggests elitist, authoritarian, or conservative attitudes. The assumption that the student is the best judge of his educational needs (and progress as well, which in turn removes the need for external evaluation) is part and parcel of the noble savage theme.

It should finally also be pointed out that while on the one hand fashionable educational theory stresses the need to reduce stultifying specialization, independent study programs open the door for unlimited (as well as premature) specialization by allowing students to do nothing but what they are interested in, uncontaminated by any external pressure that might be brought to bear to broaden or deepen existing ranges of interest or levels of curiosity. It is of course also possible that these trends will weaken before they make a full impact on higher education. Their more limited impact however is already discernible not only in the area of curricular change but also in that of admissions procedures. A highly individualized approach to student interest and performance and the abandonment of standardized criteria create special problems, as an experienced admissions official observed: "The job of selecting students for college will be made even more difficult if many high schools substitute pass/fail markings for grades and abandon rank-in-class listings, and if college board and similar national tests fall into wider disfavor. These are the trends . . . and maybe in five years we'll be assessing students by height and weight or by vague teachers' reports. People are saying now—don't look at tests and grades, look at motivation. But how do you evaluate motivation?"[41]

Future historians may read with fascination about the conferences, workshops, and meetings at which learned professors or educational experts solemnly solicited the views of young adolescents on what they deemed acceptable as part of the curriculum. For example, in 1969 school officials in a New York City school district organized a conference on curriculum reform that excluded teachers. "It is time we listened to the children," said the district's junior high school coordinator. "We have to try to make the curriculum relevant to their life styles and yet keep it an educational process. . . ." The same article quoted some student views on junior high school education:

> Chris D'Arcangelo, 13, said the schools were too structured. "You are forced to sit each day in a class you don't like and you are bored." Brad Chase, 13, cited an example: "Humanities is the study of human beings, right? To me that means just about everything—sport, fashion, soul music, the works. It could be exciting and relevant and not just deal with what the fingernail tissue is called." "There is just too much pressure," added Tanzen Flanders, a pretty, long-haired eighth grader. "You get to the point where you don't want to care anymore. . . ." Brian Briggs saw the need for better student-teacher rapport. "When the teacher comes in the room," he said, "she gets right down to business. There is no chatting, no relationship. And we get bored."[42]

There is also a connection between the rejection of authority and the often exaggerated apprehension of some students about being "swallowed up" or dehumanized by educational bureaucracy. As noted earlier the revulsion from bureaucracy is a major theme of the New Left's protest against American life as well as an important component of the counterculture. The rejection of bureaucracy (closely linked to the more generalized rejection of authority) is likely to have its roots in the experiences of childhood. The bureaucratic ethos is the perfect antithesis of that which prevails in the type of middle-class family which produced many of the alienated students. It is impersonal, hierarchical, performance-oriented, rule-governed, and it promotes standardized behavior. By contrast the type of family in question tends to be loving, accepting, and highly personalized. What enrages many students most about bureaucracy is that it does not treat them as unique (and uniquely precious) individuals.[43] The same attitude explains the violent rejection of being graded, that is, objectively evaluated with reference to some specific area of competence, rather than lovingly and unconditionally accepted as a total person.

When intense antiauthoritarianism combines with the inability to differentiate, the results are often grotesque. Thus it is becoming commonplace in contemporary critiques of educational institutions to compare them to jails and concentration camps. For example, in the famed "Student as Nigger" (the title itself an attempt to steal the aura of authentic repression from a genuinely mistreated group and transfer it to a highly privileged one), the author talks about an "Auschwitz approach to education" (supposedly prevailing in America), and asserts that "What school amounts to . . . is a 12-year course in how to be slaves." Equating the process of socialization with castration he writes: "There is a kind of castration that goes on in schools. It begins, before school years, with parents' first encroachments on their children's unashamed sexuality and continues right up to the day when they hand you your doctoral diploma with a bleeding, shriveled pair of testicles stapled to the parchment." The teacher is perceived as "flog[ging] his students with grades, tests, sarcasm and snotty superiority until their very brains are bleeding."[44] In a similar vein we are told that many students find it "painful and frightening" that the school prepares them for business and professional careers (described as "the painful and frightening sensation of being funneled into slots in business and the professions"[45]). It is only against the background of confused yet intense expectations (harbored mostly by the well-to-do students) that we can understand the frequent references to "student outrage" and the oppressed state of students. The inability to discern the difference between a school and a prison is probably based on the intolerance of restrictions of any kind, rather than on the actual discovery of similarities between the two institutions. This is all the more likely since they usually do not know what prisons are like, hence they may simply equate them with the only restrictive environment they know, the school.

The *sense* of oppression is no more a proof of its presence than the sense of powerlessness is evidence of powerlessness. There is a significant difference between failure to accomplish rapid social change or influence the course of history and total powerlessness. Naturally the more intense and impatient the desire for change and the more grandiose the vision of the transformations desired, the greater the sense of powerlessness, frustration, and oppression, when these changes are not forthcoming.

It is not difficult to relate the current forms of antiauthoritarianism and hostility to differentiation to the long-standing American value of egalitarianism and the associated suspicions of authority. Yet what we encounter today in education is surely an extreme development of these attitudes. There is a noteworthy paradox in finding side by side an excessive individualism *and* a caricature of egalitarianism which manifests itself in the wholesale rejection of differentiation, including that which is based on knowledge and experience or the lack of it.

In the final analysis, the major thrust and the most universal feature of the student unrest is its diffuse antiauthoritarian impulse. It is an ultimate paradox that this impulse is the strongest in those societies where authority at every level is the most enfeebled and hesitant. Perhaps, as Edward Shils put it, "The ineffectiveness of authority is a stimulus of aggressiveness against it. . . . Split, disunited, temporising, half-hearted authority which repeats against itself the charges made by the student radicals serves only to encourage more hostility."[46] It is at the confluence of intense expectations and the crisis of authority (resting on a still more profound crisis of values) that we find the fundamental sources of student radicalism and the associated problems of education in American society.

Redemption Through Education: The New American Dream

Student Senate President Bruce R. Balboni last night announced his resignation from the Senate and his withdrawal from the University, "effective immediately." . . .

Balboni remarked that the University was unable to answer his questions on life . . . "Questions of Who am I? Where am I going? and What shall I do with my life?"[47]

There is no other area of life in American society today that generates a greater volume of rhetoric than education. Discussions of education, and particularly of educational goals and ideals, have become the most prevailing form of preaching, the most popular format for restating (and proposing) ceremonial values. It seems as if holding forth on education has replaced religious rhetoric: vast numbers of people have no hesitation whatsoever to discuss education in a language which used to be reserved for religion and which religious functionaries would hesitate to use today for fear of being ridiculed as naïve, overly idealistic, pompous, or bombastic. Increasingly, it may be argued, displaced religious impulses have found a new focus in the area of education, particularly on the college campuses. Earlier conceptions of education as a primarily intellectual undertaking are under open attack. The revolution of rising *nonmaterial expectations* that has been sweeping America in the last decades has created new demands on education. It is expected and demanded by many that educational institutions (at the college level in particular) provide people with a new sense of meaning in life, a sustaining community and a resolution of personal and group identity problems, as well as clues to solving major social problems. Few disquisitions on education can be read today without encountering the magic words of community, identity, and meaning, followed by those of innovation, creativity, flexibility, sensitivity, and responsiveness. The major thrust of these trends is unmistakably anti- or nonintellectual. The mere dissemination of knowledge is increasingly condemned as arid, meaningless, dry, dehumanized, or soulless. The importance of emotional involvement in the learning process is being given more and more emphasis. Typical of these sentiments is the comment from an education newsletter of an innovative school of education:

> The emphasis in today's schools is on facts, skills, concepts, and lastly, affect (values and feelings). If education is to be humanized the affective areas of living and learning must be given priority in the schools.
> The basic difference among people is not what they know or what they can do, but in what their commitments are. Any important difference between given people lies in their values and feelings, not in their knowledge or their skills.[48]

Theodore Roszak, by no means an enemy of the cultivation of creativity and sensitivity, noted (in discussing the "apocalyptical yearnings" which influence educational innovation) that "Often enough such madcap brainstorming under the auspices of instructors hardly out of their teens degenerates into a semiarticulate, indiscriminate celebration of everything in sight that is new, strange and noisy; a fondling of ideas that resembles nothing so much as an infant's play with bright, unfamiliar objects."[49] Indeed an important aspect of educational reforms proposed and introduced consists in the progressive dilution or elimination of the distinction between student and teacher. In a well-known experimental high school in Philadelphia:

> Teachers and students together decide what courses will be offered. . . . There are no grades, except for pass and fail.* Teachers assess students' progress on a personal basis and students evaluate teachers' performance. . . . Equality between student and teacher is not only encouraged but pursued almost fiercely. Sometimes it is difficult to distinguish long haired, bearded teachers from teenagers. Students call instructors by their first name and in general wear their newly found equality like a badge. . . . There is no objective way so far to determine, in traditional terms, how much and how well the students are learning.[50]

Another experimental and innovative program in a college had these, by now not so novel features:

> . . . Professors . . . are being asked to look beyond their narrow scholarly specialties to guide students in a wide range of academic and personal pursuits. . . .
> . . . projects embody experiential rather than cognitive learning and the instructor who cannot be expert in all these areas, is asked to provide inspiration and support rather than bits of specialized information.
> . . . a historian . . . said that "not a single student is working in a field I have any expertise in."
> . . . the goal is to create a kind of "community of learners" in which the distinction between teacher and student is blurred. . . .

* In general, Pass/Fail is a euphemism for no evaluation, born out of the reluctance to admit openly that students are no longer evaluated, when in fact this is the case. More recently in many institutions even the word "fail" has been banished and replaced by "no pass" or "no credit."

Since the students get no grades, there is no objective way to measure the program's success.[51]

The new wave of educational theory and methodology aims essentially at abolishing (or devaluing) a series of distinctions which have characterized the educational enterprise. These are the distinction between thinking and feeling, knowing and not knowing, facts and values, teachers and students, students and nonstudents, intellectual and political activities and, finally, between the university (college or school) and the outside world. The rejection of such distinctions grows out of a confused egalitarianism, anti-intellectualism, the longing for community, and the rejection of achievement, competition, and specialization, in turn based on a general intolerance of compartments in life, whether at the individual or institutional level. Edward Shils has observed: "They [that is, the students] believe that everything is integrated with everything else and that dispassionately acquired knowledge is an impossibility . . . they refuse to acknowledge the differentiation of tasks or a division of labor among institutions. . . . The very notion of differentiation and specialization in a division of labor among individuals and institutions is repugnant to them."[52]

In line with such demands and pressures the role of the teacher is also being redefined. Gradually he ceases to be a person who teaches and evaluates students and becomes instead a cross between guidance counselor, social worker, therapist, and chaplain, or simply a humble listener at "rap sessions," or a "resource person" who might occasionally suggest some books to read on topics defined as "relevant" by the students. The vaunted quest for relevance itself often boils down to the desire to be amused, on the one hand, and on the other, to avoid the mental exertions of dealing with subjects unfamiliar. As Robert Nisbet pointed out:

> invariably what the student cry for relevance turned out to be was the all-too-familiar middle-class child's cry to be entertained, to be stimulated, above all, to be *listened to,* no matter what or how complex the subject at hand. Having become accustomed in their homes to get attention to whatever was on their minds, and of course incessant and lavish praise for their "brightness," is it not to be expected that when children go off to the university the same attention should be given their interests and needs?[53]

The major function of the "restructured" school (or college, or university), as seen by the more radical educational reformers, is no longer the attainment of specific skills, or the acquisition of knowledge or the improvement of the capacity for thinking. Rather it is to promote self-revelation and better ways of relating to people. The following fantasy is characteristic of the impulses underlying much of the contemporary spirit of educational "innovation":

> Imagine a class where every student gets an "A." Imagine the student getting an "A" even if he did not work. If he did work, he chose what work he did, how much he did, and decided himself in what ways doing this work was valuable for his own life. . . .
>
> Imagine the students—people—talked about the way work interfered with or enhanced students'—people's—relating. Imagine that people threw out reserve, inhibitions against showing feeling, courtesy or decorum, dependency on authority to explain or pathfind. Everyone had to struggle for his own meaning. People threw out texts, seating arrangements, tests. They worked out one to one their problems in relating. Imagine trusting people, with no established, ceremonial ways of thinking about people's lives, each of which really does soon end. Competition is replaced by cooperation. Isolation is replaced by communality. Anxiety and hostility are replaced by love and gentleness.[54]

Behind these strivings there is a dwindling concern not only with knowledge, skill, and performance but even work as a source of satisfaction. As Richard Hofstadter observed in 1970:

> . . . The desire to perform well, the feeling of craftsmanship, the sense of vocation . . . began to fade in the last ten, perhaps twenty years. And it seems to be fading faster and faster.
>
> Young people don't have anything they want to do. Our culture hasn't been able to perpetuate . . . the desire to do this or that or the other thing and I think this is one of the roots of dissatisfaction in college. Students keep saying that they don't know why they are there. They are less disposed than they used to be to keep order partly because the sense that they are leading a purposeful life has gone. They have the feeling that they are being processed, that they don't have anything to say about what they want their lives to say.[55]

Partly as a result of his growing preoccupation with the present, with the self, with relating to others, and with the meaning of life, the student alienated from intellectual pursuits begins to resemble the type of person sketched by Richard Hoggart and Basil Bernstein:

> Their education is unlikely to have left them with any historical panorama or with any idea of a continuing tradition . . . though they may possess a considerable amount of disconnected information, have little idea of a historical or ideological pattern or process . . . with little training in the testing of opposing views against reason . . . judgements are usually made according to the promptings of those group apothegms which come first to mind. . . . Such a mind is . . . particularly accessible to the temptation to live in a constant present. . . . Present gratifications or present deprivations become absolute gratifications or absolute deprivations, for there exists no developed time continuum upon which present activity can be ranged . . . the postponement of present pleasure for future gratification will be found difficult . . . a more volatile patterning of affectual and expressive behavior will be found. . . .[56]

Curiously enough these observations were made about characteristic British working class attitudes yet they have come to apply to many young middle-class Americans who find the system of education meaningless, the past irrelevant, and deferring gratifications intolerably frustrating.

There are two basic premises behind much of the current ferment in education. We have already referred to one: the new noble savage conception of the young. The noble savage educational philosophy avows that, in view of the essential goodness of the as yet uncorrupted young, the imposition of any discipline is inadmissible and traumatizing. What education should aim at is the preservation and cultivation of youthful innocence, joyfulness, spontaneity, creativity, and goodness, all of which are seen as far more important than substantive knowledge or skills.

The ideal of anxiety-free education (and possibly, anxiety-free life in general) is the second major premise of current educational innovation. Many fashionable critiques of education assert that its evil or most undesirable feature is that it makes children or students or both anxious: they are anxious about examinations, grades, competition, achievement, evaluation, getting into college (or graduate school)—taking for granted that anxiety has no place in human life, or at least not in the lives of the young, who ought to be protected from it as long as possible.

How did this attitude come about? On the one hand, it seems to be a straightforward extension of the psychic environment many middle-class parents try to provide for their children. Schools should continue, in this viewpoint, what is being attempted in the family. In its broader implications this ideal may also be related to the many real sources of anxiety outside the family that confront Americans today: the whole range of political, economic, domestic, and foreign policy problems, which inspire a desire to escape them. On the other hand, the ideal of anxiety-free education is also viewed sometimes as being a new point of departure for reshaping society by creating a new generation with different life goals and ambitions (which would exclude competition and achievement orientation—the two evil anxiety-producing twins).

Both the image of the new noble savage and the ideal of anxiety-free education—as indeed most problems of American education today—are inextricably tied to the deeper problems of values and value commitment in American society. Education, by a process of elimination, has become the major arena where we can witness today the most intense—and often the most confused—groping for new values, or for the revitalization of some old ones. But the problem is inherent in the nature of a secular pluralistic society, although it seems to be more intensely experienced at present than in earlier years:

> Almost everyone . . . is exposed at close range to a variety of competing legitimation systems which undermine each other's credibility and authority. Thus more and more people grow up with a haphazard collection of beliefs and values lacking depth and integrative power. Anomie, alienation and identity crises reach epidemic proportions. . . . Rational pragmatism which is its dominant intellectual outlook is obviously indispensable for the functioning of a complex, modern, scientific-technological civilization. It solves practical problems where religion or ideology fail. But what it cannot do is decide about final goals and values. It provides no clues to the nature of true manhood and womanhood, nor can it fill the daily round with a sense of ultimate purpose and meaning. In short, it does not legitimate the human enterprise. Where there is no vision the people perish; and as

secularism is the absence of visions, it teeters on the knife-edge between chaos and tyranny.[57]

In the final analysis most of the problems and criticisms of contemporary American education have less to do with education per se than with the crisis of values in American society. Education cannot replace religion as a source of meaning in life, but the attempt to do so can seriously endanger the survival of its cognitive, intellectual, and vocational functions.

Religion in American and Soviet Society

To what extent are religious beliefs an integral part of the major values of each society? This is an area in which the differences are more apparent than real. Between the openly and officially atheistic Soviet society and the avowedly God-fearing American, differences diminish when we ask, how much difference does religion make in the behavior of most people. It would appear that religion has little observable influence on the behavior of the majority in either society though the reasons for this differ. In the United States religious values, institutions, and participation remain respected and legitimate. In many American social settings a minimal degree of religious participation, or at least identification, is expected. The charge of atheism is damaging to politicians and office holders, many of whom conspicuously attend church services and invoke the name of God in their speeches. The show of religious conviction is often good "public relations." Many parents send their children to Sunday school and almost half of the population attends church with some regularity.[58] The profession of disbelief in God can disqualify people from teaching positions in some communities. Many religious organizations in the United States are powerful pressure groups influencing legislation (in such important areas of life as divorce, birth control, and education). There are over 300,000 churches in this country; billions are spent on them. Hundreds of thousands of full-time religious functionaries attend to the spiritual and other needs of close to 130 million Americans.[59]

All of this stands in sharp contrast to the situation in the Soviet Union, where most churches are closed (or used for museums showing the pernicious relics of religion), the training for the ministry is restricted to a handful,[60] and antireligious education and propaganda are a major preoccupation of the authorities. The freedom of religion (assured to all by the Soviet Constitution) is a legal fiction—people are not only strongly discouraged from religious participation, they are also deprived of adequate facilities for it. The Soviet mass media make no secret of the official attitudes toward religion. Indeed it is both surprising and contradictory that the Soviet Constitution should bother to guarantee the freedom of beliefs and practices ("survivals" of the past) which have been consistently denounced as harmful and unworthy of Soviet citizens* and against which incessant, serious struggle has to be waged.

Thus one major difference between the position of religion in the two societies is that in one (the American) it receives considerable institutional support and is upheld as a highly legitimate value while in the other (the Soviet) it receives no institutional support and is under consistent official attack. In terms of the dominant values of these two societies being religious is conformity in one and deviance in the other.

We suggest, however, that in spite of this difference, religious values do not govern or significantly affect the life of the majority in either country.† There is nothing surprising about this. Modern, urban, industrial societies have witnessed everywhere the decline of

* As in other fields of the ideological struggle there can be no peaceful coexistence with religion and no compromise with its influence: "It seems there is both good and bad in religious morality. It only remains to take the good and discard the bad and religious morality will be acceptable even for communist society. But such a view is incompatible with genuine atheism which sees its task in overcoming religion completely. . . ."[61]

† This observation is contradicted by the results of Lensky's study, which, however, was carried out in the late 1950's. Among others he found that almost half of his respondents prayed once a day (this, though, varied significantly among different subgroups in his sample, from the 68% of Negro Protestants to the 29% of white Protestants). He concluded that "religion in various ways is constantly influencing the daily lives of the masses of men and women in the modern American metropolis."[62]

Robin Williams, on the other hand, observed that "America is not irreligious, but a whole configuration of forces has pressed in the direction of a slow but pervasive withdrawal of attention and effect from the organized traditional religions. . . .

A broad hypothesis . . . is that the main result of modern secularization of organized religion is the destruction of the belief in a transcendental being, which removes both the supernatural sanctions for our ethical system and a central value focus for the established beliefs."[63]

Finally we might also mention here the results of recent (1970) Gallup Polls in which 75% of the respondents thought that religion was losing its influence in American life (the corresponding figure in 1957 was 14%).[64]

religion as a belief system that provides guidance to behavior and shapes major life goals.[65] The religious world view and explanations of the universe have become both irrelevant and unsupportable, partly at least as a result of the advances of science and technology, and also as a result of a wider contemporary awareness of the atrocities and outrages which have always been a feature of human existence and interaction. This situation holds in both American and Soviet societies, the principal difference being that in the United States religion has preserved its institutional superstructure (while the values themselves upon which these institutions rest have slowly crumbled) and its decline as a moral force has been gradual, while in the Soviet Union the decline of religion has been, at least in part, a consequence of deliberate, systematic and large-scale attack on religious institutions and beliefs.

Of course, we do not know with any precision what has been the extent of the decline of religious beliefs (as distinct from religious institutions) in the USSR. It is conceivable that there remains more religious faith in Soviet than in American society. Two factors suggest such a possibility. One is that Soviet society has preserved more features of a traditional peasant society (of which religion is usually an integral part) than the American. Secondly, the persistence of antireligious campaigns and the recurring call for their intensification[66] suggests that religion is far from eradicated, and that it remains—as Soviet spokesmen put it—a tenacious survival. It may even be the case that official pressure and harassment give religion more meaning and vitality than it would otherwise have. Occasional reports indicate remarkable revivals of certain sects like the Baptists which have grown in membership and continue to defy considerable government pressures.*

The persistence of religious institutions in the United States, although not rooted in their continued gratification of spiritual needs, has a solid sociological basis. As many observers have noted,[69] religious participation for many Americans has been an important basis

* "They not only hold conclaves in houses but also hold forth openly in public places. For example, last July a group of sectarians [Baptists] started singing religious psalms to the accompaniment of guitars and balalaikas on the suburban Azov-Rostov train. . . . Worst of all the Baptists are dragging children and adolescents into the muck. . . . How long are the sectarians going to poison the lives of many Soviet people . . . ?"[67] Equally remarkable are some Soviet figures indicating that 57% of all workers in Moscow are still married in church and 70% of them have their children baptized.[68]

of identification, an aid in the anxious struggle against feelings of rootlessness. Belonging to a religious group, community or church provided a counterweight to the weakening of ethnic and cultural identifications entailed in moving to a new society. Also important to its survival have been the "social" functions of religion, the subtle process of the secularization of religion itself. Not all of this process has been so subtle. Some of the attempts of the churches or individual clergymen to update themselves have been both grotesque and self-defeating.* The minister trying to be like "the fellow next door" may gain some personal popularity and may even function as a bait to get people to the church but, whether he wants it or not, he provides further evidence of secularization. Dancing and singing nuns, priests running "hangouts" and presiding over rock and roll sessions in churches and the like may accomplish useful social, but not religious functions. When churchmen argue that religion must keep up with the progress of science[71] and that there is no inherent conflict between religion and science, they are voicing opinions inspired by the understandable desire to salvage religion, but they are hardly convincing. The progress of science reduces the basis for belief in supernatural entities and compels further revision of the doctrines and traditions that form the foundation of religious beliefs—although the resulting disenchantment (in Weber's sense) may in turn contribute to a new thirst for moral certainties and spiritual comfort. To the extent that institutionalized religion remains a part of the American value system, it has been largely deprived of supernatural meanings and appeals, and transformed into an undemanding, comforting routine. (There remain, however, pockets of traditionalism and fundamentalism. Often these are also oriented toward *this world* engaging in right-wing political activism.)[72] The built-in secularism of American religion today is also expressed in the ease with which the religious calling can be embarked upon: perhaps we see here a reflection of the free enterprise system coupled with American egalitarianism. Setting up a church is no more difficult than setting up a business enterprise,[73] although competition has to be faced on the

* The dangers and difficulties of trying to be relevant have been illuminatingly analyzed by Peter Berger who noted that in American society "Relevance and timeliness are defined for society at large primarily by the media of mass communication. These are afflicted with an incurable hunger for novelty. The relevancies they proclaim are, almost by definition, extremely vulnerable to changing fashions and thus of generally short duration."[70]

part of the established giants in religion as in business. Thus the secularization of religion in America probably has been the major factor prolonging its institutional existence while reducing its importance as a focus of ultimate value orientation.[74]

In the late 1960's the secular trends in American religion took on a new form, which, not unlike the religious "revival" of the early 1950's, was interpreted by some observers as new evidence of the continued vitality of religious institutions and impulses. We are referring here to the new social consciousness and social activism displayed by many churches and clergymen, sometimes earning them headlines, occasional arrests, imprisonment, and the heady feeling of oneness with the young and the spirit of the times. Turning to social activism and increasing immersion in the affairs of the world, communal and political, were in part a spontaneous development usually originating with ministries on campus or in the slums. At the same time the new display of commitment, involvement, and social consciousness was also a part of a deliberate effort to prove to the young that the churches were still "relevant."* No matter how praiseworthy some of these attempts have been, many of these activities had little to do with the core concerns of religion: the supernatural and the ultimate meaning of life. As Peter Berger has pointed out ". . . the passion for social involvement was largely a way of avoiding the facing up to the problem of religious belief."[76]

As in the earlier period of religious "revival," the current striving for new relevance in religion has been accompanied by a characteristic "consumer orientation" (also discernible in education), by the desire to please the customer, to entertain him, to cater to his needs as he defines them at any given time. Liturgical innovations, like those in education, often have been designated to combat boredom. A recent one, the home mass, was described as . . . " 'not so much a new way to have a mass as a new way to have a group,' said Mrs. Rena Hansen, a liturgical expert on the staff of the National Council of Churches. 'It is a do-it-yourself experience with free responses to what a group is thinking and feeling.' "[77] In another imaginative liturgical innovation (devised by an off-Broadway playwright), the communicant's sins were represented by toilet paper (draped around his neck)

---

* A crusading religious publication addressed to the young described Jesus as follows: "All the docile, subjective, effeminate images about Jesus are not true. The Christ of the New Testament is a gutsy, contemporary, radical revolutionary. He is tough!"[75]

and subsequently flushed away in the toilet "in a symbolic declaration of absolution."[78]*

Such examples of farce, confusion, and popularity-seeking notwithstanding there has been since the early 1960's a new and earnest groping for ultimate meaning in life (especially on part of the young), and a turning away from many conventional, this-worldly concerns and preoccupations. Most of these gropings and impulses have, however, bypassed the established religious forms and institutions. Instead, they manifest themselves in aspects of the counterculture (discussed earlier), and especially in drug-induced escapism, group therapy, communal living, dabbling in Eastern philosophy and astrology, and at times in the attempts to convert formal education into a nonintellectual, quasi-religious process.

The secular religion of Soviet society is the system of beliefs and propositions embodied in Marxism-Leninism and its continuing modifications.[80] As treated in the USSR, this official creed has most of the hallmarks of a religious belief system with one important exception: the belief in God or some supernatural entity. At the same time history, the proletariat, the party, or the supreme leader seem to be the various functional equivalents of the conception of Divinity or the Sacred. Like most religions, Marxism-Leninism is also future-oriented. It offers the ultimate alleviation of all earthly suffering, deprivation, and imperfection at an unspecified future date when communist society will be attained. The principal characteristics of this social order will be the perfect harmony between society and the individual—and among all social groups of society—and the unlimited possibilities for satisfying all personal needs. While such a utopia does not answer the questions of death, it promises limitless self-realization and freedom from all worldly frustrations, which conventional religions have also sought to alleviate in their own way.

---

* Lensky's observations about the attraction of new religious movements fully apply to the contemporary American scene, especially since most Americans are conditioned by a variety of social forces and cultural values to equate "new" with good, desirable, and satisfactory: "When new religious movements are formed they typically possess spontaneity and enthusiasm, both qualities which attract converts who are disenchanted with the routinized and unexciting older faiths. Spontaneity is an inevitable byproduct of the newness of the movement and the absence of established routines. . . . In many cases a new faith is also linked with the breaking of established behavior patterns—a process which often has an exhilarating effect."[79]

The similarity of this secular religion to major Western religions is also reflected in the importance of the doctrinal base, the holy scriptures of the Soviet belief system: the writings of Marx, Engels, and Lenin. These are the sacred texts upon which the Soviet social order, past, present, and future, is allegedly based. The fact that realities belie many descriptions and propositions to be found there is immaterial in comparing their significance with those of the sacred scriptures of traditional religions. In both cases, practice deviates widely from the written heritage—as, for example, do the practices of the Christian Churches from the teachings of the Bible. Nonetheless leaders and interpreters claim to follow the teachings, and major decisions are made with reference to original doctrine. Relating policy decisions to doctrine results in its ongoing vulgarization and the compulsive quotation-mongering of Soviet leaders. Ever since the Communist Party of the Soviet Union was founded twisting doctrine to justify short term policy has been routinely combined with demands for preserving doctrinal purity. The names who laid down these doctrines are hallowed objects of compulsory reverence. This is well-illustrated in the charges of irreverence toward Lenin, one of the most damning accusations made against a dissident Soviet writer: "To what a bottomless morass of abomination must a so-called man of letters sink to desecrate with his hooligan's pen this name that is sacred to us! It is impossible to repeat the relevant passages here, so malicious is this scribble, so outrageous and filthy. These blasphemous lines alone suffice for the diagnosis that the authors place themselves outside Soviet society."[81]

More striking yet has been the veneration of the bodily remains of Lenin (and Stalin, for a short time) enshrined in the mausoleum in Red Square. Comparable cults can be found only in the religious worship of saints.

The introduction of new secular rituals represents a further similarity between Soviet secular and conventional religion. New secular holidays (May 1st, November 7th, the birthday of Lenin, and earlier that of Stalin) have been established. The so-called red corners (displaying the pictures of leaders and founding fathers, slogans, and banners) are reminiscent of small shrines. Masses of people assemble to listen to secular sermons (at speeches and rallies). All these are among the quasi-religious manifestations of the Soviet belief system.

Yet Soviet efforts to make Marxism-Leninism more "meaningful" or "vital" are no less pathetic than American efforts aimed at finding new religious content by means of the devices noted earlier. The new Soviet rituals have not taken root: "A rite without traditions, not grounded in history but imposed from above, becomes a planned state 'measure.' "[82]

Substantively this secular religion views the world as an arena of the struggle between the forces of good and evil, that is, between the historically progressive forces (the Communist party or parties, the USSR or the working classes) and their enemies (the capitalists, imperialists, reactionaries, and so on). We may single out three major propositions of this secular religion (which overlap with our discussion of Soviet values in Chapter 4). First, that work is the most important aspect and activity of human life, particularly if it is not "alienated," that is, if it is carried out in the framework of a socialized or nationalized economy that prohibits the private control of the means of production and the attendant private expropriation of its products. Second, that the industrial workers are the most valuable segment of humanity and the party the leading force of this segment, born out of it and embodying progress, social justice, and insight into all historical processes. Third, there is collectivism, the subordination of the individual to society, or the superiority of the group over the individual, with the attendant demand for self-denial.

The heydays of Soviet secular religion seem to have passed with the death of Stalin and the intense totalitarian rule associated with him. Soviet secular religion itself has become more truly secular, its demands less binding, and its objects of veneration less prominent. Secular religions, it may be argued, cannot flourish without a supreme leader, an unchallenged interpreter of doctrine, a living personification of its moral wisdom and object of worship. De-Stalinization removed this object, and none of the new leaders has played the same role. Neither has the receptivity of the Soviet masses and elites to Marxism-Leninism increased. If anything, the official value system and its daily regurgitations in the mass media, schools, and political meetings inspire increasing boredom[83] as we noted earlier in another context.

Other reasons have also been noted for the decline of Marxism-Leninism as a substitute religion. First, it has been fatefully compromised by its expropriation by Stalin and his successors and by its utilization and degradation in the service of whatever policies the Soviet leadership wished to pursue. No value system can be used for long as a mere instrument for the rationalization and legitimation of morally dubious policies without undermining its vitality and ethical content. Nor has the vulgarization and constant repetition of the doctrines helped to retain their spiritual appeal. Still more apparent have been the departures, first by Lenin, from Marxism, and later by Stalin from both Marxism and Leninism. Moreover fundamental questions have been raised about the relevance of Marxism (and Marxism-Leninism) to the social and historical conditions of the world today, Soviet society included. Thus in the words of one Western scholar, Soviet Marxism has become "an artificially preserved dinosaur" despite (or because) of the fact that "there are myriads of agitators and propagandists, a whole army of lecturers and university professors who teach a dead dogma. . . ."[84]

Death and the Value Systems

Perhaps it should not be surprising that on closer inspection both sets of values turn out to be something different from what they claim to be. The American one appears on the surface to be permeated by religious principles and is said to be founded upon respect for the supernatural.[85] In fact, the values pursued by Americans are thoroughly secular. The Soviet official value system in turn claims to be totally secular, yet it abounds in metaphysical and quasi-religious elements. The inability to "handle" death is among the important similarities between the two value systems: neither has much to say about it that is meaningful or helpful to most people.

The problem has been more frequently dealt with in the American context. American funeral practices, for example, have for some time been derided and critically commented upon[86] by writers and sociologists alike (although sociological literature includes few significant studies of the subject—in itself an interesting indication of the reluctance to face the issue). Few observers have failed to be impressed by the central preoccupation of American funeral arrangements and institutions, namely the denial of death.[87] It is among the truisms of anthropology and sociology that attitudes surrounding death in any society illuminate many facets of the culture uncon-

nected with death itself, and in particular the values which prevail
and the sense in which they do so.

The denial of death expressed in American funeral practices and
popular attitudes are among the best measures of the secularization
of American society. While religion and religious functionaries lend
a feeble and perfunctory hand to the bereaved, the emphasis is
clearly on forgetting and suppressing the frightening fact. When
death is not totally ignored or repressed, attempts are made to view
it as an extension of life, to which the perspectives and categories
of worldly existence apply. For instance, enterprises appeal to their
customers' desire for durability, sense of tidiness, and hygiene when
trying to sell corrosion-resistant and waterproof vaults (in which,
one presumes, corpses decay in a more orderly and neat manner);*
cemeteries advertise, among other things, the absence of "competing
headstones"[88] as if anxiety about status would continue to pursue us
even in death. Other funerary firms advertise their facilities in ways
which remind the reader of the descriptions of restful summer resorts where the patrons can relax in unperturbed and graceful re-
pose. Such appeals have in common the denial of both the religious
aspects and the stark physiological realities of death: on the one
hand, they wish to distract our attention from the unknown possibilities of afterlife, and on the other, from the grimness of disintegrating
matter.

The secularization of American society and its relation to death
can also be traced from the material objects used to mark burial
places. A visit to contemporary and old cemeteries provides striking
illustrations of the changed attitudes toward death, most vivid when
we compare 17th- and 18th-century graveyards in New England with
contemporary "memorial parks" near any big city. The differences
reflect not only the decline of gravestone carving as a folk art—in
itself a telling development—but above all the changed attitudes toward death. For the people of 17th- and 18th-century New England
death was a reality faced unflinchingly and earnestly.[89] We cannot,
of course, tell how literally the images and inscriptions on their

---

* "The Clark Grave Vault . . . is built to protect against water in the ground to make
the last resting place of a loved one dry. And what priceless peace of mind this brings,
throughout the years, to those who are left behind." (From *My Duty*, a pamphlet published by the Clark Grave Vault Co., Columbus, Ohio, no date. The pamphlet was advertised and obtained in the mid-1960's.)

gravestones reflected their beliefs about the other-world and whether or not the manifest rejoicing about being freed from the bondages of earthly existence was totally genuine. It is however clear that these early Americans were preoccupied with death and its aftermath and accepted it without trying to transform it into a cheerful continuation of the restful aspects of life. They certainly did not ignore its frightening dimensions. If gravestone carving is any guide to this development, it would appear that the process of taming death started in the 1820's and 30's when tombstones began to shed the images, symbols, and inscriptions directly connected with death (skulls, bones, coffins, and so on) and began to blossom with flowers, weeping willows, and other symbols more appropriately associated with life than decay. In modern American cemeteries there is hardly a hint that the people buried there are dead and hardly an expression of what religion has to say on the subject. The "funeral industry," in a presumably accurate anticipation of what the consumers want, has seen to it that we forget about the traditional associations of death: a beginning of a new state of existence which might have some relation to the way we conducted ourselves on earth, or the grim and irrevocable end to all we cherished while alive. The secularization of death is also vividly reflected in the commercial exploitation of the disposal of corpses.[90]

In the Soviet Union the treatment of death is better attuned to the dominant system of values, which is explicitly and unashamedly secular in theory, if not always in practice. We cannot observe the contradictions in its handling comparable to those in the United States where religious superstructures have persisted despite their eroding basis of belief. Death in Soviet society, from the official point of view, is at best an occasion to survey and sum up the contributions the deceased had made to society, and, if significant enough, to view his life and death as meaningful in the light of such contributions.* At the same time we may presume that the be-

---

* In official discussions only rarely does the subject come up. When it does, it is tied to religious superstition. "Yes, the 'fear of death' . . . still holds sway over people, especially those of the older generation. The craving to console oneself with the illusion of a continuation of life is so great that some are attempting even today to secure tickets to the 'heavenly kingdom.' . . . Individualism . . . is ill reconciled to the truth that the spark of life acquires relative immortality only in human society, in what we have contributed to it . . . in our labors and creative work. . . ."[91] A letter from a reader—reflecting the official view on the subject—thus disposes of the problem: "You write about

leaguered Soviet religious adherents are more earnest in their ob-
servances than Americans and consequently death is also more
meaningful to them. It is likely, for example, that in the rural areas
where traditional outlooks and styles of life have persisted more than
in the corresponding regions of the United States, rituals and attitudes surrounding death are also more traditional and unaffected by
secularization.*

From the official, ideological, philosophical point of view, the issue
of death becomes troublesome when a supreme leader dies. Lenin's
and Stalin's entombment and the preservation of their bodies as
sacred relics† indicates an interesting uncertainty about the treatment of the death of the leader. In the light of philosophical materialism, the preservation of and pilgrimage to the embalmed bodies
is both meaningless and bizarre. They represent an awkward effort
to persuade people about the imperishable essence of the dead
leader, an attempt to bridge the gap between past and present, and a
futile gesture of defiance toward death, aided by chemical preserva-
tives. The exhibition of the lifeless tissues of Lenin also suggests
an official belief in the need of the Soviet masses for a tangible reminder of the great founder of their society who towers above them
even in the permanence of his physical remains.

---

the fear of death [this was in reply to another reader's letter who related death and religion to one another]. Confirmed unbelievers cannot have it. The materialist under-
stands that there are no immortal people, that everyone will die. This is not terrible."[92]
* There are sporadic reports about surviving religious interpretations of death even in
urban areas and among the intelligentsia. Apparently Soviet authorities have not been
very successful in secularizing death, which for many Soviet citizens remains the only
major occasion to call forth the support of religion.
† Stalin's body was subsequently removed from the mausoleum (in late 1961)—an act
which further demonstrated the great symbolic significance of the preservation (or non-
preservation) of sacred remnants. The expulsion of his bodily remains concluded the
process of depriving Stalin of his quasi-saintly status.
   "On October 30, 1961 following the first public denunciation of a selection of Stalin's
crimes at the 22nd Party Congress of the Soviet Communist Party, delegates proposed
'that the sarcophagus with Joseph Stalin's body be removed from the [Lenin-Stalin]
Mausoleum. To leave it there would be blasphemy.' An aged woman delegate, D. A.
Lazurkina, rose to say: 'Yesterday I asked Ilych [Lenin] for advice, and it was as if he
stood before me alive and said: 'I do not like being next to Stalin, who inflicted so
much harm on the party.' (Stormy prolonged applause.)"[93] Interestingly enough, apparently no one in that gathering of staunch nonbelievers and philosophical materialists
found anything questionable in this fantasy of supernatural communications between
Lazurkina and Lenin's spirit!

Summary

Our survey of American and Soviet values suggested similarities as well as differences between the two sets of values. There is bound to be some similarity between major social ideals and values in all contemporary secular societies especially insofar as they reflect some of the most self-evident human needs, aspirations, and expectations. As pointed out by an American sociologist "despite cultural differences . . . men everywhere prefer health to sickness, and longevity to early death. Men everywhere prefer material well-being to poverty."[94] Besides such obvious sources of similarity, social values by definition must also stress a degree of cooperativeness and unselfishness and some form or degree of honesty or fair play, for otherwise social order could only rest on force or fraud. The latter has of course been a familiar historical reality but rarely an *ideal* enshrined in the ceremonial values of any society. At the same time very significant differences remain. Some of these can be related to the circumstances in which the two sets of values emerged. By and large American values have developed much more slowly, and few, if any, radical shifts have taken place over the centuries as far as *ideals* are concerned.[95] At the ideal level the changes which occurred have been matters of emphasis rather than substantive innovation. By contrast, the official, legitimate Soviet values—having emerged from deliberate revolutionary transformations of society—negate and stand in diametrical opposition to many of the pre-Soviet values, as in the realm of religion. There is an interesting similarity between the historical background of the official Soviet and the ceremonial American values: their sources are located in quasi-sacred written materials: the writings of Marx, Engels, and Lenin in the Soviet case; the Constitution and the Declaration of Independence in the American. Both sources are sufficiently diffuse to allow for divergent interpretations.

Because of the relative abruptness with which the Soviet values emerged, their close association with the ruling groups, and the monopoly they enjoy as a result of political enforcement, we have referred to them as *official* values. In the United States it is more difficult to sense a sharply contrasting official and popular value "system," though we can certainly discern a discrepancy between private and public, operative and professed (or ceremonial) values. This

distinction, however, derives from the perennial and universal contrast between what people believe they should be doing and what they actually do. In the USSR, the official values (corresponding in some degree to the public or ceremonial values in the United States) are more clearly articulated, deliberately applied, and enforced. This leads to more noticeable differences between official and popular values. American society differs from the Soviet not only because there is somewhat more continuity between the ceremonial and popular values but also because of the presence of numerous and relatively easily identifiable sets of subcultural values (political, religious, ethnic, cultural, criminal, and so on). In the USSR, it is more difficult to ascertain the existence of such subcultures since they have little or no organizational framework and their representatives rarely have access to the public. There are occasional exceptions to this proposition. At times written evidence about values, clearly at variance with the official ones, reaches the West. A remarkable example of this was the letter of L. Chukovskaya, a critic and prominent member of the intellectual elite, written to Sholokhov, the Stalin and Nobel Prize winning writer.[96] The letter was a passionate condemnation of Sholokhov, who found the sentences of the writers Sinyavsky and Daniel (five and seven years of forced labor, respectively) too lenient. (They were accused of ideological subversion for publishing books abroad critical of many aspects of Soviet life and values.) A rare document of political protest, the importance of the letter also lies in its eloquent reaffirmation of such "unofficial" values as an apolitical, universalistic humanism, compassion, mercy, love for the sufferer, and the autonomy of the arts and ideas. Chukovskaya linked these values with Russian and Western literary traditions, and the names of Gorky, Pushkin, Zola, Chekhov, Dostoevsky, Tolstoy, and even the early Sholokhov. Among other things, the letter stated:

> the tradition of interceding for people—the condemned, that is—
> is nothing new in Russia, and our intelligentsia is rightly proud
> of it. . . . A book, a piece of fiction, a story, a novel, in brief, a
> work of literature—whether good or bad, talented or untalented,
> truthful or untruthful—cannot be tried in any court, criminal,
> military, or civil, except in the court of literature. . . . Ideas
> should be fought with ideas not with camps and prisons. . . .
> The books of the great Russian writers have always taught and

still teach us to look not in an oversimplified way, but deeply and subtly, armed with social and psychological insight, at the complex causes of human error, misconduct, crime, and delinquency. The humanizing message of Russian literature is indeed to be found mainly in this quality of understanding. . . .[97]

Such statements indicate that there is, if not a widespread ferment, at least a quiet search for new values among some intellectuals. Sometimes such gropings reflect the desire "to re-establish certain principles of common decency . . . in the face of the Party's denunciation of such ideals as undesirable 'abstract humanism. . . .' " Frequently the same desire for spiritual renewal is reflected in an upsurge of interest in the past and the traditions of the countryside: "The feeling is widespread that in the countryside important spiritual and human values have miraculously been preserved through the upheavals of war, revolution and industrialization and that it is important to regain them for the whole nation."[98]

What are the most apparent contrasts between American and Soviet values?* There is no way of reconciling the American value of *individualism* with the Soviet value of *collectivism*. Consistent with this divergence, there is a similar contrast between the values of *private* and *public* property, again reflected in a variety of institutional arrangements. Less pronounced but still discernible is the difference in emphasis on the value of *consumption* as against *production,* the former being ascendant in the United States while the latter is stressed in Soviet society. (This is one of the areas where a fairly clear clash between Soviet official and popular values is discernible.) The American *belief in God* and Soviet-style *scientific atheism* are equally irreconcilable, although here again we have no exact knowledge of the degree to which Soviet atheism is a popular and not merely official value. Correspondingly it is not easy to assess to what extent belief in God in the United States is a value reserved for the ceremonial plane, and to what extent it is a vital, living belief. The American values of *novelty* and *youthfulness* differ probably more in degree than in kind from corresponding Soviet values. In the United States there is however far more concern with these attributes than in the Soviet Union, which in some ways remains more static and traditional than American society. Certainly novelty per se,

---

* Again it should be kept in mind that we are juxtaposing official values in the Soviet case with a combination of ceremonial-popular ones in the American case.

while deeply cherished in America, is neither a popular nor official value in the USSR.

These contrasts stand side by side with the acceptance and affirmation of a number of generalized values in both societies (as was also noted in Chapter 4). *Patriotism* is one of them. In the United States, and to a lesser extent in the Soviet Union, the more highly educated —who are more acutely aware of the defects of their society—tend to view with distaste the more extreme manifestations of patriotism. *Achievement* is of course highly valued in both societies but probably more so in America* and especially in its highly personalized, individualistic form whereas in Soviet society the achievements of the collective are extolled and the value of personal achievements is often reduced by linking them to the assistance of the collective. Americans probably feel less personal pride in their space program than do Soviet people, nor are they noticeably proud of the number of dams or hydroelectric stations in their country. There is, however, a widespread reverence for bigness in both societies. *Material abundance* and *comforts* are also highly valued by Americans and Soviet citizens alike, though here again there is more emphasis on the collective rather than privatized versions in the Soviet official value system. *Equality of opportunity* is another widely affirmed value reflected, to varying degrees, in certain institutional arrangements in both societies. The belief in the equality of opportunity represents a modified form of egalitarianism that allows for unequal rewards in situations when, it is assumed or asserted, opportunities for competing have been equalized. (This matter is more fully discussed in Chapter 6.) Both societies also display an *optimistic orientation* toward the future,† a *belief in progress* and in the corrigibility of social problems and the *perfectibility of human nature*.

---

* It would, however, be a mistake to regard the achievement orientation of Americans as purely or primarily materialistic or status-oriented. In many occupations and for many people achievement-orientation is, in some respects, a way of facing death. In a secular society where death is viewed (if and when confronted at all) as the irrevocable end, the desire to transcend death is nonetheless still present and the only possibility to do so is by creating something that will survive its creator: a book, a painting, a piece of sculpture, a building, an organization, a foundation, a trust fund, a business firm, a musical recording, some artifacts—it can be a variety of things.

† At least this was the case until recently in the United States. The intense awareness of social problems of the 1960's has dampened traditional American optimism. The optimism of Soviet society belongs, clearly, to the official values rather than popular dispositions.

Many of these similarities reveal a distant yet discernible common ancestry of beliefs and values associated with 18th-century rationalism and the Enlightenment* which influenced the authors of the Declaration of Independence and the American Constitution no less profoundly than they had Marx and Engels and through them many of the official values of Soviet society today.

* The effects of the Enlightenment were, of course, far more powerful in American than in Russian society.

It should also be noted here that the different religious traditions of the two societies— Protestantism as against the Russian Orthodox Church—left their highly divergent imprints on cultural values and popular attitudes which are still discernible.

6. Stratification
and Styles of Life

Affirmations and Limitations of Equal Opportunity

It would probably surprise most Americans and most Soviet people
that there are significant similarities between their societies with respect to the conditions of social inequality and the achievement of
social status.[1] There is an impression of far-reaching differences—less
justified in this area than in many others—created by claims on both
sides. American popular criticism of Soviet society stresses regimentation, uniformity and the extinction of both individual initiative
and genuine opportunity to rise to the top. Americans are skeptical
of the proposition that people will work hard when possibilities for
enrichment and the acquisition of private property are limited. The
impression of a dreary egalitarianism is reinforced by the homoge-
nized, bureaucratized nature of employment opportunities in the
Soviet Union, where the state is the sole employer, everybody earns
wages and salaries, and the upper limits of what can be earned appear to be inflexibly fixed.

By contrast, in Soviet eyes American society, being a capitalist one,
is characterized by extreme inequalities of wealth based upon the exploitation of the masses by the greedy capitalist minority. Americans
in general are considered to be obsessed by the pursuit of money,
and American society one in which social position and personal

worth are defined by income and the possession of material goods alone.

What many Americans and Soviet people think of their own society is no more accurate than their stereotypes of one another's. Many Americans have taken for granted that the United States offers more opportunity for social-economic advancement than any other country and that in American society the major (if not the only) obstacle to improving one's position is lack of ambition, sloth, or other defects of character. Only in the last few decades, and particularly since the 1960's, with the rediscovery of huge pockets of poverty, have such beliefs been seriously questioned. Correspondingly spokesmen for Soviet society see theirs as the most advanced and just society known in history that satisfies all personal needs (as far as resources permit) and is proceeding steadfastly toward an era of material abundance and optimal conditions for individual fulfillment.

There is, then, a surprising amount of similarity between American and Soviet claims for their respective stratification systems. Both point to the existence of equality of opportunity for virtually all, and both deny, in somewhat different ways, the legitimacy of inequality, at any rate as an immutable condition. Both recognize inequality, and particularly unequal access to opportunity, only as a transient aberration that is to be eradicated, or is already in the process of eradication. Thus the Soviet proposition that until communism is achieved each should receive in proportion to the contribution he is able to make to society, resembles the axioms of American social competition, which stress that drive, talent, ambition, and ability will be rewarded: "the [American] culture enjoins the acceptance of three cultural axioms: First, all should strive for the same lofty goals since these are open to all; second, present seeming failure is but a waystation to ultimate success; and third, genuine failure consists only in the lessening or withdrawal of ambition."[2] Robert K. Merton, the author of this statement, characterizes such sentiments as the "deflection of criticism of the social structure onto one's self among those so situated in the society that they do not have full and equal access to opportunity." In a technologically more backward society like the Soviet Union, in which access to consumer goods is far more limited, the slogan "to each according to his ability" serves similar functions. Apologists of laissez-faire capitalism in America and spokesmen for the Soviet system are thus curiously agreed in claiming that in their respective societies rewards go to those who deserve them, and that those who fare poorly have only themselves to blame.[3]

Besides the obvious social-political function of such claims, the similarities in the underlying assumptions and rationalizations concerning inequality may be traced to the origins of each society, and to the desire to establish a social order of greater equality than the old one. This is more obvious in the Soviet than in the American case, since Soviet society emerged from a deliberate revolutionary design, inspired by the Marxist utopia in which the abolition of economic exploitation—the alleged fountainhead of *all* inequality—occupied a central part. The pursuit of equality also motivated the founders and early settlers of the United States who were escaping feudalism, religious intolerance, and the lack of opportunity of their native lands.

However in both societies the ideal of social and material equality became gradually transformed into the concept of the *equality of opportunity* which emerged as an openly stated major American value while it was a more implicit admission of the deferment of the original Soviet aspirations of complete equality. In each case the concept of equal opportunity represents a retreat from the founding ideals, a compromise with social reality. In the Soviet Union the compromise was necessitated in part by lack of resources, making the satisfaction of material needs on a broad scale impossible, and rewarding the most able and useful members of society imperative. (To be sure, "able" and "useful" have often been defined on the basis of political-ideological considerations.) In both societies transmuting social and material equality into equality of opportunity made it possible to preserve some of the old as well as to develop new forms of inequality. And in both, the spokesmen for the existing social order could argue that social organization cannot be blamed if individuals *fail to take advantage* of opportunity, suggesting—with different degrees of explicitness—that conditions have been created for the deserving to rise, while those lacking in talent, ambition or industry have only themselves to blame.

In the United States equality of opportunity is impeded by several circumstances, some of which are present in most societies—historical as well as contemporary—while others are more peculiar to American society. The most general obstacle in the way of establishing equal opportunity in any society (even when such a desire is widespread and receives institutional support), is the familial transmission of inequality. This does not consist simply or primarily in passing on the material advantages of higher income and status but rather in the social inheritance of attitudes, aspirations, and expectations. It has become a commonplace observation that middle- and upper-class youth are better equipped and generally speaking more strongly motivated to compete for higher income, education, and prestige, than their lower-class counterparts, who usually do not expect to succeed and thereby reduce their chances for doing so from the start.* But, in addition to these more subtle motivational factors, institutional opportunities are *also* unequal. For instance, people with lower incomes are less likely to prolong the schooling of their children since the lower the income of the head of the family the greater the pressure for other members of the family to find a job. This applies to both American and Soviet society.

Even in societies offering social mobility, access to the means with which to improve one's social position is predetermined to a considerable degree. Education is the prime factor. The poor tend to have access to inferior schools largely because of the characteristics of their place of residence. This phenomenon is more pronounced in the United States than in the Soviet Union. In the former, residence both reflects and determines social status to a far greater extent than in the USSR. In the latter, housing patterns may not reflect status, and people of different incomes, occupations, and educational attainments often live in the same neighborhood. In the United States this is rarely the case due to the far greater availability of and wider choice in housing and because higher income can be used to buy better housing. In the USSR while rents are generally low income is often irrelevant to gaining better housing for this depends largely on bureaucratic procedures, housing being controlled and centrally al-

* This is not to say that all those better equipped for it do in fact engage in this type of competition. From the mid-1960's what appears to be an increasing number of youth of middle- and upper-class backgrounds have decided to opt out of competition rejecting the values associated with it. Should these trends gain momentum, there could be far-reaching implications for the entire stratification system and some novel patterns and rates of downward mobility may emerge.

located by governmental or municipal authorities or plant management. (There is a small supply of cooperative apartments, which can be had for sums most people cannot afford.) In contrast, the American acquires better housing primarily through private channels, by commercial transactions. Better housing in the United States also means, in most cases, home ownership, that is, living in a small house and not in an apartment building, which in turn means moving into suburbs. Housing thus reflects—through the price and appearance of the home—the financial and generally concomitant social status of the owner. Residential social segregation is rooted in the differential purchasing power of people* but it has numerous secondary results which further diminish the equality of opportunity. Along with the quality of housing, differences emerge in the quality of education, recreational facilities, libraries, municipal services, police and fire protection. High income areas, as a rule, have better schools because schools are maintained from local taxes and more lavish school budgets tend to result in better schools. At the same time studies such as the Coleman Report[4] suggested that schools alone cannot radically improve the level of education if the environment outside them remains unsatisfactory. The high levels of violence which prevail in many slum schools further diminish the opportunity for learning.

In the Soviet Union the situation is quite different. The school system is thoroughly centralized and standards are set by the Ministry of Education. School equipment, teacher-student ratio, qualification of teachers, and the like do not depend on the resources and interests of a given neighborhood or community, and local residents have little to do with decisions affecting the curriculum. A greater emphasis on vocational training offers more hope for finding employment even for the less privileged and less strongly motivated in the USSR than does the American public school system, which often fails to provide useful, marketable skills for the poor.

Yet it would be incorrect to visualize the Soviet system of education as providing complete or near-complete equality of opportunity. The greatest flaws of the Soviet system of education, and those which have the greatest bearing on social mobility, are to be found in rural areas. As in so many other spheres of life, the most crucial differences in the realm of opportunity unfold along the lines of the rural-urban

* This does not mean that income is the sole factor. Racial and ethnic prejudice and preference also play a major role in the processes of residential segregation.

distinction.* According to all available information, Soviet rural schools are markedly inferior, and the fulfillment of the requirements of compulsory education is often more symbolic than real. Such conditions reflect the relative indifference of the regime toward the rural population. They also reflect the chronic difficulty of attracting (or compelling) highly qualified people to live in such areas.

Certainly in both societies there is some sense of guilt and embarrassment over the rampant inequalities in social privilege and material rewards. While there are probably far greater inequalities in the distribution of political power in the Soviet Union than in the United States, this kind of inequality is somewhat more easily concealed than the contrast between the extremes of ostentatious wealth and abject poverty found in American society. Perhaps in part to counter such facts of life, American culture has retained its early normative injunctions against showing deference, however great the differences between the various economic strata of the population.† It is a curious feature of American stratification that the acceptance and indeed expectation of sharp economic differences and inequalities are coupled with a rejection of expressions of deference to wealth. The ideal code of behavior prescribes an easy, often unreal informality between people of totally different status. Even in hierarchical organizations people frequently call each other by their first names, those in menial occupations show little respect or deference to their employers and bosses, and the latter in turn often strive to underemphasize in manner and address their superior income and social position. It is difficult to establish to what extent this is a deliberate effort to camouflage social inequality and thereby placate the troubled consciences of those who believe in the basic egalitarianism of the society (and to provide some compensation for the disadvantaged), and to what extent it is a survival of a greater degree of equality that had actually existed in the more distant past. It is a matter of debate whether inequalities of wealth and power have increased, decreased, or remained more or less constant over time, although indications are that no great shifts have taken place in the past few dec-

* There is a striking similarity between some American measures to provide crash programs for the educationally handicapped groups—black children from urban slums or rural backwaters—and a recent Soviet program embarked upon by Leningrad University to attract more students from the provinces with the assistance of rural teachers.[5]
† This proposition does not, however, apply to the remnants of color-caste relationships, particularly in the Southern states.

ades. The same applies to social mobility, which, contrary to some impressions, has not altered significantly.[6]

The Soviet Union had no prerevolutionary tradition of egalitarianism and used to be openly hierarchical; class distinctions and social distance were accompanied, as a matter of course, by expressions of deference. This tradition and the social structure that sustained it were swept away by the October Revolution, though not completely. From the 1930's onwards, economic and social inequalities were reintroduced, helping to revive, at least partially, the habits of thinking and the attitudes that accompany status distinctions. The persisting contrasts between urban and rural ways of life have also played a part in maintaining psychological patterns of inequality. Today, there is still in Soviet society much contempt on the part of the educated toward the uneducated (and "uncultured"), of the established urban dweller toward the peasants, and a high premium is put on mental work even if it is less well paid than certain types of manual work.

The importance of the type of work performed and the attendant level of skills as a differentiating factor in Soviet society is well illustrated by certain problems of the rural areas. A Soviet weekly quoted a state farm bookkeeper recently: "Thank goodness there are still some girls with only an elementary education, otherwise we wouldn't have any milkmaids at all." A chairman of a collective farm "remarks bitterly that in all his long years as a collective farm chairman he has never married off a milkmaid. The most eligible rural bachelors—the equipment operators—do not marry them."[7]

The theoretical discussions in the press also indicate that there is some concern over inequality in Soviet society. Readers inquire about "ways to achieve social equality." Such questioning is stimulated by the rising material expectations and is in part an unintended consequence of the official propaganda of the recent years that often exaggerated the imminence of communism, that is, the stage of abundance in the development of Soviet society. The official answer designed to remedy the situation is surprisingly similar to that which is offered in capitalist societies:

> inequality in distribution can be liquidated only on the basis of development of production. Equality cannot be established through the introduction of a levelling type of distribution. . . .
> The levelling type of distribution . . . will undermine the incen-

tive for increasing the productivity of labor and will impede the development of the economy.[8]

It is difficult to say in which of the two societies inequalities are more readily accepted, since both in principle are dedicated to their drastic reduction. Some observers assert that there is among Soviet people an attitude that seems to have much in common with the widespread American admiration of success, even if it can be had only by the few. According to a former Soviet citizen "The average Russian . . . is neither angry nor vindictive about the irony of the great discrepancies in income that exist in a society that, in theory, aims at Communism. Any resentment he might feel is greatly toned down by the respect he feels for those whose status . . . happens to be above his own."[9]

This does not imply that Soviet people, and those at the lower rungs of society, accept material inequalities with complete equanimity or without grumbling. A recent discussion of the subject in the press presents striking evidence that delicate questions are being raised by some workers. They reflect above all resentment toward those whose social utility is not self-evident, that is, the bureaucrats. The discussion took the form of an official answering letters by readers whose "incorrect notions" included the suggestion that those "who do not directly produce material wealth are unnecessary." Another still more daring question went to the root of an issue that is not supposed to exist in a socialist society. A worker asked: "What would be the average monthly earnings of a worker in our branch of industry . . . if all the money from the output he has produced were to be divided only among those who have had at least something to do with its production?"[10] The answer to this question pointed out that though the worker does not receive his "unreduced labor income," "everything that has been withheld from the producer as a private individual goes in one way or another, directly or indirectly, to benefit him as a member of society"—an assertion that is based on ideological premises which do not invite further public questioning in the Soviet Union.

In the United States in recent years a growing impatience with various forms of inequalities has developed that is far more intense than the corresponding phenomenon in the Soviet Union. The intensified refusal to accept inequalities has been manifest over a wider range of issues, but more concentrated among specific segments or strata of the population. The battle against inequalities in American society is not limited to the more traditional objectives of gaining greater economic-material equality. Much of it has been aimed at barriers to educational and occupational self fulfillment, limitations on personal autonomy, participation in community affairs and at the attainment of greater personal dignity on the part of various ethnic groups, women, welfare clients, and some of the younger age groups.[11]

The Major Determinants of Social Status: Occupation, Wealth, and Political Power

In American society income is not only a fairly reliable indicator of high status position; it is also one of its preconditions. People who enjoy high status are, with few exceptions, wealthy to some degree. If they have political power it frequently derives from wealth. In American political life ample funds are required to compete effectively for political office, especially at the national level. There are of course many exceptions to this pattern, yet the fact remains that wealth is an important asset for participating in electoral campaigns.

At the same time political power can be quite irrelevant to another component of high status: prestige. Traditionally, political careers and offices have not enjoyed a high reputation in American society because of their frequent association with corruption and because of a long-standing mistrust of politics in general. In this perspective government has been seen as either a necessary (or unnecessary) evil, defined as such by the values of an individualistic, competitive society inimical to externally imposed constraints and regulations.

Thus to the extent that there is an overlap between political and economic power in the United States, economic power usually precedes the political and rarely the other way round, although political positions often lead to improving financial circumstances.[12] Still, while some political offices can lead to financial gain, they are not usually *major* avenues of enrichment or of the acquisition of economic power. This is not to say that politicians do not have an impact on the economy by their veto power or by favoring special interest groups in or outside their constituency. The present discussion, however, is primarily concerned with the relationship between economic and political resources and their effect on status.

By contrast, in the Soviet Union the highest positions in the system of stratification are based on political power which is also a source and precondition of an abundant flow of goods and services as well as the stepping stone to economic power.* Some of the most conspicuous status differences in the USSR derive from different shares of political power—a compelling refutation of the Marxist claim that social inequalities are invariably based on property.

In some measure, we can discern two partly overlapping systems of stratification in Soviet society, one based on political power and the other on special skills and the associated material and prestige rewards. The most powerful persons in Soviet society, the party elite, do not necessarily have the highest prestige among the population at large. The highest prestige is accorded to other, nonpolitical occupations, those in the sciences and the arts. This pattern applies, with some qualifications, to rewards of various kinds, for example travel privileges. Top scientists, artists, and certain athletes command higher incomes than do many individuals in the party elite and their life styles, as well as occupational security, are superior to those among the political elite. The latter probably work harder, carry greater burdens of responsibility and, while they also have access to the most sought after goods, services, and privileges, do not have the same opportunity to take advantage of them as those belonging to the nonpolitical elites. Nor does party membership in itself confer material benefits, even though it may help. Certainly a worker or kolkhoz peasant who belongs to the party is not more but less advantaged than a scientist or engineer or opera singer who does not. On the other hand, it is true that the most important and outstanding professionals tend to be party members. This, however, is more a symbolic recognition of their functional importance or preeminence already achieved than a precondition of it.

* According to George Fischer in the Soviet popular perceptions of social stratification "the Party alone ranks high in both class and power. Status, in the sense of social prestige or 'honor' goes more to Intelligentsia than to Party." He also describes the popular view of the basic class divisions in Soviet society as: "a triad of classes consisting of the intelligentsia, the Party and the People."[13] According to his tabulations the Party (that is Party elite, not rank and file membership) represent 0.5% of the population, the Intelligentsia 8% and the People 91.5% (that is, all those who cannot claim elite status either on political or functional-skill grounds).[14]

A Polish writer (now living in the U.S.), while somewhat over-stating the case, depicts this twofold system of stratification:

> there persists a belief that the upper class in a Communist society
> is made up of Party members, government officials, high-ranking
> military people and industrial managers. Nothing could be more
> mistaken. These people are the rulers, overburdened with work,
> gross, coarse, very limited . . . undemanding where a better life
> is concerned. They live modestly, work fourteen hours per day,
> are early victims of heart disease. The real upper class is made up
> of those who serve them—the cynical intellectuals, writers, artists,
> and journalists who sell a preparedness for every lie in return for
> money and lack of responsibility.[15]

It should be pointed out that this view of the upper class ignores the many scientists and engineers who are also among the privileged, not for the political-ideological services rendered, but for their economic or administrative contributions. The author also exaggerates the modesty of managers and the political elite.* Yet an important element of truth remains in his observations.

It should be borne in mind that in *neither* society is there a complete overlap between the principal components of status: access to goods and services, political power, and prestige. As already noted, in the United States there is frequently a discrepancy between wealth or income on the one hand, and political power on the other, sometimes even between prestige and wealth. Opinion surveys repeatedly[16] put the position of Supreme Court judge and physician higher than that of businessman, even though a businessman is more likely to be wealthy. It is also apparent that doctors rank high not only because of their income but because of the association of the medical profession with service and social utility. In the Soviet case it seems that the highest prestige occupations are not those that yield most power but nonpolitical occupations, noted earlier. This is most clearly reflected in the occupational aspirations and choices of secondary school students. According to a Soviet article:

> Between 70% and 90% of the young men and women graduating
> from school have thought of no path other than continuing their

* Thus, for example, recent (1972) reports of Brezhnev's possession of several imported luxury cars—including a Rolls Royce and Cadillac—hardly squares with the image of the self-denying, puritanical functionary.

studies. At the same time (influenced to a substantial degree by newspapers and books) they all chose the same occupations—physicist, radio or electronics engineer, pilot, doctor and the like—and disdain those branches of the national economy that need more young people (the entire sphere of services, for example). Many upperclassmen still consider physical labor demeaning.[17]

In Soviet society definitions of status are further complicated by the two competing criteria of prestige: the official and popular. (There is no comparable "official" scale of prestige in American society.) For example, in terms of the official values manual labor has a high prestige and the regime regularly bestows social honor on manual workers, reflecting the value put on hard work.* Yet, as indicated above, there seems little corresponding popular enthusiasm for manual labor,† particularly agricultural. Next to agriculture, service occupations have the lowest prestige and often also the lowest income. Recent efforts to make them more attractive included the following: ". . . An All-Union Rally of Young Workers in Trade and Everyday Services was held in Moscow. The banner of the Young Communist League Central Committee was ceremoniously brought onto the stage, and this was as a symbol of the fact that the YCL henceforth regards the vocation of salesclerks, waiters, tailors and shoemakers as among the romantic vocations of our times."[19] Yet such social honors often fail to correspond to the material rewards offered, and as a rule the more highly skilled and trained a person is—and thus the less likely to do work at the manual level—the higher his material rewards.

The popular value put on the jobs of the scientist, engineer, and artist is also closely tied to the desire to escape politically sensitive occupations or those more directly under political supervision, for example, in the humanities, the social sciences, and political admin-

---

* This is not to say that, from the official point of view, manual labor actually has a higher standing than mental. The exaltation of manual labor has been part of the campaign to inculcate respect for work, regardless of its nature. Soviet authorities have always been aware that only a limited number of people can become scientists, artists, and so forth, while the economy needs multitudes for the more humble occupations.

† A recent article discussing difficulties and deficiencies in factories (including the attitudes of some workers) noted regretfully that "given the present level of technology, it is not yet possible to make every worker's labor interesting and diversified. . . ."[18] Perhaps it ought to be added that the problem of monotony is only one reason for the low status of manual labor. Probably more important is the fact that much of it is not well paid and is physically fatiguing.

istration. Yet there is little evidence of difficulties in recruiting enough functionaries (mediocre as they often are) for the party and its various affiliated organizations (such as the Komsomol and the Trade Unions) since these positions offer comfortable living standards and upward mobility.[20]

In contrast with the American system of stratification, which evolved gradually and spontaneously, the Soviet system has been "set up" in a deliberate way, at least as far as the allocation of material privileges and status is concerned. This in part followed from the planned nature of Soviet society, from the centralized distribution of scarce goods and services and from the effort to provide optimal conditions for rapid industrialization. To the extent that the government controlled all material resources and rewards decisions had to be made as to "who gets what, when, how." The purposeful restratification of Soviet society began in the early 1930's and, like most major steps taken by the regime, received ample ideological justification. In 1934 Stalin said:

> By equality Marxism means not equalization of individual requirements and individual life but the abolition of classes, i.e., the equal emancipation of all working people from exploitation . . . the equal abolition for all of private property in the means of production . . . the equal duty of all to work according to their ability and the equal right of all working people to receive remuneration according to the amount of work performed (socialist society); the equal duty of all to work according to their ability and the equal right of all working people to receive remuneration according to their needs (communist society). . . . That is the Marxian conception of equality. . . .[21]

Having thus partly redefined, partly projected to the future the accomplishment of equality (that is, equal access to remuneration according to needs), Stalin produced further arguments in order to obscure the extent to which his policies diverged from the original goals and expectations of the revolution:

> every Leninist knows (that is, if he is a real Leninist) that equalization in the sphere of requirements and individual life is a piece of petty-bourgeois absurdity worthy of a primitive sect of ascetics but not of a socialist society organized on Marxian lines; for we cannot expect all people to have the same requirements and tastes. . . .[22]

This, of course, was not the real issue. Taking up a spurious defense of the diversity of personal needs, Stalin's argument was surprisingly close to those which defended inequality under capitalism on similar grounds and which criticized socialism by equating it with the ruthless leveling of all individual differences. Quite clearly the critics of Stalinist restratification had no desire to eradicate individual differences in taste and need. They wanted a rough equality in satisfying *basic* needs which all shared: the need for a decent minimum of food, clothing, shelter, and so forth. Inequalities were particularly glaring at a time of severe shortages, since having or not having enough to eat was not a matter of "tastes."[23]

Few people have a taste for depriving themselves of the necessities of life. Inequalities were not introduced in response to different personal needs and requirements but in order to secure the fuller support and cooperation of those loyal to or functionally important for the regime. Another statement by Stalin makes this abundantly clear:

> . . . What is the cause of the heavy turnover of labor power? The cause is the wrong structure of wages, the "Leftist" practice of wage equalization. . . . The consequence of wage equalization is that the unskilled worker lacks the incentive to become a skilled worker. . . . We cannot tolerate a situation where a rolling mill hand in a steel mill earns no more than a sweeper . . . where a locomotive driver earns only as much as a copying clerk.[24]

This, of course, was only part of the explanation, namely that the more highly skilled deserved to earn more because of his greater utility for society. What Stalin did not mention was that party functionaries, security police officers, and sundry administrators—whose *social* utility was less self-evident—also earned a great deal more than ordinary workers, including "rolling mill hands" and "locomotive drivers." Furthermore, the issue was never squarely faced: *how much more* should an engineer or officer or functionary earn? How much greater were their needs? How much greater their merit?

Thus from the 1930's the new elites emerged in the Soviet Union from the deliberate policy of highly rewarding experts and technicians, and from the "instinct of self-preservation" of the regime. Loyalties were no longer expected to be rooted in ideological and value commitments—rather in the material rewards and interests of those most actively engaged in administrative and coercive functions (army officers, the secret police, party functionaries, administrators). The process was somewhat similar to the creation of an aristocracy in feudal societies, but in Soviet society the rewards and privileges were not hereditary or legally granted (though in many cases they became transmitted informally from one generation to the other). There has been no comparable process of restratification by government decree in American society.

Another peculiarity of Soviet stratification is the presence of a nucleus of an elite *within each social stratum* defined by occupation. Virtually every occupation in the Soviet Union has its own elite, far better rewarded, both materially and in terms of prestige, than the rest of the group. There are elite industrial workers in all branches of industry, from miners to truck drivers and lathe operators; outstanding milk maids, tractor drivers, shepherds, sportsmen, folk artists, performers, musicians, scientists, and teachers. To be sure, the proportions vary from occupation to occupation, reflecting the importance of the occupation itself—there are many more highly rewarded scientists than highly rewarded kolkhoz peasants—nevertheless each group has its exemplars of productivity and civic virtue. These outstanding and exceptionally well-rewarded individuals in almost every occupation are supposed to illustrate that the equality of opportunity has been achieved, that no matter what trade, occupation, or calling a person is engaged in he can make the most of it: a meritorious cattle breeder can have a standard of living that equals that of an academician of science or manager of a large factory. More practically, rewarding at least a minority in each social stratum enhances "socialist competition," since rewards are given for high productivity and efficiency at work. The lesson is that if one coal miner can produce, say, five times his production quota, it should be possible for others to achieve similar results. For this reason outstanding workers receive great publicity, and they become examples used to spur productivity and sometimes to justify the increase of production quotas.

In the United States there has been no governmental effort to elevate groups within groups, or to create corresponding nuclei of elites within the broader strata of the population. The rewards, prestige, and expectations *within* occupational groups are much more uniform and the range of variation in income *within* such groups is far narrower. Thus we do not find in the United States—at least among fully employed workers—a miner who earns ten times more than most other miners earn or similarly distinguished farmhands. Neither is there much publicity given to the glories of manual labor, though there is a lingering, nostalgic respect for farm work rather than manual labor as such.

In some important respects the Soviet stratification system is more fluid than the American: material and status privileges can be lost more quickly in response to poor performance, error, or political shortcomings. This is particularly striking in the case of highly placed people who can be demoted, deprived of all privileges, and disgraced with astonishing speed, and who have no recourse to appeal, alternatives, or opportunities in a sphere other than that in which they failed. Paradoxically, the higher the status position, and the greater the associated responsibilities, the greater the level of insecurity, particularly in politically sensitive occupations, and the higher one's position—no matter in what field—the more politically sensitive it becomes. Thus while the poor performance of a peasant or worker may be ignored, in the case of a manager it is more likely to attract punitive measures and to be treated as sabotage. While under Stalin arrest might have been the likely response to poor performance, in the post-Stalin period transfer to less desirable geographical areas is the typical form of retribution, resulting in considerable loss of status, decline in standard of living, and loss of prestige. This can happen not only to prominent political figures like a Molotov or Malenkov but also to recalcitrant workers, inefficient managers, engineers, or others.[25] In the United States, while subjectively felt status-insecurity may increase with upward mobility, the objective conditions for loss of status and privilege do not. As the individual moves up, his security is enhanced and not diminished. The social position, once achieved, is unlikely to be lost or threatened, especially by administrative measures on behalf of political agencies and institutions. In the United States the advantages of status are more clearly cumulative and self-perpetuating.

Nevertheless the transmission of certain status advantages from generation to generation is a recognizable phenomenon in *both* societies: achievement and upward mobility are widely shared goals, but it is easier to maintain than to achieve high status position. This situation, well observed and documented in American society, has lately become a legitimate subject of public discussion in the Soviet Union as well. Cumulative status advantages are reflected in access to education, especially higher education. The following Soviet comments on the subject might very well have been written to describe conditions in the United States:

> It is well known . . . that the applicant's level of preparation depends not only on his natural ability, but also on the material and cultural level of the family in which he grew up, on the level of instruction at the secondary school he attended and on many other factors. . . . All other conditions being equal, therefore, greater possibilities to enter high school are enjoyed by those who come from families in comfortable circumstances; from families whose parents have had more education; from the big cities, where the qualification of the school teachers are higher on the average than they are in the villages or outlying settlements. . . . When admitting students to the institute on the basis of competitive examinations, the admissions committees keep the interests of society in mind. They do not, as a rule, make allowances for the different conditions under which the applicants were prepared and in this sense they sanction factual inequality. . . . It was not surprising that the offspring of the intelligentsia became numerically predominant among the students of the daytime divisions of these higher educational institutions.[26]

In a similar vein another article observed that:

> In the lower grades in the city of Gorky, about 80% of the pupils are the children of workers and 20% are the children of members of the intelligentsia (in this case, office workers); as a result of dropouts, however, the ratio among those graduating is reversed. In sociological language, this tendency is called inadequate social mobility. For the most part, the stratum of the intelligentsia reproduces itself.[27]

While the role played by family and education is among the similarities of the two systems of stratification, the state and political criteria have played a far more important part in determining social position in the USSR than in the United States. This is reflected not merely in the state monopoly of allocating privilege, in its control over promotion in the various hierarchies, in the state's power to endow—or to deprive—individuals of lucrative positions, but more generally in the state control of the entire economy. In the Soviet Union the range of alternatives for social mobility is limited by the fact that the individual can move up (or down) in essentially only one hierarchy, one vast organization which applies basically the same criteria in all its branches, and in which failure is not forgotten and cannot easily be erased or escaped. Thus the employee who is unsuccessful in Kiev or who feels slighted by his manager in Khabarovsk cannot make a radical break by moving to a new place of employment: his records, files, his labor passport with all relevant information will accompany him to his next place of work. There he will probably be judged and evaluated as he was at his prior place of employment. Furthermore, he may expose himself to serious disadvantage if he leaves his job on his own initiative without the consent of his superiors, though restrictions in this sphere have diminished in the post-Stalin period. The decisive fact is that the state can directly interfere with social position by withholding employment (as has happened with a number of dissenters, especially intellectuals) or by withholding *good* employment, or by transferring people to undesirable locations. In the United States political agencies are usually powerless to interfere with the individual's employment although they may be in a position to create jobs and influence the economy in various ways. While a vocal critic of Soviet society may expect to be imprisoned or lose his job, it is possible, even for the most embittered critics of American society and its political institutions to publish their exposés, go on lecture tours, appear on TV shows, and the like, and thereby maintain a comfortable, sometimes affluent standard of living. Indeed social criticism has become a flourishing minor industry in the United States.

In regard to the allocation of prestige, the scope of activities of the government in the United States is still more limited. Governmental medals and prizes are few (and not widely known), and there are no titles like those found in the Soviet Union, such as Hero of the Soviet Union, Hero of Socialist Labor, Hero of Labor, the Order of Lenin (the highest Soviet award), the Order of Maternal Glory (awarded to mothers who have borne and raised seven [III Class], eight [II Class], or nine children [I Class], the Order of Mother Hero (awarded to mothers who have borne and raised ten children), the Order of the Red Labor Banner (awarded to groups and individual workers for economic efforts), and many lesser medals and titles bestowed not only by the USSR but also by the separate Republics.[28] In the United States the irrelevance of political sanctions to prestige is exemplified by citizens who suffered little or no loss of prestige, power, or income while or after serving jail sentences (as in the case of a former mayor of Boston, price-fixing executives, trade union officials, and more recently some political activists who became lionized in some segments of society).

Finally, it is also important to note that in the Soviet Union income differences in themselves do not exhaust the range of material inequalities. A number of material privileges are expressed in non-income terms (though they may often be correlated with high income). In other words, the acquisition of certain goods and services, for example, good housing,* cars, access to certain shops, resorts, and travel abroad, is not just a matter of purchasing power. These are allocated through bureaucratic channels on the basis of merit as perceived by the political agencies. In contrast, in the United States there are virtually no goods or services which are not for sale: their acquisition is a matter of financial means. This is at once a more democratic and more undemocratic arrangement.

The Upper Classes[30] and Their Life Styles

The conspicuous display of status advantages, including conspicuous consumption, is far more in evidence in American than in Soviet society. It is a matter of opinion whether the groups in question ("society people," "beautiful people," "jet set") merit the designation of "leisure class."† Certainly some factors would seem to hinder the

* There is an especially highly structured correlation between housing space and social status made all the more striking since it is determined deliberately by the authorities and thus reflects their perception of social utility and its appropriate reward. This is how Akademgorodok, a town accommodating scientific research institutions near Novosibirsk (in Siberia), was stratified in terms of housing, reflecting a pattern characteristic of Soviet society as a whole:

Occupation	Allotted amount of dwelling space
1. Academicians, corresponding members of the Academy	cottage (a small separate house)
2. Professors, senior scientific workers	apartment (97 sq. feet per family member, plus an extra allotment of 216 sq. feet)
3. Engineers, doctors, junior scientific workers	apartment (97 sq. feet per family member, the USSR legal norms)
4. Construction workers, service personnel	apartment (at least 77 sq. feet per family member, below the USSR norms)[29]

† John Kenneth Galbraith, for example, believes that "in the United States the leisure class, at least as an identifiable phenomenon, has disappeared."[31]

flourishing of a leisure class in the United States. They include the tradition of egalitarianism, an absence of a feudal past, and a lingering distaste for unadulterated idleness and purely nonutilitarian or aesthetic pursuits. A correspondingly high value is placed on activism. At the same time other factors favor the development of a stratum approximating a leisure class. First of all, there is wealth. There are probably more truly wealthy people in the United States than there have ever been in any other society relative to the rest of the population. Furthermore, despite high taxes, passing on wealth and its associated advantages from one generation to another is entirely feasible. It is hardly a secret that large taxes can be avoided by those skilled in the art, and, for obvious reasons, the rich are the most adept in this.

There is more evidence than can be ignored to suggest that styles of life associated with the wealthy of the past (as portrayed for example by Thorstein Veblen) have not faded away, despite beliefs to the contrary. Even in an affluent society where the consumption of nonessentials is within the reach of tens of millions, only the truly rich can afford yachts, art collections, multiple homes, servants, and other costly and conspicuous goods and services. Furthermore, conspicuous consumption has become especially conspicuous only in this century with the development of the mass media that can make such consumption known to millions rapidly and regularly.

It is precisely because of an egalitarian tradition and an absence of stable, well-established status distinctions (related to feudalism in Europe) that conspicuous consumption has become, and has remained, one of the major ways of asserting the distinctiveness of a particular social position and its associated life style.[32] Moreover, conspicuous consumption and the attendant desire for publicizing it, is not limited to the "new rich"—as is often assumed—but can be found also among the "established" and "old" rich, as the reports of the *New York Times* society page indicate. (Not that conspicuous consumption is limited to the wealthy. People at all income levels are prone to increase their joys of possession and property by letting others know about them.)

The society pages of the *New York Times* are a continuing documentation of conspicuous consumption among elite groups of American society. They also reflect a surprising lack of desire for privacy. The reporters and their informants keep few secrets concerning the life style of the rich. Meticulous attention to detail prevails. The price of apartments, houses, yachts, gowns, jewelry, rentals, membership fees in exclusive clubs, the value of total assets of individuals, the number of homes owned, of guests invited, the cost of the parties, cars, servants, who wore what, where, sums donated for charity—all are revealed.

Mr. William J. Levitt calls a press conference to help the public become acquainted with various features of his new 1400 ton yacht. "The three largest private modern yachts in the world . . . are Aristotle Onassis's Christina, Charley Revsons's Ultima II and La Belle Simone" [his own—P. H.] the lean, tanned exbuilder said. . . . "All my life I wanted a yacht tailored to my needs. . . ." The stepson of the late William Vanderbilt is in the habit of giving souvenirs to guests on his boat, "black sweaters with the name of the ship hand-embroidered in white on the front. . . . 'The letters,' he said, 'cost fifty cents apiece.' That is $5 for the embroidery. The sweaters themselves are considerably more." It is reported that in an elegant New York home all soap dishes are 18th-century porcelains and in another the TV set is hidden behind a Cranach painting. In Newport, Rhode Island, "Twenty evening dresses are quite enough" for the season, we are assured. "Few men have more than three dinner jackets." Discussing boats, H. H. Tyler McConnell of Wilmington, president of the Delaware Trust Company, informed the reporter, "I have five. Three ski boats and two for sailing. That way I know at least one will always be in working condition." "While explaining her real estate, Mrs. Byrd and her husband . . . were being driven around her properties in one of their white Cadillacs. 'Yes,' she said, waving a gloved hand, 'this is my cemetery. There is my rose garden. It has 3000 bushes. . . . Down there is my 'Little Mermaid.' It's an inch larger than the one in Denmark."[33]

Next in importance to what-is-worn-by-whom and who was present at important parties and the cost of various items of consumption and display come the trappings of exclusiveness—hideaways, elite resorts, and houses. Thus, "it is the inconvenience and isolation that attract vacationers [to Fisher's Island] for the relaxed, quiet, simple, away-from-the social-whirl existence. . . ." Members of this group apparently reached the stage of considering the topic of money bad form. ("At cocktail parties it's not so much stocks and bonds, but how are your tomatoes?")[34]

The pursuit of exclusiveness has other forms, too. When money is possessed by too many, new measures have to be taken to assure distinctiveness. Exclusive resorts, clubs, residential enclaves or apartment buildings provide part of the solution. The paraphernalia of aristocratic leisure time activities offer further marks of distinction: polo, yacht racing, stables, gentleman farming, elaborately organized balls and parties, escort services, fox hunts, head gardeners, and others all duly recorded in the society columns of newspapers, magazines, and fashion magazines. European aristocracy is still sought after to ornament social gatherings. Whenever possible, old family traditions are cherished, researched, and maintained.

While there is probably no single, nationally prominent and known upper class, there is an elite of wealth in every major urban area of the United States, with its old rich, not so old rich, and new rich. There is also a stratification in terms of just *how rich* families are. Sensitive dividing lines are drawn between those with a few millions, tens of millions, or hundreds of millions.

Civic mindedness and the willing assumption of communal responsibilities are characteristic of the wealthy in most regions of the United States. A combination of "noblesse oblige," social climbing, and publicity-seeking yields important results in the form of foundations, donations, and impressive scientific, educational, and cultural institutions. The rich also participate in public life by supporting political causes and movements of various character, including leftist ones in many cases. Thus total, unadulterated idleness does not prevail even among those who can financially afford it and some form of useful activity is sought after, both as a means of combating boredom and as a sign of the conscious or unconscious submission to the activist spirit of American culture.*

The importance of upper-class life styles in American society is underscored and enhanced by the publicity they receive and the public interest that surrounds them. Despite the egalitarian traditions of American society extremely high material rewards in themselves are generally accepted as legitimate (especially if seen as the result of skill and effort) and there is an avid popular interest in the exact nature of these rewards and in the life of those thus rewarded.

* As an expert on "beautiful people" put it: "Pure hedonism . . . is unchic and the fashionable playgirl works at something like a Vogue editorship, modelling or travel agency . . . but never in jobs that interfere with gallivanting."[35]

In the Soviet Union despite striking differences in the standard of living of different strata, institutional arrangements prevent the emergence of leisure groups (no healthy adult member of society is allowed to be unemployed; nonemployment, sometimes even the lack of a regular job is equated with "parasitism," except for women with large families). Ostentation among members of the elite, and particularly the political leaders, is generally discouraged. The life style and consumption patterns of the latter are practically state secrets. In the words of a Soviet observer:

> . . . In Russia the highly privileged usually conceal themselves behind the fences of their villas and find their amusements among their own friends. As a rule they are hidden from view, too, by barriers put up by the secret and not-so-secret police. Capitalist inequality is visible . . . while the Communist tends to be out of obvious view. . . . Those fortunate Soviet citizens who have managed to accumulate wealth—such as some writers and composers, for example—usually throw a veil over their affluence. . . .[36]

On the other hand, certain inequalities and privileges are sharply etched and unconcealed:

> . . . Many of the privileges Russia's upper crust arrogate to themselves would not be tolerated for a moment under the most unrestrained capitalist economy. Theatre and airline tickets, hotel rooms, and places in resorts not sold to the pleading crowds *in case* an official or foreigner appears at the last minute to claim, by right, the best of everything. Drivers waiting all day in the cold outside Party and government buildings while officials, their masters, are at work—or enjoying themselves at the specially stocked buffets—inside. Entire stretches of the Black and Baltic sea coasts and large tracts of the most picturesque countryside reserved for official villas, and not even visible because they are protected by high fences. Caviar, foreign travel, imported furniture, private railway carriages, private hotels . . . a hundred luxuries and privileges are reserved exclusively for men of rank. And the Russian masses, struggling in shops, shivering in queues, do not protest or even question this anomaly. No Rockefeller, and not even a Rothschild, could get away with the kind of disdainful highhandedness taken for granted here.[37]

The Middle Classes

The middle classes in American society have been, from time to time (or simultaneously) the objects of praise, pride, rejection, and contempt. For some observers they have been the key to political stability, the bastion of moderation, the activists in civic affairs, the builders and savers, the quiet masses of solid citizens oriented toward modest yet essential achievements, upholders of the Protestant Ethic and the mainstay of economic prosperity and social order. Equally familiar have become the critiques and denunciations of the middle classes. They have been viewed as the supporters of the status quo, complacency, and self-righteousness; they have been depicted as hordes of anxious people bent on mindless acquisition of property and competition for hollow status symbols; denizens of joyless suburbia, confused in their value orientation, conformist in their everyday life, pedestrian in outlook, and hypocritical in their behavior. There have also been contrasting views of their power or powerlessness. Far from seeing the middle classes as a repository of political power, C. Wright Mills and his followers have judged them to be without real power, or as being reduced to sham participation in the decision-making process. Thus Mills depicts a large proportion of the middle class as composed of "the small creature who is acted upon but does not act," who is "pushed by forces beyond his control," who "never takes a stand," is "bored at work, restless at play," whose will "seems numbed, his spirit meager," self-alienated and also alienated from his work and suffering from psychological malaise which parallels the material hardships of the industrial workers of the past century.[38]*

The contrasting stereotypes still coexist, although the unfavorable ones have increasingly grown stronger in the past decades.[39] Yet there is considerable evidence to indicate that middle-class status has been the aspiration of many generations of Americans, and that those both above and below this uncertain position wish to be identified with it.

* Mills's view of the middle classes may be distorted because he generalizes from a limited segment of middle class life and experience: of that of the sales personnel or low-level corporation employee. He was also aparently influenced by the effort to postulate a parallel between contemporary and past forms of exploitation and alienation, to rediscover new forms of the loss of individual autonomy rooted in the spirit and social organization of capitalism today, as it was in the past.

Surveys show that a majority of Americans are inclined to view themselves as members of the middle class whether or not other, more
"objective" indices of class position—for example, income, occupation, education, and residence—warrant it.[40] It would seem that in
a society that is egalitarian in its self-image and lacking in a clear-cut
hierarchy of prestige* there is security in claiming "middle"-class position. At the same time "the middle classness" of American society
has become a symbol in the eyes of many radical critics (themselves
middle class as a rule) of everything that is wrong with society.

With the fragmentation of middle-class values it has become easier to define the middle class in statistical-income terms rather than
with reference to shared values and styles of life.† A description of
American middle classes at the turn of the century reads like a quaint
memento of a bygone era:

> The middle class held a sense of general identity, a calculus of
> income and family and occupation and manner that many of its
> members usually interpreted strictly. But it also retained a sense
> of values, drawn from the past and pertinent to the future, that
> persuaded some within its ranks occasionally to stretch their
> standards for identification to include potentially all who quali-
> fied, all who were virtuous.[44]

Instead of a sense of identity, fidelity to values drawn from the past,
or even definable "ranks" which have a degree of exclusiveness, income is a safer criterion in defining the middle class. It might be
proposed somewhat arbitrarily that people with (family) incomes
in the annual $12,000-25,000 range constitute the middle classes.[45]
It is, however, clear that the values, outlook, style of life, and politi-

---

* This aspect of the American stratification system has been observed by both Mills
and Parsons, not otherwise noted for their converging evaluations of American society.
To be sure, where Mills talks about the "disturbed and uneasy" enjoyment of prestige
and about "status panic," Parsons confines himself to suggesting the absence of a uniform or clear-cut system of classification and "the difficulty in establishing comparability
of different lines of achievement."[41]

Larrabee also points to the fluidity of status distinctions: "Once commerce gets its
greasy fingers on class distinction there is little enough left of it; given the effort and
incentive, there is no honor, no eminence, no ornament that cannot be cheapened and
coarsened and marketed to the millions. A hierarchy subject to merchandising is no
longer binding on the independent individual. . . ."[42]

† The difficulties associated with the use of the concept of middle class are a part of
the more general problem of analyzing modern, complex societies by means of the traditional concept of "class."[43]

cal attitudes of such a disparate group cannot be homogeneous. People even of proximate income levels may have a wide variety of educational qualifications, ranging from the barely literate to the holder of the Ph.D. Correspondingly, the middle income range also accommodates a heterogeneity of occupations: certain groups of skilled manual workers (usually excluded from definitions of the middle class), school and college teachers, civil servants, army officers, professionals, salesmen, small businessmen, and clerical workers.

The outlooks and values of the middle classes are further diversified by the impact of ethnic origins, rural-urban differences, and regional ties (or residence). If there is anything middle income groups (or middle classes) have in common with regard to their value orientation, it is the respect for education.*

The political events and trends of the past few years raise serious questions about the customary assumptions of middle-class commitment to the status quo. Most of the young radicals and self-styled revolutionaries of present day America are the sons and daughters of the middle and upper-middle classes. While this development is the result of a variety of complex social-psychological factors, it casts considerable doubt on a generalized support of the Establishment on the part of a class that has produced the most vociferously rebellious groups in recent history.

The middle classes in Soviet society do not have the same prominence as they do in the United States. Nobody in or outside the Soviet Union has asserted—either in praise or in condemnation—that the USSR is a middle-class society. The Soviet middle classes have not yet become either the foci of sociological investigations or of popular social criticism. If "middle classness" entails the possession of a comfortable home, washing machine, car, nonmanual work, and freedom from pressing material cares, then, far from being a despised station in life, it is one that is contemplated with reverence by the Soviet masses and unattained by their great majority. Nor is it

* We should perhaps add another important aspect of middle-class economic "existence" (in the Marxian sense) namely, home ownership that has considerable influence on "consciousness" (that is, outlook, attitudes and values) and might help to transcend differences in occupation and levels of education. Certain shared interests and attachments to the status quo may follow from the possession of a private dwelling—as Soviet authorities also perceived in opting for the construction of apartment buildings rather than private homes. Their reasons have only in part been economic.

without significance that the term "middle class" is not used in the Soviet Union, its validity being denied.* While wishing a social class away does not result in its actual disappearance, the result of this official attitude has been a great scarcity of published materials on the subject by Soviet social scientists, who have concentrated their attention on the celebrated working classes of Soviet society.

In Soviet discourse the term "intelligentsia" comes closest to the American concept of middle class. It differs from its American counterpart in several respects. Among other things, it does not include the self-employed strata of the population, for the simple reason that there are no such strata in the Soviet Union. Not only are there no private businesses in the USSR, but professionals are also employees of some firm or organization of the state.

It would be difficult to assign to the Soviet middle classes (whom we define as middle income groups† of nonmanual occupations) any

* The Soviet aversion to the concept probably has its roots in orthodox Marxism that postulated long ago the disappearance of middle strata from capitalist society during the process of "pauperization," when "society as a whole is more and more splitting into two great hostile camps, into two great classes directly facing each other: Bourgeoisie and Proletariat."[46] The hostility to the concept is doubtless related to the fact that the growth of the middle classes in Western, capitalist societies has upset one of the favorite assumptions of Marxism: the apocalyptic polarization of capitalist societies, destined to lead to the triumph of proletarian revolution that would sweep away the tiny crust of parasitic exloiters. Insofar as the emergence of middle classes represented a moderating influence on class conflict, they have retarded what Marxists consider the unfolding of inexorable historical laws. As far as Soviet society is concerned, it has been postulated since the 1930's that there are only two social classes in it: the workers and the peasants, supplemented by what Soviet spokesmen call the "stratum" of intelligentsia. Presumably this simplification of Soviet class structure is not unrelated to the desired vindication of Marxism, which, as we noted, denied the persistence or emergence of a relatively autonomous and distinctive middle class, even though the social setting is not a capitalist one. Finally, it might also be suggested that the fewer the classes the more plausible to claim the approach of a classless society. More recently some Soviet sociologists have presented a more complex and realistic view of Soviet system of stratification in which "the basic elements of the social structure of contemporary Soviet society consist of the working class, the kolkhoz peasants, specialists and employees."[47] In this usage specialists equal intelligentsia, that is, people of nonmanual occupations with higher training (for instance, scientists, artists, engineers, high-level administrators, and the like) while "employee" refers to those engaged in nonmanual work of a less complex nature requiring no higher education (for example, low echelon office workers, sales clerks, and so forth).[48]

† Determining what constitutes "middle income" is in itself a thorny problem in a society where the top salaries and earnings (which may include special bonuses) are not made public and in which a great many material advantages and benefits are provided outside the ordinary channels of wages and salaries. First we must note that in 1968 the monthly minimum wage was raised to 60 rubles per month (roughly the same in

reasonably coherent value system, or homogeneous style of life along the lines of the dubious stereotypes often applied to the American middle classes. As in the American case, we can only speak of the Soviet middle classes in a statistical or quantitative sense: people in the "middle" in terms of income and possibly education. According to Soviet sources, the values and outlook of the middle strata (whatever their official designation) are not different from the allegedly homogeneous "spectrum" of civic virtue presented by the population at large. Thus in a Soviet public opinion survey (addressed to a self-selected group of readers of the Soviet official youth paper, *Komsomolskaya Pravda*) in 1965 were 797 young engineers who responded to the question: "What is the goal of your life?" While the answers may not tell us much about the representative attitudes of the Soviet intelligentsia (or even of young engineers who read the paper in question) they give some indication of the outlook of a group of enthusiasts who took the trouble to respond. The professed life goals included "Service to the nation" (32 per cent), "Becoming a first class expert, the mastery of occupational skills" (32.8 per cent), "Many sided/personal/development, perfection of moral attitudes" (27.2 per cent) and the like. Seventy-six per cent of those in the sample considered to have attained their life goals.[51] (It should be added, however, that several other Soviet attitude surveys in recent years have revealed attitudes far less high-minded than those above.)

---

dollars). Average monthly wages for workers and employees (that is, everybody except peasants and probably some members of elite groups) in 1968 was 108.6 rubles per month.[49] We may, therefore, include in the middle income groups all those with *family* incomes between, say, 180-250 rubles per month. (It should be stressed that in the vast majority of Soviet families both husband and wife are employed.) Characteristic income levels are further illustrated by the income classification used in a major Soviet study of industrial workers cited earlier: workers earning less than average monthly wages made between 72-82 rubles; average earnings were between 90-100 rubles and those above average ranged between 105-124 rubles.[50] Many working-class families with both spouses working have family incomes in the middle range suggested above. Thus neither in the Soviet nor the American case is income by itself a clear differentiating factor between working class and middle class. Perhaps the crucial difference between the Soviet and American class structure, in terms of income distribution relative to the size of income groups, is that unlike the proverbial diamond shaped American diagram (which has a bulge in the middle) the Soviet diagram would be more like the pyramid, far broader at the lower levels than in the middle. As we have seen the Soviet income distribution system also permits great variations *within* the same occupations.

While the American and Soviet middle classes are similar in that probably neither has a unified or reasonably homogeneous outlook or value system (as would be appropriate for a "class" in the classic, Marxist sense of the term), there are obvious differences in their access to political power. Unlike their counterparts in America, the Soviet middle classes have no special advantages in regard to political influence or participation. They are as much excluded from the political decision-making process as are the lower income groups and the less educated strata of the population. In the United States the middle classes are an important political force for several reasons: they vote in much greater numbers than the less educated,[52] occupy more public offices, are more active in voluntary and community organizations, write more letters to newspapers or to their elected representatives, and contribute more effectively to public opinion formation. There is no evidence of "middle-class" persons performing analogous functions in the USSR. Political participation in Soviet society is organized from the top to the bottom; it is almost totally unspontaneous, popular initiatives play no part in it and—insofar as pressure groups exist—a matter of some debate in itself —only the few elite groups matter, such as the top military echelons, the most powerful industrial managers, the high-ranking security police officers, and possibly some outstanding scientists and artists. In other words, politics in the USSR is even further removed from a clear-cut class basis than in the United States. More importantly, the different strata in Soviet society, including the middle classes, have no organizations at their disposal (except of course the party elite) through which they can bring to bear political pressure.

The Soviet middle classes also differ from the American with regard to the relative importance of various occupational groups which belong to it. Thus, for instance, there is a marked difference between the status and income of engineers and physicians in the two societies. In the United States physicians have a high earning power that puts them in the upper middle class as a group; in the Soviet Union medicine is a far less lucrative occupation; it is also less prestigious, largely left to women, who make up 75 per cent of the medical professions.[53] On the other hand, engineers as an occupational group probably earn more than doctors and are accorded more prestige. The occupation of the engineer has, from the beginning of Soviet society, but especially from the 1930's, been glorified in the mass media and literature. Engineers have been assigned to the vanguard of the active builders of socialism (and communism), while physicians have been tacitly relegated to the "service" jobs, essential enough but nonproductive. We should remember that the "restratification" of Soviet society that took place in the 1930's elevated to high status (and accorded the highest rewards) to those who made the most tangible contributions to the industrial-military power of the regime: the experts in science, engineering, and administration, and the specialists in coercion (the officers in the state security organs and the military service).

Another middle-class occupational group whose income and status differ considerably in the two societies is the legal profession. Again, as a group they earn far more and they enjoy much greater prestige in the U.S. than in the USSR. This fact reflects the relative unimportance of legal institutions in Soviet life and the limited extent to which personal and social conflicts find legal expression.*

In conclusion we may note a paradox. Middle-class life, as traditionally known and relished in the United States, has increasingly become a subject of both public and private questioning and criticism. At the same time, in the USSR it is an ascendant phenomenon based on the untroubled enjoyment of a higher standard of living and the acquisition of material goods and amenities of life—the very same things which are the source of guilt feelings and unease for substantial segments of the middle classes in America.

The Working Classes: Industrial and Agricultural

The term "working class" is just as replete with ambiguities as "middle class." It can refer to industrial workers, and particularly factory workers; manual workers in any occupation; all those who work regularly but do not own the means of production; or those who earn wages rather than salaries. Finally, sometimes working class also refers to the lower classes, "lower" in terms of income, prestige, and the desirability of the work performed.

---

* The lawyer who takes his job seriously defending a political prisoner is unusual, but when he does, the results discourage others from following the example. This was illustrated by the case of a lawyer who took seriously the defense of Alexander Ginsburg, one of the intellectuals openly critical of the regime, and whose career was ruined as a result.54

In this section we will be focusing on manual workers in industry, but not limiting "industrial" to the factory setting, in recognition of the fact that in many contemporary societies much of agricultural work has also become mechanized and standardized, hence industrial.

The position of industrial workers in the two societies is significantly different. While the standard of living of American workers is much higher than of their Soviet counterparts,* their job security is lower. Unemployment is a persistent problem in the United States for approximately 3-6 per cent of the labor force (depending on prevailing economic conditions)—whereas the Soviet worker can, under all circumstances, count on employment of some kind. It may not be employment to his liking, and his choices may be limited; nevertheless, he has no fear of unemployment.

Soviet workers carry a labor passport in which the conditions of transfer and discharge are noted. Leaving one place of employment without the consent of the management may result in penalties (as noted before), although in the post-Stalin period the mobility of labor has increased considerably, often despite official policies. For example, it has been difficult to attract or compel workers to the more remote, hardship areas of the Soviet Union, such as Siberia, Central Asia, and the Far East.[56]

Soviet workers, while their right to work is guaranteed, are more helpless in the face of the "management," the management being the state. Soviet trade unions are not autonomous organizations set up to defend their members' interests but agencies of the state whose primary role is to promote efficiency in production and improve labor discipline.† They also concern themselves, within the framework of the policies determined by the government, with the welfare and working conditions in the factory. Trade unions run resorts and sanatoria for workers and often initiate housing programs for the employees of a factory or firm. They do not, however, engage in collective bargaining, since wages and salaries are fixed by gov-

* In 1969 the average monthly take-home pay of American industrial manufacturing workers was $460.09; the corresponding Soviet figure was $119.28. The "cost of the median weekly family foodbasket" was put at $31.91 in the United States and $55.83 in the Soviet Union.[55] At the same time Soviet rents represent a much smaller portion of the budget, approximately 5-10 per cent of the net income.

† The official May Day slogans in 1968 referred to the trade unions as "a school of administration and economic management, a school of communism."[57]

ernment agencies and are not subject to bargaining. Nor can Soviet trade unions organize strikes, since strikes are illegal in the Soviet Union. Nor are Soviet trade unions political pressure groups. By contrast, American trade unions are autonomous organizations which exist to promote militantly the economic, and to a lesser extent, the political interests of their members. They are independent of government control and are often opposed to government policies, for example, voluntary wage freezes. American trade unions are active politically, lobby for legislation favorable to their interests, support or oppose candidates for public office, and engage in the dissemination of political propaganda. Frequently they organize strikes to bring pressure on management and employers and to improve working conditions, income, and fringe benefits. American trade unions have been credited with significantly improving the living standards of industrial workers. At the same time, many areas of employment— for example, agriculture and commerce—remain largely outside the influence of unions, which have had little success in organizing salaried employees and agricultural laborers; nor have they made much progress in certain regions (the South, in particular).

The American working class, and certainly its skilled segment, has often been viewed as a part of the lower middle class.* Contrary to Marxist assumptions, the American working class has become increasingly nonrevolutionary, indeed rather conservative. Nevertheless in terms of voting preferences and party affiliation, most American workers traditionally have supported the Democratic party, though some segments have shown interest in the third-party movement of George Wallace in 1968 and more recently in the Republican party.

The political attitudes of Soviet workers do not seem to be different from the political attitudes of the rest of the Soviet population (with the obvious exceptions of the party elite and the critical intellectuals), and an accurate estimate of these attitudes is as difficult as of those of the population at large. There is certainly no evidence to indicate that Soviet workers are the most vocal or committed

---

* This, however, does not mean its absorption into the middle class. According to Bennett Berger: ". . . To call America a middle class society obscures more than it illumines because the differences between the upper middle class and the lower middle class are too great, both in terms of cultural style and their conomic position, to conceptualize them as different strata of the same major class"58

supporters of the regime; nor have they shown tendencies toward outspoken criticism.

In their social origins American workers also differ from Soviet workers who are in their majority derived from peasants, most of them first- and second-generation industrial workers and city dwellers. Most American workers have been removed from rural roots and origins for generations (the most important exception being rural Negroes from the South); many in fact had no such roots to begin with.

In recent years American sociologists have devoted relatively little attention to industrial workers as such.[59] Instead they focused their attention on the lower classes of urban ghettoes (especially the young, unemployed, or underemployed members of ethnic minorities) who in many instances have become a subject of the type of idealization that was earlier reserved for industrial workers, and especially for organized labor. This shift in interest and empathy followed the realization that industrial workers were neither revolutionary nor untainted by the acquisitive spirit of American society. Worst of all (from the point of view of some of their intellectual observers) they were insufficiently, if at all, alienated. By contrast the more "exotic" ethnic poor were far more excluded from society, more alienated (and with good reasons), lived dangerously, free from the confining and boring norms of middle-class respectability and in the eyes of some beholders seemed to partake of an exciting, intense group life.

Soviet sociological investigations of the working class have focused on work satisfaction (especially in relation to the high turnover of labor), time budgets and leisure-time activities, and the ways of narrowing the gap between mental and manual labor with the help of raising the occupational qualification of workers and mechanizing production.

The agricultural working classes of the two societies are even more different in social position and character than the industrial workers.* Even the terminology differs, and revealingly so. The

* They also differ numerically. In the USSR peasants in collective farms constitute 20 per cent of the total labor force to which must be added another 5-10 per cent working on state farms (the latter is in Soviet statistics usually included under "workers"). In the U.S. farm workers comprise about 4 per cent of the labor force. Workers are 55 per cent of the Soviet labor force, the remaining 25 per cent is designated as employees, a category discussed earlier. The official Soviet figures do not break down the latter into

United States has no peasants, only farmers. Certainly not all American farmers are prosperous, many in fact are marginal and poor by American standards. Still, although sizable pockets of rural poverty persist, the majority of American farmers are prosperous, in part because the less economically successful tend to drop out of farming and seek other employment. Farming also has a fairly high prestige in American society, being associated with self-reliance, independence, and the traditional personal virtues of a more stable era in American history. In addition, farmers wield a disproportionately high share of political and economic power, and influence legislation more effectively than most other social strata and pressure groups.

Peasants in the Soviet Union form a far more undifferentiated stratum. There are no independent farmers, landowners, or small-holders; the land is owned either directly by the state (*sovkhoz*) or indirectly, through its control of collective farms, which are run according to economic plans formulated at high governmental level. Peasants in Soviet society are the lowest stratum both in income and prestige, as we noted earlier. (The problems of Soviet peasants and the poorest groups in American society will be discussed in Chapter 8.)

The Middle-Class Poor, or the Phenomenon of Dropouts in American Society

Our discussion of social stratification in the United States would be incomplete without reference to the groups which might also be called the "quasi-lower classes" or "temporary lower classes." The hippie-dropout subculture could be viewed in such terms. Its life style is deliberately and self-consciously a life style of poverty, at any rate as conceived of by the middle classes. In their social origins the dropouts are, of course, anything but poor. Their poverty is not a condition they are born into, but is voluntary and often temporary, at times incongruously alleviated by expensive items of consumption such as a microbus, sports car, drugs, or stereo set. The drop-

---

specialists and low-level office, clerical, and so forth, workers. In the U.S. close to half of the labor force belongs to the equivalent of the employee category, almost equally divided between "specialist" and "nonspecialist." Industrial workers are about one-third of the American labor force.[60]

outs differ from the real poor, not only in their social origins but, even more sharply, in their attitudes and values. The real poor do not ostentatiously reject material possessions; on the contrary, they long for them. The poor do not entertain any philosophy or ideology about the virtues of their life style, the salutary effects of scarcity, or material deprivation. Least of all would they associate spiritual uplift or personality improvement with it. Throughout recorded history only those well above the poverty line have projected onto the poor those qualities of life which they found admirable and missing from their own.*

In the case of the dropouts the pursuit of certain material discomforts (for example, tattered clothing, overcrowded housing, irregular meals, inadequate diet and hygiene)[61] derives its meaning and force from the rebellion against acquisitiveness and the cult of consumption and the allegedly associated spiritual torpor. Perhaps it is not so much the belief that poverty as such is good, but rather that material comforts and the pursuit of wealth are bad that is characteristic of this subculture. In other words, the precondition of this cult of poverty is abundance: "The heady atmosphere of abundance even creates new and unheard of ostentations, like the luxury of refusing to consume at all: of being 'beat,' of designing buildings without decoration, or of going on diets."[62] Since the dropouts do not usually know the real poor they can believe that they are pure in heart, unselfish and uncorrupted; they can attribute to their way of life a spirit of community and brotherhood they find missing in the individualistic, competitive, and achievement-minded world of their middle- or upper-class elders.

Curiously enough, many of the dropouts justify (in part) their alienation from American society by the presence of poverty, especially among ethnic groups. Yet at the same time they continue to idealize the attitudes and values they assume are associated with poverty, without facing the fact that real and prolonged material dep-

---

* The admiration of the poor has deep roots in Western tradition. From the New Testament's praise of the "blessed poor" to the upper class nostalgia of 18th- and 19th-century Europe for the simple and salubrious life of the pastoral peasant, to the glorification of the Noble Savage (inhabiting earlier versions of the Third World), to Marx's somewhat less sentimental veneration of the abused but authentic proletariat, to the contemporary American romanticization of the life styles prevailing in some black and Puerto Rican subcultures (found among certain middle- and upper-class whites)—they are all manifestations of the same tradition, the same impulse.

rivations are no more likely to purify the spirit than modest physical comforts are likely to subvert moral rectitude.

The key difference between voluntary and real poverty is that the former can be renounced at will or mitigated by parental assistance, while the latter cannot.

Physical Beauty and Publicity: Two Neglected Determinants of Social Status

Oddly enough, an important aspect of stratification in the United States (and probably in most societies), namely physical characteristics (other than skin color)* and physical attractiveness in particular, are almost totally ignored by social scientists. This may have two explanations. One is the liberal bias of most American sociologists and the associated reluctance to examine the role of physical, physiological, or biological characteristics in social life because of the frequent affinity of such criteria with racism. Physical appearance and attractiveness are also difficult to measure, at any rate more so than other determinants of social status, such as income, housing, occupation, and the level of education. Yet, the prevailing conceptions of physical attractiveness, elusive as they are, doubtless play an important part in attainment of certain social statuses and in recruitment to many occupations. Nor are the criteria of such evaluations totally subjective, erratic, or idiosyncratic. Conceptions of physical beauty and attractiveness are, at any given time, standardized to a surprising extent; converging judgments are likely to be found on this subject among large segments of the population in any society.

The importance of physical appearance is illustrated by the popularity of many entertainers, actors, and actresses, which is associated with their appearance rather than with their acting or performing talent. The degree of standardization is reflected in the requirement of certain physical dimensions women entertainers and actresses in many cases possess as a precondition of success. A prominent Hollywood surgeon, specializing in plastic surgery noted: "Talent scouts are generally under orders not to bring any new kids in for screen tests unless they are a good 38." It was also reported that one doctor

---

* Skin color as a ranking criterion remains very important though less decisive than it used to be in American society. Owing to the absence of a large colored minority, the problem has no parallel in Soviet society.

in Hollywood performed 2000 operations in a year to improve physical appearances, primarily of faces and breasts, including "bust enlargement." Operations to enhance appearance were also performed on men.[63] As has often been noted, the standardization of conceptions of physical attractiveness has been furthered by the mass media.* Denis de Rougemont's observations are pertinent here:

> Nowadays . . . a man who falls passionately in love with a woman whom he *alone* finds beautiful is supposed to be a prey to nerves. . . . Admittedly, every generation forms a standardized notion of beauty. . . . But nowadays our sheep-like aesthetic tastes exert a greater influence than ever before, and they are being fostered by every possible technical and sometimes political means. A feminine type thus recedes more and more from personal imponderables and is selected in Hollywood. This influence of standardized beauty is a double one. On the one hand it preordains who shall be an appropriate subject of passion . . . on the other hand it disqualifies a marriage in which the bride is not like the obsessing star of the moment. In short, the present so-called "freedom of passion" is a question of advertising power. A man who imagines that he is yearning for "his" type, or a woman for "hers," is having his or her private wishes determined by fashionable and commercial influences.[64]

There are many indications of the importance of physical attractiveness, especially for women, in American society. Advertising is among the most conspicuous ones. Most advertising messages aimed at women (which in turn may represent the single biggest share of *all* advertising messages) promise to increase physical attractiveness and allure. There is of course also a connection between the importance of physical attractiveness and the value of youthfulness. Another phenomenon indicative of the same preoccupation is the institutionalization of beauty contests.[65] There are probably tens of thousands of beauty contests held all over the United States every year under various pretexts and in varying contexts, at local as well as on national levels, sponsored by diverse agencies, associations, and com-

---

* Paradoxically, even those who reject these mass-produced, commercialized and standardized versions of beauty, that is, members of the "counterculture" end up with a highly standardized version of their own. Sometimes the rejection of conventional standards of attractiveness is conveyed by an ostentatious neglect of personal grooming, clothing, posture, and at times even cleanliness. (Some of these gestures are also supposed to represent an homage to spontaneity.)

mercial interests.* Physical attractiveness is also in heavy demand in numerous occupations for women, not merely in the sphere of entertainment. Stewardesses, receptionists, models, hostesses, sometimes waitresses and sales personnel must measure up to certain standards of physical attractiveness, which in recruitment to such—and many other—occupations is an obvious advantage. There is also some impressionistic evidence to suggest that physical attractiveness for women is a significant factor in social mobility, that it helps to bridge gaps in family background, level of education, and intellectual attainments.[66]

For example, there are indications that a high proportion of prominent models marry rich men, and the same seems to apply to many actresses and performers. In other words, exchange relations between beauty and money are quite common, though no systematic studies of this relationship have been made. Presumably it is partly for this reason that the upward social mobility of women is somewhat greater than that of men.[67]

The importance of physical attractiveness in women is also attested to by the development of the cosmetics and fashion industry and its advertising. A paradoxical aspect of the existence of these industries (including beauty parlors and health and dieting establishments) is that they transform physical beauty from an inherent or genetically determined (or ascribed) characteristic into an achieved one. Indeed, the basic message of most advertising directed at women is that everybody can be beautiful, attractive, or alluring and that it is only a matter of effort, exercise, hard work, and wise purchases. We encounter here an unexpected manifestation of achievement orientation, a somewhat bizarre expression of the Protestant Ethic translated into exhortation and encouragement to maximize physical attractiveness through hard work.

How can we account for the extraordinary importance of physical attractiveness in American society and for the immense efforts expended in acquiring it? Certainly advertising plays an important part in stimulating and diffusing the notion that, like everything else, physical attractiveness is also a matter of effort and cash invest-

* Not surprisingly, Women's Liberation groups have been objecting to such contests. It remains to be seen what, if any, effect this movement will have on the preoccupation with physical attractiveness, which it views as closely related to the treatment of women as "sex objects."

ment. This is a highly egalitarian message that strikes a responsive chord among Americans. In addition, advertising strives to increase self-consciousness about unattractiveness, body odor, "dull hair," rough hands, less shapely breasts, and hairy legs, and so forth. The general cult of youthfulness and preoccupation with sexual attractiveness are further contributing factors. American society, moreover, is fluid, unstable, and lacking in traditional status differentiation. It is also one in which there is much insecurity and anxiety about standardization and the loss of individuality. And it is a society oriented toward consumption. Under these conditions physical attractiveness (or distinctiveness) becomes a differentiating criterion that can be acquired like income and education—or at any rate this is the belief promulgated by advertising, women's magazines, and much of the mass media. Beauty can also be a short cut to success, and insofar as it can be "achieved" it might seem easier than the "achievement" of a good family background, higher education, social skills, or contacts with influential people. For the ambitious woman (and for some men, too) physical attractiveness can be manipulated (and this has been an age-old path of feminine mobility) to attain goals which would otherwise be far more difficult to accomplish. Thus physical attractiveness becomes an achieved status in the eyes of many, not unlike high income, acquisition of skills, or higher education.*

Some of these tendencies presumably also exist in the Soviet Union but there is neither comparable cultural nor economic-commercial support for them that would make them as significant as they are in American life. Certainly among the changes of the last decade or so has been a growing fashion-consciousness on the part of Soviet women, an important indication of higher living standards. Here as in other spheres of consumption, Western and especially American styles have been eagerly followed within the limitations of the Soviet economy and incomes. The desire to be well dressed is among the efforts to combat the dreariness of Soviet living conditions; it is also one which allows for some expression of individuality not generally encouraged in Soviet society. A preoccupation with beauty and personal appearance is still frowned upon by the official moralists of the regime. Their disapproval is a legacy from the more puritanic

---

* It should be noted that there is also a new emphasis on physical attractiveness for men in American society today as indicated by advertising and the proliferation of products and services catering to it.

periods of Soviet society (that is, from the beginnings until the mid 1950's) when, for example, evil heroines in "socialist realist" fiction were often presented as extremely attractive physically, while the "good" women were usually portrayed as plain and unconcerned with their looks.

The relationships between social status and publicity differ still more profoundly in American and Soviet society. In general there are two types of such relationships. On the one hand eminence of any kind, or any widely esteemed social position, tends to bring in its wake publicity. Thus the owners of great fortunes, the claimants of scientific or artistic achievement, important statesmen or generals, beautiful women, record-breaking athletes and others will sooner or later gain publicity (even if they do not seek it), and their personalities, activities, and entire lives become objects of popular curiosity which the mass media are all too eager to satisfy. At the same time publicity has also become a stepping stone to high status. To be well known for almost any reason* is a widespread aspiration, because it sets the incumbent of "well knownness" apart from ordinary people. Moreover, being famous has its own rewards, monetary, psychological, and social—and the *source* of fame is of relatively limited importance (not unlike the source of wealth). To be well known tends to be associated with being "discovered," appreciated, and liked.

To be sure, all of this applies primarily to Western, and particularly American, society rather than the Soviet. Publicity plays an exceedingly important part in the achievement and preservation of many categories of high status in the United States. The concept of celebrity helps to understand this relationship:

> The celebrity in the distinctive modern sense could not have existed in any earlier age, or in America before the Graphic Revolution. *The celebrity is a person who is known for his well-knownness.* His qualities—or rather his lack of qualities—illustrate our peculiar problems. He is neither good nor bad, great nor

---

* Thus to gain fame and publicity people will resort to the oddest activities which are in themselves pointless, even nonsensical. They will travel for days on the New York subway to set a "new record," spend weeks in caves or in pseudograves, attempt to eat more eggs in an hour than any other mortal had done before, compete in timed beer-drinking, and strive in countless other ways to achieve "distinction" of one sort or another.

petty. He is the human pseudoevent. . . . He is morally neutral.
. . . The *Celebrity Register's* alphabetical order shows Mortimer
Adler followed by Polly Adler, the Dalai Lama listed beside TV
comedienne Dagmar, Dwight Eisenhower preceding Anita Ek-
berg, ex-president Hoover following ex-torch singer Libby Hol-
man, Pope John XXIII coming after Mr. John, the hat designer
and Bertrand Russell followed by Jane Russell. They are all
celebrities.[68]

The role of publicity (or of "the process by which fame is manufactured" as Daniel Boorstin calls it) in the attainment and further-
ance of status is to some degree uniquely American. It is among
the indicators of the fluidity and instability of the American ranking
priorities, of the changeability of the criteria used for the assignment
of status distinctions. The significance of publicity reflects the uncertainties in the American social-cultural tradition and value "system" as to what things and accomplishments are to be valued highly.
Perhaps it is a more universal symptom of the confusion associated
with the ranking of individuals in modern, mobile, secular societies.* In more traditional and stable societies the criteria for achieving prominence (insofar as it depended on achievement of any kind)
were more narrowly defined. Certain activities, accomplishments, or
occupations could under no circumstances be accorded societywide
recognition and acclaim in such societies. While achievement has for
a long time been highly valued in most Western societies, peculiar to
America is the permissiveness (or the apparent unselectivity) in valu-
ing and rewarding achievement.

Our earlier discussion of "society people" illustrates the importance of publicity in supporting high status, especially in a society
in which there are so many people of affluence that wealth in itself
no longer lends sufficient distinction to a name or a family. For a
substantial minority of the American population the attainment of
a high income does not present insurmountable difficulties. Nor is
there a clearcut hierarchy of the more and less respectable ways of
accumulating wealth. Certainly, old wealthy families enjoy more
prestige than the new rich, but the competitive nature of American

* Erich Fromm's explanation of the preoccupation with fame seems to apply here: "If
the meaning of life has become doubtful, if one's relations to others and to oneself do
not offer security, then fame is one means to silence one's doubts."[69] American society
today fully meets these conditions.

society makes the "hoarding" or exclusive possession of such prestige impossible. In any event, there are relatively few old families which have retained wealth or public eminence for many generations. The rich are to some extent "equals among equals," which gives rise not only to conspicuous consumption but also to the scramble for publicity—and, as noted earlier, it is publicity that can make consumption truly conspicuous.

Publicity comes sparingly and selectively to members of the Soviet elite. Apart from the cult of personality reserved for the supreme leader, little publicity is given to members of the political elite, and none to their private lives and families. Famous artists and performers, have more but far less than to their American counterparts. Partly for reasons of security, famous scientists are also deprived of publicity, especially those whose work has military significance.[70] On the other hand, the Soviet mass media in the last few years have singled out for attention the Soviet cosmonauts, as symbols of Soviet space achievements and superior scientific accomplishments. This policy has been part of the effort to make the space program not only an instrument of strengthening Soviet military power but also a proof of the vitality of the Soviet social system with which to boost popular morale and pride. In extolling the glory of space probes and in glamorizing the cosmonauts the Soviet regime has once more relied on using technological proficiency as a legitimating device of the social order. While astronauts also enjoy considerable publicity and some popularity in the United States, the American promotional efforts have been less systematic and institutionalized than the Soviet ones. As a recent (1969) American television documentary of the Soviet space program pointed out, the Soviet cosmonauts are the only living Soviet people of whom statues have been made. They have also been made major official heroes and models for the younger generations.

*   *   *

In the preceding discussion we observed a number of similarities between the modes of stratification in American and Soviet society, particularly the predominance of occupational-skill criteria in the ranking process. It should be remembered, however, that other criteria are also significant. They include the advantages or disadvantages of birth, political-ideological reliability (in the Soviet Union) and access to publicity (especially in the United States). Often even identical occupational positions carry different meanings and rewards in the two societies. Being a manager, engineer, writer, teacher, industrial worker or farmer in America and in the USSR represent vastly different social and subjective experiences and expectations for various cultural, historical, political, and economic reasons. The social distance between identical occupations also varies considerably. Thus, for example, the Soviet manager of a factory has far more power over the worker than his American counterpart. Moreover, in a society like the Soviet Union where at least one-third of the labor force still consists of largely unskilled peasants, education and specialized training command disproportionate authority and prestige.

The comparison of American and Soviet patterns of stratification shows that cultural traditions and political arrangements, in addition to the processes of industrialization, continue to influence the class structure and the opportunities of the individual in both societies.

7. The Person in Society: Sex Roles, Family, and Private Life

Sexual Equality and Inequality

In any society the most obvious characteristic which determines the conditions of life for the individual is his or her sex. We shall therefore first inquire into the manner in which sex differences are associated with other differences in American and Soviet societies. The equality of sexes is among the professed values and (to different degrees), the claimed achievements of both societies. There are, however, considerable differences both in regard to the origin of the claim and its actual fulfillment. In the United States the equality of women is only tenuously related to the general espousal of egalitarianism. As a rule inequality in American society has been conceived of as deriving from the limitations of opportunity imposed by religious, class, race, or ethnic origins. The desire to overcome the traditional disadvantages associated with the sexual status of women played no prominent part in the aspirations of the various generations of immigrants to the United States. Rather, the improved status of women was perceived as a natural by-product of the equal opportunity of their husbands. For most Americans the status of women continues to be seen as dependent on the status of their husbands and not on their autonomous efforts or positions outside the home. The equality of women as an ideology evolved slowly and haltingly, as have their gains in their struggle to broaden the traditional sexual role definitions. In this process American cultural values have offered limited help.

By contrast there has been far more support for the equalization of the sexes in the Soviet value system—and in its historical source, Marxism. There is an explicit concern in the writings of Marx and Engels with the exploitation of women in capitalist society, manifested in the suffocating respectability of the Victorian family, sweatshops of industry, or houses of prostitution. Marx and Engels were interested in the problem in part because it fitted well into their analysis and indictment of capitalist society. Correspondingly the process of equalization was also quite different in the Soviet Union than in the United States. Equalizing opportunities for women was among the clearly formulated demands of the October Revolution and the ideas underlying it.[1] The social order that was overthrown was, among other things, associated with the exploitation of women sanctioned by tradition. The liberation of women from the burdens and limitations imposed by a part feudal-peasant, part capitalist society (such as prerevolutionary Russia) was inseparable from the liquidation of other forms of exploitation. Women were seen as victims of capitalist property relations, of the concern with pecuniary matters typical of the bourgeois mentality. Since the equalization of women in the Soviet Union was tied to revolutionary change and revolutionary ideology, its tempo was much faster. The changes in the condition of women were thoroughgoing in areas of life which were easy to bring under formal-institutional control, such as educational and employment opportunity, but slow and incomplete in those areas more difficult to reach through legal-political intervention. The difference in the nature of equality achieved by women in the two societies may be summarized by observing that in the USSR women progressed much further *outside* the home in the attainment of occupational, educational, and political rights. By contrast, in the United States they are probably more advanced in being treated as individuals in interpersonal relations, and in regard to status and authority *within* the family. Concretely this means that in the Soviet Union more occupations are open to women than in the United States (legally as well as practically), that women have a better chance to rise within these occupations, and that they are encouraged to participate in political activities as much as men are. At the same time they are poorly represented on higher decision-making bodies.* Soviet women are also more seriously enjoined to take advantage of educational opportunities. For a university-educated woman in the USSR it is unthinkable to settle back to the role of housewife upon the birth of children and to let her training fall into disuse. It is, of course, important to bear in mind that this is partly a result of economic pressure: in a society where the standard of living is low and one breadwinner typically does not earn enough, the proportion of employed women is bound to be higher. Thus it may be argued whether or not access to equal and full employment of Soviet women is a net gain or a partial loss, a blow struck for fuller self-realization or a routinized response to economic necessity. As a Soviet worker put it in a letter to a newspaper: "I'll put it bluntly, in workingman's fashion. There are five children in our family. There are plenty of cares. But my wife goes to work. She works because my earnings do not provide for all the needs of our family. No, today work is not a spiritual need for women. Rather, it is a material necessity."[3] Yet it might also be argued that work for men, or most men, is not a spiritual necessity either (or a form of self-realization) but also an economic necessity and habit. If so, working women have made a stride toward equality.

The Soviet regime has been highly successful in breaking down the biases toward certain occupations viewed as inherently masculine, particularly in the sciences. Moreover, as noted earlier, approximately 75 per cent of the physicians in the USSR are women[4]—a fact that also reflects the lesser prestige of the medical profession, whose practitioners command relatively modest salaries. Soviet women have also gained complete, and perhaps unwanted, equality in their access to heavy manual labor, including mining, construction, and street cleaning.†

* The limitations of political equality (or perhaps the indifference of women toward politics in the USSR) is illustrated by the women's proportion among party members. Only 21.2 per cent of the party members are women, while they compose more than half the total population.[2] It is also noteworthy that there are no women members of the highest decision-making body (The Politbureau and earlier the Presidium) and relatively few among the members of the Central Committee. There are also hardly any women in the diplomatic corps or the foreign service in positions of importance. There is only one on the Council of Ministers at the Union level.

† As a leading Soviet economist observed ruefully: "Women who are no longer young are doing highway repair work. This hard work requires considerable physical effort. Alongside them stands a strong man, calmly watching their work and filling out work records. Even today this is not an unusual situation. The moral aspect and the ethical

The status of women in American society is rather ambiguous. On the one hand, generations of foreign visitors have almost unanimously expressed astonishment about the freedom and independence enjoyed by American women,* not a few among them considering them overemancipated, aggressive, and domineering. Certainly in much of their interaction with men they reflect little of the traditional submissive roles they have been assigned to in most societies through much of history. The American women's typical control over family finances is another expression of power and influence, at least in one sphere. Nor is it without significance that, unlike other, less "subtly" oppressed minority groups (for example, Negroes, Puerto Ricans, and American Indians) the life expectancy of women in the United States is eight years longer than men's.[7]

At the same time a closer look at American life reveals a wide range of disadvantage and discrimination which women are subjected to and large areas of inequality. Perhaps the most significant examples can be found in the areas of income and employment. Though it is no longer legal, women are often paid less than men for the same job; they also find it difficult to advance to managerial or executive positions and are rarely recruited for training programs for such positions.[8] There is also informal discrimination against women in a variety of occupations, from engineering and forestry through law to horse-racing and medicine, among many others. Such informal discrimination is usually an outgrowth of traditionl conceptions and

aspect, so to speak, and the economic aspect here are all cause for concern."[5] Visitors to the Soviet Union have also frequently commented upon the unusually heavy concentration of women among street cleaners.

* Tocqueville, of course, was among those who had something to say on the subject: "In the United States the doctrines of Protestantism are combined with great political liberty and a most democratic state of society, and nowhere are young women surrendered so early or so completely to their own guidance. Long before an American girl arrives at the marriageable age, her emancipation from maternal control begins; she has scarcely ceased to be a child when she already thinks for herself, speaks with freedom, and acts on her own impulse. . . . She is full of reliance on her own strength, and her confidence seems to be shared by all around her. . . . It is rare that an American woman, at any age, displays childish timidity or ignorance." But he also observed that "In America the independence of woman is irrevocably lost in the bonds of matrimony. If an unmarried woman is less constrained there than elsewhere, a wife is subjected to stricter obligations." He also noted that ". . . the Americans do not think that man and woman have either the duty or the right to perform the same office . . ." and, most significantly, that "In no country has such constant care been taken as in America to trace two clearly distinct lines of action for the two sexes and to make them keep pace with the other, but in two pathways that are always different."[6]

stereotypes about the proper role of women and the nature of femininity. The latter usually implies an allegedly innate incapacity to master certain skills or perform certain tasks defined as manly or masculine. Women also face disadvantages in education. These are twofold. On the one hand, informal discrimination operates in admission policies to certain types of institutions and areas of learning. On the other hand, at least until very recently, women themselves tended to avoid occupations like engineering, forestry, law, business administration, and medicine, which were generally viewed as unsuited for women; in turn their avoidance of these occupations was seen as proof of their incapacity to master the requisite skills. The further education of women has also been hampered by their familial obligations: child care and housework, which characteristically have made it impossible to make (occupational) use of the education already obtained, let alone pursue it further. As we move higher in the level of education the ranks of women thin out: while they enter college in approximately the same numbers as men, only one-third of the B.A.'s and M.A.'s are earned by women and only one-tenth of the Ph.D.'s.[9] It is safe to say that American society and culture assign little importance to the equal rights of women to work. At least until recently work for women has been viewed more as a temporary economic necessity, than an ideal or a potentially important form of self-fulfillment. It is also widely felt in American society that social status and decent material circumstances are to be reflected in the male's ability to provide for the whole family without the wife's employment.* These attitudes are expressed in the severe limitations of institutional assistance to working women, especially those with children. There are hardly any child care institutions, and still fewer supported or subsidized by the government, municipal, state, or federal. Although more than one-third of the labor force is composed of women, "Across the country, licensed day care is available to some 185,000 children only. . . ."† At the same time, "Almost 3

---

* Given the fact that over 40 per cent of the labor force consist of women it is reasonable to assume that in many cases economic necessity is more than temporary and that the second income plays an important part in the family budget.

† One would guess that this is fewer than that which is available in *any one* of the small Scandinavian countries with populations roughly one-twentieth (or less) of that of the United States. It should also be noted here that, contrary to widespread beliefs, Soviet child care facilities are quite limited, too: ". . . As of 1960 preschool institutions enrolled no more than about 14% of the eligible age group on a permanent basis, with another 8 or 9% in the summer season."[10]

million mothers of children under 6 work outside the home. . . ."[11]
The absence of child care institutions is not the only impediment
women face in finding or training for a job. Significantly, working
women cannot even deduct from their taxes the wages paid to a baby
sitter. Uniquely among the highly urbanized and rich societies, the
social security and welfare system of the United States makes no
effort to provide assistance to pregnant women or mothers with small
children—unless they are destitute welfare cases. Legally defined (or
routinely granted) maternity leaves and benefits are almost unknown
in America. (In the Soviet Union pregnant women who work, and
most do, are given 8 weeks' leave with pay before and after the birth
of their child and after that period are given time off to nurse the
baby. They are also assured of retaining their job while on leave.[12])
The Presidential Report on the Status of Women in the United
States (cited above) observed that

> The general federal system of social security makes no provision
> for compensating a working wife for loss of income due to child-
> bearing. Forty-six of the 50 states also ignore it. Yet in about 70
> other countries, governmental action has provided for such pro-
> tection, mostly as part of broader programs of insurance against
> income loss due to sickness or temporary disability. No more than
> a third of American women have such insurance from either pri-
> vate or public sources. . . .[13]

Here again the message of American culture is clear to women who
want to work (or have to) and be mothers at the same time: they may
do so at their own risk, so to speak, and can expect little help or
sympathy from society.

The inequality of women is further reflected in their lack of
power and influence in most sectors of life (other than the family,
neighborhood, and voluntary organizations) and in many instances
of residual legal inequalities.[14] This is especially visible in politics.
There are two women senators in the United States Senate (of 100
senators) and 11 representatives in the House of Representatives (of
435 members). "Only 2 women have held cabinet rank in the federal government; only 6 have served as ambassadors or ministers . . .
no women are on the Supreme Court or the courts of appeals. . . .
Of 307 federal district judges, only 2 are women."[15]

Many further examples could be cited. Indeed discrimination

against women could easily rank as a social problem but for the fact that it has not been perceived to be one. Until recently the inequalities of women have not been defined as socially problematic* in part because the facts of discrimination were not fully known (or were ignored) and in part because such discrimination was defined as just or natural by society at large and the majority of women as well. This outlook may, however, be changing with the recent emergence of women's liberation movement and the attendant rise of public awareness of their problems.[16]

There is some similarity between discrimination against women and ethnic minority groups, Negroes in particular.[17] The practices of discrimination, insofar as admitted, are accompanied by stereotyping, and the stereotypes are justified by biological factors: skin color in one case, sex in the other. The exclusion of women from many activities, occupations, or decision-making positions is usually justified by reference to their inherent uniquely feminine qualities, or to their "natural" subordinate status in relation to men. With women as with blacks, discrimination and inequality often form a vicious circle and become self-fulfilling. If women believe that it is against their nature to learn to fly planes or to run for political office or to become mathematicians, there will be few women pilots, senators, or mathematicians. This in turn can be used to justify existing stereotypes about the attitudinal and intellectual proclivities of women, who, as statistics testify, gravitate toward occupations associated with the traditional feminine roles, such as teaching, nursing, or social work. Also as with Negroes, most of the discrimination against women is informal and illegal. Despite such similarities there are also important differences between the consequences and comparative disadvantages of sexual as distinct from ethnic discrimination. Most importantly there is no clear correlation between being a woman per se and a lower social status (or between sex and social class) whereas such a correlation has been well established as far as

---

* This is not to say that concern with women's rights is a new phenomenon. Yet for several decades before the late 1960's the issue was largely dormant. It should also be pointed out that earlier attacks on the inequality of women were narrower in scope than the recent liberation movement's, some spokesmen of which define even matters like the vaginal orgasm as politically relevant. (According to them the "myth of vaginal orgasm" is part of the male conspiracy to deprive women of their autonomy—in this case by making them believe that men are essential for the sexual gratification of women.)

blacks are concerned.* A well-housed, well-clothed, and educated middle-class woman in a comfortable suburban home may be bored, relatively isolated, depressed, and arrested in her self-development, but such deprivations are of a different order than, for example, those visited upon the impoverished black slum dwellers of *both* sexes. Yet it may be also true that *among* the otherwise disadvantaged blacks women are *more* deprived and exploited, and that being poor *and* a woman is often a double disadvantage.†

Beginning in the middle of the 1960's small groups of American women—mostly educated and middle class—began to show signs of intense dissatisfaction with their culturally sanctioned roles, in particular the "housewife drudge" and the "sexmate."[18] Although women's liberation groups often emerged in association with or in the context of left-radical movements, the men and women supposedly dedicated to the same goals and ideals did not for long cooperate. Members of the SDS and other radical groups (white and black) have been accused of "male chauvinism" (and "sexual fascism") as frequently as members of the Establishment,[19] indicating that such attitudes transcend manifestly shared political philosophies and commitments. At the same time many militant and vocal groups within the women's liberation movement retained the radical rhetoric and outlook of the male-dominated New Left and its mood of total alienation from democratic institutions and procedures, as well as the belief that capitalism is the source of all social evils, including discrimination against women.

Although discrimination against women is not sanctioned in any area of Soviet life and although the authorities are committed to eradicating it completely, inequalities and disadvantages persist in the lives of Soviet women, manifesting themselves in the private rather than public realm. Soviet women continue to carry the full burden of household work (called the "second shift" in Soviet dis-

* It may be argued that this is so because the social position of women remains largely determined by their husbands or fathers, a circumstance that does reflect a more subordinate status. This however does not alter the above proposition concerning the relationship between sex and class and race and class.

† However, it could also be argued that the position of Negro men has been worse than that of Negro women in regard to access to work, if value is being placed on being employed, regardless of the nature of the work that is available. It would be also untenable to insist that a lower-class Negro male is better off than a white middle-class woman or for that matter a black middle-class woman. Nor is a lower-class white male, needless to say, more privileged than a white woman of higher social status.

course), thereby preserving an important traditional prerogative of males. Study after study shows that because household work is not shared, Soviet women have considerably less free time (and even sleep less) than Soviet men, usually two-thirds to half of that enjoyed by men.[20]

Passages from a well-known Soviet novel conjure up the mood of weariness and exertion encountered at the end of the work day by Soviet women who wish to meet their traditional obligations toward their family:

> Many of the women in the trolley, like Ludmilla Afanasyevna, were carrying not handbags but big bags like small suitcases that could hold a live piglet or four large loaves of bread. At every step and with every shop that flashed by the window Ludmilla Afanasyevna's thoughts turned more and more to her housework and her home. Home was her responsibility and hers alone, because what can you expect from men? Her husband and son, whenever she went to Moscow for a conference, would leave the dishes unwashed for a whole week . . . they just saw no sense in this repetitive, endless self-renewing work. . . . Today was Friday. On Sunday she absolutely must get through a lot of washing that had piled up. This meant that dinner for the first half of the week had to be got ready and cooked, come what may, on Saturday evening (she prepared it twice a week). As for putting the wash to soak, that had to be done today, whatever time it meant getting to bed. Even though it was getting late, now was the only time left to go to the main market. . . . She was standing in line behind two men when suddenly there was a hubbub in the shop. People were pouring in from the street, forming lines at the delicatessen counter and at the cashier. Ludmilla Afanasyevna started, and without waiting to collect her goods in the grocery department hurried across to a line-up at the delicatessen counter and at the cashier. So far there was absolutely nothing to be seen behind the curved glass cover of the counter, but the jostling women were absolutely confident. Minced-ham sausage was going to be sold, one kilo for each buyer.
> What a stroke of luck! It was worth going back of the line a bit later for a second kilo.[21]

The woman in the narrative was a highly skilled physician with an important position in a hospital.

It should be added that the Soviet authorities are not unaware of these problems. Men are from time to time admonished in the press for not helping women in the house,[22] and the importance and desirability of producing more labor-saving devices and household services (for example, laundries, self-service shops, canned or frozen foods), are constantly stressed. Freeing women from onerous housework is among the desired goals of the regime even though progress has been very limited. Some experimental gestures in this direction were made in the designs of the so-called "house of future" or "new way of life" apartments. They had no kitchens (only so-called kitchen compartments), but dining rooms on each floor and, of course, professional catering. Press reports and discussions made it clear, however, that these apartment houses were both extremely costly* to build and to maintain (they had various other unusual facilities such as swimming pools, Finnish sauna, social center, winter gardens, hairdressing shop). Thus they are unlikely to become prototypes pointing to new trends in the organization or reduction of housework in Soviet society.[24]

While we noted earlier that compared with American women, Soviet women achieved a far greater equality of opportunity in the occupational realm, there is evidence to indicate that in this area too they still face considerable disadvantages, that sex remains an important differentiating factor in attitudes toward work and work satisfaction. Thus a major Soviet sociological study referred to earlier noted that

> . . . Interest in the content of the work is significantly more pronounced among men (42.2% among men and 28.4% among women). . . .
>
> Among young female workers, 54.7%, as against 43.2% of males, did not choose their jobs but acted in response to 'circumstances.' In the group of heavy manual labor, 80% of women workers entered this line of work in response to 'circumstances,' generally despite their desire to work in a more skilled and . . .

---

* One article pointed out "It is obvious that the building can be tenanted only by highly paid working people. But if this is the case, then, in the first place the meaning of the experiment is lost, for socialist society is not oriented upon a limited group of people who can enjoy greater benefits than others, by virtue of their material status. And in the second place, it is practically impossible to conduct the experiment in these circumstances, for the planners themselves expect to include among the tenants some whose earnings are relatively low—the staff of service personnel (and it is not small— 350 people, including the families, or 16% of the entire population of the building!). Or is full service excluded for these people?"[23]

more mechanized job. . . . On the whole, the level of demands, in terms of the content of labor and the amount of wages, is significantly lower among women than among men. . . .

Numerous data from this and other social studies indicate that the female worker finds herself, up to the present time, in considerably less favorable conditions, relative to the man, for the development of the personality. . . .

As we have seen, female workers frequently have a lower level of general education and occupational skill; since they are generally employed at less skilled jobs, they have at their disposal relatively fewer opportunities for creative work in industry. Women, over the sample as a whole, give lower indices for degree of initiative on the job. . . . The shortening of the workday . . . does not greatly increase the amount of free time enjoyed by the woman with a family. She still devotes the lion's share of the additional nonworking time td housework, while the man receives a perceptible addition to his leisure and can use this as he sees fit.[25]

The persistence of certain traditional forms of sex differentiation is also indicated by the discrepancy between male and female attitudes toward drinking and law breaking. Relying on Soviet sources an American student of Soviet deviant behavior noted that "Drinking remains, by and large, a male activity" and, commenting on juvenile delinquency, that "Data on the sex of offenders . . . shows the same underrepresentation of females observed in other societies. Generally, girls make up less than five per cent of juveniles handled by the courts." Equally revealing of prevailing cultural assumptions is that insofar as Soviet authorities blame inadequate parental supervision for juvenile delinquency the prime solution is seen in the reduction of the *mothers'* working hours.[26]

The Family

In comparing the American and Soviet family we face not only the usual problem of having more information—statistical and sociological—about the American family but also that of generalizing about the family in each of these complex, highly differentiated societies. In fact most generalizations about the American family have been based on the model of the American middle-class family (often suburban) that captured the imagination of American social scientists, journalists and advertisers in the post-World War II decades. This was the norm and the prototype.

No corresponding models or stereotypes have yet evolved in the Soviet Union unless we include the official ones extolling the Soviet socialist family and its unique virtues. Given an even greater ethnic and regional diversity and a comparably differentiated class structure, it is as difficult to generalize about the Soviet as about the American family. Three factors however impinge on the character of the family in both societies. They are: 1) The levels of modernization (interpreted here to include physical and social mobility, the ideology of free choice, the technology of communications, educational and employment opportunities for women, persistence or disappearance of religious belief and practice, the ease or difficulty of divorce, and the availability of birth control). 2) The standard of living (in particular access to private apartment or house and to household labor-saving devices and services, the possibility of automobile ownership and the like). 3) Public-political pressures and policies (including the presence or absence of an official "family policy," ideological assumptions about the desirability of the institutions of the family itself, and the presence or absence of extrafamilial alternatives or supplements in child rearing).

The survivals of a traditional peasant society are still perceptible in Soviet family life. For example, it is common for three generations to live together—a practice that cannot be attributed *solely* to the housing shortage or the desirability of free domestic help even in a society where most mothers work and there is a shortage of kindergartens and day care centers. The traditional aspects of the family also survive in collective farms, where the family retains many of its economic functions and where the household is the membership unit.[27] The survival of traditional attitudes is apparent in the findings of the Soviet sociologist Kharchev, who reported that 80 per cent of the respondents (in a sample of young couples drawn from Leningrad) sought parental consent before marrying and almost 78 per cent obtained it.[28] It will also strike many American readers as anachronistic that among Soviet parents obedience from their children is still a fairly widespread expectation, as is respect for adults, including the aged.

At the same time, the Soviet (as the American) family has been weakened by high rates of social and physical mobility (including job assignments which may separate a couple for years) and by the decline of the traditional religious supports of family life.

More difficult to assess is the influence of the standard of living on family life and stability. There is little doubt that a combination of the survivals of peasant tradition and conditions of material scarcity do not constitute an ideal setting for the emergence of romantic patterns. Such patterns presuppose not only the legitimacy of highly individualistic criteria in selecting marriage partners but also considerable freedom from material need. Nonromantic, practical factors are likely to carry more weight when they have a greater survival value. A peasant or farmer is more likely to appreciate a sturdy wife who can help with his work than a doctor of philosophy or a stockbroker. A man or woman of comfortable means can afford to disregard the occupation or dowry of his or her potential spouse. In a society that suffers from a chronic shortage of housing people contemplating marriage are very apt to consider what type of housing one's bride or bridegroom can look forward to. In other words, the less people can take material goods and services for granted, the more likely they are to be materialistic. The possession of a car (even an expensive one) is unlikely to be a major attraction in an affluent society; not so in one in which the car is at the pinnacle of the material, indeed "spiritual," aspirations of tens of millions of people. The exclusive or overwhelming emphasis on personal-emotional compatibility is a luxury the poor can less afford than those better off. Correspondingly, freedom from parental matchmaking is more likely in a society where the young can look forward to greater economic security and earlier independence from their parents.

The predominance of romantic criteria is also less plausible in a society where not only goods and services, but also leisure, is in short supply. Because life is difficult, because men and women spend much time in making a living and managing their households, there is also much less free time at every level of society. Even young people have less leisure, resulting from the regime's policy of providing a profusion of organized activities, both work and recreation, to minimize idleness or the misuse of free time. Further differences between the American and Soviet family can be observed in their respective exposure to political-ideological factors and pressures.

In the United States no political attempts have been made (or seriously considered) to alter the structure or functioning of the family (black or white) or to bring it under political control. The family, at least until recently, has been assumed to be a semisacred, inviolable, and imperishable social institution which the government had no intention and little power to tamper with.

A brief review of Soviet family policies and ideologies over a period of time presents us with a very different picture. The development of Soviet official attitudes toward the family shows interesting paradoxes. We would expect a totalitarian regime which has tried to "atomize" society (that is, to bring the citizen into a direct, immediate contact with the state) to mount an implacable campaign against the family, that bulwark of privacy and focus of apolitical attachments and values. The myth persisted in the West (well beyond the time when there was some evidence to support it) that the Soviet regime had embarked, and proceeded far along, the destruction of the family. Actually, the more totalitarian the Soviet regime became, the more committed it was to the maintenance and strengthening of the family. How can we account for this?

In the early and mid-1920's when Soviet society was in its truly revolutionary stage many of its leaders and supporters were seriously anticipating the withering away of the family, some among them favoring the acceleration of the process. At the time a genuinely radical break with the past seemed incomplete without abolishing one of its most deeply entrenched and traditional institutions, the family. The equalization of the sexes, another objective of the regime, also appeared to be obstructed by the family. (It was assumed by some leaders that the family could not survive the complete equalization of the sexes—a sound sociological suspicion supported to some degree by the parallel processes of equalization and growing instability of the American family.) Hostility toward the family was also rooted in the views of Marx and Engels, who considered the bourgeois family an exploitative institution par excellence, a microcosm of large-scale economic exploitation tied to the division of labor,* private prop-

* Interestingly some women's liberationists in the U.S. have recently proposed a new but strictly and contractually specified division of labor among spouses codified in the marriage contract. It is a proposal at once trendy and quite conservative in its implications. Its novelty lies in the implied repudiation of the model of marriage (widespread in modern, secular societies) which is, at least initially, romantic, emotionally diffuse and resting on mutual trust.

If marriage becomes a contractual relationship, as it used to be in more traditional societies, in which the duties of the spouses was sketched at least in broad outlines and financial arrangements were spelled out, it ceases to be a romantic one based on trust.

erty, and egotistic individualism. Marx and Engels, as well as many of their followers, believed that the major functions of the family in class society were economic. These, however, could be taken care of by other appropriate institutions under socialism. Monogamous marriage reminded Marx and Engels, and many of the early Bolsheviks, of private property relations, acquisitiveness, and possessiveness. It is important to realize that this antagonism toward the family was based, to a large extent, on the image of the Victorian bourgeois family, in the life of which pecuniary considerations had indeed played an important part. To Engels in particular, bourgeois marriage was akin to lifelong prostitution: the exchange of sexual favors and household work for financial support and social status. The bourgeois family was said to be an adjunct to prostitution: the double standard and the prostitution of the poor were the price paid for the stability of respectable family life. Among the early Bolsheviks, then, there was considerable hostility toward the family.

Nothing shows the change in attitudes better than a comparison of the views expressed by the revolutionaries of the 1920's and the functionaries of later days. Reflecting the spirit of the twenties, Madam Kollontai said:

> There is no escaping the fact: the old type family has seen its day.
> . . . The family is ceasing to be a necessity . . . as it was in the past; on the contrary it is worse than useless since it needlessly holds back the female workers from more productive and serious work. . . . On the ruins of the former family we shall soon see a new form rising. . . . The Workers' state has need for a new form of relation between the sexes. The narrow and exclusive affection of the mother for her own children must expand until it embraces the children of the great proletarian family. In place of the individual and egotistic family there will arise a great universal

---

The ideal that marriages be based on mutual trust and emotional attraction is hardly compatible with spelling out the specific duties of the spouses (for instance, who will cook, take care of the laundry, look after the children, when and how often, and the like). The contractual specification of such obligations reflects the fear, on the part of women proposing such arrangements, of being exploited by their husbands and perhaps a deeper ambivalence toward marriage and men as well. Whereas the romantic and still dominant assumptions about marriage imply that the spouses can rely on one another without minutely spelling out who does what, when.

The current idea of the marriage contract also reflects a fundamental lack of comprehension of the fact that enduring *and* satisfying *personal* relationships of mutuality and complementarity cannot be secured by the constraints of a written contract.

family of workers. . . . This new relation will assure to humanity all the joys of so-called free love ennobled by a true social
equality of the mates, joys which were unknown to the commercial society of the capitalist regime.[29]

By 1936 the official views on the family and free love were quite
different:

> When we speak of strengthening the Soviet family, we are speak-
> ing precisely of the struggle against the survival of a *bourgeois* at-
> titude towards marriage, women and children. So-called "free
> love" and all disorderly sex life are bourgeois through and
> through and have nothing to do with either socialist principles or
> the ethics and standards of conduct of the Soviet citizen. Socialist
> doctrine shows this and it is proved by life itself.[30]

In all probability the early Soviet attacks on the family were not
the outcome of careful totalitarian calculation aimed at the destruction of a potentially hostile social institution. Rather, these attacks
were motivated by the idealistic objective of maximizing the freedom
of the individual, seen as hampered in self-realization by the family.
It is worthwhile to underscore the difference: in the West, particularly in the United States, the family has been seen traditionally not
only as the "cradle of human nature" but also as a bulwark of freedom and individualism. In early Soviet thinking it was seen exactly
in the opposite light: the stronghold of oppressive, exploitative personal relations which mutilate rather than liberate the individual.

From the early 1930's, however, the Soviet regime has become increasingly committed to the preservation of the family—a commitment seemingly inconsistent with the nature of totalitarianism. The
Soviet support of the family offered for some Western sociologists in-
controvertible proof of the resilience of this basic institution; it appeared that even a totalitarian system had to make peace with it.*

*According to Barrington Moore, the survival of the family in the USSR had no such
far-reaching theoretical significance:

"The Soviets, the argument runs, were compelled to adopt the family as a device
to carry part of the burden of making Soviet citizens, especially after they perceived
the undesirable consequences of savage homeless children, largely the outcome of the
Civil War. [However] . . . with their very limited resources and with other, more
pressing objectives they had no genuine alternatives. Steel mills had to be built before
creches, or at least before creches on a large enough scale to make any real difference
with regard to child care. In the meantime, the services of the family . . . had to be
called upon. . . . The Soviet experience does not constitute by itself very strong evidence in favor of the 'functional necessity' of the family."[31]

This is noteworthy since the Soviet family was not basically different in structure and functions from those in capitalist societies. We make this point because of the Soviet claim that the "socialist family" is totally different from the capitalist one—an implicit justification of its preservation. It would be far more accurate to say that the *ideal* socialist family is very similar to the ideal family of the capitalist societies including the United States: based on authentic emotional commitment, fidelity, devotion to children, companionship, and friendship between the spouses. There are only two major differences between the American and Soviet family ideal: the official Soviet ideal includes political-ideological compatibility and participation of women in socially useful, that is, productive work. The role of homemaker, mother, and companion has been the mainstay of ideal womanhood in America, at least until recently. Sexual compatibility and satisfactions are also more heavily emphasized in the American ideal, whereas they are generally ignored in the Soviet one. The official family ideals, if not the actual policies, have changed little since the 1930's. The Soviet regime has never seriously tried to destroy the family. On the other hand it would not be quite true to say either that it has made peace with it. Rather, the Soviet regime has chosen to neutralize the family as an agent of (potentially deviant) political socialization.

Leon Trotsky viewed the preservation of the family as one of the retreats from the regime's original ideals, a contradiction related to the insufficient material basis upon which the Soviet system tried to create the new social relationships: "The real resources of the state did not correspond to the plans and intentions of the Communist Party. You cannot 'abolish' the family; you have to replace it. The actual liberation of women is unrealizable on the basis of 'generalized want.' "[32] Trotsky, too, noted that Soviet society could not provide the material basis for removing the housekeeping and child care functions of the family. But more importantly, he was also sensitive to the ideological-political implications of the changed policies: "The most compelling motive of the present cult of the family is undoubtedly the need of the bureaucracy for a stable hierarchy of relations and for the disciplining of youth by means of 40 million points of support for authority and power."[33]

Trotsky's point brings into sharp focus the relationship between the increasingly totalitarian character of the regime under Stalin and the new official attitude toward the family. In terms of ideology and social control the issue was: what are the alternatives to the family if it is destroyed? In theory one alternative would have been the provision of new institutions for child care, household functions, and stable emotional-sexual relations. This, as indicated above, was not feasible for practical reasons. The resources of the new state did not permit costly new departures. The other alternative would have been a chaotic increase of personal freedom, a most unstable constellation of sexual-emotional relationships, and the likelihood of severe social disorganization. Although a totalitarian society may aspire to do away with the family as long as it is a competing source of socialization, it has certainly no interest in allowing "free love," or less regulated human relationships to take its place. Contrary to some Western notions about the family as a source of resistance to political controls, the family has proved more compatible with totalitarianism than extrafamilial love and sexual relations and the attendant fluidity of human relations. It is not impossible that Soviet leaders might have sensed that authoritarianism, rigidity, and uniformity in political relations and institutions are incompatible with the tolerance of freedom, diversity, and mobility in interpersonal relations. It is difficult to maintain a social order in which there is unlimited freedom in one sphere (the personal-emotional-sexual) and severe limitations on freedom in others, such as the political and economic.* The deprivation of freedom might proceed more smoothly if there are no pockets of it left in some areas of life that can provide standards of comparison. Free love and sexual-emotional excesses are also discouraged by totalitarian rulers for more tangible reasons. They make undue alternative demands on the energies and interests of the citizen. By contrast the family as a rule does not deplete sexual energies; rather it is a framework in which sexual-emotional relations can more easily be stabilized.

As far as ideological interference on the part of the family is concerned, under Stalin Soviet parents learned that it was unwise to try to inculcate values into their children that might contradict the official ones, those disseminated outside the family. Concurrently the Soviet schools, pioneer and Komsomol organizations have taken

* The same point was made by Alexander Gerschenkron: ". . . the dictators are likely to assume that looseness in matters of sex may loosen behavior in other areas, and in particular may affect the political discipline of the ruled."34

over the tasks of political socialization. This does not mean that the regime has written off the family completely as an ally or auxiliary socializing agency in the civic-political realm. Soviet families have always been encouraged to support the official values of society and assist in their inculcation. Yet occasional official complaints suggest that most families prefer to remain neutral and apolitical in their child-rearing activities:

> It is not enough to see to it merely that the children study well and are models of behavior in the school or the street. It is the parents' sacred duty to instill in their children from an early age such precious qualities as conscious love of the socialist homeland, devotion to the cause of communism, honesty, diligence and the desire to serve the people loyally and defend the gains of the Revolution. This calls for constant and concerned penetration into the spiritual world of the children and patient and comprehensive upbringing work, for which Sundays open up especially great opportunities. . . . Few fathers and only some mothers talk with their children on civic themes, apparently believing that our Soviet reality itself molds one's communist world view. Some parents even forget to ask their son or daughter what assignments he or she is fulfilling in the Young Pioneer detachment or the Young Communist League group and rarely take an interest in the children's public activity in school.[35]

The socializing influence of the family has been still further reduced as children spend more time in other social settings—such as the school and youth organizations—and as parents do not have enough time to spend with their children because of the demands of their work and their own participation in public and quasi-public activities. Finally the influence of the family weakens when there is insufficient privacy for undisturbed interaction between its members—a condition provided by crowded housing and the general difficulty of attaining privacy in Soviet society.

Under these circumstances the family ceased to be an ideological threat to the regime, or a source of competing values and norms. It is possible that improving standards of living will increase the importance of the family as a unit of shared recreation, consumption, and intimacy.

While the problem of family versus state (or the political neutralization of the family) does not exist as such in the United States, there are certainly other factors which tend to weaken the influence of the family. In almost every urban-industrial society, family instability has increased, probably in part because of the decline of familial functions, the reduction of the services it provides. As Robert Nisbet has pointed out:

> Historically the family's importance has come from the fact of intimate social cohesion united with institutional significance in society, not from its sex or blood relations. In earlier ages, kinship was inextricably involved in the process of getting a living, providing education, supporting the infirm, caring for the aged and maintaining religious values.[36]

In American society the institutional significance of the family has been eroded especially fast. Its socializing functions have been undermined not by political institutions or the ideological jealousy of the authorities, but by the growing belief that the experience of one generation is irrelevant for the next. It is the same belief that has also begun to weaken the influence of educational institutions, whose control by adults is being increasingly contested. (For further discussion of the generational conflict see Chapter 8.)

The Upbringing of Children

Few areas of life provide better indicators of cultural stability or confusion than approaches to the upbringing of children. Patterns in child rearing also provide insight into the whole complex of social values and institutions which are not directly linked to the family and the process of socialization.

As can be expected, both the prevailing practices and the theories of child rearing differ significantly in the two societies. Most importantly, taking care of children—at any rate in early childhood—is a predominantly private affair in the United States, where the authority and legitimacy of the nuclear family remain uncontested. In the Soviet Union familial responsibility is shared with and often subordinated to public or societal authorities; extrafamilial agencies play a far greater part in the raising of children. The activities of the various socializing institutions are far more systematically and successfully coordinated—under the aegis of political authority—than in the United States.

In American society the upbringing of children is surrounded by more anxiety, attention, and uncertainty than in the Soviet Union. One possible reason for this is the lack of authoritative guidance. The confusion in bringing up children extends beyond "methodology," beyond the fads and fashions of bottle or breast feeding, schedules or the lack of them. The basic problem parents face is how to teach their children moral and ethical principles which they themselves firmly believe in. Obviously, unless parents are committed to some set of values they cannot lay claim to any moral authority. This, of course, is a problem faced above all by suburban middle-class families and in general by the most mobile and least traditional segments of American society.

Among American parents (and especially among the middle classes) there is a strong belief in the essential goodness and innocence of children[37] and a corresponding preoccupation with the cultivation of spontaneity. In Soviet society such a preoccupation is rare. There is rather an abhorrence of spontaneity—political in origin—which permeates the official approach to child rearing and is most pronounced in the institutional setting. As an authoritative Soviet manual summed it up: "We cannot risk our children's future by allowing their upbringing to be determined by spontaneous drift. The school and parents [note the order] must hold the reins of upbringing in their own hands and take all measures necessary to insure that children obey their elders."[38] It is in order here to recall that though the Soviet official system of values is overtly optimistic, both political practices and techniques of institution building betray a streak of profound pessimism about human nature.

The American self-consciousness about how to bring up children is also reinforced—at least among the more educated segments of the population—by the popularization of Freudian theory, in particular by the belief in the impact of early childhood experiences on the adult personality. Soviet parents and authorities on child psychology labor under no such pressures. Psychoanalytic theories remain proscribed and officially viewed as anti-Marxist, obscurantist products of decadent bourgeois culture—a hostility that spans many decades, and which began with Lenin's objections to Freud, conveyed in his famous conversations with Clara Zetkin.[39] The Soviet official value system, with its overt emphasis on rationalism, cannot accept the idea that the basic processes of personality formation take place at an un- or preconscious level.

There are further differences. Soviet patterns of child rearing are more authoritarian than the American ones and certainly far more oriented toward the inculcation of discipline and impulse control. As Urie Bronfenbrenner, the leading American expert on Soviet child rearing, has observed:

> It would be a mistake to conclude that the affection and solicitousness which Russians, in particular Russian mothers, lavish on children implies permissiveness or indulgence with respect to conduct. On the contrary, much emphasis is placed, no less by parents than by professional educators, on the developments of such traits as obedience and self-discipline.

He quotes from a widely used Soviet manual on the subject:

> The child must obey the adult when the latter says anything to him—this is the first thing the child must be taught. The child must fulfill the demands of his elders. In following the orders, instructions and advice of grownups the child manifests obedience. By becoming accustomed to obey from early childhood, to react to the demands of adults as something compulsory, the child will begin successfully to fulfill later demands made of him in family and school.[40]

It should not be surprising, then, that Soviet children are both a good deal less spontaneous and less unruly than their American counterparts. This naturally has important implications for social stability, conformity, and deviance:

> The greatest offense a child can commit in a kindergarten is to be different . . . the young boy or girl gradually acquires what is an extremely important faculty in Soviet society. He develops an understanding of which questions one can ask or discuss, and which ones must be avoided. Few nations make it easy for the individual who wants to swim against the current of prevailing mores, but the Soviet Union makes it almost impossible. . . .[41]

Significant differences have been observed between those Soviet children who had and who did not have a kindergarten experience:

> . . . primary school teachers are quick to admit that the children who have been educated at home until the age of seven are as a rule more interesting—more intellectual, better mannered and even more affectionate.[42]

American-style permissiveness and the cult of free expression are yet to be duplicated in Soviet society on a significant scale, either in the family or in the kindergarten or school. While in the United States permissiveness is combined with the encouragement of independence, initiative, and self-reliance, in the Soviet Union the stress on self-discipline is taught in conjunction with a sense of responsibility toward the group, the collective. The major disciplinary technique is shaming. At the adult level this process is also manifest in criticism and self-criticism sessions (discussed in Chapter 2). It is, however, likely that such techniques (for instance, public ridiculing, reprimand, and scorn) make a deeper impact on children than corresponding rituals make on adults.

Not only is the Soviet child's environment more constraining outside the family, there is also less permissiveness and less egalitarianism within the Soviet family itself. Soviet parents compared with American ones seem to fuss less about their children: about their growth rates, comparative intelligence, character and body development. Their approach is more casual and matter of fact. Interestingly enough, both the surviving traditional ways of upbringing and those of a more recent official-ideological inspiration assist the parents. They both provide more clear-cut prescriptions (than are available in the United States) on how to handle children, at least while they are small. Soviet parents must also maintain tighter controls because of the difficult living conditions, especially overcrowded housing, which make it imperative that children be less indulged and less "expressive" in consideration of the adults who cannot easily avoid their company in the home. In American society the standards of child care, physical and mental health, and correct development are changeable to a startling degree.[43]

Much has been said here and elsewhere about the permissive ways of the American family. In this respect, as in many others, contemporary practices have their beginnings in the past; thus in the 1830's Tocqueville observed:

> In America the family, in the Roman and aristocratic significa-
> tion of the word, does not exist. All that remains of it are a few
> vestiges in the first years of childhood, when the father exercises,
> without opposition, that absolute domestic authority which the
> feebleness of his children renders necessary and which their inter-
> est, as well as his own incontestable superiority, warrants.[44]

Yet another major difference in the upbringing of children in the two societies is to be found in the nature of extrafamilial agencies and institutions and their relationship to the family. Increasingly in American society the influence, authority, and socializing role of the family has been supplemented or replaced by the peer group, the ethos of the "teen-age culture." The latter, as a rule, represent a degree of deviance and discontinuity, a form of rejection of the world of adults, their institutions and values. It is true that sometimes peer groups are imitative caricatures of the adult world incorporating, for example, the striving for status, the cult of aggressiveness, competition, material ostentation, and other aspects of adult society. Increasingly, however, they accommodate or generate values and attitudes which are antithetical to those of the adult world. Thus they provide a measure of countersocialization, rather than vehicles for the transmission of cultural patterns.

In Soviet society there is far less disjunction between the peer group and adult society.[45] Teen-age culture is a less discernible entity, in part because there are no commercial interests to benefit from its existence. From kindergarten onward there is a high degree of coordination and cooperation among the various socializing agencies in the Soviet Union, which are not allowed to work at cross purposes with one another. By contrast, not only is there a conflict between the family and peer group in America, there is an even stronger clash between the school and peer group and also sometimes between the school and family. Nor are youth organizations as important and ubiquitous in the United States as they are in the USSR. There membership is virtually obligatory, while in this country joining such groups is a matter of choice and there is a range of clubs and organizations—religious or secular, political or nonpolitical—to choose from.

The peer group in the Soviet Union does not have the same autonomous existence and pervasive influence as in the United States. This is probably also related to the different conceptions and patterns of friendship which manifest themselves at an early as well as a more mature age. (It has only been recently that the beginnings of a youth culture have been observed in the Soviet Union in major urban centers.)

Finally, there also seem to be differences in the size of the typical family unit in the two societies which bear on the upbringing of

children. Soviet children—rather paradoxically—derive some benefits from the housing situation which makes it unavoidable for many
families to have three generations sharing an apartment. In particular the importance of the "babushka," the grandmother or some
other older female relative, is considerable in carrying part of the
burden of housework and looking after children. There are no figures available on the number of Soviet households where this is the
case, but it is a common practice and probably involves about half
(or one-third) of the Soviet families, even with slowly improving
housing conditions. To what extent these old ladies transmit traditional values to the children is not known, but there is little reflection in the behavior of Soviet adults of such influences. Probably
the effects of this type of socialization evaporate upon contact with
the more powerful and authoritative socializing institutions of the
school, pioneers, and Komsomol.

Sexual Morality, Divorce, and Birth Control

Even in societies where sociological inquiry is *not* subject to political control and ideological legitimation (as is the case in the U.S.),
the prevailing forms of sexual conduct are difficult to ascertain. Quite
possibly, more has been written and published on these matters in
the United States than in any other society at any time, yet much
remains unknown. For example, it is difficult to know how much of
the "Sexual Revolution" is a behavioral reality and how much a creation of the mass media, some social scientists and journalists who are
overeager to characterize every form of change as revolutionary.
While in 1964 *Time* Magazine in its article on "The Second Sexual Revolution," asserted that there was only a "tattered remnant"
of a sexual code, and that people in the 1960's were "adrift in a sea
of permissiveness," in 1966 it was reported in the *New York Times*
(in an article summarizing the results of many studies and opinions
of experts) that "nonvirginity among college women [was put] at
20% or less."[46] The article quoted John H. Gagnon, a senior trustee
at the Institute for Sex Research at Indiana University, who observed
that "the rules on speaking about sex have changed and . . . because Americans talk more about it they conclude there is more of
it."

A study of the sex life of a group of middle-aged, upper middle-class Americans found that

> . . . this [culturally] pervasive accent on sex seems not to have much shaped the habits and tastes of the Significant Americans in line with the ubiquitous image. Many remain clearly ascetic where sex is concerned. Others are simply asexual. For still others sex is overlaid with such strong hostility that an *anti*-sexual orientation is clear. . . . The overriding fact seems to be that for the majority, by the middle years, sex has become almost nonexistent. . . .[47]

Have things changed drastically since the mid-1960's? Conceivably they have. For example, if it is true, as was reported in 1970[48] that 10 per cent of high school students in California were estimated to have venereal disease—then, unless standards of medical care have deteriorated, promiscuousness must be on the rise. It is certainly plausible that there has been a relaxation of sexual constraints in American society in the 1960's. The Youth Culture, as we noted in Chapter 4, is hedonistic, disdains self-restraint, and glorifies all forms of self-expression. Millions of young (and not so young) Americans have joined the battle against real or felt personal-social isolation. Sexual relations do hold out the hope for breaking out of isolation and for intensifying personal relationships. On the other hand, drug use relegates sex to a secondary place in the hierarchy of pleasures. (Nor does promiscuousness per se deepen the significance or the intensity of the act.)

Despite all the publicity the topic receives few well-established facts are available on the sexual behavior of Americans. The level of premarital activity and adultery, the number of prostitutes and the volume of their business, the ages when most women (or men) lose their virginity, the number of "group marriages" and "cooperative families," and the types of communal living arrangements which include or exclude some form of casual polygamy*—these and other similar matters remain unknown. We do know, of course, that censorship is rapidly retreating across the land, and that the mass media and entertainment allow forms of sexual display which were prohib-

* Students of the subject have variously given estimates of "mate swapping" as ranging from the participation of 2½ million to 8 million couples, as well as one to ten million people.[49]

ited not long ago; that an increasingly (and sometimes incredibly) wide range of sexual services and goods (including, for instance, electrical vaginal stimulators) are for sale. At the same time in the same society some political groups wage war on antiseptic sex education in secondary schools; the sale of contraceptives is restricted in many states, and abortion is banned in most. Robert Welch, leader of the John Birch Society, probably spoke for a good number of Americans when he said that "The Communist design to promote sex education . . . is a final assault upon the family as a fundamental block in the structure of our civilization. . . . The program is also designed to destroy one whole generation of American youth."[50] Similarly, it was proposed in Monmouth County, New Jersey, that unwed mothers (or at least those on welfare) be prosecuted for criminal adultery or fornication.[51] The examples of such contradictions could be multiplied. The dedicated opponents of what they perceive to be sexual license or permissiveness are just as determined to establish a relationship between sexual libertarianism and the evils of communism as Herbert Marcuse and his followers are convinced of the relationship between the evils of sexual repression and capitalism.

It has been claimed that many Americans approach sex in a spirit more appropriate for work than play, that they are unspontaneous, anxious, technique- and "achievement"-oriented as if suffering from a combination of bad conscience and misplaced work ethic. A study of sex manuals concluded "That sex involves effort is a pervasive theme" and that "Sex . . . is considered a kind of work. . . ."[52] Such an approach toward sex might also be linked with competitiveness and manipulativeness. The competitive person, in work as in play, measures himself against other people or against certain standards or norms. He wants to maximize his performance in whatever he does. Not making the most of any opportunity is felt to be threatening. Moreover, insofar as sexual activity has become for more and more people not just a means of satisfying biological and emotional needs but also a more generalized form of self-expression, the intensity of gratification becomes crucial. The comments made by a critic of Norman Mailer's literary approach to sex speak to this point:

> There is something faintly touching and not a little bit absurd in attributing to poor coitus a burden of such momentous gravity. Indeed, Mailer's characters display the sort of elaborate . . . awareness of themselves and the symbolic significance of their

every genital thrust which renders the possibility of their experiencing true passion or release highly unlikely.[53]

While most Americans are undoubtedly less metaphysical about sex than Norman Mailer and his heroes, a cruder manipulative approach has an appeal to all those who believe that most things in life can be reduced to techniques—a belief that has deep roots in American culture and appears in forever new guises (such as the recent expectation that a sense of community can be accomplished in small, more or less randomly selected groups of people who mechanically bare their souls—and sometimes their bodies as well—to one another). Manipulativeness is, of course, also built into such a venerable American institution as dating. An advertisement for a booklet by Ann Landers, guidance counselor for millions of Americans, offers to help the reader "To learn how to keep your boyfriend in line without losing him, send for Ann Landers' booklet: 'Necking and Petting' and how far to go." To be sure, neither manipulativeness nor compulsiveness exhaust the range of attitudes toward sex. There has also been a growth of "permissiveness with affection" and a more casual, yet noninstrumental approach toward sex, the origins of which can be traced to the 1920's.

It is not easy to make broad generalizations about sexual mores and practices in American society. There is much diversity—some of it class- and age-patterned, some of it regional—but there is doubtless a growing tendency toward permissiveness and the relaxation of standards (other than those of personal gratification) governing sexual behavior.

A sociologist (in 1968) saw the present American sexual situation in the framework of a well-worn historical parallel:

> There is a haunting similarity between the situation of modern America and that of ancient Rome at the height of its imperial powers. . . . The harsh ascetic standards of the founding period were crumbling in favor of an opportunistic code . . . among the sources of pleasure none was pursued with greater intensity than those of a sexual nature.[54]

The picture is quite different in the Soviet Union. Most striking is the absence of an observable preoccupation with sex, vast and intense in America but barely noticeable in Soviet society.

The libertarian sexual ethic of the 1920's notwithstanding, the roots of Soviet puritanism go deep. It did not originate with the Stalinist reconstruction of Soviet society. Lenin's views on sex, more bourgeois and conservative than revolutionary, were the forerunners of the neo-Victorian respectability fully restored under Stalin. Lenin impatiently rejected the preoccupation with sex and early sexual experimentation which prevailed among some segments of the revolutionary youth. He deplored concern with matters sexual and expressed, for example, a middle-class distaste for the efforts of German communists to organize prostitutes, calling it "a morbid deviation." Most of all, he objected to the dissipation of energy which he felt was inherent in excessive sexual activity:

> "The youth movement is also affected with the modern approach to the sex problem and with excessive interest in it." Lenin emphasized the word "modern" with an ironical, depreciative gesture: "I have been told that sexual questions are the favorite study of your youth organizations too. . . . Young people particularly need the joy and force of life. Healthy sport, swimming, racing, walking, bodily exercises of every kind and many-sided intellectual interests . . . that will give young people more than eternal theories about sexual problems. . . . The revolution demands concentration, increase of forces. . . . It cannot tolerate orgiastic conditions. Dissoluteness in sexual life is bourgeois. . . . Self control, self discipline is not slavery not even in love.[55]

It would be tempting to tie these views of Lenin to his great fear of and preoccupation with the spontaneity of the Russian masses. "Sexual excesses" might have been viewed as one of the aspects of the Russian national character the Bolshevik leaders were determined to stamp out. At the same time it is also quite possible that Lenin's attitude toward sex was a reflection of a purely personal (puritanic) disposition.

Whatever the private sexual concerns of Soviet citizens, they are hardly reflected either in the mass media, entertainment, or published materials. Nor is it very likely that under the smooth surface there lies a seething popular obsession with sex. Prudishness and modesty appear to be fairly widely distributed popular attitudes, although, as will be shown later, there is also some recent evidence to the contrary. Some of these attitudes may be attributed, at least in part, to the persistence of the values of a traditional peasant society. Not only is close to half of the population still rural, but even those in the cities are in large measure first generation urbanites. Still more significant is the fact that, according to recent calculations, "only one eighth of all Soviet women may be considered more or less completely urbanized."[56] Again, these are only impressions and surmises. There has been no Soviet Kinsey, or Ira Reiss, no Masters and Johnson. It would be difficult to conceive of a Soviet social scientist (except in the 1920's) making a statement as the following *and* getting it published:

> Even if the result of further research is to the effect that an increase in sexual promiscuity and sexual license is symptomatic of the decline and breakdown of the traditional officially monogamic family unit as the exclusive marital form, we must look further to social policy and social philosophy, and, rather than decrying and resisting those changes, look for new ways to cope with them and ways to develop novel types of family structures and family policies with new and hopefully expanded means of sexual fulfillment. . . .[57]

From the early 1930's until the 1960's there was hardly any public discussion of matters relating to sex in the USSR. Not only were no inventories made about the frequency and form of sexual activities of the citizens, but references to sex were practically eliminated from fiction, movies, and theater as well. Before 1955 abortions were illegal and contraceptives often unobtainable or in short supply and of limited variety. More recently some official concern has developed over the effects of the long suppression of public discussion of sex. Poor marital relations, coarseness toward women, and even sexual crimes have been attributed to ignorance about sex, still sometimes called "a delicate subject"! The loss of virginity of a fifteen-year-old girl not only resulted in criminal proceedings against the perpetrator ("for corrupting morals of a minor") but also in the observation that such problems arise in part "because adolescents have no communication with their elders on this subject."[58] Another article provides interesting clues to both the persistence of Victorian moral standards and the youthful deviations from them. Again a man was "accused of debauching minors":

> A picture was unfolded before the court showing how in the course of a few months the most sacred thing in a woman's life

was trampled on, how girls went beyond the purity of the first
timid kisses, the freshness of feelings, their joyous youth, and went
from childhood directly into the depth of depravity. . . . [The
article concluded:] In the relations between the sexes we have dis-
carded much that was hypocritical and that had been implanted
by religion and the pedagogy of private boarding schools. But
somewhere and in some way, it seems to me, we have gone over-
board. Some young people have interpreted the lifting of harmful
prohibitions as a lifting of all prohibitions.[59]

Interestingly enough the same article also accused the mothers of the
two girls (aged fifteen and sixteen) of failure "to guard their daughters." When a leading Soviet daily newspaper talks about "some
young people" in a critical context such as the above it is likely that
the author had in mind large numbers of people.* Thus we cannot
rule out the possibility that there is much premarital sexual activity,
at least in some segments of Soviet society, a possibility supported by
the high rates of illegitimacy. While precise, nationwide statistics
are, as usual, unavailable, there are suggestive bits of information:
"A Soviet legal specialist estimated that there were 11 million illegitimate children in the USSR in 1947, a year in which 3,312,000 unmarried mothers were receiving grants for support of their children."[60]

Although, as noted earlier, a Soviet Kinsey Report is yet to be
written, we do have some interesting figures concerning sexual attitudes in the USSR. Unfortunately, as is often the case with Soviet
empirical investigations, there is little information provided about
the method of sampling, the size of the sample, and the method of
eliciting the information. The study we are referring to probed attitudes toward premarital sexual relations. The sample consisted of
students and professional people (the latter defined as "scholarly and
scientific personnel of Leningrad academic and research institu-

* In this respect the Soviet and American mass media often play diametrically opposed
roles. In the Soviet Union the mass media frequently understates social problems, at
least those which have significant ideological implications. One might say that reportage
on such problems resembles the proverbial iceberg. "Some people" mentioned suggests
a vast number who go unmentioned. In the American mass media the situation is often
very different. Social problems, especially those which can be presented in a lurid,
sensational manner, are often overdramatized and exaggerated. In this manner, however, a commercially oriented mass media may perform the useful function of muckraking or societal self-criticism, no matter what the underlying motives are.

tions.") They approved or disapproved of premarital sexual relations in the following proportions:

	STUDENT		PROFESSIONAL	
	Men	Women	Men	Women
	Per cent		Per cent	
Approve	58	38	62	55
Condemn	16	27	14	7
Indefinite	31	35	24	38

It was also found that in a sample of 500 *unmarried* students (it was not clear whether or not this was in the same sample reported above) 85 per cent of the men and 47 per cent of the women had sexual experience, presumably intercourse. (The actual questions were not reproduced.)[61]

Figures such as the above would suggest that popular attitudes, among some segments of the population, are certainly less puritanical than the tone of many official discussions would suggest.* In the dissertation cited above, other surveys undertaken by the author were also reported. These dealt with the permissibility of premarital sex with a loved one, as against a mere acquaintance. The results were not surprising: far larger proportions of the respondents favored sex with love than without (a finding consistent with a large body of research in the United States). Remnants of the double standard did show up: "men are more liberal toward their own sexual behavior than toward that of women, and women are more liberal toward male sexual behavior than toward their own"[63]—again a fairly widespread pattern in this country. Apparently the samples used in these studies were heavily weighted toward the educated groups from Leningrad (although one of the surveys mentioned included blue-collar workers as well, without indicating their proportions). This weighting naturally raises questions concerning their generalizability to the population as a whole or even to the urban population.

It is somewhat less difficult to make comparisons between family instability, and divorce in particular, in the two societies. One thing is clear: there has been a striking increase over the past decade in

---

* According to one Western observer, "Behind the appearance of modesty and decorum . . . Russia is considerably more permissive than any Western society I know. . . . Lovemaking is extraordinarily casual, in the emotional as well as physical sense. There is almost total freedom, with very little talk about it, and less guilt."[62]

Soviet divorce, as a result, in part, of easier divorce procedures.* It also appears that many reasons adduced to explain the high divorce rates in the USSR are similar to those which have been proposed to account for divorce in the United States. Soviet divorce rates are also similar to those in this country and are among the highest in the world. The following figures indicate changes in divorce rates (per thousand population) in the two countries:

	1940	1950	1955	1960	1965	1967	1968	1969	1970[65]
U.S.	2.0	2.6	2.3	2.2	2.5	2.7	2.9	3.2	no inf.
USSR	1.1	0.4	no inf.	1.3	2.8	2.7	2.7	2.6	2.6[66]

More research has been done in the U.S. about the factors associated with family instability, since divorce rates have been high for decades. The explanations of the upsurge in Soviet divorce rates are less well established, although they include the institutional facilitation of divorce that took place in 1965.

Thus until recently both American and Soviet society maximized the institutional obstacles of divorce although in the U.S. there are great variations among states concerning divorce procedure. It is not easy to assess in which society divorce is more difficult at present. Given sufficient financial resources required for travel, legal advice, or both, it is fairly easy (if time-consuming) to obtain divorce in the U.S. In the Soviet Union the major hurdles were more bureaucratic than financial, although there were also fees to be paid. The changing Soviet divorce laws have faithfully reflected the fluctuating family policies of the regime. The 1920's was the famed period of "postcard divorce," replaced by the new stringent regulations in 1936 and 1944, which were eased in 1965. In part because American divorce laws have changed relatively little over the last few decades (except for a few states), it is likely that the rising rates of divorce in the U.S. had little to do with legal facilitation, but reflected other social conditions. Correspondingly, the growth of divorce in the Soviet Union in the recent years reflects more than merely the greater legal opportunity. The increase of Soviet divorce is associated with factors at work in both societies: the continuing decline of traditional family

* This means the abolition of large fees, reduction of prolonged waiting periods, and doing away with public (press) announcement of the intent to divorce. In uncontested cases and at the request of both parties, marriages can now be dissolved through the registry without legal proceedings. There still is, however, a one month waiting period before a wedding and three months' before divorce is granted.[64]

controls, the desire for more choice in every area of life, improved opportunities to focus attention on the personal-emotional aspects of a relationship and—in the Soviet case—the transition from a highly repressive to a somewhat more permissive social order. In both societies the existing arrangements for divorce constitute what might be called a "cultural lag"; they are greatly out of step with the values and attitudes of large portions of the populations. This is especially marked in the United States, where a very high popular toleration of divorce is juxtaposed with an archaic legal structure which has produced proliferating patterns of circumvention. The institutional obstruction of divorce has different sources in the two countries. In the U.S., it is clearly a survival of religious values; in the Soviet Union—in addition to the factors discussed earlier—it is related to the right of the state and the collective to exercise supervision over the personal life of the citizen. Practical considerations also play a part; the Soviet state is not anxious to take over the upbringing and care of children who are products of broken homes and parental irresponsibility. In many Soviet articles discussing family problems a great emphasis is put on the need to enforce court rulings on alimony.

The comments of Soviet sociologists probing the causes of divorce have a familiar ring. For example:

> People of different cultural and moral levels and of different backgrounds and ways of life mix. They leave behind them traditional forms of control by the family, by the public opinion of the village street, by relatives. No social or material factors hinder them from marrying—and from soon realizing that they had been hasty. . . .
>
> Research has been and is being conducted in different parts of the country, but the results are amazingly similar. Two-thirds of those questioned cite spiritual and moral differences as the cause of disruption of marriage.* Economic conditions turn out to have an ever smaller effect (about 5%) on the family. And almost 100%

---

* Many of which doubtless spring from class differences. Perhaps the phenomenon can be explained in part by Trotsky's scathing observations made decades ago: "One of the very dramatic chapters in the great book of the Soviet will be the tale of the disintegration . . . of those Soviet families where the husband as a party member, trade unionist, military commander or administrator, grew and developed and acquired new tastes in life and the wife, crushed by the family, remained on the old level. The road of the two generations of the Soviet bureaucracy is sown thick with the tragedies of wives rejected and left behind."[67] Naturally the disruptive effect of such circumstances is not confined to Soviet society.

of the husbands and wives consider love, mutual respect and sharing of cultural interests to be the foundation of family life. . . .
    Young men and women today make greater moral demands of
marriage. They seek to embark upon married life at an earlier age
than ever before and very often the romantic ideas of married life
are wrecked upon its prose—an inability to run a household, to
keep to a family budget, to give in to one another when disagree-
ments arise.[68]

This article also pointed out that, as in the United States, high rates
of divorce do not indicate loss of confidence in the family, since most
of those divorced remarry. On the other hand, drunkenness plays a
far more important part in the break up of marriages in the USSR
than it does in the United States.

But no matter how important personal compatibilities are, no
matter how much a rise in expectations has contributed to family
instability in Soviet society, more tangible circumstances of life continue to play a part. This fact was pointed out by A. G. Kharchev,
the most eminent Soviet family sociologist:

> . . . it would be one-sided at best to assert that the solidity and
> well-being of the family collective depends solely on the moral
> complexion of those who start the family. Without exception all
> the readers who sent letters to the editor about the article "The
> Family Is a Cell of Society" agree that many conflicts, disorders
> and misunderstandings in family life occur because of poor or-
> ganization of everyday life, and that people responsible for living
> arrangements and services to the population still fall far short of
> squaring accounts with the Soviet family.[69]

Equally interesting and sociologically plausible are the observations
offered by V. Perevedentsev, a well-known Soviet economist who often
writes about sociological topics:

> . . . divorce was highest among the intelligentsia and the lowest
> among the collective farmers. . . .*
> Because so many women now have good jobs they no longer are
> dependent economically on their husbands. . . .
> . . . the rising number of divorces has caused society to be more
> tolerant. . . .[70]

* Soviet collective farmers are the most tradition-bound segment of the population,
which explains their low divorce rates, while the intelligentsia encompasses a wide
variety of white-collar occupations (including those with modest incomes) who tend to
be urban and mobile both socially and geographically.

The factors generally associated with marital instability in the United States have often been stated. Religious sanctions against divorce have lost much of their force, as have familial pressures with the decline of the extended family; the threat of economic insecurity and the total dependence of women on men have also diminished (probably one of the motives that prompted many women in the past to stay married); the practical "services" provided by the family have become fewer with the narrowing of its functions; greater social and geographic mobility provides opportunities for more people of more varied, and potentially more incompatible, backgrounds to meet and marry; greater economic security has made early and more ill-considered marriages possible; improvements in the material conditions of life together with the growing meaninglessness of religious values have increasingly predisposed people to seek private, personal, emotional fulfillment (offered by the family) and to make, correspondingly, greater psychological demands on it.[71] And, of course, despite many persisting restrictions, divorce is also becoming somewhat easier in the United States as exemplified by the recent changes in California law, which now permits couples to dissolve their marriages on grounds of "irreconcilable differences."

As these conditions are likely to persist in American society the divorce rate will remain high, and may even continue to grow. Similarly, in Soviet society where several of these trends are also present, a high divorce rate will continue and possibly increase.

In matters of birth control Soviet policies followed the familiar zigzag from early permissiveness to the totalitarian policy of encouraging population growth beginning in the 1930's and back to the somewhat more permissive policies of the last fifteen years during which abortion has become both legal and widely available. The greater variety of birth control techniques and devices available in the United States reflect a more advanced medical technology and a developed "consumption economy," rather than a more enlightened public policy toward family planning (as contraception is still called euphemistically).* While birth control is widely practiced in both

* In the Soviet Union the limited range and availability of contraceptive devices was suggested by a study published in 1965 which found that in a sample of small town and rural women who required abortions, 52 per cent used no form of contraception and only 5 per cent used diaphragms and/or jelly. The pill was not even mentioned.[72]

societies it continues to be hedged in by various restrictions, especially for the unmarried. In the United States, the main resistance comes from the Catholic Church, a force with which Soviet birth control advocates do not have to contend. In both societies it is the more highly educated strata who are most willing to use birth control; those who have the largest families are, or have been frequently found among the lower socioeconomic groups. In American society, however, particularly in the years following World War II, it was something of a fashion among middle- and upper-middle-class families to have three to five children, a number well above the then national average of children per family. This was not a reflection of the lack of contraceptives, but rather an attempt, facilitated by material affluence, to find fulfillment in the family, especially on the part of women.

Birth rates in the Soviet Union have significantly declined over the past decades: 1940—31.2 (per thousand of population); 1950—26.7; 1960—24.9; 1968—17.2 (thus approximating American rates which were 24.1 in 1950, 23.7 in 1960, and 17.5 in 1968).[73] The reasons for the decline of Soviet rates presumably include improved access to birth control methods, the persistence of overcrowded housing, and the growth of material expectations which accompany the process of urbanization and secularization.

Equally noteworthy are the regional variations within the USSR: in Azerbaijan and Turkmenia, for example, the rate in 1962 was over 40 per 1000 while it was 16 per 1000 in the Baltic Republics.[74] The figures reflect the persistence of tradition in parts of the Soviet Union. According to another Soviet source, these geographical (and associated cultural) variations "have been in existence for a long period of time and remain virtually unchanged." Low birth rates or, according to the same article, a preference for having no more than one or two children, are viewed as a threat to society, confronting it with the problem of an aging population and the associated "reduction in manpower reserves." The author's recommendation is the following:

> . . . It would be best for society and the family itself if each family were to have two or three children. Children are not only the hope and future support of their parents but also the future of our state. Therefore, the raising and care of children should be

regarded not as merely the private concern of married couples but as socially useful labor. . . .[75]

Another article written by V. Perevedentsev voices the official apprehension that declining birth rates could undermine or weaken the world power status of the USSR by reducing her share of the world population.[76]

In the final analysis in both American and Soviet society it is still the context of the family in which most people expect to find their major emotional gratifications and source of security.* This is a curious situation in view of all the real and alleged problems which beset the family, including the role conflicts of spouses, the possibilities of rejection of the parents by children, and the awareness of the predictable routinization of sexual and emotional pleasures in marriage etc. Why should it be that despite such problems (and notwithstanding very high divorce rates) people continue to pursue happiness in the family? Perhaps it is in large part by default of other institutions that the family persists as a continued source of attraction, and also by the sheer weight of convention. But more important may be the circumstance that other groups and relationships have proved still more transient and unsatisfactory as sources of emotional sustenance. (As Nisbet put it "In this now small and fragile group we seek the security and affection denied everywhere else."[77])

Friendship†

The forms and functions of friendship in the two societies differ in many respects. It should not be surprising if different social environments have a different influence even in the more intimate realms of life where friendship belongs.

Friendship implies selectivity and intimacy. It is a highly individualized relationship generally *unsupported* by widely shared normative prescriptions. Contemporary societies provide especially few guidelines for the selection of friends in contrast with other relation-

---

* Even those who reject traditional forms of family, members of hippie and other communes in America, talk about *their* "family," thereby paying tribute to an institution they otherwise hold in low respect.

† Friendship patterns have been hardly studied by either American or Soviet social scientists. Therefore, more than in most other parts of this book, a highly impressionistic discussion of the topic is inescapable.

ships of solidarity and support. Ethnic, kinship, religious, and neighborly ties—and the solidarity they imply—are clearly normative. We are supposed to show respect and affection toward our parents, protect our children, assist our neighbors, and feel somewhat more solidarity toward those who share our religious, ethnic, or political affiliations or backgrounds. By contrast, the selection of friends is left almost entirely to the individual and contemporary Western culture supplies few criteria for choosing them, no suggestions as to their most desirable number, little guidance concerning the nature of the relationship and the obligations entailed. The need for friendship, however, seems to arise in proportion to the growing meaninglessness or lack of kinship and community ties.*

In American society the term "friendship" is applied to relationships which in the Soviet Union (and much of Europe) would be called acquaintanceships. Many students and observers of American society, native and foreign alike, have suggested that the friendships of Americans tend to be superficial, short-lived, and limited in intimacy. Friendships in America do not often become life-long exchanges of solidarity and moral and emotional support. The very fact that people often have a large circle of friends rules out deeper personal involvement. The contrast with the Soviet patterns of friendship is quite pronounced. In Soviet society (as in many other European countries) people more typically have only a small circle of friends with whom the ties are more enduring, intimate, and intense. These friendships usually start early in life, are highly selective, and not easily interchangeable. Their development is slow, gradually increasing in intensity and mutual expectations. Trust plays a very important part in them. Why do American friendship patterns seem different?

Two factors seem to be paramount in shaping American attitudes toward friendship: one is mobility, and the other is freedom or what might be called the structural permissiveness of American society. The effects of mobility—both geographic and social—are the more obvious. People who frequently change their social environment are

---

* If novels are any guide to social realities it would seem that the emphasis on and preoccupation with friendship becomes conspicuous in the early 19th century with the emergence of the romantic movement in Europe. This would seem to support the above proposition since the early 19th century also saw the beginnings of the accelerated decline of traditional society in Europe.

under pressure to avoid getting seriously involved with others except those in their immediate family. Nor do people who move frequently have enough time to build up deep friendships. Even if there is actually enough time, the anticipation of departing from a geographical or social locale prompts caution in developing involvements which could be painful to break off. Adaptation to such circumstances results in keeping friendships superficial* and in focusing on those aspects of the personality which are most widely distributed among large numbers of people with whom the mobile person is likely to become acquainted. Therefore, the "friends" of the typical American have to be easily interchangeable at short notice. He must be able to find qualities which are less unique; hence friendships come to be based less on highly personalized criteria of congeniality than on the most commonly shared values and attitudes. A direct consequence of geographic and social mobility is the decisive importance of propinquity in the determination of friendship patterns. When people are mobile it is most convenient to find friends among one's neighbors both at the place of residence and work. The fact that the place of residence also reflects socioeconomic status makes it easier to operate on the premise that there will be shared values and styles of life.

Another characteristic of many American friendships is their functionalization, that is, subordination to values other than the inherent, irreducible psychological gratification of maintaining a reciprocal relationship of intimacy and solidarity. More often than not, and particularly in upper socioeconomic levels, the selection of friends is based on considerations other than personal affinities. When people *periodically* select friends because they live next door to them or work at the same place, they are obviously not making their choices on the basis of highly personalized affinities. The functionalization of friendship also means its coordination with occupational or career goals, the choosing of "friends" on the basis of their potential contribution to career opportunities or prestige in the community. It is paradoxical that while the Soviet regime has pur-

* Americans might have dozens of "friends" but hardly any of them are close enough to open up with on any topic that touches the core of the personality. A psychiatrist reported that "One of the problems we face today is the scarcity of good friends. . . . Almost without exception when I ask a young person who his best friend is, he can't tell me."78

posefully striven to functionalize (in a political sense) personal relationships and has largely failed, in the United States functionalization has been accomplished spontaneously.

The facility for easy and superficial friendships in America is enhanced by a poorly developed sense of privacy and by egalitarianism,
the pervasive feeling that one person is, on the whole, as good as
another (at least within one's status group). The quest for popularity,
or the indiscriminate pursuit of approval on an ever-widening scale,
is another factor that dilutes the meaning of friendship. Exclusive
relationships, and the high degrees of selectivity they imply, are incompatible with the pursuit of popularity. The preoccupation with
success also often reduces involvement in friendships since it leads
to extreme competitiveness.* At the same time, success is rewarded
by popularity and respect which furnish emotional gratifications
that partially preempt the need for friendship. Among males the
fear of homosexuality is also sometimes viewed as a factor detrimental to the development of intimacy.[79] The closely knit nuclear family
and a more equal partnership between man and wife too may function as substitutes for friendships.

The permissiveness pervading American society also affects the
nature of friendship, which becomes especially clear in comparison
with conditions prevailing in the Soviet Union. In the United States
people approach one another with a relatively high degree of confidence and openness—within a given social level, at any rate—and this
is not totally unrelated to political factors. Under conditions of relative political freedom the value of personal intimacy and solidarity
diminishes; there is less need to draw sharp dividing lines between
friend and enemy, those who can or cannot be trusted. Americans
as a rule do not worry about the range of topics they can *safely* discuss with friends or acquaintances. Americans do not expect to get in

---

* Differing levels of competitiveness between Americans and Russians (and Soviet citizens in general) have often been observed. Competitiveness—even if originally arising in
the occupational sphere—spills over into the personal and does little to nurture deep
and enduring friendships. The achievement orientation of Americans also contributes
to a lessened interest in the total personality of those they are dealing with. By contrast
the demand for a strong personal involvement, for the greater personalization of important and close social relationships, has been viewed as an element of the Russian
national character. Some have called it "The Russian preoccupation with elemental
humanity," others have explained it as an expression of an overabundance of emotional resources, or the sentimental side of the Russian character.

trouble with the authorities for their views, especially when expressed in private. In the Soviet Union life is harsher and interpersonal trust a more rare and cherished commodity. The pressure of external conditions cements friendships; solidarity on a small scale develops more readily in face of the difficulties people experience. Friendship has survival value. Perhaps it is easier to share certain types of deprivation than prosperity. Also, external supervision and control produce their antidote in techniques of concealment. Under Stalin, in particular, the official concern with the political reliability of the citizen produced its counterpart in the citizen's concern with the reliability of his friends and hence their interchangeability could not readily be assumed or expected. Friendship was more demanding and necessitated careful selection.*

While we have no solid information about the effects of social and geographical mobility on friendship in the Soviet Union, it appears that these effects are less corrosive than in the United States. This at least in part may be attributed to the different patterns of geographical mobility in the USSR. The movements of Soviet citizens are determined to a lesser extent by their own desires than those of Americans. Residents of major urban areas have stronger ties to their cities because of the obvious disadvantages of life in the countryside. Except for the backward rural areas, Soviet citizens are more closely attached to their place of birth; moving from one place to another on purely personal initiative is a more costly and difficult matter than in the U.S. Spontaneous population movements, while they have been occurring in the post-Stalin period, are discouraged by the regime. On the other hand, changing the place of residence under administrative pressure has been common throughout the history of the Soviet Union. Such involuntary moves range from assignment to a new post (with or without punitive implications) to various forms of exile or forced resettlement. "Volunteering" to move to undesirable regions to be opened up (for example, the Virgin Lands campaign under Khrushchev) is another form of semicompulsory geographical mobility. Yet the advantages of physical mobility are less evident for most Soviet citizens than for their American counterparts, for whom the association between movement and opportu-

* The reports of those returning after recent extended visits to the USSR suggest that these conditions have not changed fundamentally in the last decade. Political criteria and caution continue to influence friendship patterns, especially among intellectuals.

nity is closer. Among other things the difficulty of finding good housing in a new location is a strong deterrent to unauthorized moves for the Soviet citizen.

We know much less about the effects of *social* mobility on friendships in the Soviet Union (and about expectations concerning social mobility), though it can be presumed that Soviet citizens are as unlikely to maintain friendships across class lines as are Americans. Certainly the findings of the Harvard Project (based on interviews with former Soviet citizens) indicate that friendships cutting across socioeconomic differences were not widespread during the period studied.[80]

It is among the seeming paradoxes of Soviet life that in a regimented and closely supervised society friendships may flourish in greater depth and intensity than in a much more free, unorganized, and permissive society like the American one.* If this proposition could be firmly substantiated, it would be an indicator of both the success and failure of totalitarianism. The failure lies in the inability of the regime to atomize society completely and to reintegrate the "atoms" into officially structured and supervised collectivities. The success lies in *partial atomization* which enhances the importance of very small, informal, and intimate units—such as small groups of friends. Official policies would probably favor the political functionalization of friendships and the concomitant reduction of the strictly personal element in them. Not unlike romantic heterosexual involvements, friendships represent potentially competing forms of social relations which may remove the individual from the realm of politicized or public preoccupations and activities, or reduce his concern with them. Friendships can also be the bulwark of privacy and the source of incipient anti- or asocial attitudes. From the official, ideological point of view, friendships are desirable if they take place within the framework of the collective and help to solidify it. Ideally, friends (as well as members of a family) ought to be the guardians of each other's ideological-moral integrity and subordinate friendship to commitments to society.

These official-ideological preferences do not mean, of course, that

---

* "The very qualities of human intimacy and intensity are, in part, a kind of overcompensation at the family and precinct level for studied inhumanity at higher, more official levels"—observed James H. Billington, the historian, discussing personal relationships in the Soviet Union.[81]

they have been translated into effective policies. To the extent that the Soviet regime has increasingly concentrated its attention on overt conformity (rather than on a genuine transformation of private lives and beliefs), official concern with the potentially disruptive or subversive aspects of private attachments has been quite limited.

It is difficult to say to what extent friendship patterns in America have been affected by the newly intensified pursuit of communal intimacy evident in some areas of American life today. It is unlikely, however, that the new cult of intimacy has made friendship more enduring or selective, because the cult itself is rather unselective and group-oriented. If many Americans, especially among the young, have a greater need for intimacy, they express it in short-term relationships that may be intimate and gratifying, but short-term nevertheless. There is also an element of unselectivity in the forms of communal living or subcultural togetherness;* rarely does prolonged familiarity or a trial period precede the establishment of such communities. These subcultures, urban or rural, tend to be "crash pads" rather than communities, characterized by the constant coming and going of new people.[82] Thus mobility and restlessness continue to influence even those relationships which are manifestly dedicated to depth and intimacy. Perhaps a misplaced "achievement orientation" has also penetrated the drive for close personal relationships. The grasping for instant community, instant intimacy, and instant emotional gratification is unlikely to add depth to either friendship or any other personal relationship.

National Character and Ideal Character

The role of national character or modal personality in the shaping of a given social system is among the unsettled issues of the social sciences. It is one of the many chicken-or-egg dilemmas which can

---

* As there is in the wide variety of other temporary, ersatz "communities" and ersatz intimacies which sprung up in the form of T-Groups, support groups, encounter groups, sensitivity training, and similar efforts. All of them testify to the belief that intimacy and community can be achieved quickly, in a few easy steps and stages among a collection of interchangeable individuals. They also reflect the persisting American article of faith that everything can be reduced to techniques, that attitudes and feelings are as manipulable as is matter. The existence of such groups also testifies to the difficulties many Americans have in developing or maintaining one-to-one relationships and to their corresponding preference for less involving (group) ties in situations which are split off from the rest of the life of the participants.

only be resolved by introducing the magic word of "interaction" or "interdependence" which we apply to relationships in which we find it difficult or impossible to specify causation. In spite of this, these concepts have achieved a qualified acceptance in the social sciences and are, moreover, deeply rooted in nationalistic sentiment in almost every society. It is generally believed that there is *some* kind of relationship between the "typical" American and American society, between the "typical" Russian and Soviet social institutions. If indeed, as is generally assumed, national character refers to characteristics that are common in a given society and are of a relatively enduring nature[83] then there is reason to believe that such widely distributed traits do exert influence on social institutions.

At the same time both American and Soviet social scientists recognize, although for different theoretical reasons, the limited usefulness of these concepts. For example, David Riesman has noted that if personality determined social institutions it would be difficult to explain the rise of political democracy in 17th-century New England since the Puritans' personality showed close resemblance to what contemporary social scientists defined as the authoritarian personality.[84]

Two Soviet authors, while cautiously acknowledging the legitimacy of the concept of national character (after all, "K. Marx noted distinctive features of the Russians") stated that "psychological traits arising from national identity are less basic than class characteristics." They claim that in the hands of "ethnopsychologists" (like Margaret Mead, Geoffrey Gorer, and Clyde Kluckhohn) the concept of national character merely "veils" racism.[85]

In addition to such theoretical problems, discussions of American and Soviet national character are complicated by the ethnic heterogeneity of the respective populations, and especially the Soviet (see page 344). Since Russians are the politically and culturally predominant among the various Soviet ethnic groups, and since far more information is available about the Russian character than that of any other Soviet ethnic group, the following discussion will contrast the Russian (rather than a composite Soviet) national character with the American.

It is plausible that there is more congruence between American national character and American social institutions than between these two in the Soviet Union. Several observers, in fact, have characterized the Soviet system as an ongoing struggle between the modal Russian character and deliberate social innovation; in this view, many features of Soviet society have been derived from the conflict between widely distributed personality traits and the institutions imposed upon them.[86] The traditional Russian national character is often equated with the modal personality of the Russian peasant, which inspired the mistrust of the early leaders of the Bolshevik movement, Lenin among them. Indeed, the existence of this modal personality can be inferred from the attitudes of Lenin and his collaborators and successors. In particular, Lenin's abhorrence of spontaneity—and his political measures to suppress it—are consistent with findings of psychological and anthropological research on the Russian national character. Indirect support of the Russian national character can also be found in its opposite, namely, the Soviet elaborations of the ideal personality type, the "new Soviet man" pictured in Soviet literature, mass media and ideological discussions.[87] The behavior of some segments of the Soviet elite probably is the closest approximation in reality of this new synthetic culture hero.

Let us first examine the principal characteristics of the traditional Russian national character, which is still discernible and influences many aspects of Soviet life. According to the literature on this subject, the following features stand out: spontaneity;* strong need for emotional gratification; tendency toward moodiness, or extreme swings of moods; impulsiveness; difficulty to defer gratifications; lack of discipline; self-indulgence; disorderliness; unpredictability; and group orientation.[89]

In the light of such observations it may be of some significance (despite the smallness of the sample) that in a study carried out in the early 1960's a majority of seventeen-to-twenty-year-old technical school students named "lack of self-control," "hot temper" and "impatience" as the first three character traits they wished to overcome. Among those they wished to develop were—again in order of frequency—"persistence," "strength of will," "bravery," and "self-control."[90]

* The evidence as to the extinction or survival of spontaneity in Russians is contradictory. A reader of a Soviet newspaper wrote that "Soviet citizens still bore the heritage of the Stalin era when people 'forgot how to associate with strangers in public places and preferred to shut themselves up among their families. . . .'" The Leningrader (also) spoke out against "rehearsed informality" at poetry readings in youth cafés and observed that those attending these places had "no live spontaneity."[88]

Gorky's discussion of the Russian peasant includes some interesting speculation about some of the factors that might have contributed to a predisposition to apathy and lack of initiative:

> In the West the individual is used to seeing around him . . . the monumental outcome of his ancestors' labor. From the canals of Holland to the tunnels of the Italian Riviera and the vineyards of Vesuvius, from the great works of England and the mighty Silesian factories, the entire soil of Europe is covered with grandiose manifestations of human will—the will which has set itself the proud aim of conquering the forces of Nature and harnessing them to human reason. In the West, a person imbibes this impression with his childhood and this develops in him a consciousness of human worth, of respect for human labor, and an awareness of his own significance. . . . Such thoughts and such feelings and values can never arise in the soul of the Russian peasant. . . . Around him not a tangible trace of labor and artistry to be found in the West.[91]

While these words were written in 1922, the attitudes and situations described are by no means extinct. To be sure, the Russian peasant today can see around him the fruits of human labor in far greater abundance, yet rural indolence, sloth, inefficiency, and apathy continue to characterize the Soviet countryside. Deficient work discipline, low level of motivation and labor productivity continue to retard the development of Soviet agriculture despite a comparatively high level of mechanization and despite the numerous schemes of reorganization. The historical conditions described by Gorky also help to explain the immense emphasis which the Soviet regime has put on the value of work, planning, and the inculcation of a new sense of dignity and mastery over nature.

The New Soviet Man, the regime's ideal prototype, is the antithesis of the traditional Russian character. According to Henry Dicks: "The 'New Man' . . . is the one who overcomes his anarchic spontaneity in favor of leader-like abstinence from immediate impulse gratification; he who suppresses sentiment and private feeling through systematic thought and planned purposeful activity in wholehearted pursuit of the party line."[92] It is among members of the party elite that the closest approximation of this ideal might be found: "The Party elite do love their work to an extent paralleled in Western history only by militant religious orders. . . . Family, recreation, outside interests . . . are utterly subordinate to the demands of one's 'mission.' "[93]

The gulf between the elites on the one hand and the peasant or peasant-derived masses on the other is among the factors which make it difficult to generalize about a dominant Soviet Russian modal personality. However, the characteristics of the official ideal, the "New Soviet Man," are readily summarized: he is totally dedicated to the policies pursued by the party leadership at any given time (whether a member of the party or not); puts the public ahead of the private interest; sensitized to the political dimension of any issue, situation or relationship; self-disciplined, industrious, and hard-working; bent on constant self-improvement relying on the criteria supplied by the ideological authorities; somewhat puritanical in his moral standards, he makes high demands on himself and his fellows; he is familiar with the prevailing interpretations of Marxism-Leninism and is an ardent Soviet patriot. He combines rigidity with flexibility; he is adamant and inflexible in always following the party line obediently, but he has to be highly flexible to do so in view of its frequent and sometimes contradictory changes. He has respect for learning and education in part because a more educated citizen is more useful to his society but also because he believes in the "all round development of the personality" (not wholly unlike the American notion of the well-rounded person) that is required by the transition to communism.

No one has ever attempted an estimate of the quantitative distribution of such personality types in the Soviet population. That they exist cannot be doubted; that their number is small, and has not grown significantly over time, is also probable. Many of the most deeply committed idealists in Soviet society perished in the civil war and purges, and other revolutionaries were replaced by—and sometimes transformed into—functionaries.

The regime's long standing campaign against the Russian traditional character has obscured the fact that even the traditional Russian character has traits which have been distinctly functional from the regime's point of view. They include the propensity to guilt and shame, the capacity to endure suffering, fatalism (which facilitates manipulation from above), and respect for authority. Even emotionalism is of value when it is harnessed to the objectives of the regime.

The Soviet author Andrey Amalrik (jailed a number of times) has cited some other attitudes helpful for the political system:

> . . . The ideas of self government, of equality under the law for all and of personal freedom—and the responsibility that goes with these—are almost incomprehensible to the Russian people. The average Russian will discern, even in the idea of pragmatic freedom, not the possibility of securing a good life for himself but the danger that some clever chap or other will make good at his expense. The very word "freedom" is understood by most people as a synonym of the word "disorder," as an opportunity of executing with impunity some kind of anti-social or dangerous actions. As for respecting the rights of the individual as such, such an idea simply evokes bewilderment. One can feel respect for force, authority, or even ultimately for education, but that human personality of itself should represent any kind of value—this is a preposterous idea in the popular mind.[94]

Interestingly enough, alongside the long-standing official denigration of the pre-Soviet characteristics (associated with the Russian peasant), there has been a quiet resurgence, primarily among intellectuals, of respect for and even idealization of the peasant. In part a reaction to the official pressures toward politicizing everything, and in part a reaction to the results of modernization, a new value is being put (in these circles, at any rate) on the timeless peasant qualities: apolitical goodness, simplicity, endurance, and wisdom. The phenomenon did not escape the attention of the guardians of the official values:

> Today's writers on rural life . . . are more interested in analysis of the peasant's soul. . . .
> There have been numerous articles and discussions of "lyrical" rural writing . . . about "the poetry of peasant labor." Such expressions as "the voice of the soul," "the majesty of the Russian soul," "the shrine of the people's life," "the patriotism of the Russian soul" and the like have been turning up in magazine and newspaper articles.

Criticizing a particular short story, the article goes on: "this is a story that makes the highest virtue of meekness, blind faith in authority and infinite patience in bearing hardship. The hero . . . can work year after year without getting anything in return, and wait passively for justice to triumph."[95] Another article made broader charges:

> Unfortunately not all our writers and artists understand the essence of the Soviet national character. . . .
>
> . . . [some] writers about rural life portray the Russian national character without reference to its contemporary, Soviet features. The characters of V. Likhonosov's story . . . could easily have lived, and the action could have taken place, in non-Soviet times. There is no indication in either of these works that the Soviet way of life has changed the character of the Russian peasant. Such writers idealize the patriarchal way of life . . . and portray its representatives, the older villagers, as practically the only ones who are kind and decent.[96]

The same tendency in character portrayal also pervades the writings of the most influential (though largely unpublished in the USSR) living Soviet writer, Alexander Solzhenitsyn.* His most appealing characters are often uneducated, simple people, especially of peasant background and old or middle-aged rather than young and urban.[97]

Another version of the alienation from the politicized and collectivistic ethos was reflected in a remark of a Soviet intellectual quoted in *Message from Moscow:*

> "People are suddenly realizing that no ideology or sweeping theory is of any importance at all." "Then what is important?" "It sounds banal. Self improvement. Individual effort. Study and thought for one's moral development. The classical liberal virtues. Being honest and loyal and kind to the ten people closest to me rather than professing my good intentions to world history of social movements . . . we have realized that a man's principal duty is not to perfect society or the world, but himself. Making his own work, his own understanding, his own personal relationships good or virtuous in the sense those words have had throughout civilized history. Of course, these have always been the most important

---

* Solzhenitsyn's literary fame among Soviet readers rests primarily on his only novel published in the Soviet Union, *One Day in the Life of Ivan Denisovitch,* a concentration camp story. In addition numerous typed copies of his other manuscripts have been circulating among Soviet intellectuals and occasionally foreign editions of his writings are smuggled in and also widely circulated. Recurrent official criticism of his writings and attitudes (including his expulsion from the Writers Union) and his being awarded the Nobel Prize have further enhanced his reputation among Soviet intellectuals.

things in every society, but we Russians are rediscovering this after decades of obsession with social forces and progressive movements."[98]

It remains to be seen to what extent these apolitical ideals and models will gain popularity and further erode the dubious appeals of the official ones.

The "fit" between the American modal personality and American social organization seems less problematic than the corresponding relationship in Soviet society. The most characteristic American social institutions and practices can be related more directly to the American modal personality. They were certainly not formed as responses *against* that character structure as has been suggested in the Soviet Russian case. And while there are differences between the average or typical American and the character of the American elites, these differences are more quantitative than qualitative. There is, furthermore, a more clearly ascertainable congruence between the American character and the dominant American social values. Perhaps the major explanation of the relatively high degree of congruence between "culture and personality" through much of American history is that American society was established by a fairly homogeneous group who shared a set of values and wished to translate them into social reality. While subsequent generations of settlers and immigrants represented different values and attitudes, there continued to be converging motives among those who came to America voluntarily. Another factor lending a degree of homogeneity to the American national character has been the shared experience of responding to opportunity.* This opportunity consisted of the rich, untapped resources of the land, a relatively small population, freedom of movement, the relative freedom from tradition, the absence of feudal ties and restrictions, and the lack of pressure of a long established community.

That there is a discernible American character has been the widely held finding of generations of visitors from abroad and of historians and social scientists, both American and foreign. These characterological traits come into a sharp focus when contrasted with those of

* A rather jaundiced historical interpretation of the American character is suggested by Philip Slater. He perceives a negative selection process operating among those who came to the United States, rootless and unscrupulous people unable to cope with the challenges of their original environment.[99]

Europeans, including Russians. Thus several years ago when a sample of ex-Soviet citizens was compared with a group of Americans matched for sex, age, and occupation, the following differences were noted:

> These Russians are expressive and emotionally alive. They exhibit fewer defense mechanisms than do Americans of comparable age and occupational position. The issue between isolation and conformity is less pronounced than among Americans. Russians . . . show greater fear of external authority. In general, they express fear, depression and despair more frequently and openly than Americans. . . . They accept the need for impulse control, but are nevertheless more prone to excessive indulgence. They are, however, seldom punitive toward themselves or others for giving way to impulses. They are less perseverant than Americans and more acceptant of the passive sides of their nature. While a little "puritanical" about verbal discussion of sex, the Russians exhibited little conflict in this area and showed less confusion about their sex identification than did Americans. . . . American stress upon autonomy, social approval, and personal achievement appears little. . . . [They] demand and expect moral responses (loyalty, respect, sincerity) from their group. Americans care more about just being liked. . . . Americans are more optimistic, former Soviet citizens more pessimistic. In spite of the passion of the Russians for close social interaction, they exhibit considerable mistrust of others. . . . Americans are appreciably more worried about their failures in achievement, lapses in approved etiquette, inability to meet social obligations. Russians are shamed most deeply by dishonesty, betrayal, and disloyalty. Americans are less aware of other individuals as unique entities as opposed to performers of familiar roles. The Russians value identification with and participation in the larger collectivity more than Americans. At the same time they are less timid about expressing their individuality within the group. . . . Russians and Americans both love material things, especially gadgets. . . . The elite group [the Soviet] are notably less expressive emotionally. . . .[100]

Many of the major differences between Russian and American character are captured in the above quotation. In the latter case, however, there are additional traits deserving comment. It is certainly true, as noted, that Americans have usually been considered highly optimistic, and their activism is sometimes viewed as part of the optimistic belief that effort will bring results; yet intense activism might *also* be viewed as an expression of profound despair, an effort to divert attention from issues and questions which are either deeply disturbing or unanswerable. In any event, it appears that in recent years American optimism, even as a personal quality, has been declining. It may be conjectured that optimism and such other American characteristics as intense activism, competitiveness, and openness may altogether disappear before this century is over, if the current crisis atmosphere in American life continues unabated.

There are tensions between certain components of the American character. For instance, a high value is placed on *both* individualistic and conforming behavior. (Interestingly enough in some spheres of private life, there is less pressure to conform in Soviet society, according to some Western visitors to the USSR.*)

Materialism and idealism are another combination of traits which do not seem to go well together. There is undoubtedly a preoccupation among Americans with objects, gadgets, money, and quantity. Yet it might be asked: *compared to whom* are Americans materialistic? Americans appear more acquisitive than some other peoples because it is easier for them to acquire things. However, the examples of Western Europeans, the Japanese and even the Soviet people have made it clear that there is nothing unique about such American attitudes. Cars, TV sets, washing machines, refrigerators, and so on have the same allure for other people as they have for Americans and probably more so, since by now more and more Americans can take such goods for granted. Still there is a certain preoccupation with money and income which is a marked American trait. Income, as has been frequently observed, is valued and evaluated not primarily for what it can buy, but rather as a symbol of personal worth: it is a rational device of quick appraisal. For example, when the mass media informs the public about a new appointment or election to an office, the salary that goes with the job is usually mentioned—an unheard of practice in most countries. If Americans appear more materialistic than other people this may be in part

* "In all aspects of 'private' life there is a remarkable absence of conventional standards and pressure to conform. One is not looked down upon if one is ugly, smells strongly, looks or behaves oddly . . . slurps one's soup, or otherwise departs from the standards of glossy magazines. . . . In Russia, the conventions permit far greater individual freedom than what the state can grant or take away."[101]

because there is more point in being materialistic in America since material objects are produced in greater profusion and are more obtainable by more people. At the same time, Americans are far less *attached* to their property than people in countries where the standard of living is lower. The very ease with which Americans discard and exchange material objects indicates that many objects per se are not considered valuable beyond their short term functions. Material objects do, of course, also serve as symbols of social status, particularly when new (or *very* old) and expensive. Whatever the degree and uniqueness of the materialism of Americans, it is also frequently noted that they are idealistic. Among expressions of idealism are cited the multiplicity of philanthropic organizations, the preoccupation with saving lives (as illustrated by rescue operations in peace and war), and even American involvement in the two world wars and many foreign aid programs. Americans often tend to regard international relations as extensions of personal relations, or at any rate, not fundamentally different from them.

Beliefs in equality and in success (or achievement) also clash.[102] Success is inconceivable without those who are not (or who are less) successful; thus there is tension between the American beliefs that people are inherently equal and that one should be successful.

Still more glaring is the contradiction between the professed "puritanism" of many Americans and their concurrent preoccupation with sex. While sexual satisfaction is indisputably one of the major goals of a large number, perhaps the vast majority, of Americans, the search for sexual stimulation and gratifications is conducted against the background of surviving puritanical values and mores. There are still many state laws against statutory rape (that is, sexual intercourse with a woman under a specified age), fornication, and even birth control. Legally divorce cannot be obtained on the basis of mutual consent in most states (although this in fact is usually the actual ground); colleges until recently assumed the function of moral guardianship for adult students. Illegitimacy is generally censored, and teachers have been dismissed for proposing that sexual intercourse is permissible between emotionally involved adults even if they are not married. It is very likely that in this, as in some other areas of life, we are confronted with what Soviet authors would call "survivals" from the past. At least some segments of the population cling to them the more tenaciously the more insecure they are in a world which provides them with fewer and fewer guideposts as to what is right or wrong.

Finally there is a conflict between the American respect for formal education and suspicion or even contempt for intense preoccupation with learning for its own sake. The tradition of anti-intellectualism in American society has been widely observed, alongside the ambivalent reverence for science. It is still true that the respect for education is of an instrumental nature for the most part: not a respect for learning as such, but a respect nurtured by the experience that education is helpful for one's earning power. Another basis for the respect for education is the desirability of being well-rounded, that is, generally—if superficially—knowledgeable. Anti-intellectualism has several historical and cultural sources: the surviving respect for simple, frontier virtues; the preference for action over talk and theory; the pragmatic rejection of abstraction and reflection; the egalitarian hostility toward snobbishness that sometimes accompanies an overdose of learning and refinement.*

Interestingly enough, while both American and Soviet people believe that profound differences exist between their political and social institutions, many people in each society also believe in the similarity between the good "average American" and the good "average Russian"—each saddled with "bad" governments which get between the goodness of "ordinary" people. (To be sure, Soviet people are less likely to engage publicly in such reflections, as far as the "badness" of their own government is concerned.) While such beliefs are comforting enough (insofar as they allow us to retain a hopeful view of human nature, abstracted from social institutions), it is as unrealistic to divorce completely the nature of political institutions from the character of the governed as it is to postulate a perfect harmony between the two.

* There are of course other, more recent forms and sources of anti-intellectualism in American life, many of them to be found, as we have seen, on the campuses.

8. American and Soviet Social Problems

The acknowledged presence of social problems tells as much about a society as its aspects which are objects of pride and satisfaction. This is particularly true in view of the increasing recognition of the inseparability of the problematic from the unproblematic in social life, and the finding that things highly valued in society not only coexist with, but often generate, phenomena that are feared and rejected.[1] Thus social problems inform us about the values of society and about its moral-ethical standards, since definitions of "problematic" involve the use of standards of good and bad, satisfactory or unsatisfactory, efficient or inefficient.

Nothing seen as unalterable is conceived of as "problematic." Therefore, what is defined as a social problem also reflects the prevailing beliefs in change and changeability in regard to both human nature and social institutions. The very concept "social problem" is of comparatively recent origin and indicates a growing belief in the possibilities of eradicating undesirable or unsatisfactory features of human nature and social life. The more intolerant a society is of the imperfections and defects of human and social existence the more problems it has—not unlike an individual. For example, in rich and highly productive societies hunger is seen as a social problem, something which should not exist, rather than an inevitable condition. In a primitive, tribal society hunger may not be seen in the same light, but on the contrary as a part of normal human existence about which little can be done—hence not a problem. The same applies to floods, droughts, and other natural disasters which, depending in part on the level of technological and scientific development, may not be seen as "problems." Types of behavior seen as problematic are closely related to beliefs in the perfectibility of social order and human nature—beliefs which need not be, but usually are, associated with the level of technological development. In short, expectations are at the root of the definitions of situations and behavior as "problematic."

Since social problems, once defined as such, elicit institutional responses the way in which they are handled informs us about a variety of social institutions, for example, welfare services, agencies of crime control, correctional institutions, and systems of planning. This in turn provides further information about society as a whole.

Comparative Definitions

Despite many differences in the values and institutions of contemporary urban-industrial societies, there is increasing agreement on what constitute social problems. This agreement is in part produced by the shared drive for efficiency. Social problems generally entail some form of inefficiency on the part of some group or the individual, limiting participation in some important arena of life: work, education, the family, predictable social intercourse. If, indeed, there is any kind of convergence between the United States and the Soviet Union, it can be found in the realm of social problems.[2]*

* Soviet spokesmen acknowledge neither the similarity between the social problems in the two societies, nor the resemblance between their origins:
"All these attempts [at ideological subversion by bourgeois propaganda, that is—P. H.] are based on the conception that capitalism and socialism are supposedly two societies that are coming closer to one another and have common problems that stem from human nature and the development of modern technology and are not dependent on the difference in social forms. All this bears the poisonous seeds of apoliticism, the desire to implant a philistine neutralism in people. . . . Neutralism in ideology has been and remains a form of support of bourgeois ideology." Elsewhere in the same article the author admits and explains social problems in Soviet society in the following way:
". . . problems do exist and very complex ones at that. It is known that the countryside still lags behind the city in the level of mechanization of production and in the standards of everyday life. The rate of housing construction still does not satisfy the requirements of the population. There are serious shortcomings in everyday services

To be sure, by the same token there is also convergence between the United States and Great Britain, or the U.S. and West Germany, the U.S. and Japan, or among other countries which have created large, complex, and secular urban environments detrimental for the maintenance of efficient systems of informal social control and lacking in strong commitment to ultimate values. This is not to say that the political and ideological factors peculiar to American and Soviet society, respectively, are unimportant in the perception and definition of social problems. They are, and this is well illustrated by the case of religion. In the USSR it is the *survival* of religion that is officially defined as a serious social problem; in the U.S. its *decline* is a cause for public concern and lament. The evaluation of the mass media and TV in particular provides another example of contrasting definitions of what is socially problematic. In America there is an inclination on the part of many social scientists, some government officials, thoughtful parents, and better educated people in general to consider prolonged exposure to the mass media as unwholesome, especially for the young. In the Soviet Union the authorities hardly consider exposure to a governmental mass media either a waste of time or a potentially insidious influence on character development.*

In both American and Soviet societies the prevailing emphasis

---

and in the organization of trade. There are still swindlers, speculators and hooligans in our country, and there are also people who fall under the influence of the ideology of bourgeois society. . . . [However] socialism is the first phase of communism and . . . such a society still retains in all respects—economic, moral, intellectual—the birthmarks of the old society from whose womb it sprang. . . . The Communists have not promised the complete eradication of all problems from the life of society, and surely they bear no historical responsibility for the origin of these problems or for the many flaws and calamities in the life of society that have been created by the age-old rule of private property and age-old oppression. . . . But we do bear responsibility for how well we understand and solve the urgent problems of social development. . . ."[3]

By contrast the problems of American society are described as "Incurable Sores" in an article of the same title which stated that "the sickness of American society is the sickness of capitalist society which is historically doomed to perish."[4]

* It is of course an altogether different matter when it comes to the foreign mass media and its products which occasionally gain admittance to the Soviet Union: "Foreign films steeped in bourgeois morality are often shown on the screens of our movie theaters. . . . The press, the public and movie-goers have expressed serious anxiety over this. . . ."[5] The official assertion that "public anxiety" exists over foreign movies is hardly supported by evidence. On the contrary, the Soviet public shows an avid interest in foreign movies, plays, orchestras, books, and newspapers—in fact in most things foreign, as visitors commonly testify.

on activism and mastery predisposes to the perception of and impatience toward social problems, although the evaluation of their gravity depends on cultural and value factors peculiar to each. For example few people in America—either among officials and experts or the public at large—expect that a totally crimeless society can ever be achieved in which no serious infringements of law would occur. (At the same time there is widespread concern about the constant increase of crime, its visibility and destructive and violent manifestations.) Even in the relatively optimistic American outlook on society and human nature, the perfectibility of human beings (as of social organizations) is seen by most people as limited. Sociological and psychological insights provide support for these views. The belief in the coexistence of good and evil (or of the uncontrollable, asocial, and destructive impulses *and* rational controls) within the same personality is commonplace, at least in the Western world. Sociologists have demonstrated the same coexistence, on the societal level. Law-abiding behavior and law-violating behavior of various kinds are closely related. Things highly valued may lead, in the least expected ways, to things widely detested.[6] Sociologists have also stressed that crime serves some positive functions in society: it reminds people, particularly when the criminal is apprehended and punished, of the values of society he had violated, thereby increasing solidarity among the noncriminal majority.[7]*

Crime in the Soviet Union is also defined as a serious social problem—to the extent that its existence is acknowledged. While its explanation and interpretation presents certain theoretical difficulties, crime is viewed as eradicable, at least in Soviet (or other social-

---

* On the other hand Durkheim, and many of his functionalist followers, neglected the possibility that the high incidence of crime can also lead to an erosion of moral standards, to a decline of strong reactions against it. Most people get tired of moral indignation if its display is occasioned every day. Indeed it would seem that rather than cementing social solidarity (as it might in a small-scale, relatively homogeneous, and relatively crime-free society), the high rate of crime, and especially its well publicized nature, has led, at least in the United States, to a growing, resigned acceptance of crime, to its being taken for granted. The same applies to politically motivated acts of violence: "As campaigns gradually mount in intensity and the rights and liberties of others are infringed on an ever more massive scale, so the threshold of that which is deemed wrong rises to a level at which even physical and mental intimidation of unpopular individuals, destruction of public institutions, and damage to private property are felt justified, and the penalization of such acts—reference always being made, of course, to the just aims of the 'idealists' who perpetrate them—is considered repressive."[8]

ist) society. This approach to crime is paralleled by the Soviet view of other social problems, all of which are seen as eradicable and subject to social engineering. The official beliefs of Soviet society admit to few, if any limits to the perfectability of human nature and social institutions.

In the selection of specific social problems we have used two major criteria. The first is the traditional, Western social scientific conception of what constitutes social problems: in brief, activities and attitudes disruptive of social participation (or threatening to physical survival) or impinging on the predictability of social interaction, or both, as well as *situations* which lead to the same results.* The second criterion is the prevailing perception of what constitute social problems within American and Soviet society, respectively. As we have indicated, the two criteria do not invariably overlap. Many aspects of social life seen as problematic in the United States are not seen in the same light in the Soviet Union and vice versa. There are certain problems which are apparent and acknowledged in both societies, for example, juvenile delinquency and water pollution. There are, however, others which exist (on a significant scale) only in one of them. Among the latter, are racial tension and drug addiction in the United States and crimes against state property, housing shortage, and the persistence of religion in the USSR.

Crime and Delinquency

Crime is a serious social problem in both societies, but probably more so in the United States, where no attempt is made to conceal its magnitude. On the contrary, it is often exaggerated and emphasis is put on its most spectacularly gruesome aspects.[9] Characteristically, it is presented in the American mass media in either a matter of fact or a sensational way.† In neither manner of reporting do the

* The Merton-Nisbet volume, cited earlier, considers the following social problems: crime; juvenile delinquency; mental disorder; drug addiction; suicide; prostitution; population problems; race and ethnic relations; family disorganization; work disorganization; disorganization in the military; community disorganization; traffic, transportation, and urban problems; disasters, war, and poverty.

† When reproached about this, representatives of the mass media tend to claim that the lurid exposés of crime, violence, or aberrant sex serve moral ends and that they are committed to "telling the truth" no matter how unpleasant. Thus a measure of respectability is imparted to the commercial exploitation of violence and sex by claiming a latent moral message.

descriptions of crimes stress the moral culpability of the criminals nor the probability and justice of punishment, the lesson prospective criminals presumably should learn. In the Soviet Union, the reporting of criminal acts in the mass media is almost invariably accompanied by their condemnation and by descriptions of the apprehension of the wrongdoers. The Soviet press hardly ever reports unsolved criminal cases, especially major ones. Even this mode of crime reporting is a comparatively new development. Until the 1960's, crime, as well as many other social problems, was not an officially approved subject for public discussion. The alleged or implied absence of crime was one of the indicators of the superiority of a socialist society.

In the present discussion of crime in Soviet society we are considering only the "ordinary" type to which no or little political and ideological connotation is attached. The number of certified "political criminals" declined since the death of Stalin and—as we noted in Chapter 3—political repression has become more selective. The decline of Soviet political crimes over a period of time* may be explained on two grounds: sociological and ideological. The prolonged existence of the Soviet regime resulted in the natural (and unnatural) extinction of its genuine opponents, both those willing and able to take action against it and those passively hostile. New generations (with a few exceptions) became increasingly incapable of thinking about political alternatives worth fighting for or forms of unauthorized political action possible to pursue. The prolonged absence of opportunity for any form of organized political activity other than those sanctioned by the regime largely removed the objective conditions for political crimes.[11] Moreover, after more than

---

* By contrast there has been an increase in "political crimes" in the United States, or, more accurately, a growing attempt to redefine crime against property (and, in theory, only business or government property) as a political or even revolutionary act committed by some segments of the radical counterculture to wreck the "System." Thus quite ordinary stealing (renamed as "ripping off") is dignified and provided with an ideological justification. By coincidence, these revolutionary activities also help to alleviate, or in some cases totally reduce, the need to work.[10]

Another development to be mentioned in this context is the effort (on the part of some radicals) to define ordinary and often totally apolitical criminals in jail as political prisoners if they belong to certain minority groups such as blacks, Puerto Ricans, Mexican-Americans, and American Indians.

At the same time (as we noted elsewhere in this book) there has also been an increase in crimes more indisputably political, such as attacks on policemen, bombings, and arson.

half a century of the Soviet political system, the spokesmen of the regime have developed an understandable preference for representing those, politically opposed to it, as isolated malcontents and deviants, and for stressing their alleged personal pathologies and defects of character rather than their political motivation and ideology.* At the same time, in line with the generally more pragmatic policies of the post-Stalin and post-Khrushchev leadership, the admission of the existence of ordinary, nonpolitical crimes became legitimate. Several factors might have contributed to this development. One was perhaps a greater sense of security of the new leaders than possessed by their predecessors. Correspondingly, they might have considered the Soviet public more mature and thus ready to be exposed to the official acknowledgement of the existence of social problems like crime. It is also possible, indeed probable (though in the absence of comparative figures difficult to prove), that ordinary crime has increased in the last decade which makes its existence more difficult to deny.

The probable increase of crime might be attributed to the overall slackening of repression and discipline, to higher standards of living (leading to the familiar phenomenon of the sudden rise of expectations), looser social controls over the younger age groups, and greater physical mobility within Soviet society. Whatever the explanation there is reason to believe that crime, at least in comparison with some other social problems, has become a greater source of frustration and concern for the Soviet leadership over the last decade. The 1961 introduction of the death penalty for economic crimes provides considerable support of this supposition, since no society—unless there is a radical shift in value orientation—is likely

---

* This point raises a more general dilemma of totalitarian social controls: how much or how little publicity should be given to acts of deviance or instances of dissent? When is it more prudent to suppress any evidence of them and when is it edifying to deplore them in public and thereby teach a lesson?

On the one hand, publicizing deviance, political or other types, creates an awareness of it which might not have existed before; shared propensities to deviance and discontent might be discovered, "infections" spread, and possible models provided inadvertently. On the other hand, when total silence envelops deviance and discontent their roots might be more difficult to ferret out; under the crust of enforced conformity and the apparent serene acceptance of the status quo more serious alienations might fester and contaminate. The denial of publicity to such attitudes prevents them from being exposed in a didactic manner; without publicizing acts of deviance and discontent their dangerousness or repugnance cannot be impressed upon the populace.

to make punishment more severe for a particular form of misbehavior unless it has become more widespread.

Although crime has become in the Soviet Union a legitimate topic for public discussion, social research, and ideological exhortation, its basic dimensions remain unknown.[12] At the time of this writing there are still no official (or unofficial) crime statistics available that would provide information of the regional or national distribution of various types of offenses and the handling of the offenders, and so forth. What we have are occasional, scattered figures (that is, percentages without the number of cases) about the incidence of a particular type of crime in a particular area. (Connor cited a table of percentages of extremely broad and rather vague categories of crimes for the USSR as a whole, compiled by one Soviet criminologist, which are of rather limited usefulness or reliability.) Without such data the comparisons with crime in the United States must, by necessity, be largely speculative.

From various sources of information three major facets of Soviet crime can be pieced together: it is preponderantly directed against property (and state or public property, for that matter); the majority of the offenders seem to be young; and a high (though again unspecified) proportion of it is committed in states of alcoholic intoxication. Soviet crime is, then, in at least one fundamental respect, similar to the American variety: its bulk consists of property violations. Statistical evidence in the United States shows the overwhelming preponderance of property crimes[13] over any other type, with the exception of traffic offenses. Traffic violations, unless resulting in the loss of life or serious injuries, are excluded in the United States from the range of criminal activities in popular awareness. Not unlike crimes against property—which are usually related to the high value put on material acquisition and success—traffic violations can also be better understood against the background of certain American values. If time, speed, efficiency, and activism are valued excessively, it is not surprising that people will take, metaphorically and literally, short cuts to attain these goals.

One should assume that traffic violations in the USSR constitute a relatively small part of the overall crime statistics in view of the limited number of motor vehicles.[14] We do not know, however, what is the ratio of violations per drivers or per passenger miles. It is not impossible that the figures would exceed those in the United States where roads and safety regulations are better, and where driving habits have been internalized by generations. There are some indications that car accidents are becoming more numerous in the Soviet Union, beginning to give rise to some official concern. (In 1969, 16,000 people were killed in automobile accidents in the largest of the constituent Republics of the Soviet Union, an extremely high figure considering the small number of cars.)[15]

While we can easily account for the different dimensions of traffic violations in the two societies and the related volume of accidents, crimes against property require more complex explanations in view of their high levels in *both* countries. Assuming a functional relationship between social structure and the prevailing forms of crime it may seem puzzling that countries whose social structures and many dominant values are as different as those of the United States and USSR may produce the same types of crime in comparable quantities. If we accept the still prevailing sociological explanation of American crimes against property as deriving from the success-oriented ethos of the United States—where material aspirations inculcated exceed opportunities provided for their gratification (an explanation that relies heavily on the concept of relative deprivation) —can we extend the same explanation to the Soviet Union? Surely the Soviet Union is not an "acquisitive society": there are institutionalized limits on acquiring private wealth and property. The official value system is far removed from the dominant American values: material success is not a major index of personal worth, material goods and services are not postulated to be the most important goals in life. In other words, the official Soviet values do not generate pressures, *comparable to the American,* to engage in law-breaking activities in order to achieve material wealth. This is true even if a decent standard of living for everybody is an officially supported objective. Success in Soviet society has indicators other than material possessions. Consumption per se is not such an important component of status, as it is in the United States. In the United States, and capitalist societies in general, the contrasts between standards of living and levels of consumption are highly visible, often conspicuously and deliberately displayed, thereby providing bases of comparison for all. Such contrasts exist to a much lesser degree in the Soviet Union. As we noted in Chapter 6, inequalities of material wealth and styles of life are far less visible: members of certain elite groups, especially the political ones, self-consciously segregate themselves from the rest of society who have no exact information about their styles of life. Few in the Soivet Union have any idea how the apartments of members of the elite are furnished, how they spend their leisure, how much their houses or cars cost, what their incomes are, and so forth. In the USSR the low visibility of the life style of the elite groups is also facilitated by the persisting traditionality of Soviet society. Rural areas are often substantially isolated from urban ones; peasants and even workers rarely communicate with or come into contact with members of the elite groups; models of high and elaborate consumption are not readily available.

Thus we cannot in the Soviet case satisfactorily explain crimes against property with reference to the pressure of dominant values* or by the ready availability of conspicuous models of lavish consumption which invite and stimulate imitation. Certainly the improvement in the standard of living has created such models on a moderate scale and their presence is probably a part of the explanation, as they contribute to the growth of expectations. But perhaps the full explanation of crimes against property is to be sought in the other direction, in the persistence of low living standards and the illicit efforts to improve them. In the USSR crimes against property are not generated by the fantasies and unreasonable expectations inculcated by the value system (not that all crimes are so motivated in the United States either) but are prompted by the modest desire to improve one's living standards, to supplement one's income.†

That in all probability, the majority of these crimes are committed against public or state property rather than private property reflects not only the greater abundance and availability of such property, but also the likelihood that people feel less inhibited about taking from abstract-impersonal entities than from individual per-

---

* "Dominant" as defined in our discussion of values in Chapters 4 and 5.

† B. A. Viktorov, USSR Deputy Minister of Internal Affairs made these remarks about stealing public property: "The majority of thefts are quite small in scale, but they grow like snowballs and as a whole they cause the national economy serious loss. We have been thinking . . . whether in a number of branches, in, for example the food and meat and dairy industries, we should not introduce a system of allowing a worker to buy at cost the goods he produces, and of course, in amounts that do not exceed his family's needs."16 The reflections of the Deputy Minister are revealing and their message obvious in the context. Allowing the workers to buy these goods at cost would be preferable to the present practice of helping themselves to them. Of particular interest is the fact that the industries singled out were food, meat, and dairy.

sons. One of the most strongly held aspirations of the Soviet regime (and perhaps its most obvious failure) has been to instill respect for public property.[17] For the average Soviet citizen what is public is impersonal, or at best, belonging to some distant group, the proverbial "they" of a hierarchical society, and to convince him of his personal involvement in the national economy remains a difficult task. Civic pride, community spirit, collectivism—qualities the regime has tried to foster over a period of half a century—have yielded few results so far as respect for public property is concerned. The errors of planning and the known instances of mismanagement of various sectors of the economy have helped to foster the feeling that what belongs to the public belongs to nobody.

Significantly, most Soviet crimes against property are committed at the place of employment, where goods and temptations are most readily available. To what degree such pilfering is also an expression of repressed hostility against the regime can only be guessed, but not substantiated. It is more than likely that little political sentiment enters into such crimes; they are basically rational and utilitarian. Surviving peasant traditions may also facilitate the violations of public property. Attitudes toward the landlord, toward the proverbially mismanaged Russian estates, might have been plausibly transferred to similarly (or even more) mismanaged state and collective farms,* and even to factories.

If our impressions are correct in regard to the second major characteristic of Soviet crime, namely, the preponderance of younger age groups among lawbreakers, the explanation is likely to be similar to that which is used to account for the corresponding phenomenon in other societies. Most juvenile offenders are not professional or habitual criminals. Juvenile delinquency for the most part is a passing stage of life tied to adolescent rebellion, restlessness, and

* In an autobiographical account a former exile in the Soviet countryside made these observations as a field guard at harvest time: "There is not much guarding an unarmed, disabled old man can do. But it's not so much the guarding that's important, as the regulations. It is forbidden to leave the grain unguarded. If the higher powers should find a grain heap unguarded, then the local leaders might have to go to prison. Not as if the grain would not have been pinched. Some pinched by the satchel, some by the pocketful, others in the water barrels in which water is taken to the tractor drivers. They stole in daylight, when the field guard has a statutory right to sleep. No thieves came by night. But had they come the field guard could have done nothing other than keep quiet. And had the robbers ordered him to do so, he would have helped them haul up the grain sacks on their wagon. . . ."[18]

relative freedom from social obligations and routine.[19] In comparison with adults the young in most societies, including the Soviet, have more discretionary time and fewer established ways of spending it. Like youth everywhere, the Soviet young people also have more physical energy than their elders, a factor of some importance since many criminal activities demand considerable physical exertions and mobility.

The close association between intoxication and law violations appears to be another major characteristic of Soviet crime, as conveyed by various Soviet sources.* We do not know to what degree this is exaggerated. Tying drunkenness, a type of behavior popularly excused and largely sanctioned by Russian culture, to criminal offenses (less readily excused) could assist in the campaign against alcoholism. Positing such a relationship might also seem desirable from an ideological point of view. Crimes committed in a state of intoxication are obviously less rational, more unmotivated. According to the official Soviet view there are simply no valid reasons in Soviet society to behave criminally, especially to choose criminal methods for improving one's standard of living. Wrongdoings under the influence of alcohol constitute less serious violations of public order, since they can be viewed more as acts of foolishness than criminality proper. Nonetheless, one cannot doubt the reality of a close association between crime and drunkenness, probably closer than in the United States. The explanation may lie in the greater strictness of the Soviet system of controls, internalized as well as legal. It may take a greater psychic effort for a Soviet citizen to become nonconformist in a lawbreaking manner than for an American because the former lives in a far more organized and repressive social environment. Therefore, the tendency to conform may at

---

* For example A. Gertsenzon, the noted Soviet criminologist observed that "it is common knowledge that drunkenness is one of the most important conditions conducive to the commission of crimes. In 1967 and 1968 the writer of these lines made a selective sociological-legal study of criminal cases and sentences handed down for crimes such as murder, rape, and malicious hooliganism, as well as larceny, robbery, and swindling. Despite the seemingly great difference between these crimes, the provocative role of alcohol was highly characteristic of all of them. Intoxication turns out to be characteristic not only of the criminals but also of their victims. This is true of the victims of murder, rape and robbery."[20]

It was also reported that "A justice of the Soviet Supreme Court revealed that 80% of all juvenile lawbreakers here committed their crimes while they were drunk. . . ."[21]

times have to be subverted with the assistance of an outside agent, alcohol.

Another characteristic manifestation of crime in the USSR—which has its well-known counterpart in the United States—is referred to as "hooliganism," or "malicious mischief and hooliganism." Hooliganism is a catchall phrase applied to a cluster of misbehaviors, mostly crimes against a person and public order. Hooliganism (sometimes used synonymously with vandalism) is very similar to what an American sociologist has called "malicious, negativistic, nonutilitarian" delinquency.[22] It can entail assault, provoking fights, using rude and abusive language, wanton destruction of property,* and (public or private) drunkenness. In other words, hooliganism represents actual or potential violence, a threat to public order and personal safety; it reflects the free-floating aggression most frequently found among groups of young lower-class males. Despite the apparent frequency of hooliganism it is likely that crimes of serious violence are less common in the USSR than in the United States. This guess is based on many factors. One is the difference between access to lethal weapons in the two societies. In the Soviet Union the American ease of access to firearms would evoke incomprehension. For political-ideological reasons, the Soviet state guards its monopoly over the control of weapons with great care. There are no constitutional assumptions about the right of the citizen to arm himself. Even hunters in the Soviet Union must submit applications which are carefully screened by the police before they can obtain licenses to own hunting rifles.* Political reliability is among the

* Interestingly enough forms of vandalism, all too familiar to American urban dwellers, are also reported from the Soviet Union, though again we have no statistical information about their magnitude comparable, say, to the gloomy annual reports of the New York City Board of Education stating the costs of thousands of school windows to be replaced. The Soviet transport organizations, similarly, do not report the number of seats slashed. On the other hand, there are press reports which suggest striking qualitative similarities: "In a new city borough, hundreds of young apple trees were set out along a wide boulevard. . . . But not a single fruit has ripened in the apple orchard. As early as June swarms of vandals raid the orchard. . . . They tear off the fruit while it is still green and in the process break the branches and trample the ground under the trees. It is difficult even to think of a place where vandals do not leave their dirty traces. It is they who throw burning matches into mailboxes, tear pages out of library books, and hoot from the gallery [at the theater]. . . . They can underhandedly darken people's joy, spoil their mood and poison their recreation."[23]

* Even "keeping a dagger at home without a permit is a crime" although in a survey of 218 Muscovites 79% were uninformed about this law.[24]

factors which presumably govern the granting of such permits. Such restrictions on access to firearms are undoubtedly among the factors which explain why armed robbery (often leading to murder in the U.S.) is virtually unknown in the Soviet Union.

As far as organized crime is concerned it is apparently limited to certain economic crimes. Soviet press reports have revealed the existence of elaborate criminal organizations engaged in defrauding the state or consumers or both by systematically embezzling, black marketing, or simply stealing state property. A high level of organization of some of these activities is also suggested by the fact that in some instances the systematic stealing of public property went on for years, in one recently reported instance, for eight years.[25] The elaborately bureaucratic organization of Soviet economy itself invites the development of elaborate efforts designed to thwart controls. Among such criminal ventures have been illegal "underground" manufacturing establishments which employed mental patients.[26] Such "enterprises" seem to be the closest approximations of organized crime.

We know a great deal more about crime in the United States. We have extensive statistics, thousands of studies, and the overabundant reports of the mass media. Whatever the inaccuracies or even distortions of these sources, it can safely be said that we know as much about the forms, quantitative dimensions, and sources of crime in the United States as probably has ever been known of crime in any society. The abundance of information in itself gives the impression that there is more crime in the United States than in the USSR or, for that matter, than anywhere else in the world. While it is likely that there is in fact more crime in the United States than in the Soviet Union, we cannot be completely certain: Soviet sources do not reveal the necessary information, and, possibly, Soviet authorities themselves have no clear idea about the volume of crime. It is not too far-fetched to assume that in an enormous, geographically and ethnically diverse country, where the communications network is unevenly developed, the collection of local crime statistics is deficient and reporting to the higher authorities tardy. It is even more probable that the bulk of petty crimes against state property is either never discovered or goes unreported. At the same time, to the extent that some traditional (peasant) values and quasi-traditional communities persist in the USSR, it can also be expected that they exercise a restraining influence on crime. Informal social controls tend to operate effectively in most rural communities.* Even in large urban areas the Soviet citizen spends more of his life in clearly defined institutional contexts than the American does, which increases the effectiveness of social controls. Economic crimes apart, there is reason to believe that there is less crime in a highly controlled and organized society, like the Soviet Union, than in a permissive and somewhat chaotic one like the United States.

Crime in the United States, and particularly its steady increase, has received a great deal of social-scientific and popular attention. The aspects of crime in America which have been of major concern include the high proportion of juveniles involved; the physical violence associated with lawbreaking; the concentration of many types of crime among disadvantaged ethnic groups; the great social and financial costs of crime and law enforcement; and finally, the presence of highly organized criminal enterprises (or crime syndicates) which have proved so far largely impervious to the attacks of various law enforcement agencies.[28] Virtually all experts agree that the high rates of crimes against property, as well as the often associated "functional" violence, are correlated with the American expectations of material success and facilitated by loose social controls, both formal and informal. The laxity of informal social controls is usually seen as the by-product of the mobility and heterogeneity of American society. However, in making the comparison with the Soviet Union it must also be pointed out that in American society the formal, institutional devices of crime control are *also* much weaker than is often realized. This is worth stressing because the major thrust of sociological theorizing about crime in the United States tends to focus on the inadequacy of the informal social controls which are inherent in the community. While such controls are doubtless increasingly ineffective, the additional inefficiency of administrative-police and judiciary control is often neglected. This weakness in turn reflects the American political and legal structure which is pluralistic, decentralized, and relatively permissive. For example,

* But Soviet rural areas are not immune from crimes, as the following, possibly unusual, report indicates: "How we used to live during the war! And after the war, too. We never hung padlocks on our cellars or hen-houses then; it never occurred to anyone that we had to do so. But now! Thieves have even stolen chinaware from an old woman. . . . It's shameful to lock up every little thing. That is not our way, that is not the peasant's way."[27]

there are no controls over population movements within the country and very little control of movement across the borders. By contrast in the USSR every change of residence has to be registered with the police, certain areas require permission before they can be entered, getting permission to go abroad is extremely difficult, and illegal exit is virtually impossible. In addition certain groups of the population —for example, agricultural workers and many former prisoners—are not free to move to a different location unless granted special permission. Under such circumstances the apprehension of criminals is a great deal easier. A person cannot get "lost" in the Soviet Union as easily as he can in the United States; the legally required possession of personal identity papers (internal passport) makes this almost impossible. Despite the size of the Soviet Union people cannot move at will from one place to another and assume a new name, a new identity. By contrast, the often limited and deficient collaboration between American local, state, and federal law enforcement agencies adds to the loopholes that actual and would-be offenders can take advantage of. And escaping abroad and especially to a neighboring country is a correspondingly easy task for American fugitives from the law.

Of all types of criminal behavior in the two societies juvenile delinquency seems to have the closest similarities. In both cases the contributing factors appear to be frustrated expectations of some type (in the American case greatly inflamed by the mass media), an excess of discretionary time, inadequate parental supervision, poor integration into the community,* and the defects of the school sys-

---

* As a Soviet author put it: "Children who are noted for bad behavior in school are not, as a rule, bound by ties of friendship with the class collective. Moreover they are often isolated and this weakens . . . their sense of moral responsibility to their comrades for their behavior. . . . 72% of the minors against whom proceedings were instituted did not attend school, i.e., they stood outside a healthy children's collective. . . . A large percentage of law violations were recorded in areas of new construction projects, where, of course, school and class collectives have not yet taken shape where the adolescent has no friends or comrades whose opinion or judgment he would value and whose censure would be unbearable for him. . . ." While these observations do not account for the opposite phenomenon, the presence of *groups* of delinquents, they do bring into focus deviance resulting from the absence of strong informal social controls.

The author quoted has essentially the same explanation for crime among young workers: ". . . the reason for the large percentage of crime among working adolescents is not only the weakness of supervision, the presence of free evening time, but also and to a large extent the circumstance that young workers do in fact live outside a healthy

tem. In this realm the Soviet Union seems to have made great strides in catching up with the United States. Boredom, cynicism, hedonism, and frivolousness among Soviet youth are reported with increasing frequency.* A growing number of young people in the USSR fail to spend their free time fruitfully, are disrespectful of their elders (who often allegedly pamper them†), are bored with school and communal activities, alienated and mistrustful of the adult world and looking for "kicks" in a spirit of escapism reminiscent of their American counterparts. As noted before in the United States many of these problems are intensified and concentrated among members of certain ethnic groups (especially Negroes and Puerto Ricans), whereas in the Soviet Union ethnicity does not seem to be correlated with juvenile delinquency.

There are a number of major differences, as well as some similarities, between the explanations and theories of crime in American and Soviet societies. Generally speaking there is a greater diversity of explanations in the United States, a diversity which reflects the different orientations within the social sciences consistent with the degree of pluralism in the society at large. Not surprisingly the Soviet explanations move within more limited perimeters. They are characterized by a curious duality. On the higher theoretical level crime is viewed as basically extrinsic and incidental to Soviet society and its institutions. Unlike capitalist societies where crime is an or-

---

collective of peers. . . ."29 This of course raises the question—unexplained elsewhere in the article—as to why do "in fact" young workers live outside "a healthy collective of peers."

* A study of young lawbreakers found the following attitudes: "The lawbreakers in the second group [unlike the repentant ones in the first] do not experience pangs of conscience. After committing the crime they fear only punishment. If the crime remains undetected these adolescents are tranquil, satisfied, even happy. . . . The third group consists of adolescents who consciously pit themselves against society. Not only do they fail to experience conflict between negative needs and moral motives, but their violations of the law finds support in their conscious antimoral convictions. They satisfy their strongly developed antisocial needs by following a cynical 'morality' of their own: 'Only fools don't steal'; 'if you don't steal, you can't live'; etc. Their conviction of these 'amoral principles' is often accompanied by a sense of pride in their 'fearlessness' and a flaunting of their criminal behavior."30

† As exemplified in an all too didactic confession of a young criminal: "I learned early to spend money. I grew up without a father and my grandmother spoiled me. As I grew older, I demanded more money. I learned to smoke, treated my pals to vodka and played cards. No matter how much my grandmother gave me, it never seemed enough. I took up theft. And here I am."31

ganic, inherent phenomenon, tied to the social structure and values (and to competition in particular), crime in the Soviet Union is an unnatural phenomenon, alien to it. Nonetheless it does exist, though it is often claimed, without statistical substantiation, that its volume has been steadily decreasing. The most characteristic and self-contradictory feature of many Soviet explanations of (Soviet) crime, is the attempt to locate its sources outside Soviet society. To a large extent this is due to ideological restraints which do not permit sociological analysis to direct attention to any institutional-structural defect in Soviet society. Locating the sources of crime outside Soviet society is accomplished by recourse to two concepts: "survivals" and "contamination." Survivals refer to customs, traditions, and attitudes which originate in pre-Soviet times, in the past and the exploitative social order characteristic of it. Crime, hankering for private property, sexual depravity, antisocial acts of any description, as well as religious beliefs, belong to the category of survivals. Soviet theoreticians from the 1930's onwards have been asserting that institutional transformations in themselves are insufficient to change attitudes and therefore massive educational and propaganda efforts were required to inculcate desirable behavior patterns.[32] The new line amounted to an implicit retreat from orthodox Marxist economic determinism which proved unsuitable to explain and excuse many social problems which persisted well after the fundamental institutional changes took place.* The basic problem was that although the entire social environment—which, according to Marxism-Leninism determines consciousness (or attitudes)—had been radically transformed, people had not changed substantially enough to abstain from crime. The proposition that consciousness lags behind institutional change has served to some extent to fill the gap in theoretical explanations.[34]

It is noteworthy (and indicative of the limited explanatory powers of the concept of survivals) that no empirical inquiries have been undertaken to specify the conditions necessary for the elimination of survivals (or the conditions which favor them most). Soviet social

---

* This is how S. P. Pavlov, head of the Young Communist League (Komsomol) made the point: "It would be a big mistake to think that the very fact of living in the land of the Soviets, in the conditions of socialist reality, presupposes a communist world outlook in a young person."[33] If so, then—contrary to Marx's proposition—existence no longer determines consciousness, at least not in Soviet society.

scientists have not conducted studies of groups most and least likely to be the victims of survivals, of the relationship between age and the propensity to be effected by survivals, of the relevant socioeconomic factors and the relationship between different types of survivals and other attitudes. Such questions presumably have not been asked because the answers might have undermined the whole theory by showing that the undesirable phenomena denoted by the concept are generated by Soviet society itself and not by the past.

Western capitalist societies and the "contaminating" influences emanating from them are represented as the other major sources of crime. These influences, according to Soviet statements, are twofold. First, such societies provide corrupting examples of behavior, especially by means of the mass media, which particularly affect the suggestible young. Secondly, there is also a deliberate effort on part of the political-ideological protagonists in these societies to subvert and corrupt Soviet people, first and foremost, Soviet youth.[35] Beyond accusing the Western mass media of being an instrument of these efforts, little else is offered by way of explanation concerning the nature of and processes involved in this type of subversion and contamination.

We suggested earlier that Soviet approaches to crime are characterized by a curious duality. At one level we find the highly ideological and rather unrealistic explanations designed to locate the sources of Soviet crime outside Soviet society, either in the past or abroad. However, when Soviet discussions of crime descend from the theoretical level to the analysis of actual cases they become, perhaps by necessity, far more realistic and sociological. It is of particular interest that both American and Soviet discussions of crime ultimately and inescapably raise the issue of informal social controls and their breakdown in modern, urban, secular, and mobile societies. In 1969 an unusually specific Soviet report of criminological research addressed itself to the comparison of the types and rates of crime in rural and urban areas. Some of the findings were these:

> The study established that crime among minors is significantly more widespread in the city than in rural localities. . . . For each year studied, the crime rate among minors in Vladimir is three to five times as high as in the rural localities of Yuryev-Polsky District. . . . In the process of the study significant similarities were discerned in several indices of crime among minors

in the city and in rural localities. The similar indices include, first of all, the structure of crime (about 60% of the crimes among minors were thefts of state and public property and hooliganism). The following data also coincided: a) the prevalence of group crimes among minors (78% in the city, 70.4% in rural localities); b) the percentage of juveniles who committed crimes in a state of alcoholic intoxication (66.6% in the city, 64.6% in the country-side); c) an identical breakdown of the juvenile offenders by age and occupation; the ages 16 and 17 predominated both in the city and the countryside; the highest percentage of crimes (more than half) were committed by working teenagers; d) the fact that in most cases the juveniles lived in families with two parents before committing the offense; e) the low educational level of the parents (84% of the fathers and 78% of the mothers in the city and 84% of the fathers and 83% of the mothers in the countryside had an elementary school education).

Theft and robbery are more widespread in the city than in the countryside (14% and 3.6% respectively, in the city and 9.4% and 0.9% in the countryside). . . .

The findings of the study confirmed that in most cases both parents work. . . .

14.3% of the urban teenagers had friends with records of mis-conduct. . . . Among the rural schoolboys, only 4.2% had friends of this sort.[36]

Evidently there is a third, and most surprising, approach to crime in the Soviet Union today. It has been criticized, though rather mildly and without ideological fervor:

N. Struchkov and B. Utevsky . . . while denying innate criminal-ity, affirm the existence of innate "socially negative instincts" such as, for example, cruelty, callousness, vindictiveness, malice, men-dacity, etc. which in their opinion lie at the basis of crime. Ya. Iorish . . . makes the theoretical assumption that there are people with a biological disposition to crime. He deems it pos-sible to include malicious hooligans, for instance, among such individuals.[37]

Somewhat similar has been the approach of two other Soviet crimi-nologists who sought the clue to crime in the personalities of the of-fenders, or at any rate wished to redress the balance between so-called external or objective and personality factors. Some of their comments are significant:

> it was not living conditions and material circumstances that pre-vented lawbreakers from attaining the proper education and level of culture. On the contrary they had all the possibilities for this but did not wish to make use of them because their impoverished interests were oriented . . . to drink, lead dissipated lives. . . . People sometimes draw the conclusion that everything depends upon these objective conditions and that the individual bears the least responsibility. . . . Fatalism of this sort does not withstand criticism. . . . It is not conditions of material life that drive the "safeguarders of the traditions of capitalism" to the path of crime. Everything turns on the level of consciousness and culture of these individuals, on their unwillingness to study, work and take recreation as do Soviet people, and on their desire to live as parasites. . . ."[38]

It is not surprising that such explanations of crime are becoming more acceptable in Soviet society since, from an ideological stand-point, it is preferable to hold the individual responsible, rather than the purposefully created social environment guided and legitimated by (allegedly) infallible social-political forces.

As the above and other examples indicate, not all Soviet discus-sions of criminal behavior invoke or stress the concept of survivals.[39] The limited number of concrete studies (or at any rate the limited number reported) and the more frequent journalistic treatments of the subject end up, interestingly enough, by singling out the same factors associated with crime that are central to the Western studies and theories of crime. They are the following:

1. The family environment (broken homes, lack of parental super-vision, drinking parents, parents with limited education);
2. The indifference of the community (in the Soviet context this can mean neighbors, school authorities, youth, party, trade union organization; the collective at the place of work);
3. Low level of formal education of the delinquent;
4. Various forms of escapist tendencies (heavy drinking, hanging around in the street, waste of time);
5. Disruptive social change (World War II and its effects on the upbringing of children);

6. Bad examples: the influence of more experienced adult criminals;
7. The offender's desire for an easy life and luxuries (but not his poverty per se).

Crime in Soviet society, then, seems in no way fundamentally different in its origin from crime in many other contemporary societies. To the extent that Soviet society has become urbanized and secularized, many of the sources of crime are highly similar to those in the United States. At the same time it is likely that—with the exception of crimes against public property—there is a lesser volume of crime in all categories in the Soviet Union than in the United States. If this is the case, the difference can be explained without undue difficulty. There are two major impediments of crime: the fear of authority and limited expectations. Both are more prevailing in the Soviet Union than in the United States.

Responses to Crime

While the professed aims of crime control are virtually identical in the two countries—namely crime prevention and the rehabilitation of the apprehended criminal—the trends in the actual institutional response show considerable divergence, especially over time.

The Soviet Union started out in the 1920's with penal policies that emphasized not punishment but character reform. This approach rested on the optimism and idealism that pervaded the Soviet political elite and intelligentsia in the years following the revolution, a period of bold experimentation and radical social change. It was a time when Lenin's words about the necessary withering away of crime in a socialist society still had a ring of plausibility.[40] It was widely believed that the structural-institutional changes that took place, and above all the liquidation of private ownership of the means of production, removed the conditions which generate crime and that the socialist transformation of society would deprive people of the motivation to engage in antisocial activities of any kind. This outlook afforded Soviet policy-makers the optimism which in turn generated a lenient and humane approach toward nonpolitical offenders. The leniency and rejection of vindictiveness rested on the traditional Marxist belief in the social-environmental determination of crime. If society is responsible there was no point and no justice in punishing individuals; the criminal is to be treated like the victim of a passing disease. This is how a sympathetic Western visitor of the period observed these Soviet attitudes:

> Crime according to Soviet law is the outcome of antagonisms existing in a society divided into classes: it is always the result of faulty social organization and bad environment. The word punishment is not approved of: it has been replaced by the phrase "measures of social defense. . . ." Sentences are short and once the sentence has been served the miscreant is readmitted into everyday life with no . . . scar of shame, no brand of having been a "convict. . . ." Soviet criminology seems to assume that the "criminal" is not a criminal. He is not to be treated as an outcast. . . . He is an "unfortunate" sick, weak or maladjusted and must be trained to become a functioning member of society. This theory is carried out in practice in the communes run by the OGPU.*[41]

Thirty-six years later the 1969 "Principles of Corrective Legislation" does not shy away from the word and concept of punishment. It includes "Measures of Punishment Applicable to Individuals Deprived of Freedom" that entails

> confinement of inmates of corrective labor colonies in punitive cell blocks . . . confinement of prison inmates in punitive dungeon cells . . . the transfer of inmates of standard-regime, intensified-regime and strict-regime corrective labor colonies to cells up to six months; the transfer of inmates of special-regime colonies to solitary confinement for up to one year. . . .[42]

Even the principles of handling minors incorporates a punitive streak: "The basic means for correcting and reforming inmates of labor colonies for minors are: the penal regime, socially useful labor, general education and technical-vocational schooling and political upbringing work."[43] It is noteworthy that the enumeration of the means of correction begins with "the penal regime," that is, with the punitive element of the process.

Articles and letters in the press indicate a highly punitive attitude among certain segments of the "opinion-makers" and also the public at large:

* OGPU was at the time the abbreviated name of the Soviet political police or "state security organs" which at present are known as KGB.

> In our country there are no objective, chronic social causes of crime. Therefore, our criminal legislation should proceed on the assumption that crime can have no place in a socialist country. . . .
>
> A thief in our country must be punished for the very fact that he stole, because it is forbidden to steal, regardless of the object stolen or its value.
>
> The simple Russian words "it is forbidden" must be elevated in our country to an indisputable height and must have the character of a sacred taboo. . . .
>
> The Criminal Code must be more severe. More types of crimes— for example bribery, embezzlement and pilfering of socialist property, escape from prison, etc.—should be punishable by death than is the case. . . .
>
> Prisons must and can no longer be regarded as an institution for upbringing and reformation measures. Prison is a place of isolation and punishment for socially dangerous . . . elements in our society. . . .[44]

In all fairness it must be pointed out that such views are not officially accepted. They were in fact strongly criticized by a legal scholar even though he himself admitted that "for the time being it is still necessary to punish criminals, and, if society's interests require it, to punish them severely, harshly, relentlessly."[45] Reflecting the same mood of public punitiveness, another article noted that: "This dispute [about the nature of punishment] is not new. It has been going on for years. In this time, there have been the decrees of 1961 and 1966 increasing liability for crime and hooliganism but nonetheless the letters [to the newspaper] again sound a call for making punishment still more severe. . . ."[46]

The changes in the Soviet approach toward crime reflect (as do other trends), over time the progressive totalitarianization of the system, the retreat from the early idealism, and the ideological shift from economic to political determinism. And while ordinary, non-political criminals continue to be better treated than political ones, the past decades have been marked by increasingly harsh penalties for them, too. Among these, the introduction of the death penalty for economic crimes (in 1961) is but one vivid manifestation of the punitive spirit. Considerable lip service is still paid to the goal of rehabilitation, yet often it seems implied that such changes can best be accomplished by strictness. When surveying the period from the 1920's to the 1960's, it appears that Soviet penal policies moved from an emphasis on character reform and the responsibility of society to a stress on punishment (and deterrence) and the responsibility of the individual.* Even in cases when the individual's responsibility for misbehavior is said to be shared by his collective, his place of employment, the mass organizations, or neighbors, in the final analysis these considerations do not significantly alter the nature of punishment. The shrill note of vindictiveness is persistently heard in the Soviet press: loafers, parasites, hooligans, and economic criminals are condemned; the judicial authorities are chastised at times for being too gentle, for overusing parole, for allowing a too permissive regime in prisons or corrective labor camps, and for letting parents send money to their children "under correction."

American penal policies have been moving in a different direction. While in the 1920's the United States was lagging behind the Soviet Union in applying the principle of rehabilitation, today it is generally acknowledged that punishment, at least in principle, is not a primary objective of penal policy.[48] The movement against the abolition of capital punishment—culminating in the 1972 Supreme Court decision making the death penalty unconstitutional—has made corresponding progress, and (as also noted in Chapter 3) there has been a downward trend in the use of capital punishment which some states have abolished and none applied since 1968. Again, these are the figures:

Executions in USA[49]

1930-39	1940-49	1950-59	1960-62	1968
166	127	72	48	0

The diffusion of the findings of the social sciences, psychology and psychiatry in particular, has contributed to a less punitive approach toward crime control in the United States and to the viewing of the

* "The first criminal code, adopted in 1922, provided up to one year's deprivation of freedom as punishment for hooliganism. The Criminal Code of 1926 raised the penalty for malicious hooliganism to two years' deprivation of freedom. In 1935 the punishment was raised to five years' deprivation of freedom. In the first quarter of 1965 the people's court of Moscow's Leningrad Borough . . . sentenced 65% of the persons convicted of hooliganism to deprivations of freedom, many of them for terms of three to five years."[47]

criminal more as a maladjusted, sick or socially wronged individual in need of treatment than a willfully evil and hence punishable figure. To be sure such a conception of the criminal is not accepted by many segments of the public at large and many politicians or by those staffing the law enforcement machinery, in particular policemen and prison guards. And even when a nonpunitive, reform-oriented approach toward criminals is upheld, its implementation is lacking for the most part.

It is difficult to assess progress made along these lines in view of the heterogeneity of the American law enforcement machinery. Penal policies vary from state to state, from North to South, from urban to rural areas, and even with the ethnic status and social class of the offender. The administration of justice in the United States is influenced by factors which are not present in the Soviet Union. The degree to which ethnicity affects law enforcement has been widely noted and it is reflected in the proportional overrepresentation of Negroes in prisons and among those arrested by the police.[50] Socioeconomic status, expressed in the financial ability to purchase competent legal defense, is another significant factor which appears to distort the distribution and quality of legal punishment.[51] The chances for a middle-, upper-middle-, or upper-class individual to be arrested, and if so to be sentenced, and if sentenced to serve a prison sentence are considerably smaller than for his lower-class counterpart.

In this brief survey of American penal policies the recently intensified movement for prison reform should also be noted. The prison uprisings of the early 1970's have sharply increased public awareness of the defects of prisons and detention centers, leading at once to demands for humanizing (or even abolishing) prisons *and* to make them more tightly controlled to discourage uprisings and especially the taking of hostages by prisoners. It remains a matter of dispute to what extent such rebellions reflect the general rise of expectations in American society reaching into prisons, political agitation among prisoners, the fact, argued by prison officials, that increasingly inmate populations are composed of the more violent and determined criminals (since lesser offenders are more and more frequently on probation or paroled), or simply a protest, born of despair, against the dehumanizing futility of prison life.

The lesser punitiveness of the American system of law enforce-

ment is also related to certain social and cultural trends. Notwithstanding the cries for law and order, American society of the 1960's
was characterized by a growing ethical relativism, the decline of old
certainties and values which are the mainspring of any harshly
punitive system of justice. Unless there is strong belief in social
values, their violation will not provoke the sense of outrage which
seeks severe punishment, a phenomenon Durkheim observed. When,
for example, state property is enshrined, as in the Soviet Union, its
private expropriation will bring forth demands for the severe punishment of the wrongdoers. When private property was venerated,
as in, say, 19th-century England or the United States, its violators
were treated without mercy. But today private property in American
society is no longer surrounded with the same reverence as it used
to be, nor has state property been elevated to a new pedestal. Consequently, crimes against property are dealt with less harshly than
in the Soviet Union. In a society (such as the United States) that
has a bad conscience about the treatment of minority groups, qualifications enter into the administration of justice. Poverty, for example, is no longer prima facie evidence of poor character (as it was
once regarded) but rather an extenuating circumstance. Just as in
Soviet society the alleged perfection of social institutions increases
the responsibility of the individual, conversely in the United States
the growing awareness of the faults of social institutions—and an
attendant growth of a sociological environmentalism—predisposes toward greater leniency* toward those who break the law. The overall
decline of authority in American society provides further pressures
toward milder punishment. Changes in penal policy are further suggested by the decline of the prison population from a ratio of 132
(per 100,000 of the civilian population) in 1940 to 99.1 in 1967 and
by the related growth of probation and parole.[52] It should be noted,
however, that such changes continue to coexist with serious defects
of the correctional system and with instances of the brutal mistreatment of prisoners.[53]

A comparison of American and Soviet public attitudes toward
punishment (which often differ from the official attitudes), suggests
a number of similarities. In American society attitudes toward pun-

* Another more striking manifestation of the same tendency is the claim, put forward
by some radical social critics, that every black person in prison is, by definition, a political prisoner in a society which treats black people unjustly at every level.

ishment are differentiated along political and socioeconomic lines even though political crime as such is hardly an issue. White middle-class and upper-middle-class liberals of the relatively secure suburbs favor leniency toward the rioters or muggers of the central city, while the lower middle-class and working-class residents or neighbors of these areas favor their strict punishment. So do most slum dwellers.[54] Thus the demand for "law and order" has two sources. On the one hand, there are fears deriving from racial prejudice (and reinforced by statistics showing that most crimes of violence are committed in the slums and by blacks and Puerto Ricans), but on the other hand, there are highly realistic apprehensions rooted in the experience of insecurity prevailing in most urban areas. In the Soviet case, public punitiveness is in part a reflection and result of an authoritarian spirit and intolerance toward deviance that permeates society as a whole and has been selectively cultivated by the highest authorities themselves.

There is apparently a further similarity in the attitudes toward crime expressed in the reluctance of many American and Soviet citizens to become involved with or supportive of the law enforcement process. The unwillingness to help the police in apprehending criminals, to help those assaulted, and to report crimes, is a well-known, much publicized phenomenon in American society.[55] Less well known are some corresponding attitudes in the Soviet Union. An interesting indication of their existence is a statement by the Chairman of the Criminal Cases Colloquium of the USSR Supreme Court:

> It is necessary to wage an insistent struggle against the widespread and tenacious opinion that to be a witness is supposedly something shameful. What a strange delusion! To appear in our Soviet court; to testify truthfully, honestly and candidly about everything one knows positively about a case; to help the court . . . all this is honorable, important to the state and socially useful.[56]

American and Soviet approaches toward crime control differ primarily in relation to the societal values backing up the institutional practices. There is an impression of a growing inability at various levels of American institutions to cope with crime, from apprehending the criminal to sentencing and segregating him. Law enforcement in the Soviet Union seems to be more swift and decisive—in part following from the nature of a totalitarian political system—but in neither societies is there much, if any, evidence of successful rehabilitation programs.

Violence in the United States

It seems to us that violence in the United States, although touched upon under other topics (notably political extremism and crime) is a phenomenon that needs to be examined separately. No analysis of American society of the 1960's can omit violence as a social problem in its own right. Indeed, violence is a problem of which there is a seemingly unprecedented public awareness, even self-consciousness.[57] The propensity to violence is an element in American life that enters into and magnifies many of its other problems, notably crime and political conflict.

The varieties of violence and the situations and types of behavior in which they are manifest are almost endless. The following classification is an attempt to distinguish the major types of violence in American society:

1. Criminal violence which includes homicide, assault, rape, and robbery, all of which have shown striking increases between 1960-68: 36, 65, 67, and 119 per cent, respectively.[58]

2. Political violence, which in the 1960's had four major expressions: assassinations, bombings, campus disturbances, and ghetto riots. Of these the slum riots are not a purely political phenomenon, but partake of both political and criminal content in that looting is frequently associated with them. Nor is campus violence completely political for it involves various elements of apolitical, stylized and expressive behavior.

3. Voyeuristic violence is involved in the production and consumption of violence in the mass media, certain forms of entertainment and some spectator sports. The phenomenon of voyeuristic violence also helps to explain the reluctance of people to interfere with fights or go to the aid of those attacked, and the encouragement given by passive bystanders to rampaging mobs and sometimes to individuals about to commit suicide.

4. Violence as a form of self-expression probably enters into all categories of violent behavior but more spectacularly in some than others. It plays an important part, for example, in student disturb-

ances. In these more importance is often attached to the performance and experience of specific acts of violence than to their results. Violence as self-expression derives its appeal from its affinity with self-assertion and liberation from internalized inhibitions or externally imposed restraints. Often it is viewed as self-purification.[59] Violence as a form of self-assertion also enters into the actions of various extremist groups (such as the Weathermen), into gang fights and possibly bombings or other destructions of property which may have no clear political message.

5. Finally, there is random violence which probably also incorporates elements of the self-expressive type. This form of violence is in some ways the most disturbing* since the motives for engaging in it cannot be readily comprehended; random violence, like virtue, is its own reward and its appeal stems from the murky underworld of sadism and cruelty.† It is difficult to avoid using the word "pathological" when one considers such crimes. The murder or torture of people (especially of the old or very young or the helpless) is repugnant enough when indulged in for discernible reasons (for example, robbery). But when such activities are undertaken for the sheer pleasure of inflicting imaginatively devised forms of suffering, sociological explanations falter and detachment is difficult to maintain.[62] Presumably similar crimes also occurred in the past (in America as elsewhere) but we knew less about them since the means for

* According to Jules Feiffer, "Random violence gets more attention today than any other domestic problem, having replaced civil rights as the newest hot issue that we intend to do nothing about." The fascination with random violence has many causes but one among them is similar to the sources of interest in other social problems, as again, Feiffer points out: ". . . the desire to expose the hidden festering roots of contemporary society is mixed with the desire to be made rich by the society one is exposing."[60]

Indeed exposé literature of various types (usually a mixture of popular sociology, commercial sensationalism, and a dash of masochistic soul-searching) has in itself become a minor social problem, because of the possibility that too much public catharsis might become a substitute for action and social policy.

† While such attitudes appear to be primarily characteristic of American society they are by no means unknown in the Soviet Union. A newspaper article on cruelty included the following incidents: ". . . near Moscow, one Volkov, a mechanic, poured gasoline on a bull and set the animal on fire . . . in Moscow the pensioners Yevdokia Zinovyevna and Anna Alekseyevna put needles and poison in food and gave it to animals . . . the manager of the Quiet Nook Young Pioneer Camp in Kostroma destroyed all the birds' nests in the forest adjoining the camp . . . right here is one of the sources of juvenile delinquency . . . it begins with senseless cruelty to a puppy, to a bird, and later perhaps in turn to a person. . . ."[61]

disseminating such information were lacking, or even if available, publicity about them was constrained by prevailing standards of decorum or morality.* Thus it is difficult to draw enlightening sociological conclusions from cases like that of the mass murders of Richard Speck in Chicago, the children in New York who set the Bowery bums on fire, or the bizarre depredations of the Manson "family" in California. The perpetrators of such acts are often defined as mentally ill people, but whether or not we have more of them today than in earlier times we do not know, nor do we know how their numbers compare with those in the Soviet Union or what outlets their counterparts might find there for similar impulses. It is, however, quite certain that both the random and the more "rational" or purposeful types of violence are facilitated in the United States by the easy availability of firearms—in itself an indication of what might be called the culture of violence.[63]

Violence in American society may have distinct historical and sociological explanations. The circumstances and attitudes which provide a backdrop for understanding the propensity to violence in America include individualism, impatience, mobility, preoccupation with success and achievement, and the belief that shortcuts to the latter can be found. Egalitarian and individualistic Americans have little respect for or fear of authority, an attitude which readily combines with indifference and contempt toward law.[64] The violent streak in the American character has also been traced to the traditions of frontier days when self-reliance and muscle power, as well as the skilled use of firearms, were often preconditions of physical survival or prosperity. There is also an affinity between violence toward humans and violence toward nature. Perhaps what is distinctive about American violence is the attitude of sweeping obstacles out of the way, be they humans, animals, or trees. In this respect a source of propensity to violence is the belief in the achievability of almost anything, the belief in the fruits of aggression.

In the 1960's several factors converged to make violence a more serious problem. First, the mass media have thrived on reporting and

---

* This might be one of the few merits of censorship; in the so-called socialist countries, the USSR included, this type of sensationalism cannot flourish and the readers are not treated to blow-by-blow descriptions of horrifying crimes and photographs of the victims (though details about victims of political violence in other countries may be published for propaganda purposes).

embellishing it and have helped to spread models of violent behavior. Secondly, the easy availability of efficient and inexpensive firearms has facilitated the gratification of violent impulses and the commission of crimes.* Thirdly, there has been an actual increase in certain violent crimes in urban areas (thus public concern had been grounded in reality). Fourthly, the discontent of urban Negroes has increasingly taken violent expression, notably in riots, but also in attacks on policemen and firemen and in some instances on schools and teachers. Fifth, student violence on college campuses has also erupted during the decade and shattered widespread American stereotypes of serenity, fun, or diligent scholarship associated with the campus. Finally, entering into these several expressions of violence has been a growing belief (especially among the young) in untrammeled self-expression and passionate commitment which often takes violent forms. An observation about American literature can be readily generalized to many aspects of American society today:

> [The] image of violence . . . arise[s] from an international disenchantment with the view that life is essentially decent, rational and peaceful. . . . American writers have wrought a synthesis between such rebellious antirationalism and the older native tradition of the individualistic hero who seeks to prove himself by violent acts.[66]

Two questions in particular require further attention: It there more violence today in the United States than previously? Is there anything about American violence that distinguishes it from violence in other societies?

The *Report of the Commission on Violence* states that:

> even excluding the American Revolution and the Civil War, there have been periods in the American past when relative civil commotion—as measured by deaths, injuries and property damage—has exceeded that of the 1960's. A statistical study of American newspapers over the past 150 years confirms the historical impression that America experienced several periods of greater relative turbulence during the 19th century.

* ". . . There are now about 90 million firearms in the United States. Half of the Nation's 60 million households possess at least one gun. In the decade since 1958 . . . nearly 30 million guns have been added to the civilian stockpile. . . . Annual rifle and shotgun sales have doubled since 1963. Annual handgun sales have quadrupled."[65]

The most violent urban riot in American history remains the New York draft riot of 1863. The largest vigilante movement was the San Francisco Vigilance Committee of the 1880's.

Proportionately more death occurred as a result of racial lynching and labor violence around the turn of the century than in the contemporary period.*[67]

The belief that violence in the 1960's has assumed unheard-of proportions is in part created by the mass media, without which we simply would not know—beyond our immediate neighborhood or community—who murdered whom and how, who was most recently kidnaped for how much ransom, what sort of riots took place in slums and on campuses, what are the national crime statistics, how criminals behave in their private lives, what they look like, what are the most favored ways of doing away with people, and so forth. More significantly, without television and the movies we would not have so many of the vivid visual images of violence which create such a powerful awareness of it. Despite their claims to the contrary, the mass media are more than neutral reporters or bookkeepers of violent events. The preference for the gruesome, exciting, dramatic, shocking, or bizarre—for the violent—is built into the fabric of mass media in pluralistic societies where they are competing under commercial pressures for the attention of the audience. Violence is newsworthy not only for the reasons noted above, but also because, for the majority of the public, it still represents relatively unusual and hence interesting behavior. It is a measure of the growing commonness of violence that some successful publications find it necessary to devote special efforts to depicting its more unusual varieties to

* While there might not have been more violence in the U.S. in the 1960's than in other periods, there has been more violent crime in the United States than in numerous comparable societies: "A comparison of reported violent crime rates in this country with those in other modern, stable nations shows the United States rape rate clear leader. Our homicide rate is more than twice that of our closest competitor, Finland, and from 4 to 12 times higher than the rates in a dozen other advanced countries, including Japan, Canada, England and Norway. Similar patterns are found in the rates of other violent crimes; averages computed for the years 1963-67 show the United States rape rate to be 12 times that of England and Wales and double that of Canada, our aggravated assault rate is double that of England and Wales and 18 times that of Canada."[68]

maintain what might be an otherwise sagging public interest in, for example, ordinary murders.*

But the preoccupation of the mass media with violence is not the only explanation for the contemporary awareness of it. There is a morbid fascination with violence in American society today which is a part of the broader syndrome of social masochism, or what Spengler called "culture pessimism." This is the pervasive feeling that everything is wrong and doomed and the violent behavior of groups and individuals (whatever their motives), is only one among the multiple manifestations of an underlying malaise, for some, the only redeeming force. Satire captures this mood more accurately than scales of anomie or alienation:

> Many Americans will be disappointed if there is no apocalypse this year. It has been forecast, promised and talked about for so long that the nation seems to have developed a need for it. . . .
>
> It is a rare evening when a search of the TV channels does not flush a panel of distinguished firebrands shrouded in crocodile gloom about the imminence of doomsday. . . .
>
> Everything at last is thinkable and, in the best American tradition, convertible into fun.[70]

Thus the belief in the pervasiveness and intensification of violence is also related to a national mood of self-punitiveness (at any rate among large segments of the middle classes, academics, and the so-called opinion-makers). They see various forms of violence as a reaction to the corruption and injustice in American society, a punishment visited upon us by the judgments of history and sociology.

It would seem then that violence plays a complex part in American of it as something we brought upon ourselves for allowing the various life today. On the one hand, there is the awareness and expectation is a growing revulsion and indignation about violence and some of its most conspicuous expressions: crime in the streets and riots. Hence, we have the "law and order" issue in politics and criticism of

---

* Thus the *National Enquirer* and its numerous competitors specialize in compiling written and photographic records of exceptionally brutal and unusual forms of violence, such as baby-killing or cannibalism. Similar trends are evident in movies where innovative portrayal of violence manifests itself in "modernizing" it through James Bond-type science fiction technology and in the presentation of uninhibited "simple" brutality of the "New Western" movies featuring Clint Eastwood ("A Fistful of Dollars," and the like) and his colleagues.[69]

the courts for "pampering" criminals, public misgivings about apparently permissive correctional policies (for example, the granting of paroles), growing investment in police forces and rapidly growing popularity of guard dogs* and firearms for self-protection. And finally there is also a voyeuristic approach and tacit approval of certain types of violence, as well as its occasional glorification by political extremists.† As an observer has noted, many types of violence require a "supportive audience, . . . a combination of people personally willing to use violence and an audience to which they play and which will offer them encouragement and moral support."[74]

Poverty and Living Conditions

Paradoxically poverty is seen as a social problem in the United States, but not in the Soviet Union. It is an American social problem to a large extent *because* the standard of living is high and consequently expectations are also higher. In the Soviet Union, against the background of generally low living standards, poverty is not a social problem, but rather a normal state of affairs. Moreover, as noted earlier, in Soviet society the contrasts between poverty and richness are far less visible. People are used to low living standards, shortages, lining up for consumer goods, to crowded housing conditions, and the many discomforts of everyday life. Poverty in the United States is more debilitating, not only because of the expectations generated by the American value system but also because of the spectacular local and ethnic concentrations of it. In the Soviet Union there are no "depressed areas" as such (unless one regards the countryside in general as one), no ethnic groups we know of whose standard of living is almost automatically lower than that of the majority, and most important, there is no unemployment (which lends a particularly demeaning tone to poverty in the United States). Unemployment is a social problem that has no counterpart in Soviet society, where the state provides employment and where the lower rate of mechaniza-

* "The sale and rental of guard dogs and trained attack dogs has jumped 50 to 100 percent in the last two years. . . ."[71] Equally ominous has been the spread of violence in secondary schools necessitating the deployment of special guards in many schools of large cities.[72]

† As a former self-appointed spokesman of love and brotherhood, Timothy Leary, in his more recent militant-activist reincarnation, put it: "To shoot a robot genocidal policeman is a sacred act."[73]

tion supplies additional economic pressures for the maintenance of a fully employed labor force.*

Poverty in the United States is, to a certain extent, a psychological and social deprivation rather than a predominantly economic one. While the living conditions of the poor are indeed degrading, and their physical deprivations also very real (and not just a matter of "relative deprivation") there are many aspects of poverty in the United States which would not be considered undue hardships in the Soviet Union. For example, lack of adequate plumbing and central heating, overcrowded housing, lack of household appliances, and a monotonous diet may be considered as relatively normal, if undesirable, in the Soviet Union. It is a further peculiarity of poverty in America that many who are poor nevertheless may possess cars (old ones to be sure), refrigerators, washing machines, and television sets[76] while living in dilapidated substandard housing.†

There is another circumstance that makes poverty in America a particularly severe problem, namely, its self-perpetuating and cumulative character. As many studies have shown, poverty is not a temporary, not even a one-generation status, but rather it is transmitted from generation to generation and it resists change.[78] "Equal opportunities" do not help the "hard-core" poor. They are not caught up in the overall improvements of the standard of living. Even technological progress works against the poor, the unskilled, the uneducated, who are not prepared for the jobs of an advanced industrial society.

A puzzling aspect of the problem of poverty in America is the inability or unwillingness of a rich, resourceful, and enterprising society to eradicate it. The philosophical relics of a more crudely and

---

* It is among the more attractive aspects of the Soviet social-economic system that it is difficult to fire workers and consequently enterprises often have a labor force far above their needs. Not surprisingly the productivity of labor is much lower than in the United States and several other industrial nations.[75]

† The poor are also encouraged to consume but often in an exploitative manner. As has been documented, "the poor pay more" and installment buying plans are particularly ruinous for them. This was observed in 1903, well before the current concern with the problems of the poor: "When the poor man would borrow, he is often exposed to the impositions of a class of unscrupulous money lenders, who violate the laws against usury, but hope to escape punishment or loss through the ignorance of their customers. . . . Bled dry at last and unable to pay such extortionate interest and the principal, too, their goods are seized and the members of the household become objects of charity."[77]

openly competitive social order help to account for the lack of compassion American society at times exhibits toward the poor, the sick, and the old. These attitudes are reflected in the welfare system. It has a thinly disguised punitive character and provides grudging and minimal public assistance to many who are unable to fend for themselves. These problems are well known and widely discussed, yet as in many other instances, thorough analyses have not produced solutions. The defects of the welfare system are illustrated by some of the results of recent cutbacks in welfare payments in New York State (which is among the most generous):

> A family of ten in Brooklyn is suffering from a 12% cut in food money, including the elimination of special diet grants to strengthen them against the father's tuberculosis.

> A blind man on the East side has seen his daily-needs budget cut by more than half, including the elimination of 24 cents a day to feed his guide dog.

> A crippled polio victim in Harlem, whose previous $191-a-month allotment has been cut by $60, has missed physician's appointments because his carfare was eliminated.

> A welfare mother who has worked for almost two years, has earned a high school diploma and hopes for a career as a social worker, has suffered a cut of $140 a month, mainly in fees for the babysitter who tends her five children and one grandchild.[79]

It should also be noted that the budgetary difficulties of the welfare program exist in a society that spends approximately three billion dollars per year on pets.[80] On the other hand, the total costs of welfare nationally, and in some states like New York, are considerable. In 1970 13.4 million Americans received 12.8 billion dollars in welfare payments from federal and state governments.[81]

We know much less about the specifics of the Soviet welfare system and how the sick, old, or blind live in the Soviet Union, but it is likely that, in the absence of a general assumption of high living standards, cases of gross and obvious neglect are more infrequent and the welfare system somewhat more equitable and better organized. This is not to suggest that assistance and benefits are lavish or particularly generous:

> With the exception of a few lump-sum payments, benefits in the Soviet scheme are related to previous earnings rather than to need

or contributions. In almost no case, however, do benefits equal the amount the beneficiary earned when he was an active member of the labor force. In this respect the Soviets seem to adhere to the famous principle of "less eligibility" enunciated by the English Poor Law commissioners in 1834 (and since then applied to the social-security systems of all capitalist countries) which expressed the view that publicly assured income should never exceed the earnings of the lowest category of independent worker.[82]

Nevertheless the Soviet welfare (and value) system at least does not call into question the right of a citizen for public assistance. On the contrary, the Soviet Constitution declares that "citizens of the USSR have the right to material security in old age as well as in the event of sickness and loss of capacity to work. This right is ensured by the wide development of social insurance of workers and employees at the expense of the state, free medical aid and the provision of a wide network of health resorts for the use of the toilers."[83] This sense of openly assumed societal responsibility is certainly among the factors that remove from the Soviet welfare system some of the qualities of grudging reluctance and suspicion that are directed at the client of the welfare system in America. The Soviet welfare system has also been more generous in regard to unwed mothers, dispensing free medical aid and providing maternity benefits. At the same time, the bulk of these benefits do not reach peasants working on collective farms who have to rely on mutual aid societies, that is, funds which reflect the level of income and wealth of the particular collective farm to which they belong. This is one among the many disadvantages of working on the *kolkhoz*, although approximately one-third of the labor force does so. According to one source, the Soviet state spends about twice as much in social welfare payments on workers as on peasants.[84]

There is yet another respect in which the Soviet welfare system differs from the American which, until recently, had little concern with helping the recipient to enter or re-enter the labor force:

Helping people to enter or re-enter productive life, even on a partial basis, seems to be the main driving force behind all [Soviet] welfare endeavour and the measure of its success. So insistent and pervasive is this objective that one cannot help wondering whether those human needs which can be met only by relationship and pursuits that are nonproductive in a conventional sense are neglected. One also wonders how much genuine appreciation there exists for the plight of those who, through no fault of their own but because of imperfect knowledge and skill of their therapist, cannot become productive. . . .[85]

Because of the Soviet control over information-gathering and the mass media (including their representatives from abroad), as well as the movements of visitors to the USSR in general, we have few, if any, vivid, visual images of poverty in the Soviet Union. The absence of such images and impressions also helps to explain why visitors prefer to use terms like "low standards of living" or "primitive living conditions" rather than alluding to poverty as such. In part this is probably also a result of a subconscious acceptance of Soviet claims about Soviet society, as if somehow it would be inappropriate to talk about poverty in a society that *calls itself* socialist. The idea of Soviet poverty also conflicts with a widely held Western image, indeed stereotype, of the Soviet Union as a country which, at the expense of civil liberties and political freedom, has virtually abolished poverty and ushered in an era of social justice if not abundance. Yet there is little doubt that there are countless people in the Soviet Union whose life-style, diet, clothing, and housing are such that in the United States they would be defined without hesitation as poor.*

A major manifestation of what would undoubtedly be defined as poverty in America is to be found in Soviet housing conditions characterized by overcrowding, poor workmanship, and insufficient plumbing. Probably about half of the families in the Soviet Union share bathrooms and kitchens and an unshared apartment is a prize most people do not take for granted.[87] Although apartment construction is a major undertaking, supply does not seem to catch up with demand. The quality of new housing seems generally deplorable, as the monotonously recurring articles in the press and letters from readers indicate. Rare is the apartment that is livable without additional repairs, even in newly built houses. The following complaint is characteristic: "Immediately after the housewarming in my apartment, a leak was discovered in the ceiling, the reason for which has not been established to this day. And two years have now gone by. . . ." Another reader reported that in his newly built apartment

* According to Sakharov, the famous Soviet nuclear scientist, "40% of the Soviet population is in difficult economic circumstances."[86]

house "The tenants on the upper stories go upstairs and down with buckets. And this is in Leningrad, on the beautiful Smirnov Prospect, almost at the city's center."[88]

It is no mystery why there are housing problems in the Soviet Union. In the first place, ever since Soviet industrialization began in the late 1920's there has been an influx from the rural areas to the cities, new industrial towns, and construction sites. Although industrialization has slowed down in the last twenty years, the rural migration has continued in response to difficult living conditions in the countryside and the general undesirability of agricultural work.* Secondly, during World War II much of European Russia—that is, the most densely populated areas of the Soviet Union—was devastated. Thirdly, housing has not been, at any time in the history of Soviet planning and resource allocation, a top priority.

The primitive housing and living conditions in the countryside and on new construction projects also contribute to yet another Soviet social problem: the high turnover of labor and the uneven distribution of the population.[90] Young people are especially eager to avoid or escape assignments to the rural and non-European parts of the country. A research project on this subject found that

> a young person's mood changes drastically depending on the length of his stay at a construction project. The poll question "Are you satisfied with life at the construction project?" was answered in the negative in one group by 19% of those who had worked one year; 35%, two years and as many as 53%, three years.[91]

The various disadvantages of rural life may be itemized as follows:

1. Physical isolation; villages and small towns are the prime victims of the highly inadequate road network of the Soviet Union. Astonishingly enough, "Out of 52 province, territory and autonomous-republic centers in the European part of the Russian Federation, 16 cities, including Ulyanovsk, Volgograd, Kirov, Saransk, and Izhevsk are still not connected to Moscow by hardtop roads."[92] Needless to say, if major administrative and population centers, such as the

---

* As a recent Soviet article summed it up: "There is no doubt that one of the most important reasons for the desire of young people to go to the cities is the extreme backwardness of everyday life in the countryside."[89] This also applies to small towns with populations between 3000-5000 according to the same source.

above, are not well linked with one another, villages and small towns are in a far worse position.* Such localities are no better served by railway lines.†

2. Physical isolation is further intensified in the rural areas by an almost total lack of telephones in private homes:

> There are only 5.1 million telephones‡ belonging to the entire system of the Ministry of Communication as of 1966, and only 800,000 of these are in rural areas. . . . Most farms have a telephone in the administration office and in the local "office of communications" but this is about all. . . . Even when a community has a telephone it cannot always make a connection quickly with the outside world.[97]

3. Workers on collective and state farms earn a good deal less than factory workers. State farm workers averaged 70 rubles per month (one ruble equals 1.1 dollars at the official exchange rate) compared with the average monthly wage of 90 rubles for all workers in 1965; however, collective farm workers earn significantly less, from 20 to 40 rubles per month, according to various Soviet sources.[98]

4. Not only do peasants earn less, they also have a much more limited supply and narrower range of consumer goods and services;§ moreover, until recently a rural surcharge (about 7 per cent) existed on manufactured goods and foods sold in rural areas, justified by higher distribution costs.[100]

5. Working conditions are also undesirable in rural areas; in the

---

* "The 235,000 miles of hard surface highways in the USSR are less than one-tenth the paved highway mileage in the United States, even though Soviet territory is two and one-half times larger than that of the U.S."[93]

† There were 135,000 km.—or about 86,000 miles of railroad tracks in the entire Soviet Union in 1970.[94] In the U.S. there are 428,883 miles of railroad tracks, much of it unused now.[95]

‡ By 1970 the number of telephones in the Soviet Union rose to almost 11 million of which almost 9.5 million were described as "automatic" in the Soviet statistical yearbook. In the same year there were 120 million phones in the U.S.[96] (According to some experts on Soviet communications Soviet figures include nondial phones as well.)

§ For instance, in Vologda Province (European Russia), one-third of the collective farms had no electricity. Moreover, "At that time (1963) each Vologda collective farm had from 30 to 40 villages but as a rule only the collective farms' central farmsteads and livestock sectors were electrified. Thousands, many thousands of villages lived by the light of Kerosene lamps." The article also noted that ". . . of all the electric power generated by the country's power stations only 4% went to the countryside."[99]

summer men work as much as 70 hours per week and women (household work included) about 77.[101] Moreover, Soviet agriculture is not highly mechanized and, consequently, many jobs are physically demanding and fatiguing.

6. There is also a particular stigma attached to living on the *kolkhoz* manifested in the official refusal to issue internal passports—required for travel and change of residence—to kolkhoz peasants. Such restrictions can only be evaded if a person leaves the *kolkhoz* before age sixteen or if he obtains permission from the *kolkhoz* officials to leave. The latter is difficult because of the shortage of labor.[102]

7. Finally the quality of rural schools is also notoriously poor; the chances of a rural child's receiving higher education are far lower than those of his urban counterpart. Rural schools are badly equipped, often understaffed, and unattractive to teachers.* The published complaints of a rural school principal were probably not atypical: "The 36 eight-year and secondary schools in our district cannot claim as many as ten buildings that meet standard specifications. Some are housed in converted homes—decrepit log cabins in which school desks are crowded together. Our school has 400 pupils and no gym."[104]

For all these reasons the age structure of rural areas is becoming increasingly unbalanced with a growing middle-aged and old population and fewer younger age groups. This further decreases agricultural productivity and undermines morale.[105] There is, indeed, some similarity between the vicious circle of poverty in the United States and of the hopelessness of Soviet rural areas. However, in the Soviet case a move to the city is probably a more decisive improvement than similar moves are for the American poor.

Ethnic Minorities

Historical and cross-cultural experience shows that few societies are immune to ethnic prejudice and discrimination. Unfavorable popu-

---

* This point was also discussed in Chapter 6. There is, however, one more interesting figure that ought to be mentioned in relation to schooling differences: "Whereas 45% of all urban children up to six years of age are in preschool institutions, the figure for rural localities is only 10%."[103] Needless to say, the American figures on preschool attendance of children would be far lower than the Soviet, certainly under 10 per cent for the whole country. On the other hand, the majority of American mothers do not work outside the home, whereas the majority of Soviet mothers do.

lar reactions against African students in the Soviet Union[106] suggest that this applies to Soviet society as well.*

Although the Soviet Union incorporates a wide range of ethnic groups (Russians comprising approximately half of the total population) it has no problems comparable in magnitude to the racial conflict in the United States, which, by the early 1960's has become the gravest single social problem of American society. Since there is an unusually rich literature, as well as widespread popular awareness of this problem, it should suffice to sketch only its major dimensions. The racial problem in American society has three basic components:

The actual practices of discrimination and their historical results are in sharp conflict with major American cultural values which affirm and promise equality of opportunity for all. Such a glaring discrepancy between theory and practice, or ideal and actual conditions, undermine the authenticity of the entire value system and the social institutions supposedly based upon it.† Although it is a commonplace that most societies do not live up to their professed values and ideals, seldom is the gap so massive and obvious as is the case with the position of the American Negro (as well as other minority groups such as the American Indian, Puerto Ricans, and Mexican-Americans) and seldom are the consequences of falling short of such ideals so spectacularly destructive.

The second major aspect of the racial problem consists of a vast array of social problems (in themselves not racial) associated with a large portion of the black population. They include poverty, crime, juvenile delinquency, dropping out of school, drug use (and other forms of escapist behavior), violence, family instability, problems of physical and mental health, malnutrition, unemployment, higher infant mortality, and lower life expectancy.[108] It is well established that the incidence of these phenomena is higher proportionally among Blacks than among whites. They reflect both persisting discrimination (for example, in employment and housing) and also the

---

* ". . . There is . . . enough pure racial comment about skin, smell, inherent inferiority and abnormal sexual appetite to satisfy any small-town sheriff in the American South."[107] This observation was made in Moscow in the late 1960's concerning Soviet attitudes toward colored students.

† This, however, only applies if the discrepancy is perceived. For centuries it was not, or not to a significant extent. Widespread awareness of this gap between the American ideals of social equality and the realities of Negro life emerged as late as the 1950's, a delay that in itself is a fascinating and puzzling historical and sociological problem.

genuine handicaps of a stratum of the population that has faced severe discrimination for centuries, a stratum that suffered all the ill effects of slavery and the self-fulfilling prophecies of asserted racial inferiority.[109] No group of people can be subject to economic exploitation, political repression, social discrimination, and the denial of educational opportunity for centuries without negative consequences. "The mark of oppression" does not disappear once legal barriers to equal status are struck down, nor do compensatory measures and policies yield rapid and dramatic results.

The third aspect of the problem is that the Negro population of the country, or a significant portion of it, no longer accepts low status and limited opportunities and thus the apparent equilibrium between those subject to repression and those imposing it has come to an end. The result is social conflict manifesting itself in a range of phenomena from slum riots and the existence of black revolutionary groups to voter registration drives in the South, struggle over community control of schools in Northern cities, Black Studies programs in many schools, demands for more black workers in certain trades and industries, and more recently the pressure for ethnic quotas (usually referred to as "affirmative action programs"). The latter have been most vigorously pursued in educational institutions, municipal and government jobs. Such compensatory efforts, which do imply preferential hiring practices, aroused resentment and apprehension among the white population.

Ethnic discrimination is a problem that societies can avoid confronting when the oppressed acquiesce in their status, the oppressors go about the business of oppression with an untroubled conscience, and the techniques and institutions of oppression function efficiently. None of these conditions is met in the United States of the 1970's. The exploited no longer accept their lot as legitimate or unalterable, the powerholding elites (at any rate on the national level) no longer affirm the legitimacy of discrimination,* and for these and other reasons, the machinery of suppressing discontent is no longer efficient.†

---

* It is another question how energetically they take action to end discrimination and its consequences. Important to the discussion is that its legitimacy is denied.

† Thus, for example, not even the police raids on the Black Panther offices can be considered *efficiently* repressive since they generated much unfavorable publicity and various investigations of police behavior. Nor can a system of repression be considered truly efficient that allows political interviews—involving the denunciation of the gov-

Thus the black-white conflict has become the most bitter and apparently the most insoluble conflict of American society in recent years,[110] permeating almost all social, economic, cultural, and political institutions and processes. Its solution would be costly in both financial and psychic terms, requiring untold billions of dollars to rebuild slums and improve education, medical care, job training, and employment opportunity for Negroes and other minorities. At times such improvements come into conflict with the economic benefits and social status enjoyed by other groups (for example, white building workers), especially when scarce resources or services are to be allocated. Frequently the compensatory programs and policies (often initiated by white elite groups) are criticized on the grounds of "reverse discrimination" by those unfavorably effected by such policies especially working and lower-middle-class groups.

At the same time only the most embittered and blind critic of American society can deny that significant improvements in the life of the black population have taken place over the last two or three decades. They have been particularly noticeable in three areas: legal rights, education (and especially higher education), and political participation. There has also been an upsurge, on the part of some of the most educated and articulate segments of the white population (upper-middle-class, intellectual, and student groups), of a desire to contribute to the solution of this problem which is at the root of a pervasive sense of shame, guilt, and social criticism.

The problem of national minorities in the Soviet Union is of an altogether different nature and magnitude than in the United States.*

---

ernment—to be televised with one of its alleged arch enemies, as was the case for example with Bobby Seale, a Black Panther leader, who was interviewed on NBC from the San Francisco jail in December 1969. It might be said that, in general, Black radicals have an easier access to nationwide television than members of many other minority groups or minority political movements—with the possible exception of photogenic campus radicals, black or white. (Angela Davis, another prominent revolutionary, has received probably still more, largely favorable, publicity, both before and after her trial which ended in her acquittal. Her case once more illustrated how difficult it is for the government in a pluralistic and legalistic society to curtail its avowed political opponents.)

* The proportion of ethnic groups is also very different in the two countries. About half of the Soviet population are Russians, around 20 per cent Ukrainians and in addition "there were 17 nationalities numbering from one to eight millions, 29 numbering from 100,000 to a million and dozens of smaller groups."[111] In the U.S. about 85 per cent of the population are white of European descent, while over 10 per cent are Negroes

There is no group comparable in accumulated disadvantage to the American Negro (with traditions of slavery and high visibility) and no long standing victimization of any ethnic group on the same scale. The Soviet official policy toward most national minorities has assured a measure of cultural and territorial autonomy. At the same time, unconditional loyalty toward the Union is demanded and the slightest tendency toward nationalistic self-assertion or even consciousness is viewed and treated with much severity.[112] Nationalities accused or suspected of unreliability during World War II were dealt with harshly: entire ethnic groups were deported from their native territory to Central Asia and the Far East and their "autonomous territories" abolished. Some of these groups were "rehabilitated" and allowed to return to their lands, some were not.[113] Much reshuffling of populations has taken place, and in many instances Russian settlers were encouraged to move into non-Russian republics or autonomous territories, thus altering the ethnic balance. Russians are "more equal" than other ethnic groups, reflected in their domination of the major decision-making bodies of the USSR, the Council of Ministers, and the Politbureau of the Party.

Faithful to the Leninist principle that "ideas are weapons," Ukrainian intellectuals suspected (or actually "guilty") of concern with the survival of Ukrainian cultural and ethnic identity were subjected to official harassment in the 1960's. This included secret and semisecret trials, prison and corrective labor camp sentences, exile, house searches, threats, interrogations, and an official propaganda campaign against "bourgeois nationalism" or "anti-Soviet nationalistic agitation." Incriminating evidence of such attitudes included unpublished articles and books, as well as some published before Soviet times.[114]

Such arrests and jailings (involving dozens, perhaps hundreds of Ukrainian intellectuals) do not necessarily mean that there has been a sharp upsurge of nationalist sentiment or that there is an organized mass (or even elite) movement. It does mean, however, that there is a handful of articulate Soviet citizens who challenge the system on the basis of its own professed values and principles. The nationality

and the remaining 5 per cent consist of American Indians, Mexican-Americans, Puerto Ricans, and recent Cuban refugees. This, of course, is not to suggest that the European-derived majority has been ethnically homogeneous, or that the ethnic differences within the white majority were inconsequential for American society.

problems are apparently linked with other abuses of power, as the
following inventory of complaints of a Ukrainian dissenter suggest:

> The true friendship of peoples also requires a broad amnesty for
> the prisoners who are still (after 15, 18, 20 years!) rotting in
> prisons and camps for participating in actions against Stalin and
> Beria . . . in order to prevent the release of these people, the
> USSR has retained the barbarous 25-year-prison term. This term
> is being served mainly by Ukrainians, Lithuanians, Latvians,
> Estonians, Byelorussians, and Moldavians. . . .

> The genuine friendship between peoples is thwarted by the prac-
> tice of settling Russian populations in . . . other national repub-
> lics. Thus in the Ukrainian SSR [Soviet Socialist Republic] the
> Russian population systematically increases from year to year and
> the Ukrainian one decreases. Similar national migrations occur in
> Lithuania, Latvia, Estonia, Byelorussia, Moldavia, Kazakhstan,
> Kirghizia and other national republics. . . . For instance, the ap-
> pearance in the Ukraine of large numbers of Russians (retired
> officers, retired KGB officials and other privileged categories of
> citizens), who . . . take over all better positions, jobs and profes-
> sions, forces the native Ukrainian populace into low-paying
> work. . . . In 1958 when the Chechens and Ingushes* returned
> to their homeland they were met in the city of Grozny by the Rus-
> sian populace with the slogans "Keep Chechens and Inguses out of
> the Caucasus!," "Long live the Stalinist nationality policy!" . . .

> No less disturbing is the system of passport registration. . . . In
> keeping with this system a person must live where the military
> officials permit him to. He has no right to move freely around the
> country. . . . An inhabitant of the Ukraine, for example, has no
> right to move and live in Kiev, Odessa or L'vov [all are cities in
> the Ukraine]. A Lithuanian may not move to Vilnius and Kaunas
> [Lithuanian cities]. . . . The present discriminatory residence-
> permit system opens the way to colonizing the towns of national
> republics with outsiders, primarily with Russians.[115]†

Dissenting Ukrainian intellectuals also pointed to the unequal and
limited opportunities for Ukrainian children to study in their own

---

* Two ethnic groups deported after World War II for alleged collaboration with the
German troops but "rehabilitated" under Khrushchev.

† Elsewhere in the same source it is noted that "500,000 Russians settled in the Ukraine
during 250 prerevolutionary years, and approximately seven million came here during
the years since."[116]

language, to the declining number of such schools and to "the relega-
tion of the Ukrainian language to a secondary position in higher
education."[117]

Possibly of all "nationality groups" the position of the Jews is in
some ways the most precarious. Several factors contribute to this.
First is the unfortunate combination of religion and cultural-national
identity that enters into the definition of the Jew. While the Soviet
state has, from the beginning, been engaged in an open campaign
against religion (including Judaism), the fact that according to the
Soviet doctrine Jews also form a nationality group makes them more
suspect.* Yet although "Jew" is stamped into the identity papers of
some Soviet citizens (as is "Uzbek" or "Russian"), Soviet Jews are
not accorded any of the privileges of the recognized nationality
status.

> They [Jews] have no recognized language, no educational system
> of their own, no press, radio, poetry, literature, or history; in
> short, nothing at all. . . .
> The most important of these missing elements is of course the
> language and the educational system. In this respect Jews live in a
> total wasteland. About three and a half million Jews in the Soviet
> Union (half a million of whom speak Yiddish according to Soviet
> records, and tens of thousands of whom had a Hebrew education
> in their youth) are deprived not only of schools where the Hebrew
> alphabet is taught, but even of a class where Yiddish or Hebrew
> teaching is allowed, if only once a week or once a month.[119]

In particular there is no territorial basis for the Jewish nationality,
although there was a feeble and symbolic effort to provide one in
1928.[120] There are other contradictions attached to the "nationality"
status of Jews. Thus, for example, while it is perfectly legitimate to
admit, indeed to emphasize, the contributions and sacrifices different
Soviet nationality groups made to the defense of the Soviet Union
during World War II, Jewish contributions—and even the Jewishness of the victims of the Nazis—are de-emphasized. On these occa-

---

* "Because of the semantic affinity between the term 'Jewish religion' and the term
'Jewish nationality' the Jew in Russia is the butt of endless attacks against the Jewish
faith. He reads continually that the Jewish religion is barbaric, polluted, exploitative,
and reactionary. These negative attributes, related to something to which he is willy-
nilly attached, are the only traits by which he can identify himself, his origin, his past.
Were he to believe all that is said about the Jewish religion, he would be bound to
regard himself and his forefathers as being of doubtful, corrupt and tainted origin."[118]

sions Jews become "Soviet citizens." There is no official indication that Soviet Jews were killed by the Nazis at Babi Yar or at Fonar, the collective grave of the Jews of Vilna.[121]

Not only are Jews discriminated against as a nationality, they are also treated differently from other religions. Attachment to Judaism is viewed more unfavorably than other types of religious practices and attitudes. Correspondingly synagogues have been closed down more rapidly than other churches and in general the regime places more obstacles in the way of Jewish religious practice and training. The attendance at Jewish religious services is associated in the press with antiregime activities, black marketeering and speculation, circumcision has been virtually outlawed and its practitioners are punished for illegal surgical activities, and the authorities will not provide ground for Jewish cemeteries when old ones fill up. Moreover, the tone of the Soviet antireligious tracts has, as a rule, been nastier in relation to Judaism than toward other religions. There are also other forms of discrimination alleged: "In Odessa where there is a Jewish population of 150,000, there is not a single Jewish school. . . . In Odessa where the Jewish population amounts to 25%, only 3% to 5% of the Jews study in institutions of higher learning. This is the norm which secretly exists in the admission to institutions of higher learning."[122]

There are no Jews at the top Party and government positions, a fact all the more striking since many of the early leaders of the Party were Jewish. Many of them perished in the purges in the 1930's; important Jewish intellectuals were liquidated or demoted in the postwar campaign against the "cosmopolitans," a term that was often used at the time as an euphemism for Jew as "Zionist" is used today. At the same time Jews remain proportionally overrepresented among rank-and-file Party members, an indication of the fact that enough of them are considered loyal and important enough to be tolerated in the Party.[123] Further, there is a large number of Jewish professionals, especially scientists in Soviet society. Thus, the picture of discrimination is not consistently dark; there are sufficient numbers of loopholes for a large proportion of assimilated Jews to find a niche in Soviet life. At the same time, the Soviet government (except during the 1920's) has been less determined to stamp out anti-Semitism than the Federal government in the United States has been to combat racial prejudice, at least since the mid-1950's. In fact, the Soviet government has, on many occasions, catered to popular and traditional anti-Semitism by depriving the Jewish minority of cultural and religious facilities, by informal and tacit discrimination against Jews in many occupations and political positions and by giving wide publicity to the trials of Jewish economic criminals.[124]

Part of the explanation of these policies and attitudes is to be found in the traditional Russian and Ukrainian anti-Semitism that has persisted both among the masses and the leaders, Stalin and Khrushchev included. In a society dedicated to fostering unanimity, homogeneity and conformity the traditional stereotypes about Jews and Jewishness—clannishness, individualism, questioning, inquisitiveness, scheming, intellectual concerns, irreverence, and the like—make them an easy and obvious target both of the authorities and the masses. Soviet policies toward, Israel and the Arab world provide further explanation. The existence of Israel represents an invitation for divided loyalties as well as a potential source of attraction and an alternative homeland for Soviet Jews. This in itself explains official hostility toward Israel even without the Soviet foreign policy which has made its goal the penetration of the Middle East by maintaining good relations with the Arab countries.

Old Age

The definition of old age as a social problem is one of the best indicators of a society entering modernity. Old age, no matter how unpleasant, debilitating, and painful, was not in itself a social problem in the past. Two developments make it a social problem today. One is the numerical increase of the old people in relation to other age groups, which results from improvements in the standard of living, medicine, and public health. The other development consists of the changes in the structure of the family. Old age and the social role of the old become problematic with the decline of the extended family and the preponderance of the nuclear family. The latter, and the social institutions associated with it (compulsory schooling, nurseries, a place of work away from the home, and a generally expanded division of labor and specialization) drastically reduce the social and personal usefulness of the old. In modern societies the old become progressively excluded from the familial division of labor, whether it relates to work, household activities, or the upbringing of children. Significantly they are also physically removed from the younger generations whose first symbolic assertion of independence consists of moving into a home of their own if they can afford to do so. To the extent that the United States is more modernized than the Soviet Union, these processes are accelerated there. Moreover, in the United States the popular value system also supports the social isolation and implicit denigration of the old. The American obsession with youthfulness, novelty, energy, aggressiveness, innovation, and change leaves little room for the fruitful integration of the older generation with the younger ones. Old age commands little if any respect in American society. The old are under great pressure to behave as if they were young. The notion that the experience of the old has some value is incomprehensible for most Americans, who fail to see what relevance past experience could have in a rapidly changing environment. Recruitment and retirement policies in American industry closely reflect these attitudes. In many occupations people over forty-five find it impossible to enter new employment.

As is the case with other serious social problems, old age has a variety of ramifications and related problems. Most fundamental, of course, is that being old is a prelude to being dead. It is a period in which people must, in some manner, confront and anticipate death. At a time when a secular culture is ignoring, evading, or denying death, or at any rate is incapable of offering any philosophical comfort in relation to it, old age is doubly bereft of serenity and dignity. Physical infirmity and decrepitude are other endemic problems of old age, although they are somewhat ameliorated in modern societies where more people retain better health and have more mechanical devices at their disposal with which to compensate for the loss of physical vigor. Yet in American society where aggressiveness, efficiency, and competitiveness are prized, physical incapacitation, even if slight, is more painful to bear than in societies which put less premium on these qualities.

A tragic and avoidable aspect of old age in American society is its association with poverty and social isolation. At the age when people's earning power declines or disappears, retirement and social security benefits do not, as a rule, compensate for lost salaries or wages, inflation whittles away savings and, until recently, medical expenses were an unmitigated threat to meagre retirement incomes.

In a sense, cultural values are faithfully mirrored in the pauperization of so many of the old; if they were more appreciated or respected, Americans would not allow them to become impoverished.
The extent to which any society takes care of its old shows exactly
how much the aged are valued or devalued.[125]

Old age reveals the emptiness of lives which was earlier concealed
by the routines of work, social life, and active recreation. For most
people, few things are more difficult to handle than being put into a
position of having unstructured, unlimited time at their disposal. To
be sure, this does not apply so much to the impoverished old as to
those whose old age is better provided for materially. The life styles of
many old people afford distressing insights into and illustrations of the
ultimate difficulty of bringing life to a dignified, and in some manner,
meaningful conclusion. Leisured old age, almost like a laboratory experiment, reveals and culminates meaningless lives, which were more
concealed in the past when the old were less visible, because less segre-
gated from the rest of society and less anxious to appear young and active. The recently developed retirement communities in the United
States symbolize and embody these trends and problems, even though
only a small, though growing, proportion of the old can afford them.
They are a historically new and unique American effort to solve the
problem of old age by the physical removal of the old from close
and regular contact with other age groups. These communities put the
seal, so to speak, on the separation of the generations and the super-
fluousness of the old; paradoxically they also represent the ultimate
fulfillment of the American dreams of freedom, fun, and leisure. "Leisure villages" and retirement communities are commercial enterprises
where every service is provided by the management and where the de-
teriorating old are placed in a physically attractive, secure environment in the like-minded company of others over fifty-five, the usual
age of admission. Such communities are in some ways distorted mirror
images of American society, of its major values and preoccupations.
Thus for example in Sun City ". . . the formula for happiness, or
'pure happiness' . . . is, roughly, that happiness equals activity plus
friendliness."[126] Egalitarianism is prized although there is awareness of
financial differences and possibilities for differential spending. Sun
City is "a community dedicated to self-indulgence on an unprecedented scale, a place in which the distinction in value among various
kinds of activities has all but disappeared."[127] In such places the

struggle against boredom and loneliness seems to assume gigantic proportions and the consequences of being deprived of family solidarity and work routines become painfully evident.[128] Yet in a sense the Sun Cities of America are not only caricatures of American culture, they are also caricatures of Communist society at its most utopian stage: people are freed from the onerous task of earning a living, they are preoccupied with what are considered leisure time activities (or the "all-round development of the personality"), they live in self-contained communities, develop their own associations and organizations, exercise both the body and mind, and conduct undiscriminatingly friendly (comradely) social relations.

Whatever such possibilities for some of the old, for many the "golden years" or "freedom years" are a period of neglect, frustration, often economic deprivation, social isolation, and exclusion from a wide range of activities. Retirement is dreaded by most people, despite the enticements and encouragements of insurance companies, retirement communities, and some leisure industries.[129]

Old age does not appear to be a major social problem in the Soviet Union at present. If nothing else, housing patterns and shortages continue to hold together the older and younger generations to a far greater extent than in the United States. The old are not isolated socially because they share homes (apartments as a rule) with the young,* and even play important roles in running the household and looking after the children. Their presence is also necessitated by the far higher proportion of working mothers in the USSR than in the United States. Further, the persistence of the traditional values of a peasant society, even among those transplaned into the cities, helps to maintain a measure of respect toward the old. By virtue of their comparative leisure the old in the Soviet Union have, in addition, greater opportunities to participate in communal-public affairs (encouraged by the authorities for all age groups) which are also a source of certain status and self-respect, an index of some degree of social usefulness. Old age will not be a serious social problem in the Soviet Union as long as the living standards remain comparatively low, housing overcrowded, the proportion of women in the labor force high, and certain attitudes of a traditional peasant society survive.

* In the United States only about 4 per cent of households with both husband and wife present contained any parents of either husband or wife.[130]

This is not to say that there are no problems at all associated with old age in the Soviet Union. First, not unlike American society, Soviet society too expresses its estimate of the importance of the old by providing them with pitiful pensions, though perhaps with better health services. But there are other problems peculiar to Soviet society, mostly centering around the scant institutional care available, although apparently more and more are in need of it:

> The trouble is that for many years, right up to 1952, no new old-age homes were built. . . . Only 110 old-age homes with space for 30,000 people have been built in the last 14 years . . . [in the Russian Republic].
> . . . Some province executive committees are reducing the allocations for old-age home construction.
> . . . In the Kalmyk Autonomous Republic an old-age home for 100 people has been under construction for eight years.
> . . . In recent years collective farms have altogether ceased building homes for elderly collective farmers. There are only 160 such homes in the republic accommodating a total of 2000 people.
> . . . And yet the need for them in the villages is no smaller but greater than in the cities.[131]

The same article (from which the above is quoted) made reference to "letters written by old people complaining about the difficult and sometimes humiliating conditions in which they are compelled to live." Its major thrust was that more old-age homes are needed urgently because of the growing proportion of old people in the population and the frequent difficulty of the young in providing adequate care for the old who need professional, regular medical attention.

Youth

Although in American society the problems of the old are far more numerous and debilitating than those of the young, significantly less attention is given to them by the mass media, social scientists, or public policy-makers. The reasons for this are both cultural and pragmatic. The old are, so to speak, on the way out. Their power is negligible or waning, they will neither riot nor demonstrate, and even as voters they will not be around for a long time. Besides, as already noted, old age is something to be repressed and forgotten rather than dwelled upon in American society. Nevertheless the public attention lavished on the "youth problem" is not totally irrational. There is a youth problem, or a set of problems which derive in some measure from a "generation gap."[132] The latter need not be interpreted too literally. It may involve varying degrees and forms of rebellion, or even grotesque exaggeration (amounting to rejection) of adult norms, values, and attitudes. Even if in many instances the young merely insist on realizing the values their elders affirmed but did not live up to, rather than rejecting these values altogether, this still creates (or signifies) conflict, and estrangement between the generations.

This, of course, is hardly a new phenomenon. The extent of the contemporary generation gap cannot be evaluated meaningfully without comparative historical data on youthful attitudes toward adults and authority. In any event, there is a widely shared and consequential belief that in American society today there is more estrangement and lack of continuity between the generations than in earlier decades.* This estrangement involves an apparently wide-

---

* For example, one cannot read the findings of a study by David Riesman from the mid-1950's without a strong awareness of change at least among a section of college students. Here are some of the findings and comments, characterizing the "found generation":

". . . they [the students in the samples] have already made up their minds as to exactly who they are and exactly where they want to go on the superhighway of their chosen corporation or profession."

"No one voices objection to service on political grounds or as a pacifist . . . a great many see the period of military service as a kind of postgraduate training, helpful to their careers. . . ."

". . . It is the company's role to develop and train, never to threaten or fire. This, indeed, is part of the benevolent world these men foresee. . . ."

"The career they want is to find the good life, for which their corporation or profession [would] serve as the good provider."

"It is this vision of life on a plateau that perhaps most distinguishes the Class of 1955 from that of 1931. . . . The Class of 1955 . . . would appear to expect to go on successfully adapting as they have already done, but not to change in any fundamental way, save that the family will take the place of the fraternity."

". . . There is very little evidence in the interviews that the respondents had to struggle for anything they want—or have wanted anything that would cost them a struggle they have very few dreams, these young men . . . contentment is the main thing. . . ."

"They were all asked about the political future—a boring topic for most of them."

". . . The Class of 1955 is at peace with its parents. . . . They do not regard them as Philistines to be overcome by fight or flight"[133]

Whether or not these attitudes have survived or to what extent is difficult to say

spread rejection of many hitherto dominant cultural values and tends to be associated with a rejection, or at least a suspicion, of adults and authority. These attitudes are in turn related to an amorphous groping for a (new) meaning to life, for community, love, and some vague quasi-religious fulfillment.[134] The striving for limitless and highly personalized self-expression and the simultaneous craving for submergence in a sustaining community are among the contradictory components of this quest. These attitudes could lead to (or deepen) not only the discontinuity in the relationships and values of the generations, but also to a loss of social cohesion and a possible threat to the unimpaired survival of institutions such as the family, the school, and the university. Thus, for example, the prospects for the successful socialization of children (entailing a reasonably well integrated personality, and some control over immediate impulse gratification) do not seem to be very good in hedonistic, utopian communities.* or on the part of parents whose restlessness and mobility would exceed even the current already high levels. Attitudes associated with quasi-religious communitarianism could also lead to a drastic drop in the number of those interested in or willing to undergo the discipline of mastering the natural sciences or engineering. We may in a few years or decades face a serious shortage of scientists, engineers, technicians, skilled craftsmen or qualified administrators without whom the high standards of living and amenities of an urban-industrial society cannot be maintained. And it should be pointed out that few of even the most embittered, alienated, and vocal critics of industrial society propose to eke out an existence in rural backwaters without the benefits of cars, roads, electricity, central heating, plumbing, canned goods, ready-made clothes, contracep-

---

(though it is not very likely that many of them had), since few college seniors would express them today with such innocent candor. College seniors today, or those among them who talk about these matters, would speak of conscience, commitment, community, change, the problems of the nation and the environment, and the like. Few would confess to indifference to social problems or public affairs, few would admit to a benevolent view of big corporations and the military, few would reflect an uncritical position of their parents, few would admit to being at peace with themselves, few would without flinching profess the goals of personal success or contentment. In doing so, however, they would also be responding to the expectations of the adult world around them. In a curious, circular way, the young may simultaneously reject their elders and live up to their expectations!

* This is not to imply or suggest that the American family as it exists today does a good job along these lines, or that all utopian communities are hedonistic.

tives, stereo sets, and the rest.* And yet this would be a prospect if the anti-industrial, antiscientific components in the radical rejection of American society and culture intensify. Such developments would also have implications for national security and the international role of the United States. That is, if the radicals succeeded in seriously weakening the "military-industrial complex" the results might be unwelcome even for them. What is perhaps most characteristic of these youthful attitudes is the coexistence of a self-indulgent individualism with a globalistic, collectivistic idealism. These attitudes often lead to more tangible problems. Escapist behavior (discussed later in this chapter) is one of them; family instability another. Both in a sense flow from the intolerance of frustration. Political-revolutionary activism is another manifestation of "the youth problem," as are the campus disturbances which often resulted in the decline of academic-professional standards, and possibly, in the long run, in the overall reduction of the levels of competence of both the educated and the educators.

It is sometimes said that the youth problem is really an adult problem just as the black problem is a white problem and the woman problem a man problem. While there is an element of truth in this, it would be misleading to suggest a parallel between, say, the problems and difficulties of white middle-class teenagers and

---

* This, of course, also applies to the various dropouts from society and advocates of some form of free, communal existence unfettered by the customary routines of a materialistic society. Few of the retreatist communes or hippie subcultures or "street people" escape the contradictions of their life style and professed values. For people of comfortable middle-class backgrounds it is difficult, at least for a sustained period, to live up to the values of poverty, simplicity, autonomy, and independence. As Hans Toch has pointed out: "The hippie's temporary self-exile into the gutter can be an unconvincing performance to a ghetto audience. . . . The hippie, like his cousin the New Left, has a penchant for assuming that he is spiritually related to people who view him as a freak. . . . Hippies see any demand for a better life as crassly materialistic and hopelessly middle class. . . . [Yet] The hippies after all accept—even demand—social services while rejecting the desirability of making a contribution to the economy. Their cry for services presumes that society contains individuals and agencies (medical clinics, the ACLU, the custodians of public parks) that are necessary for survival. . . . On the other hand, the aspect of society that calls for productivity is characterized as the 'Establishment,' and comprises brutal police, compromising liberals, draft boards, men in flannel suits, hucksters, hypocrites, multiversities, the military-industrial complex and other assorted evils. This artificial split (which ignores the functional link between, say, the ACLU and 'compromising liberalism') is designed to justify 'dropping out.' What it supports, however, is a new type of social membership—consuming but noncontributing."[135]

residents of the black ghetto, or between the privations of the young and the poor in general. However, it would be safe to say that the adult's floundering and bewilderment* find reflection in the angry or confused groping of the young. Perhaps adults are merely more resigned to chaos, confusion, and meaninglessness in life and society, and to the absence of ready remedies, whereas the young balk at this and long for simple certainties and definitive solutions. More relevant to youth problems is the peculiar unease of American adults, middle-aged and older, about not being young any longer. This unease, almost a guilty conscience, and the associated veneration of youth† have contributed to the collapse of authority (or its hesitant apprehensive exercise, tantamount to collapse) and evoke, more often than not, contempt rather than camaraderie from the young.

The youth problem in Soviet society is a good deal less pressing than in the United States, despite the wishful exaggerations and projections of many Western commentators and the mass media. According to their clichés the "swinging" Soviet youngsters contentedly dancing in the styles of the mid-1950's in the decorous atmosphere of a university gymnasium become the equivalents of the rebellious American young who can do pretty much as they please. The dimensions of the youth problem in the Soviet Union are inherently limited by the institutional obstacles to developing a life style of alienation and the formation of retreatist subcultures. Active alienation—along the lines of political activism, protest, and dissent as practiced by the radical youth in America—is, of course, unthinkable at present. There must be minimal conditions to be met for such attitudes, behavior or movements to develop and persist. The young in the Soviet Union do not protest or criticize openly for the same reason the older generations do not engage in such activities: because to do so seems pointless and dangerous, or because the motives, im-

---

* A somewhat poetic, but no less characteristic, example of adult uncertainty and fear of imposing values (or merely an absence of values to draw on) was provided by a member of a hippie community, who pointing to his baby daughter, said: "We are waiting for these kids to talk so we can find out the next step. We are waiting for instructions."[136]

† The culturally prescribed idealization of the young is so deeply embedded in American culture that even a distinguished anthropologist and self-conscious student of that culture, such as Margaret Mead, cannot completely escape it, as some of her recent observations on this subject suggest.[137]

pulses, and faculties of criticism and questioning are simply not present. In other words, youth in the Soviet Union in its overwhelming majority is conformist by training and early socialization, and submissive by necessity. As to the passive alienation of the retreatist, hippie-variety, once more Soviet conditions are most unfavorable. Even the life styles of passive alienation require a large measure of societal permissiveness or at least indifference, plus a material-financial base, much leisure, freedom from work routines and freedom of assembly and association (that is, to "hang out" legitimately). A retreatist, bohemian, or hippie subculture (let alone actual communes) can hardly develop in a society where work is a "sacred obligation," where not being employed is equated with deviance and leads to being defined as a "parasite"—which in turn can and often does bring about administrative and legal punishments such as exile, a sentence in a corrective labor camp, or assignment to a place of work with a reduced wage. Nor are Soviet universities hospitable environments for the development of such subcultures; they do not shelter deviant attitudes, behavior, comportment, or modes of dress, as they do in the United States and Western countries in general. Social controls (that is, political controls) in Soviet institutions of higher education are as strict, if not more so, as in other settings, and expulsion for antisocial behavior is a risk few Soviet students are willing to take.

This does not mean that alienation or retreatism among the Soviet young is totally unknown, but rather that its manifestations are less perceptible and that it is limited to very few. What bothers the Soviet authorities are the tendencies toward youthful political apathy and apolitical attitudes. Although there is no lack of passive compliance, Soviet leaders want more active political participation in approved channels, and active affirmation of the system, fearing perhaps that compliant apathy may eventually lead to something worse. The official ideal is the type of conformity that is rooted in positive affirmation. Most conspicuous among the apprehensions of the leadership is that the younger generations will go soft, become too hedonistic and demanding of the good things of life, unaware of the hardships of the past and contaminated by Western standards and ideals of consumption, entertainment and art. The following characteristic admonition reflects these official concerns:

it is important that the heroes of the Pantheon of the Revolution remain eternally living examples for young people. . . . As is known the unhealthy longing for "deheroization" of the revolutionary past and the truly heroic present, the downgrading of Soviet man and his labor and struggle, and the reappraisal, without serious justification, of entire periods of history and the role of outstanding individuals therein . . . objectively lead to a disruption of the spiritual, class and political continuity between the generations and prepares the soil for alien influences.[138]

The same article (in *Pravda*) also referred to "backward views among some of our young people, especially a consumer attitude toward life." Significantly, such attitudes were contrasted with the timely heroism of Soviet border troops repulsing Chinese invaders along the Ussuri River.

While apolitical attitudes and an overeagerness to consume are the more typical expressions of the Soviet youth problem, as seen by the authorities, there are also occasional reports about deviant subcultures of sorts. One such isolated case was described in the Soviet press:

Base interests gradually brought these dissipated fellows together. . . . The need for tape recording so-called pop music gave rise to great interest in the broadcasts of foreign radio stations hostile to us. Thus what seemed at first glance harmless buffoonery and the desire thoughtlessly to imitate all kinds of "hippies" and the Beatles led these young fellows into the filthy morass of moral dissipation and alienation from real life . . . they preferred to loaf, to be a burden on others. It took a long time to prove them [there is no indication in the article of the form this persuasion took—P. H.] that in our time one cannot live as a deadbeat, that our society does not tolerate parasites or apostates from the established rules of the socialist community. . . .[139]

A milder manifestation of the same underlying problem—that is, heightened individualistic expectations leading to indifference toward the public interest—is to be found in the area of occupational choices. Evidently (as also pointed out in Chapters 5 and 6) there is a growing discrepancy between what many young Soviet high school graduates would like to do and what they can, and are expected to do, by way of study or occupational choice. In particular (as noted earlier in this chapter) they do not wish to till the land and prefer to flock to the big cities, regulations permitting; they wish to avoid manual occupations if possible, but if not, will select the most glamorous and lucrative among them. Above all, they strive for higher education and the concomitant status and income.

There is no doubt that the youth problem is more troublesome in American than in Soviet society even though there is some official concern in the USSR with its potential for creating political discontinuity. Yet Soviet society is far more stable than the American; it does not offer many alternatives, competing values, and cultural styles; its centers and sources of authority have yet to be seriously shaken or induced to engage in a soul-searching self-examination.

The Varieties of Escapism

"Escapism" or "escapist behavior" is difficult to define; there is an immense variety of escapist behavior and many forms of it cannot be considered socially problematic. There are, however, certain widespread forms of escapism which clearly have negative social consequences.

What provides a unifying strand to the many kinds of escapist behavior is the underlying desire to reduce awareness of personal or social realities. Suicide is, of course, the ultimate escape, and certain kinds of mental illness might also be viewed in similar terms. Among the best examples and most widespread forms of escapism (also of a socially problematic nature) are heavy drinking and drug addiction. Both rely on chemical substances to alter consciousness. Both interfere with the performance of familial and social obligations, work, intellectual effort, and disciplined activity. Although there is, initially, a social element in both drinking and drug cultures, in many cases gradually both heavy drinking and drug-taking lead to a privatized, isolated, asocial existence. Generally heavy drinkers and drug addicts are not well-functioning members of society. Both are incapacitated to varying degrees depending on the nature or stage of their addiction and the stimulants or depressants used. Not every type of escapist behavior relies, however, on alcohol or drugs. For example, gambling is a popular form of escapism that can assume obsessional dimensions. So can watching television programs or reading pornography or even some forms of routinized work itself.*

While every society and every individual need, in a broad sense, to rely periodically on escapist behavior of some kind to cast off the routine, unrewarding aspects of existence, a Sunday walk in the woods or a game of cards is hardly a menace to either society or the individual. If, however, a large number of people in a given society decided to do nothing but walk in the woods or play cards this would constitute something of a social problem. Escapism, then, becomes a social problem when it is widespread and has observably deleterious effects on those engaging in it, with respect to their mental or physical health, or their capacity to relate to others, or both. Whenever a large number of people engage in such activities, be it drug-taking, heavy drinking, or compulsive gambling, sociologists are apt to look for widespread patterns of frustrations from which they want to escape and for the linkages between the personal problems experienced and their social setting.

In both American and Soviet society there is a great deal of escapist behavior which suggests widely felt conflicts and frustrations. Again we have far more complete information—both statistical and qualitative—about escapism in the United States than in the Soviet Union.

Although the underlying motives for escapism are likely to be similar everywhere, social institutions, resources, and norms have much to do with the forms it will assume. Two factors are especially influential in this regard: the standard of living and level of technology, on the one hand, and political and social controls on the other. There is a wider range of escapist activity in the United States than in the Soviet Union because there is a far wider range of escape mechanisms in a consumer-oriented, permissive society than in a strictly controlled puritanical one, characterized by endemic scarcities. In the Soviet Union even the mass media are nonescapist but purposeful, didactic, and heavily politicised. Not many Soviet

---

* It is difficult to eliminate value judgments from the definition of escapism (as it is from that of social problems in general). Thus "interfere[nce] with the performance of familial and social obligations, work, intellectual effort, and disciplined activity" (p. 360) may be a laughable criterion for some members of the counterculture who may define good life and authenticity as deriving from the *absence* of such obligations and activities. For them drug taking may be an encounter with, rather than escape from, reality.

citizens rely on them for transcending—however fleetingly—the dreariness of their daily routines. In American society the mass media, and television in particular, cater to the escapist impulse above all. Certain forms of escapism are peculiar to an affluent society. The indigent cannot engage in drag racing in cars costing thousands of dollars, or own motorboats and snowmobiles. Drug-taking is also tied to substantial financial means and those not prosperous enough to pay for their habit from legitimate sources become criminals or prostitutes to finance it—a fact that greatly aggravates drug-taking as a social problem, creating associated patterns of deviant behavior such as theft, robbery, and other crimes.

In an officially puritanical society where escapism, with its antisocial implications, is strongly discouraged, the escapist impulse finds fewer outlets than in an affluent, hedonistic, and consumer-oriented society where the provision of such services is highly lucrative. On the other hand, certain types of harmless escapism are promoted by the authorities in the Soviet Union as eagerly as they are by the commercial promoters in the United States, such as spectator sports. There are also considerable efforts made by the Soviet government to steer the citizen's leisure-time activities into wholesome and constructive channels, such as participation in amateur drama groups, orchestras, hobby groups, and attendance at plays and concerts. There are very few corresponding efforts in American society where the political authorities are not, to any significant extent, involved in the provision or supervision of cultural, recreational, or entertainment activities. (Outdoor recreation is an exception in that parks are provided by the government.)

In ranking the seriousness of social problems associated with escapism it is tempting to consider drug addiction the gravest in the United States, although the less publicized social costs of alcoholism may be just as great. Drug addiction may justify greater concern because drugs cost more than alcohol and, therefore, their regular consumption is more likely to lead to criminal activities. It seems that two groups in the United States are particularly susceptible to drugs: the most deprived (such as slum dwellers) and the bored middle- and upper-middle-class youth.* There are significant differences in their

* Apparently almost any form of escapism can acquire instant acceptability among many American high school students for whom few, if any, internalized values and moral standards provide resistance. This is also relevant to the "pushing" of drugs: "School

respective patterns of drug use. Those in the former group tend to take the more addictive and more dangerous drugs; most middle-class youth seem to favor marijuana, which is less dangerous (or, according to some, totally harmless) and nonaddictive. Since enormous profits are made from drug-peddling, the consumption of drugs has a solid commercial basis—another obstacle to control and prevention. It is easy to understand the popularity of drugs as escape mechanisms. Though they may be expensive, they are easy to acquire and easy to use; they produce (for many people) instant results, instant euphoria, regardless of sex, age, race, color, religion, level of education, or social background. (The same also applies to alcohol.)

There are no indications that drug addiction is a serious problem in the Soviet Union, one reason for this, we may assume, being the limited availability of drugs. The Soviet government is, of course, in a far better position to control possible drug traffic than the American by virtue of its generally tight control over the borders. There seem to be some exceptions such as Georgia, (and some areas in Central Asia) where apparently drugs are locally produced and enjoy considerable popularity. While according to Soviet custom there are no published statistics on whatever is troublesome, the recent doubling of sentences for drug use and peddling in Georgia suggests that there is a growing problem. Nevertheless, a Soviet newspaper concluded an article on the subject by proclaiming that "drug taking is not characteristic of the Soviet way of life and is a foreign bacteria that has penetrated the healthy body of our society."[142]

On the other hand, alcoholism is acknowledged to be a major problem in Soviet society and not even the authorities claim that it is a "foreign bacteria." If the publicity accorded to any social problem is a measure of its gravity, alcoholism is probably a greater prob-

---

and rehabilitation officials say it is almost impossible to convince a youthful pusher who has $200 in his pocket and is wearing an $80 pair of alligator shoes and a $50 cashmere sweater that selling narcotics is wrong. . . . They [the pushers] say 'I am making five times as much as you (teachers) do. Why should I quit?"[140]

It is interesting to note here that television has (like many college administrators) taken a sympathetic view of young drug takers as reflected in a large number of drug plays: ". . . a close analysis of 24 of these plays reveals that their dominant perspective is a strange one: they add up, collectively to an anti-Establishment cartoon, in which the 'heavies' tend to be liquor-guzzling, pill-taking, profit-making, Protestant-ethic-advocating, middle-class 'squares' . . . while the drug takers—also mostly white middle class—are cast as acutely suffering, often idealistic 'victims' of this 'society.' "[141]

lem in the Soviet Union than in the United States. To be sure, publicity need not be a correct measure of the magnitude of a social problem, for often it is not the frequency but rather the nature of the problem that determines the publicity it will evoke. Very serious violations of the moral or normative order, no matter how rare, are likely to receive more attention than far more widespread but less significant violations. This, however, does not apply to Soviet alcoholism since excessive drinking ranks relatively low in the hierarchy of the violations of either the official or popular norms. Thus we can safely assume that the publicity is due to the spread or magnitude of this form of misbehavior and its effect on production and family life.

A report in *Pravda* (1968) highlights various aspects of the problem:

> Almost all the letters [from the readers of the newspaper], and there are hundreds of them, express the same complaint: My husband (or son, or father) comes home from work drunk every day. From work! Evidently gangs of drinkers form in workers' collectives. Before the eyes of the public. Often they drink right in the shop or in the office of an institution.

> The sociological laboratory of the Kirgiz State Institute of Physical Culture jointly with officials of the republic militia administration, conducted an investigation into the circumstances contributing to the spread of drunkenness in the city of Frunze. They questioned about 400 persons who have been brought to sobering-up stations. . . . Most of them had taken to drinking . . . in early youth, as soon as they began working . . . 32% had begun drinking at the age of 18, 23% at the age of 19 or 20, and 42% after 20. . . .

> Only 6% of those questioned drank alone; 11% drank at home, with members of the family; 1.5% drank with neighbors in the apartment building; but 58% drank with comrades at work and 21% with comrades at work plus friends who worked elsewhere![143]

Officials are understandably concerned with the effects of heavy drinking, indeed alcoholism, among the young. Antialcohol propaganda is among the measures favored:

> we should give some thought to effective forms of anti-alcohol propaganda among the young people. . . .
> First of all there are the psychiatric hospitals. Let the teenagers

see the people who have lost all human characteristics, people in the stages of the most complex psychic derangement. Let him acquaint himself with the case histories of illnesses and the medical records of the sick, let him examine photographs taken of them in the past in which they still appear to be perfectly normal people. . . . One must show the teenager habitués of the sobering-up stations and the inmates of correctional colonies. Let him learn about the fates of many of them. . . .[144]

We have no statistical basis for comparing alcoholism in the two countries. Soviet publicity, as well as the new measures advocated and introduced for treatment of alcoholics,[145] offers one clue to its comparative magnitude. Another is the permissiveness of the popular value system. Russian popular values clearly sanction heavy drinking and little moral revulsion is provoked by drunkenness, which, on the contrary, is viewed as a legitimate form of entertainment and recreation. It would appear that in the Soviet Union the social and escapist aspects of drinking merge somewhat more harmoniously than in the U.S. where excessive drinking often tends to take on a more ominously self-destructive character perhaps in part a result of the legacy of puritanical values. Moreover, while in Soviet society drinking cuts across all age groups, in the United States it is somewhat less common among the young, many of whom seem nowadays to favor drugs over drinks.

Other factors must also be considered. In theory the greater affluence of Americans compared with the far more limited purchasing power of Soviet citizens might be viewed as facilitating alcoholic indulgences. This, however, does not seem to be a significant factor. People have been known to spend a great deal of money on alcohol (or drugs, or other means of escape) in preference to other needs, regardless of their level of income.* The proverbial drabness of Soviet life, the petty difficulties and discomforts of everyday living, the relative dearth of opportunity for other leisure-time activities, plus Russian cultural traditions favoring drinking, combine to create strong pressures to rely on alcohol as a time-tested and simple method of release and relaxation. Even in the absence of comparative figures it is probable that alcoholism is a more severe social problem in the

---

* A worker in a letter written to a Soviet newspaper declared that no less than one-third of the entire family income, with four of its members working (170 of a total of 510 rubles) goes for vodka. He considered these figures typical.[146]

Soviet Union than in the United States. The major explanation is most likely to lie in the fact that opportunities for escapism are more varied and more abundant in American society which makes the singular reliance on alcohol alone less imperative.

Mental Illness

Limited comparative evidence and sociological speculation suggest that mental illness may be a more serious social problem in the United States than in the Soviet Union. Although the absence of publicity in the USSR does not necessarily correspond to the absence of a social problem, in the 1960's the regime has been willing to give publicity to social problems which had no direct political significance, origin or ramification, yet little has been said about mental illness. To the extent that urbanization, social mobility, social isolation, and decrease in family size and solidarity are associated with mental disorder,[147] it is understandable why mental illness should be more widespread and visible in the United States than in the Soviet Union, where the persisting ethos of a traditional peasant society cushions the impact of modernization. The latter, as we noted earlier, has not been as pervasive in the realm of popular values and interpersonal relations as is often assumed. In fact, it appears that a line of defense against the onslaught of forced modernization developed precisely in the realm of intimate personal relations. While widespread, ingrained, individualistic competitiveness is seen as one of the major factors associated with neurosis in the United States,[148] competitiveness is neither a major social value nor a predominant attitude among Soviet people. The Soviet Union is a more group-oriented society, and the traditional popular attitudes and the official values fostering collectivism strengthen one another. The official encouragement for labor competition, for example, has by no means been internalized by the vast majority, and even if it were, it would cause far less anxiety than does the kind of competition and competitiveness which have prevailed in American society.

In the United States, competitiveness, individualism, and intense achievement-orientation have created a setting for strong conflicts within the self. Expectations are high, probably unduly so, and there has traditionally been a widespread and often exaggerated yet persistent belief in the opportunities American social structure affords for personal success.* Consequently when failure occurs, it is plausible to attribute it to personal defects, incompetence, low motivation, insufficient drive, or poor mental abilities. By contrast, the relative harshness of the Soviet institutional environment, its lesser emphasis on individual success (officially claimed to be inseparable from collective help) and numerous restrictions on personal freedom, initiative, and opportunity—all these help to create a personality type less prone to anomie, with relatively low expectations and a more permissive superego. The high degree of regimentation and organization of Soviet society further helps to foster the feeling that there are few things for which the individual is truly and solely responsible.† To put the difference in other terms: in Soviet society the individual has fewer choices than he does in the United States. Nor do the excesses of privacy threaten many people in the Soviet Union. This fact is also significantly reflected in the handling of mental disorder. While in the United States the tendency is to segregate the mentally ill, to remove them from society into institutions, in the Soviet Union this happens less frequently.[151] Outpatient clinics rather than mental hospitals are the rule. By contrast, ". . . approximately 600,000 adults are confined in mental hospitals of the United States on any given day and . . . according to current estimates one person in twelve will spend some time in a mental hospital before he dies."[152] Belief in the therapeutic power of participating in the life of the collective, as well as the desire to avoid the depletion of the labor force, lie behind the Soviet approach.

Finally we should also note the putative links between mobility (geographic and social) and the problems of personal identity which loom so large in the American consciousness and often form the

---

* Even in the 1960's, despite the growth of self-denigration within the United States and the numerous manifestations of anti-Americanism almost everywhere abroad (at least in the mass media), about three million new immigrants arrived from all over the world.[149] Quite possibly, without restrictions tens of millions might have come. A generally high standard of living, scorned by some domestic critics of American society, has continued to be an attraction. Likewise the political freedoms available in the United States retained their appeal for those who experienced life in police states.

† An example of this outlook is reflected in the feelings of a former labor camp inmate subsequently exiled: "As he had not picked the place [of his exile] no one could throw him out. The authorities had planned it all for him; he had no need to worry about whether he was missing a chance of living somewhere else or whether he ought to look for a better set-up. He knew he was treading the only road there was, and this gave him a cheerful sort of courage."[150]

backdrop to the predisposition to certain types of mental illness. That mobility has some adverse effects on psychic stability is both a common-sense proposition and one supported by social scientific studies.[153] As noted earlier the mobile person is deprived of fulfilling, stable, long-range personal relationships (except with members of his small family who accompany him) but in addition mobility of both types also tends to result in exposure to conflicting values and life styles and in the alternation or disruption of stabilizing routines. Downward social mobility is particularly damaging, in most cases, to self-esteem, and there is in general a higher correlation between lower social status and mental illness than between higher social position and the same. While recent figures do not indicate an overall increase in geographic mobility* in the U.S., impressionistic evidence suggests that it might have increased among the younger age groups in conjunction with the pursuit of new life styles and the restlessness that has characterized large segments of American youth in the 1960's. A personal account of a highly mobile member of the counterculture quoted below illustrates the connections between geographic mobility, problems of identity, and personal instability (even after allowances are made to the unique personality factors involved) which may be more widespread than currently realized:

> Reflecting how strange it is that so much of what one considers "oneself" disappears, evaporates when one does not have a *home*. A place of inclusion and exclusion, where things are known and available, and the moment-by-moment passing of daily life can be taken for granted . . . there is an aspect of identity which is lost when the identifiable place is lost, and the traveling self is not the self at home. . . . I have lost most "traits" and "characteristics" of personality which I and others have in the past known me by. I am without energy and incapable of making plans, never know the time and can never talk to somebody without looking around distractedly, looking for something which I have not been able to name yet. When you are traveling, all of your ideas are in doubt.[155]

Bearing in mind that geographic mobility in the U.S. is more a matter of choice than in the Soviet Union (where much of it is initi-

* In 1965-66, 19.3 per cent of the entire population moved; in 1968-69 it was 18.3 per cent.[154]

ated by the authorities in connection with job assignments), one can better understand why—in its more extreme forms—it is among the factors which contribute to certain types of mental disorder.

The Mismanagement of the Physical Environment

The mismanagement and destruction of the physical and natural environment has only recently entered into the inventory of social problems but has rapidly achieved a preeminent status in both the United States and the Soviet Union.* It is a problem that is obviously social in nature: it is man-made and has wide-ranging effects on human life. Its major sources are overpopulation in many localities, lack of planning and foresight, the misuse of technology and science (or ignorance about their long-term effects), and a rapacious, predatory attitude toward nature and material resources. We are all familiar with the manifestations of this mismanagement: water and air pollution, the extinction of wild life, soil erosion, the accumulation of waste material, the loss of land usable for outdoor recreation, and the immense aesthetic damage done to the cities and the countryside by their haphazard "development."

The roots of these problems are to be found in shared attitudes in both countries, in particular in the fetish of growth, bigness, and development common to both the capitalist and Soviet-communist mentality. Apparently this attitude is deeply rooted in Western culture and thought and transcends differences in contemporary political structure and ideology.[156] To be sure, in each case the "metaphor of growth" is influenced by more specific attitudes, values, and circumstances. In the American case the opportunities for geographical expansion and financial betterment, in a framework of values that sanctified private enterprise (and private greed), have intensified the worship of growth and development. Difficult early struggles with nature in the American wilderness lent a heroic dimension to a set

---

* Contrary to the belief that environmental problems are among the exclusive sins of capitalism, a belief questionable not only because there is pollution in "socialist countries" (including the Soviet Union) but also because there are striking differences among capitalist countries, some of which have adopted far more stringent conservation policies than others. It is, however, true that among the highly industrialized and urbanized capitalist nations the United States has been up till now the most negligent, especially in relation to the magnitude of the damage done to the environment.

of attitudes which have completely lost their relevance in twentieth-century America, in which men with the aid of technology have effortlessly subjugated nature. Marxism puts as high a premium on work, on mastery over nature, as does the most puritanic acquisitive capitalism.* Mastery over both the forces of nature and of society is enshrined in Soviet Marxist thought. Peculiar circumstances in Russia added intensity to these underlying themes and motives. The huge land mass of tsarist and Soviet Russia was to be galvanized to life and great power status by industrialization. Industrialization was required both in support of the visions of a communist society of abundance and for assuring military security and international political weight to the country; industrialization was also necessary for making the power of the government effective domestically, especially in relation to the communications and transportation network. Finally, there are the geographical parallels: the Soviet Union, like the United States, is an enormous country with seemingly inexhaustible resources of land, timber, fresh water, minerals, and the like. In the USSR, as in the United States, until recently, it seemed misplaced to worry about exhausting abundant natural resources. Another Soviet condition reduced concern with conservation planning: the sense of urgency and emergency that accompanied, indeed propelled, the drive to industrialize. The consequences began to show only recently, or rather, only recently has there been official public attention paid to them.[158]

In some respects the Soviet Union has fared better than the United States. It has been saved from the ravages of the automobile, one of the prime threats to the environment and urban amenities and aesthetics in the United States. As we noted earlier in this chapter, the motor vehicle is not a major form of transportation in the Soviet

* The profound attachment to the idea of growth, development, and mastery at the societal level is, perhaps, reflected on the individual level in the cult of being busy, admiration of activism, and abhorrence of idleness, nonactive leisure, and reflection. It is as if stability (or the lack of growth) at the societal level would correspond to individual stagnation or failure, as if it were feared that in a state of stability or equilibrium a yawning chasm of unanswerable questions would open up—for both society and the individual. The busy person is the ideal in both American and Soviet society: he is seen as important and respectable; in turn his self-image benefits from being in demand. Being ceaselessly active and achieving at the individual level corresponds to growth and development on the societal. Both have the quality of mindless compulsion, both tend to become ends in themselves, and both have some relationship to what Leites called "the fear of goal-fulfillment."[157]

Union, neither of passengers nor of goods.* The scarcity of cars removes or reduces an important source of air pollution, urban congestion, and urban destruction (such as we witness when freeways and expressways reduce American cities to exit ramps and parking lots), and has spared the Soviet Union from urban-suburban sprawl. This notoriously disfigures the American countryside, creating environments that are neither rural nor urban but an unappealing mixture of both. Soviet open spaces are also better protected because the population lives predominantly in apartment houses. Uncontrolled development along American lines is not feasible because people must rely on public transportation and they cannot afford to or are not allowed to build homes in great numbers and at locations of their choice.

Another source of environmental mismanagement in the United States—namely zoning regulations, their absence or abuse evolved from the ethos of 19th-century capitalism and the type of individualism associated with it. Underlying the ineffectiveness of zoning regulations in many localities is the belief that everybody has the right to build almost wherever and whatever he wants to, and that it would be an unconscionable interference with individual rights to prescribe the type of dwelling (or commercial building) or location where one may build. Belief in the preeminence of commercial over most other considerations further contributes to the ugliness that has spread over the American landscape. Since commercial establishments pay more taxes (as do owners of jerry-built apartment complexes and developments) few local officials worry about conservation or aesthetics.

Having recognized the problem of environmental mismanagement, the Soviet government is in a far better position to do something about it than the American since the latter is confronted with the multiplicity of legal, political, and attitudinal obstacles inherent in a pluralistic society which puts high value on private enterprise,

---

* Thus Trotsky's rhetorical question, raised in the mid-1930's remains relevant and unanswered in the early 1970's as well: "How many years are needed in order to make it possible for every Soviet citizen to use an automobile in any direction he chooses, refilling his gas tank without difficulty en route? In barbarian society the rider and the pedestrian constituted two classes. The automobile differentiates society no less than the saddle horse."[159] There is every indication that Soviet people would willingly exchange lesser air pollution for more cars, reflecting the same kind of popular preferences which have prevailed in the U.S.

profit, and individual freedom. In the Soviet case, once a high-level decision is made in matters like urban planning or environmental protection there are fewer hindrances in the way of implementing it.

In the United States, even though public concern and indeed alarm with the state of the environment have rapidly increased in the last decade, translating these concerns into reality will be costly, complicated, and protracted.

Religion in the Soviet Union

Religion is a social problem in the Soviet Union in every sense of the term: it is considered an undesirable form of behavior or attitude and one which is to be brought under control, indeed completely eliminated by corrective measures (see also Chapter 5). Defining the survival or existence of religion as a social problem is one of the best examples of the normative character of social problems. In many other societies, American included, religious behavior is considered desirable and praiseworthy.

Religion in Soviet society is, justifiably, considered a survival from the past. Soviet society does not give rise to religious institutions. The regime's hostility toward religion derives from its official value system based on Marxism-Leninism that views religion as an opiate of the masses, as an escape mechanism on the one hand and a tool of oppression on the other. For the oppressed it helps to divert attention from the privations of this world, from the point of view of the oppressors it is a useful device in minimizing the importance of worldly rewards and justice. According to orthodox Marxism, religion is bound to disappear in a nonexploitative, rational social environment which people can understand and control and, therefore, no longer need the escape mechanism religion represents.

What, apart from such ideological-philosophical considerations, impels the Soviet regime to view religion as a blemish and a social problem? Probably the most important reason for official hostility is the potential for privatization and withdrawal facilitated by certain religious values. Deep religious commitments may weaken social-political commitments or compete with them; they may contribute to the citizen's renouncing or reducing his role as a citizen, to limiting his participation in society and public affairs; they can create indifference or critical sentiment toward official values and the code of behavior derived from them. Religious commitments are also potentially inaccessible to external control and limit the manipulability of the citizen. From the standpoint of a system that desires total commitment and loyalty, even a compartmentalization of worldly political and other worldly nonpolitical attachments is intolerable.

This discussion of social problems, lengthy as it has been, clearly is limited. Not only have many problems been completely neglected (for example, unemployment and sexual deviance), but the analysis of such major problems as mental illness and environmental mismanagement has been pursued only very briefly. Our "inventory," however, includes the principal social problems faced by the two societies, as well as the similarities and differences between them with respect to definition, prevalence and efforts to cope with them. In both societies, as we have seen, several social problems have derived from or have been closely related to the decline of informal social controls, the growth of physical, social, and psychic mobility, secularization, and the unforeseen (and unwelcome) consequences of the development of science, technology, and industry.

9. Conclusions:
A Comparative Evaluation

Differences and Similarities—Failures and Achievements

It should be clear from all that was said in these pages that differences between American and Soviet society outweigh the similarities. As a rule, the further removed an area of life is from the influence of political ideologies and institutions the more likely it is that parallels might be found. However, this does not mean that the differences are purely or largely a result of political factors. In addition, there are vast historical dissimilarities, a great many things which did (or did not) happen in one or the other of the two countries, the profound and persisting influence of culture and tradition, the proverbial weight of the past.

A brief—and necessarily inadequate—summation of the principal differences between the United States and the USSR may be provided by labeling one as an imperfectly (or incompletely) pluralistic and the other as an imperfectly (or incompletely) totalitarian society. On the one hand, totalitarianism is not as "total" as was thought when the concept was most widely used; on the other, the realities of pluralism are far removed from the degree of participation in the political process suggested by its ideal type. There remains, however, a vast difference between two societies, one of which does not fully live up to its democratic ideals and another that does not conform to the theoretical model of a totalitarian polity. These differences include the almost total absence of free expression (let alone assembly and organization) in the USSR, as against a historically rare degree of free expression in the United States. Significantly, even those who insist that American society is repressive[1] belie their own assertion by their behavior, that is to say, by their sustained and vocal public criticism of the major institutions and values of American society and by having easy access to the media of communication to disseminate these viewpoints. A Soviet citizen, and especially a Soviet dissenter, would be baffled by the nature of repression his American "counterparts" are talking about between (or during) well-paid and popular speaking engagements, the publication of best-selling books of social criticism, and nationwide television denunciations of the "system."

If there is repression in the United States it has certainly failed to intimidate many people and especially its allegedly intended victims: the radicals of the Left. In the Soviet Union the range of free expression is limited even in private, while politically or ideologically deviant views rarely find public expression. Soviet people have developed an extraordinary sense of self-censorship: not raising certain questions or discussing certain topics has become second nature for most of them. In short, while in the United States (in many circles) dissent is flaunted, fashionable, prestigious, and often lucrative, in the Soviet Union it is marginal, secretive, and truly dangerous.

There are also enormous differences in the exposure to political propaganda of the population. For the most part American society has been relatively apolitical, except for electoral campaign periods. Even today the extent to which the government can disseminate its own political propaganda is surprisingly limited, while antigovernment or "antiestablishment" propaganda flourishes in certain sectors of society—especially on campuses and in some black slums—with little hindrance. The government has no exclusive control over any segment of the mass media which during the 1960's have in fact become increasingly critical of many government policies.* If "capitalists" control the mass media its content hardly reflects a congruence of their interests and those of the government. Soviet propaganda, as we discussed in Chapter 4, is a gigantic undertaking comparable in

---

* Daily observation of nationwide evening news programs over the last 4-5 years leaves this writer with the impression that the various critics of the U.S. Government (including news reporters and commentators) are actually given more television time than government spokesmen or officials, including the president and members of the cabinet.[2]

volume (though not in diversity or substance) to American advertising ("if all the most insistent and obnoxious advertisements for deodorants and detergents, motor cars and headache remedies were imagined to be emanating from the 'creative departments' of a single corporation, and that corporation had a monopoly of insight, virtue and the qualities necessary to achieve happiness and the 'American way of life,' one might get an idea of the effect of the Party's incessant message"[3]). And, one might add, if the corporation had the authority to demand and receive respectful attention toward these messages.

The quality of life in the United States and the Soviet Union is, of course, also vastly different, resulting, to a large extent, from the differences between an economy of scarcity and an economy of abundance, indeed of wastefulness. This does not mean (as noted in the previous chapter) that there is no poverty in this country but it does lend a different tone even to poverty. Many poor people in the United States have access to consumer goods which middle-income Soviet citizens cannot obtain.

The two societies also differ in their degrees of urbanization. America is an almost completely urban society; almost half of the Soviet population still lives in rural areas, and the majority of urban residents are only one generation removed from their peasant background.

There are important differences between the prevailing belief systems of the two societies. The Soviet is characterized by a combination of modified Marxism-Leninism and traditional Russian peasant values; the American by a mixture of a surviving Judeo-Christian ethic and acquisitive liberalism, *and* a radical-political, or hedonistic-escapist reaction *against* that mixture.

Life in the two societies also differs significantly in regard to the possibilities for "dropping out"—that is, withdrawing from the dominant patterns of life, from the social division of labor, and established routines, in regard to the freedom to define one's life style in ways which differ from the prevailing norms and customs. Such options are an important aspect of "negative freedom," that is *freedom from* restraint, compulsion, and conformity. This freedom allows people (within certain limits) to do as they please with their lives, whether or not their conception of the "good life" agrees with that of the majority or the dominant groups. Such freedom means that the individual can decide for himself what he does with his private life, choosing to work or not to work, to move wherever he wishes to move, to associate with whomever he wants to, to dress as he sees fit, to seek out his own forms of escape, recreation, entertainment, and relationships with other people. Dropping out also means that the dropouts have some financial means enabling them to relinquish tiresome routines associated with making a living for most people. Those without regular, routinized employment must somehow support themselves: either they must have private incomes or support, or part-time jobs must be available and lucrative enough to get by. Even setting up the most primitive "commune" dedicated to humble manual work presupposes some capital: land, equipment, and housing must be bought or improved or both. And, of course, there must be private owners of land willing to sell. All these conditions are met in the United States, instances of public hostility toward "hippie types" notwithstanding. It is easy to drop out of college, abandon regular work, the traditional family, or a fixed place of residence. Hence those alienated from the "system" have options; they can develop sustaining subcultures and communities for experimenting with new life styles, avoiding conformity or adjustment to the dominant culture and institutions. This mode of escaping the pressures of the dominant values and institutions has been more popular than actually leaving the country—another option that is open to those who feel oppressed, uncomfortable, or alienated in American society.

As we have pointed out, disaffected Soviet citizens are, as a rule, in no position to leave the country either legally or illegally. Dropping-out American-style is also impossible for a variety of reasons, especially because as noted earlier the authorities equate the lack of regular employment with "parasitism," a ground for deportation to labor colonies or exile to inhospitable regions. Second, all employment is state-controlled and part-time work is rarely available or well enough paid to allow large numbers of people to subsist on it. Third, Soviet authorities would not tolerate an attempt by any self-selected group of people to set up communes or communities—if indeed such an idea would occur to Soviet citizens, a rather remote possibility. Nor could, of course, people buy land from the state or be given housing for such purposes. There is only one legitimate "community" in the Soviet Union: Soviet society as a whole and the derivative collectivities of the place of work and study, or of the party and youth organization. Dropping-out, in the eyes of the authorities, is almost as reprehensible as actively opposing the system. A totalitarian state does not wish to allow such forms of withdrawal for the citizen.*

Finally and most importantly, American and Soviet society differ with respect to the potential for change, fluidity, and instability. The Soviet Union is justly perceived as stable, and its citizens do not anticipate dramatic changes. If in the United States many people consider the rate of change dizzying and its direction ominous, in Soviet society at least some people are dismayed by the lack of change, by the substantial continuity, the lack of innovation and the prospects of a continued stability and monotony. Most Soviet citizens, however, probably find the type of stability attained relatively satisfying.

A brief summary of similarities may begin with such prominent social problems as crime, juvenile delinquency, and family instability which are conspicuously present in both societies. It is not inconceivable that in the long run the stability of Soviet society may be eroded by such problems, in particular those involving the family. There are also striking similarities between the two societies in regard to the mismanagement of natural resources and the failure to eradicate various kinds of pollution. There is a high rate of physical and social mobility in both societies (although geographic mobility is more controlled in the USSR) and certain similarities between the systems of stratification, especially with respect to the importance of education and occupational achievement. Both societies are highly bureaucratized, although in the Soviet case bureaucratization is far more pervasive and monolithic. Finally both countries are military superpowers—a condition that has significant implications for their economy, their use of resources, utilization of labor, domestic politics, and ties with other nations.

The major accomplishments and failures of the two societies may be summed up with the help of the concepts of negative and positive freedom. The former refers to "freedom from" (or to freedom as "noninterference"); the latter is associated with "freedom to," with

---

* According to a recent report, the shortage of labor in remote parts of the USSR provide some limited opportunities for the appearance of a Soviet version of retreatism. There are apparently some nomadic drop-outs from various occupations who escape political participation and collective pressures by doing manual labor on state and collective farms periodically, thereby avoiding both regular work and fixed residence, and sometimes family problems.4

positive rights. In actual political practice the concern with negative freedom tends to characterize liberal-pluralistic societies. In these the power of the government has traditionally been limited because of a fear of the abuse of power and the related belief in the relatively limited obligations of the government. In contrast, totalitarian societies are philosophically and politically committed to "positive freedoms," to sweeping social transformations, to the reconstruction of social institutions. This is not to say that in pluralistic societies there is no concern with positive freedoms; welfare states from Scandinavia to the United States are attempting (with varying determination and generosity) to compensate for socioeconomic disadvantage, no longer leaving the poor and old and uneducated entirely to their own devices. At the same time totalitarian societies make no "concessions" to the ideals of negative freedom. They do not acknowledge any restraint on their power and authority, that ". . . there must be some frontiers of freedom which nobody would be permitted to cross . . . that there are frontiers . . . within which men should be inviolable . . ." or "an area within which I am not frustrated."[5] Totalitarian systems and movements deny that there is a legitimate boundary between the public and private domain (or between the personal and political), or even that there is a private domain as such.

The appealing features of positive freedom are associated with the idea of helping people, improving or equalizing opportunities, promoting self-realization and security, speeding up otherwise sluggish historical-social processes, and preventing or alleviating ignorance, apathy, or poverty. The questionable aspects of positive freedom have to do, above all, with the temptation to compel and coerce people in their own (unperceived) interest to do what presumably is good for them, and with the inclination to interfere in private lives by extending the definition of the public-political domain. Thus a one-sided preoccupation with positive freedom has often led—as in the Soviet case—to the expansion of political power (in proportion to its almost limitless responsibilities), to paternalism and manipulation, to doctrinaire commitments and intolerance. In the words of Isaiah Berlin:

> The common assumption of these thinkers [who stress positive freedoms] . . . is that the rational ends of our "true" natures must coincide, or be made to coincide, however violently our poor, ignorant, desire-ridden, passionate empirical selves may cry

out against this process. Freedom is not freedom to do what is irrational, or stupid, or wrong. To force empirical selves into the right pattern is no tyranny, but liberation. . . .

Or . . . I may conceive of myself as an inspired artist, who molds men into patterns in the light of his unique vision . . . humanity is the raw material upon which I impose my creative will; even though men suffer and die in the process, they are lifted by it to a height to which they could never have risen without my coercive—but creative violation of their lives. This is the argument used by every dictator, inquisitor and bully who seeks some moral, or even aesthetic justification for his conduct. I must do for men . . . what they cannot do for themselves, and I cannot ask their permission or consent, because they are in no condition to know what is best for them. . . .

If you fail to discipline yourself, I must do so for you; and you cannot complain of lack of freedom, for the fact that Kant's rational judge sent you to prison is evidence you have not listened to your own inner reason, that, like a child, a savage, an idiot, you are not ripe for self direction or permanently incapable of it.

The drawbacks of the concern with negative freedom are equally perceptible. They may manifest themselves in the enshrinement of societal irresponsibility and civic indifference, sometimes in the unstated assumption that every member of society has an equal chance to compete (for scarce goods and values), in the possibility of chaos resulting from the lack of regulation and planning, in allowing social ills to persist for fear of undue interference with spontaneous or natural social processes, in the freedom of choice degenerating into freedom to abuse others. Again, these issues have been dealt with by Berlin:

The extent of a man's or a people's liberty to choose to live as they desire must be weighed against the claims of many other values, of which equality, or justice, or happiness or security or public order are perhaps the most obvious examples. For this reason it cannot be unlimited. . . .

At the same time negative freedom has some unique appeals: Pluralism with the measure of "negative" liberty it entails seems to me a truer and more humane ideal than the goals of those who seek in the great, disciplined, authoritarian structures the ideal of "positive" self-mastery by classes or peoples, or the whole of mankind. It is truer because it does, at least, recognize the fact that human goals are many, not all of them commensurable, and in perpetual rivalry with one another. . . .

. . . It is more humane because it does not (as the system builders do) deprive men in the name of some remote, or incoherent ideal, of much that they have found to be indispensable to their life. . . .[6]

There are numerous historically identifiable institutions and practices connected with the emphasis on one or the other type of freedom in the United States and the Soviet Union, respectively. The tradition of weak and corrupt government (at any rate at the local level), the ravages of unbridled competition, the excesses of individualism, the reluctance to help those who cannot help themselves, the untroubled acceptance of racial discrimination, the despoliation of the physical environment, the fading away of the distinction between self-determination and violence, the elevation of property rights above human rights, the perpetuation of inequalities of wealth and status from one generation to another, a permissiveness toward irresponsible and exploitative commercial and business practices—these are some of the failures in American life which can, to a considerable extent, be traced to an excessive veneration of negative freedom, or to classical liberalism.

It is also clear that the vices and virtues of Soviet society are related to the orientation toward positive freedom. Indeed the whole phenomenon of totalitarianism may be viewed as a perversion of the concern with positive freedom, as "the vivisection of actual human societies into some fixed pattern dictated by our fallible understanding of a largely imaginary past or a wholly imaginary future."[7] For example, the creation of economic security by eliminating unemployment may be viewed as a step toward fuller self-realization. Similarly, economic planning is an attempt to maximize security at the societal level, to subordinate productive forces to rational principles, and to speed up the attainment of material abundance. But the same orientation provides the political elite with powerful levers of social control and facilitates their becoming the infallible guardians of public morality and unchallenged arbiters of personal lives.

The issue can also be presented in terms of ends and means. A totalitarian society of the Soviet type is propelled (at least, to begin with) by visionary, millennial ends; such a system soon becomes unconcerned with the means of attaining its self-evidently good and desirable objectives. In a liberal democratic society like the United States, the situation is the opposite in many respects. A concern with means, procedures, legality, or traditional norms often impedes necessary social change and reform. Is it possible without violating the Constitution to disarm the American public? Can effective measures be taken against slumlords who don't keep up their buildings without violating their property rights? Is it possible to deal with organized crime within the law, when wealthy criminals with good lawyers can remain free for years? How can polluting business firms be dealt with legally yet effectively? And how can laws themselves be enforced without violating the rights of the accused or the suspects? How can both property and civil rights be reconciled by legislating open housing? How can occupational and educational opportunities be enlarged with or without quotas? These and similar questions are related to the American liberal tradition, the kernel of which is the concern with negative freedom, and the attendant reluctance to interfere with individual rights.

American society has, however, made some efforts in the past three decades to redress the balance between positive and negative freedoms—a trend hardly in evidence in the Soviet Union.

Ideal and Actual—Theory and Practice

Societies are often evaluated by using standards of historical comparison or by reference to certain ethical or moral values. They may also be evaluated in terms of some tangible accomplishment (or the lack of it): on the basis of production figures, per capita income, rates of infant mortality, size of armed and police forces, the number of people in jail, death sentences imposed and carried out, the network of roads, numbers of tourists coming and going, and many other indicators of prosperity, poverty, freedom, or oppression.[8] Such comparisons are valuable but suffer from many limitations. For instance, certain vital statistics may be lacking or suppressed (such as, figures on death sentences and prison populations in a secretive society), or they may be uncollected or falsified. Other figures, even if available and reliable, often fail to capture the quality of life in a given society. In the final analysis, satisfaction or dissatisfaction with life depends on elusive factors, in particular the perceived relationship between ideals and their realization, in other words, on expectations. For this reason, societies should also be assessed against the background of *their own* values and stated aspirations. Using this yardstick, hardly any society can escape criticism since none lives up fully to its ideals or ideal patterns.[9]

Not surprisingly, most critiques of both American and Soviet societies stem from the realization that ideal and actual, theory and practice do not mesh. For many reasons this realization is incomparably stronger in American than in Soviet society. First, Americans have higher expectations; that is to say, they believe more wholeheartedly in the possibility of translating social ideals into practices. Such beliefs spring both from the actual experience of the economic, social, and political accomplishments of American society and also from a certain innocence of unpleasant historical realities—such as foreign invasions, large-scale revolutions, lost wars or marked institutional discontinuity. At least until recently, probably more Americans believed in the solubility of most personal and social problems than the citizens of any other nation.* National character and historical experience provide a basis for understanding the differences between the levels of American and Soviet expectations. An intense and recurring realization of the gaps between ideal and actual is also facilitated in the United States by the uncensored mass media and public interest in the lurid and scandalous. The American mass media thrive on the ventilation of the contradictions between "ought" and "is," as do many intellectuals and youth whose social criticism (and alienation) is anchored precisely in the contrasts between American ideals and social practices.

The principal conflict between ideal and actual in American society pertains to economic and social inequality, the persistence of racial-ethnic discrimination, and poverty in general. These are the most painful contradictions because of the specific beliefs and promises embedded in American culture concerning the attainment of success, abundance, social justice, and equality.

Equally conspicuous is the lack of congruence between the American ideals of individual freedom, autonomy, and self-determination and the realities of many impersonal secondary associations, the bu-

---

* David M. Potter pointed out that "Americans have always been especially prone to regard all things as resulting from the free choice of a free will. Probably no people have so little determinism in their philosophy. . . ."[10] It remains to be seen how seriously these attitudes have been damaged by the frustrations of the 1960's and 1970's.

reaucratization of large areas of life and the growing general difficulty of the individual to assert himself and make an impact on his environment.* The conflict between such aspirations and realities is particularly frustrating since expectations concerning autonomy, identity, and self-determination have spread and intensified in recent times. In the words of Andrew Hacker:

> In the past, ordinary people thought of themselves in unpretentious terms, acknowledging their limitations and accepting stations relatively consonant with their capacities. But the emergence of individuality has changed self-conceptions, creating discontents of a sort that were unlikely to occur to men and women of earlier times. Once persuaded that he is an "individual" entitled to realize his assumed potentialities, a citizen will diagnose himself as suffering quite impressive afflictions.
>
> The intensity with which Americans now explore their egos arises from the conviction that even an average presonality is a deep and unparalleled mechanism. . . . Hence also the stress on individual "powerlessness," and the constrictions that large institutions impose on self-discovery and self-development. While these terms of discourse are not of a recent invention, their employment by so large a part of society is certainly new. Alienation, powerlessness and crises of identity come into being only if citizens decide to invest their personalities with potentialities ripe for liberation. As soon as people make such decisions about themselves, regulations once taken for granted appear as oppressive instruments of government and society.
>
> Thus, most of those who describe themselves as "alienated" lack any credentials for so tragic a predicament. . . .
>
> . . . Indeed, most of the feelings of exasperation about contemporary American life come from the fact that many more people now feel deserving of protections and privileges once accorded to only a few.[11]

Another set of contradictions emerges when the ideals of physical, economic, and social security (which brought many people to this

* There is one important shortcut to maximizing individual or group efficacy today in the United States, namely, publicity. No single technique or mechanism is more effective in making people feel that they matter, and in reducing the sense of isolation, anonymity, and ineffectiveness. As we have seen, access to publicity has been democratized to a great extent: money, status, or political power (conventionally defined) are no longer the only or even major means of obtaining it. A vast range of unusual, violent, dramatic, or bizarre behaviors can elicit generous publicity.

country) are contrasted with the realities of physical insecurity (in crime-ridden and polluted cities), status anxiety, inflation, or unemployment. Similarly, the promise of community and brotherhood has been unmet for millions who face social isolation and identity problems.

Finally, there is the general discrepancy between the ideals of efficiency—supposedly achieved by technology, scientific management, professionalization, and applied rationality—and the reality of growing chaos in many areas of life. In particular, urban development, transportation, and the use of natural resources have become increasingly inefficient, as have both formal and informal social controls.

Ideologically defined ideal patterns abound in Soviet society. The Revolution that took place over half a century ago was inspired by the most ambitious modern blueprint to right all wrongs—in Russia and the world at large. The tales of a blissful future never stopped in the Soviet Union, not even during the darkest periods of police state oppression and material deprivation. The regime itself provided the most authoritative, and oft repeated, ideals against which social and political realities could be measured. Yet not many Soviet citizens chose to engage in such a painful and seemingly pointless stock-taking. The handful of those who did include Trotsky and the uncounted idealists and revolutionaries who perished in labor camps or jails, a few political refugees who managed to escape, and some surviving second-generation idealists within the Soviet Union.* Foreign students of Soviet life and history have also analyzed the nature and degree of departure from the ideals of the October Revolution and those of Marx, Engels, and Lenin.

Perhaps the most fundamental conflict between Soviet ideals and reality has been the failure of the elimination of private ownership of the means of production to lead to either a greater autonomy of the individual or the growth of democratic political practices—or for that matter, to socioeconomic equality. Not only has the state ownership of the economy proved to be compatible with the persistence (or emergence) of a class structure, it has also deepened political inequalities, magnifying the gaps between haves and have-nots in terms of access to power. While it is probably true that there are more spec-

* For example, Pyotr Ivanovich Yakir, a historian belonging to the small circle of dissenting intellectuals, is the son of General Iona E. Yakir, who was executed during the purges in 1937.

tacular economic inequalities in the United States than in the Soviet Union, there is little doubt that political inequalities in Soviet society are far greater than in America and many other European societies.

Second, public control and planned development of the economy has failed to raise the standard of living in any rapid, spectacular manner; on the contrary, many of the gains of industrialization have been achieved by keeping living standards low.

Third, civil rights and liberties have become more circumscribed (if not totally extinguished) than they were in many periods under the tsars. Intellectual and artistic freedom and creativity have suffered greatly. Little progress has been made toward implementing the humane values of Marxism. For most people most of the time life has been bleak, regimented, plagued by shortages of goods and services, and haunted by apprehensions of the police state; millions of citizens have had an opportunity to substantiate these apprehensions, many of them failed to survive the process.[12]

It is difficult to make a comparative assessment of the magnitude of the discrepancies between ideals and social realities in the two societies. The gap seems greater in the Soviet case (though felt less) because the regime set out (a mere fifty years ago) in a more deliberate, determined, and programmatic fashion to attack injustice and scarcity. Although many of the ideals and promises of the United States originate in a more distant past, there is a startling and widespread awareness of them even today among American people. The Soviet system has never ceased to reiterate its claims and promises, harnessing the mass media to the task. The reminders of the promises of America have been more scattered and inconsistent. There has been no comparable American timetable, so to speak, for attaining utopia, no claim of catching up with this or that society more advanced than the United States, no specifying that when the production of steel, oil, or electrical energy reaches a certain level, a qualitatively different new society will materialize. Nor have there been attempts to purposefully create a "New American Man"—an equivalent of the Soviet drive to upgrade human nature. Above all, there has never been any sustained and comprehensive planning in America designed to achieve far-reaching idealistic social goals. Poverty programs and "new deals" were not ambitious schemes in social engineering, but rather pragmatic attempts to patch up society, even though accompanied by ceremonial rhetoric.

More recently many Americans have discovered that the attainment of certain ideals and goals was not as fulfilling as had been anticipated. We are witnessing today among large segments of the American population a pained disappointment over the gratification of material desires. The ideals of affluence and physical comfort when attained by millions have turned sour for many. Among the youthful members of the middle and upper-middle classes, the current disparagement of the dominant rewards and values of society tends to combine with a heightened sensitivity about, and a new preoccupation with, the gaps between ideal and actual and a search for spiritual self-realization. Although such discrepancies may be smaller in American society than in the Soviet, they are felt more intensely and by far more people. Many Americans, especially among the young and college-educated, appear more and more unwilling to believe that conditions can significantly improve, that the gap between ideal and reality may narrow without some largely unspecified but dramatic social change.* Not infrequently a rigid posture of estrangement precedes the observation of actual social wrongs, which, when identified, serve to bolster the already firmly held pessimistic view of American life and institutions.

This is especially true and understandable with respect to the racial problem. As Dennis Wrong has pointed out:

> The fact that the circumstances of blacks have improved, however modestly and starting from whatever low levels, needs stressing because I have found that the presentation of the statistical evidence is greeted by students—and not only by students—with amazement and incredulity. Lacking any historical perspective and having so recently "discovered" the unfavorable position of blacks in American society, students find it very hard to believe

---

* While immersion in campus life and exposure to the mass media are the major sources of such impressions, at least one national opinion survey suggests that despair is not totally, or unambiguously, representative of the mood of the country: "The national mood is one of seeming paradox: grave apprehension about the state of the nation juxtaposed against a tempered sense of personal achievement and optimism."[13] The explanation of the seeming paradox may lie in the fact that many of the problems and issues which worry people—for instance, crime, drugs, war, riots, inflation—have yet to effect the majority directly or painfully enough.

that *any* progress can have taken place. . . . Suspicious of statistical abstraction by contrast with "lived experience" and raised in comfortable suburbs where there was little visible evidence of poverty or the squalor of black ghettos, they often seem to feel that the sheer existence of the latter refutes any quantitative indications of improvement. There is also the tendency, common to liberals as well as to those students who define themselves as radicals, to evaluate the present by the ideal standard of full equality, whereas statistical trends inevitably compare the present with the past. As a result, one finds a strong disposition to dismiss the evidence in toto as an apologia for evil, or even as a pack of self serving lies put out by the "Establishment."[14]

While it may take several more decades before large portions of the Soviet population develop a strong awareness of the gaps between ideal and actual in their society, such an awareness is already profoundly affecting American social institutions. The probable consequences are difficult to predict. On the one hand, American society might become its own gravedigger by continuing to inculcate expectations and values into the young to which it cannot live up. On the other hand, the more modest dreams of social improvement often remain unrealized unless people believe in and pursue the unattainable ones.

Expectations and Alienation—Stability and Change

The key to the stability of the Soviet system lies in its management of expectations rather than in the powers of the KGB*—although there is some connection between the two. This is a curious paradox. Soviet people have been told of approaching utopia for over fifty years and yet there has been no appreciable growth of a utopian mentality among them. They have not made effective demands on the system to deliver the spiritual and material goods it has promised.

* This is not to suggest that widely shared value orientations are the principal foundation of the cohesion and stability of the Soviet political order. The Soviet case is best characterized by Randall Collins's general observation: ". . . It is possible for an organized group, especially one with great *force,* to dominate other groups without the groups sharing common values. The fact that some kinds of understandings and expectations may grow up between ruling and ruled groups may contribute to the stability of their relationship, but force is still the basis of domination."[15] The above also helps to better understand the issue of the legitimacy of the Soviet system and the (false) dichotomy of coercion versus persuasion discussed in Chapter 5.

Quite to the contrary, expectations have remained at such a relatively modest level that people are appreciative if there is a regular supply of carrots or onions on the market, or if once in a while they can see a movie made in the West. The accounts of visitors to the Soviet Union confirm and reconfirm this point. For example:

> One of the reasons Russians work badly is that they are surprisingly content with their lot. . . . It is true there is very little of real value to buy, and the prices are outrageous; but it is also true that most Russians do not want much in the way of material goods. *(But they want little because they cannot imagine themselves having more—and so the circle goes around)* . . . [my emphasis].
>
> Russian workers have this remarkably low level of expectation and ambition partly, at least, because they don't live in a competitive society where advertised riches are constantly dangled before their eyes. . . . Their frame of mind is still that of a Russian peasant, to whom the notion of wordly success and riches is as far-fetched as a holiday in Nassau.

The low level of expectations is, more striking outside the economic sphere. A Soviet intellectual observed:

> The fascist American presidential candidate Wallace was quoted in a newspaper here not long ago. He compared Russians to fleas under glass: if you keep them there long enough they stop jumping, even when you remove the glass. Much as I detest Wallace, that is a rather fair description of the Russian people. We are *tamed,* we don't *think* of jumping. And the ironic proof is that such a quotation could appear in a Soviet newspaper. . . .[16]

The manipulability of Soviet people and their low level of critical thinking were observed in a similar fashion by Valentyn Moroz, an imprisoned Soviet dissenter:

> A human being deprived of the ability to differentiate independently between good and evil becomes a sheep which feels anger only on orders and sees only the evil that is pointed out to it. Cogs read in newspapers that black people are forbidden to live in Capetown or Johannesburg, that Africans are forbidden to live in South African cities without permits, and they consider this lawlessness. But their frozen brains cannot compare facts and draw the conclusion that registration in cities, familiar to them since birth, is just as much of a violation of Article 13 of the Declara-

tion of Human Rights . . . and that in our times the legalized
"Pale" is not just for Jews, as before, but for all the people.[17]

Thus Soviet citizens are thankful that people are no longer arrested purely for the suspicion that they *might* harbor antiregime
views; nowadays those subject to official mistreatment are in fact critical of the system.

Two explanations of these attitudes might be offered. First, that
for far too long daily experience belied and made mockery of the
utopian pretension and promises of the regime, preventing the
buildup of expectations. From a psychological standpoint the lowest expectations had the greatest survival value. Second, even after
the economic and political improvements of the post-Stalin period,
there is still a very long way to go in satisfying modest expectations
before the latter "get out of hand" and become politically or economically troublesome. In other words, the expectations of most Soviet citizens will remain realizable (though probably unrealized) for
a long time to come. It is within the realm of possibility—even in a
dubiously managed socialist economy—to provide a regular supply
of vegetables, to make small refrigerators accessible to the middle
classes (or even to the upper strata of workers) and automobiles to
the elite groups, to provide every family with running water, and a
separate kitchen and bath. Likewise, the application of police state
methods can be limited to genuine dissenters, and changes in the top
leadership can be carried out without a bloodbath. In the meantime,
periodic crackdowns are *also* possible (the past few years have shown
that Soviet liberalization is neither an inexorable nor an irreversible
process) and make it less likely for people to be carried away on the
tides of rising expectations. Real and alleged external threats, too,
remain a mainstay of propaganda and command acceptance, whether
reference is made to "German Revanchism," "American Imperialism" or the "Maoist Clique" across the long Asian borders. Such
threats, taken seriously by a country devastated by World War II,
can always be used to bolster sagging discipline and to tighten the
reins, political or economic.* The manipulation of expectations is

* By contrast, in many circles of American society (and especially the academic-intel-
lectual) it has become a hallmark of political sophistication to make light of and ridicule
the possibility that any external force or power could threaten the security of the country. Such a disbelief is in part a result of geographical factors which spared America
the experience of foreign invasion; it also is a reflection of the upsurge of neo-isolation-

also illustrated by the official practice of bolstering the satisfaction of Soviet citizens by describing the dire conditions prevailing elsewhere, especially in the United States. Thus Suslov, a member of the Politbureau, in an "election campaign" speech discussed the inaccessibility of higher education in America, the costs and inadequacy of American medical care, the faults of Lyndon Johnson's programs, the fraudulence of American campaign promises, the number of the unemployed, and the problems of crime, among others.[18]

It is difficult now to conceive of an American politician campaigning on the platform of how bad things are in the Soviet Union (or elsewhere), quoting figures on Soviet wages, the price of consumer goods, number of automobiles per population, housing conditions, estimates of people in concentration camps, and the like. The audience of the American politician, or campaign orator, expects him to tell how good things could be and that there is no limit to improving life. He must make his promises (fraudulent or not) in the light of ideals and possibilities as yet unrealized. The Soviet propagandist tries to cheer up his audience by telling them how bad things are elsewhere and that in comparison with other countries conditions are pretty good in the USSR.

Although expectations are generally low, there is now in the USSR a small group of malcontents who dream of democratizing the Soviet Union and wish to implement the Constitution; some of them insist on taking seriously the humanistic messages of Marx and Lenin. Certainly, people like Amalrik, Bukovsky, Daniel, Ginzberg, Grigorienko, Sinyavsky, Solzhenitsyn, Yakir, and others, less known in the West, do have high expectations. They demand not only that the Soviet economy provide greater material abundance,* but also ask for elusive, unheard-of freedoms. Many of them believe in them strongly enough to face years of penal servitude or incarceration in

---

ism (bred by the Vietnam fiasco). Finally, the belittlement of external threats is also closely related to the animosity toward the military establishment, whose reason for existence (and enormous budgets) is predicated on the possibility of external threat. Indeed the major thrust of recent revisionist historiography is that America is to be blamed for all her misadventures in foreign policy and that threats to her security have been imaginary or artificially conjured up.

* Some of them even reject the goals of material abundance unless associated with other values and freedoms. For example, Vyacheslav Chornovil declared: "The greatest material saturation, without the unfettering of thought and will, is not communism. It is merely a large prison with a higher ration for prisoners."[19]

special mental hospitals. Whatever their courage and idealism, their capacity to disrupt, subvert, or incite is minuscule.* Then, of course, there is also the KGB and the weight of the entire Soviet state and party apparatus. There is no reason to underestimate the power of the KGB and the relationship between its existence and the modesty of political expectations of the Soviet masses. The existence of such a police force makes deviant political behavior more a matter of existential and moral choice than an activity expected to contribute to political change. The odds are overwhelming that a person will not escape retribution for any sustained political dissent. At best he will be a party to a cat and mouse game in which the KGB occasionally extends a period of supervised grace preceding arrest.

If a relatively low level of expectations is the key to the stability of Soviet society, it is the intensification of expectations that underlies the turmoil in the United States of the 1960's and 1970's.[21] To be sure a high level of expectations has been built into American culture and woven into the fabric of society from its earliest beginnings. Those who peopled this continent (slaves excepted) came in the expectation of religious and political freedoms, greatly improved material conditions, social status, and the attainment of happiness of various kinds. Many of these expectations have been met, many have not, and new ones have also been generated.†

As noted earlier, the fulfillment of material desires seems to have contributed widespread feelings of futility and guilt in the 1960's. Affluence— simultaneously taken for granted and rejected—has been a heavy burden to bear for many young, (as well as some older) white, middle- and upper-middle-class Americans. There has been an upsurge of nonmaterial expectations, a widely publicized quest

* As Henry Kamm has pointed out, ". . . For every Sinyavsky or Daniel, or Larisa Daniel, or Pavel Litvinov, or Alexander Ginzburg, or Yuri Galanskov, or Pyotr Grigorienko, or Pyotr Yakir or Natasha Gorbanevskaya—the heroic and lonely few . . . —there are hundreds of others who see the same wrongs but have not found the tongue and the heart to say so, and thousands who also see them but pretend that they don't, and hundreds of thousands who hate those who say so, because to say so is rocking the boat and the rulers reward a peaceful, well behaved citizenry with more bread, and it is bread most Russians want and not freedom."[20]

† As Banfield puts it: ". . . Because we set our standards and expectations to keep ahead of performance, the problems are never any nearer to solution. Indeed, if standards and expectations rise *faster* than performance, the problems may get (relatively) worse as they get (absolutely) better. . . . We may mistake failure to progress as fast as we would like to, for failure to progress at all. . . ."[22]

for meaning, community, and identity which are difficult (if not impossible) to gratify. Many of these expectations overlook the nature of the contemporary social world. There is, for instance, little chance of running a modern industrial society without bureaucracy; of keeping 200 million people (in the United States) from colliding with one another without rules and without those who enforce them. Likewise, brotherhood and love on a large scale cannot be conjured up merely by an intensely held desire for them; nor can community be achieved without deeply shared purpose, value and function; or specialization be abolished without also abolishing knowledge and competence. Most importantly, such expectations ignore the overwhelming probability that it is not possible to banish *all forms* of scarcity and frustration from human life.[23] It is paradoxical that much of the present intolerance of deferred gratification (personal, social, and political) associated with the New Left has been generated by American capitalism itself, its technology and merchandizing. All messages of American advertising can be reduced to one basic formula: "There is a quick and easy solution for every need and problem." From hairy legs to a negative self-image, everything can be alleviated by the appropriate purchase of goods, services, or techniques.* The radical activists of recent years seem to have taken this to heart. They, too, assume that every human and social problem is quickly soluble and that all good things in life are compatible: unrestrained individualism with a warm community, material wealth

---

* A similar point has been made by Daniel Boorstin: "Our national hypochondria is compounded by distinctively American characteristics. The American belief in speed, which led us to build railroads farther and faster than any other nation, to invent 'quick lunch' and self-service to save that terrible ten-minute wait, to build automobiles and highways so we can commute at 70 miles per hour, which made us a nation of instant cities, instant coffee, TV dinners and instant everything, has bred in us a colossal impatience. Any social problem that cannot be solved instantly by money and legislation seems fatal"[24]

In the 1960's the traditional American belief in the solubility of all problems moved from the commercial-material-acquisitive, to the political-sociological sphere. As Norman Podhoretz has pointed out: "As the activist faith spread, so too did the disposition to blame every conceivable trouble on 'the society' and to demand remedial action by the state, whether or not the trouble was social in its causes. . . . In 1970 some of us who came a decade earlier to radicalism via the route of ideas rather than the route of personal grievance are convinced that it has become more important to insist once again on the freedom of large areas of human experience from the power of politics, . . . than to acquiesce in the surly tyranny of the activist temper in its presently dominant forms"[25]

with spiritual freshness and spontaneity, anarchy with self-development, lack of discipline with creativity, hedonism with puritanism, the cultivated hatred of one group with the love of another (or with that of mankind).[26]

The high levels of expectations which prevail in important segments of American society are closely related to two prevailing impulses in American life today: the almost desperate quest for community* and the rejection of authority, and a cluster of related "evils," such as organization, discipline, differentiation, and hierarchy.[28]

Perhaps the most pessimistic outcome to be envisaged for American society is its internal decay or destruction through a series of conflicts between those whose expectations are frustrated and those who take pride in their society and their personal accomplishments, those who want revolutionary change and those intent on crushing it. Should such conflicts materialize (or intensify), idealistic, educated, and committed youth might play a leading part in the largely unwitting destruction of democratic institutions in their impatience with their defects, unaware how historically rare and precious such institutions are, with all their flaws. As Nathan Glazer has put it: "There has been built up among the youth, aided by irresponsible intellectuals and the sensation-seeking mass media, feelings of such despair and distrust and so great an ignorance of this country, that any position, regardless of how fantastic, now has the chance of being given wide credence."[29]

A sense of crisis which permeates the most alienated segments of the American population, is sometimes used in a more cynical and manipulative manner to generate disrespect toward democratic procedure. ("To harp on the idea of crisis is in effect to declare a state of emergency in which extraordinary measures become necessary; at

* Many of the current forms of the quest for community are not too far removed from what Fromm has characterized as the "escape from freedom" in his analysis of the mass psychological preconditions of the rise of nazism in Europe. Although no leader worship has emerged among alienated radicals, there is an unmistakable affinity between their overwhelming desire for community, for escaping the self through close (if crude) contacts with other people, and the submersion into crowds which the supporters of nazism also relished. It is also significant that, despite a dominant disposition toward anarchy and indiscipline among many radicals, there are also signs of some acceptance of regimentation and deindividuation, as indicated by the popularity of stilted movement jargon, clenched-fist salutes, shouting slogans, rallies, marches, and the predilection for "uniforms," of their own.[27]

that point the enemies of democracy converge from all sides offering solutions unavailable to the antiquated, rotten or unresponsive system"[30]). Another expression of crisis-mongering is the legitimation-by-silence of the apocalyptic rhetoric fashionable during much of the 1960's, especially on the campuses.

> . . . We listen to the rhetoric as if it were the statement of a position, of one side of an issue, and we respond by disagreeing perhaps, but by accepting the premise of apocalyptic crisis. The reward we hope for is not too much violence. . . . We have listened . . . to incredibly loose talk about the obsolescence and rottenness of our society and all our institutions, and have come to parrot it in order to propitiate a sizable number of young.[31]

Even if much, or most of this type of rhetoric is rejected or fails to make a direct impact, the cumulative, residual effects have been considerable making a positive appraisal of any aspect of American society psychologically difficult. Thus the vehemence and well-publicized nature of the radical critique has had at least a disarming effect, especially among college students, academics, literary intellectuals, and journalists, creating a vague sense of unease even among those who do not share either its premises or accept its specific charges.

In a misunderstanding of political realities, many alienated radicals believe that regimented dictatorships (such as Cuba, China, North Vietnam, North Korea, or a generally undefined and unknown "Third World") offer more freedom and self-fulfillment for the individual than chaotic, permissive, and pluralistic America. The radical critique of American society loses much of its force when one realizes that much of it is applicable to all organized societies, and especially all modern industrial societies. Utopian expectations thrive in a vacuum of historical knowledge and evade the guideposts provided by comparative standards of judgment. This is the most obvious to those who were not spared appropriate historical experiences, like a Czech writer ("Class 1968"), who observed bitterly:

> . . . children of your permissive, affluent society, throwing tantrums because Father gave them only education, security and freedom—but not Utopia. . . . They seem to have no idea of the cost

or the value of the privileges they receive abundantly and *gratis.* They dismiss them as "bourgeois". . . .

In the West it seems possible to grow quite old without having to grow up—you have so much slack, so much room, so much padding between yourself and reality. . . . You simply have not faced up to the fact that you can't build Utopia, without terror, and that before long, terror is all that's left.[32]

Another foreign-born observer, Walter Laqueur, noted in a similar vein that "The use of terms such as genocide, Gestapo, Auschwitz, is disturbing, for it betrays a lack of historical perspective, a provincialism and narrow-mindedness so monumental as to make rational discourse impossible."[33]

Besides the sheer ignorance of history and the world outside the United States, the intensity of value commitments and the resulting selectivity in moral judgment help to explain how, ardent critics of bureaucracy and police repression in the United States can become the admirers, again, of countries like Cuba, China, or North Korea (and, in the case of Angela Davis, even of the Soviet Union).

To be sure, the social injustices of American society do not diminish because similar or greater injustices abound elsewhere in this world, including the countries our revolutionaries admire and look upon as models for the reconstruction of America. Yet it is also true that societies, not unlike individuals, must be judged by a combination of two standards: an ideal one and another that might be called comparative-historical. The United States and the Soviet Union must be measured both against ideals and promises and against historical realities, past and present. Some familiarity with the known limits of creating good societies, and especially the limits of providing social or collective solutions to personal problems, must temper the rejection of American society. The spectacle of totalitarian societies and political and religious movements which have tried to translate into reality various utopian designs ought to be even more sobering. The results of historical attempts at redemption through politics should give pause to those who long for revolution without bothering to ponder or spell out the substitutes they would propose for present institutional arrangements. On the other hand, the attractions of the *idea* of revolution are not hard to understand. As Raymond Aron has put it: "A revolution seems capable of changing everything, since no one knows precisely what it will change. . . . Revolution provides a welcome break with the everyday course of events and encourages the belief that all things are possible. . . ."*[34]

Contrary to the spreading and often implicit belief that this is the worst of all possible societies, by almost any standards of judgment, American society is as rich in collective achievements as it is in human and institutional defects. As Peter Berger has written: "Once one looks at American society with eyes that are freed of Utopian distortions it appears as a society with remarkable humane achievements. Even more importantly, it appears as a society with a remarkable capacity to reconstruct itself in response to moral challenge and human needs."

Berger also reminds us of the age-old dilemma of ends and means, which would-be revolutionaries typically ignore: "The reality of revolution as against the romantic fantasies about it, is as ugly as the reality of war, and in some instances uglier."[36]

The current, almost reflexive, disparagement of American society on the part of so many intellectuals has well-established historical roots. The alienation of intellectuals is a venerable tradition in American life, as is its counterpart, anti-intellectualism. In Richard Hofstadter's words:

> The tradition of alienation turned into a powerful moral imperative . . . Alienation is seen not as a risk he [the intellectual] must have the integrity to run, but as an obligation which preconditions all his other obligations. Alienation has ceased to be merely a fact of life and has taken on the character of cure or prescription for the proper intellectual regimen. . . .
>
> Once one has accepted the idea that alienation is an inevitable consequence of the assertion of certain artistic or political values, it is easy to slip into the assumption that alienation has a kind of value in itself. . . .[37]

These tendencies and attitudes were given a powerful boost by the war in Vietnam† and the new public awareness of the race problem.

---

* An equally insightful comment was made by Ernest Gellner: "The mystique of violence . . . fits in perfectly with a vision of revolution which is expressive and not at all instrumental: to think of consequences of a revolution would be as sordid as drawing up a financial marriage settlement. Spontaneity is all."[35]

† This applies to some of the old leftists. In many instances all that is left of their commitments is what they started with: the estrangement from American society, which in the first place led to their interest in, or admiration of other social systems, such as the

There are some further paradoxes associated with present-day alienation. In the past alienation usually entailed dissent, deviance, a critical spirit, an independent mind, and a sense of autonomy. Today alienation has become a new form of conformity, a well-established subculture, indeed, an establishment in its own right with its own journals, publishing houses, news services, speakers' bureaus, organizations, films, records, festivals, and best-selling books. This subculture has its own uniformities and taboos and is just as highly patterned as the dominant culture it rejects. Those who belong to it are distinguished by taking for granted whatever is good, decent, or at least acceptable in American society, while feeling with an exceptional intensity all that is not. (As George Kennan notes: "Such exaggeration of admittedly existing evils has regularly formed the initial ideological basis for fanatical political movements, including the totalitarian ones."[39])

Another aspect of the malaise of American society in the 1960's and the early 1970's is a *sense* of powerlessness that permeates almost every major stratum and segment of society—an indication of politics having become more subjective, and unconnected with the more clear-cut issues of measurable social-economic interest and deprivation. Not only do those strata of the population feel powerless which have good reason to do so, for example poor blacks; such feelings are also in evidence among the privileged upper-middle-class young. In turn the middle classes—alleged supporters and mainstays of the Establishment—feel anything but powerful, regarding themselves as the somewhat martyred carriers of the burden of social order in their capacities as taxpayers, voters, and participants in community organizations, observers of the law and victims of inflation. Similar sentiments are voiced with greater intensity and bitterness by the "lower-middle" working class populations, who often feel betrayed by politicians who court the riot-prone groups, sneered at by the liberal-intellectual establishment and all but ignored by

---

Soviet. As the realization grew that the USSR had fallen short of original expectations, interest in her (and some other Communist societies) declined and thus the positive aspects of the commitment evaporated. Some critics like Herbert Marcuse got around this problem by suggesting that "The Soviet system is worse in actuality but better in potentiality."[38] Such realizations, however, did not reduce the rejection of American society, rather they intensified it, as this rejection represented the only continuity between early commitments and latter-day disillusionments.

the mass media which seek out more glamorous and lively subjects, such as the colorful student rebels or the "exotic" slum dwellers. In addition, many people also feel powerless because of age (both the young and the old) and because of sex (women). Almost every major stratum of the population simultaneously attributes power and influence to some other group: the blacks to whites, militant feminists to men, the lower middle-class whites to the students and ghetto residents, the radical students to the Establishment, the middle classes to the manipulators of the mass media, the alienated intellectuals to the "silent majority."

Neither powerlessness nor alienation is much of an issue in Soviet society. Powerlessness is taken for granted among the population at large. Alienation is not a pressing public or private concern. There is little self-consciousness about it; a certain amount of alienation is probably taken for granted—as a more or less natural condition.

It must be pointed out, however, that we know a great deal less about alienation in Soviet society than in the American. What is known suggests that except for a handful of intellectuals, Soviet alienation is not angry but resigned, not action-oriented but passive and fatalistic. It entails an untroubled acceptance of exclusion from the important social-political decision-making processes. This type of alienation can also be found in the United States, primarily among such groups as (a decreasing number of) Southern Negroes, many old people, and the rural poor. Yet increasingly alienation in America has become angry and activist. Even those who claim to be totally powerless and ineffective—for example, many college students and elements of the black community—are often engaged in political activity with an intensity that seems to contradict the stated belief in its ineffectiveness. A genuine belief in personal ineffectiveness is expressed in abstention, withdrawal, and privatization, as is the case in Soviet rather than American society.

It is perhaps understandable for the author of a comparative study to detect more change in the more change-conscious of the two societies—especially if he happens to live in it. Thus it seems to me that the United States has changed in more ways than the Soviet Union since World War II and especially in the last decade. The nature of these changes is exemplified by the total obsolescence in the early 1970's of the perceptive comments on American life made in the late 1950's by a sociologist. Read today these observations of American society (made in a critical spirit) have a quaint, almost nostalgic quality:

> Consent and affirmation fill the press, are found on every other page of serious and scholarly journals, envelop the classroom, and fall instinctively from the mouth of ordinary men and women.
> So pervasive is the atmosphere, so unconscious is assent, that 18th-century philosophers coming upon this . . . would suspect a trick. . . . The central article of faith in America, at the moment of my visit, was that it was a society the problems of which were exclusively technical matters of detail. . . .
> Spontaneity . . . was hard to find. . . .
> The serious young American students . . . are instinctive patriots convinced of the general superiority of their country's ways. . . .
> The Jewish community's self satisfaction . . . only matched that of the rest of America.[40]

There is no dearth of "harder" data with which to back up such subjective assessments of change. Agreement on the facts of change poses a far lesser difficulty than their evaluation. Despite the problems and frustrations associated with changes of various kinds, many Americans continue to cling to the deep-seated belief that change is usually beneficial, and status quo remains a bad word especially in public discourse.

Change has meant improvement in many areas of life in America, but certainly not in all; correspondingly, some changes to come may not be benevolent. Technological-ecological problems may become insurmountable; racial-political conflict may further intensify, authoritarianism of both the Right and the Left may overwhelm democratic values and processes; the country may become internationally isolated and demoralized. Family instability may assume such proportions that the socialization process could become seriously impaired for still greater numbers of people. ("A virtual laissez-faire surrounds the institution of marriage. Americans may marry anyone they choose, using whatever criteria they happen to find convenient at the time . . . couples feel no need to ask advice of any sort concerning the suitability of their intended mates. . . . If marriage leaves much to be desired in the lives of most Americans, the difficulties increase with children. For if men and women no longer understand how to be husbands and wives, they show even more uncertainty as parents. This lack of assurance is intensified by the lack of advice they can regard as authoritative.")[41]

The gloomy prospects to unfold may also include the decline of the great power status of the United States and associated domestic problems, political, economic, and psychological. It is even conceivable, though obviously far-fetched at present, that American military power and the willingness to use it could fall to such a comparatively low level that the country might become subject to nuclear (or non-nuclear) military blackmail in the years or decades following the end of the war in Vietnam.[42] That this could come about is not altogether fanciful in view of current trends and moods among many of the young. The issue is not whether or not the younger generations are radical or revolutionary. Certainly most of them are neither. Yet the future elites of this country, those in the best colleges and universities—and the nonradicals among them—have become increasingly isolationist in global outlook, disinterested in foreign affairs, indifferent toward (and incomprehending of the whole concept) of an international balance of power, and often intensely hostile to all institutions and policies associated with the military.[43] A generation has grown up to which any external threat to the country (especially from a Communist power, or powers) is mythical and inconceivable.* It is a generation that is unlikely to send many of its best minds to the military academies, the Pentagon, or the State Department, a generation that can see no other threat to American soicety than some of its unresolved domestic social and spiritual problems.[44]

On the other hand, there may also be more cheerful prospects ahead. The Vietnam war may, despite all discouraging evidence, come to an end before long, and as a result perhaps domestic tranquility will be restored; improvements in the position of Black Americans may move from statistics to felt gratifications; political extremism may lose its bite and anger; external threats may remain insignificant. Of course, we do not know what the future holds. Sociological speculations offer no better key to the future than common sense. Prediction is hazardous, but we should be grateful for

---

* These attitudes are largely the result of the Vietnam war, but also of the remoteness of World War II from this generation and its disbelief that there is (or has ever been) a rational basis for an anti-Communist (anti-Soviet or anti-Chinese) foreign policy.

that: there is both hope and a promise of freedom in the indeterminacy of social and historical processes.

In speculating about the future of Soviet society the major temptation for the Western observer is to succumb to the familiar combination of wishful thinking and projection from the trends and experiences of Western societies. Until recently these predictions and projections crystalized around two propositions: that Soviet society is becoming more affluent and that—partly as a result of this—more liberal, democratic, and pluralistic.* A variant on this theme has been that Soviet society, being more complex, is also more resistant to regimented political patterns and, further, that with the rising level of education there will be less tolerance of a police state. All these viewpoints rest on the exaggeration of change that has so far taken place. Those who have followed Soviet developments closely, inside or outside the USSR, are less likely to subscribe to these beliefs. For example, Tibor Szamuelly, a political scientist who had spent many years of his life in the Soviet Union, has pointed out that:

> The conviction that the system will *have* to change, that it is bound to undergo major transformations, stems from a variety of causes. One of these is the belief—deeply ingrained in the Western mentality—in the inevitability of constant change, of permanent movement: the belief in progress, in short. Another factor is our perfectly understandable reluctance to accept the awful prospect of living with a faceless, impersonal and brutal totalitarian system for as far into the future as we can see. Finally, one must take into account the difficulty . . . of appreciating and assimilating a genuinely new concept which overturns hallowed traditional certitudes: in this case, the idea that totalitarianism, a revolutionary form of government invented in the 20th century, may have become as stable and as lasting a political system as democracy, absolutism, autocracy, oriental despotism, theocracy or any other long-lived type of government, past or present.

The belief that there is an unbreakable bond between science, technology, and rationality, and that rationality in turn must lead to democratic political arrangements, has been at the root of the faith

* The Czech invasion and the better publicized instances of persecution of Soviet intellectuals gave some pause to those who cherish such views, but probably not even these events have had a significant impact on them.

in convergence among industrial societies. This is all the more curious since few people would argue that such a benevolent relationship
exists in the United States, where we have become well aware of the
harm done by technology to nature and to the manmade environment. Again, as Szamuelly points out, it is the height of culture-
bound myopia to assume "as self evident that to be 'rational' is to
conform to what we in the West regard as standards of rationality."

There are several indicators of continuity, barely noticed in the
West, which testify to the stability of the Soviet system. For instance,
in 47 years there have been only 3 incumbents to the most important
position in the Soviet Union, the First Secretary of the Central Committee of the Party; there have been only 8 prime ministers since
1917; since the purges of the 1930's, of the 71 members elected to
the Central Committee, 12 have remained on it for 30 years; many
important economic expert-civil servants (ministers) have been on
their jobs since the 1930's, 40's, and 50's. Nearly two-thirds (46) of
the important regional party secretaries appointed under Khrushchev are still in office. Szamuelly's conclusion, I believe, is persuasive:

> In the dictatorship of the Communist Party Russia found a
> unique instrument of the stabilization and perpetuation of its tra-
> dition. Communist elitism coalesced with Russian bureaucratic
> despotism to form modern totalitarianism. The absolute, unlim-
> ited and undivided dictatorship of the Party, unchanged through
> all the vicissitudes of Soviet history, provides the basis for the
> stability of Soviet society.[45]

Soviet intellectuals themselves, or at least those willing to discuss
such matters candidly with foreigners, do not entertain the hopes
current in the West about liberalization, as the following comments
suggest:

> I have heard this hypothesis [i.e., the inevitability of liberaliza-
> tion and democratization—P.H.] often enough in the West, but
> never in Russia, neither from those who operate the dictatorship
> nor those who suffer under it. . . .
> "The only place I encounter strong optimism about liberaliza-
> tion," said a middle-aged [Soviet] teacher, "is in the Western
> press." The notion that protests against the writers' trials are the
> forerunners of a great movement toward freedom is wishful
> thinking. It's a Western analysis based on Western conditions and

has little to do with Russian history and the Russian environment. . . . There are no liberals at the top. Not in in Politburo.
. . . Czechoslovakia will bounce back one day. . . . Russia will
stay true to her character. Which means keeping tyranny roughly
like this, with periodic witch-hunts more or less like this one.[46]

Perhaps we should brace ourselves, if not to cataclysmic developments, to the persistence (or slow deterioration) of an unappealing
status quo in both American and Soviet society. The Soviet Union
may not, in our lifetime, become significantly more free and "live-
able," and the United States may gradually shed its democratic values and institutions as the forces of despair, anarchy, and extremism
(right and left), gather strength over time.

It is hard to end a book—both for its readers and its author—on
such a note of unrelieved gloom. Yet, there is little, if any, historical
or social scientific evidence to show that diversity, pluralism, and the
prevalence of personal freedoms (such as still exist in the U.S.) have
much survival value for a society or, on the other hand, that a system
that stifles free expression and certain types of initiative cannot endure.[47] We cannot assume that it is only a matter of time before
people in a regimented society such as the Soviet become intolerant
of the restrictions on their lives. Nor can we confidently expect a
massive upsurge of social consciousness among prosperous Americans
that would motivate them to reduce their level of consumption and
material comforts in order to contribute to the resolution of certain
social problems and a strengthening of social cohesion.[48] It would
be equally unrealistic to expect the rapid erosion of the certainties
of alienation among other groups of Americans, committed to the
perversely comforting belief that existing American social, political,
and economic institutions are responsible for every human frustration and indignity known and imagined.

In short, the respective virtues and vices, failures and achievements
of the United States and the Soviet Union provide a most uncertain
guide to predicting the future of these societies.

If attempts at rational speculation and extrapolation from observable trends and conditions offer little ground for a more optimistic
conclusion of a book of this kind, a reminder of the limitations of
personal insight, sociological knowledge, and accessible experience
may allow some questioning of pessimism. Perhaps today an academic sociologist in the U.S. is not in the best position to perceive

and appraise with equal clarity and sensitivity both the distressing and hopeful aspects of observable social realities and their complex potentialities. He is immersed in what has become in some ways the most alienated and alienating of all social settings in contemporary American society, the campus. It is possible that those of us contemplating with gloom and foreboding the domestic problems and unfriendly external forces facing the United States—including the Soviet Union—may have overlooked important social processes, dormant or ripening under the obtrusive surface of crisis or behind the obvious drama of social-political conflict.

Notes

Chapter 1

1. See also Anatol Rapoport: *The Big Two—Soviet-American Perceptions of Foreign Policy*, New York, 1969, p. 9.
2. There has been no book-length comparison of the United States and the Soviet Union by sociologists except for P. Sorokin: *Russia and the United States*, New York, 1944. A comparison of the political institutions of the two countries has been undertaken, however, in Zbigniew Brzezinski and Samuel P. Huntington: *Political Power USA/USSR*, New York, 1964.
3. Walt W. Rostow: *Stages of Economic Growth*, London, 1960; Isaac Deutscher: *The Great Contest*, New York, 1960; Raymond Aron: *Industrial Society*, New York, 1967; Pitirim Sorokin: "The Mutual Convergence of the US and the USSR" in *The Basic Trends of Our Times*, New Haven, 1964. For a critique of Sorokin's earlier views on convergence (which, however, is also applicable to his above cited revival of these views) see Alex Inkeles: "Russia and the United States: A Problem in Comparative Sociology" in Philip S. Allen, ed.: *Pitirim A. Sorokin in Review*, Durham, 1963. For a discussion of the uniformities created by industrialization which has implications for convergence see Alex Inkeles: "Industrial Man," *American Journal of Sociology*, July 1960. See also Peter Wiles: "Convergence: Possibility and Probability," in A. Balinsky et al., eds.: *Planning and the Market in the USSR: The 1960's*, New Brunswick, 1967; Gordon Skilling: "Soviet and American Politics: The dialectic of Opposites," *Canadian Journal of Economics and Politics*, May 1965. A surprisingly unqualified support of the convergence thesis (and of an ahistorical technological determinism) was expressed by John K. Galbraith in an interview in *The New York Times Magazine*, December 18, 1966, p. 92. See also *The New Industrial State*, Boston, 1967. For what might be called a moderate convergence thesis which stresses "basically similar cultural roots" see Talcott Parsons, "Communism and the West," in A. Etzioni, ed.: *Social Change*, New York, 1964. For critical discussions of convergence see Bertram D.

Wolfe: "A Historian Looks at the Convergence Theory" in Paul Kurtz, ed.: *Sidney Hook and the Contemporary World*, New York, 1968, and Ian Weinberg: "The Problem of the Convergence of Industrial Societies: A Critical Look at the State of a Theory," *Comparative Studies in Society and History*, January 1969. Mihajlo Mihajlov, the Yugoslav writer, believes that convergence need not be benevolent and that totalitarianism and high levels of technological-scientific development can be reconciled. "Thought on Society: I," *New York Times* (hereafter referred to as *NYT*), July 26, 1971, p. 25. For a survey of convergence theories (by an author sympathetic to some of their varieties) see Alfred G. Meyer: "Theories of Convergence" in Chalmers Johnson, ed., *Change in Communist Systems*, Stanford, 1970. See also Irving Louis Horowitz: *Three Worlds of Development*, New York, 1972, pp. 52-53, and Maurice Duverger: *The Idea of Politics*, Chicago, 1970, pp. 230-31.

4. Claude Cockburn: *Crossing the Line*, London, 1958, p. 123.

5. Proponents of convergence are, however, not always optimistic. For some gloomy visions of modern industrial societies, and the U.S. and the USSR, in particular, see Herbert Marcuse: *One Dimensional Man: Studies in the Ideology of Advanced Industrial Societies*, Boston, 1964; C. Wright Mills: *The Origins of World War III*, New York, 1958; Barrington Moore, Jr.: "Reflections on Conformity in Industrial Society," *Political Power and Social Theory*, Cambridge, Mass., 1958. Two excellent critiques of Marcuse and the views represented by him are George Lichtheim: "The Threat of History," *New York Review of Books*, February 20, 1964, and Julius Gould: "The Dialectics of Despair," *Encounter*, September 1964. For Soviet criticism of convergence see Yu. Zamoshkin: "Teoria yedinovo industrialnovo obshchestva na sluzhbe antikommunizma" (The Theory of a "Single Industrial Society" in the Service of Anticommunism), in *Marksistkaya i burzhuaznaya sotsiologia sevodnia* (Marxist and Bourgeois Sociology Today), Moscow, 1964. See also "Against Imperialist Ideology," *Pravda*, transl. *Current Digest of the Soviet Press* (hereafter referred to as *CDSP*), July 21, 1965; "Admissions and Ditsortions," *Izvestia*, transl. *CDSP*, April 26, 1967; "The Invincible Power of Marxist-Leninist Ideas," *Pravda*, transl. *CDSP*, July 5, 1967. A pre-Soviet Russian thinker who detected similarities between the United States and Russia was Herzen. Some of his views have a contemporary ring. See A. Kucherov: "Herzen's Parallel Between the United States and Russia" in John S. Curtiss, ed.: *Essays in Russian and Soviet History in Honor of G. T. Robinson*, New York, 1963.

6. A somewhat, though not totally, different point of view on the usefulness of various models was presented by Alex Inkeles, "Models and Issues in the Analysis of Soviet Society" in his *Social Change in Soviet Russia*, Cambridge, Mass., 1968.

7. The two major publications to come out of the project were Alex Inkeles and Raymond Bauer: *The Soviet Citizen*, Cambridge, Mass., 1959, and Raymond Bauer, Alex Inkeles, and Clyde Kluckhohn: *How the Soviet System Works*, Cambridge, Mass., 1956.

8. The major revelation came from Khrushchev himself; see further N. S. Khrushchev: "Special Report to the 20th Party Congress," *New Leader* pamphlet, 1962. See also A. V. Gorbatov: *Years of My Life*, New York, 1965; A. Solzhenitsyn: *One Day in the Life of Ivan Denisovich*, New York, 1963; I. Ehrenburg: *Memoirs 1921-1941*, Cleveland, 1964. According to a Yugoslav author some 10,000 short stories, and memoirs dealing with concentration camp themes have been submitted to Soviet literary journals. M. Mihajlov: *Moscow Summer*, New York, 1965, p. 66.

9. It might be noted here that at least one critic thought that the major publication

of the Harvard Project (Inkeles and Bauer, *op cit*.) did not sufficiently emphasize the totalitarian aspects of Soviet society and instead stressed those it had in common with other industrial societies. See further S. V. Utechin in *Soviet Studies*, January 1963, p. 322. For some classical formulations of the concept see C. Friedrich, ed.: *Totalitarianism—Symposium*, Cambridge, Mass., 1954. For recent discussions of its applicability see Alfred Meyer: *The Soviet Political System*, New York, 1965, esp. pp. 470-72; also Alfred Meyer: "The Comparative Study of Communist Political Systems," *Slavic Review*, March 1967; Alex Inkeles: "Models in the Analysis of Soviet Society," *Survey*, July 1966; H. Seton-Watson: "Totalitarianism Reconsidered," *Problems of Communism*, July 1967; Paul Hollander: "Observations on Bureaucracy, Totalitarianism and the Comparative Study of Communism," *Slavic Review*, June 1967; Allen Kassof: "The Administered Society: Totalitarianism Without Terror," *World Politics*, July 1964; Donald Treadgold, ed.: *The Development of the USSR*, 1964, contributions by Brzezinski, Meyer, and Tucker.

10. Reinhard Bendix: *Citizenship and Nationbuilding*, New York, 1964, p. 8.

11. For a different conception of the tasks and nature of history see J. H. Plumb: *The Death of the Past*, Boston, 1970, p. 106.

12. Wilbert E. Moore: *The Impact of Industry*, Englewood Cliffs, 1965, esp. Chap. 2, and Bendix, *op. cit.*, esp. pp. 299-301. For discussions of the relationship between science, technology, rationality, and political liberality see Bertram D. Wolfe: "Reflections on the Future of the Soviet System," *Russian Review*, April 1967, and Zbigniew Brzezinski: "The Patterns of Autocracy," in C. Black, ed.: *The Transformation of Russian Society*, Cambridge, Mass., 1960, esp. pp. 108-10. For an affirmation of the belief in the liberalizing impact of the mass media in the Soviet Union see Ithiel de Sola Pool: "The Changing Soviet Union—The Mass Media as Catalyst," *Current*, January 1966.

13. *The Collected Essays of George Orwell*, New York, 1968, Vol. III, p. 145-47.

14. Geoffrey Gorer, *The American People*, New York, 1964, rev. ed., p. 224.

15. *NYT*, February 27, 1967, p. 47.

16. The Soviet policy in the Middle East and Cuba and the resulting clash of interests illustrate that there is more to the tension between the two countries than inadequate information or hostile stereotypes. Indeed, peaceful competition involves such old-fashioned stakes as oil, military bases, harbor facilities, and political control of governments. For an interesting discussion of some of the persisting realities of the cold war see Edmund Taylor: "The Political War Intensifies," *The Reporter*, June 29, 1967.

17. Sorokin, *Russia and the United States*. Sorokin's views cannot be ascribed entirely to the spirit of wartime cooperation as is illustrated by his essay published 20 years later on convergence (Sorokin, *op. cit.*, 1964). The following provide better examples of books born out of the spirit of wartime friendship: Albert Rhys Williams: *The Russians*, New York, 1943; Edmund Stevens: *Russia Is No Riddle*, New York, 1945; Edgar Snow: *Stalin Must Have Peace*, New York, 1947. For an incisive analysis of distorted Western (including American) views of Soviet society see "Western Images of the Soviet Union," *Survey*, April 1962.

18. For example: Inkeles and Bauer, *op. cit.*; Bauer, Inkeles, Kluckhohn, *op. cit.*; Merle Fainsod: *How Russia Is Ruled*, Cambridge, Mass., 1953; Merle Fainsod: *Smolensk Under Soviet Rule*, Cambridge, Mass., 1958; Barrington Moore, Jr.: *Soviet Politics: The Dilemma of Power*, Cambridge, Mass., 1950; Barrington Moore, Jr.: *Terror and Progress USSR*, Cambridge, Mass., 1957; Alex Inkeles: *Public Opinion in Russia*, Cambridge, Mass. 1951.

19. As at least one study has shown, the differences between the militant foreign policies of Stalin and the more accommodating ones of his successors have been greatly exaggerated; see Marshall Shulman: *Stalin's Foreign Policy Reappraised*, Cambridge, Mass., 1965.

20. The "revisionist" view of the cold war, usually combined with an intensely critical stance toward American society as a whole, has many distinguished and less distinguished representatives. For some examples see H. S. Commager: *Freedom and Order: A Commentary on the American Political Scene*, New York, 1966; William J. Fulbright: *The Arrogance of Power*, New York, 1966, Ronald Steel: *Pax Americana*, New York, 1967; Charles Oglesby and Richard Shaull: *Containment and Change*, New York, 1967; R. Niebuhr: "The Social Myths in the 'Cold War,' " *Journal of International Affairs*, No. 1, 1967; David Horowitz, ed.: *Containment and Revolution* with a preface by Bertrand Russell, Boston, 1967; Richard J. Barnet and Marcus G. Raskin: *After Twenty Years*, New York, 1965 (a book that was characterized as making "recent history appear like a gigantic misunderstanding caused essentially by American shortsightedness." See also Henry A. Kissinger: "Answers Aren't Easy" *NYT Book Review*, June 27, 1965); Jason Epstein: "The CIA and the Intellectuals, "*The New York Review of Books*, April 20, 1967; and John Leo: "Revisionist Historians Blame US for Cold War," *NYT*, September, 1967; see also Joyce and Gabriel Kolko: *The Limits of Power*, New York, 1972. For rebuttals of the "revisionist" approach see Arthur Schlesinger, Jr.: "The Origins of the Cold War," *Foreign Affairs*, October 1967; Joseph R. Starobin: "Origins of the Cold War: The Communist Dimension, *Foreign Affairs*, July 1969. See also Adam Ulam: *Expansion and Coexistence*, New York, 1968.

21. See, for example, Irving Louis Horowitz: "The Conflict Society," in Howard Becker, ed.: *Social Problems*, New York, 1966, p. 733. The view of the Cold War as a distraction from domestic problems is also expressed by David Riesman: "The Cold War and the West" in *Abundance for What?*, Garden City, 1964, p. 93.

22. See Erich Fromm: *May Man Prevail?*, Garden City, 1961.

23. *Look Magazine*, May 30, 1967, p. 75.

24. This unease and its sources have been thoroughly examined in "Liberal Anti-Communism Revisited, A Symposium," *Commentary*, September 1967. Significantly, of the 21 participants only 10 would admit, with or without qualifications, of being anticommunist. Seven expressed views that might be classified as antianticommunist and four were sufficiently vague as to defy classification. For discussions of the liberal's fear of being identified as anticommunist see esp. the contributions by S. Hook, R. Pickus, A. Schlesinger, Jr., S. Spender, and D. Trilling. See also George F. Kennan: "The Ethics of Anti-Communism, *University—A Princeton Quarterly*, Spring 1965; also Harvey B. Schecter: "The Liberals Have Helped the Radical Right," *NYT Magazine*, April 29, 1962. For a book-length exposition of the antianticommunist position see Michael Parenti: *The Anti-Communist Impulse*, New York, 1969.

25. *Encounter*, November 1962, p. 47.

26. Susan Sontag: *Trip to Hanoi*, New York, 1968, p. 87.

27. This view is shared to some degree by a wide variety of political thinkers and writers, including Walter Lippman, William Fulbright, Henry Steele Commager, Hans Morgenthau, Erich Fromm, Graham Greene, Norman Mailer, Jules Feiffer, and a multitude of social critics at home and abroad.

28. See *Trail of the Dinosaur*, Port Washington, 1955.

29. For a further discussion of this attitude see Tibor Szamuelly's contribution to "In-

tellectuals and Just Causes," *Encounter*, September 1967, pp. 13-15. Orwell's observations quoted in the article are of special interest.

30. H. Stuart Hughes: "Jean Paul Sartre: The Marxist Phase," *Ramparts*, March 1967, p. 47. In a similar vein Hannah Arendt also pointed out that "calls for Mao, Castro, Che Guevara, and Ho Chi Minh are like pseudo-religious incantations for saviors from another world; they would also call for Tito if only Yugoslavia were farther away and less approachable." See her *On Violence*, New York, 1969, p. 21.

31. "Mirror images . . ." by U. Bronfenbrenner in Harry G. Shaffer, ed.: *The Soviet System in Theory and Practice*, New York, 1965; Raymond Bauer: "Accuracy of Perceptions in International Relations," *Teachers College Record*, Vol. LXIV, January 1963; David Riesman: "Dealing with the Russians over Berlin," *The American Scholar*, Winter 1961-62, Vol. XXXI, No. 1; Ralph K. White: "Images in the Context of International Conflict—Soviet Perceptions of the US and USSR," in Herbert C. Kelman, ed.: *International Behavior*, New York, 1965.

32. N. S. Khrushchev: *For Victory in Peaceful Coexistence*, New York, 1960.

33. For a compilation designed to provide factual (?) as well as ideological basis for a highly negative portrait of the United States (and some other Western countries) see *Spravochnik propagandista mezhdunarodnika* (Handbook of the International Propagandist), Moscow, 1966. This book has a section of statistical highlights on the various gloomy aspects of these societies ranging from "child labor in Italy," to the "catastrophic decline" of birth rates in Japan, to the poor health of Americans and inequalities among Britons. For a similarly tendentious compilation see also *Strani sotsializma i kapitalizma v cifrah* (The Countries of Socialism and Capitalism in Figures) Moscow, 1966; and *Cifri i fakti SSSR—SSha* (USSR—USA, Figures and Facts), Moscow, 1961; for an American compilation of Soviet official perceptions of the United States see parts of Alan F. Westin et al., eds.: *Views of America*, New York, 1966. For an interesting description of Soviet television coverage of life in the United States see Edith Efron: "The Land of the Shanty and the Home of the Oppressed," *TV Guide*, January 13, 1968. For indications of a more sophisticated Soviet view of the U.S. see William Zimmerman: "Soviet Perceptions of the U.S." in A. Dallin and T. B. Larson, eds.: *Soviet Politics Since Khrushchev*, Englewood Cliffs, 1968; see also Paul Aron, ed.: *Soviet Views of America*, White Plains, 1969; see also *SSha* (USA), a Soviet journal devoted to a highly ideological though better informed analysis of American society published for the edification of the Soviet elites.

34. Frederick C. Barghoorn: *The Soviet Image of the United States*, New York, 1950, p. 277; for a more recent discussion of such distortions see Max Beloff: "Soviet Historians and American History" in John Keep, ed.: *Contemporary History in the Soviet Mirror*, New York, 1964.

35. The most authoritative statement on this subject was made in the 1961 Program of the Communist Party of the Soviet Union: "A grim struggle is going on between two ideologies—communist and bourgeois—in the world today. . . . The more victories the socialist system achieves the deeper the crisis of world capitalism and the sharper the class struggle the more important becomes the role of Marxist-Leninist ideas . . ." *The Program of the Communist Party of the Soviet Union*, New York, 1965, pp. 57-58. On the irreconcilability of the ideological struggle see also *Marksistkaya i burzhuaznaya sotsiologia sevodnia* (Marxist and Bourgeois Sociology Today), Moscow, 1964, p. 3.

36. Richard Pipes: *Some Operational Principles of Soviet Foreign Policy*, Memorandum prepared at the request of the Subcommitte on National Security and International

Operations of the Committee on Government Operations, U.S. Senate, Washington D.C., 1972, p. 14.

37. An interesting effort to penetrate elite thinking and also to explain the tendency to projections can be found in Nathan Leites: *A Study of Bolshevism*, Glencoe, 1953.

38. Adam B. Ulam: "Reflections on the Revolution," *Survey*, July 1967, p. 12.

39. See, for example, Mihajlov, *Moscow Summer*, p. 154.

40. Lewis M. Feuer: "Meeting the Philosophers," *Survey*, April 1964, p. 16.

41. For an example of the Soviet projection of political indoctrination to the United States see "Brains on the Assembly line," *Pravda*, transl. *CDSP*, July 15, 1964; on the Soviet system of political indoctrination see E. Mickiewicz: *Soviet Political Schools*, New Haven, 1967; Frederick C. Barghoorn: *Politics in the USSR*, Boston, 1966, and Gayle D. Hollander: *Soviet Political Indoctrination: Developments in Mass Media and Propaganda Since Stalin*, New York, 1972.

42. *Life Magazine*, November 10, 1967, pp. 81-82.

43. Two Soviet visitors reported to have encountered American children who actually cringed at the sight of Soviet people, so deep were the scars of anti-Soviet indoctrination! see further A. Svetlikov and M. Kuchtarev: *Strana Gde Zhivut Nespokoino* (The Country Where They Live Without Tranquility), Moscow, 1964, p. 33; for a similar travelogue see V. Krivoruchenko: *Mesyats v Shtatakh* (A Month in the States), Moscow, 1964; for an example of a Soviet visitor's impressions in English see "Why the Statue of Liberty Looks to the East," *NYT Magazine*, December 25, 1966.

44. B. A. Viktorov: *Spioni pod maskoi turistov* (Spies Masked as Tourists), Moscow, 1963. It is indicative of its importance that 200,000 copies of this booklet were printed (Soviet books usually show on the back page how many copies have been printed); also relevant here is George Bailey: "Cultural Exchange as the Soviets Use it," *Reporter*, April 7, 1966. "Vigilance and the struggle against ideological subversion" were also prominent themes of the 1968 May Day Celebrations; see also Robert F. Byrnes: "American Scholars in Russia Soon Learn about the KGB," *NYT Magazine*, November 16, 1969.

45. "They Are Afraid," *Komsomolskaya pravda*, transl. *CDSP*, August 9, 1967.

46. Sylvia R. Margulies: *The Pilgrimage to Russia—The Soviet Union and the Treatment of Foreigners*, Madison, 1968.

47. "Let's Talk About Tourism," *Sovetskaya Rossia*, transl. *CDSP*, May 28, 1969, p. 12. Many articles in the Soviet press are devoted to the necessity of combating positive descriptions or stories of Western life and countries. For example, "Not on Instructions, But By Conviction," *Pravda*, transl. *CDSP*, August 28, 1968, p. 10. Here the citizens are admonished to rebut and rebuff, on their own initiative, information favorable to the West that may circulate among gullible elements of Soviet society.

48. Leopold Tyrmand: *Notebooks of a Dilettante*, New York, 1970, pp. 86-87.

49. Yu. Zamoshkin: *Krizis burzhuaznovo individualizma i lichnost* (The Crisis of Bourgeois Individualism and Personality), Moscow, 1966, pp. 252-53.

50. E. G. F. Orekhov: "Dollar Democracy," *International Affairs*, February 1965; V. Kononov: "The Ideology of Big Business," *Pravda*, transl. *CDSP*, September 27, 1967, p. 21.

51. Zamoshkin, *Krizis burzhuaznovo individualizma i lichnost*, pp. 250-70.

52. "Russian Tourists Combine Sightseeing with Work," *NYT*, June 22, 1969. In 1970, 66,365 Americans visited the Soviet Union and 5,268 Soviet citizens came to the United States, of whom 3500 were on official business (*NYT*, July 28, 1971, p. 2.

53. For example, Maurice Hindus: *The Kremlin's Human Dilemma*, Garden City, 1967;

Wright Miller: *Russians as People,* New York, 1961; Maurice Hindus: *House Without a Roof,* Garden City, 1961; Alexander Werth: *Russia Under Khrushchev,* Greenwich, 1962; Markoosha Fisher: *Reunion in Moscow,* New York, 1962; An Observer: *Message from Moscow,* New York, 1969, Chap. V.

54. Personal communication from a Russian-speaking visitor to the Soviet Union, 1969-70 academic year.

55. This and other subsequent examples of the Soviet citizen's misconceptions of American life come from an unpublished survey (carried out by the author) of the experiences of several hundred American travelers in the Soviet Union in the summer of 1966.

56. Examples of such views may be found in Alayne P. Reilly: *America in Contemporary Soviet Literature,* New York, 1971.

57. On the social critical disposition of American television journalism see Edith Efron: *The News Twisters,* Los Angeles, 1971.

58. *NYT News of the Week in Review Section,* November 30, 1969, p. 6.

59. Tyrmand, *op. cit.,* p. 70.

60. Quoted in "The Ginsburg and Galanskov Trail," *Problems of Communism,* July-August 1968, p. 42.

61. Jacques Barzun: "The Man in the American Mask," *Foreign Affairs,* April 1965, p. 427.

Chapter 2

1. William Kornhauser: *The Politics of Mass Society,* Glencoe, Ill., 1959, p. 39.

2. Frederick Engels: *The Origin of the Family, Private Property and the State,* as quoted by V. I. Lenin: *The State and the Revolution,* Moscow (no date), p. 11.

3. For Soviet discussions of the retention of the state and the prospects of its disappearance see F. Burlatsky: *The State and Communism,* Moscow: (no date, early 1960's); D. Chesnokov: "The Educative Role of the Soviet State," *Pravda,* transl. *CDSP,* March 22, 1967, p. 6. The classical discussion is of course Lenin's *State and Revolution* which presents Lenin's most unrealistic (and totally unfulfilled) expectations and predictions concerning the character of the Soviet state, its transformation, and "withering away."

4. Richard Lowenthal: "Development vs. Utopia in Communist Policy" in Chalmers Johnson, ed.: *Change in Communist Systems,* Stanford: 1970, p. 86.

5. Engels, in Lenin, *op. cit.,* pp. 26-27.

6. Rosa Luxemburg: *The Russian Revolution,* Ann Arbor, 1961, p. 77.

7. See, for example, A. Hamilton, J. Madison, and J. Jay: *The Federalist,* Cambridge, Mass., 1961, papers 41-51.

8. See further, for example, B. Goldwater: *The Conscience of a Conservative,* New York, 1963; F. Hayek: *The Constitution of Liberty,* Chicago, 1960.

9. See, for example, E. H. Carr: *The New Society,* Boston, 1963, pp. 26-39; for a more general discussion of the two types of freedoms, positive and negative, see further Isaiah Berlin: *Two Concepts of Liberty,* Oxford, 1963.

10. See also Alfred G. Meyer: *Leninism,* Cambridge, Mass., 1967, p. 19.

11. For an excellent discussion of the differences between commitment to a communist or democratic party see also Gabriel Almond: *The Appeals of Communism,* Princeton, 1954, Chaps. 1 and 2.

12. *Ibid.,* p. 27.

13. Quoted in Fainsod, *How Russia Is Ruled,* Cambridge, p. 205.

14. Lenin stated in his article "Urgent Tasks of Our Movement," in the first issue of

the underground paper *Iskra,* that the party must be composed of people "who shall devote to the revolution not only their spare evenings, but the whole of their lives." Quoted in B. D. Wolfe: *Three Who Made a Revolution,* New York, 1964, p. 155.

15. N. Leites: *The Operational Code of the Politburo,* New York, 1951.

16. The operation of this process ("Nomenklatura") is described in Merle Fainsod, *Smolensk Under Soviet Rule,* pp. 45, 64-66, 73-74, 99-100. See also Bohdan Harasymiv: "Nomenklatura: The Soviet Communist Party's Leadership Recruitment System," *Canadian Journal of Political Science,* December 1969.

17. Jan Triska, ed.: *Soviet Communism: Programs and Rules,* San Francisco, 1962, pp. 156-59.

18. See Fainsod: *Smolensk Under Soviet Rule,* pp. 39-47 and Fainsod: *How Russia Is Ruled,* pp. 191-202.

19. In 1958 there were somewhat less than a quarter million paid Party functionaries in the Soviet Union. See further Leonard Schapiro: *The Communist Party of the Soviet Union,* New York, 1960, pp. 572-73. A more recent estimate put their number at 100,000-125,000. See H. Gordon Skilling and Franklyn Griffiths, eds.: *Interest Groups in Soviet Politics* Princeton, 1971. p. 49.

20. B. Mochalov (Secretary of the Party Committee of Moscow University): "Party Work In Instiuttions of Higher Education," *Kommunist,* transl. *CDSP,* September 28, 1966, pp. 3-4. For another article critical of apolitical attitudes among scientists and the intelligentsia see "Party Concern For the Upbringing of the Scientific-Technical Intelligentsia," *Kommunist,* transl. *CDSP,* January 22, 1969, pp. 3, 4. For an early critique of the bureaucratization of the party see Leon Trotsky: *The Revolution Betrayed,* New York, 1937.

21. For another detailed discussion of the functions of the Party see T. H. Rigby: *Communist Party Membership in the USSR, 1917-1967,* Princeton, 1968, pp. 11-18.

22. Fainsod: *Smolensk Under Soviet Rule,* pp. 166, 167, 171-72.

23. For a discussion of the unique features of Soviet bureaucracy, and especially its deviation from Western social scientific models of bureaucracy, see further Paul Hollander: "Politicized Bureaucracy: The Soviet Case," *Newsletter on Comparative Studies of Communism,* May 1971, pp. 12-22.

24. Raymond Aron: "Social Structure and the Ruling Class," *British Journal of Sociology,* June 1950. Appropriately enough, Aron noted that "a unified elite is the end of freedom." This has been also borne out by developments in the Soviet Union following Stalin's death. To the extent that a small-scale fragmentation of elites has begun, and in particular to the extent that some members of the intellectual and scientific elite decreased their identification with the party, demands for a greater freedom of expression have grown, and indeed the freedom of expression itself has somewhat expanded.

25. See further Rigby, *op. cit.,* pp. 341, 348, 449.

26. Inkeles and Bauer, *op. cit.,* pp. 323-24. More recently, and particularly under Khrushchev, there has been an effort to diminish somewhat these imbalances in the composition of the party, to increase the worker and peasant membership. However, ". . . the emphasis is still on enrolling 'leading' workers and collective farmers, and the definitions of both workers and collective farmers are apparently elastic enough to embrace many foremen, brigadiers and other administrative and specialist personnel who are not themselves engaged in physical labor." (Fainsod, *How Russia Is Ruled,* 1963, p. 276.) For two more recent Soviet articles on the composition of the membership see "The CPSU [The Communist Party of the Soviet

Union] in Figures (1961-1964)," *Partiinaya Zhizn*, transl. *CDSP*, August 11, 1965, p. 14 and "CPSU in Figures" *Partiinaya Zhizn*, transl. *CDSP*, November 15, 1967, p. 10. See also Rigby, *op. cit.*, Chaps. 9, 10, 13, and 14.

27. "On Results of Admissions to Party and Changes in the Composition of CPSU [Communist Party of the Soviet Union] in 1967" *Partiinaya Zhizn*, transl. *CDSP*, May 8, 1968, p. 12.

28. A somewhat similar point is made by Paul Cocks in his discussion of the two official views of the party: a moral entity on the one hand and an organizational structure on the other. See his so far unpublished study: *Controlling Communist Bureaucracy: Ethics, Rationality, and Terror* (1972).

29. I. Pomelov: "The Communist Party in a Socialist Society," *Pravda*, transl. *CDSP*, March 15, 1967, p. 8.

30. Speech by writer A. O. Avdienko to the Seventh Congress of Soviets in 1935 (at that time the cult was just beginning), quoted in T. H. Rigby, ed.: *Stalin*, Englewood Cliffs, 1966, p. 111.

31. A most remarkable document of the consequences of his "cult" has been Khrushchev's speech at the 20th Party Congress in 1956. See N. S. Khrushchev: *The Crimes of the Stalin Era*, New York, 1962 (annotated by Boris I. Nikolaevsky).

32. See, for example, "Stirring Pages in the Annals of the Great Patriotic War," *Kommunist*, transl. *CDSP*, January 27, 1969.

33. "The Soviet Union consistently pursues a Leninist foreign policy," *Pravda*, transl. *CDSP*, January 5, 1966, p. 19; "V. I. Lenin foresaw that the popular masses of non-Russian nationalities . . . would themselves realize the necessity of mastering the Russian language . . . ," *ibid.*, p. 33; "V. I. Lenin repeatedly called the attention of scholars, specialists and organizers . . . to the necessity of conducting concrete social research," *Izvestia*, transl. *CDSP*, January 12, 1966, p. 16; "V. I. Lenin taught us to fight against religion. . . . ," *ibid.*, p. 35; "V. I. Lenin also emphasized the necessity of concrete . . . study of the laws of population," *Literaturnaya gazeta*, transl. *CDSP*, January 19, 1955, p. 12. "According to Lenin free time is necessary not only for rest and self-development but also for the utilization of human rights and those pertaining to family life and citizenship." Quoted in *Voprosy teorii i praktiki partiinoi propagandy* (Questions of the Theory and Method of Party Propaganda), Moscow, 1971, p. 198.

34. Peter Kenez: "Notes on the 1969-70 Moscow Movie Season," mimeographed, 1970.

35. Kornhauser, *op. cit.*, pp. 76-78.

36. "Grechko Book Depicts Brezhnev as a Hero in World War II," *NYT*, March 23, 1969, p. 13.

37. *Bolshaya Sovetskaya Entsiklopedia* (The Great Soviet Encyclopedia), Moscow, 1950, p. 516. The article on criticism and self-criticism (four pages long) contained no less than 38 references to Stalin, including copious citations, one of which we quoted.

38. For a discussion of such safety-valve functions of critical letters in the press see Alex Inkeles: *Public Opinion in Soviet Russia*, Cambridge, Mass., 1958, pp. 217-19.

39. "Kritika i Samokritika—Nashe Ispytannoe Oruzhie" (Criticism and Self-Criticism—Our Tested Weapon), *Kommunist*, No. 1, January 1961, p. 81. For descriptions of actual criticism and self-criticism sessions see Joseph Novak: *No Third Path*, Garden City, 1962, Chap. 1. See also Paul Hollander: "Criticism and Self-Criticism in Soviet Society" in *Marxism, Communism and Western Society: A Comparative Encyclopedia*, New York, 1972.

40. For a discussion of the number and kind of officials and representatives who gain

office through elections in the United States see Robert E. Lane: *Political Life,* Glencoe, 1959, pp. 45-46.

41. See, for example, "Millionaire Gives Most of $708,300 to Aid McGovern," *NYT,* June 25, 1972, p. 32. A few days later it was also reported that some other rich fund-raisers became disillusioned with McGovern on account of his tax proposals.

42. Emmette S. Redford, David B. Truman, Andrew Hacker, Alan F. Westin, and Robert C. Wood: *Politics and Government in the United States,* New York, 1965, p. 238. See also Fred I. Greenstein: *The American Party System and the American People,* Englewood Cliffs, 1965, p. 10.

43. Jerome M. Gilison: "Soviet Elections as a Measure of Dissent: The Missing One Percent," *American Political Science Review,* September 1968, No. 3, p. 817.

44. For a further discussion of this and other aspects of Soviet elections see Alfred G. Meyer: *The Soviet Political System,* New York, 1965, pp. 269-74.

45. Quoted in Fainsod, *How Russia Is Ruled,* p. 382.

46. Captions to a photograph of young accordion players in *Vechernia Moskva,* March 18, 1962, p. 3.

47. Emile Durkheim: *The Elementary Forms of Religious Life,* New York, 1961, pp. 22, 473.

48. Y. Frantsev: *Communism and the Freedom of the Individual,* Moscow (no date, early 1960's).

49. "Anti-Allende Rally Is Held in Santiago," *NYT,* December 17, 1971, p. 9. Castro was of course referring to the rally the leftist government organized following that of the opposition party.

50. Durkheim, *op. cit.,* pp. 465, 474-75. For a thorough discussion of the corresponding phenomena in Nazi Germany see Hamilton T. Burden: *The Nurenberg Rallies: 1923-39,* New York, 1967.

51. George Feifer: "Russia—Da, China—Nyet," *NYT Magazine,* December 4, 1966, p. 157.

52. Henry Kamm: "Brezhnev Sets the Clock Back," *NYT Magazine,* August 10, 1969, p. 18.

53. *Message from Moscow,* pp. 207-08.

54. M. Garin, A. Druzenko, and M. Ovcharov: "This Is What Young Working People Are Like Today," *Izvestia,* transl. *CDSP,* June 19, 1968, p. 22. See also on the low attendance of seminars on party history, philosophy, and dialectics; Alex Inkeles: *Social Change in Soviet Russia,* Cambridge, Mass., 1968, p. 273.

55. "Party Life: How can time be found?" *Pravda,* transl. *CDSP,* May 28, 1969, p. 21.

56. Leonid Vladimirov: *The Russians,* New York, 1968, p. 40.

57. *"Trud* Glazami Chitatelia" (*Trud* Through the Eyes of the Readers), *Zhurnalist,* July 1968, p. 48. Another survey found that "articles on economics and on the work of Soviets and propaganda articles came at the bottom of the list of 'regularly read. . . .'" See "The Reader and the Newspaper," *Izvestia,* transl. *CDSP,* July 31, 1968, p. 17.

58. "Nixon Talent Scout Asks Casey Stengel for Help," *NYT,* December 6, 1968.

59. Marvin E. Olsen: "Social and Political Participation of Blacks," *American Sociological Review,* August 1970.

Chapter 3

1. Gerhard A. Ritter: "Student Rebellion and Industrial Society," *Survey,* Summer 1970, pp. 138-39.

2. "Minutemen Upset by GOP Loss, Set New Drive," *NYT*, November 12, 1964. For a major study of American right-wing movements see Seymour Martin Lipset and Earl Raab: *The Politics of Unreason*, New York, 1970.

3. "Trend of the New Left Alarm Intellectuals of 'Old Left' at Conference Here," *NYT*, May 8, 1967.

4. Daniel Bell: "The Dispossessed" in D. Bell, ed.: *The Radical Right*, Garden City, 1964, p. 5.

5. "Birchite Scholar Center of Dispute," *NYT*, March 15, 1964.

6. "Red Net Grows, Rightists Hear," *NYT*, August 10, 1965.

7. "Rightists Attack Mental Aid Plan," *NYT*, March 28, 1965.

8. See also the same title by Richard Hofstadter, New York, 1965.

9. See also "Minutemen Upset. . . ."

10. C. Vann Woodward: "Cranks and Their Followers," *NYT Book Review Section*, November 14, 1965.

11. "Trail Blazer Seeking 1968 Democratic Nomination for President" (Advertisement) *NYT*, July 19, 1967.

12. "Carmichael to Take Part in War Protest April 15th," *NYT*, March 30, 1967.

13. *Report of the National Advisory Commission on Civil Disorders*, New York, 1968, p. 202.

14. Tom Milstein: "A Perspective on the Panthers," *Commentary*, September 1970, p. 36.

15. Sandra Levinson and Carol Brightman, eds.: *Venceremos Brigade—Young Americans Sharing the Life and Work of Revolutionary Cuba*, New York, 1971, pp. 311, 373, 392.

16. *Ibid.*, pp. 310, 318-19.

17. For an elaboration of some of these characteristics see Edward Shils: "Plenitude and Scarcity," *Encounter*, May 1969, and Leopold Labedz: "Students and Revolutions," *Survey*, July 1968; for sympathetic analysis of some of these attitudes see Kenneth Keninston: "You have to Grow Up in Scarsdale to Know How Bad Things Really Are," *NYT Magazine*, April 27, 1969.

18. Aldous Huxley: "Words and Behavior" in his *Collected Essays*, New York, 1953, p. 254.

19. For further discussions of the New Left see T. B. Bottomore: *Critics of Society— Radical Thought in North America*, New York, 1968; Nathan Glazer: "The New Left and Its Limits," *Commentary*, July 1968; Christopher Lasch: *The Agony of the American Left*, New York, 1969; Irving Louis Horowitz: "Radicalism and the Revolt Against Reason," Introduction to *The Social Theories of Georges Sorel*, Carbondale, 1968; Bennett M. Berger: "Self-hatred and the Politics of Kicks" in his *Looking for America*, Englewood Cliffs, 1971.

20. Walter Laquer: "Reflections on Youth Movements," *Commentary*, June 1969, pp. 37-38.

21. On the intellectual-historical antecedents and roots of these attitudes see Marshall Berman: *The Politics of Authenticity—Radical Individualism and the Emergence of Modern Society*, New York, 1970.

22. Nathan Glazer: "Blacks, Jews and Intellectuals," *Commentary*, April 1969.

23. Levinson and Brightman, eds.: *Venceremos Brigade*, pp. 21, 125, 127, 170, 172, 69, 219.

24. See Walter Goodman: "Yessir Boss, Said the White Radicals—When Black Power Runs the New Left," *NYT Magazine*, September 24, 1967; also Martin Peretz: "The American Left and Israel," *Commentary*, November 1967.

25. See further Bell, ed., *op. cit.*; also Edward Shils: *Torment of Secrecy*, Glencoe, 1956.

26. See, for example, Arnold M. Rose: *The Power Structure*, New York, 1967, p. 68; see also William McPherson: *Parallels in Extremist Propaganda*, doctoral dissertation, Harvard University, 1967.

27. Andrei D. Sakharov: *Progress, Coexistence and Intellectual Freedom*, New York, 1968, pp. 63-64.

28. "525 More FBI Agents Asked in Peak Budget Backed by Nixon," *NYT*, July 8, 1969; also Tom Wicker: "What Have They Done Since They Shot Dillinger," *NYT Magazine*, December 28, 1969, esp. p. 6.

29. Rigby: *Communist Party Membership in the USSR, 1917-1967*, p. 342; see also "Structure of Soviet Intelligence," *NYT*, November 10, 1967, p. 14.

30. See D. Dallin and B. Nicolaevsky: *Forced Labor in Soviet Russia*, New Haven, 1947.

31. See S. Wolin and R. M. Slusser, eds.: *The Soviet Secret Police*, London, 1957.

32. *Message from Moscow*, p. 65.

33. "Account of Soviet Prison Brutality Is Smuggled Out," *NYT*, April 28, 1969, p. 10; "KGB Is Said to Harass Ukrainian Intellectuals," *NYT*, February 8, 1968; V. Moroz: "A Report from the Beria Reserve," *Problems of Communism*, July-August 1968, p. 90.

34. See P. Barton: "An End to Concentration Camps?" *Problems of Communism*, March-April 1962.

35. For an excellent summary of these activities see further Chap. 10 in Robert Conquest: *The Great Terror*, New York, 1968.

36. For a detailed discussion of Soviet border and travel controls see Paul Hollander: "Grenzen Controllen als Integraler Teil des Sowjetsystems" (Border Controls: An Integral Part of the Soviet System), *Osteuropa*, October 1969; also Robert Conquest, ed.: *The Soviet Police System*, New York, 1968, esp. pp. 30-40, 55-59.

37. For examples of how the Soviet press depicts those who want to leave or have left the Soviet Union see "The Troublemaking Berezins and their Benefactors," *Izvestia*, transl. *CDSP*, October 28, 1964, p. 24; or "Weeds," *Izvestia*, transl. *CDSP*, November 18, 1964, pp. 26-27.

38. See, for instance, the case of the Soviet exchange scholar in England as reported in the *NYT* September 17, 18, and 19 issue of 1967 and the *Guardian* (of London) September 18, 19, and 20, 1967. See also the case of the Soviet sailor forcibly removed from a U.S. Coast Guard vessel in November 1970 off Cape Cod.

39. See also "Article 64, Treason" in Harold J. Berman, ed.: *Soviet Criminal Law and Procedure—The RSFSR Codes*, Cambridge, Mass., 1966, p. 178.

40. *The U.S. Book of Facts, Statistics and Information* (Officially Published by the U.S. Govt. as Statistical Abstracts of the U.S.), New York, 1967, p. 168; the figure for 1967 comes from *Pocket Data Book—USA 1969*, Washington D.C., 1969, p. 129.

41. "A check of 12 cities indicates that many of those arrested in race riots last summer were later released, received suspended sentences or were allowed to plead guilty to lesser charges. In some communities . . . penalties were eased despite early warnings by city officials that those taken into custody would be punished to the full extent of the law." "Many Arrested in Racial Riots Get Light Sentences," *NYT*, November 27, 1967, p. 52.

42. Alex Inkeles: "Fifty Years of the Soviet Revolution" in his *Social Change in Soviet Russia*, pp. 58-59.

43. *U.S. Book of Facts*, p. 163.

44. See, for example, Anatoly Marchenko: *My Testimony*, New York, 1969, and V. Chornovil, *The Chornovil Papers*, New York, 1968.

45. Inkeles, *Social Change in Soviet Russia,* p. 58.

46. Skilling and Griffiths, eds, *op. cit.,* p. 122, offers further evidence on this.

47. "Transcript of the Trial of Iosif Brodsky," *The New Leader,* August 31, 1964, p. 17.

48. Title Two of the Internal Security (McCarran) Act of 1950—so far not invoked—does provide legal opportunity for *preventive* detention.

49. J. Gliksman: "Social Prophylaxis as a Form of Soviet Terror," in C. J. Friedrich, ed.: *Totalitarianism,* Cambridge, Mass., 1954.

50. This point is discussed in Z. Barbu: *Democracy and Dictatorship,* New York, 1956; see esp. pp. 3-11.

51. See, for example, the characteristic title of a Soviet booklet: Kh. M. Akhmetshin: *Okhrana Gosudarstvennoy Tayni—Dolg Sovetskikh Grazhdan* (The Preservation of State Secrets: The Duty of the Soviet Citizen), Moscow 1954.

52. For instance, Viktorov, *op. cit.*

53. Thus the *NYT Travel Section* found it advisable to publish "Advice from The State Department—Hints for Americans Touring Russia On How to Avoid 'Incidents,'" April 16, 1967 issue.

54. See *NYT,* April 25, 26, 27, 28, 29, 1966 on the CIA. Of similar significance are other "exposes" in book form. For example, Omar V. Garrison: *Spy Government—The Emerging Police State in America,* New York, 1967; and Clark R. Mollenhoff: *The Pentagon,* New York, 1967.

55. V. Moroz, "A Report from the Beria Reserve," *Problems of Communism,* July 1968, pp. 86, 87, 89.

56. "Letter of Soviet Farm Chairman Protesting Trial of Dissidents," *NYT,* March 8, 1968.

57. For Grigorienko's petitions see *Problems of Communism,* July 1968, pp. 31-32, 59-60, 93-95, and for a protest by his wife after his arrest, pp. 72-73. Another unusual dissenter has been a Communist Party member since 1917, the writer Kosterin who actually returned his membership card—an unheard of act of defiance in the USSR. See further "Defiant Russian Quits the Party," *NYT,* October 29, 1968.

58. Document by Vyacheslav Chornovil, *Problems of Communism,* July 1968, p. 8.

59. Moroz, *Problems of Communism, op. cit.,* July 1968, p. 86.

60. Yakhimovich, *NYT,* March 8, 1968.

61. "The Defense Counsel: Rights and Problems," *Literaturnaya gazeta,* transl. *CDSP,* February 17, 1970, pp. 4, 5.

62. Skilling and Griffiths eds., *op. cit.,* p. 124.

63. For some aspects of this controversy see Alfred Meyer: "The Comparative Study of Communist Political Systems," *Slavic Review,* March 1967, and Paul Hollander: "Observations on Bureaucracy, Totalitarianism and the Comparative Study of Communism," *Slavic Review,* June 1967; also Alex Inkeles: "Models in the Analysis of Soviet Society," *Survey,* July 1966, and "Introduction" in Paul Hollander, ed.: *American and Soviet Society: A Reader in Comparative Sociology and Perception,* Englewood Cliffs, 1969, pp. 5-9.

64. C. Wright Mills: *The Power Elite,* New York, 1956; for more recent but a good deal less original and forceful expositions of the same thesis see J. M. Schweitz: "The Shadow Knows . . . ," and Bruce C. Johnson: "The Democratic Mirage" both in the *Berkeley Journal of Sociology,* XIII, 1968.

65. For instance, H. Gordon Skilling: "Interest Groups and Communist Politics," *World Politics,* April 1966; also Albert Parry: *The New Class Divided,* New York, 1966; for an analysis that upholds the totalitarian model of Soviet decision-making see

also Jeremy Azrael: *Managerial Power and Soviet Politics,* Cambridge, Mass., 1966; see also Paul Hollander, review of A. McFarland: "Power and Leaders in Pluralist Systems," *American Sociological Review,* January 1970. The most far-reaching attempt to impute pluralism to the Soviet political system can be found in Jerry F. Hough: "The Soviet System: Petrification or Pluralism?" *Problems of Communism,* March-April 1972; his and similar analyses however do not adequately resolve questions such as: "How were the specialists trained? How are they selected and promoted? What means does the system afford for independent influence? . . . The evidence offered here indicates that unlike the situation in pluralistic systems —in which the experts can be found in the various parties, in and out of the government—the Soviet model encompasses a bureaucratic hierarchy who use the opportunities to capture the specialists' talents for the central leadership's ends." Roy D. Laird: *The Soviet Paradigm—An Experiment in Creating a Mono-Hierarchical Polity,* New York, 1970, p. XIX. Although Laird is also uneasy about the continued use of the concept of totalitarianism his concept of "monohierarchical polity" is extremely close to the former (see, for example, his comments on p. XXVI and 92).

66. George Fischer: *The Soviet System and Modern Society,* New York, 1968, pp. 13, 15.
67. K. S. Karol: "Conversations in Russia," *The New Statesman,* January 1, 1971, p. 8.
68. Samuel P. Huntington: "Political Modernization: Europe vs. America," *World Politics,* April 1966, p. 411.
69. For example, Richard Pipes: *The Premises of American and Russian Foreign Policy,* Paper presented at the American Historical Association Meeting, Washington 1969.
70. The best source of definitions and discussions of totalitarianism remains Carl Friedrich, ed.: *Totalitarianism;* Cambridge, Mass., 1954. Two distinguished historical analyses are: Hannah Arendt: *The Origins of Totalitarianism,* New York, 1958, and J. L. Talmon: *The Origins of Totalitarian Democracy,* New York, 1961; for an excellent recent survey of various totalitarian ideas and ideologies see A. James Gregor: *Contemporary Radical Ideologies—Totalitarian Thought in the Twentieth Century,* New York, 1968. For more recent reappraisals see Carl J. Friedrich, Michael Curties, Benjamin R. Barber: *Totalitarianism in Perspective,* New York, 1969.
71. "Totalitarian Elements in Pre-industrial Societies" in Barrington Moore, Jr.: *Political Power and Social Theory,* Cambridge, Mass., 1958.
72. The Soviet Union ranks among the lowest of the industrial nations in the ratio of telephones per population: with a total of 5.7 million phones (see also *Narodnoye Khozyaistvo SSSR v 1967,* Moscow 1968, p. 596). Another source estimated the number of Soviet phones to be 8.4 million in the same year; the number of American telephones was 98.7 million (See also *The World's Telephones,* 1967, p. 2.)
73. "Soviet Olympians Fall Below the Medal Quota," *NYT,* October 26, 1968.
74. *Message From Moscow,* p. 219.
75. A recent work on the subject defines pluralism as "referring to the dispersal of power among many elites, as opposed to its exercise by a single elite." Andrew S. McFarland: *Power and Leadership in Pluralist Systems,* Stanford, 1969, p. XI. For a discussion of the concept by a sociologist see Brigitte Berger: *Societies in Change,* New York, 1971, Chap. 10.
76. See further Gabriel Almond and Sidney Verba: *The Civic Culture,* Boston, 1965, Chaps. V, VI, VII.
77. "Idaho Missile Base Has Phone Failure in Protest on Bill," *NYT,* January 26, 1964.

78. "Johnstown Mayor Fights U.S. and Army—and Wins," *NYT*, January 16, 1966.

79. "Dubois Clubs Win in Radio Disputes—FCC Orders Station to Air Reply to Attack on Group," *NYT*, February 3, 1968.

80. "Critic of Johnson Reports Inquiry—Secret Service Questioned Him, TVA Aide Says," *NYT*, December 28, 1965.

81. "Mark Rudd Seeks a Draft Deferment as a Revolutionist," *NYT*, November 16, 1968; the article reported that he asked his draft board "to grant him an occupational deferment as a 'revolutionist.' "

82. "Antiwar Group Asks Ft. Dix For Permit to Stage Show," *NYT*, October 26, 1968.

83. "Fort Dix Acquits War-Protest G.I.," *NYT*, October 2, 1968; see also "3 Militants Form G.I. News Service to 'Expose' Army," *NYT*, June 8, 1970 p. 4. Two of the founders were still serving in the army at the time of forming the news service. See also "Army Sets Rules on Troop Dissent—Tells Officers to Use Only 'Minimum Restraints,' " *NYT*, September 12, 1969.

84. Tyrmand, *op. cit.*, p. 201.

85. "15 Veterans Leave the Statue of Liberty, Claiming Victory in Take-Over," *NYT*, December 29, 1971, p. 32.

86. "Prisoner Allowed Ramparts," *NYT*, March 22, 1970, p. 48.

87. "Seattle Mayor Says He Refused to Raid Panthers," *NYT*, August 5, 1970, p. 37.

88. "A Dealer Defends Bomb Book Sales," *NYT*, August 5, 1970, p. 37.

89. "Intruders Found at Nixon Homes" *NYT*, March 12, 1970, p. 32.

Chapter 4

1. For example, Talcott Parsons: *Societies—Evolutionary and Comparative Perspectives*, Englewood Cliffs, 1966; F. S. C. Northrop: "Ideological Man in His Relation to Scientifically Known Natural Man," in F. S. C. Northrop, ed.: *Ideological Differences and World Order*, New Haven, 1963, pp. 407-9. The elucidation of the relationship between values and institutions is also the basic concern of Emile Durkheim: *The Elementary Forms of Religious Life*, New York, 1961, see also in particular, "Conclusions."

2. Jerome D. Frank: *Healing and Persuasion*, New York, 1963, p. 38.

3. T. B. Bottomore: *Sociology, A Guide to Problems and Literature*, Englewood Cliffs, 1963, p. 33.

4. For a related discussion on the discrepancies between personal motivation and social behavior, see also Bert Kaplan, ed.: *Studying Personality Cross-Culturally*, New York, 1961, pp. 663-65.

5. Barrington Moore, Jr.: *Social Origins of Democracy and Dictatorship*, Boston, 1966, p. 486.

6. Not so in homogeneous, small-scale societies ". . . held together by common understandings as to the ultimate nature and purpose of life." Robert Redfield: *The Primitive World and Its Transformations*, Ithaca, 1953, p. 4. It is precisely the lack of such common understandings stemming from the heterogeneity and complexity of societies like the U.S. and the USSR that the "poor fit" arises.

7. A similar point is made in C. Kluckhohn et al.: "Values and Value Orientations in the Theory of Action," in T. Parsons and E. Shils, eds.: *Toward a General Theory of Action*, New York, 1962, p. 397.

8. For some authentic discussions of the Soviet system of controlling free expression, and censorship in particular, see "Text of Solzhenitsin's Demand for End of Soviet Censorship," *NYT*, June 5, 1967; also "Document by V. Moroz," in *Problems of*

Communism, July-August 1969, pp. 84-87; for inside stories of how the Soviet press and its censorship functions, see Vladimirov, *op. cit.*, pp. 79-107.

9. See also Efron, *op. cit.*, pp. 143-71.

10. *Pocket Data Book op. cit.*, p. 323.

11. Frederick Barghoorn: *Soviet Foreign Propaganda*, Princeton, 1964, p. 261. For other estimates combining Soviet and Chinese propaganda expenditures see John C. Clews: *Communist Propaganda Techniques*, London, 1964, pp. 23-25.

12. For systematic discussions of the goals and organization of Soviet propaganda see further Alex Inkeles: *Public Opinion in Soviet Russia*, Cambridge, 1958. Barghoorn, *The Soviet Image of the U.S.*, and *Politics in the USSR*, Chaps. III, IV, V; G. Hollander, *op. cit.*, esp. Chaps. 1, 6 and 8.

13. This is not to say that American advertising always avoids political involvement. Advertising and public relations firms frequently serve the needs of political clients, particularly at election times. This, however, has nothing to do with subservience to government or political groupings. The services are provided on a strictly businesslike basis and the political principles of the client are of little concern. This has been vividly demonstrated by a public relations firm in California which, in turn, assisted liberal-republican Senator Kuchel and conservative-republican Governor Regan. (*NYT Magazine*, 1966, November 20 issue quoted an advertising executive who stressed his industry's unconcern with issues of morality: "Advertising Is a Science, an Art, a Business?" by Victor S. Navasky, pp. 52-53, 162-77.)

14. See also Jules Henry: *Culture Against Man*, New York, 1965, pp. 19-22.

15. The dominance of such values has been noted by Robin Williams, Jr.: *American Society*, New York, 1965, pp. 417-21; Max Lerner: *America as a Civilization*, New York, 1957, pp. 690-91; Seymour M. Lipset: *The First New Nation*, New York, 1963, pp. 112-14; Margaret Mead: *And Keep Your Powder Dry*, New York, 1965, pp. 80-98.

16. Paul Fettis: "1500 Advertisements a Day," *The Observer* (London), September 22, 1963.

17. G. Hollander, *op. cit.*, p. 154.

18. *Voprosy Teorii i Praktiki Partiinoi Propagandy, op. cit.*

19. Boorstin refers to this as the "half-intelligibility" of American advertising, Daniel J. Boorstin: *The Image*, New York, 1961, pp. 222-23. See also Milton Rokeach: "The Consumer's Changing Image," *Transaction*, July 1964, esp. pp. 10-12.

20. Richard Hoggart: *Speaking to Each Other*, London, 1970, Vol. I., p. 210.

21. *Message from Moscow*, p. 27.

22. "Social Activism Grips Soap Opera," *NYT*, December 11, 1969, p. 111.

23. An illuminating discussion of this and other aspects of totalitarian propaganda is to be found in George Orwell: "The Prevention of Literature," *Collected Essays*, London, 1961; on the techniques of personification and abstraction see Aldous Huxley: "Words and Behavior," in his *Collected Essays*, London, 1960.

24. Allen Kassof: "The Administered Society," *World Politics*, July 1964; Philip E. Mosely: "Soviet Myths and Realities" in Mosely, ed.: *The Soviet Union—A Foreign Affairs Reader*, New York, 1963, pp. 436-40; Bauer and Inkeles, *op. cit.*, p. 381.

25. G. Hollander, *op. cit.*, p. 193.

26. Richard Hoggart: *The Uses of Literacy*, Boston, 1961, p. 227. Russell Baker has made the same point about the claims of American advertising: "Without even thinking about it, we automatically discount 80 or 90 per cent of the typical advertising assertion for mendacity. This saves us from apoplectic seizure each time we rediscover that the new miracle product performs no miracles at all." ("Ob-

server: An Evolutionary Failure," *NYT,* August 31, 1967.) Baker's point probably
retains its validity even in the early 1970's when the Federal Trade Commission
began questioning some extravagant advertising claims.

27. Thomas Meehan: "Cruise Director on the Titanic," *NYT Magazine,* January 2,
1972, pp. 10-11.

28. Soviet propaganda would fulfill economic functions if its exhortations to work
harder were observed. The history of Soviet wage differentiation is the most telling
evidence that they were not. We might also note here that recently there have been
some discussions in the Soviet press about limited advertising in the USSR. There
is, however, very little of it. On the subject of socialist advertising, see "Discussing
Problems of Everyday Life: How Are You Served? Advertising Has the Floor,"
Izvestia, September 21, 1966, transl. *CDSP,* October 12, 1966, pp. 22-23.

29. *Success Digest for the Entire Family,* New York, 1966.

30. For a succinct discussion of the self-improvement literature, see Robert K. Merton,
Social Theory and Social Structure, Glencoe, 1959, pp. 137-39. See also Richard
Weiss: *The American Myth of Success—From Horatio Alger to Norman Vincent
Peale,* New York, 1969.

31. For example, the works of Seymour Martin Lipset, Robert K. Merton, Margaret
Mead, Talcott Parsons, and Robin Williams, Jr.

32. The popular attitudes toward the expert, as indicated by the stance taken by these
advertisements, is a contradictory one. On the other hand, it seems that Americans
are overawed by the authority of expertise, especially if it is "scientific." On the
other hand there is also a residue of the populist disbelief that anything can be
beyond the grasp of the common man. Writing in 1930, Bertrand Russell commented on the latter saying that there is in America an ". . . unwillingness to admit that there is anything in science which only experts can understand." Bertrand
Russell: *In Praise of Idleness,* New York, 1960, p. 122. The desire to capitalize on
the popular reverence toward science can also be inferred from the policy of *quan-
tifying* the various techniques advertised. Copywriters take great pains to number
everything: 8 easy steps, 9 fatal errors, 11 easy ways . . . and so forth.

33. The gullibility of Americans as consumers is also attested to by the existence of
publications wishing to protect them from the multiplicity of frauds perpetrated
by those who gave a literal interpretation to the freedom of the marketplace. To
mention only a few examples of such publications: Dexter Masters: *The Intelligent
Buyer and the Telltale Seller,* New York, 1966; Walter Wagner: *The Golden
Fleecers,* New York, 1966; Curt Gentry: The *Vulnerable Americans,* New York,
1966; James Gollin: *Pay Now and Die Later (What Is Wrong with Life Insurance),*
New York, 1966; Philip G. Schrag: *Counsel for the Deceived—Case Studies in Consumer Fraud,* New York, 1972. Perhaps it is heartening that not only commercial
abuses are lucrative in American society but also the writing of books which expose them.

34. For example, studying in the Famous Writers' School "will pay the student in
achievement, personal fulfillment and often in increased income as well." The
financial appeal, as the foregoing shows, is not totally neglected but somewhat
played down. Another ad of the same institution said that ". . . writing provides
a wonderful means of emotional release and self-expression, to say nothing of the
extra income it can bring" illustrating again the best-of-all-possible-worlds-syn-
drome. The Famous Writers' School, Westport, Conn., pamphlet and newspaper
advertising has appeared in many issues of the Sunday *NYT Magazine and Book
Review Section.* Under legal pressure these ads have been modified more recently.

35. Karen Horney: *The Neurotic Personality of Our Time,* New York, 1937, p. 288.

36. See, for instance, Geoffrey Gorer: *The American People,* New York, 1964, pp. 106-19, 138. Practicality and romanticism clash in other areas too where the thirst for adventure is quenched by "contrived experience." Travel is a case in point: "The modern American tourist . . . expects that the exotic and familiar can be made to order . . ." (Boorstin: *The Image, op. cit.,* pp. 79-80.

37. "Selling oneself" as an aspect of many nonmanual occupations is discussed extensively by C. Wright Mills in *White Collar,* New York, 1951, esp. Chap. 8.

38. Wright Miller: *The Russians as People,* New York, 1961, pp. 72-73, 85-86.

39. The concept originates in Theodore Roszak: *The Making of a Counter Culture,* Garden City, 1969.

40. See "Hippie Morality" in Bennett Berger: *Looking for America.*

41. Jonathan Kozol: "Moving on to Nowhere," *NYT,* March 24, 1972, p. 39.

42. "There is so much talk of self—of self-fulfillment, self-realization, self-determination —and so little of one's devotion and responsibility to particular others—I don't mean mankind; I mean particular others." The remark made in the context of a discussion of certain characteristics of Women's Liberation movement has a more general applicability to broad segments of the counterculture, although probably not to those who have chosen communal living which is difficult to envision without responsibility to particular others. Joseph Adelson: "Is Women's Lib a Passing Fad?" *NYT Magazine,* March 19, 1972, p. 98.

43. Albert Goldman: "Grab the Money and Run!" *NYT Arts and Theater Section,* February 23, 1970, p. 23.

44. Elia Katz: *Armed Love,* New York, 1971, p. 164.

45. P. Filonovich: *O Kommunisticheskoi Morali—Popularniy Ocherk* (On Communist Morality—A Popular Outline), Moscow, 1963; for other representative examples see: Z. V. Strukov: *Kommunizm i Vsestoronnoye Razvitie Lichnosti* (Communism and All-Round Development of the Personality), Moscow, 1960; *Moralniy Kodeks Stroitelya Kommunizma* (The Moral Code of the Builder of Cummunism), Moscow, 1964; *Stroitelstvo Kommunizma i Dukhovniy Mir Cheloveka* (The Building of Communism and the Spiritual World of Man), Moscow, 1966.

46. J. Triska, ed.: *Program of the Communist Party of the Soviet Union* (with a special preface to the American edition by N. S. Khrushchev), New York, 1963, p. 122.

47. For example, "Rear Young People in the Spirit of Revolutionary Ideals," *Pravda,* November 18, 1965, transl. *CDSP,* December 22, 1965, pp. 5-6: "The Student and the Social Sciences," *Komsomolskaya Pravda,* April 20, 1966, transl. *CDSP,* May 18, 1966, pp. 5-7: "Direct the Organizational and Political Work of the Young Communist League Toward Rearing Convinced and Fervent Fighters for Communism," *Komsomolskaya Pravda,* May 18, 1966, transl. *CDSP,* June 15, 1966. While urging the improvement of propaganda and ideological training, Pavlov, the First Secretary of the YCL, gave evidence of the stress on tradition by suggesting that Pavel Korchagin, a hero of socialist realist fiction from the 1930's in *How the Steel Was Tempered,* remain the model for Soviet youth. Korchagin has been the improbable one-dimensional, fiercely puritanic "positive hero" of a novel that won official acclaim under Stalin, a young man who in the service of socialism contracted almost every conceivable illness and bodily ailment, who totally subordinated his personal life and pleasures to the goals of the Collective. The voice of doctrinaire fanaticism was also evident in Pavlov's demand ". . . to maintain young people's unwavering certainty of the absolute superiority of our socialist system."

48. Filonovich, *op. cit.,* p. 3.

49. Herbert Marcuse: *Soviet Marxism*, New York, 1961, p. 216 see also Crane Brinton: *A History of Western Morals*, New York, p. 405.
50. Adam Ulam: "The Price of the Revolution," *Commentary*, October 1968, p. 81.
51. Filonovich, *op. cit.*, p. 49.
52. M. L. Chalin: *Moral Stroitelya Kommunizma* (The Morality of the Builder of Communism), Moscow, 1963, pp. 24-25.
53. Triska, ed., *op. cit.*, p. 121.
54. *Ibid.*, p. 122.
55. Erich Fromm: *The Sane Society*, New York, 1955, p. 142.
56. Filonovich, *op. cit.*, pp. 165-66, 169.
57. *Ibid.*, pp. 45-46.
58. For example, Bauer, Inkeles and Kluckhohn, *op. cit.*, pp. 172-73, 270-74. On the apathy of peasants: Alfred G. Meyer: *The Soviet Political System*, New York, 1965, pp. 54-58.
59. Bauer and Inkeles, *op. cit.*, pp. 282-83.
60. Paul Hollander: "Models of Behavior in Stalinist Literature," *American Sociological Review*, June 1966.
61. Filonovich, *op. cit.*, p. 153.
62. *Ibid.*, p. 155.
63. *Ibid.*, p. 157.

Chapter 5

1. On the integration of various forms of socialization see Urie Bronfenbrenner: *Two Worlds of Childhood—U.S. and USSR*, New York, 1970. For an overview of Soviet education, see further George Z. F. Bereday et al., eds., *The Changing Soviet School*, Boston, 1960; George Z. F. Bereday and Jan Pennar, eds., *Politics of Soviet Education*, New York, 1960; George S. Counts: *The Challenge of Soviet Education*, New York, 1957. For a unique personal account of exposure to Soviet education see Wolfgang Leonhard, *Child of the Revolution*, Chicago, 1958.
2. Barrington Moore, Jr., "Thoughts on the Future of the Family" in his *Political Power and Social Theory*, pp. 166-69.
3. This is one of the major arguments of David Riesman, *The Lonely Crowd*, New Haven, 1961. See also Eric Larrabee and Rolf Meyerson, eds., *Mass Leisure*, Glencoe, 1958.
4. See Ellen Propper Mickiewicz: *Soviet Political Schools*, New Haven: 1967, p. 10. See also G. Hollander, *op. cit.*
5. This is an understatement as can be readily discovered, for example, by perusing G. K. Shakhnazarov, et al., *Social Science, A Textbook for Soviet Secondary Schools*. English edition, Washington, D.C., 1964. See also *Social Science in Soviet Secondary Schools—Syllabus of the New Course*, Washington, D.C., 1966.
6. "All Union Pedagogical Council," Editorial in *Pravda* transl. *CDSP*, July 24, 1968, p. 9.
7. Fred M. Hechinger: "Education: Triumphs and Doubts" in Harrison E. Salisbury, ed.: *The Soviet Union: The Fifty Years*, New York, 1967, pp. 110-11.
8. There is a sobering discussion on the relationship between Soviet education, rationality, and liberal attitudes in Z. Brzezinski: "Totalitarianism and Rationality" in his *Ideology and Power in Soviet Politics*, New York, 1962, pp. 13-16. On the economic and political functionalization of Soviet education see also Nicholas DeWitt, "Recent Trends in Soviet Education," Alex Inkeles and Kent Geiger, eds., *Soviet Society, A Book of Readings*, Boston, 1961, esp. p. 439.

9. Only relatively recently have specifically political-ideological texts been introduced, such as William J. Miller, Henry L. Roberts, and Marshall D. Shulman: *The Meaning of Communism*, New York, 1963; and Alfred J. Rieber and Robert C. Nelson, *A Study of the USSR and Communism*, New York, 1962.

10. See, for example, Thomas Fitzsimmons, Peter Malof, John C. Fiske, *USSR*, New Haven, 1960, pp. 106-7.

11. Hechinger, *op. cit.*, p. 116.

12. Urie Bronfenbrenner, "Soviet Studies of Personality Development and Socialization," in Raymond Bauer, ed.: *Some Views on Soviet Psychology*, 1962, pp. 63-86.

13. V. Khvostov: "School Will Prompt Choice of Vocation," *Izvestia*, transl. *CDSP*, October 6, 1970, p. 10. This and other articles complained about the growing disinterest, even contempt, on the part of the young toward manual labor. It was reported from Magnitogorsk, a large industrial center, that according to a poll of 10th-graders, 5.7 per cent planned to work; 17.7 per cent planned to combine work and study and 70 per cent planned to study full time in institutions of higher education; see also "Man and His Work: Learn in Order to Know How," *Izvestia*, transl. *CDSP*, August 18, 1970, p. 24. For a book-length treatment of the subject, see M. N. Rutkevich, ed.: *The Career Plans of Youth*, White Plains: 1969.

14. "What Vocation Should One Choose?" *Pravda*, transl. *CDSP*, June 22, 1966, p. 36. See also "Provide Jobs for Adolescents," *Komsomolskaya Pravda*, transl. *CDSP*, September 7, 1966, p. 12; "As Yet There Are Applicants for Admission," *Pravda*, transl. *CDSP*, October 12, 1966, p. 11.

15. The importance of social life in high schools is reflected in such headlines, "Glen Rock Parents Make Senior Ball Success," *NYT*, June 19, 1963. On this occasion "42 fathers of the graduates served as waiters," providing thereby a final symbolic relinquishment of paternal authority. See also Grace and Fred M. Hechinger, *Teenage Tyranny*, 1967, pp. 21-25, etc. and James Coleman, *The Adolescent Society*, New York, 1961, pp 11-58.

16. Much of this section follows closely an article of the author. See Paul Hollander, "How Political Is the Student Revolution?" *Youth and Society*, December 1971.

17. Tyrmand, *op. cit.*, p. 47.

18. Nathan Glazer: "On Being Deradicalized," *Commentary*, October 1970, p. 79. For another excellent summary of the contradictions of the youth culture see John W. Aldridge: *In the Counrty of the Young*, New York, 1969, pp. 11-13.

19. Quoted in Fred M. Hechinger: "We Were Very Together," *NYT*, June 2, 1969, Editorial Page.

20. For a good description of one such occasion, exemplifying the characteristic mixture of political protest and entertainment, idealism and hedonism, excitement and torpor, see "America Is Hard to Find Weekend Ends at Cornell," *NYT*, April 20, 1970, p. 46. According to the report the weekend cost $20,000.

21. "Twenty Years Later—A Second Preface," p. XIX. in David Riesman: *The Lonely Crowd*, New Haven: 1969.

22. Ernest Gellner: "The Panther and the Dove: Reflections on Rebelliousness and Its Milieux" in David Martin, ed.: *Anarchy and Culture—The Problem of the Contemporary University*, New York: 1969, pp. 142-43. See also Robert Brustein: *Revolution as Theatre*, New York, 1971.

23. Tyrmand, *op. cit.*, p. 143; concerning the double standards applied by some intellectuals to student violence, see also Sidney Hook: "Campus Terror: An Indictment," *NYT*, October 22, 1970.

24. Lewis F. Feuer: *Marx and the Intellectuals*, Garden City, 1969, pp. 222-23.

25. Kurt Tausky: *Some Societal Aspects of Marijuana Use Among College Students.* Paper presented at the University of Maine, Orono, June 1970, pp. 8, 9.

26. E. V. Kohak: "Requiem for Utopia—Socialist Reflections After Czechoslovakia," *Dissent,* January-February, 1969, p. 41.

27. John Kifner: "Vandals in the Mother Country," *NYT Magazine,* January 4, 1970, pp. 16, 17.

28. Feuer, *op. cit.,* p. 227; a similar appeal of violent imagery is reflected in this wishful remark: "Amerika we will rip you up—tear your guts apart from the inside." Quoted from Venceremos Brigade, *op. cit.,* p. 385.

29. Liberation News Service dispatch printed in *The Guardian,* January 10, 1970, quoted in *Encounter,* April 1970, p. 37.

30. *Dump Truck—The Supplement to the Harvard Crimson,* November 12, 1969, p. 7.

31. Richard E. Hyland in the October 22, 1969 *Special Supplement to the Harvard Crimson,* quoted in *Encounter,* April 1970, p. 30.

32. Hans Speier: "Risk, Security and Modern Hero Worship," in his *Social Order and Risks of War,* New York, 1952, pp. 126, 127, 128.

33. I. Horowitz: "Radicalism and the Revolt Against Reason Then and Now," Preface to *The Social Theories of George Sorel,* Carbondale, esp. p. XII. See also Feuer, *Marx and the Intellectuals,* p. 220.

34. "Violence in Young Laid to Inarticulate Students," *NYT,* December 14, 1969, p. 13.

35. An excellent case study of such a situation was presented by Robert Brustein in his article "When the Panther Came to Yale," June 21, 1970, *NYT Magazine.*

36. This state of affairs has not been limited to college campuses. Many urban high schools experienced similar problems and sometimes far more serious eruptions of violence than the colleges, including attacks on teachers. The following story is probably characteristic of the making of educational policy in our times, at least in some large cities, without exemplifying the worst outbreaks of violence: "The acting chairman of the English department at Boys High School in Brooklyn has gone on sick leave after an incident in which a group of students barred him from his office. . . . They reportedly told him not to go to his office and criticized him for allegedly not 'relating' to his students. . . . It is known that he aroused displeasure among some students when he withdrew his predecessor's permission to use office equipment for duplicating and distributing student handbills and literature. . . . Last night the school's acting principal . . . said he 'would not encourage Mr. Soman to come back' as a result of the 'unfortunate incident,'" *NYT,* December 14, 1971, p. 46.

37. Seymour Martin Lipset: "Youth and Politics" from Robert K. Merton and Robert Nisbet eds.: *Contemporary Social Problems,* New York, 1971, p. 763-70.

38. Riesman, *op. cit.,* p. XIV.

39. For some influential examples of this attitude, see Edgar Z. Friedenberg: *Coming of Age in America,* New York, 1967; also by Friedenberg: *The Vanishing Adolescent,* Boston, 1964; also John Holt: *How Children Fail,* New York, 1964; also by Holt: *How Children Learn,* 1967; and *The Underachieving School,* New York, 1969. For a critical discussion of viewing the young as "victims or visionaries," see Joseph Adelson: "Inventing the Young," *Commentary,* May 1971.

40. See for example a recent report on the "grade inflation": "Flunking Is Harder as College Grades Rise Rapidly," *NYT,* March 13, 1972, p. 1. Another factor associated with this "grade inflation" but rarely discussed in public is the impact of the student evaluation of teachers. When such evaluations are used by college ad-

ministrators in relation to faculty promotion, tenure or pay raise—as they increasingly are—a new relationship between teacher and student is created hardly conducive to a fair evaluation of student performance on part of the teacher. The quest for popularity, consciously or otherwise will enter into student evaluation. One time-honored route to popularity is to go easy on grading.

41. "Youth 'Don't Know What They Are Looking For' Says College Admissions," *NYT*, August 24, 1970, p. 23.

42. "Students Dissent Dropout Problem," *NYT*, November 19, 1969, p. 25.

43. Children who "had been raised with warmth and affection all around them and expected the same relationship in their dealings with school, the authorities, the police. Not finding it they judged everything about them corrupt, demanding destruction." Oscar and Mary F. Handlin: *Facing Life—Youth and Family in American History*, Boston, 1971, p. 265; see also Peter L. Berger and Richard John Neuhaus: *Movement and Revolution*, Garden City, 1970, p. 37.

44. Jerry Farber: "The Student as Nigger," reprinted in the *Massachusetts Daily Collegian*, April 11, 1969, p. 7.

45. *NYT Book Review Section*—review by Sara Davidson of three books on high school radicalism (no date, 1970), p. 3.

46. Edward Shils: "Plenitude and Scarcity," *Encounter*, May 1969, p. 47.

47. "Senate President Leaves University," *Massachusetts Daily Collegian*, November 20, 1969, p. 1.

48. "The School of Education Expands," *Massachusetts Daily Collegian*, September 10, 1970, p 16. For cogent discussions of grading and evaluation see also Steven D. Krasner: "A Defense of Conventional Grading" *PS* Fall, 1970, pp. 651-52; also "On Grading" in Nathan Glazer: *Remembering the Answers*, New York, 1970, pp. 245-49 and Louis G. Geiger and Helen M. Geiger: "The Revolt Against Excellence," *AAUP Bulletin*, September 1970, pp. 297-301.

49. Roszak, *op. cit.*, p. 46.

50. "Students Flock to Philadelphia 'School Without Walls,'" *NYT*, January 23, 1970; for other articles discussing educational innovation and voicing criticism of schools, see "Teaching Methods Challenged," *NYT*, September 7, 1970, pp. 1, 15, and "Study Calls Public Schools 'Oppressive' and 'Joyless,'" *NYT*, September 20, 1970, pp. 1, 70. The latter derives from Charles E. Silberman: *Crises in the Classroom*, New York, 1970.

51. "Tufts Plan Questions Tradition," *NYT*, February 26, 1972, pp. 25, 35.

52. Shils, "Plenitude and Scarcity," pp. 45, 46. For another discussion of the rejection of differentiation in education and in general see Franklin L. Ford: "Roles and the Critique of Learning," *Daedalus*, Summer 1970.

53. Robert Nisbet: "Who Killed the Student Movement?" *Encounter*, February 1970, pp. 11-12.

54. Bart Kaplan: "The Living," *Massachusetts Daily Collegian*, December 19, 1969.

55. Richard Hofstadter: "The Age of Rubbish," *Newsweek*, July 6, 1970, p. 21.

56. Quoted in Seymour Martin Lipset: "Working Class Authoritarianism" in his *Political Man*, Garden City, 1963, pp 109, 111-12.

57. George Lindbeck: "Ecumenism and the Future of Belief," *Una Sancta*, 1968, Vol. 25, No. 3, p. 11.

58. Though, according to a survey, "Belief in God [is] down"; the decline, however, is very slight, with 97 per cent of those interviewed indicating "some degree of belief in God." The corresponding proportion was 99 per cent in 1952. See *NYT*, June 6,

1966. See also the *Yearbook* of the National Council of Churches of Christ in the United States, New York, 1966, pp. 197, 221. On the other hand, church attendance dropped from 49 per cent (of adults) in 1958 to 42 per cent in 1969. See also "Decrease Found in Church Goers," *NYT*, December 28, 1969, p. 56.

59. See the *Yearbook*, pp. 196, 197, 214, 215, 223. Also, R. M. Williams, Jr., *op. cit.*, p. 376.

60. Walter Kolarz, *Religion in the Soviet Union*, New York, 1961, p. 37. The following figures illustrate the institutional limitations on Soviet religion: 20,000 Orthodox churches (1955) (estimated 20-30 million believers); total number of theological students in 1955, 1500, an optimistic estimate (p. 90); only two church periodicals, no religious literary publications. The restrictions on Jewish religious practices are still more severe as has been well documented. See, for example: "A Report and Analysis of the Status of Soviet Jewry," in *Congress*, December 5, 1966; also D. Weiss: "A Culture in Torment," in *Dissent*, July-August 1966. It should be pointed out that the occasional currents of liberalization since the mid 1950's did not include an increased support or toleration of religious practices on part of the authorities.

61. "Do Not Flirt With God," *Izvestia*, October 1963, transl. *CDSP*, November 20, 1963, p. 33; see also "Rear Militant Atheists," *Pravda*, March 6, 1964, transl. *CDSP*, April 1, 1964, p. 30; "Don't Engage in Cap-tossing!" *Komsomolskaya Pravda*, May 29, 1965, transl. *CDSP*, June 23, 1965. In these "Notes of an Atheist Lecturer," the author sets out to demolish the illusion that "religious belief is harmless," p. 15. For a few revealing case studies of the variety of measures employed by the authorities in the struggle against religion, see "Religious Dissent" in *Problems of Communism*, July-August 1968, pp. 96-114.

62. Gerhard Lenski: *The Religious Factor*, Garden City, 1963, pp. 58, 320.

63. R. M. Williams, Jr., *op. cit.*, pp. 383, 384.

64. "Religion Is Found to Lose Influence," *NYT*, March 5, 1970, p. 67; also "70% In Survey See Religion on Wane," *NYT*, June 1, 1969.

65. For example, Erich Kahler, *The Tower and the Abyss*, London, 1958, pp. 195-97; Kingsley Davis, *Human Society*, New York, 1960, pp. 535-36; Pitirim Sorokin, *Social and Cultural Dynamics*, Boston, 1957, pp. 272-75. For an empirical study on the same subject, see Rodney Stark and Charles Y. Glock: *American Piety: The Nature of Religious Commitment*, Berkeley and Los Angeles, 1968.

66. For example, "On measures for intensifying the atheistic indoctrination of the population," *Partiinaya Zhizn'*, transl. *CDSP*, March 25, 1964.

67. "Disrespect for the Law Is Intolerable," *Pravda*, transl. *CDSP*, March 9, 1966, pp. 34-35; also "Some Questions on Religion and the Church," *Izvestia*, transl. *CDSP*, September 21, 1966, pp. 5-6. The article gives unwitting evidence of the upsurge of the activity of the Baptists in the USSR and particularly of their attempt to rid themselves of the government-controlled "religious center"—an intention that provoked the wrath of the Soviet authorities. For a more general discussion of the tenacious footholds of religion in Soviet society see, Robert C. Tucker: "Religious Revival in Russia"; in Alex Inkeles and Kent Geiger, eds., *op. cit.*, pp. 424-28.

68. Cited in Lewis Feuer: "The Intelligentsia in Opposition," *Problems of Communism*, November-December 1970, p. 14.

69. For example, Will Herberg, *Protestant, Catholic, Jew*, Garden City, 1955.

70. Peter L. Berger: *A Rumor of Angels*, Garden City, 1969, p. 29.

71. *Zygon, a Journal of Religion and Science*, has recently been established to bridge

the gap between religion and science, as its editorial stated, *Zygon*, Chicago, March 1966, Vol. I, no. 1, pp. 1-10.

72. For example, "The Bible Is the Prime Textbook in Every Lecture Course at Bob Jones University," *NYT*, April 26, 1965.

73. The inventiveness and energy Americans betray in founding religions and producing a vast flood of "religious popular culture" is documented in Louis Schneider and Sanford Dornbusch, *Popular Religion*, Chicago, 1958.

74. The secularization of religion in the United States is vividly illustrated by such newspaper reports: "39 Young Nuns Get Airline Charm Course," *NYT*, Dec. 23, 1966; "California Priest Offers a Prayer for Golfers" (which included: "Oh God, the Author and Exemplar of poise, power, perseverance, and pointedness give us a portion of Your smoothness and accuracy on the golf course"), *NYT*, July 19, 1966; "Fort Dix Chaplain Conducts Informal Chapel for Men" ("with emphasis on informality and fun"), *NYT*, January 1, 1967; "Clerics Debate Uses of Leisure —Puritan Work Ethic Called a Hindrance in This Era," *NYT*, June 26, 1966; " 'Theology of Fun' Is Suggested For Church in 'Religious Ghetto,' " *NYT*, February 1, 1967; "Theologian Calls for Church Jazz—Says It Might be a 'Symbol for Renewed Affirmation,' " *NYT*, December 3, 1961; "Church Unite Frug and Religion," *NYT*, April 26, 1966. For further examples of the same trend, see Dan Wakefield: "Slick-Paper Christianity" in Maurice Stein, Arthur J. Vidich, and David Manning White, eds., *Identity and Anxiety*, New York, 1960, pp. 410-15. For a discussion of the relationship between secularization and bureaucratization in the churches see Charles H. Page: "Bureaucracy and the Liberal Church," in *Review of Religion*, Vol. XVI, No. 3-4, March 1952. The secular characteristics of religion in America are explained by the presence of a "civil religion" by Robert N. Bellah in his "Civil Religion in America," in Willam G. McLoughlin and Robert N. Bellah, eds.: *Religion in America*, Boston, 1968, pp. 3-23.

75. *Student Action* (the student voice of Campus Crusade for Christ), Winter 1971, p. 4. For a journalistic report of the same movement, see "The New Rebel Cry: Jesus Is Coming!" *Time Magazine*, June 21, 1971.

76. "Religion in the Age of Aquarius," *NYT*, December 25, 1969, p. 41.

77. "A Spiritual Revival Outside the Church," *NYT*, *News of the Week Section*, November 2, 1969.

78. "Barefoot Worshippers Blindfolded for Communion at St. Clements," *NYT*, January 27, 1969, p. 23.

79. Lenski, *op. cit*, p. 333.

80. For discussions of Marxism-Leninism as a secular religion, see for example, Raymond Aron: *The Opium of Intellectuals*, London, 1957; Jules Monnerot, *Sociology and Psychology of Communism*, Boston, 1960; Waldemar Gurian: "Totalitarianism as a Political Religion," in Carl J. Friedrich, ed., *Totalitarianism*, New York, 1964, pp. 119-29; Nicholas Berdyaev, *The Origin of Russian Communism*, Ann Arbor, 1960. For a discussion of the preservation of elements of Christianity in Marxism see J. H. Plumb, *op. cit.*, pp. 98-100.

81. "Turncoats," *Izvestia*, transl. *CDSP*, February 2, 1966.

82. Nikita Struve: "Pseudo-Religious Rites Introduced by Party Authorities," in William C. Fletcher and Anthony J. Strover: *Religion and the Search for New Ideals in the USSR*, New York, 1967, p. 47; for a recent Soviet discussion of secular rituals by the Latvian Republic's Minister of Culture, see "Ceremonies in Our Everyday Life," *Izvestia*, transl. *CDSP*, November 23, 1971, pp. 8-9.

83. For example, "Thirteen Days Around the Clock at Meetings," *Molodoy Kommunist*, No. 2, February 1965, transl. *CDSP*, May 5, 1965, p. 7. See also Merle Fainsod, *How Russia Is Ruled*, p. 594.

84. Max Hayward: "Summary" from Fletcher and Strover, eds., p. 133.

85. Alexis de Tocqueville, *Democracy in America*, Vol. I, New York, 1958, pp. 314-16. Harriet Martineau, *Society in America*, Garden City, 1962, pp. 333-34.

86. The satirical and critical treatments include, Evelyn Waugh: *The Loved One*, Boston, 1948, and Jessica Mitford: *The American Way of Death*, Greenwich, 1963. For a social-psychological treatment of the subject explored in the hospital setting, see Barney G. Glaser and Anselm L. Strauss, *An Awareness of Dying*, Chicago, 1965.

87. For example, Herman Feifel, ed.: *The Meaning of Death*, New York, 1959, pp. 115-16.

88. Advertisement for Pinelawn Memorial Park, *New York Post*, Summer, 1961. However, the versatile funerary enterprise also offers "prestige above-ground burial arrangements" described in their booklet "The New Garden Mausoleum at Pine Memorial Park," Farmingdale, New York.

89. Allan I. Ludwig: *The Graven Images, New England Stonecarving and Its Symbols, 1650-1815*, Middletown, 1966, p. 77.

90. For the year 1960 funeral costs per adult population of the U.S. averaged $1450 (based on the total of $2 billion expended), see further Mitford, *op. cit.*, pp. 31-32.

91. "There Are No Two Truths," *Izvestia*, transl. *CDSP*, April 15, 1964, p. 16.

92. "Reader Continues Discussion: Man Is great!" *Izvestia*, transl. *CDSP*, May 27, 1964.

93. Quoted in Robert Conquest: "De-Stalinization and the Heritage of Terror" in Alexander Dallin and Alan F. Westin, eds.: *Politics in the Soviet Union—7 Cases*, New York, 1966, p. 39.

94. Wilbert Moore, "The Utility of Utopias," *American Sociological Review*, December 1966, p. 771. This is also the burden of the findings in Hadley Contril: *The Pattern of Human Concerns*, New Brunswick, 1965. For another position on this subject see Dorothy Lee: "Are Basic Needs Ultimate?" Clyde Kluckhohn and Henry A. Murray, eds., *Personality in Nature, Society and Culture*, New York, 1962, pp. 335-41.

95. This is one of the major arguments of S. M. Lipset, *The First New Nation*, New York, 1963. An interesting empirical confirmation of the stability in American values is found in Fred I. Greenstein, "New Light on Changing American Values: A Forgotten Body of Survey Data," *Social Forces*, Vol. 42, May 1964. The controversy on the subject is dealt with in Talcott Parsons: "The Link Between Character and Society," in Parsons, *Social Structure and Personality*, Glencoe, 1964, pp. 183-235. For yet another perspective on this subject see Stuart Chase: "American Values— A Generation of Change, *Public Opinion Quarterly*, Fall, 1965. See also Riesman, "Second Preface," *op. cit.*

96. "Text of the Soviet Writers' Petition to the Kremlin and of Letter of Protest," *NYT*, November 19, 1966, p. 6.

97. *Ibid.* Similar sentiments and values can also be found in the writings of Solzhenitsyn, Pasternak, Sinyavsky, Daniel, and other dissenting intellectuals.

98. Peter B. Reddaway: "The Search for New Ideals in the USSR: Some First Hand Impressions," in Fletcher and Strover, eds.: *op cit.*, pp. 85, 87.

Chapter 6

1. For recent comparisons of certain aspects of social stratification in capitalist and Communist societies see Frank Parkin: *Class Inequality and Political Order*, Lon-

don, 1971; Seymour Martin Lipset: "Mobility and Class Consciousness" (unpublished manuscript) and Paul Hollander, ed.: *American and Soviet Society,* Englewood Cliffs, 1969, pp. 123-53.

2. Robert K. Merton: *Social Theory and Social Structure,* Glencoe, 1957, p. 139.

3. See also Stanislaw Ossowski: *Class Structure in the Social Consciousness,* New York, 1963, p. 114. A similar point was also made in Seymour Martin Lipset: *The Political Man,* Garden City: 1963, p. XXV.

4. James S. Coleman et al.: *Equality of Educational Opportunity,* Washington, D.C., 1966.

5. See "University for Rural Schoolchildren," *Pravda,* May 28, transl. *CDSP,* June 19, 1968, p. 23. Also "How to Equalize Opportunities," *Pravda,* transl. *CDSP,* July 16, 1969, p. 34.

6. See, for example, Charles H. Page: "An Introduction Thirty Years Later," in his *Class and American Sociology,* New York, 1970, pp. XLVI-LII. For a survey of literature on stratification critical of insufficient emphasis on economic inequalities see John Peace, William H. Form & Joan Huber Rytina: "Ideological Currents in American Stratification Literature," *American Sociologist,* May 1970.

7. Aleksandr Yanov: "The Kostroma Experiment," *Literaturnaya Gazeta,* transl. *CDSP,* January 31, 1968, p. 11.

8. L. Nikiforov: "The Reader Asks to Be Told: On Social Equality and Levelling," *Pravda,* transl. *CDSP,* February 21, 1968, p. 7; see also V. Kelle: "Questions of Theory: The Perfecting of Social Relations Under Socialism," *Pravda,* transl. *CDSP,* April 26, 1967, p. 10.

9. Vladimirov Leonid: *The Russians,* New York, 1968, p. 137.

10. "The Components of Your Income," *Sovetskaya Rossia,* transl. *CDSP,* April 26, 1967, p. 10.

11. See, for example, Herbert J. Gans: "The Equality Revolution," *NYT Magazine,* November 3, 1968.

12. See, for example, Gerhard E. Lenski: *Power and Privilege,* New York, 1966, p. 333.

13. G. Fischer, *op. cit.,* p. 4.

14. *Ibid.,* p. 5.

15. Tyrmand: "A Reporter at Large," *The New Yorker,* November 11, 1967, p. 93.

16. Robert W. Hodge, Paul M. Siegel, and Peter H. Rossi: "Occupational Prestige in the United States: 1925-1963" in Reinhard Bendix and Seymour Martin Lipset, eds.: *Class, Status and Power,* 2nd ed. New York, 1966.

17. V. Kantorovich: "A Science Kindred to Us," *Literaturnaya Gazeta,* transl. *CDSP,* July 20, 1966, p. 14; for further reports on the distaste for manual labor see also William Taubman: *The View From Lenin Hills,* New York: 1967, p. 27; Fred M. Hechinger: "Education: Triumphs and Doubts" in Harrison E. Salisbury, ed.: *The Soviet Union: The Fifty Years,* New York, 1967, p. 104; and Albert Parry: *The New Class Divided,* New York, 1966, pp. 235-40. For an excellent summary and analysis of relevant Soviet studies see Murray Yanowitch and Norton T. Dodge: "The Social Evaluation of Occupations in the Soviet Union," in *Slavic Review,* December 1969; G. Osipov, chairman, of the Soviet Sociological Association has also warned about the danger of overeducating young people in relation to the opportunities available; see also his "Problems and Judgements Man, Labor and the Collective," *Pravda,* transl. *CDSP,* January 29, 1969, p. 19. See also "Russian Youth Scorns Blue Collar," *NYT,* June 20, 1971, p. 3; a major sociological study concerned with work satisfaction reached similar conclusions and cautioned about "a disproportion between the growing intellectual expectations and the possibili-

ties of carrying them out in laboring activity. *Hence one of the most important social problems of indoctrination is the formation in people of an optimal structure of value orientation.*" In other words people should be socialized so that their expectations will not exceed their opportunities. See A. G. Zdravomyslov, V. P. Rozhin, and V. A. Iadov: *Man and His Work,* White Plains, 1970, p. 291.

18. "This Is What Young Working People Are Like Today," *Izvestia,* transl. *CDSP,* June 19, 1968, p. 22.

19. "From Experiment to Practice," *Pravda,* transl. *CDSP,* June 12, 1968, p. 12.

20. It is nevertheless noteworthy that in a poll on occupational preferences it was found that "among the seventy occupations listed . . . none was in the realm of politics." G. Fisher, *op. cit.,* p. 174.

21. Quoted in Robert V. Daniels, ed.: *A Documentary History of Communism,* New York, 1960, Vol. II, pp. 36-37. For some further comments on the ideological implications of these policies see R. Lowenthal *op. cit.,* esp. pp. 55-56, 74-75.

22. *Ibid.,* p. 36.

23. Leon Trotsky: *The Revolution Betrayed,* New York, 1965, see esp. pp. 115-43; and Wolfgang Leonhard: *Child of the Revolution,* Chicago, 1958, esp. pp. 476-79. For evidence about the preferential food distribution to party officials in 1934 see Merle Fainsod: *Smolensk Under Soviet Rule, op. cit.,* p. 118.

24. Quoted in Daniels, *op. cit.,* p. 26.

25. For some case studies see Joseph Novak: *No Third Path,* Garden City, 1962, pp. 40-47.

26. M. N. Rutkevich: "The Social Sources of Replenishment of the Soviet Intelligentsia," *Voprosy Filosofii,* transl. *CDSP,* September 20, 1967, p. 15.

27. Kantorovich, *op. cit.,* p. 14.

28. *A Russian-English Dictionary of Social Science Terms* compiled by R. E. F. Smith, London, 1962, pp. 485-89.

29. Michael Frolic: "Soviet Urban Sociology," *International Journal of Comparative Sociology,* December 1971, p. 238. The author quoted the descriptions of the housing situation in Akademgorodok from a Soviet study of housing patterns in Siberia.

30. The section to follow focuses on the life style of the upper classes in part because the topic is rarely dealt with by sociologists and in part because other elite groups (e.g. politicians, intellectuals, and so forth) have been discussed in other parts of the book. For systematic treatments of elite groups in modern societies see T. B. Bottomore: *Elites and Society,* London: 1964, and Suzanne Keller: *Strategic Elites,* New York, 1963.

31. John Kenneth Galbraith: *The Affluent Society,* New York, 1958, p. 263.

32. Seymour Martin Lipset: "Equal or Better in America," *Columbia University Forum,* Spring 1961, Vol. IV, No. 2, p. 18.

33. "Levittown on Water that Rivals the Taj Mahal—and It Floats" *NYT,* July 15, 1972, p. 18; "Greek King Spurns Newport Yachts for Cruiser," *NYT,* September 14, 1967. At Truman Capote's celebrated party it was reported that the masks worn by the guests ranged in price from $65 to $600. "Behind the Masks of Truman Capote's Party," *NYT,* November 29, 1966; "Very Often There Is No Place Like Home Except the Metropolitan Museum," *NYT,* November 22, 1964; "Anything Goes for Daytime at Rhode Island Resort," *NYT,* August 9, 1965; "Rehoboth Beach: Beyond the Boardwalks Citadels of Wealth," *NYT,* July 9, 1967; "Richness Like Most Other Things in Texas, Is a Matter of Size," *NYT,* February 4, 1968.

34. "Fisher's Island: Simple Vacation Hideaway for the Quiet Rich," *NYT,* August 20,

1967. For other examples of the quest for not entirely unpublicized seclusion see "For the Citizens of Affluent Centre Island Life Rolls Merrily Along," *NYT*, January 1, 1967; and "Sugar Bowl: Getting There Can Be Half the Fun for Its Skiers," *NYT*, January 7, 1968.

35. "Setting Fashion Trends In Their Work and Play," *NYT*, December 14, 1964.

36. Vladimirov, *op cit.*, p. 237. On the Soviet policy of concealing inequalities of income see also: Isaac Deutscher: *The Unfinished Revolution*, New York, 1967, p. 58. In comparing inequalities in American and Soviet society Bottomore pointed out that income differentials are less objectionable to many people if they are not based on unearned income, such as property ownership. See further T. B. Bottomore: *Classes in Modern Society*, New York, 1966, p. 70.

37. *Message from Moscow*, p. 109. Another visitor observed along these lines: "What astonished me in Russia was that even the regime's opponents seemed to accept calmly a 'socialist' society which is split up into classes and in which glaring privileges and contrasting standards of life exist." K. S. Karol, *op. cit.*

38. C. Wright Mills: *White Collar—The American Middle Classes*, New York, 1951, pp. XII, XVI-XVIII.

39. According to Murray Friedman "The culture had become frankly hostile to Middle Americans"—a view that is widely shared and contributes to the new sense of powerlessness among the middle classes. See also his *Overcoming Middle Class Rage*, Philadelphia, 1971, p. 23.

40. See, for example, Milton Gordon: *Social Class in American Sociology*, New York, 1963, pp. 196-98.

41. *The Collected Essays of C. Wright Mills*, ed. by I. L. Horowitz, New York, 1963, p. 314; and Talcott Parsons: *Essays in Sociological Theory*, New York, 1964, pp. 332, 428.

42. Eric Larrabee: *The Self-Conscious Society*, Garden City, 1960, p. 30.

43. Robert Nisbet: "The Decline and Fall of Social Class" in *Tradition and Revolt*, New York, 1968.

44. Blum, John Morton, *The Promise of America*, Boston, 1966, p. 76.

45. Mayer and Buckley consider families with incomes between $10,000 and $25,000 belonging to the upper middle class. See Kurt B. Mayer and Walter Buckley: *Class and Society*, New York, 1970, p. 83.

46. Marx and Engels: *Communist Manifesto*, Moscow, 1955, p. 53.

47. M. N. Rutkevich and F. R. Filippov: *Sotsialnie Peremeshchenia* (Social Transformations), Moscow, 1970, p. 57.

48. *Ibid.*, p. 52-53; for an overview and summary of recent trends in Soviet literature on stratification see Zev Katz: "Sociology in the Soviet Union," *Problems of Communism*, May-June 1971, pp. 28-33.

49. *Pravda and Izvestia*, trans., November 1, 1967, p. 11.

50. Zdravomyslov et al., *op. cit.*, pp. 112-13.

51. V. G. Baikova, A. S. Duchal, A. A. Zemtsov: *Svobodnoye Vremya i Vsestoronnoye Razvitie Lichnosti* (Free Time and the All-Round Development of the Personality), Moscow, 1965, pp. 183-84.

52. See, for example, William H. Flanigan: *Political Behavior of the American Electorate*, Boston, 1968, p. 20.

53. Mark G. Field: *Soviet Socialized Medicine*, New York, 1967, p. 118.

54. *Message From Moscow*, pp. 67-69.

55. Keith Bush: "A Comparison of Retail Prices in the United States, the USSR and

Western Europe in April, 1969," *Radio Liberty Research Paper, No. 33*, New York 1969, pp. 2, 4. It should be noted that the typical Soviet family spends close to half of its income on food.

56. V. Perevedentsev: "Where It Is Crowded and Where It Is Deserted," *Literaturnaya gazeta*, transl. *CDSP*, April 6, 1966.

57. "CPSU Central Committee's Slogans for May Day," *Pravda, Izvestia* transl. *CDSP*, May 8, 1968, p. 10; for a study of the loss of autonomy of Soviet trade unions, see also Jay B. Sorensen: *Life and Death of Soviet Trade Unionism 1917-1928:* New York, 1969.

58. Bennett Berger: *Working Class Suburb*, Berkeley, 1960, p. 97.

59. Notable exceptions include Ely Chinoy: *Automobile Workers and the American Dream*, Garden City, 1955 (not exactly a recent work); Arthur B. Shostak: *Blue Collar Life*, New York, 1969; Arthur B. Shostak and William Gomberg, eds.: *Blue Collar World*, Englewood Cliffs, 1964; and Mira Komarovsky: *Blue Collar Marriage*, New York, 1967; see also "The World of the Blue Collar Worker," *Dissent*, Winter 1972.

60. *Narodnie Khoziaistvo SSSR v 1970—Statisticheskii Ezhegodnik* (The National Economy of the Soviet Union in 1970, A Statistical Yearbook), Moscow, 1971, p. 22; *Pocket Data Book USA 1971* Washington, D.C., 1971, p. 138.

61. The results of the latter produced some startling news: "Doctors who work in free clinics around the country said . . that the youthful counterculture—with its close communal living, sharing of clothing and beds and poor hygienic conditions—was giving the louse a new lease on life." See "Infestations of Lice Increasing; Communal Living a Key Factor," *NYT*, September 5, 1971, p. 28.

62. Larrabee, *op. cit.*, p. 41.

63. Dick Hobston: "Oh To Be 30 Again!" *TV Guide* September 23, 1967, pp. 12, 13, 14; see also "Average People Joining the Parade of Face Lifts," *NYT*, April 18, 1969; and "More and More 'Average' Americans Are Visiting Plastic Surgeon in Search of the Body Beautiful," *NYT*, April 13, 1969.

64. Denis de Rougemont: *Love in the Western World*, Garden City, 1957, pp. 293-94.

65. Frank Deford: *There She Is: The Life and Times of Miss America*, New York, 1971.

66. C. Wright Mills: "Plain Talk on Fancy Sex" in *Collected Essays, op. cit.*

67. Lenski, *op. cit.*, p. 417.

68. Boorstin: *The Image—A Guide to Pseudo-Events in America*, New York, 1964, pp. 57-58.

69. Erich Fromm: *Escape from Freedom*, New York, 1965, p. 66.

70. Parry, *op. cit.*, pp. 110-14.

Chapter 7

1. Kent Geiger: *The Family in Soviet Russia*, Cambridge, Mass., 1968, pp. 11-71.

2. "On Results of Admissions to Party and Changes in the Composition of the CPSU," *Partiinaya zhizn*, transl. *CDSP*, May 8, 1968, p. 12.

3. "Whose Job Is the Kitchen," *Literaturnaya gazeta*, transl. in *CDSP*, September 6, 1967, p. 7; on the general relationship between women's equality and their employment, see also Williams, Jr., *op. cit.*, p. 71.

4. Mark Field, *op. cit.*, p. 118.

5. L. Kantorovich: "A Specialist's Opinion: Utilizing the Capacities of Each," *Trud*, transl. *CDSP*, June 5, 1968, p. 3.

6. Tocqueville, *op. cit.*, Vol. II, pp. 208, 212, 223, 225.

7. In 1968 life expectancy at birth for men was 66.6 years and 74.0 for women. There was however a difference between white and black rates, although even among blacks life expectancy of women was almost eight years longer than that of men: white male 67.5; white female: 74.9; black male: 60.1; black female: 67.5. Source: *Pocket Data Book*, p. 64.

8. *American Women—Report of the Presidential Commission on the Status of Women*, New York, 1965, pp. 30, 45-46, 56.

9. *Ibid.*, pp. 27, 91.

10. Geiger, *op. cit.*, pp. 192-93.

11. *American Women*, p. 36.

12. David & Vera Mace: *The Soviet Family*, Garden City, 1964, p. 255.

13. *American Women*, pp. 63-64.

14. Leo Kanowitz: *Women and the Law—The Unfinished Revolution*, Albuquerque, 1969.

15. *American Women*, pp. 72-73; see also Martin Gruber: *Women in American Politics*, Oshkosh, 1968.

16. See further, for example, Caroline Bird: *Born Female—The High Cost of Keeping Women Down*, New York, 1968; also Kate Millet: *Sexual Politics*, Garden City, 1970. For a critique of Millet's book and of certain characteristics of the Women's Liberation Movement, see also Irving Howe: "The Middle Class Mind of Kate Millet," *Harpers*, December 1970.

17. See also Marlene Dixon: "Why Women's Liberation?" *Ramparts*, December 1969, esp. p. 59.

18. Donna Keck: "The Art of Maiming Women," *Women—A Journal of Liberation*, Fall 1969. Interestingly enough, a somewhat similar typology of the roles of American women was proposed in a well-known essay of Parsons many years ago. See: "Age and Sex in the Social Structure of the United States" in Talcott Parsons: *Essays in Sociological Theory Pure and Applied*, Glencoe, 1949, esp. pp. 225-28.

19. See Dixon, "Why Women's Liberation"; also Susan Brownmiller: "Sisterhood Is Powerful," *NYT Magazine*, March 15, 1970, p. 128.

20. See, for example, G. Hollander, *op. cit.*, pp. 177-78; also P. Hollander: "Leisure: The Unity of Pleasure and Purpose" in A. Kassof, ed.: *Prospects for Soviet Society*, New York, 1968.

21. Alexander Solzhenitsyn: *Cancer Ward*, New York, 1969, pp. 91-92.

22. For instance, "Argument with a He-man." Reprinted in P. Hollander, ed.: *American and Soviet Society*, Englewood Cliffs, 1969, pp. 204-6.

23. "House of the New Way of Life: A Building with Privileges?" *Literaturnaya gazeta*, transl. *CDSP*, February 12, 1969, p. 16.

24. See also "The Building in Which We Shall Live," *Literaturnaya gazeta* transl. *CDSP*, February 5, 1969, pp. 16-18.

25. *Man and His Work*, pp. 155, 260, 261, 303, 304.

26. Walter D. Connor: *Deviance in Soviet Society—Crime, Delinquency and Alcoholism*, New York, 1972, pp. 40, 87, 98.

27. Stephen P. Dunn and Ethel Dunn: *The Peasants of Central Russia*, New York, 1967, pp. 47-48.

28. Hollander, ed., *op. cit.*, p. 177.

29. Quoted in Robert V. Daniels, ed.: *A Documentary History of Communism*, New York, 1960, pp. 195, 197. Vol. I.

30. *Pravda*, editorial quoted in Daniels, *op. cit.*, p. 45, Vol. II (Italics added).

31. B. Moore, Jr.: "Thoughts on the Future of the Family" in his *Political Power and Social Theory*, pp. 162, 183.
32. Leon Trotsky: *The Revolution Betrayed*, New York, 1965, p. 145.
33. Ibid., p. 153.
34. *Continuity in History and Other Essays*, Cambridge, Mass., 1968, p. 306. The importance of congruent authority patterns for political stability is stressed by Harry Eckstein in his *Division and Cohesion in Democracy*, Princeton, 1966.
35. "The Parents Are at Home Today," *Pravda* (editorial), transl. *CDSP*, February 26, 1969, p. 43.
36. Robert Nisbet: *Community and Power*, New York, 1968, p. 59.
37. Geoffrey Gorer has pointed out that American society is one of the very few societies which fully subscribes to the belief in the basic goodness of the newly born and which seeks to explain any subsequent unpleasantness of character by external conditions. See his "Are We 'By Freud Obsessed'?" *NYT Magazine*, July 30, 1961.
38. Quoted in Urie Bronfenbrenner: "Soviet Methods of Upbringing and Their Effects," paper delivered at Cornell University at a Conference on May 16, 1968, p. 9.
39. Clara Zetkin: "Lenin on the Woman Question" in *The Emancipation of Women From the Writings of V. I. Lenin*, New York, 1966.
40. Bronfenbrenner, *op. cit.*, pp. 4, 5; for a systematic comparison of American and Soviet patterns in this area see his *Two Worlds of Childhood: U.S. and USSR*, New York, 1970. For a major source of Soviet principles of upbringing see Anton S. Makarenko: *The Collective Family: A Handbook for Russian Parents*, Garden City, 1967.
41. Leonid Vladimirov: *The Russians*, New York, 1968, p. 35.
42. *Ibid.*, pp. 35-36. The Soviet dispute about the merits and demerits of public vs. private upbringing was recently reflected in a new defense of the public sector against criticism; see "Childhood: Family and Nursery," *Pravda*, transl. *CDSP*, February 5, 1969, p. 32.
43. See, for example, R. M. Williams, Jr., *op. cit.*, p. 81; here the author reports how successive editions of the U.S. Government publication *Infant Care* underwent substantive changes in a few decades.
44. Tocqueville, *op. cit.*, p. 202.
45. See also Bronfenbrenner, *op. cit.*, 1968, p. 32.
46. *Time Magazine*, January 24, 1964, p. 54; and "A U.S. Sex Revolt? It's Mostly Talk," *NYT*, July 11, 1966. A gradual change toward permissiveness (and particularly toward permissiveness with affection), rather than a sexual revolution is frequently viewed as characteristic of our times, see, for example, Erwin O. Smigel and Rita Seiden in their "Decline and Fall of the Double Standard" in *Sex and the Contemporary American Scene, The Annals*, March 1968.
47. John F. Cuber with Peggy B. Haroff: *The Significant Americans—A Study of Sexual Behavior Among the Affluent*, New York, 1965, pp. 171-72.
48. On CBS evening news, July 21, 1970. See also "VD: The Epidemic" *Newsweek* January 24, 1972.
49. Duane Denfield and Michael Gordon: "The Sociology of Mate Swapping," and Gilbert D. Bartell: "Group Sex Among Mid-Americans," both in *The Journal of Sex Research*, May 1970, pp. 95 and 114.
50. "Nixon Naming of Three Decried by Welch," *NYT*, January 7, 1969.
51. "Curb on Child Aid Backed in New Jersey—Welfare Board in Monmouth Favors Plan to Prosecute Parents of Illegitimates," *NYT*, September 15, 1966.
52. Lionel S. Lewis and Dennis Brisset: "Sex as Work" in Edward McDonagh and

Jon E. Simpson, eds.: *Social Problems: Persistent Challenges,* New York, 1965, pp. 76, 77.

53. Robert Boyers: "Attitudes Toward Sex in American High Culture," *The Annals,* p. 39.

54. Theodore N. Ferdinand: "Sex Behavior and the American Class Structure: A Mosaic," *The Annals,* p. 77.

55. *The Emancipation of Women—From the Writings of V. I. Lenin,* New York, 1966, pp. 104, 107, 108.

56. William M. Mandel: "Soviet Women and Their Self Image," paper presented at the Far Western Slavic Conference in May, 1970, p. 1.

57. James R. and Lynn G. Smith: "Co-Marital Sex and the Sexual Freedom Movement" *The Journal of Sex Research,* May 1970, p. 142.

58. "If It Were Only An Isolated Case," by Candidate of Jurisprudence V. Baskov, Moscow Assistant Prosecutor, *Izvestia,* transl. *CDSP,* October 21, 1964.

59. "Grandfathers and Grandmothers," *Izvestia,* transl. *CDSP,* December 4, 1968, pp. 11 and 12.

60. Geiger, *op. cit.,* p. 259.

61. S. I. Golod: "Sociological Problems of Sexual Morality," *Soviet Sociology,* Summer 1969, pp. 12, 13; this article is a translation of the dissertation abstract submitted by the author to the Philosophical Faculty of Leningrad University in 1968. The limited information concerning sampling, referred to in the text, may be a result of selective translation in this case.

62. *Message From Moscow,* p. 115.

63. Golod, *op. cit.*

64. Theodore Shabad: "Simplified Soviet Divorce Law Expected to Bolster Family Life," *NYT,* December 28, 1965, p. 7; and also "Report of Marriage and Family Law," *Pravda* and *Izvestia,* transl. *CDSP,* July 24, 1968, pp. 16 and 17.

65. *Pocket Data Book,* p. 68; and *Statistical Abstract of the U.S. 1970,* Washington, D.C., 1971, p. 60.

66. *Narodnoye Khozyaistvo SSSR v 1970 g.* (The National Economy of the USSR in 1970), Moscow, 1971, p. 52. It should be noted that this publication does not provide figures for the same years as the *Pocket Data Book.*

67. Trotsky, *op. cit.,* p. 156.

68. I. Kasyukov and A. Mendeleyev: "Sociologist's Opinion: Must a Family Man Have Talent?" *Nedelya,* transl. *CDSP,* April 19, 1967, p. 25.

69. "Once More on the Family" in P. Hollander, ed., *op. cit.,* p. 194.

70. "Soviet Population Expert Deplores Rising Divorce Rate," *NYT,* September 7, 1969.

71. See, for instance, William J. Goode: *World Revolution and Family Patterns,* New York, 1963, esp. pp. 81-86.

72. Cited in David M. Heer: "Abortion, Contraception & Population Policy in the Soviet Union," *Soviet Studies,* July 1965, p. 82.

73. *Pocket Data Book,* p. 59; *Narodnoye Khozyaistvo SSSR v 1970 g,* p. 47.

74. Henry P. David: *Family Planning and Abortion in the Socialist Countries of Central and Eastern Europe,* New York, 1970, p. 42.

75. Valentei and G. Kiseleva: "The Family, Children and Society," *Pravda,* transl. *CDSP,* October 29, 1969, p. 10.

76. V. Perevedentsev: "Continuation of a Controversy," *Literaturnaya gazeta,* transl. *CDSP,* April 10, 1968, p. 9.

77. *Power and Community,* p. 62.

78. "Lack of Close Friendships Called a Disturbing Problem," *NYT,* May 12, 1966.

79. Geoffrey Gorer: *The American People*, New York, 1964, p. 125.

80. Inkeles and Bauer: *The Soviet Citizen*, pp. 200-202.

81. James H. Billington: "Beneath the Panoply of Power, the Intelligentsia Hits Out at the Old Order," *Life Magazine*, November 10, 1967, p. 70.

82. Such aspects of commune life are evoked by the following account: "It was 11 p.m. when I entered the commune. The whole bottom floor was filled with people I had never seen before, and who didn't know me. The walls had been covered with luminous paint and the house looked like it had been taken over by the psyche-delic crowd. It was strange. Here I had come home, and I had no home. I felt very strongly that I had nothing to say to these people. . . .

I felt I wanted to cry. This was where I had to live; this was my family but my family didn't exist anymore. The place looked like a crash pad. I got this feeling of a fantastic lack of awareness and lack of seriousness, an indifference and selfish-ness—even a fantastic decadence.

There was a girl dancing aimlessly. Everyone seemed stoned, and the music was turned up full volume. . . . There were many people hiding in their rooms, hid-ing from other people, from the society that gave them no spiritual suste-nance . . .

. . . The people in my commune . . . took nothing seriously. They were obsessed with being free in a way that was purposeless. They were suspicious of any form of discipline, anything that interfered with pure spontaneity."

Venceremos Brigade, pp. 399-400. It should be noted that these were the first im-pressions of a political, rather than "life-style radical" returning from sugarcane-cutting in Cuba to his commune in the U.S.

83. Alex Inkeles and Daniel J. Levinson: "National Character: The Study of Modal Personality and Sociocultural Systems" in Gardner Lindzey, ed.: *Handbook of So-cial Psychology*, Cambridge, 1956, pp. 980, 981.

84. David Riesman: "The Study of National Character: Some Observations on the American Case," *Harvard Library Bulletin*, Winter 1959, p. 13. For a more general discussion of historical development and national character see David M. Potter: *People of Plenty*, Chicago, 1965. See also Seymour Martin Lipset and Leo Lowen-thal, eds.: *Culture and Social Character*, New York, 1961; David Riesman: *op. cit.*; Philip E. Slater: *The Pursuit of Loneliness*, Boston, 1970.

85. P. M. Rogachev and M. A. Sverdlin: "On the Concept of 'Nation,'" *Voprosy istorii*, transl. *CDSP*, June 15, 1966, p. 17.

86. See, for example, Henry V. Dicks: "Some Notes on the Russian National Char-acter," in Cyril Black, ed.: *The Transformation of Russian Society*, Cambridge, Mass., 1960; Chap. 15 in Raymond A. Bauer, Alex Inkeles and Clyde Kluckhohn: *How the Soviet System Works*, New York, 1960; and Nathan Leites: *A Study of Bolshevism*, Glencoe, 1953, especially pp. 237-40.

87. See, for example, Raymond A. Bauer: *The New Man in Soviet Psychology*, Cam-bridge, Mass., 1952; P. Hollander: "Models of Behavior in Stalinist Literature," *American Sociological Review*, June 1966; Abram Tertz (Andrey Sinyavsky): *On Socialist Realism*. New York, 1960.

88. "A Comrade Calls for Camaraderie," by Theodore Shabad, *NYT*, December 28, 1964.

89. For further discussions on the Russian national character see also Margaret Mead: *Soviet Attitudes Toward Authority*, New York, 1951; Geoffrey Gorer and John Rickman: *The People of Great Russia*, New York, 1960; and Alex Inkeles: "Modal

Personality and Adjustment to the Soviet Socio-political System" in his *Social Change in Soviet Russia,* Cambridge, 1968.

90. V. I. Selivanov: "Voleviye Cherty Novogo Rabochego" (Volitional Traits of the New Worker) in K. K. Platonov, ed.: *O Chertakh Lichnosti Novovo Rabochevo* (On the Characteristics of the Personality of the New Worker), Moscow, 1963.

91. Maxim Gorky: "On the Russian Peasantry," Berlin, 1922 (Mimeographed). transl. by V. Boss.

92. Dicks, *op. cit.,* p. 640.

93. Inkeles, Bauer, Kluchhohn, *op. cit.,* pp. 200-201.

94. Andrei Amalrik: "Will the USSR Survive Until 1984?" *Survey,* Autumn 1969, p. 62.

95. "Polemical Notes: Pages on Rural Life," *Novy mir,* transl. *CDSP,* May 1969, p. 16.

96. "The National Character and Literature," *Literaturnaya gazeta,* transl. *CDSP,* May 1969, p. 17.

97. See, for example, his *Matryona's House,* the heroes in his *One Day in the Life of Ivan Denisovitch,* and many characters in *Cancer Ward* and *The First Circle.*

98. *Message From Moscow,* pp. 238, 239.

99. Slater, *op. cit.,* p. 14.

100. Clyde Kluckhohn: "Studies of Russian National Character" in Alex Inkeles and Kent Geiger, eds.: *Soviet Society—A Book of Readings,* Boston, 1961, pp. 615-16.

101. *Message From Moscow,* p. 98.

102. This point is elaborated in Seymour M. Lipset: *First New Nation,* Garden City, 1963, esp. Chap. 3.

Chapter 8

1. Robert K. Merton: *Social Theory and Social Structure,* 1964, pp. 68-82. Merton here discussed latent and manifest functions without explicit reference to social problems but pointing to the difficulties of moral evaluation of complex social phenomena. See also Merton's "Epilogue" in R. Merton and R. Nisbet, eds.: *Contemporary Social Problems,* New York, 1966.

2. See also Paul Hollander, ed., *op. cit.,* pp. 217-20.

3. G. Smirnov: "Questions of Theory: Socialist Humanism," *Pravda,* transl. *CDSP,* January 1, 1969, pp. 14, 15.

4. *Pravda,* trans. *CDSP,* February 7, 1968, p. 21.

5. "No one can be passive in the ideological struggle," *Sovetskaya Rossiya,* transl. *CDSP,* March 5, 1969, p. 7.

6. This is also the message of "Juvenile Delinquency and Subterranean Values" by David Matza and Gresham M. Sykes, *American Sociological Review,* October 1961. The best known exposition of this relationship is found in Merton's chapters on anomie in his *Social Theory and Social Structure* cited; but essentially the same point had been made earlier by Donald R. Taft in his *Criminology,* New York, 1942, Chap. XV; see further especially the concept of a "crimogenic" society.

7. Emile Durkheim: *The Division of Labor in Society,* New York, 1965, Book One, Chap. 2.

8. Gerhard A. Ritter: "Student Rebellion and Industrial Society," *Survey,* Summer 1970, p. 142.

9. As Daniel Bell observed "Crime stories are . . . circulation builders." See also "The Myth of Crime Waves" in his *The End of Ideology,* New York, 1961, p. 151.

10. Michael Drosnin: "Ripping Off, The New Life Style," *NYT Magazine,* August 8, 1971.

11. The limited awareness of political alternatives is discussed in Allen Kassof's "The Administered Society: Totalitarianism Without Terror," *World Politics*, July 1964, esp. pp. 572-75.

12. For a major Western attempt to present a relatively coherent picture of Soviet crime, see Walter D. Connor: *Deviance in Soviet Society—Crime, Delinquency and Alcoholism*, New York, 1972.

13. J. E. Hoover: *Crime in the United States, Uniform Crime Reports*, Washington, D.C., 1969, p. 92.

14. In 1964 there were 900,000 cars in the USSR (see D. Barry: "Russians and Their Cars," *Survey*, October 1965, p. 98). Even with the projected increase of production in the late 1960's it is unlikely that there were more than two million cars in 1970. According to an article in late 1969 there were "about 1 million" privately owned passenger cars in the country ("Auto ABC," *Izvestia*, transl. *CDSP*, December 10, 1969, p. 12).

15. "Traffic on Highways in the USSR," *Radio Liberty Dispatch*, April 13, 1970, p. 1.

16. "The Militia and the Public," *Literaturnaya gazeta*, transl. *CDSP*, March 5, 1969, p. 14.

17. See also Connor, *op. cit.*, pp. 152, 240, 256, 262.

18. Jozsef Lengyel: *From Beginning to End*, Englewood Cliffs, 1968, p. 132.

19. See Matza and Sykes, *op. cit.*; also David Matza: *Delinquency and Drift*, New York, 1964, and Barbara Wooton: *Social Science and Social Pathology*, London, 1960, Chap. 3.

20. A. Gertsenzon, "A Jurist's Comments: Eradicate the Evil!" *Izvestia*, transl. *CDSP*, June 11, 1969, p. 23.

21. "80% of Youth Crimes Tied to Intoxication in Moscow," *NYT*, October 23, 1969, p. 11; see also Connor, *op. cit.*, pp. 46-48.

22. Albert K. Cohen: *Delinquent Boys*, New York, 1955.

23. "Vandals," *Pravda*, transl. *CDSP*, May 21, 1969, p. 29.

24. "What Is the Law?" *Izvestia*, transl. *CDSP*, November 13, 1968, p. 24.

25. "The Inspector's Powers," *Izvestia*, transl. *CDSP*, October 9, 1968, p. 23.

26. In this famous case a "production therapy workshop" of a psychoneurological clinic in Moscow was the setting, and the labor of the patients was used to manufacture woolens. According to the newspaper report "The gang members processed 460 tons of wool in the underground shop! . . . In one way or another, 52 factories, artels [a type of artisans' cooperative] and collective farms were connected with the gang of robbers. . . . 3 million rubles was stolen. . . ." "There Will be No Mercy for Thieves!" *Izvestia*, transl. *CDSP*, November 13, 1963, p. 26.

27. "Village Assembly," *Literaturnaya gazeta*, transl. *CDSP*, March 5, 1969, p. 12.

28. See Gus Tyler: *Organized Crime in America*, Ann Arbor, 1962; also Donald Cressey: *The Theft of a Nation*, New York, 1969.

29. "The Psychology of Juvenile Lawbreakers," *Sovetskaya yustitsiya*, transl. *CDSP*, February 14, 1968, p. 9. It is hardly known in the United States that there is also a dropout problem in the Soviet Union and that dropping out of school and delinquent episodes are correlated in Soviet society too: "The study of criminal cases shows that in the overwhelming majority . . . minors who have taken the path of crime have a low level of general education and a narrow range of interests, dropped out of school between the ages of 13 and 15. . . ." "Crime Prevention is the Main Thing: One Guarantee for Reducing Crime Among Minors," *Sovetskaya yustitsiya*, transl. *CDSP*, May 21, 1969, p. 8.

For further discussions of Soviet juvenile delinquency see Walter D. Connor:

"Juvenile Delinquency in the USSR: Some Quantitative and Qualitative Indicators," *American Sociological Review*, April 1970; and Paul Hollander: "Reflections on Soviet Juvenile Delinquency" in Paul Hollander, ed., *op. cit.* For a major source on Soviet criminology see Peter H. Solomon, Jr.: "A Selected Bibliography of Soviet Criminology," *The Journal of Criminal Law, Criminology and Political Science*, 1970, No. 3.

30. "The Psychology of Juvenile Lawbreakers," *op. cit.*, p. 10.

31. "Money and Young People," *Pravda*, transl. *CDSP*, February 14, 1969, p. 10.

32. For a discussion of the decline of economic determinism in relation to crime causation see Raymond Bauer: *The New Man in Soviet Psychology*, Cambridge, Mass., 1952, esp. pp. 37-43.

33. "Address by S. P. Pavlov . . . ," *Komsomolskaya Pravda*, transl. *CDSP*, January 26, 1966, p. 10.

34. J. Stalin: *Problems of Leninism*, Moscow, 1940, pp. 515-39.

35. For example, "Antisocial Phenomena, Their Causes and the Means of Combating Them," *Kommunist*, transl. *CDSP*, September 28, 1966, p. 10.

36. B. S. Vorontsov: "Problems of Criminology: On Crime Among Minors in the City and Rural Localities," *Sovetskoye gosudarstvo i pravo*, transl. *CDSP*, May 21, 1969, pp. 10, 11, 12.

37. "Questions of Soviet Law: The Nature of Lawbreaking," *Izvestia*, transl. *CDSP*, August 7, 1968, p. 24.

38. S. S. Ostroumov and V. E. Chugunov quoted in P. Hollander, ed.: *American and Soviet Society*, pp. 271, 273-74.

39. See, for example, G. M. Minkovsky: "Some Causes of Juvenile Delinquency in the USSR and Measures to Prevent it," *Sovetskoye gosudartsvo i pravo*, transl. *CDSP*, August 17, 1966; see also M. D. Shargorodsky: "The Causes and Prevention of Crime," *Soviet Sociology*, Vol III, No. 1, 1964.

40. V. I. Lenin: *State and Revolution*, Moscow (no date), e.g., p. 163.

41. Ella Winter: *Red Virtue*, New York, 1933, p. 206.

42. "The Principles of Corrective Labor Legislation of the USSR and the Union Republics," *Pravda* and *Izvestia*, transl. *CDSP*, August 13, 1969, p. 7. The harsh sentencing for crimes against state property was exemplified by the case of a man who was given 11 years for stealing goods worth 11,000 rubles; see also "From the Courtroom, Let Himself Go and Came a Cropper," *Izvestia*, transl. *CDSP*, November 26, 1969, p. 27.

43. "Statute Governing Labor Colonies for Minors," *Vedomosti Verkhovnovo Soveta SSSR*, transl. *CDSP*, July 3, 1969, p. 3.

44. "On the Simple Words 'It is Forbidden,'" *Literaturnaya gazeta*, transl. *CDSP*, August 21, 1968, p. 13.

45. B. Nikiforov: "On the Complex Concept of 'Punishment,'" *Literaturnaya gazeta*, transl. *CDSP*, August 21, 1968, p. 14.

46. "Return to What Was Printed," *Izvestia*, transl. *CDSP*, January 31, 1968, p. 24.

47. "The Individual Circumstances and Responsibility," *Literaturnaya gazeta*, transl. *CDSP*, July 14, 1965, p. 9.

48. See, for example, Hans Toch, ed.: *Legal and Criminal Psychology*, New York, 1961, pp. 171-91.

49. *United States Statistical Abstracts*, Washington, D.C., 1969, p. 158.

50. See, for example, Thomas F. Pettigrew: *A Profile of the Negro American*, Princeton, 1964, Chap. 6.

51. By contrast the kind of legal defense available is hardly a factor in the Soviet sys-

tem of justice. It is the prevailing political conditions which determine sentencing, not the capabilities of lawyers. On the irrelevance of income to the type of legal resources available see George Feifer: *Justice in Moscow*, New York, 1965, p. 79.

52. *The American Almanac—The U.S. Book of Facts, Statistics and Information for 1971*, New York, 1971, p. 157; see also *Task Force Report: Corrections*, Washington, D.C., 1967 Chaps. 3 and 6 (on probation and parole).

53. For an extreme case of such brutalities in recent times see Tom Burton and Joe Hyams: *Accomplices to the Crime—The Arkansas Prison Scandal*, New York, 1970.

54. See, for example, "Harlem Likened to the Old West," *NYT*, January 8, 1969, p. 48.

55. See, for example, Stanley Milgram and Paul Hollander: "The Murder They Heard," *The Nation*, June 15, 1964.

56. "The Witness and the Administration of Justice," *Izvestia*, transl. *CDSP*, March 19, 1969, p. 24.

57. For scholarly explorations of the subject see Hans Toch: *Violent Men*, Chicago, 1969; also Marvin Wolfgang and F. Ferracuti: *Subculture of Violence*, London, 1967; Ralph Turner: "The Public Perception of Protest," *American Sociological Review*, December 1969; Hugh David Graham and Ted Robert Gurr, eds.: *Violence in America—Historical and Comparative Perspectives*, New York, 1969; *Report of the National Advisory Commission on Civil Disorders*, New York, 1968; Jerome H. Skolnick: *The Politics of Protest*, New York, 1969; also Richard Maxwell Brown, ed.: *American Violence*, Englewood Cliffs, 1970; also "Collective Violence," *Annals of the American Academy of Social and Political Science*, September 1970; Richard Hofstadter and Michael Wallace, eds.: *American Violence: A Documentary History*, New York, 1971.

58. "Excerpts from Report by the Commission on the Causes and Prevention of Crime," *NYT*, November 24, 1969, p. 51.

59. The case of the Weatherman activists provides the best illustration of such attitudes, much in evidence despite the political motives proclaimed: "The fantasy of violence was joined with another strand of the radical movement in America: an existential emphasis on personal authenticity as a criterion of valid politics. . . . Revolution reflected a taste for absolutism almost religious in its intensity . . .
. . . Life in the collectives took on a frenzied, brutal, savage air as the Weathermen tried to root out their fear of violence. . . .
The Weathermen talked of themselves as barbarians sent to destroy a decadent society, the twentieth-century equivalent of the Vandals and Visigoths who harried and finally destroyed the Roman Empire. They had stopped talking about politics; now they talked only of violence and savagery, of ripping, tearing, smashing, destroying." Thomas Powers: *Diana: The Making of a Terrorist*, Boston, 1971, pp. 124, 143, 167-68.

60. Jules Feiffer: "Our Age of Violence," *NYT Art & Theater Section*, April 23, 1967.

61. "On Moral Themes: Inhuman," *Izvestia*, transl. *CDSP*, August 23, 1967, p. 23.

62. For a rather comprehensive sampling of many forms of gruesome violence see "A Special Section on Violence," *Esquire*, July 1967. It also exemplifies the mixture of motives which lead to such exposés, as discussed by Feiffer earlier.

63. Otto N. Larsen: "Controversies about the Mass Communication of Violence" in *Patterns of Violence*, The Annals of the American Academy of Political and Social Science, March 1966, p. 45.

64. See Taft, *op. cit.*

65. "Excerpts from the Firearms Statement by the National Commission on Violence,"

Perspective" in S. N. Eisenstadt, ed.: *Comparative Social Problems*, New York, 1964.

152. John A. Clausen: "Mental Disorders" in Merton-Nisbet, eds., *op. cit.*, p. 26.

153. See, for example, Clausen, *op. cit.*, in Merton-Nisbet, *op. cit.* (1971 edition), p. 53.

154. *Pocket Data Book*, p. 51.

155. Elia Katz: *Armed Love*, New York, 1971, pp. 165-66. Apart from mobility there are apparently other aspects of the lives of the alienated which create difficulties for the maintenance of stable relationships, especially marital ones. Kenneth Kenniston, discussing marital relationships among Movement people noted: "Even marriage, as contrasted to intense but not binding love relationships, seems extraordinarily difficult within the New Left. No one knows what the actual rate of marriage failure is in the Movement, but the figure of 50 per cent was often cited. In discussions of this topic, several young radicals ventured that 'people with stable politics have stable marriages.'" Kenneth Kenniston: *Young Radicals—Notes on Committed Youth*, New York, 1968, p. 261.

156. According to Nisbet, "Developmentalism is one of the oldest and most powerful of all Western ideas." Robert Nisbet: *Social Change and History*, New York, 1969, p. VII (preface).

157. Nathan Leites: *The Study of Bolshevism*, Glencoe, 1953, p. 102.

158. For a typical Soviet discussion see: "The Earth, People, Today and Tomorrow," *Literaturnaya gazeta*, transl. *CDSP*, August 30, 1967, p. 12. See also Marshall Goldman: *The Spoils of Progress, Environmental Pollution in the Soviet Union*, Cambridge, Mass., 1972.

159. Trotsky, *op. cit.*, p. 57.

Chapter 9

1. For an analysis of the recent claims and realities of repression in America see Walter Goodman: "The Question of Repression," *Commentary*, August 1970. For an example of the difference betwen the myth and reality of repression see Edward Jay Epstein: "The Panthers and the Police: A Pattern of Genocide?" *The New Yorker*, February 13, 1971.

2. For a critical analysis of these and other aspects of television news reporting see Edith Efron: *The News Twisters*, Los Angeles, 1971.

3. *Message from Moscow*, p. 26.

4. *NYT*, August 17, 1970, p. 11.

5. Isaiah Berlin: "Two Concepts of Liberty," in *Four Essays on Liberty*, New York, 1969, pp. 161, 164, 165. For an excellent analysis of the same and related issues see also A. James Gregor: *Contemporary Radical Ideologies*, New York, 1968, esp. Chaps. I and VIII.

6. Berlin, *op. cit.*, pp. 148, 150-151, 153, 170, 171.

7. *Ibid.*, p. 171.

8. An informative quantitative and qualitative comparison of Soviet society with other contemporary societies can be found in Cyril E. Black: "Soviet Society: A Comparative View" in Allen Kassof, ed.: *Prospects for Soviet Society*, New York, 1968, pp. 14-53.

9. For a somewhat related discussion see Marion Levy, Jr.: *The Structure of Society*, Princeton, 1952, pp. 123-25, 159-60.

10. Potter, *op. cit.*, p. 111.

11. Andrew Hacker: *The End of the American Era*, New York, 1971, pp. 167-68, 32.
12. For another summary of the unfulfilled promises of the Bolshevik Revolution see "Fifty Years of the Soviet Revolution" in Alex Inkeles: *Social Change in Soviet Russia*, pp. 49-55.
13. Albert H. Cantril and Charles W. Roll, Jr.: *Hopes and Fears of the American People*, New York, 1971, p. 51.
14. Dennis H. Wrong: "Portrait of a Decade," *NYT Magazine*, August 2, 1970, p. 30. For a more detailed discussion of the extent and nature of black gains and the responses to them see also Daniel P. Moynihan: "The Schism in Black America," *Public Interest*, Spring 1972.
15. Randall Collins: "A Comparative Approach to Political Sociology" in Reinhard Bendix, ed.: *State and Society*, Boston, 1968, p. 51.
16. *Message from Moscow*, pp. 102-103, 209.
17. *Problems of Communism*, July 1968, p. 88.
18. "Suslov-Voters' Meeting with M. A. Suslov," *Pravda, Izvestia*, transl. *CDSP*, July 21, 1970.
19. *Problems of Communism*, p 81.
20. Henry Kamm: "Brezhnev Sets the Clock Back," *NYT Magazine*, August 10, 1969, p. 28.
21. "Tensions and frustrations are bound to arise when 200 million human beings demand rights and privileges never intended for popular distribution. . . .
. . . Moreover, most of the sensations of injustice about which ordinary citizens complain arise from overinflated hopes concerning what an ordinary person may experience throughout his life." Hacker, *op. cit.*, pp. 8, 160.
22. Edward C. Banfield: *The Unheavenly City*, Boston, 1968, p. 21.
23. Edward Shils has written the most penetrating piece on this subject: "Plenitude and Scarcity," *Encounter*, May 1969.
24. "A Case of Hypochondria," *Newsweek*, July 6, 1970, p. 28.
25. Norman Podhoretz: "Laws, Kings and Cures," *Commentary*, October 1970, p. 31; Another manifestation of the same trend noted by Podhoretz, has been the tendency to absolve the individual—or certain types of individuals—from responsibility for their behavior: "The new mythology sees entities called the Establishment, the Power Structure, Society (with capital S), and, of course, the System as the origins of goods and evils, of the causes of our conduct, and, hence, as 'responsible' to and for us. The logic that attributes blame to the System reduces the responsibility of the individual enmeshed in it. . . . The behavioral sciences have helped shift the load of responsibility from individuals to environments. Their message allocates responsibility for conduct to causes beyond the control of the actor . . . Modern morality attributes behavior to circumstance; it thereby converts sin to sickness and erases fault." Quoted from Gwynn Nettler: "Shifting the Load," *American Behavioral Scientist*, January-February, 1972, pp 372, 373.
26. Concerning the last point Riesman observed (in his discussion of the youth culture) that "Tolerance and openness are extended only to small, marginally connected networks, whose norms include intolerance toward others outside the networks." "Twenty Years After—A Second Preface" *op. cit.*, p. xix.
27. See also Marya Mannes: "Where Is Youth's Individualism?" *NYT*, October 22, 1970, editorial page.
28. There is an illuminating discussion of how this is tied to a general revulsion from differentiation and to a critique of *all* learning in Franklin Ford's article "Roles and the Critique of Learning" in *Daedalus*, Summer 1970.

29. Nathan Glazer: "Blacks, Jews and Intellectuals," *Commentary* April 1969, p. 39; for some further illustrations and discussion of such attitudes see also Ronald Berman: *America in the Sixties, An Intellectual History*, New York, 1968, esp. pp. 110-20.

30. Norman Podhoretz: "The Idea of Crisis," *Commentary*, November 1970, p. 4.

31. Alexander M. Bickel: "The Tolerance of Violence on the Campus," *New Republic*, June 13, 1970, pp. 15, 16.

32. Erazim V. Kohak: "Requiem for Utopia," *Dissent*, January 1969, p. 41.

33. Walter Laqueur: "The Cry Was, 'Down With Das System,' " *NYT Magazine*, August 16, 1970, p. 33; see also Arnold Reichman: *Nine Lies About America*, New York, 1972.

34. Raymond Aron: *The Opium of the Intellectuals*, London, 1957, pp. 42-43.

35. Ernest Gellner: "The Panther and the Dove . . ." in David Martin, ed.: *Anarchy and Culture*, New York, 1969, p. 141.

36. "On Revolution—Rhetorical and Real" in Peter L. Berger and Richard John Neuhaus: *Movement and Revolution*, Garden City, pp. 51, 59; on the various manifestations of the utopian temper in American politics see John H. Bunzel: *Anti-Politics in America*, New York, 1967.

37. Richard Hofstadter: *Anti-intellectualism in American Life*, New York, 1963, pp. 417, 420, 424.

38. Quoted in George Kateb: "The Political Thought of Herbert Marcuse," *Commentary*, January 1970, p. 57.

39. George F. Kennen: "Con III Is Not The Answer," *NYT*, October 28, 1970, p. 43.

40. Norman Birnbaum: "America, A Partial View," *Commentary*, July 1958, pp. 43, 44, 47, 48.

41. Hacker, *op. cit.*, pp. 174, 181.

42. Needless to say such gloomy views are not universally shared. George Kennan, for example, does not believe that the Soviet Union remains much of a threat to the United States or Western Europe. See "Interview with George F. Kennan," *Foreign Policy*, Summer 1972.

43. Discussing the problems of isolationism and globalism Kingman Brewster, Jr. noted that "For the first time in our history a very substantial number of future leaders of the country are disenchanted with the inherited role of the U.S. in the world." "Reflections on Our National Purpose," *Foreign Affairs*, April 1972, p 407.

44. At the same time, and in addition, "The most talented young Americans are continuing to avoid careers involved in any way with production and economic affairs, and they are also now avoiding careers in the physical sciences (other than medicine)—these are regarded as lacking in meaning." Riesman, *op. cit.*, p. XVIII.

45. Szamuelly: "Five Years After Khrushchev," *Survey*, Summer 1969, pp. 51-52, 53, 60, 61, 65.

46. *Message from Moscow*, pp. 84, 90.

47. Once more Isaiah Berlin's observation puts the matter into the necessary historical perspective: "It may be that the ideal of freedom to choose ends without claiming eternal validity for them, and the pluralism of values connected with this, is only the late fruit of our declining capitalist civilization: an ideal which remote ages and primitive societies have not recognized, and one which posterity will regard with curiosity, even sympathy, but little comprehension. This may be so; but no sceptical conclusions seem to me to follow. Principles are not less sacred because their duration cannot be guaranteed. Indeed, the very desire for guarantees that our values are eternal and secure in some objective heaven is perhaps only a crav-

ing for the certainties of childhood or the absolute values of our primitive past."
Berlin *cited* p. 172.

48. "With the artifacts of prosperity so readily at hand, private activities become all
the more enjoyable, weakening any tendency to undergo sacrifices for social
ends. . . .

. . . A preoccupation with private concerns deflects a population from public
obligations. The share of energy devoted to common concerns gradually diminishes,
and a willingness to be governed is less evident." Hacker, *op. cit.*, pp. 5, 6.

Bibliography

Abramov, Fyodor. *The New Life—A Day on a Collective Farm*. New York: Grove Press, 1963.

Akhmetshin, Kh. M. *Okhrana Gosvdarstvennoy Tayni—Dolg Sovetskikh Grazhdan* (The Preservation of State Secrets: The Duty of the Soviet Citizen). Moscow: 1954, Izd. Iuzid. Lit. (Legal Publishing House).

Aldridge, John W. *In the Country of the Young*. New York: Harper's Magazine Press, 1969.

Almond, Gabriel and Verba, Sidney. *The Civic Culture*. Boston: Little, Brown, 1965.

———. *The Appeals of Communism*. Princeton: Princeton University Press, 1954.

Amalrik, Andrei. *Involuntary Journey to Siberia*. New York: Harcourt Brace Jovanovich, 1970.

American Women—Report of the Presidential Commission on the Status of Women. New York: Scribner's, 1965.

Arendt, Hannah. *On Violence*. New York: Harcourt Brace and World, 1969.

———. *The Origins of Totalitarianism*. New York: Macmillan, 1958.

Aron, Paul, ed. *Soviet Views of America*. White Plains: International Arts and Sciences Press, 1969.

Aron, Raymond. *Industrial Society*. New York: Praeger, 1967.

———. *The Opium of Intellectuals*. London: Secker and Warburg, 1957.

Azrael, Jeremy. *Managerial Power and Soviet Politics*. Cambridge: Harvard University Press, 1966.

Baikova, U. G.; Duchal, A. S.; Zemtsov, A. A. *Svobodnoye Vremya i Vsestoronnoye Razvitie Lichnosti* (Free Time and the All-Round Development of the Personality). Moscow: Misl Publishing House, 1965.

Banfield, Edward C. *The Unheavenly City*. Boston: Little, Brown, 1968.

Barbu, Zevedei. *Democracy and Dictatorship*. New York: Grove Press, 1956.

Barghoorn, Frederick C. *Politics in the USSR*. Boston: Little, Brown, 1966.

——. *Soviet Foreign Propaganda*. Princeton: Princeton University Press, 1964.

——. *The Soviet Image of the United States*. New York: Harcourt Brace, 1950.

Barnet, Richard J. and Raskin, Marcus G. *After Twenty Years*. New York: Random House, 1965.

Bauer, Raymond. *The New Man in Soviet Psychology*. Cambridge, Mass.: Harvard University Press, 1952.

——; Inkeles, Alex; and Kluckhohn, Clyde. *How the Soviet System Works*. Cambridge, Mass.: Harvard University Press, 1956.

Beichman, Arnold. *Nine Lies About America*. New York: Library Press, 1972.

Bell, Daniel. *The End of Ideology*. New York: Collier, 1961.

——, ed. *The Radical Right*. Garden City: Doubleday, 1963.

Bellah, Robert N. "Civil Religion in America," in William G. McLoughlin and Robert N. Bellah, eds. *Religion in America*. Boston: Houghton-Mifflin, 1968.

Bellow, Saul. *Herzog*. New York: Viking Press, 1964.

——. *Mr. Sammler's Planet*. New York: Viking Press, 1970.

Beloff, Max. "Soviet Historians and American History" in John Keep. ed., *Contemporary History in the Soviet Mirror*. New York: Praeger, 1964.

Bendix, Reinhard. *Citizenship and Nation Building*. New York: Wiley, 1964.

Bennis, Warren G. and Slater, Philip E. *The Temporary Society*. New York: Harper and Row, 1968.

Bensman, Joseph and Vidich, Arthur J. *The New American Society—The Revolution of the Middle Class*. Chicago: Quadrangle Books, 1972.

Berdiaev, Nicholas. *The Origin of Russian Communism*. Ann Arbor: University of Michigan Press, 1960.

Bereday, George Z. F. *The Changing Soviet School*. Boston: Houghton Mifflin, 1960.

—— and Pennar, Jan, eds. *Politics of Soviet Education*. New York: Praeger, 1960.

Berger, Bennett M. *Looking For America*. Englewood Cliffs: Prentice-Hall, 1971.

——. *Working Class Suburb*. Berkeley: University of California Press, 1960.

Berger, Brigitte. *Societies in Change*. New York: Basic Books, 1971.

Berger, Peter L. *A Rumor of Angels*. Garden City: Doubleday, 1969.

Berger, Peter L. and Neuhaus, Richard John. *Movement and Revolution*. Garden City: Doubleday, 1970.

Berlin, Isaiah. *Four Essays on Liberty*. New York: Oxford University Press, 1969.

Berman, Harold J., ed. *Soviet Criminal Law and Procedure—The RSFSR Codes*. Cambridge, Mass.: Harvard University Press, 1966.

Berman, Marshall. *The Politics of Authenticity—Radical Individualism and the Emergence of Modern Society*. New York: Atheneum, 1970.

Berman, Ronald. *America in the Sixties—An Intellectual History*. New York: Free Press, 1968.

Bird, Caroline. *Born Female—The High Cost of Keeping Women Down*. New York: McKay, 1968.

Black, Cyril E. "Soviet Society: A Comparative View" in Allen Kassof, ed., *Prospects for Soviet Society*. New York: Praeger, 1968.

Blum, John Morton. *The Promise of America*. Boston: Houghton Mifflin, 1966.

Bolshaya Sovetskaya Entsiklopediya (The Great Soviet Encyclopedia). Moscow: 1950.

Boorstin, Daniel J. *The Image*. New York: Harper & Row, 1961.

Bottomore, T. B. *Classes in Modern Society*. New York: Random House, 1966.

——. *Critics of Society—Radical Thought in North America*. New York: Random House, 1968.

——. *Elites and Society*. London: C. A. Watts, 1964.

————. *Sociology, A Guide to Problems and Literature.* Englewood Cliffs: Prentice-Hall, 1963.

Brinton, Crane. *A History of Western Morals.* New York: Harcourt Brace & World, 1959.

Bronfenbrenner, Urie. "Mirror Images . . ." in Harry G. Shaffer, ed., *The Soviet System in Theory and Practice.* New York: Appleton-Century, 1965.

————. *Two Worlds of Childhood—U.S. and U.S.S.R.* New York: Russell Sage, 1970.

Brown, Richard Maxwell, ed. *American Violence.* Englewood Cliffs: Prentice-Hall, 1970.

Brustein, Robert. *Revolution as Theatre,* New York: Liveright, 1971.

Brzezinski, Zbigniew. "The Patterns of Autocracy" in C. Black, ed., *The Transformation of Russian Society.* Cambridge, Mass.: Harvard University Press, 1960.

————. "Totalitarianism and Rationality" in his *Ideology and Power in Soviet Politics.* New York: Praeger, 1962.

———— and Huntington, Samuel P. *Political Power USA/USSR.* New York: Viking Press, 1964.

Bunzel, John H. *Anti-Politics in America.* New York: Knopf, 1967.

Burden, Hamilton T. *The Nurenberg Rallies: 1923-39.* New York: Praeger, 1967.

Burlatsky, F. *The State and Communism.* Moscow: Progress Publishers, no date.

Burton, Tom and Hyams, Joe. *Accomplices to the Crime—The Arkansas Prison Scandal.* New York: Grove Press, 1970.

Cantril, Albert H. and Roll Jr., Charles W. *Hopes and Fears of the American People.* New York: Universe Books, 1971.

Cantril, Hadley. *The Pattern of Human Concerns.* New Brunswick: Rutgers University Press, 1965.

Caplowitz, David. *The Poor Pay More.* New York: The Free Press, 1963.

Carr, E. H. *The New Society.* Boston: Beacon Press, 1968.

Chalin, M. L. *Moral' Stroitelya Kommunizma* (The Morality of the Builder of Communism). Moscow: Izd. Urs, and Aon, 1963.

Chinoy, Ely. *Automobile Workers and the American Dream.* New York: Doubleday, 1955.

Chornovil, Vyacheslav. *The Chornovil Papers.* New York: McGraw-Hill, 1968.

Clark, Kenneth. *Dark Ghetto.* New York: Harper & Row, 1965.

Clausen, John A. "Mental Disorders" in Robert K. Merton and Robert Nisbet, eds. *Contemporary Social Problems.* New York: Harcourt Brace and World, 1966.

Clews, John C. *Communist Propaganda Techniques.* London: Methuen, 1964.

Clinard, Marshall. *Sociology of Deviant Behavior.* New York: Holt, Rinehart & Winston, 1963.

Cockburn, Claude. *Crossing the Line.* London: MacGibbon & Kee, 1958.

Cocks, Paul. *Controlling Communist Bureaucracy: Ethics, Rationality and Terror* (unpublished manuscript), 1972.

Cohen, Albert K. *Delinquent Boys.* New York: The Free Press, 1955.

Coleman, James. *The Adolescent Society.* New York: The Free Press, 1961.

Coleman, James S. et al. *Equality of Educational Opportunity.* Washington, D.C.: U.S. Office of Education, 1966.

Collins, Randall. "A Comparative Approach to Political Sociology" in Reinhard Bendix, ed. *State and Society.* Boston: Little, Brown, 1968.

Commager, H. S. *Freedom and Order: A Commentary on the American Political Scene.* New York: Braziller, 1966.

Connor, Walter D. *Deviance in Soviet Society—Crime, Delinquency and Alcoholism.* New York: Columbia University Press, 1972.

Conquest, Robert. "De-Stalinization and the Heritage of Terror" in Alexander Dallin and Alan F. Westin, eds. *Politics in the Soviet Union—7 Cases.* New York: Harcourt Brace and World, 1966.

————. *The Great Terror.* New York: Macmillan, 1968.

————. *The Soviet Deportation of Nationalities.* London: Macmillan, 1960.

————, ed., *The Soviet Police System,* New York: Praeger, 1968.

Counts, George S. *The Challenge of Soviet Education.* New York: McGraw-Hill, 1957.

Cressey, Donald. *The Theft of a Nation.* New York: Harper & Row, 1969.

Cuber, John F. and Haroff, Peggy B. *The Significant Americans—A Study of Sexual Behavior Among the Affluent.* New York: Appleton-Century, 1965.

Dallin, D. and Nicolaevsky, B. *Forced Labor in Soviet Russia.* New Haven: Yale University Press, 1947.

Daniels, Robert V., ed. *A Documentary History of Communism.* New York: Random House, 1960.

David, Henry P. *Family Planning and Abortion in the Socialist Countries of Central and Eastern Europe.* New York: The Population Council, 1970.

Davis, Kingsley. *Human Society.* New York: Macmillan, 1960.

Decter, Midge. "Anti-Americanism in America" in *The Liberated Woman and Other Americans.* New York: Coward, McCann and Geoghegan, 1971.

Deford, Frank. *There She Is: The Life and Times of Miss America.* New York: Viking Press, 1971.

Deutscher, Isaac. *The Great Contest.* New York: Oxford University Press, 1960.

————. *The Unfinished Revolution.* New York: Oxford University Press, 1967.

DeWitt, Nicholas. "Recent Trends in Soviet Education" in Alex Inkeles and Kent Geiger, eds. *Soviet Society, A Book of Readings.* Boston: Houghton Mifflin, 1961.

Dicks, Henry V. "Some Notes on the Russian National Character" in Cyril Black, ed. *The Transformation of Russian Society.* Cambridge, Mass.: Harvard University Press, 1960.

Dunn, Stephen P. and Dunn, Ethel. *The Peasants of Central Russia.* New York: Holt, Rinehart & Winston, 1967.

Durkheim, Emile. *The Division of Labor in Society.* New York: The Free Press, 1965.

————. *The Elementary Forms of Religious Life.* New York: Collier, 1961.

Duverger, Maurice. *The Idea of Politics.* Chicago: Regnery, 1970.

Eckstein, Harry. *Division and Cohesion in Democracy, A Study of Norway.* Princeton: Princeton University Press, 1966.

Efron, Edith. *The News Twisters.* Los Angeles: Nash, 1971.

Ehrenburg, Ilya. *Memoirs 1921-1941.* Cleveland: World, 1964.

Eliav, Arie L. *Between Hammer and Sickle.* New York: The New American Library, 1969.

Fainsod, Merle. *How Russia Is Ruled.* Cambridge, Mass.: Harvard University Press, 1953.

————. *Smolensk Under Soviet Rule.* Cambridge, Mass.: Harvard University Press, 1958.

Feifel, Herman, ed. *The Meaning of Death.* New York: McGraw-Hill, 1959.

Feifer, George. *Justice in Moscow,* New York: Delta, 1965.

Feuer, Lewis F. *Marx and the Intellectuals.* Garden City: Doubleday Anchor Books, 1969.

Field, Mark G. "Soviet and American Approaches to Mental Illness: A Comparative

————. *The Uses of Literacy*. Boston: Beacon Press, 1961.

Hollander, Gayle D. *Communications and Social Modernization in Soviet Society*. Ph.D. Dissertation, M.I.T., 1968.

————. *Soviet Political Indoctrination: Developments in Mass Media and Propaganda Since Stalin*. New York: Praeger, 1972.

Hollander, Paul, ed. *American and Soviet Society: A Reader in Comparative Sociology and Perception*. Englewood Cliffs: Prentice-Hall, 1969.

————. "Criticism and Self-Criticism in Soviet Society" in *Marxism, Communism and Western Society—A Comparative Encyclopedia*. New York: McGraw-Hill, 1972.

————. "Leisure: The Unity of Pleasure and Purpose" in A. Kassof, ed. *Prospects for Soviet Society*. New York: Praeger, 1968.

Holt, John. *How Children Fail*. New York: Pitman, 1964.

————. *How Children Learn*. New York: Pitman, 1967.

————. *The Underachieving School*. New York: Pitman, 1969.

Hoover, J. E. *Crime in the United States, Uniform Crime Reports*. Washington, D.C.: U.S. Dept. of Justice, 1969.

Horney, Karen. *The Neurotic Personality of Our Time*. New York: Norton, 1937.

Horowitz, David, ed. *Containment and Revolution*. Boston: Beacon Press, 1967.

Horowitz, Irving Louis, ed. *The Collected Essays of C. Wright Mills*. New York: Oxford University Press, 1963.

————. "The Conflict Society" in Howard Becker, ed. *Social Problems*. New York: Wiley, 1966.

————. "Radicalism and the Revolt Against Reason" Introduction to *The Social Theories of George Sorel*. Carbondale: Southern Illinois University Press, 1968.

————. *Three Worlds of Development*. New York: Oxford University Press, 1972.

Huxley, Aldous. "Words and Behavior" in his *Collected Essays*. New York: Harper and Brothers, 1953.

Inkeles, Alex. "Modal Personality and Adjustment to the Soviet Sociopolitical System" in his *Social Change in Soviet Russia*. Cambridge, Mass.: Harvard University Press, 1968.

————. *Public Opinion in Soviet Russia*. Cambridge, Mass.: Harvard University Press, 1958, revised edition.

————. *Social Change in Soviet Russia*. Cambridge, Mass.: Harvard University Press, 1968.

————. "Russia and the United States: A Problem in Comparative Sociology" in Philip S. Allen. *Pitrim A. Sorokin in Review*. Durham, N.C.: Duke University Press, 1963.

———— and Bauer, Raymond *The Soviet Citizen*. Cambridge, Mass.: Harvard University Press, 1959.

———— and Levinson, Daniel J. "National Character: The Study of Modal Personality and Sociocultural Systems" in Lindzay Gardner, ed. *Handbook of Social Psychology*. Cambridge, Mass.: Addison-Wesley, 1956.

Kahler, Erich. *The Tower and the Abyss*. London: Jonathan Cape, 1958.

Kanowitz, Leo. *Women and the Law—The Unfinished Revolution*, Albuquerque: University of New Mexico Press, 1969.

Kaplan, Bert, ed. *Studying Personality Cross-Culturally*. New York: Harper & Row, 1961.

Kardiner, Abram. *The Mark of Oppression*. New York: Norton, 1951.

Katz, Elia. *Armed Love*. New York: Holt, Rinehart & Winston, 1971.

Keller, Suzanne. *Strategic Elites.* New York: Random House, 1963.

Kenniston, Kenneth. *Young Radicals—Notes On Committed Youth,* New York: Harcourt Brace and World, 1968.

Kharchev, A. G. *Brak i Semia* (Marriage and Family). Moscow: Izd. Mysl, 1964.

Khrushchev, Nikita S. *For Victory in Peaceful Competition with Capitalism.* New York: Dutton, 1960.

Killian, Lewis. *The Impossible Revolution?* New York: Random House, 1968.

Klapp, Orrin E. *Collective Search for Identity.* New York: Holt, Rinehart & Winston, 1969.

Kluckhohn, Clyde. "Studies of Russian National Character" in Alex Inkeles and Kent Geiger, eds. *Soviet Society—A Book of Readings.* Boston: Houghton Mifflin, 1961.

—— et al. "Values and Value Orientations in the Theory of Action" in T. Parsons and E. Shils, eds. *Toward A General Theory of Action.* New York: Harper Torchbooks, 1962.

Koestler, Arthur. *Trail of the Dinosaur.* Port Washington, New York: Kennikat Press, 1955.

Kolarz, Walter. *Religion in the Soviet Union.* New York: St. Martin's Press, 1961.

Kolko, Gabriel and Joyce. *The Limits of Power.* New York: Harper & Row, 1972.

Komarovsky, Mira. *Blue Collar Marriage.* New York, Random House, 1967.

Korhauser, William. *The Politics of Mass Society.* Glencoe: The Free Press, 1959.

Krivoruchenko, V. *Mesyats v Shtatakh* (A Month in the States). Moscow: Molodaya Gvardia, 1964.

Kucherov, A. "Herzen's Parallel Between the United States and Russia" in John S. Curtiss, ed. *Essays in Russian and Soviet History in Honor of G. T. Robinson.* New York: Columbia University Press, 1963.

Laird, Roy D. *The Soviet Paradigm—An Experiment in Creating a Monohierarchical Polity.* New York: The Free Press, 1970.

Lane, Robert E. *Political Life.* Glencoe: Free Press, 1959.

Larrabee, Eric and Meyerson, Rolf, eds. *Mass Leisure.* Glencoe: The Free Press, 1958.

——. *The Self-Conscious Society.* Garden City: Doubleday, 1960.

Lasch, Christopher. *The Agony of the American Left.* New York: Knopf, 1969.

Lee, Dorothy. "Are Basic Needs Ultimate?" in Clyde Kluckhohn and Henry A. Murray eds. *Personality in Nature, Society and Culture.* New York: Knopf, 1962.

Leites, Nathan. *The Operational Code of the Politburo.* New York: McGraw-Hill, 1951.

——. *A Study of Bolshevism.* Glencoe: Free Press, 1953.

Lemon, Richard. *The Troubled American.* New York: Simon & Schuster, 1969.

Lengyel, Jozsef. *From Beginning to End.* Englewood Cliffs: Prentice-Hall, 1968.

Lenin, V. *State and Revolution.* Moscow: Foreign Language Publishing House (no date).

Lenski, Gerhard. *The Religious Factor.* Garden City: Doubleday Anchor Books, 1963.

——. *Power and Privileges.* New York: McGraw-Hill, 1966.

Leonhard, Wolfgang. *Child of the Revolution.* Chicago: Regnery, 1958.

Lerner, Max, *America as a Civilization.* New York: Simon & Schuster, 1957.

Levinson, Sandra and Brightman, Carol, eds. *Venceremos Brigade—Young Americans Sharing the Life and Work of Revolutionary Cuba.* New York: Simon & Schuster, 1971.

Levy, Marion, Jr. *The Structure of Society.* Princeton: Princeton University Press, 1952.

Lewis, Lionel S. and Brisset, Dennis. "Sex as Work" in Edward McDonagh and Jon E. Simon, eds. *Social Problems: Persistent Challenges.* New York: Holt, Rinehart & Winston, 1965.

Lion, Jill A. *Long Distance Passenger Travel in the Soviet Union.* Cambridge, Mass.: M.I.T. Center for International Studies Monograph, 1967.

Lipset, Seymour Martin. *The First New Nation.* New York: Basic Books, 1963.

———. *Political Man: The Social Basis of Politics.* Garden City: Doubleday, 1960.

———. "Youth and Politics" in Robert K. Merton and Robert Nisbet, eds. *Contemporary Social Problems.* New York: Harcourt Brace Jovanovich, 1971.

——— and Lowenthal, Leo, eds. *Culture and Social Character.* New York: The Free Press, 1961.

——— and Raab, Earl. *The Politics of Unreason.* New York: Harper & Row, 1970.

Lowenthal, Richard. "Development vs. Utopia in Communist Policy" in Chalmers Johnson, ed. *Change in Communist Systems.* Stanford: Stanford University Press, 1970.

Ludwig, Allan I. *The Graven Images, New England Stonecarving and Its Symbols, 1650-1815.* Middletown: Wesleyan University Press, 1966.

Luxemburg, Rosa. *The Russian Revolution.* Ann Arbor: University of Michigan Press, 1961.

Mace, David and Vera. *The Soviet Family.* Garden City: Doubleday, 1964.

Mack, Raymond W. "Race Relations" in Howard Becker, ed. *Social Problems,* New York: Wiley, 1966.

Madison, Bernice. "The Organization of Welfare Services" in Cyril Black, ed. *The Transformation of Russian Society.* Cambridge, Mass.: Harvard University Press, 1960.

———. *Social Welfare in the Soviet Union.* Stanford: Stanford University Press, 1968.

Marchenko, Anatoly. *My Testimony.* New York: Dutton, 1969.

Marcuse, Herbert. *One Dimensional Man: Studies in the Ideology of Advanced Industrial Societies.* Boston: Beacon Press, 1964.

———. *Soviet Marxism.* New York: Vintage Books, 1961.

Margulies, Sylvia R. *The Pilgrimage to Russia—The Soviet Union and the Treatment of Foreigners.* Madison: University of Wisconsin Press, 1968.

Markarenko, Anton S. *The Collective Family: A Handbook for Russian Parents.* Garden City: Doubleday, 1967.

Marksistkaya i Burzhuazhnaya Sotsiologiya Sevodnya (Marxist and Bourgeois Sociology Today). Moscow: Izd. Nauka, 1964.

Martineau, Harriet. *Society in America.* Garden City: Doubleday Anchor Books, 1962.

Marx and Engels, *Communist Manifesto.* Moscow: Foreign Languages Publishing House, 1955.

Masters, Dexter. *The Intelligent Buyer and the Telltale Seller.* New York: Knopf, 1966.

Matza, David. *Delinquency and Drift.* New York: Wiley, 1964.

Mayer, Kurt B. and Buckley, Walter. *Class and Society.* New York: Random House, 1970.

McFarland, Andrew S. *Power and Leadership in Pluralist Systems.* Stanford: Stanford University Press, 1969.

McPherson, William. *Parallels in Extremist Propaganda.* Doctoral Dissertation, Harvard University, 1967.

Mead, Margaret. *And Keep Your Powder Dry.* New York: Morrow, 1965.

———. *Culture and Commitment—A Study of the Generation Gap.* Garden City: Doubleday, 1969.

———. *Soviet Attitudes Toward Authority.* New York: Morrow, 1951.

Merton, Robert K. *Social Theory and Social Structure.* Glencoe: Free Press, 1959.

———— and Nisbet R., eds. *Contemporary Social Problems*. New York: Harcourt, Brace and World, 1966.

Meyer, Alfred G. *Leninism*. Cambridge, Mass.: Harvard University Press, 1967.

————. *The Soviet Political Systems*. New York: Random House, 1965.

————. "Theories of Convergence" in Chalmers Johnson, ed. *Change in Communist Systems*. Stanford: Stanford University Press, 1970.

Mickiewicz, Ellen. *Soviet Political Schools*. New Haven, Yale University Press, 1967.

Mihajlov, Mihajlo. *Moscow Summer*. New York: Noonday Press, 1965.

Miller, William, Roberts, Henry L., and Shulman, Marshall D. *The Meaning of Communist*. Morristown: Silver Burdett, 1963.

Miller, Wright. *The Russians as People*. New York: Dutton, 1961.

Millet, Kate. *Sexual Politics*. Garden City: Doubleday, 1970.

Mills, C. Wright. *The Origins of World War III*. New York: Simon and Schuster, 1958.

————. *The Power Elite*. New York: Oxford University Press, 1956.

————. *White Collar*. New York: Oxford University Press, 1951.

Mitford, Jessica. *The American Way of Death*. Greenwich: Fawcett Publications, 1963.

Mollenhoff, Clark R. *The Pentagon*. New York: Putnam's, 1967.

Monnerot, Jules. *Sociology and Psychology of Communism,* Beacon Press, Boston, 1960.

Moore, Jr., Barrington. "Reflections on Conformity in Industrial Society" in *Political Power and Social Theory*. Cambridge, Mass.: Harvard University Press, 1958.

————. *Social Origins of Democracy and Dictatorship*. Boston: Beacon Press, 1966.

————. *Soviet Politics: The Dilemma of Power*. Cambridge, Mass.: Harvard University Press, 1950.

————. *Terror and Progress USSR*. Cambridge, Mass.: Harvard University Press, 1957.

————. "Thoughts on the Future of the Family" in his *Political Power and Social Theory*. Cambridge, Mass.: Harvard University Press, 1958.

Moore, Wilbert E. *The Impact of Industry*. Englewood Cliffs, Prentice-Hall, 1965.

Moralniy Kodeks Stroitelya Kommunizma (The Moral Code of the Builder of Communism). Moscow: Izd. Poleticheskoi Literaturi, 1964.

Mosely, Philip E., ed. *The Soviet Union 1922-62: A Foreign Affairs Reader*. New York: Praeger, 1963.

Myrdal, Gunnar. *An American Dilemma*. New York: Harper & Row, 1962.

Narodnoye Khozyaistvo SSSP v 1970 (The Economy of the USSR in 1970). Moscow: Central Statistical Administration, 1970.

Nelson, Robert C. and Rieber, Alfred J. *A Study of the U.S.S.R. and Communism*. New York: Putnam's, 1962.

Neugarten, Bernice L. "The Aged In American Society" in Howard S. Becker, ed. *Social Problems*. New York: Wiley, 1966.

Nisbet, Robert. *Community and Power*. New York: Oxford University Press, 1968.

————. *Degradation of the Academic Dogma*. New York: Basic Books, 1971.

————. "The Decline and Fall of Social Class," *Tradition and Revolt*. New York: Random House, 1968.

————. *Social Change and History*. New York: Oxford University Press, 1969.

Northrop, F. S. C. "Ideological Man in His Relations to Scientifically Known Natural Man" in *Ideological Differences and World Order*. New Haven: Yale University Press, 1963.

Novak, Joseph. *No Third Path*. Garden City: Doubleday, 1962.

————. *The Future Is Ours Comrade*. New York: Dutton, 1964.

Nove, Alec. *The Soviet Economy*. New York: Praeger, 1969.

Observer. *Message from Moscow*. New York: Knopf, 1969.

Oglesby, Charles and Shaull, Richard. *Containment and Change*. New York: Macmillan, 1967.

Orwell, George. "The Prevention of Literature" in his *Collected Essays*. London: Secker & Warburg, 1961.

Osborn, Robert J. *Soviet Social Policies: Welfare, Equality and Community*. Homewood: Dorsey Press, 1970.

Ossowski, Stanislaw. *Class Structure in the Social Consciousness*. New York: The Free Press, 1963.

Page, Charles H. "An Introduction Thirty Years Later" in *Class and American Sociology*. New York: Schocken Books, 1970.

Parenti, Michael. *The Anti-Communist Impulse*. New York: Random House, 1969.

Parkin, Frank. *Class Inequality and Political Order*. London: McGibbon & Keel, 1971.

Parry, Albert. *The New Class Divided*. New York, Macmillan, 1966.

Parsons, Talcott, "Age and Sex in the Social Structure of the United States" in *Essays in Sociological Theory Pure and Applied*. Glencoe: The Free Press, 1949.

————. "Communism and the West" in A. Etzioni, ed. *Social Change*. New York: Basic Books, 1964.

————. *Essays in Sociological Theory*. New York: The Free Press, 1964.

————. "The Link Between Character and Society" in *Social Structure and Personality*. Glencoe: The Free Press, 1964.

————. *Societies—Evolutionary and Comparative Perspectives*. Englewood Cliffs: Prentice-Hall, 1966.

———— and Lidz, Victor. "Death in American Society" in E. Shneidman, ed. *Essays in Self Destruction*. New York: Science, 1971.

Pettigrew, Thomas F. *A Profile of the Negro American*. Princeton: Van Nostrand, 1964.

Plumb, J. H. *The Death of the Past*. Boston: Houghton Mifflin, 1970.

Pocket Data Book—USA 1969. Washington D.C.: U.S. Bureau of the Census, 1969.

Potter, David M. *People of Plenty*. Chicago: University of Chicago Press, 1965.

Powers, Thomas. *Diana: The Making of a Terrorist*. Boston: Houghton Mifflin, 1971.

The Program of the Communist Party of the Soviet Union. New York: International Publishers, 1965.

Rapoport, Anatol. *The Big Two—Soviet-American Perceptions of Foreign Policy*. New York: Pegasus, 1969.

Redfield, Robert. *The Primitive World and Its Transformations*. Ithaca: Great Seal Books, 1953.

Redford, Emette S.; Truman, David B.; Hacker, Andrew; Westin, Alan F. and Wood, Robert C. *Politics and Government in the United States*. New York: Harcourt Brace & World, 1965.

Reich, Charles. *The Greening of America*. New York: Random House, 1970.

Reilly, Alayne P. *America In Contemporary Soviet Literature*. New York: New York University Press, 1971.

Report of the National Advisory Commission on Civil Disorders. New York: Bantam Books, 1968.

Richmond, Mary E. *Friendly Visiting Among the Poor—A Handbook for Charity Workers*. New York: Macmillan, 1903.

Rieber, Alfred J. and Nelson, Robert C. *A Study of the USSR and Communism*. New York: Putnam's, 1962.

Riesman, David. "The Cold War and The West" in *Abundance for What?* Garden City: Doubleday, 1964.

——. *The Lonely Crowd*. New Haven: Yale University Press, 1950, 1969.

Rigby, T. H. *Communist Party Membership in the USSR, 1917-1967*, Princeton: Princeton University Press, 1968.

——, ed. *Stalin*. Englewood Cliffs: Prentice-Hall, 1966.

Rimlinger, Gaston V. "Social Security Incentives and Controls in the U.S. and U.S.S.R." in R. Bendix, ed. *State and Society*. Boston: Little, Brown, 1968.

Romm, Ethel Grodzins and many named and unnamed writers of these uncensored excerpts from the underground and Movement Press. *The Open Conspiracy—What America's Angry Generation Is Saying*. New York: Giniger, 1970.

Rose, Arnold M. *The Power Structure*. New York: Oxford University Press, 1967.

Rostow, Walt W. *Stages of Economic Growth*. London: Cambridge University Press, 1960.

Roszak, Theodore. *The Making of a Counter Culture*. Garden City: Doubleday, 1969.

Rougemont, Denis de. *Love in the Western World*. Garden City: Doubleday Anchor Book, 1957.

Rubin, Ronald I., ed. *The Unredeemed: Anti-Semitism in the Soviet Union*. Chicago: Quadrangle Books, 1968.

Russell, Bertrand. *Bolshevism: Practice and Theory*. New York: Harcourt Brace and Howe, 1920.

——. *In Praise of Idleness*. New York: Unwin Books, Barnes & Noble, 1960.

——. *Power: A New Social Analysis*. London: Allen and Unwin, 1962.

Rutkevich, M. N., ed. *The Career Plans of Youth*. White Plains: International Arts and Sciences Press, 1969.

—— and Filippov. *Sotsialnie Peremeshchenia* (Social Transformations). Moscow: Izd. Mysl, 1970.

Sakharov, Andrei D. *Progress, Coexistence and Intellectual Freedom*. New York: Norton, 1968.

Schapiro, Leonard. *The Communist Party of the Soviet Union*. New York: Random House, 1960.

Schneider, Louis and Dornbusch, Sanford. *Popular Religion*. Chicago: University of Chicago Press, 1958.

Schrag, Philip G. *Counsel for the Deceived—Case Studies in Consumer Fraud*. New York: Pantheon, 1972.

Selby, Jr., Hubert. *Last Exit to Brooklyn*. New York: Grove Press, 1964.

Seligman, Ben, ed. *Aspects of Poverty*. New York: Crowell, 1969.

Selivanov., V. I. "Voleviye Cherty Novogo Rabochego" (Volitional Traits of the New Worker) in K. K. Platonov, ed. *O. Chertakh Lichnosti Novovo Rabochevo* (On the Characteristics of the Personality of the New Worker). Moscow: Academy of Sciences of the USSR, Institute of Philosophy, 1963.

Shakhnazarov, G. K. et al. *Social Science, A Textbook for Soviet Secondary Schools*, English Edition. Washington D.C.: U.S. Dept. of Commerce, Office of Technical Services, Joint Publication Research Service, 1964.

Shils, Edward. *Torment of Secrecy*. Glencoe: The Free Press, 1956.

Shostak, Arthur B. *Blue Collar Life*. New York: Random House, 1969.

—— and Gomberg, William, eds. *Blue Collar World*. Englewood Cliffs: Prentice-Hall, 1964.

Shulman, Marshall. *Stalin's Foreign Policy Reappraised.* Cambridge, Mass.: Harvard University Press, 1965.

Silberman, Charles E. *Crises in the Classroom.* New York: Random House, 1970.

Skilling, Gordon H. and Griffiths, Franklyn, eds. *Interest Groups in Soviet Politics.* Princeton: Princeton University Press, 1971.

Skolnick, Jerome H. *The Politics of Protest.* New York: Ballantine Books, 1969.

Slater, Philip E. *The Pursuit of Loneliness.* Boston: Beacon Press, 1970.

Slusser, R. M. and Wolin, S., eds. *The Soviet Secret Police.* London: Methuen, 1957.

Smith, Homer. *Black Man in Red Russia.* Chicago: Johnson, 1964.

Smith, R. E. F. *A Russian—English Dictionary of Social Science Terms.* London: Butterworth's, 1962.

Snow, Edgar. *Stalin Must Have Peace.* New York: Random House, 1947.

Social Science in Soviet Secondary Schools—Syllabus of the New Course. Washington D.C.: U.S. Dept. of Health, Education and Welfare, 1966.

Solzhenitsyn, Alexander. *Cancer Ward.* New York: Farrar, Straus and Giroux, 1969.

———. *The First Circle.* New York: Harper & Row, 1968.

———. *One Day in the Life of Ivan Denisovitch.* New York: Praeger, 1963.

———. *"We Never Make Mistakes"—Two Short Novels.* Columbia: University of South Carolina Press, 1963.

Sontag, Susan. *Trip to Hanoi.* New York: Farrar, Straus and Giroux, 1968.

Sorensen, Jay B. *Life and Death of Soviet Trade Unionism, 1917-1928.* New York: Atherton, 1969.

Sorokin, Pitrim. "The Mutual Convergence of the U.S. and the USSR" in *The Basic Trends of Our Time.* New Haven: College and University Press, 1964.

———. *Russia and the United States.* New York: Dutton, 1944.

———. *Social and Cultural Dynamics.* Boston: Porter Sargent, 1957.

Speier, Hans. "Risk, Security and Modern Hero-Worship" in *Social Order and Risks of War.* New York: George W. Stewart, 1952.

Spravochnik Propagandista Mezhdunarodnika (Reference book of the International Propagandist). Moscow: Izd. Polit. Lit., 1966.

Stalin, J. *Problems of Leninism.* Moscow: Foreign Languages Publishing House, 1940.

Stark, Rodney and Glock, Charles Y. *American Piety: The Nature of Religious Commitment.* Berkeley & Los Angeles: University of California Press, 1968.

Steel, Ronald. *Pax Americana.* New York: Viking, 1967.

Stevens, Edmund. *Russia Is No Riddle.* New York: World, 1945.

Strani Sotsialisma i Kapitalizma v Tsifrakh (Socialist and Capitalist Countries in Figures). Moscow: Izd. Polit. Lit., 1961, 1966.

Stroitelstvo Kommunizma i Dukhovniy Mir Cheloveka (The Building of Communism and the Spiritual World of Man). Moscow: Izd. Nauka, 1966.

Strukov, Z. V. *Kommunizm i Vsesteronnoye Razvitie Lichnosti* (Communism and All Round Development of the Personality). Moscow: Izd. Znanie, 1960.

Struve, Nikita. "Pseudo-Religious Rites Introduced by Party Authorities" in William C. Fletcher & Anthony J. Strover. *Religion and the Search for New Ideals in the U.S.S.R.* New York: Praeger, 1967.

Svetlikov, A. and Kuchtarev, M. *Strana Gde Zhivut Nespokoino* (The Country Where They Live Without Tranquility). Moscow: Molodaya Gvardia, 1964.

Taft, Donald R. *Criminology.* New York: Macmillan, 1942.

Talmon, J. L. *The Origins of Totalitarian Democracy.* New York: Praeger, 1961.

Task Force Report: Corrections. Washington D.C.: U.S. Govt. Printing Office, 1967.

Taubman, William. *The View From Lenin Hills.* New York: Coward-McCann, 1967.

Tertz, Abram (Andrei Sinyavski). *On Socialist Realism.* New York: Pantheon, 1960.

Toch, Hans, ed. *Legal and Criminal Psychology.* New York: Holt, Rinehart and Winston, 1961.

———. *Violent Man.* Chicago: Aldine, 1969.

Tocqueville, Alexis de. *Democracy in America.* Vintage Books, New York, 1958.

Treadgold, Donald, ed. *The Development of the USSR.* Seattle: University of Washington Press, 1964.

Triska, Jan, ed. *Soviet Communism: Programs and Rules.* San Francisco: Chandler, 1962.

Trotsky, Leon. *The Revolution Betrayed.* New York: Merit Publishers, 1965.

Tyler, Gus. *Organized Crime in America.* Ann Arbor: University of Michigan Press, 1962.

Tyrmand, Leopold. *Notebooks of a Dilettante.* New York, Macmillan, 1970.

Ulam, Adam. *Expansion and Coexistence.* New York: Praeger, 1968.

———. *The Fall of the American University.* New York: Library Press, 1972.

———. *The Rivals: America and Russia Since World War II.* New York: Viking, 1971.

———. *The Unfinished Revolution.* New York: Random House, 1960.

Updike, John. *Rabbit Redux.* New York: Knopf, 1971.

———. *Rabbit Run.* New York: Knopf, 1960.

The U.S. Book of Facts, Statistics and Information (officially published by the U.S. Govt. as statistical abstracts of the U.S.). New York: Esselen Special Edition, 1967.

The U.S. Book of Facts, Sattistics and Information. New York: Grosset & Dunlap, 1971.

United States Statistical Abstracts. Washington D.C.: Dept. of Commerce, 1969, 1970, 1971.

Viktorov, B. A. *Spioni Pod Maskoi Turistov* (Spies Masked as Tourists). Moscow: Voennie Izd., Ministertsva Oboroni (Military Publishing House of the Ministry of Defense), 1963.

Vladimirov, Leonid. *The Russians.* New York: Praeger, 1968.

Voprosy Teorii i Praktiki Partiinoi Propagandy (Questions of the Theory and Method of Party Propaganda). Moscow: Izd. Polit. Lit., 1971.

Wagner, Walter. *The Golden Fleecers.* New York: Doubleday, 1966.

Wakefield, Dan. "Slick-Paper Christianity" in Maurice Stein, Arthur J. Vidich and David Manning White, eds. *Identity and Anxiety.* New York: Free Press, 1960.

Waugh, Evelyn. *The Loved One.* Boston: Little, Brown, 1948.

Weiss, Richard. *The American Myth of Success—From Horatio Alger to Norman Vincent Peale.* New York: Basic Books, 1969.

Werth, Alexander. *Russia Under Khrushchev.* Greenwich: Fawcett, 1966.

Westin, Alan F. et al., eds. *Views of America.* New York: Harcourt Brace and World, 1966.

White, Ralph K. "Images in the Context of International Conflict—Soviet Perceptions of the U.S. and USSR" in Herbert C. Kelman, ed. *International Behavior.* New York: Holt, Rinehart and Winston, 1965.

Wiles, Peter. "Convergence: Possibility and Probability" in A. Balinsky et al., eds. *Planning and the Market in the USSR: The 1960's.* New Brunswick: Rutgers University Press, 1967.

Williams, Albert Rhys. *The Russians.* New York: Harcourt Brace, 1943.

Williams, Jr., Robin. *American Society.* New York: Knopf, 1970, Third edition.

Winter, Ella. *Red Virtue.* New York: Harcourt Brace, 1933.

Wolfe, Tom. *Radical Chic and Mau Mauing the Flak Catchers.* New York: Bantam Books, 1971.

Wolfe, Bertram D. "A Historian Looks at the Convergence Theory" in Paul Kurtz, ed. *Sidney Hook and the Contemporary World.* New York: John Day, 1968.

———. *Three Who Made a Revolution.* New York: Dial, 1948.

Wolfgang, Marvin and Ferracuti, F. *Subculture of Violence.* London: Social Science Paperbacks, 1967.

Wolin, S. and Slusser, R. M., eds. *The Soviet Secret Police.* London: Methuen, 1957.

Wooton, Barbara. *Social Science and Social Pathology.* London: Allen and Unwin, 1960.

Yearbook of the National Council of Churches of Christ in the United States. New York, 1966.

Young, Jr., Whitney. *To Be Equal.* New York: McGraw-Hill, 1964.

Zamoshkin, Yury. *Krizis Burzhuazhnovo Individualizma i Lichnost* (The Crisis of Bourgeois Individualism and Personality). Moscow: Izd. Nauka, 1966.

———. "Teoria "endinovo industrialnovo obschchestva" na sluzhbe antikommunizma" (The Theory of a "Single Industrial Society" in the Service of Anticommunism) in *Marksistkaya i Burzhuaznaya Sotsiologiya Sevodnia.* Moscow: Izd. Nauka, 1964.

Zdravomyslov, A. G.; Rozhin, V. P.; and Iadov, V. A. *Man and His Work.* White Plains: International Arts and Sciences Press, 1970.

Zetkin, Clara. "Lenin on the Woman Question" in *The Emancipation of Women From the Writings of V. I. Lenin.* New York: International Publishers, 1966.

Zimmerman, William. "Soviet Perceptions of the U.S." in A. Dallin and T. B. Larson, eds. *Soviet Politics Since Khrushchev.* Englewood Cliffs: Prentice-Hall, 1968.

Articles, Papers, and Pamphlets

Adelson, Joseph. "Inventing the Young." *Commentary,* May 1971.

———. "Is Women's Lib a Passing Fad?" *NYT Magazine,* March 19, 1972.

———. "What Generation Gap?" *NYT Magazine,* January 1970.

"Advice from the State Department—Hints for Americans Touring Russia on How to Avoid 'Incidents.' " *NYT Travel Section,* April 16, 1967.

Amalrik, Andrei. "Will the USSR Survive Until 1984?" *Survey,* Autumn 1969.

Aron, Raymond. "Social Structure and the Ruling Class." *British Journal of Sociology,* June 1950.

Bailey, George. "Cultural Exchange as the Soviets Use It." *Reporter,* April 7, 1966.

Barry, Donald. "Russians and their Cars." *Survey,* October 1965.

Bartell, Gilbert D. "Group Sex Among Mid-Americans." *The Journal of Sex Research,* May 1970.

Barton, P. "An End to Concentration Camps?" *Problems of Communism,* March-April 1962.

Barzun, Jacques. "The Man in the American Mask." *Foreign Affairs,* April 1965.

Bauer, Raymond A. "Accuracy of Perceptions in International Relations." *Teachers College Record,* Vol. 64, January 1963.

————. "The Pseudo-Charismatic Leader in Soviet Society." *Problems of Communism.* June-July 1953.

Berger, Peter L. and Brigitte. "The Assault on Class." *Worldview,* July 1972.

Bergson, Abram. "Development Under Two Systems: Comparative Productivity Growth Since 1950." *World Politics,* July 1971.

Bickel, Alexander M. "The Tolerance of Violence on the Campus." *New Republic,* June 13, 1970.

Billington, James H. "Beneath the Panoply of Power the Intelligentsia Hits Out at the Old Order." *Life,* November 10, 1967.

Birnbaum, Norman. "America, A Partial View." *Commentary,* July 1958.

Boorstin, Daniel J. "A Case of Hypochondria." *Newsweek,* July 6, 1970.

Boyers, Robert. "Attitudes Toward Sex in American High Culture." *The Annals of the American Academy of Social and Political Science* (abbreviated hereafter as *The Annals*), March 1968.

Brewster, Jr., Kingman. "Reflections on Our National Purpose." *Forgein Affairs,* April 1972.

Brodsky, Iosif." The Trial of Iosif Brodsky." *New Leader,* August 31, 1964.

Bronfenbrenner, Urie. "Soviet Methods of Upbringing and Their Effects." Paper delivered at a conference at Cornell University on May 16, 1968.

Brossard, Chandler. "Our Most Devastating Critic: Friedenberg." *Look,* May 30, 1967.

Brownmiller, Susan. "Sisterhood Is Powerful." *NYT Magazine,* March 15, 1970.

Brustein, Robert. "When the Panther Came to Yale." *NYT Magazine,* June 21, 1970.

Bush, Keith. "A Comparison of Retail Prices in the United States, the U.S.S.R. and Western Europe in April, 1969." *Radio Liberty Research Paper,* No. 33, 1969.

Byrnes, Robert F. "American Scholars in Russia Soon Learn About the KGB." *NYT Magazine,* November 16, 1969.

Chase, Stuart. "American Values—A Generation of Change." *Public Opinion Quarterly,* Fall 1965.

Chornovil, Vyacheslav. "Document by V. Chornovil." *Problems of Communism,* July-August 1968.

Cohen, Carl. "Democracy and the Curriculum." *The Nation,* March 17, 1969.

Connor, Walter D. "Juvenile Delinquency in the USSR: Some Quantitative and Qualitative Indicators." *American Sociological Review,* April 1970.

Crowther, Bosley. "Movies to Kill People By." *NYT Arts & Theater Section,* July 9, 1967.

Davis, David Brian. "Violence in American Literature." *The Annals,* March 1966.

Denfield, Duane and Gordon, Michael. "The Sociology of Mate Swapping." *The Journal of Sex Research,* May 1970.

Dixon, Marlene. "Why Women's Liberation?" *Ramparts,* December 1969.

Drosnin, Michael. "Ripping Off the New Life Style." *NYT Magazine,* August 1970.

Efron, Edith. "The Land of the Shanty and the Home of the Oppressed." *TV Guide,* January 13, 1968.

————. "Who Is the Heavy? TV Looks at the Drug Problem." *TV Guide,* March 20, 1971.

Epstein, Edward Jay. "The Panthers and the Police: A Pattern of Genocide?" *The New Yorker,* February 13, 1971.

Epstein, Jason. "The CIA and the Intellectuals." *The New York Review of Books,* April 20, 1971.

Feifer, George. "Russia-Da, China-Nyet." *NYT Magazine,* December 4, 1966.

Feifer, Jules. "Our Age of Violence," *NYT Art & Theater Section,* April 23, 1967.

Ferdinand, Theodore N. "Sex Behavior and the American Class Structure: A Mosaic." *The Annals,* March 1968.

Ferris, Paul. "1500 Advertisements a Day." *The Observer,* September 22, 1963.

Feuer, Lewis M. "The Intelligentsia in Opposition." *Problems of Communism,* November-December 1970.

―――. "Meeting the Philosophers." *Survey,* April 1964.

Ford, Franklin L. "Roles and the Critique of Learning." *Daedalus,* Summer 1970.

Friedberg, Maurice. *Why They Left: A Survey of Soviet Jewish Immigrants.* New York: The Academic Committee on Soviet Jewry, 1972.

Frolic, Michael. "Soviet Urban Sociology." *International Journal of Comparative Sociology,* December 1971.

Gans, Herbert J. "The Equality Revolution." *NYT Magazine,* November 3, 1968.

Geiger, Louis G. and Helen M. "The Revolt Against Excellence." *AAUP Bulletin,* September 1970.

Gilison, Jerome M. "Soviet Elections as a Measure of Dissent: The Missing One Percent." *American Political Science Review,* September 1968.

Glazer, Nathan. "Blacks, Jews and Intellectuals." *Commentary,* April 1969.

―――. "The New Left and Its Limits." *Commentary,* July 1968.

―――. "On Being Deradicalized." *Commentary,* October 1970.

Goldman, Albert. "Grab the Money and Run?" *NYT Arts & Theater Section,* February 23, 1970.

Golod, S. I. "Sociological Problems of Sexual Morality." *Soviet Sociology,* Summer 1969.

Goodman, Walter. "The Question of Repression." *Commentary,* August 1970.

―――. "Yessir Boss, Said the White Radicals—When Black Power Runs the New Left." *NYT Magazine,* September 24, 1967.

Gorer, Geoffrey. "Are We 'By Freud Obsessed'?" *NYT Magazine,* July 30, 1961.

Gorky, Maxim. "On the Russian Peasantry." Berlin, 1922 (mimeographed), transl. by V. Boss.

Gould, Julius. "The Dialectics of Despair." *Encounter,* September 1964.

Greenstein, Fred, I. "New Light on Changing American Values: A Forgotten Body of Survey Data." *Social Forces,* Vol. 42, May 1964.

Grigorienki, P. "Petition by P. Grigorienko." *Problems of Communism,* July-August 1968.

Harasymiv, Bogdan. "Nomenklatura: "The Soviet Communist Party's Leadership Recruitment System." *Canadian Political Science Review,* December 1969.

Heer, David M. "Abortion, Contraception and Population Policy in the Soviet Union." *Soviet Studies,* July 1965.

Hobson, Dick. "Oh To Be 30 Again!" *TV Guide,* September 23, 1967.

Hofstadter, Richard. "The Age of Rubbish." *Newsweek,* July 6, 1970.

Hollander, Paul. "Observations on Bureaucracy, Totalitarianism and the Comparative Study of Communism." *Slavic Review,* June 1967.

―――. "Grenzen Controllen als Integraler Teil Des Sowjetsystems" (Border Controls: An Integral Part of the Soviet System). *Osteuropa,* October 1969.

———. "How Political Is the Student Revolution?" *Youth and Society*, December 1971.

———. McFarland, A. "Power and Leadership in Pluralistic Systems." *American Sociological Review*, January 1970 (review).

———. "Models of Behavior in Stalinist Literature." *American Sociological Review*, June 1966.

———. "Politicized Bureaucracy: The Soviet Case." *Newsletter on Comparative Studies of Communism*, May 1971.

Hough, Jerry F. "The Soviet System: Petrification or Pluralism?" *Problems of Communism*, March-April 1972.

Howe, Irving. 'The Middle Class Mind of Kate Millet." *Harpers*, December 1970.

———. "New Confrontation Politics Is a Dangerous Game." *NYT Magazine*, October 20, 1968.

———. "New Styles of Leftism." *Dissent*, Summer 1965.

Hughes, H. Stuart. "Jean Paul Sartre: The Marxist Phase." *Ramparts*, March 1967.

Huntington, Samuel P. "Political Modernization: Europe vs. America." *World Politics*, April 1966.

Inkeles, Alex. "Industrial Man." *American Journal of Sociology*, July 1960.

———. Models in the Analysis of Soviet Society," *Survey*, July 1966.

"In Quest of Justice." *Problems of Communism*, Part I, July-August 1968; Part II, September-October 1968.

Johnson, Bruce C. "The Democratic Mirage." *Berkeley Journal of Sociology*, Vol. XIII, 1968.

Kamm, Henry. "Brezhnev Sets the Clock Back." *NYT Magazine*, August 10, 1969.

Karol, K. S. "Conversations in Russia." *The New Statesman*, January 1, 1971.

Kassof, Allen. "The Administered Society: Totalitarianism Without Terror." *World Politics*, July 1964.

Kateb, George. "The Political Thought of Herbert Marcuse." *Commentary*, January 1970.

Katz, Zev. "Sociology in the Soviet Union." *Problems of Communism*, May-June 1971.

Keck, Donna. "The Art of Maiming Women." *Women—A Journal of Liberation*, Fall 1969.

Kenez, Peter. "Notes on the 1969-70 Moscow Movie Season," mimeographed 1970.

Keninston, Kenneth. "You Have to Grow Up in Scarsdale to Know How Bad Things Are." *NYT Magazine*, April 27, 1969.

Kennan, George F. "Con III Is Not the Answer." *NYT*, October 18, 1970.

———, "The Ethics of Anti-Communism." *University—A Princeton Quarterly*, Spring 1965.

———. "Interview with George F. Kennan." *Foreign Policy*, Summer 1972.

Khrushchev, N. S. "Special Report to the 20th Party Congress." *New Leader* Pamphlet, 1962.

Kifner, John. "Vandals in the Mother Country." *NYT Magazine*, January 4, 1970.

Kissinger, Henry A. "Answers Aren't Easy." *NYT Book Review*, June 27, 1965.

Kohak, E. V. "Requiem for Utopia—Socialist Reflections After Czechoslovakia." *Dissent*, January-February 1969.

"Kritika i Samokritika—Nashe Ispytannoe Oruzhie" (Criticism and Self-Criticism—Our Tested Weapon). *Kommunist*, No. 1, January 1961.

Krasner, Steven D. "A Defense of Conventional Grading." *PS* (Bulletin of the American Political Science Association) Fall 1970.

Kristol, Irving. "About Equality." *Commentary*, November 1972.

Labedz, Leopold. "Students and Revolution." *Survey*, July 1968.

Laqueur, Walter. "The Cry Was 'Down With Das System.'" *NYT Magazine*, August 16, 1970.

———. "Reflections on Youth Movements." *Commentary*, June 1969.

Larson, Otto N. "Controversies About the Mass Communication of Violence." *The Annals*, March 1966.

"Liberal Anti-Communism Revisited, A Symposium." *Commentary*, September 1967.

Lichtheim, George. "The Threat of History." *The New York Review of Books*, February 20, 1964.

Life Magazine, November 10, 1967 issue devoted to the 50th Anniversary of the October Revolution.

Lindbeck, George. "Ecumenism and the Future of Belief." *Una Sancta*, Vol. 25, No. 3, 1968.

Lipset, Seymour M. "Equal or Better in America." *Columbia University Forum*, Spring 1961.

——— and Dobson, Richard B. 'The Intellectual as Critic and Rebel: With Special Reference to the United States and the Soviet Union." *Daedalus*, Summer 1972.

———. "Mobility and Class Consciousness" (unpublished manuscript), 1972.

———. "Youth and Politics," in Robert K. Merton and Robert Nisbet, eds. *Contemporary Social Problems*. New York: Harcourt Brace Jovanovich, 1971, Third Edition.

Mandel, William M. "Soviet Women and Their Self Image," paper presented at the Far Western Slavic Conference, May 1970.

Matza, David and Sykes, M. "Juvenile Delinquency and Subterranean Values." *American Sociological Review*, October 1961.

Meehan, Thomas. "Cruise Director on the Titanic." *NYT Magazine*, January 2, 1972.

Meyer, Alfred. "The Comparative Study of Communist Political Systems." *Slavic Review*, March 1967.

Milgram, Stanley and Hollander, Paul. "The Murder They Heard." *The Nation*, June 15, 1964.

Milstein, Tom. "A Perspective on the Panthers." *Commentary*, September 1970.

Moore, Wilbert. "The Utility of Utopias." *American Sociological Review*, December 1966.

Moroz, V. "Document by V. Moroz" ("A Report from the Beria Reserve"). *Problems of Communism*, July-August 1968.

Moynihan, Daniel P. "The Schism in Black America." *Public Interest*, Spring 1972.

My Duty, a pamphlet published by the Clark Grave Vault Co., Columbus, Ohio.

Navarsky, Victor S. "Advertising Is a Science, An Art, A Business?" *NYT Magazine*, November 20, 1966.

Nettler, Gwynn. "Shifting the Load." *American Behavioral Scientist*, January-February 1972.

The New Garden Mausoleum at Pine Memorial Park, Farmingdale, L.I., N.Y.

"The New Rebel Cry: Jesus Is Coming!" *Time Magazine*, June 21, 1971.

"The New Seven Deadly Sins." *Esquire*, December 1966.

Niebuhr, R. "The Social Myths in the 'Cold War,'" *Journal of International Affairs*, No. 1, 1967.

Nisbet, Robert. "Who Killed the Student Movement?" *Encounter*, February 1970.

Nyangira, N. "Africans Don't Go to Russia to Be Brainwashed." *NYT Magazine*, May 16, 1965.

Olsen, Marvin E. "Social and Political Participation of Blacks." *American Sociological Review*, August 1970.

Orekhov, E. G. F. "Dollar Democracy." *International Affairs*, February 1965.

Page, Charles H. "Bureaucracy and the Liberal Church," *Review of Religion*, No. 3-4, March 1952.

Pease, John; Form, William H. and Rytina, Joan Hubert. "Ideological Currents in American Stratification Literature," *American Sociologist*, May 1970.

Peretz, Martin. "The American Left and Israel." *Commentary*, November 1967.

Pipes, Richard. *The Premises of American and Russian Foreign Policy*, paper presented at the American Historical Association Meeting in Washington, 1969.

——. *Some Operational Principles of Soviet Foreign Policy*, memorandum, Washington, D.C.: U.S. Govt. Printing Office, 1972.

Podhoretz, Norman. "The Idea of Crisis." *Commentary*, November 1970.

——. "Laws, Kings and Cures." *Commentary*, October 1970.

Pool, Ithiel de Sola. "The Changing Soviet Union—The Mass Media as Catalyst." *Current*, January 1966.

"A Report and Analysis of the Status of Soviet Jewry. *Congress*, December 5, 1966.

Riesman, David. "Dealing with the Russians over Berlin," *The American Scholar*, Winter 1961-62, Vol. 31, No. 1.

——. "The Found Generation." *The American Scholar*, Autumn 1956.

——. "The Study of National Character: Some Observations on the American Case," *Harvard Library Bulletin*, Winter 1959.

Ritter, Gerhard A. "Student Rebellion and Industrial Society." *Survey*, Summer 1970.

Rokeach, Milton. "The Consumer's Changing Image." *Transaction*, July 1964.

Schecter, Harvey B. "The Liberals Have Helped the Radical Right." *NYT Magazine*, April 29, 1962.

Schlesinger, Jr., Arthur. "The Origins of the Cold War," *Foreign Affairs*, October 1967.

Schweitz, J. M. "The Shadow Knows . . ." *Berkeley Journal of Sociology*, Vol. XIII, 1968.

"The Second Sexual Revolution." *Time Magazine*, January 24, 1964.

Seton-Watson, H. "Totalitarianism Reconsidered." *Problems of Communism*, July 1967.

Shargorodski, M. D. "The Causes and Prevention of Crime." *Soviet Sociology*, Vol. III, No. 1, 1964.

Shils, Edward. "Plenitude and Scarcity." *Encounter*, May 1969.

Sheley, Joseph F. "Mutuality and Retirement Community Success: An Interactionist Perspective in Gerontological Research." *Aging and Human Develoment* (forthcoming).

Skilling, Gordon. "Interest Groups and Communist Politics." *World Politics*, April 1966.

——. "Soviet and American Politics: The Dialectic of Opposites." *Canadian Journal of Economics and Politics*, May 1965.

Smigel, Erwin and Seiden, Rita. "Decline and Fall of the Double Standard." *The Annals*, March 1968.

Smith, James R. and Lynn G. "Co-Marital Sex and the Sexual Freedom Movement." *The Journal of Sex Research*, May 1970.

Solomon, Jr., Peter H. "A Selected Bibliography of Soviet Criminology." *The Journal of Criminal Law Criminology and Political Science*, 1970.

Sosnovy, Timothy. "The Soviet Housing Situation Today." *Soviet Studies*, July 1959.

Starobin, Joseph R. "Origins of the Cold War: The Communist Dimension." *Foreign Affairs*, July 1969.

Success Digest for the Entire Family. New York: Executive Research Institute, 1966.

Szamuely, Tibor. "Five Years After Khrushchev." *Survey*, Summer 1969.

———. "Intellectuals and Just Causes." *Encounter*, September 1967.

Tausky, Kurt. *Some Societal Aspects of Marijuana Use Among College Students*. Paper presented at the University of Maine, June 1970.

Taylor, Edmund. "The Political War Intensifies." *The Reporter*, June 29, 1967.

Toch, Hans. "Anatomy of a Hangup—Last Word on the Hippies." *The Nation*, December 4, 1967.

"Traffic on Highways in the USSR." *Radio Liberty Dispatch*, April 13, 1970.

Trilling, Calvin. "Wake Up and Live." *The New Yorker*, April 4, 1964.

Trilling, Diana. "Norman Mailer." *Encounter*, November 1962.

"Trud Glazami Chitatelya" (Trud Through the Eyes of the Readers). *Zhurnalist*, July 1968.

Turner, Ralph. "The Public Perception of Protest." *American Sociological Review*, December 1969.

Tyrmand, Leopold. "A Reporter At Large." *The New Yorker*, November 11, 1967.

Ulam, Adam B. "The Price of the Revolution." *Commentary*, October 1968.

———. "Reflections on the Revolution." *Survey*, July 1967.

"VD: The Epidemic." *Newsweek*, January 24, 1972.

Weinberg, Ian. "The Problem of the Convergence of Industrial Societies: A Critical Look at the State of a Theory." *Comparative Studies in Society and History*. January 1969.

Weiss, D. "A Culture in Torment." *Dissent*, July-August 1966.

"Western Images of the Soviet Union." *Survey*, April 1962.

Westley, William A. "The Escalation of Violence Through Legitimation." *The Annals*, September 1970.

Whyte, Martin K. "Rural Russia Today." *Transaction*, January 1970.

Wicker, Tom. "What Have They Done Since They Shot Dillinger?" *NYT Magazine*, December 28, 1969.

Wolfe, Bertram D. "Reflections on the Future of the Soviet System." *Russian Review*, April 1967.

Woodward, C. Vann. "Cranks and Their Followers." *NYT Book Review Section*, November 14, 1965.

"The World of the Blue Collar Worker." *Dissent*, Winter 1972.

Wrong, Dennis H. "Portrait of a Decade." *NYT Magazine*, August 2, 1970.

The World's Telephones. AT&T Company, 1967.

Yanowitch, Murray and Dodge, Norton T. "The Social Evaluation of Occupations in the Soviet Union." *Slavic Review*, December 1969.

Index

(n stands for substantive note)

Soviet Constitution of 1936, 68, 107, 186, 337
Speck, Richard, 330
Speier, Hans, 171
Spengler, Otto, 336
Stalin, Joseph, 7-8, 9, 13, 20, 45-46, 49-52, 50n, 52n, 54n, 55-57, 55n, 56n, 62n, 90, 95, 97-99, 105, 108, 110n, 158, 191-93, 196, 196n, 214-15, 217, 262, 273, 290, 290n, 305-6, 346, 349; post-Stalin, 20, 55n, 159, 192, 219, 232; Prize, 198; de-Stalinization, 56-57, 105
Standard of living, 257, 261, 334-41, 349
State Department, 91, 401
Struchkov, N., 319
Students for Democratic Society (SDS), 84, 88n, 252
Success, 132-45, 146, 367
Suslov, Mikhail, 391
Szamuelly, Tibor, 402-3

Terror, 56, 129, 159
Third World, 19, 40, 89, 167n, 236, 395
Toch, Hans, 35-36
Tolstoy, Leo, 198
Tomsky, Nikolai, 54n
Totalitarianism, 6, 8, 18, 37, 44, 104, 110-17, 260, 262, 287, 374, 378, 379, 396, 398, 403
Tocqueville, Alexis de, 248n, 267
Travel, 18, 28, 31-32, 43-44, 99-101, 377
Trilling, Diana, 16-17n
Trotsky, Leon, 54n, 261-62, 278n, 371n, 385
Tyrmand, Leopold, 164, 166n

Ulam, Adam, 25
Unemployment, 18, 30, 42, 232, 234, 385, 391
Urban, 163, 318, 321, 331, 355, 366, 376, 385
Utevsky, B., 319
U.S. Nazi party, 93n

Values, 118-201, 350, 368, 372, 388
Veblen, Thorstein, 221

Venceremos Brigade, 85-86n, 89
Verba, Sidney, 114
Vietnam War, 13, 15n, 17, 33, 81, 85, 87, 90-92, 104n, 114, 165, 167, 391n, 397, 401, 401n; North Vietnam, 19, 44, 83, 100, 104, 167, 395
Viktorov, B. A., 309n
Violence, 77, 82-83, 95-96, 101n, 109, 171, 206, 304n, 328-34

Wallace, George, 16, 77, 233, 389
War, 19, 104, 304n, 383
Warren, Earl, 78; Commission, 27
Weathermen, 87, 104, 167-70, 329
Weber, Max, 188
Welch, Robert, 16, 77, 271
Welfare, 336-37, 379
Williams, Robin, 186n
Wilson, Woodrow, 80
Women, 210, 237-43, 245, 257-58, 325, 341n, 399
Women's Liberation, 336-37, 379
Woodward, C. Vann, 80
World War II, 7, 12, 56n, 60n, 64, 90, 95, 256, 314, 320, 339, 345, 346n, 347, 390, 399, 401n
Wrong, Dennis, 387-88

Yakhimovich, 106, 107n
Yakir, Iona E., 385n
Yakir, Pyotr I., 385n, 391, 392n
Yezhov, 54n
Young Communist League, 161, 213, 263, 317n
Young Pioneers, 69, 161, 262-63, 269
Youth, 5n, 205, 205n, 210, 229, 234, 257, 261, 270, 304-21, 339, 350, 353-60, 368, 383, 387-88, 394-95, 399; organizations, 43, 69, 161, 378

Zetkin, Clara, 265
Zhdanov, 54n
Zhukov, Yuri, 54n
Zinoviev, 54n
Zola, Emile, 198